CHOICES

*A Basic Writing Guide
with Readings*

CHOICES

A Basic Writing Guide with Readings

THIRD EDITION

Kate Mangelsdorf ◆ **Evelyn Posey**

The University of Texas at El Paso

BEDFORD/ST. MARTIN'S
Boston ◆ New York

For Bedford/St. Martin's

Developmental Editor: Ben Morrison
Senior Production Editor: Michael Weber
Senior Production Supervisor: Dennis J. Conroy
Marketing Manager: Brian Wheel
Art Direction and Cover Design: Lucy Krikorian
Text Design: Joan Greenfield
Copy Editor: Denise Quirk
Photo Research: Alice Lundoff
Cover Photo: © Janez Skok/Corbis
Composition: Stratford Publishing Services
Printing and Binding: R.R. Donnelley & Sons Company

President: Joan E. Feinberg
Editorial Director: Denise B. Wydra
Editor in Chief: Nancy Perry
Director of Marketing: Karen R. Melton
Director of Editing, Design, and Production: Marcia Cohen
Managing Editor: Erica T. Appel

Library of Congress Control Number: 2002107337

Manufactured in the United States of America.

9 8 7
J I H G

For information, write: Bedford/St. Martin's, 75 Arlington Street, Boston, MA 02116
(617-339-4000)

ISBN: 0-312-39796-8 (Student Edition)
0-312-39814-X (Instructor's Annotated Edition)

To the memory of Anne P. Mangelsdorf

In our early years of teaching developmental writing, we searched for a textbook that would actively lead students through each step of writing an essay. Our ideal text would be complete, offering a rhetoric, a reader, and a handbook. It would also let students choose their own topics and enable them at the outset of the course to write whole essays. It would offer many models of the writing process, allow students to read and write about their own cultural contexts, and help them use computer technology to enhance their writing. This book would also teach critical thinking, would engage students in collaborative learning activities, and would help students apply what they learn in class to other classes and the workplace. Above all, it would respect the wealth of knowledge and experience that developmental students bring into their writing classroom.

Because we were never able to find such a book, we decided to write *Choices: A Basic Writing Guide with Readings*. Now in its third edition, *Choices* offers developmental students comprehensive step-by-step instruction for writing expressive, informative, and persuasive essays. It showcases the writing process, presents a wide variety of engaging assignments, and maintains a respectful tone. It strengthens students' reading, thinking, and writing skills; validates their diverse and unique cultural experiences; and helps them use computers and the Internet for communication and learning. Most importantly, it builds students' confidence by encouraging them to think of themselves as writers with important ideas to communicate in college and in the workplace. This approach works because, rather than simply talking about how to write, it gets students actively involved in writing.

THE ORGANIZATION

Choices is divided into four sections: Part One, "The Writing Process"; Part Two, "Writing to Share Ideas"; Part Three, "Writing for Different Situations"; and Part Four, a grammar handbook with exercises.

Part One presents three introductory chapters that help students view writing as a purposeful, creative endeavor. Chapter 1 introduces two important themes of the book: how reading can improve writing and how computer technology can enhance writing and learning. Chapter 2 presents the stages of the writing process and follows one student through each stage. Chapter 3 focuses on the elements of good paragraphs, giving students the opportunity to learn and practice the essential building block of the essay.

Each of the six chapters in Part Two, "Writing to Share Ideas," presents a writing assignment, reading selections, and a guide to writing an expressive, an informative, or a persuasive essay on a particular theme. Instructors can select the chapters that best fit their goals and students' interests. Each chapter includes the following elements and shows how one student carried out the assignment:

Writing Assignment

- A photograph and quotation introduce students to the chapter's writing assignment. The assignment at the beginning of the chapter tells students the type of essay they will be expected to write.

Gathering Ideas

- Students begin by reading and responding to three essays by professional writers that present models for writing and that offer ideas for students to explore.
- Students then gather ideas about the three topics in the chapter's readings, thus gaining a rich source of materials for their own essays through activities such as prewriting, consulting with others, questioning, and reflecting.

Drafting

- In preparation for drafting, students select one of the three topics about which they have gathered ideas, or they combine two or more of the topics.
- To help students write a discovery draft, the chapter includes an example of how one student writer moved from gathering ideas to drafting.

Revising

- The "Revising" section of each chapter presents the core of the rhetorical instruction. Explanations are concise and are supported by numerous activities and models from both student and professional writers.

- Students use peer review to critique each other's drafts, guided by assignment-specific questions that reinforce the chapter's instruction.
- Students revise their drafts, using instructions in the chapter and their own classmates' suggestions. The chapter also presents a revised version of the student draft as a model.

Editing

- Students edit their drafts by learning and practicing elements of grammar, spelling, and punctuation and by referring to the handbook in Part Four. During the editing process, they record errors (with corrections) in an Editing Log, so they can avoid them in the future. Again, an edited version of the student essay that appeared in draft and revised form models the editing process.

Publishing

- Students publish, or share with their audience, their final essays. Depending on the chapter's assignment, they might share their essay with friends or family, submit it to their school or local newspaper, or send it via e-mail to readers around the world.

Chapter Checklist

- Each chapter includes a chapter checklist, providing an opportunity for students to check off what they have learned in that chapter.

Reflecting on Your Writing

- Finally, students reflect on their writing experience and complete a Writing Process Report, identifying their strengths, weaknesses, and plans for continued improvement.

Additional Readings

- Each chapter concludes with three additional professional models, on the same topics as the earlier chapter readings, to provide students with more ideas for their writing.

The four chapters in Part Three, "Writing for Different Situations," provide instruction in and support for the writing assigned in

Part Two as well as in various academic situations. This part covers journals (Chapter 10), research (Chapter 11), timed writing tests (Chapter 12), and portfolios (Chapter 13).

As students work on assignments in Parts One, Two, and Three, they can easily refer to Part Four, a concise handbook of grammar, usage, punctuation, spelling, and mechanics. The handbook is meant to be a practical resource, showing students how to identify and correct problems rather than explaining grammatical concepts and terms at length. Numerous activities provide practice in correcting common errors, and boxed material as well as two separate sections highlight guidelines and grammar for multilingual students.

THE FEATURES

Step-by-Step Guidance through the Writing Process

Each of the six chapters in Part Two walks students through the steps of the writing process: gathering ideas, drafting, revising, editing, and publishing (sharing their work with others). The chapters provide abundant writing activities at every stage. The emphasis throughout is on helping students communicate effectively to a specific audience rather than simply practicing a particular mode of writing.

A Choice of Writing Topics

In each of the six chapters in Part Two, activities following the readings prompt students to gather ideas about three potential topics for their essays, a feature that inspired the title of the text, *Choices*. This approach to choosing a topic allows students to select the ones that interest them most, ensuring that they do their best work because they care about the topic.

Models of the Writing Process

Each chapter in Part Two shows how one student writer carried out the assignment at every stage, producing three complete drafts — discovery, revised, and edited. Students thus have an example for every stage of the writing process rather than a single completed sample.

A Progression of Topics and Skills

The chapters in Part Two are progressive in three ways. First, the chapters present rhetorical skills in a progression, moving from expressive to informative to persuasive writing; by the end of Part Two, students are prepared to do rudimentary primary and secondary research. Second, the themes move from personal matters to the cultural and social issues that are often the subject of academic writing. Third, in each chapter the progression of the writing process—gathering ideas, drafting, revising, editing, and publishing—strengthens students' writing skills through consistent practice.

Advice on Writing with a Computer

Throughout the text, computer and Web tips in boxes offer on-the-spot information about how to use word processing, how to use e-mail in collaborative writing, and how to use the Internet and the World Wide Web to facilitate research or locate writing resources. Many of the Web tips refer students to the *Choices* Web site, where they will find additional instruction, resources, and the opportunity to practice grammar skills by using Exercise Central. We also seek to increase students' awareness of the benefits and hazards of computer technology. For example, one writing topic in Chapter 8 addresses the issue of free expression on the Internet, and the student model in Chapter 9 is about identifying problems in a college computer lab.

Integrated Reading and Writing Instruction

Because good writers are also good readers, we provide instruction in reading as well as writing. Chapter 1 shows students how to read as writers read—to discover ideas, learn rhetorical strategies, and expand their vocabulary. Students practice these skills throughout Part Two. Each reading selection is followed by questions about content and rhetoric. Students are also asked to define unfamiliar vocabulary by guessing the meaning through context or turning to a dictionary. When new rhetorical strategies are presented, many examples are drawn from the chapter's readings.

Emphasis on Diversity

Students are invited at every opportunity to make connections between their own cultural experiences and their writing. In Chapter 5, "Examining Cultures," the assignment asks them to write about their cultures; in addition, writing models, reading selections, and rhetorical examples throughout the text represent a diversity of cultural backgrounds, encouraging students to add their own voices to the exchanges within the classroom community.

Opportunities for Collaboration

In sharing knowledge, we become better critics of our own and others' writing, and we discover how to work with others. Toward these ends, *Choices* offers more than fifty collaborative activities; some of these can be carried out electronically using e-mail and the Internet. Throughout Part Two, for example, students form peer groups to work on their drafts. These collaborative activities help make the classroom a community of writers.

Emphasis on Critical Thinking

Good critical thinking skills enable students to make effective decisions as writers. Therefore, we emphasize critical thinking in each writing assignment. We also pose questions after each reading to encourage students to reflect on the content and the writer's rhetorical strategies. The critical thinking skills taught in each chapter gradually become more advanced. By the end of the book, students can distinguish fact from opinion and can recognize logical fallacies—skills that help bring success in life as well as in higher education.

Help with Primary and Secondary Research

As college students, developmental writers need to gather information from a variety of print and electronic sources without being overwhelmed by an endless research process. To this end, Chapter 6 introduces students to locating, summarizing, and citing sources. For more in-depth help with research, students can be directed to Chapter 11, which explains how to conduct interviews, surveys, and observations; how to locate, evaluate, and cite library and Internet sources; how to take notes and avoid plagiarism; how to summarize, paraphrase, and quote information; and how to follow the MLA documentation style. This instruction is presented in the context of specific writing assignments, making research a purposeful activity rather than an academic exercise.

WHAT'S NEW

The many excellent suggestions that we have gathered from students and instructors who used the first two editions of *Choices* have helped us to strengthen the text's proven features and add others that will make the text even more useful in the classroom.

A New Chapter: "Investigating the Workplace"

Because so many students also work while attending college or are thinking about their future careers, a new chapter (Chapter 6), "Investigating the Workplace," invites them to write and think about this important part of their lives. This chapter encourages students to explore various occupations, analyze the language used in the workplace, and solve potential workplace problems.

New Readings

More than half of the professional model essays that begin each chapter in Part Two have been replaced with more interesting, effective models. To provide an even wider variety of sample essays, three additional readings now conclude each of these chapters. A total of thirty-six readings in Part Two now offers students a wide variety of model essays and instructors greater flexibility as they plan assignments.

New How-To Boxes

Through bulleted lists and practical advice, these boxes quickly review the key concepts in each chapter. Students can use these boxes to check their understanding, remember important points, or apply the chapter discussion to their own writing. Instructors who wish to prepare transparencies can download the How-To boxes from the *Choices* Web site at <www.bedfordstmartins.com/choices>.

New Material on Polishing Sentences and Editing Common Errors

Each chapter in Part Two includes new instruction and practice in sentence coordination and subordination, including additional sentence combining activities. Each chapter in Part Two also includes more instruction on editing common grammar, spelling, and punctuation errors, expanding the opportunities for students to locate and correct these errors.

Expanded Section for Multilingual Writers

As in the previous edition, instruction for multilingual writers appears throughout the handbook. In addition, coverage has been expanded to two separate sections at the end of the handbook, now including comparisons of English with other languages and dialects, characteristics of English discourse, and ways to build vocabulary.

Enhanced Computer Tips

With updated advice for students who are writing on computers, these boxes help students use computer software to their advantage at each stage of the writing process and in a variety of writing situations.

Expanded Web Tips

For those students connected to the Internet, tips on using the World Wide Web suggest additional ways to research their topics and collaborate during all stages of the writing process. Special care has been taken to refer students to the special features of the *Choices* Web site, which has been expanded to provide additional resources for developmental writers.

More Helpful Chapter Checklists

Chapter summaries have been converted to Chapter Checklists, providing a more interactive way for students to review the chapter contents by checking off whether they have learned and practiced each of the skills covered in the chapters.

INSTRUCTIONAL RESOURCES

To make *Choices* even easier for instructors to use in the classroom, we have prepared the following ancillaries for the third edition:

- The Instructor's Annotated Edition of *Choices* provides on-the-spot teaching advice, as well as resource tips and answers to activities and exercises. At the end of the Instructor's Annotated Edition, a separate "Resources for Instructors" section provides information on the text's approach as well as practical guidelines for teaching writing and evaluating student writing. Topics featured in the "Polishing" and "Editing" sections throughout the book are now listed here to simplify finding them quickly. Sample syllabi suggest how to plan semester or quarter courses at different levels, and a list of the readings in the text, classified by method of development, facilitates locating specific rhetorical models. For this third edition, information on teaching writing to multilingual students has been added.
- Exercise Central is the largest collection of grammar exercises available. It is thorough, simple to use, and convenient for both students and instructors. Multiple-exercise sets on every topic, at a variety of levels, ensure that students have as much practice

as they need. Customized, immediate feedback for all answers turns skill practice into a learning experience, and a reporting feature allows both students and instructors to monitor and assess student progress. A link to Exercise Central is available at the Web site for *Choices*, and cross references from the book guide students to the appropriate exercises.

- The World Wide Web connects students to each other and to the world, making our classrooms global communities. It is for this reason that we have created a companion Web site for this book at <www.bedfordstmartins.com/choices>. The companion site includes a variety of online assignments, FAQs for writing and teaching, and links to Exercise Central and other resources.

ACKNOWLEDGMENTS

Choices reflects years of collaboration with students, teachers, and editors, and we are especially grateful to the many students at The University of Texas at El Paso who helped us pilot the new materials for this book. Our special thanks go to Jesus Ramirez, Sandra Cordero, and Leslie Lozano, who allowed us to use their writing. Instructors Cheryl Baker-Heller and Diane Fox gave us valuable insights and suggestions. Herminia Hemmitt, Erica Loya, and Karla Jaramillo helped with the details of copying and mailing manuscript copy. Elizabeth Mangelsdorf contributed her excellent photographs to the project.

We would like to thank the following instructors who responded to a detailed questionnaire about their use of the text: Patricia Ann Baldwin, Pitt Community College; Melissa Batai, Triton College; Virgina Brackett, Triton College; Rafael Castillo, Palo Alto College; Avon Crismore, Indiana-Purdue University; Debra Deroian, Bristol Community College; Michael Dinelli, Chaffey College; Rick Dollieslager, Thomas Nelson Community College; Julia L. Fennell, Community College of Allegheny County; Ruth Ann Gambino, Palo Alto College; Robin Grissom, Indiana-Purdue University; JoAnne James, Pitt Community College; Leela Kapai, Prince George's Community College; Mary Ann Lee, Longview Community College; Carol Ludovissy, Northeast Iowa Community College; Linda Kissler, Westmoreland County Community College; Jill A. Makagon, Kapiolani Community College; Mark James Miller, Allan Hancock College; Joe Nordern, Lamar University; Sharon Owen, University of Texas at El Paso; Leslie Prast, Delta College; Dorothy Reade, North Harris College; Jane Leach Rudawski, Minneapolis Community and Technical College; Nancy Shaffer, University of Texas at El Paso; Gloria Shearin, Savannah State University; Ingrid Shreck, Chaffey Community College; Susan Spence,

University of Texas at El Paso; John Stacy, Barstow College; Kathy Stein, University of Texas at El Paso; Helen Szymanski, College of DuPage; Margaret Waguepack, Amarillo College; Ted Walkup, Clayton College; Teresa Ward, Butte College; June Wenzel, Parkland College; James Willis, Delta College; and Marilyn Wilton, Clovis Community College.

We also thank the following reviewers for many suggestions that were incorporated into the text: Cathryn Amdahl, Harrisburg Area Community College; Diane Armstrong, Ventura College; Jean D. Chamberlain, Mississippi University for Women; Susan Guzmán-Treviño, Temple College; Martina Kusi-Mensah, Montgomery College (Texas); Heather Mitchell, Montgomery College (Texas); Donald Masterson, State University of New York at Oswego; Amanda McBride, Durham Technical Community College; Mary Mears, Macon State College; Michael D. Roberts, Fresno City College; William Sweigart, Indiana University Southeast; and Nancy A. Teel, Roxbury Community College. For helpful comments on the new section for multilingual writers, we would like to thank Mark Picus, Houston Community College–Central and Bob Hemmer. Finally, we are grateful to Sandy Fuhr of Gustavus Adolphus College for her comments on the new chapter on research.

We need to thank Juliett Tubbs for developing materials for the *Choices* Web site. For helpful comments on the Web site, we would also like to thank the following reviewers: Dianne Armstrong, Ventura College; Amy Braziller, Red Rocks Community College; Beth Camp, Linn-Benton Community College; Martina Kusi-Mensah, Montgomery College; Amanda McBride, Durham Technical College; Heather Mitchell, Montgomery College; Michael Roberts, Fresno City College; Ingrid Schreck, Chaffey College; and William Sweigart, Indiana University Southeast.

Additional thanks go to Marcia Muth, a knowledgeable, patient, and evenhanded editor who made completing this book a pleasure. At Bedford/St. Martin's, Ben Morrison's support, insight, creativity, and sense of humor in supervising this project are greatly appreciated. We also thank Michael Weber for ably guiding the text through the production process.

Kate Mangelsdorf
Evelyn Posey

BRIEF CONTENTS

CONTENTS

CHAPTER 3

Crafting Paragraphs   57

Part Two: Writing to Share Ideas   97

CHAPTER 4

Showing the Ways We Change   99

CHAPTER 5

Examining Cultures   167

CHAPTER 6

Investigating the Workplace 239

CHAPTER 8

Debating the Limits of Free Expression   373

CHAPTER 9

Identifying Issues, Proposing Solutions   447

Part Three: Writing For Different Situations   505

CHAPTER 10

Keeping a Journal   *507*

CHAPTER 11

Conducting Primary, Library, and Internet Research   *521*

CHAPTER 12

Taking Timed Writing Tests   567

CHAPTER 13

Assembling a Writing Portfolio   593

The Writing Process

1. Composing Ourselves, Writing for Others

2. The Writing Process

3. Crafting Paragraphs

Writing is an important way to communicate—in class, in the workplace, and for personal enjoyment. With the growing popularity of computers, many of us are writing more than ever by communicating electronically via the Internet. As a result, good writing skills are a must.

In Part One, you'll discover why writers write and how they go about getting their ideas on paper. You'll discover your own writing process and begin to use it to communicate the important ideas you have to share. You'll also learn how to write effective paragraphs, an important step when putting your ideas in writing.

We are all apprentices in a craft where no one ever becomes a master. —ERNEST HEMINGWAY

CHAPTER 1

Composing Ourselves, Writing for Others

In this chapter you will

- examine different purposes for writing.
- learn how to analyze your audience.
- learn the importance of standard written English.
- explore the composing process.
- discover the importance of a writer's space and routine.
- learn how to read to improve your writing.

What comes into your mind when you think of a writer? You might remember a writer you studied in school, such as William Shakespeare, Langston Hughes, or Emily Dickinson. Or you might think of the stereotypes we have of writers. One stereotype is of a newspaper writer who pounds out a late-breaking story on a computer minutes before a deadline. Another common stereotype of a writer is someone who wears a beret, lives in a cold attic, composes brilliant poems on scraps of paper, and dies before receiving any recognition. Or maybe you picture a writer you like to read, such as Maya Angelou, Stephen King, or Dave Barry. Our favorite writers can inspire us, teach us, entertain us, scare us, and make us cry.

WRITING ASSIGNMENT

Your first assignment is to "compose yourself" as a writer. Think back over your life to discover the moments that helped you become a literate person—that is, a person who can read and write, comprehend and communicate.

You might want to get your ideas flowing by writing for a few minutes nonstop in response to each of the following questions:

- What would you consider to be some of the most important reading and writing events in your life? Consider not only formal writing assignments for school or work, but letters, journals, and e-mail messages.
- What languages have you used for writing? Do you prefer writing in one language or another? How would you compare your literacy in these languages?
- Who was most influential in your development as a reader and writer? How did this person influence you?
- Can you recall any times when you felt inadequate as a reader or writer? What was the event? Why did you feel this way? What changes did you make as a result?
- Do you think your reading and writing skills will develop and change? How? Why?
- What three words best describe you as reader? Discuss these three words.
- What three words best describe you as a writer? Discuss these three words.

Use your best ideas to write a story for your classmates and instructor about how you became a literate person and how you plan to develop your reading and writing skills.

But writers are more common than you might at first imagine. A consumer who writes a letter to the electric company is a writer. So is a student who completes a report for a course, a child who writes her name for the first time, a father who records the birth of his baby in a journal, and an engineer who writes a proposal to build a bridge. A lover who sends a valentine is a writer, and so is an angry voter who composes a letter to the city council. A writer is anyone who uses written language to communicate a feeling, a fact, or an opinion.

In our world of computers, fax machines, and electronic mail, more of us are required to write. The title of this chapter, "Composing Ourselves, Writing for Others," refers to the people we write for—ourselves and others. Composing ourselves means that we write to create and express ourselves. Just as a writer of music uses various sounds to compose and play a piece of music, we use words to discover and communicate our identities. Our words reveal what we think, believe, and feel. Writing for others means that we also write to affect the way others think, believe, and feel. Thus, composing ourselves and writing for others are closely connected facets of writing. We all need to communicate our ideas and feelings to the world. At the same time, we all use writing to discover and explore our thoughts.

Online Writing Assignments

The *Choices* Web site provides additional writing assignments to be completed online. Go to <www.bedford stmartins.com/choices/> and click on "Assignments."

A WRITER'S PURPOSE

Whenever you write, whether for yourself or others, you have a *purpose.* Most writing—including the kind you'll do in this textbook—is primarily expressive, informative, or persuasive.

Expressive Writing

In *expressive writing,* writers communicate their thoughts, feelings, and personal history. When you keep a diary, write a letter to a friend, or tell about something that happened to you, you're writing expressively.

In the following example of expressive writing, student Scott Weckerly describes the morning he left home for college.

The impact of saying good-bye and actually leaving did not hit me until the day of my departure. Its strength woke me an hour before my alarm clock would, as for the last time Missy, my golden retriever, greeted me with a big, sloppy lick. I hated it when she did that, but that day I welcomed her with open arms. I petted her with long, slow strokes, and her sad eyes gazed into mine. Her coat felt more silky than usual. Of course, I did not notice any of these qualities until that day, which made me all the sadder about leaving her.

This sample paragraph is expressive because it describes Weckerly's thoughts and feelings at an important time in his life. When he tells us that the reality of his departure didn't sink in until that morning, we understand what he was thinking. By describing his reactions to his dog, we know he was sad about leaving home. In re-creating an important incident in his life, Weckerly's writing is expressive.

Informative Writing

We write not only to express ourselves but also to convey information. *Informative writing* explains: it tells how something works or how to do something, what something looks like, how two things are alike or different, the cause of an event or its outcome. Informative writing typically uses facts, examples, or statistics. Most writing we encounter is informative. Nutritional labels on food containers are informative, as are directions on how to set up a computer or administer CPR. Textbooks, including the one you're reading now, are also in this category. Most sections of the newspaper are informative.

The following example of informative writing is from the *New York Times*.

It has been five years since the attitude-laden rhythm-and-blues pop harmony group TLC released a follow-up to its 10-million-selling album "Crazysexycool." But yesterday its new record, "Fan Mail" (Arista/LaFace), went to No. 1 on the pop charts.

—Neil Strauss, "TLC Returns from the Brink"

This piece of writing is informative because the author uses facts and statistics to compare the sales of TLC's previous album with the sales of its current album.

Persuasive Writing

Persuasive writing differs from expressive and informative writing because it attempts to change a reader's opinion or convince a reader to take a particular action. Newspaper editorials and advertisements are two types of persuasive writing. The *Times Picayune* wants you to support the school bond issue, and Ben and Jerry's wants you to buy its brand of ice cream. Some of the world's most memorable writing is persuasive, such as these words from President John F. Kennedy's 1961 inaugural address: "Ask not what your country can do for you; ask what you can do for your country."

Martin Luther King Jr.'s famous "I Have a Dream" speech is another example of persuasive writing. His purpose was to motivate civil rights workers to continue striving for racial equality. Here's an excerpt:

> Go back to Mississippi, go back to Alabama, go back to South Carolina, go back to Georgia, go back to Louisiana, go back to the slums and ghettos of our northern cities, knowing that somehow this situation can and will be changed. Let us not wallow in the valley of despair.

As with many persuasive pieces, King's audience is urged to believe something—in this case, that the battle for civil rights will be won. At the same time, the audience is told to do something: King wants the marchers to return home to continue the fight.

A Primary Purpose

While most writing is primarily expressive, informative, or persuasive, rarely is a piece of writing entirely one type. Much of the time, all three types occur in a single piece. In the following essay, "Mind/Body Programming," psychologist Joan Borysenko explains the concept of conditioning. What is an essay? An essay is an arrangement of the author's best thoughts written in complete sentences and paragraphs; it's usually a few pages in length. Borysenko's essay has expressive, informative, and persuasive sections. As you read the essay, think about its primary purpose.

JOAN BORYSENKO
Mind/Body Programming

Every time you miss your exit on the highway because you are daydreaming, then "wake up" to discover yourself miles farther down the road, you are demonstrating the power of the unconscious mind. Once something is learned, we don't have to think about it consciously. The task simply repeats itself as soon

1

as we initiate the program—in this case, by putting the key in the ignition. The rest of driving is second nature because our nervous system has been conditioned—or imprinted—with the driving pattern.

Because of our conditioning, we are all creatures of habit.   2
Most people get anxious before taking an exam partly because they have become habituated to feeling anxious at exam time, whether or not the situation at hand is actually threatening. Once threatened by an exam, a neural connection is established. The next time an exam comes up, the probability is that we'll reactivate that same conditioned circuit.

Physiological conditioning is a kind of rapid learning that   3
evolved to help us master cause-and-effect situations that might determine survival. We all are familiar with Pavlov's famous experiment. A dog is given meat powder, which naturally makes him salivate. A bell is then rung every time the meat powder is presented. After a time the dog salivates merely at the sound of the bell. We see the same mechanism operating in ourselves when we're working away contentedly, then glance up at the clock, notice it's lunch time, and suddenly become hungry.

The mind's power to affect the body through conditioning   4
became crystal clear to me when I was six or seven years old. My Uncle Dick, a confirmed cheese hater, was eating Sunday dinner with us. For dessert there was a cheesecake camouflaged with ripe strawberries. It was so good that he ate two pieces. About an hour later my mother expressed her surprise at Uncle Dick's delight in the dessert, since she knew how much he hated cheese. At the sound of the word cheese, Uncle Dick turned pale, began to gag, and ran for the bathroom. Even as a child it was obvious to me that the problem was not the cheese itself, but some mental conditioning about cheese that produced such a violent reaction.

Many people who receive chemotherapy for cancer get sick   5
to their stomachs from the medication. Soon, through conditioning similar to Uncle Dick's, they begin to get sick before they actually receive the drugs. Some people begin to get nauseous the night before treatment. Others may get nauseous coming to the hospital or even upon seeing their doctor or nurse. They have involuntarily learned to get sick as a conditioned response to the thoughts, sights, and smells of the chemotherapy situation.

What we've learned from Soviet studies following Pavlov's   6
model is that the immune system itself can be conditioned. In this country Dr. Robert Ader and Dr. Nicholas Cohen at the University of Rochester injected rats with an immunosuppressant

drug called cyclophosphamide and at the same time added a new taste—saccharin—to the animals' drinking water. The saccharin acted like Pavlov's bell. After a while the rats were suppressing their immunity at the taste of saccharin alone.

Dr. G. Richard Smith and Sandra McDaniel did a fascinating study of the suppression of immune reactions in humans. Once a month for five months, volunteers who had reacted positively in a tuberculin skin test came into the same room with the same arrangement of furniture and the same nurse. Each time they saw a red and green vial on the desk, and each time the contents of the red vial—tuberculin—were injected into the same arm, and the contents of the green vial—a salt solution—were injected into the other. 7

Month after month the same procedure was followed, and month after month the volunteers had the same reaction to the tuberculin—a red swollen patch on the same arm. There was never any reaction to the injection of the salt solution in the other arm. 8

On the sixth trial the contents of the vials were switched without the volunteers' knowledge. And this time the volunteers had almost no reaction to the tuberculin. Their expectation that nothing ever happened after the injection from the green vial apparently was enough to inhibit the immune system's powerful inflammatory response to tuberculin. 9

Conditioning is a powerful bridge between mind and body. . . . The reason is that the body cannot tell the difference between events that are actual threats to survival and events that are present in thought alone. The mind spins out endless fantasies of possible disasters past and future. This tendency to escalate a situation into its worst possible conclusion is what I call awfulizing, and it can be a key factor in tipping the balance toward illness or health. Perhaps you're hung up in traffic, sure to be late for an important 9 a.m. meeting. Or it's midnight and your child is still out, or the doctor tells you she wants to repeat a test, or so on in endless variation. The flood of "what ifs" and "if onlys" engages the various human emotions, which can influence virtually all bodily functions. 10

The way our minds work—the degree to which we awfulize—also depends on previous conditioning. The responses of our parents and other influential role models shape our own reactions to life. Awareness of our conditioning is the first step toward unlearning attitudes that have outlived their usefulness. Such awareness opens our ability to respond to what is happening now rather than reacting out of a conditioned history that may be archaic. . . . 11

HOW TO Know Your Purpose for Writing

- *Expressive:* You write to communicate your thoughts, feelings, and personal history.

- *Informative:* You write to explain something that you learned: how it works, what it looks like, the cause or outcome of an event.

- *Persuasive:* You write to convince others of your opinion.

Although all three purposes can appear in one piece of writing, the *primary purpose* is the one that you consider the most important reason for writing that piece.

ACTIVITY 1

Identifying the Primary Purpose. Answer these questions about Borysenko's essay.

1. Where does Borysenko use expressive writing in her essay?

   _____

   _____

   _____

2. Where does Borysenko use informative writing?

   _____

   _____

   _____

3. Where does Borysenko use persuasive writing?

   _____

   _____

   _____

4. What is Borysenko's primary purpose in this essay?

_____

_____

_____

5. Give an example of conditioning in your own life.

_____

_____

_____

ACTIVITY 2

Identifying Purpose. Identify the following paragraphs as primarily expressive, informative, or persuasive.

1. From the *Comtrad Industries Catalog:*

   We are so confident that the 900 MHz cordless phone is the best phone on the market that we challenge you to compare it to any other. For a limited time, you can buy the 900 MHz phone at the factory-direct introductory price of $399. Try it for 30 days. If you don't agree that this phone gives you incredible clarity and convenience, return it for a full refund.

   Purpose: _____

2. From Frommer's *Australia* by Elizabeth Hansen:

   Is Paul Hogan in *Crocodile Dundee* a typical Aussie? Some Australians might like you to think so, but facts show that less than 15% of the population lives in rural areas. Instead, the average Australian lives in one of eight capital cities and has never seen native fauna anywhere but in a zoo or wildlife park.

   Purpose: _____

3. From *Silent Spring* by Rachel Carson:

   The thin layer of soil that forms a patchy covering over the continents controls our own existence and that of every other animal of the land. Without soil, land plants as we know them could not grow, and without plants no animals could survive.

Purpose: _____

4. From the *American Association of Retired Persons Bulletin:*

We must create a more positive and accurate image of aging and help people recognize that people are living longer, more productive lives. As a nation, we must let go of our obsession with the number of years in life and focus instead on the life in those years.

Purpose: _____

5. From *One Writer's Beginnings* by Eudora Welty:

Of course it's easy to see why they both overprotected me, why my father, before I could wear a new pair of shoes for the first time, made me wait while he took out his thin silver pocket knife and with the point of the blade scored the polished soles all over, carefully, in a diamond pattern, to prevent me from sliding on the polished floor when I ran.

Purpose: _____

ACTIVITY 3 (GROUP)

Discovering Purposes for Writing. Bring to class three pieces of writing composed by you or someone else. For example, bring a letter you wrote to a friend or relative, an article from your campus newspaper, the recording notes to a CD, a flier from an election campaign, or your favorite recipe. Identify each piece of writing as primarily expressive, informative, or persuasive. Form a group with several classmates and exchange your pieces of writing. Do you and your classmates agree on the primary purpose of each piece?

FAQs

The *Choices* Web site includes frequently asked questions about topics in each chapter of the textbook. Go to <www .bedfordstmartins.com/choices/> and click on "FAQs."

A WRITER'S AUDIENCE

Whether your purpose is to express yourself or to inform or persuade others, your *audience* influences what you write. A writer's audience consists of those who will read the writing—yourself, family members, friends, classmates, instructors, colleagues at work, or political leaders. The possibilities are limitless.

Writing to an audience is not the same as speaking to an audience. In fact, writing has some advantages. Have you ever said something you wished you could take back? This is less likely to happen when you write because you can revise your words before your audience sees them. If you're shy, you might prefer to communicate through writing rather than face-to-face.

Writing is also different from speaking because your audience isn't actually in front of you. When you speak, your audience can smile, frown, or ask you questions. When you write, however, you must envision, or picture in your mind, how your readers will respond to your words. To envision your audience, ask yourself these questions:

- Who are my readers? Sometimes your reader is someone very specific, such as your sociology professor who will read your term paper or fellow students who will see your flier about an upcoming event at the student union. At other times, your readers will be the general educated public, such as subscribers to the local newspaper who read your letter to the editor.

- What do my readers know about my topic? Your readers' knowledge of the topic is important because you don't want to bore them by telling them what they already know. Instead, you want to tell them something new—where they might go for spring break, how to fix their VCR, whom they should vote for in the next election.

- What do my readers need to know about my topic? Answering this question can help you decide how much information you need to give your readers. For instance, if you're explaining how to change a tire, will your readers know what a tire jack is? Or must you describe it and explain how to use it?

- How do my readers feel about my topic? If your readers know nothing about your topic or might even find it dull, you'll want to find a way to get their interest. Or your readers may be opposed to your message. If you're writing a letter asking your supervisor for a raise, don't assume that he or she will automatically agree with you. Instead, try to anticipate your supervisor's reasons for not giving you a raise and take them into account when you make your case.

ACTIVITY 4

Analyzing Your Audience. Imagine that you're writing to a close friend or family member asking for a loan to buy a car. Analyze your audience using these questions.

1. What does my reader already know about my financial situation?

   _____

   _____

2. What does my reader know about why I need a car?

   _____

   _____

3. What does my reader not know that he or she needs to know?

   _____

   _____

4. How will my reader feel about my request?

   _____

   _____

   Now, imagine that you're writing to a loan officer at a bank asking for a loan to buy a car, and answer these same four questions.

1. What does my reader already know about my financial situation?

   _____

   _____

2. What does my reader know about why I need a car?

   _____

   _____

3. What does my reader not know that he or she needs to know?

_____

_____

4. How will my reader feel about my request?

_____

_____

Answer one more question.

5. How and why do your answers differ when your reader changes?

_____

_____

_____

ACTIVITY 5

Getting to Know Your Readers. Sometimes your readers will be your classmates, so you'll want to get to know them. To start, use these questions to interview a classmate about his or her first name. Then trade places so your classmate can interview you.

1. Who gave you your name, and why?
2. Do you know the history, origin, or definition of your name? What is it?
3. Do you have any nicknames? What are they?
4. How do you feel about your name?
5. If you could change your name, what would you change it to? Why?

After you and your classmate interview each other, write non-stop for five minutes about your classmate's name. Introduce your classmate to the rest of the class by reading what you have written. Your classmate should then introduce you to the class in the same way.

STANDARD WRITTEN ENGLISH

You may identify yourself as an English-speaking person, but actually you speak a dialect of English. A dialect is a variety of a language, and every language has many dialects. Dialects are characterized by pronunciation, word choice, and sentence structure. People speak different dialects based on where they live and their ethnic backgrounds. Here are some examples of dialects.

1. From *The Quilters: Women and Domestic Art.* Rosie Fischer is talking in 1974 about her life on a farm in Rowlett, Texas:

   Well, anyway, I was dreaming on havin' all kinds of pretty things in my home after I married. Well, I found out right quick that livin' out on a farm, what with all the chores that had to be done, a person didn't have a whole lot of time for makin' pretty things.

2. From Robert Kimmel Smith's *Sadie Shapiro's Knitting Book,* a novel about a Jewish widow from Queens:

   "Listen, darling," Sadie said patiently, "we all have our ways and that's it. . . . I lived with my son Stuart and his wife for three years after my Reuben died, he should find eternal peace. And what happened? My daughter-in-law and I drove each other crazy. I'm a neat person, I think you can tell that, but she. . . . Well, I wouldn't exactly call her a slob, but the best housekeeper in the world she isn't. Not that I want to talk badly about her, mind you. But by me you don't wash a floor with a mop. That's not what I call clean."

3. From "Black Children, Black Speech," an essay by Dorothy Z. Seymour:

   "C'mon, man, les git goin'!" called the boy to his companion. "Dat bell ringin'. It say, 'Git in rat now!' " He dashed into the school yard.

   "Aw, f'get you," replied the other. "Whe' Richuh? Whe' da muvvuh? He be goin' to schoo'."

   "He in de' now, man!" was the answer as they went through the door.

Northern, southern, and midwestern dialects have developed from the languages spoken by European immigrants. The structure of African American spoken English is similar to several West African languages. In the Southwest and California, dialects such as Chicano English have developed as a result of Mexican immigration.

All these dialects are different from standard English, which is taught in American schools and used in business, government, and the media. The written version of standard English is standard written English, or SWE for short.

The following examples show the differences between standard written English and three dialects.

AFRICAN AMERICAN SPOKEN ENGLISH	He always be walkin' dere.
SWE	He always walks there.
CHICANO ENGLISH	They put his broken arm a cast.
SWE	They put his broken arm in a cast.
CREOLE ENGLISH	In Main Street have plenty shop.
SWE	Main Street has plenty of shops.

Standard written English is generally considered the appropriate language to use in school and business. However, no language is better than another; languages are just different. Standard written English is a tool that will help you advance in college and in your workplace. It doesn't replace the other regional or ethnic dialects you might speak; it just adds to them.

ACTIVITY 6 (GROUP)

Thinking about Standard Written English. Working in a group of several students, discuss the following questions. Ask one member of the group to summarize your discussion for the rest of the class.

1. Why are you learning standard written English?
2. What is your attitude toward SWE and your experience with it?
3. In your opinion, is too much or too little value placed on SWE? Why?

 ESL Links

The *Choices* Web site includes links to useful ESL sites. Go to <www.bedfordstmartins.com/choices/> and click on "ESL Links."

A WRITER'S COMPOSING PROCESS

It's easy to think of writing as simply putting words on paper. In reality, however, we use a particular *writing process* or method of writing. Generally, here is the writing process that many writers follow:

- Gathering ideas to write about
- Drafting to explore ideas
- Revising one of these drafts
- Editing the draft for SWE, grammar, spelling, and punctuation
- Publishing, or sharing, the final draft with an audience

Whether you pass through every stage of this process depends partly on your audience and purpose. If you're jotting down a grocery list for your spouse, for instance, you might write "salad dressing," knowing that he or she will understand that you mean creamy low-fat ranch dressing because that's the kind both of you like. You don't worry about spelling or neatness, nor do you write a draft of your list and then revise it. Your purpose is to convey simple information to someone who will easily understand it.

But imagine yourself writing a letter to your city council because you think there should be a stoplight at a busy intersection near your house. You gather ideas by talking to the city traffic manager about how many cars use that intersection each day and how many accidents occurred there in the past year. You also interview neighbors whose children must cross the intersection on their way to and from school. Next, you write a draft of your letter and read it to a friend, who suggests how it can be improved. Then you rewrite the letter, perhaps several times, taking out unnecessary details and more forcefully restating your point in your conclusion. Finally, you edit the letter for correct grammar, spelling, and punctuation. This writing process might take several days, but in the end you have a well-written letter that might end up saving lives.

Your writing process—how you go about writing—changes each time you write. Sometimes you can simply write down what you're thinking, and that is sufficient. Other times you need to gather ideas, write and revise several drafts, and edit your final draft to eliminate errors. In this textbook you'll learn about this longer writing process because it applies to most college writing assignments. You'll also learn different strategies for each stage of the writing process—gathering ideas, drafting, revising, editing, and publishing.

Comparing Your Writing Process. One way to become a better writer is to exchange ideas about how people write. Compare your answers to the following questions with your classmates' answers. What can you learn from your classmates' writing processes?

1. In the writing I have done in the past, did I gather ideas, draft, revise, edit, and share my work? If not, what was my process?

   _____

   _____

   _____

2. What would I like to change about my writing process?

   _____

   _____

   _____

A WRITER'S SPACE AND ROUTINE

As a student, you probably prefer to take the same seat in your classes, even though you have the freedom to sit elsewhere. This seat has become your territory, and you're unsettled if you find another person sitting there. When you write, you probably also prefer being in your own territory—a space where you write best. Do you prefer a study room in the library or a chair at the kitchen table? Although you may find yourself jotting down ideas while on the bus or eating lunch, it's best to write in a setting that allows you to concentrate, where others in your life know you shouldn't be interrupted.

Developing routines can also make you a better writer. Do you prefer to write early in the morning or late at night? Do you prefer to work on a computer or to write in longhand? Do you need to read over your class notes before you get started? Do you like to take frequent breaks, or do you prefer to write nonstop until you complete a draft? The more you write, the more you'll find out which routines work best for you.

ACTIVITY 8

Thinking about Your Ideal Place and Time to Write. Respond to the following questions. If you need more room, use a separate piece of paper. When you're through, share your responses with your classmates. Then compile a list of different writing spaces and routines.

1. Where and when do I currently write?

   _____

   _____

   _____

2. What do I use to write—pen and paper, computer?

   _____

   _____

   _____

3. When I am in my writing space, what do I see in front of and on both sides of me? What do I hear, smell, feel, and taste?

   _____

   _____

   _____

4. What do I like about my writing space and routine? How could I improve one or both?

   _____

   _____

   _____

5. What is my ideal place to write? What is my ideal writing routine?

_____

_____

_____

READING TO IMPROVE WRITING

Many of us read a newspaper to keep up with what's going on around us, and it's always fun to read a book and then compare it with the movie version of the same story. Some people read during their commute to and from work to make the ride pass more quickly. At times reading occupies a particularly special place in our lives. Nancy Mairs, a writer whose physical disability prevents her from traveling, uses reading to explore exotic sites, as she describes in her essay "On Having Adventures."

> With Peter Matthiessen I have trekked across the Himalayas to the Crystal Mountain. One blistering July I moved with John McPhee to Eagle, Alaska, above the Arctic. David Bain has hiked me along a hundred and ten miles of Philippine coast, and Edward Abbey has paddled me down the Colorado River. I've ridden on the back of Robert Pirsig's motorcycle, climbed ninety-five feet to George Dyson's tree house, grown coffee in Kenya with Isak Dinesen. With wonder I contemplate the actions of these rugged and courageous figures.

The advantages of reading multiply when you read as writers read—to learn how to improve their writing. When you examine a piece of writing to learn how the author communicates a certain idea, you're like an athlete who watches a game to observe the moves of the players. Examining the writing strategies of a particular author helps you use these strategies in your own writing. If you read like a writer, you can learn ways to organize, develop, and express your ideas in your own writing.

Suppose you can't decide how to begin an informative paper on whales for your biology course. Around the same time, you read an article on hallucinogenic drugs in *Outside* magazine called "One Toad over the Line," written by Kevin Krajick. Here is its beginning:

> It's big, it looks like a cowpie with eyes, and many people believe it can bring them face to face with God. It's the Colorado

River toad, a once obscure amphibian whose fame has spread in recent years thanks to the venom secreted by its skin. When dried and smoked, the venom releases bufotenine, a substance that one California drug agent calls "the most potent, instantaneously acting hallucinogen we know."

From this paragraph you learn two strategies for beginning an essay. First, a startling comparison ("a cowpie with eyes") can get your audience's attention. Second, stating the topic of an essay (in this case, the hallucinogen bufotenine) at the beginning helps your audience understand right away what your piece is about.

HOW TO Be an Active Reader

1. Preview the text.
   - Think about the title and what it means to you.
   - Think about whether you recognize the author's name.
   - Read any headings, captions, charts, and lists.

2. Read the text.
   - Read carefully, underlining the most important points.
   - Circle and look up the meanings of words you don't know.
   - Briefly list the main points in the margin.

3. Write to comprehend and remember.
   - List or outline the most important points.
   - Write your personal reactions to what you have read.
   - Review these notes before class.

ACTIVITY 9

Sharing Favorite Books. Make a list of your favorite books or magazines. You might want to list them in different categories. For example, you could classify books as science fiction, romance, or horror, and magazines as music, fashion, or sports. As a class, compile a list of recommended readings.

Reading can also improve your vocabulary. Suppose that one of your favorite authors is the suspense novelist Mary Higgins Clark. Here's an excerpt from Clark's *While My Pretty One Sleeps,* a book about a fashion designer named Neeve:

> To Neeve's dismay, as she crossed Thirty-seventh Street she came face to face with Gordon Steuber. Meticulously dressed in a tan cashmere jacket over a brown-and-beige Scottish pullover, dark-brown slacks and Gucci loafers, with his blaze of curly brown hair, slender, even-featured face, powerful shoulders and narrow waist, Gordon Steuber could easily have had a successful career as a model. Instead, in his early forties, he was a shrewd business-man with an uncanny knack of hiring unknown young designers and exploiting them until they could afford to leave him.

The word *meticulously* might not be familiar to you, but from the context of this passage you can guess that it means "carefully" or "precisely." From this passage you can also guess that *uncanny* means "unusual" or "remarkable," and that *exploit* means "to use." Verify your guesses by looking up unfamiliar words in a dictionary.

HOW TO Make Vocabulary Cards

- As you read, circle words you don't know and can't guess from the context.

- Look up each word in a dictionary.

- Write one word each on one side of a three-by-five-inch index card.

- On the other side, write the definition and a sentence using the word.

- Review regularly, using these vocabulary cards to test your memory.

ACTIVITY 10

Collecting New Words. Read an article that interests you in your campus or local newspaper. Circle any words that are unfamiliar to you. Based on your understanding of the article, guess the meaning of each unfamiliar word. Then test your accuracy by looking the words up in a dictionary.

Keep a list or make vocabulary cards of new words and their meanings so you can refer to them when you read and write. Try to add at least five words a week to your list or cards.

Online Dictionaries

The *Choices* Web site includes dictionaries. Go to <www .bedfordstmartins.com/choices/> and click on "Annotated Web Links" and then choose one of the online dictionaries.

CHAPTER CHECKLIST

- ☐ You can have three purposes for writing:
  - ☐ Expressive writing communicates thoughts, feelings, or personal history.
  - ☐ Informative writing conveys information.
  - ☐ Persuasive writing seeks to change the reader's opinion or to convince the reader to take a particular action.
- ☐ Most writing is a combination of the expressive, informative, and persuasive types, but each piece will have a primary purpose.
- ☐ Your audience affects what you write. Identify your audience—your readers—and take into account what they know about your topic, what they don't know about your topic, and how they feel toward your topic.
- ☐ A dialect is a variety of a language. Every language has many dialects.
- ☐ Standard written English (SWE) is taught in American schools and used in business, government, and the media. It is important to learn SWE for writing in college and in the workplace.
- ☐ Most writers follow a writing process that consists of gathering ideas to write about, drafting to explore ideas, revising, editing, and publishing (or sharing the final draft with readers).
- ☐ You should find your best place to write and develop an effective routine for writing.
- ☐ Through reading you can learn writing strategies and improve your vocabulary.

Yes, it's hard to write, but it's harder not to. —CARL VAN DOREN

CHAPTER 2

The Writing Process

In this chapter you will

- learn about the stages of the writing process.

- discover your own writing process.

- follow one student through the writing process.

- reflect on your writing.

Imagine that you are taking a course in criminal justice, a field that includes law enforcement, courts of law, and the prison system. Your instructor gives you the following essay assignment. (As you might remember from Chapter 1, an essay is an arrangement of the author's best thoughts written in complete sentences and paragraphs. It's usually a few pages long.)

> Write a two-to-three-page essay in which you explain a problem in the criminal justice system. Suggest a solution for the problem.

What is your reaction to this assignment? Just the thought of it may cause you to tense up. How do you organize a paper like this? How do you find the right words to communicate what you have to say?

Writing in her journal, Amanda expressed her fears about the assignment:

> *I don't know enough about the criminal justice system to write this paper! How do I find information? How can I fill up the pages? How hard of a grader is this instructor? Because of my job, I don't have much time to work on it. I'll have to figure out how to do a good job on this assignment.*

Understanding how writers find ideas, organize them, and complete a writing assignment can help to relieve the fears associated with writing.

WRITING ASSIGNMENT

How do you react to writing assignments? Do you share any of Amanda's fears? Most students approach writing assignments with some degree of anxiety. Take a few minutes to reflect on your fears by writing about them. Then consider what you might do to overcome those fears.

Write a short essay for your instructor and fellow classmates in which you describe the steps you plan to take to overcome your anxiety about writing. Remember, to become a skilled writer, you need motivation, instruction, and practice. You may want to organize your essay around these ideas.

Other Students' Ideas

Read students' responses to this assignment on the *Choices* Web site. Go to <www.bedfordstmartins.com/choices/> and click on "Student Writing."

THE WRITING PROCESS

In Chapter 1, you learned the stages of the writing process:

- gathering ideas
- drafting
- revising
- editing
- publishing

You also learned that writers become more skilled through commitment, study, and practice. But how do they transform their commitment and practice into a polished piece of writing to be shared with readers and turned in for a grade? What do they do first, next, and last?

Polished writing is best completed over a period of time. Let's look at each stage of the writing process in more detail.

Gathering Ideas

The first stage, *gathering ideas,* includes all that you do before you actually begin to write a draft. Sometimes called *prewriting,* this stage involves activities such as writing, talking, reading, and thinking. In this stage, you first select a topic and narrow it to a manageable size.

SELECT A TOPIC. In many writing situations, someone—often an instructor or supervisor—will give you a general topic. Your job is to narrow that topic so that it's more manageable. In the criminal justice assignment, for example, you would need to decide on a problem in the criminal justice system to write about, and then think of a solution to that problem.

PURPOSE. In Chapter 1, you learned that most writing is primarily expressive, informative, or persuasive. Since the criminal justice assignment asks you to explain a problem in the criminal justice system, your purpose would be primarily informative.

The purposes for writing are explained on pp. 5–12.

AUDIENCE. As you begin to think about the assignment, you also want to keep your reader in mind. After all, you're writing this essay to communicate something of interest, so you want to be sure the reader gets your message. The more you know about your reader, the easier it will be for you to write.

Turn to p. 13 for more help understanding your audience.

You would use the questions you learned in Chapter 1 to analyze your audience for the criminal justice assignment.

HOW TO Choose a Topic

Make a list of possible topics. Then answer the following questions:

- How much does this topic interest me?

- How much do I know about this topic?

- If I select this topic, how much, if any, research will I have to do? Is this research available to me? Can I complete the research in enough time to write the paper?

- Is the topic focused enough to be explained in detail, given the word or page limit?

- How well does this topic satisfy the audience? For instance, if the reader wants an informative essay, will this topic lead to an informative essay?

Use your responses to these questions to decide on a good topic.

- Who is my reader?
- What does my reader know about my topic?
- What does my reader need to know about my topic?
- How does my reader feel about my topic?

METHODS FOR GATHERING IDEAS. Once you know your topic, purpose, and audience, you can begin to gather ideas to write about. You could use any of the following ways to help you create ideas.

Brainstorming. When you brainstorm, you list all the thoughts that come into your head on a topic. You don't consider whether your ideas are good or bad; you just write them down. For the criminal justice assignment, you could brainstorm a list of problems in the criminal justice system, such as overcrowded prisons or innocent people being jailed.

In addition to brainstorming by yourself, you can brainstorm in a group with other people. In this case, you would name a topic and then ask each group member to call out ideas on it. Asking others to brainstorm with you greatly increases the number of ideas you have to choose from for your essay.

Here is student writer Jerry's list on problems in the criminal justice system.

> *some problems*
>> *should kids be tried as adults*
>> *does it make them more responsible*
>
> *another problem*
>> *racial profiling*
>> *can it be prevented*
>> *prisoners being released and doing more crimes*
>> *no schools in prison*
>> *you just get out of prison and do more crimes*
>> *how to stop this?*

Freewriting. Freewriting means writing without pausing for a specific period of time or until reaching a certain page limit. You don't stop, go back, or correct freewriting. You can focus on one topic or go on to new ones as they pop into your mind. Freewriting helps you develop fluency as a writer.

Here is Crystal's freewriting about the use of DNA evidence in the court system:

> *Heard on the news that they released another prisoner because DNA evidence showed he was innocent. He'd been in jail for eleven years! How sad. DNA evidence is so much better than any other way of seeing if someone is guilty. They gather DNA evidence from a tiny piece of skin. It's like fingerprints. Everyone has their own DNA. I hope more innocent prisoners can be released. They should be given money for the time they had to spend in jail.*

Use Your Computer to Brainstorm or Freewrite
If you can't resist correcting your writing, try using invisible writing. Simply turn down the brightness on your monitor so that you can't see what you're writing. This forces you to stay in touch with your thoughts instead of worrying about what you have already written. Save your work.

Clustering. Clustering is similar to brainstorming, but instead of listing your ideas, you draw a cluster of those ideas. To begin clustering, you write your subject in the center of a blank page and draw a circle around it. Then, as ideas about the topic come to mind, you write them down, put circles around them, and draw lines from them to the center circle. As you think of additional details, you circle and join them to their main ideas. Clustering can thus help you organize your ideas as well as generate ideas.

The diagram Figure 2.1 shows how student writer Lee used clustering to gather ideas about problems in the criminal justice system.

Questioning. The six questions that journalists use to gather details about the news can also help you discover ideas about your topic.

- Who?
- What?
- When?
- Where?
- Why?
- How?

Reading. The more you read about your topic, the more information you'll have for your paper. Reread your textbook or lecture notes. Then go to the library or access the World Wide Web to do further reading on your topic.

Read about learning logs on pp. 514–17.

Consulting with Others. Consulting with people who know about your topic is an excellent way to gather additional information and interesting details for your paper. Also, you can enliven your writing by using quotations from the discussion.

HOW TO Consult with Others

- Prepare questions to ask. You might begin with the journalists' *who, what, when, where, why,* and *how* questions. Avoid *yes-no* questions.

- Listen carefully and take notes.

- Ask questions when you don't understand something.

- Go over your notes with the person to fill in any gaps in your understanding.

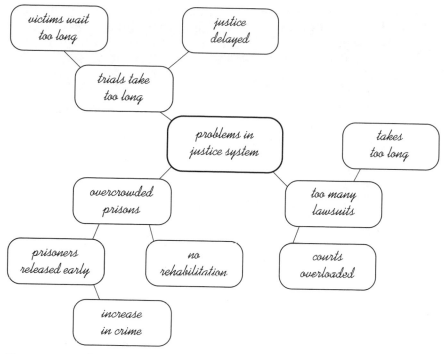

Figure 2.1. Lee's Clustering

The first step is finding someone to consult with. For the criminal justice assignment, you could talk to a family member or friend involved in the criminal justice system, such as a police officer or an attorney. You could also consult with someone who has been a victim of a crime or has been accused of committing a crime.

Relating Aloud. Relating aloud simply means talking about your topic with others. Tell friends or classmates about what you plan to write and get their feedback. Do you need more details? Do they ask questions that indicate you need to supply background information? Talking through what you plan to write is also a good way to realize that you have more to say than you think.

Reflecting. After you have tried some of the other ways of gathering ideas, reflect on your topic for a few hours or days, letting your ideas percolate before you begin to write.

Having narrowed your subject to a manageable topic that interests you and that you think will interest your reader, and having gathered ideas to begin writing, you are now ready to begin drafting.

HOW TO Gather Ideas

Use one or more of these strategies:

- *Brainstorming:* List all thoughts that come to mind about a topic.

- *Freewriting:* Write without stopping for a certain period of time (five to ten minutes) or a certain page length.

- *Clustering:* Write down your topic in the middle of a page and circle it. Write down more specific ideas, circle them, and draw lines to connect them to the larger idea.

- *Questioning:* Ask a series of questions about the topic, such as Who? What? When? Where? Why? How?

- *Reading:* Read and take notes on your topic.

- *Consulting with Others:* Ask a knowledgeable person about your topic.

- *Relating Aloud:* Talk about your topic with others.

- *Reflecting:* Think about your ideas for a few hours or days.

Drafting

In this stage of the writing process, you'll write a discovery draft. A *discovery draft* is a draft for getting your ideas down on paper without too much concern about sentence structure, word choice, grammar, spelling, or punctuation. Drafting styles vary widely. Some writers draft quickly and spend considerable time revising; others draft more slowly and write fewer drafts. You may write out your discovery draft by hand, type it, or use a computer word processor.

NARROW THE TOPIC. When starting your discovery draft, you might realize that your topic is too broad to be sufficiently developed. For instance, suppose that you want to write about how advertising on television has changed. As you start to write, you realize you could probably write a book on that topic. To narrow the topic, ask yourself questions such as "what kind of advertising?" "what time period should I cover?" and "what change, in particular, do I want to focus on?" Questions like these help you narrow a broad topic so you can go into more depth.

HOW TO **Narrow a Topic**

Break the topic into parts by asking these questions:

- What particular thing happened?

- Who is involved?

- What is the time period?

- What type is it?

- Where does it happen?

- Why does it happen?

- How does it happen?

- What is the result of it?

Practicing Narrowing Topics. Assume your sociology instructor has asked you write a three-page essay about how technology has changed American life. Using the questions in the preceding "How To" box, rewrite the following topics to make them narrow enough for a three-page essay.

EXAMPLE   Broad topic: How cars have changed American life

Narrowed topic: The influence of cars on the creation of suburbs in the 1950s

1. How computers have changed our lives

   _____

2. Recent changes in telephone technology

   _____

3. How technology has changed the home

   _____

4. Negative effects of technology

_____

5. How travel has changed in recent years

_____

_____

_____

THESIS STATEMENT. As you begin your discovery draft, you should first think about your *thesis statement,* the sentence or sentences that reveal to your reader the main point of the essay. This thesis statement will probably change as you refine your ideas when revising.

A good thesis statement

- announces the topic of your essay.
- shows, explains, or argues a particular point about the topic.
- gives the reader a sense of what the essay will be about.

Let's look at some examples of good thesis statements.

On one of the worst days of my life, I was told I needed back surgery, I got in a car accident, and I found out I'd been fired.

Community policing, where police officers work directly with a particular neighborhood, has helped to lower our city's crime rates in three areas: vandalism, burglaries, and assaults.

In order to lower the number of drunk drivers on the road, our legislature should pass a law requiring that all first-time offenders spend at least one night in jail, pay a $500 fine, and be required to perform community service.

These thesis statements are effective because they do three things: they announce the topic; they show, explain, or argue a particular point about the topic; and they give a sense of what the essay will be about.

Compare the following effective and ineffective thesis statements.

POOR My daughter was arrested last week for shoplifting.

STRONG Because of my daughter's arrest for shoplifting, I have made several important changes in how I raise my children.

POOR   Some people think that having more female police officers is good.

STRONG The increase in the number of female police officers has
helped the police deal better with domestic violence and
child abuse cases.

In the first example, we learn the topic, but a particular point isn't
being made. In the second example, the point being made is too
vague for the reader to predict what the essay will be about.

From a reader's point of view, a good thesis statement makes an
essay easier to understand. From a writer's point of view, an effective
thesis statement gives you a lot more to say than an ineffective one.

HOW TO Write a Thesis Statement

Ask yourself these questions about your topic:

• What point do I want to make about my topic?

• How can I show, explain, or argue this point?

• How can I break this point down, so that I can develop one
  idea about it in each section of my essay?

ACTIVITY 2

Evaluating Thesis Statements. Identify the following thesis statements as poor or strong. Then rewrite the thesis statements that need
improvement. (Keep in mind that a good thesis statement states the
topic; shows, explains, or argues a particular point about the topic;
and helps the reader predict what the essay will be about.)

1. Soap operas are some of the best shows on television.

   _____

   _____

   _____

2. A successful marriage requires patience, good communication, and a sense of humor.

_____

_____

_____

3. There have been too many budget cuts at this university.

_____

_____

_____

4. Studying a foreign language should be required in high school.

_____

_____

_____

5. If you have time on your hands, do community volunteer work.

_____

_____

_____

6. Even though I didn't make the Olympic ski team, my years of training taught me important skills such as discipline, time management, focus, and persistence.

_____

_____

_____

As you draft, use your thesis statement as a guide. (Keep in mind that you are free to change it later.) After all, your discovery draft is for exploring your ideas. The most important thing is to write.

Look back at the ideas you have gathered to see which ones appear most promising. Some writers prefer to organize their ideas before they begin to write, whereas others prefer to discover what they have to say while writing the discovery draft.

Where should your thesis statement appear in your essay? Usually the thesis is given in the first or second paragraph. Knowing the main idea from the start gives your reader a road map for reading the whole essay.

HOW TO Organize an Essay

- *Introduction:* Hook the reader, give background information, and state the thesis.

- *Body Paragraphs:* Give the main point of each paragraph in a topic sentence. Use details, facts, and examples to support each topic sentence.

- *Conclusion:* Refer back to the thesis. Explain the importance of the subject.

Draft Your Essay

Using your word-processing program, try to write an entire draft of your paper in one sitting, using the freewriting or brainstorming that you already saved in a file. If you reach a place where you need additional information, write "Add information here" in bold type to remind yourself to add material to this part of your paper.

Revising

When you revise, you improve your discovery draft. You want your reader to understand what you have to say and to be interested in reading your paper. At this stage you improve the content and organization of your draft. You also revise your sentences and words so that they communicate clearly. While you may write only one discovery draft, you may revise it many times. The more you revise, the better your essay will be.

HOW TO Revise an Essay

Ask yourself these questions as you revise:

- Have I followed all the instructions for this assignment?

- Do I begin the essay in a way that encourages my reader to continue reading?

- Is my thesis statement effective?

- Do I include enough main ideas to support my thesis statement?

- Do I support each main idea with details?

- Do I vary my sentences and use the appropriate words?

- Do I end the essay clearly?

One good way to revise is to set your paper aside for a day or two, reread it, and then rewrite it as you see fit. An even better way is to enlist the help of others, a strategy that is often called peer review. Ask a friend or classmate to read your paper and suggest ways it could be improved.

HOW TO Give and Receive Feedback
on Your Writing

When you're giving suggestions for revision to someone else, follow these guidelines:

- Always say something positive about the piece.

- Be specific. Don't say, "You need to improve the organization." Say, "Why don't you combine your second and third paragraph?"

- Don't make the feedback personal. Focus on the writing, not the writer. Don't say, "I can't believe you really believe that!" Say, "I was confused by your claim. Do you mean the death penalty should be used for all convicted drug felons?"

(continued on page 41)

(continued from page 40)

When you're receiving feedback on your paper, follow these guidelines:

• Write down the suggestions you receive.

• Ask questions to clarify what the readers are suggesting.

• Don't take the suggestions personally. Remind yourself that your classmates are discussing your writing, not you. The more suggestions you receive, the better your essay will be.

Use the Cut-and-Paste Function to Revise

As you revise, use the cut-and-paste function of your computer word processor to move sentences or blocks of text. The easiest way to do this is to highlight the text you want to move and drag it to the new location. Print different versions to compare which is more effective.

Editing

When you edit, you check your revised draft for errors in grammar, spelling, and punctuation. Since you have already devoted a great deal of time and effort to communicating your ideas, you don't want to spoil the paper with distracting errors. The more your readers are forced to notice errors in your writing, the less attention they'll pay to what you have to say.

As you edit, keep an *editing log.* In a section of your notebook, record the errors you discover as you edit.

• Date your entry and give the title of your essay.
• Copy the sentence with the error.
• Identify the type of error.
• Rewrite the sentence, correcting the error.

Here, for example, is an entry from student writer Luke's editing log:

3/20—"Abolish Mandatory Prison Sentences"

INCORRECT   Mandatory prison sentences don't give judges flexibility. Because they can't change the sentence to fit the crime.

ERROR   Sentence fragment

CORRECT   Mandatory prison sentences don't give judges flexi-
            bility because they can't change the sentence to fit
            the crime.

HOW TO Edit Your Essay

- Use a dictionary to check your spelling.

- Use a handbook, such as the one in Part Four of this textbook, to check on questions about grammar, spelling, and
  punctuation.

- Ask another student to read your essay for errors in grammar,
  spelling, and punctuation that you might have missed.

- Keep an editing log.

Use the Spell-Check and Grammar-Check to Edit

Be careful when you use the spell-check and grammar-
check features of your computer's word-processing program.
While spell-check helps you to spot typos and words that
you have misspelled, it won't spot all errors. For instance,
it won't notice if you use *their* when you're supposed to use
there. Grammar-check also has limitations. For example,
it tends to label all long sentences as incorrect, when in
fact the length of a sentence has nothing to do with its
grammatical correctness.

Publishing

In the final stage of the writing process, you share your revised
and edited essay with your audience. You may just submit the paper
to your instructor for a grade. But if you're proud of what you have
written, you may wish to share it with your classmates as well.

At times you may share your writing in a more public way. For
example, you may submit it to your local or campus newspaper for
possible publication. Many magazines are also interested in publishing
essays and articles submitted by their readers. If in your essay you propose a change of some kind, you might want to use the essay as the
basis of a letter that you send to a public official who can take action.

ACTIVITY 3

Reviewing the Writing Process. Review an essay assignment that you recently completed by answering these questions.

1. What was the subject of my essay?
2. How did I narrow it to a manageable topic?
3. What was the purpose, and who was the audience?
4. How did I gather ideas for this assignment?
5. What was my thesis statement?
6. How did I revise the paper so that it communicated my ideas more clearly?
7. What errors did I discover when I edited?

HOW TO Use the Writing Process

Gathering Ideas

- Brainstorm, freewrite, cluster, ask questions, read, consult with others, relate aloud, or reflect.

- Select and narrow a topic.

- Discover a purpose for writing.

- Analyze your audience.

Drafting

- Write a tentative thesis statement.

- Get your ideas down on paper.

- Don't be concerned about sentence structure, word choice, grammar, spelling, and punctuation.

Revising

- Focus on helping your audience understand your essay.

- Improve your organization and supporting details.

- Strengthen the introduction, thesis statement, and conclusion.

(continued on page 44)

(continued from page 43)

- Polish sentence structure and word choice.

- Use peer review.

Editing

- Correct errors in grammar, spelling, and punctuation.

- Use a dictionary and the Handbook in Part Four.

- Don't rely on spell-check and grammar-check to catch all errors.

- Keep an editing log.

Publishing

- Share your final draft with your audience.

DISCOVERING YOUR OWN WRITING PROCESS

To discover your own writing process, experiment with the various ways of gathering ideas, drafting, revising, and editing. The methods that work best for you will lead you to discover your preferred writing process.

You'll probably find that your writing process does not exactly follow the stages in the order outlined in this chapter, but that you prefer to move back and forth among the various stages. For example, while revising your essay you may discover you need more information. To get that information, you have to return to the gathering ideas stage. You may discover, too, that you prefer to stay in the revision stage for quite a while, producing perhaps three or four revised drafts. Figure 2.2 illustrates the recursive nature of the writing process.

A description of ways of gathering ideas begins on p. 30.

 Use Your Computer Wisely

As you learn more about your writing process, keep in mind that your best writing tool is between your ears. The computer has no ideas, no imagination, no feeling. You bring these qualities to your writing.

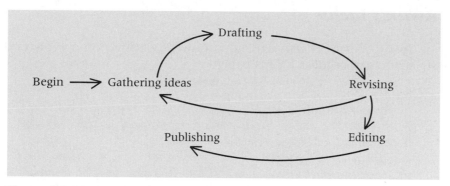

Figure 2.2. The Recursive Nature of the Writing Process

Other Students' Writing Processes

Consult the *Choices* Web site to read how other students describe their writing processes. Go to <**www .bedfordstmartins.com/choices/**> and click on "Student Writing."

ACTIVITY 4

Freewriting about the Writing Process. Use these questions to do some freewriting on your writing process.

1. Which methods of gathering ideas have I used most successfully?
2. Which other methods of gathering ideas am I willing to try?
3. How do I draft best?
4. How do I prefer to revise and edit?
5. In what ways have I shared my writing with others in the past?

ONE STUDENT'S WRITING PROCESS

On the following pages you'll follow Kwan Lu, a student writer, as he writes his essay for the criminal justice assignment given at the beginning of this chapter. As you follow Kwan through the writing process, think about your own writing process and how it resembles or differs from his. You recall the assignment:

> Write a two-to-three-page essay in which you explain a problem in the criminal justice system. Suggest a solution for the problem.

Kwan's Ideas

In his journal, Kwan explained how he decided on a topic and started to gather ideas for his paper:

If you would like to start a journal, turn to Chapter 10 for more information.

Feb. 9

A couple of weeks ago I started working as a clerk in a law firm. When I got the essay assignment in my criminal justice class, I remembered that I had overheard one of the attorneys talking about a couple getting a divorce who were seeing a mediator. I asked the attorney to explain what a mediator was. She gave me a lot of information. I took notes on what she said. When I got home, I decided to do some clustering before I lost interest in the topic.

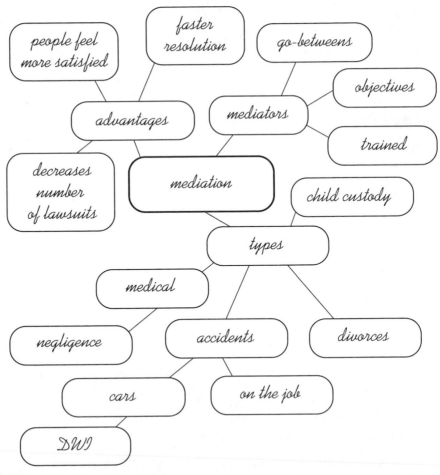

Figure 2.3. Kwan's Clustering

Kwan's Drafting

Using his notes from the interview with the attorney and his clustering (Figure 2.3), Kwan wrote the following discovery draft. (Note that the draft includes the types of errors that typically appear in a first draft.)

Mediation, Not Lawsuits

There are many lawsuits in our court system that are unnecessary. People just want revenge or money no matter what. One way to get rid of so many lawsuits is to have people who are fighting go to a mediator. A mediator tries to get people to agree on a solution before the case ends up in court. For instance, a wife is angry at her husband because he's been unfaithful. He wants to share custody of the kids, she decides she wants full custody so he'll never see his kids again. She knows he's an OK father, she just wants to get back at him. If they go to a mediator, the mediator might be able to make the wife see that she isn't think of what's right for the kids. She might agree to share custody of the kids. A mediator can help with other kinds of disagreements such as a family that is fighting with another family or a person injured in a car accident who wants money from the person who hit her car. Mediation can keep cases that are unnecessary from filling up the courts and keeping other important cases from being heard.

After finishing his discovery draft, Kwan thought about his audience. Although he planned to show his final draft to some of the attorneys he worked for, he knew his primary audience was his criminal justice instructor. Kwan decided that his instructor wanted an essay that would be easy to follow; after all, he had over a hundred students who would be turning in essays. This meant that his essay had to be well organized, with a good thesis statement. Because the primary purpose of the essay was informative, he would have to include a great deal of information to show the instructor he was knowledgeable about the topic. In addition to reflecting upon his audience and purpose, Kwan asked several students in the criminal justice class to read his discovery draft and give him suggestions for revision.

Kwan's Revising

In his journal, Kwan explained how he revised his essay.

Feb. 13
Before I revised my essay, I wrote a thesis statement: "Unnecessary lawsuits could be prevented if more people would use the services of a mediator." I based the rest of the essay on this thesis statement. I used a standard essay format—introduction, body paragraphs, and a conclusion. I decided that I needed to show my readers that unnecessary lawsuits do exist, so I gave several examples of them. Then, to show my audience (mainly the instructor) that I know all about mediation, I decided to explain how a mediator works. I also worked hard on my introduction because sometimes people form their opinion of the essay based on the introduction. The conclusion and the title gave me problems. I'm still not happy with them.

Here is Kwan's revised draft. (You may spot errors that Kwan will correct when he edits his draft.)

Mediation, Not Lawsuits

Introduction is developed.

Evolution and change are everyday occurrences. In the past, our legal system was simple. Trials happened quickly and the guilty were punished. Recently however the legal system has become more complicated. It can take months for a trial to be held because the courts have too many cases to settle. One of the biggest problems the legal system **Thesis is clearer.** faces is unnecessary lawsuits. Unnecessary lawsuits could be prevented if more people would use the services of a mediator.   1

Problem is described.

Currently, our court system is clogged with lawsuits that are a result of people being injured, disabled, or even killed because of other people's negligence. Many of todays cases have been caused by the actions that people take when they drive under the influence of alcohol or drugs. If people are seriously hurt or killed because of this behavior, the victims and their families often consider a lawsuit. At this time, the victims are angry,   2 sad, and hurt. They often want revenge. They don't consider the time, energy, and money that go into a lawsuit. Because they are overwhelmed by their emotions. They might not realize that they will have to relive the crime when they testify in the courtroom. While they may deserve some money, a lawsuit probably isn't the best way to get it.

At times, people sue other people for silly reasons. Some families have fights that last for years, and if one family member says something insulting to another family member, the whole matter can end up in court. Sometimes people file a lawsuit simply to get money, even when their injury is small. Perhaps this was the case when a woman sued McDonald's because she burned herself from spilling coffee. Divorces often result in unnecessary court hearings. For instance, a wife might sue her husband for sole custody of the children, she claims that her husband is a bad father, but the real reason she wants sole custody is that he had an affair. In a case like this, the children suffer because of the anger and imaturity of their parents.

There's a solution for the problem of unnecessary lawsuits: a mediator. This is a person who is trained to help people solve disagreements; often they have a background in both counseling and law. People in a fight (such as a couple getting a divorce) are sent to the mediator to see if their conflict can be resolved before they end up in a costly court battle. Mediators, who have no prior opinion or knowledge about the dispute, try to calm down both sides enough so that they can discuss the issues and come to a resolution agreeable to both sides. Usually, the mediator and the people involved in the disagreement will meet in the same room if the two sides get too emotional, the mediator will separate them and act as a go-between. The resolution might include the agreement that one person will pay another a certain amount of money.

Examples support main idea of the paragraph.

3 Topic sentences are used in all body paragraphs.

Examples clarify the writer's main point.

4

Solution is described in detail.

More examples make the writer's ideas clear.

A couple getting a divorce might agree to share custody of their children. Two fighting families might agree to stop insulting each other in public.

Conclusion refers to the topic of the essay.

Mediation won't stop all lawsuits. Not all people in a fight will come to an agreement, and some lawsuits involve injuries too great to be settled out of court. However, mediation works well in many cases. Because some attorneys believe they make more money through court cases, they don't always send their clients to a mediator. I believe this is a mistake. Many people should try to resolve their differences through mediation before they end up in a long, expensive, and painful court case.

5

Kwan's Editing

Kwan describes editing his essay in his journal.

Feb. 15
I used my spell-checker to catch a lot of misspelled words. I used the grammar-checker a few times. I showed the draft to a friend who's really good in English, and he caught some problems with sentence structure. Then I proofread my paper by reading it from the end to the beginning. I added my errors to my editing log so that I'd remember them the next time I wrote a paper.

Here is Kwan's edited essay. (The underlining indicates where he corrected errors during the editing stage.)

Correct essay format used.

Kwan Lu

Professor Heath

Criminal Justice 100

12 November 2002

Mediation, Not Lawsuits

Evolution and change are everyday occurrences. In the past, our legal system was simple. Trials happened quickly and the guilty were punished. <u>Recently, however, the</u> legal

1

system has become more complicated. It can take months for
a trial to be held because the courts have too many cases
to settle. One of the biggest problems the legal system
faces is unnecessary lawsuits. Unnecessary lawsuits could
be prevented if more people would use the services of a
mediator.

Currently, our court system is clogged with lawsuits   2
that are a result of people being injured, disabled, or
even killed because of other people's <u>negligence</u>. Many of
<u>today's</u> cases have been caused by the actions that people
take when they drive under the influence of alcohol or
drugs. If people are seriously hurt or killed because of
this behavior, the victims and their families often
consider a lawsuit. At this time, the victims are angry,
sad, and hurt. They often want revenge. <u>They don't consider</u>
<u>the time, energy, and money that go into a lawsuit because</u>
<u>they are overwhelmed by their emotions</u>. They might not
realize that they will have to relive the crime when they
testify in the courtroom. While they may deserve some
money, a lawsuit probably isn't the best way to get it.

At times, people sue other people for silly reasons.   3
Some families have fights that last for years, and if one
family member says something insulting to another family
member, the whole matter can end up in court. Sometimes
people file a lawsuit simply to get money, even when their
injury is small. Perhaps this was the case when a woman
sued McDonald's because she burned herself from spilling
coffee. Divorces often result in unnecessary court
hearings. <u>For instance, a wife might sue her husband for</u>
<u>sole custody of the children; she claims that her husband</u>
<u>is a bad father, but the real reason she wants sole custody</u>
<u>is that he had an affair</u>. In a case like this, the children
suffer because of the anger and <u>immaturity</u> of their
parents.

There's a solution for the problem of unnecessary   4
lawsuits: a mediator. <u>This is a person who is trained to
help people solve disagreements; often he or she has a
background in both counseling and law</u>. People in a fight
(such as a couple getting a divorce) are sent to the
mediator to see if their conflict can be resolved before
they end up in a costly court battle. Mediators, who have
no prior opinion or knowledge about the dispute, try to
calm down both sides enough so that they can discuss the
issues and come to a resolution agreeable to both sides.
<u>Usually, the mediator and the people involved in the
disagreement will meet in the same room. If the two sides
get too emotional, the mediator will separate them and act
as a go-between</u>. The resolution might include the agreement
that one person will pay another a certain amount of money.
A couple getting a divorce might agree to share custody of
their children. Two fighting families might agree to stop
insulting each other in public.

Mediation won't stop all lawsuits. Not all people in a   5
fight will come to an agreement, and some lawsuits involve
injuries too great to be settled out of court. However,
mediation works well in many cases. Because some attorneys
believe they make more money through court cases, they
don't always send their clients to a mediator. I believe
this is a mistake. Many people should try to resolve their
differences through mediation before they end up in a long,
expensive, and painful court case.

Here is Kwan's editing log:

2/15 — "Mediation, Not Lawsuits"

INCORRECT	Recently however the (1)
ERROR	missing commas
CORRECT	Recently, however, the

INCORRECT   negligance (2)

ERROR   misspelled word

CORRECT   negligence

INCORRECT   todays (2)

ERROR   possessive without an apostrophe

CORRECT   today's

INCORRECT   Because they are overwhelmed by their emotions. (2)

ERROR   Sentence fragment. Connect it to the previous sentence.

CORRECT   They don't consider the time, energy, and money that go into a lawsuit because they are overwhelmed by their emotions.

INCORRECT   For instance, a wife might sue her husband for sole custody of the children, she claims that her husband is a bad father, but the real reason she wants sole custody is that he had an affair. (3)

ERROR   comma splice

CORRECT   For instance, a wife might sue her husband for sole custody of the children; she claims that her husband is a bad father, but the real reason she wants sole custody is that he had an affair.

INCORRECT   imaturity (3)

ERROR   misspelled word

CORRECT   immaturity

INCORRECT   Usually, the mediator and the people involved in the disagreement will meet in the same room if the two sides get too emotional, the mediator will separate them and act as a go-between. (4)

ERROR   Run-on sentence

CORRECT   Usually, the mediator and the people involved in the disagreement will meet in the same room. If the two sides get too emotional, the mediator will separate them and act as a go-between.

Kwan's Publishing

Writing in his journal, Kwan summed up his feelings about the final draft of his assignment.

Mar. 1
I had no idea what grade this essay would get. I was hoping for a B.
I was shocked when I got an A! All that revising really paid off. That
gave me the guts to show it to the attorney I had interviewed. She
said she was impressed by it. My confidence in my writing has im-
proved a lot. I almost look forward to my next writing assignment.

ACTIVITY 5

Improving Kwan's Essay. Discuss the following questions with your classmates.

1. How effective is the title of Kwan's essay? What title would you suggest instead?
2. Does Kwan's introduction make you want to read the essay? Why or why not?
3. How effective is Kwan's thesis statement?
4. What details did Kwan add to the revised draft to improve his essay?
5. Give an example of a sentence that Kwan revised so that it was easier to understand.
6. How effective is Kwan's conclusion? What more would you suggest he add?
7. What else could Kwan do to improve his essay?

CHAPTER CHECKLIST

- ☐ There are five stages in the writing process: gathering ideas, drafting, revising, editing, and publishing.
- ☐ The writing process is recursive; that is, you often need to go back and forth among the stages.
- ☐ The techniques for gathering ideas include brainstorming, freewriting, clustering, questioning, reading, consulting with others, relating aloud, and reflecting.
- ☐ As you prepare to write, consider your purpose and audience.
- ☐ When you draft, focus on getting your ideas down on paper. Use an effective thesis statement as a guide.
- ☐ When you revise, aim to improve your writing and to communicate your ideas effectively and clearly.
- ☐ Skilled writers usually revise a draft several times.

☐ When you edit your writing, eliminate distracting errors in grammar, spelling, and punctuation, which if left uncorrected may prevent your reader from focusing on your message.

☐ Publish your finished work by sharing it with others.

REFLECTING ON YOUR WRITING

Reflect on your writing process by completing the following process report, describing your strengths and weaknesses as a writer and your plans for improvement.

If you are keeping a journal, you may wish to keep your process report in it. You may also wish to start your own writing portfolio by gathering examples of your writing in a folder. If you have a portfolio, consider adding your process report to it.

If you would like to start a portfolio, see Chapter 13.

Writing Process Report

Date:

Strengths:

Weaknesses:

Plans for improvement:

Once you complete your process report, freewrite on what you now know about your writing process and what you still hope to learn.

Good writers are those who keep the language efficient. That is to say, keep it accurate, keep it clear. —EZRA POUND

CHAPTER 3

Crafting Paragraphs

In this chapter you will

- write about a favorite photograph.

- compose topic sentences.

- learn about paragraph unity, development, and organization.

- practice writing special types of paragraphs.

- reflect on your writing.

Just as a football game is divided into quarters, so is an essay divided into paragraphs. The quarters of a football game divide the game into shorter time periods so spectators won't get bored or confused. Similarly, paragraphs serve to divide information into chunks so readers can more easily follow your ideas. Paragraphs separate the main ideas of an essay into easily understood sections. They tell your readers where one main idea ends and another begins. They also help your readers make connections between these ideas. This chapter will focus on important elements of good paragraphs: topic sentences, unity, development, and organization. You'll also learn to write special types of paragraphs, such as introductions and conclusions.

WRITING ASSIGNMENT

Photographs can convey powerful emotions and meanings. Think of the photo of the three New York City firefighters raising the American flag amid the rubble at the World Trade Center in September 2001. It captures the mood of the nation at that time. Photographs of our family and friends can be just as powerful, illustrating truths about our lives that we might not otherwise know.

Find a photograph that is meaningful to you in some way. It can be a photograph of an important family occasion, such as a wedding or birthday, or it can be a photograph that depicts a special place or a gathering of friends. Alternatively, you can select a photograph of a historical event that captures your attention or a person who interests you. Write a paragraph for your instructor and classmates in which you describe the photograph and explain what it reveals. Assume that your readers do not have a copy of the photograph.

Use the writing process when you compose your paragraph. As you read in Chapter 2, the writing process consists of

- gathering ideas.
- writing a discovery draft.
- revising your draft to improve the organization.
- editing your draft to eliminate errors in grammar, spelling, and punctuation.
- publishing your draft by sharing it with your audience.

TOPIC SENTENCES

When it comes to paragraphs, the phrase "one thing at a time" is useful to remember. The "one thing" that you explain in a paragraph is stated in a *topic sentence*. To write an effective topic sentence for each paragraph in your essay, follow these guidelines:

To review the characteristics of a strong thesis statement, turn to p. 36.

- Break up your thesis statement into several specific supporting ideas.
- Write a complete thought for each of these specific ideas.

A topic sentence functions as a mini-thesis for each paragraph. Here are some examples of thesis statements and the topic sentences that might follow from them.

THESIS STATEMENT   Hiking is excellent exercise because it strengthens muscles, offers a chance to enjoy nature, and relieves stress.

TOPIC SENTENCES

- Hiking provides a strenuous workout for many parts of the body, especially leg and back muscles.
- Whether in the desert or in the woods, hikers enjoy beautiful scenery and clear air.
- A hike in a beautiful area takes people completely away from the daily grind of school, family, and work.

These are effective topic sentences because they support the thesis statement that hiking is excellent exercise.

Here is another set of topic sentences that supports the thesis statement.

THESIS STATEMENT   If this university continues to increase tuition year after year, it will no longer be an asset to our community.

TOPIC SENTENCES

- As a result of tuition increases, families on limited incomes will not be able to send their children to college.
- Students who have already spent several years in college—and who have invested thousands of dollars in their education— will be forced to drop out.
- High school students will lack the motivation to study because they'll feel that college costs too much.
- Companies will decide not to locate here because they won't be able to find well-educated workers.

These topic sentences are effective because they explain the effect that tuition increases will have on the community.

Consider one more set of examples.

THESIS STATEMENT   Before I moved to the United States, I lived in Japan, a very different country and culture.

TOPIC SENTENCES

- Housing is much more spacious in the United States than it is in Japan. Even small apartments in this country are large by Japanese standards.

- Americans are informal, and even strangers use first names, whereas people in Japan are reserved and formal.

- People in the United States emphasize individuality, whereas people in Japan emphasize conformity to a group.

HOW TO Write a Topic Sentence

- Write several complete thoughts that make a point about your thesis statement. These are your topic sentences.

- Check that these topic sentences tell something informative and interesting about your thesis statement.

- Check that you can add details to show or explain these topic sentences.

- Check that you are writing on the topic assigned.

ACTIVITY 1

Writing Topic Sentences. Write several topic sentences for each of the following thesis statements.

1. No two people could be more different than Matt and Jerry, but they are my two closest friends.

_____

_____

_____

_____

_____

2. Living with your parents when you're an adult has its disadvantages, but so does living on your own.

_____

_____

_____

_____

3. Personal management skills are important for students holding a full-time job while working toward a college degree.

_____

_____

_____

_____

4. Today's communications technology—from cellular telephones to e-mail—make life more stressful, not more efficient.

_____

_____

_____

_____

5. Because anyone can use it, the Internet can be a dangerous place for children and adults alike.

_____

_____

_____

_____

_____

Should your topic sentence appear at the beginning, middle, or end of the paragraph? A topic sentence can fall anywhere in the paragraph. Most often, however, it comes first. Just as placing the thesis statement at the beginning of an essay helps guide the reader through the paper, putting the topic sentence at the beginning of the paragraph helps guide the reader through the paragraph. Or, to put it another way, giving the main idea at the beginning is like giving the reader a hook on which to hang the details that follow.

In the following paragraph, the topic sentence (italicized) comes first. The author, Garrison Keillor, states in the topic sentence that when he was a child, denim jeans represented freedom to him. In the rest of the paragraph, he gives facts and examples to support this idea.

> *Thus denim came to symbolize freedom to me.* My first suit was a dark brown wool pinstripe bought on the occasion of my Aunt Ruby's funeral, and I wore it to church every Sunday. It felt solemn and mournful to me. You couldn't run in a suit, you could only lumber like an old man. When church was over, and you put on denim trousers, you walked out the door into the wide green world and your cousin threw you the ball and suddenly your body was restored, you could make moves.
>
> —Garrison Keillor, "Blue Magic"

Sometimes, however, you may need to provide background information or explain the connection between two paragraphs before the topic sentence can be presented. In either case, the topic sentence may fall in the middle of the paragraph. In the following paragraph, the topic sentence (italicized) is given after the first sentence, which explains the connection between this paragraph and the previous one.

I don't mean that some people are born clearheaded and are therefore natural writers, whereas others are naturally fuzzy and will never write well. *Thinking clearly is a conscious act that writers must force upon themselves, as if they were working on any other project that requires logic: adding up a laundry list or doing an algebra problem.* Good writing doesn't come naturally, though most people obviously think it does. Professional writers are constantly being bearded by strangers who say that they'd like to "try a little writing sometime"—meaning when they retire from their real profession, which is difficult, like insurance or real estate. Or they say, "I could write a book about that." I doubt it.

—William Zinsser, "Simplicity"

Occasionally, placing a topic sentence at the end of a paragraph can dramatize the main idea. In the following example, the topic sentence (italicized) appears at the end. By giving several specific examples before stating the generalization, the writer emphasizes the main point of the paragraph.

Most black Americans are *not* poor. Most black teenagers are *not* crack addicts. Most black mothers are *not* on welfare. Indeed, in sheer numbers, more *white* Americans are poor and on welfare than are black. *Yet one never would deduce that by watching television or reading American newspapers and magazines.*

—Patricia Rayborn, "A Case of 'Severe Bias'"

ACTIVITY 2

Writing Your Own Topic Sentence. Brainstorm for several minutes about the photograph you have chosen to write about. In addition to describing the photograph, jot down ideas about what the photograph means to you. Then, write a topic sentence that summarizes your thoughts about the photograph. Remember that you may change this topic sentence if your ideas change during the process of revising.

PARAGRAPH UNITY

Once you have an effective topic sentence, you need to make sure that all other sentences within the paragraph relate to the topic sentence. This is called *paragraph unity*. Paragraphs that lack unity contain sentences that distract and confuse readers because they aren't on the topic. These are called irrelevant sentences. In the following paragraph, several irrelevant sentences have been added (in italics); notice how these irrelevancies distract you from the topic of the paragraph.

> I went to high school in the Fifties, when blue denim had gained unsavory cultural associations—it was biker and beatnik clothing, outlaw garb, a cousin to the ducktail, a symbol of Elvis, and as such, it was banned at our school. *Elvis Presley was my favorite singer at the time.* Every September, we were read the dress code by our homeroom teacher: you could wear brown denim, or grey, or green, but not blue. *Blue is my favorite color.* Why? "Because," she explained. *She lived a block away from me.* There have to be rules, and blue denim was a statement of rebellion, and we were in school to learn and not to flaunt our individuality. So there.
>
> —Garrison Keillor, "Blue Magic"

During the drafting stage, you may include irrelevant sentences as you focus on getting your thoughts down on paper. When you revise, however, you need to eliminate them in order to achieve paragraph unity. Reread your paragraphs and topic sentences, and delete any statements that are off the topic.

ACTIVITY 3

Improving Paragraph Unity. Place a checkmark next to the sentences that do not relate to this topic sentence: *I had defied a direct order, but I didn't expect my dad to do anything about it.*

___ My dad looked like he was trying to recover from a gunshot wound.

___ Gun control is a topic I would like to write about some day.

___ His eyes fluttered and his mouth gaped. "You're saying no to me?" was all he could say.

___ "Yea, I'm saying no to you."

___ I felt like a newborn colt, prancing around, kicking, testing my limits.

___ Riding horses is one of my favorite hobbies.

___ "Well, pack your bags and leave," he shouted.

___ Uh-oh, I hadn't expected that.

___ My Samsonite bag is stored on the top shelf of my closet.

___ "Okay, I will."

ACTIVITY 4

Identifying Irrelevant Statements. Identify and delete the irrelevant sentences that have been added to the following paragraph from a reading in Chapter 4. Then check your work against the original paragraph on the page indicated.

From "Prison Studies" (p. 113):

It had really begun back in the Charlestown Prison, when Bimbi first made me feel envy of his stock of knowledge. Bimbi had always taken charge of any conversation he was in, and I had tried to emulate him. But every book I picked up had few sentences which didn't contain anywhere from one to nearly all of the words that might as well have been in Chinese. I have since been to China, a fascinating country. When I just skipped those words, of course, I really ended up with little idea of what the book said. So I had come to the Norfolk Prison Colony still going through only book-reading motions. Norfolk is a large prison, and old. I'll always remember one guard who reminded me of my older brother. Pretty soon, I would have quit even these motions, unless I had received the motivation that I did.

DEVELOPING PARAGRAPHS

To make your paragraphs interesting and convincing, you need to develop them in detail. Writers use supporting details in their writing to

- increase interest.
- help the reader understand their thoughts.
- support their main ideas.

Eight common methods for developing paragraphs are description, narration, comparison and contrast, classification, process, examples, definition, and cause and effect.

Description

When you use *description* in your writing, you allow your readers to become more involved. The key is to go beyond describing experiences in general ways ("We had a great time; that day really changed me") to describing them in enough detail that your readers relive those moments with you.

Notice how one writer, Benjamin Alíre Saenz, improves the following sentences from his short story "Ceballeros" by adding description in the revised version.

ORIGINAL

He was getting good grades in everything except chemistry. And the teacher hated him. His brother wrote to him and told him to calm down, told him everything would be all right.

REVISED

He was getting good grades in everything except chemistry. If he didn't pass, he'd have to go to summer school because it was a required course. All those good grades, and it had come down to this. He was a borderline student in that class and he knew it, but there wasn't any time. There wasn't any time.

And the teacher hated him. He could feel the teacher's hatred, the blue-eyed wrestling coach who favored athletes and nice-looking girls.

His brother wrote to him and told him to calm down, told him everything would be all right. "Just graduate and go to college. Do whatever it takes, just don't join the army."

To use description, start with a general statement and add details to make it more specific. Use these questions:

- Who is involved?
- What happens?
- When and where does it happen?
- Why does it happen?
- How does it happen?

Here's an example of a general statement to which detailed observations have been added.

ORIGINAL

My cousin's wedding was really beautiful.

REVISED

My cousin Veronica's wedding took place in the flower garden of Haven Park on a sunny June day. Veronica and Samuel took their vows surrounded by red, pink, and yellow roses. In addition to the three bridesmaids and the best man, my four-year-old son, Jason, was the ring bearer. I've never seen Jason smile so much.

Other family members were both smiling and crying. My aunt Liz had tears streaming down her face as she watched Veronica

and Sam walk through the garden arm in arm. Even my uncle
Albert, usually so stern, had tears in his eyes.

ACTIVITY 5

Using Description. Add description to make the following paragraphs more interesting and vivid. Use the journalists' questions of
who, what, when, where, why, and *how.*

1. The first time I baby-sat for my brother's children was a disaster.
   One of them kept throwing things around. The other one wouldn't
   stop crying. I was relieved when my brother and his wife returned
   home.

   _____

   _____

   _____

   _____

   _____

   _____

2. I was so happy when the Little League team I coach won the city
   tournament. The final play was very suspenseful. The score was
   tied. The parents were probably more nervous than the players.
   But no one could have been happier than the kids when they won.

   _____

   _____

   _____

   _____

   _____

   _____

3. One of my favorite pastimes is backpacking in the mountains. I love the fresh air and the scenery. At night my friends and I lie awake and look up at the stars. One night we even saw a shooting star.

_____

_____

_____

_____

_____

Narration

Narration is writing that tells a story based on either fact or fiction. You use narration when you want to develop ideas by relating a series of events. In most cases, you will organize events in chronological order. Occasionally, however, you might use a flashback. You might also use dialogue to make a narrative more immediate and real.

CHRONOLOGICAL ORDER. Generally, stories are told in the order in which they actually happened, called *chronological order.* Imagine that you want to narrate a story about your family's ritual of taking a family photograph at the start of every new year. Here's how you might organize a narrative paragraph in chronological order.

> On picture-taking day, we all rush around trying to get ourselves to look as good as possible for the camera. In the bathroom, my mother puts makeup on my stepfather's nose to hide the redness caused by a cold. I hear my stepsister tell my parents she refuses to be in the picture because her hair is too puffy. My brother rushes into the kitchen to clean up the grape juice he spilled on his shirt, while I look through the cupboards in the utility room for shoelaces. Finally, we're ready to make our trip to the photographer's studio.

FLASHBACK. An alternative way to organize a narrative is to use a *flashback:* you begin the story in the middle, flash back to the beginning, and then resume telling the story in the middle again. You often see this technique used in movies: the picture becomes fuzzy and a scene from an earlier time appears. The flashback technique is useful when you want to contrast then and now or highlight a key scene. Here's how the paragraph about the picture-taking ritual might be organized using the flashback technique.

> In the photograph, my family appears calm and relaxed. Our hair is perfectly combed, and our clothes are neatly pressed. The expressions on our faces seem calm and happy. But as I stare at the photograph, I recall the chaos that preceded the snap of the camera. My stepfather had such a terrible cold that my mother had to put makeup on his nose to cover the redness. My stepsister didn't want to be in the picture because her hair was too puffy. My brother had spilled grape juice on his shirt, and I had broken my shoelace. To make matters worse, we had a flat tire going to the studio. But when I look at this photograph, I know it was all worthwhile.

DIALOGUE. In a narration, *dialogue* consists of the actual words that people say, indicated by quotation marks. Use dialogue when you want to highlight an important scene or portray a certain person through his or her own words.

Dialogue can make a narration more interesting and fast paced. Consider this narrative paragraph:

> I couldn't have survived my first semester in college without my roommate, Lisa. She encouraged me to study harder, helped me find a job, and introduced me to new friends. One night, while I was studying for my calculus exam, I became so frustrated I yelled and threw the calculus book across the room. Lisa comforted me. That's the kind of roommate she was.

Here's the same paragraph, expanded to five paragraphs to include dialogue. Notice that the dialogue makes the scene more vivid.

To learn how to punctuate dialogue correctly, see pp. 692–93 in the Handbook.

> I couldn't have survived my first semester in college without my roommate, Lisa. She encouraged me to study harder, helped me find a job, and introduced me to new friends. One night, while I was studying for my calculus exam, I became so frustrated that I yelled as loud as I could, "I can't take it anymore!" Then I threw the calculus book across the room.
>
> Lisa, who was studying for her psychology exam, looked up at me from across the room. "What's wrong with you?"
>
> "I can't do this! I know I'm going to flunk!"

"Calm down," she said, putting her book down. "Let me see if I can help." She spent the next hour explaining the problems to me.

That's the kind of roommate she was.

Comparison and Contrast

When you *compare,* you identify the similarities between two or more things; when you *contrast,* you identify the differences between things. Sometimes the focus is on one or the other, but at other times both similarities and differences are included.

Writers use *comparison and contrast* to clarify relationships. How are people, places, or ideas alike? How are they different? For example, in the following paragraph, the author writes about the voluntary separation between black and white students at his high school. He contrasts the distance he now feels from his black friend with the closeness he felt when they were younger:

> Ten years ago, we played catch in our backyards, went bike riding, and slept over at one another's houses. By the fifth grade, we went to movies and amusement parks, and bunked together at the same summer camps. We met while playing on the same Little League team, though we attended different grade schools. We're both juniors now at the same high school. We usually don't say anything when we see each other, except maybe a polite "Hi" or "Hey." I can't remember the last time we talked on the phone, much less got together outside of school.
>
> —Brian Jarvis, "Against the Great Divide"

Classification

Writers use *classification* to organize their ideas and thereby to aid their readers' understanding of those ideas. When you classify, then, you categorize something into types on some particular basis. For example, you might classify cars on the basis of their type or size (sports car, compact, midsize, and full-size) or on the basis of their country of origin (Volvos and Saabs from Sweden, Hyundai and Kia from Korea). You might also classify cars on the basis of their resale value, safety record, popularity as indicated by sales, or some other basis you deem important.

In the following paragraph about the camera collection of Cheng Jianguo, a student from China, the writer classifies cameras first by type and then by name.

Cheng mainly collects China-made cameras. The brands of Chenguang, Tiantan, Changhong, Huashan, Changle, Yuejin, Haiou and others vividly show the development of China's camera industry. In addition, he has also gathered many different types of foreign cameras, some produced early in this century. They include the Leica and Roland from Germany, Minolta and Fuji models from Japan, and Kodak and Browning cameras from the United States as well as models from the former Soviet Union and Czechoslovakia.

—*Beijing Review,* "Camera Collector Cheng Jianguo"

ACTIVITY 6

Using Description, Narration, Comparison and Contrast, and Classification. Following are several topic sentences. For each one, first decide whether you will use description, narration, comparison and contrast, or classification as the primary method of development. Then use that method to develop the topic sentence into a brief paragraph.

1. I'll never forget the first time I tried to drive a car.

   Primary method of development: _____

   _____

   _____

   _____

   _____

   _____

   _____

2. My mother has the cleanest kitchen I've ever seen.

   Primary method of development: _____

   _____

   _____

_____

_____

_____

_____

3. Both my boss and my partner are total introverts.

   Primary method of development: _____

   _____

   _____

   _____

   _____

   _____

   _____

4. Rock music can be divided into various categories.

   Primary method of development: _____

   _____

   _____

   _____

   _____

   _____

   _____

Process

Writers use a technique called *process* to explain how something works or how to do something. Cookbooks and repair manuals come to mind when we think of process writing, but bookstore shelves are filled with all sorts of other "how to" books explaining processes— from how to use a computer to how to arrange your closet.

In a paragraph about your favorite hiking trail, for instance, you might explain the process of preparing to hike the trail and locating the trailhead, as Laurence Parent does in the following paragraphs about hiking to Wheeler Peak in New Mexico.

> Be sure to get a very early start on this hike. To minimize problems with storms, you ideally want to be on the summit before noon. Snow flurries are possible even in mid-summer. Be sure to take rain gear and extra warm clothing. Lightning and hypothermia are real threats on Wheeler Peak and the exposed summit ridge.
>
> At just short of one mile you will pass marked Trail 63, the Long Canyon Trail to Gold Hill, coming in from the left. Ignore it and continue climbing up the northeast valley. Just past the trail junction, the trail hits an old road. Turn left onto the road and follow it the rest of the way up the valley.
>
> —Laurence Parent, *The Hiker's Guide to New Mexico*

Examples

In writing, *examples* are used to clarify, explain, and support ideas. Two of the most common types of examples are facts and expert testimony.

FACTS. Facts provide support for your ideas. Unlike opinions or guesses, facts are statements that can be objectively verified as true. For example, the statement "Golden retrievers are beautiful" represents the opinion of the writer. In contrast, the statement "A golden retriever is a breed of dog" is a fact that can be verified in an encyclopedia or other reliable source. Facts may include names, dates, numbers, statistics, and other data relevant to your topic or idea. Notice in the following paragraph that facts are used to support the idea that Asian Americans are a diverse group.

> Asian Americans are an especially diverse group, comprised of Chinese, Filipino, Japanese, Vietnamese, Cambodians, Hmong, and other groups. The largest Asian-American groups are Chinese

Americans (24 percent), Filipino Americans (20 percent), and Japanese Americans (12 percent). Other groups, such as Vietnamese, Cambodians, Laotians, and Hmong, are more recent arrivals, first coming to this country in the 1970s as refugees from the upheavals resulting from the Vietnam War. In the 1980s, Koreans and Filipinos began immigrating in larger numbers. The majority of Asian Americans live in the West.

—Bryan Strong and Christine DeVault,
The Marriage and Family Experience

EXPERT TESTIMONY. Statements made by knowledgeable people are considered *expert testimony.* Examples supported by expert testimony make your writing more convincing. For example, citing the surgeon general's warning that cigarette smoking greatly increases your risk of lung cancer is more convincing than offering the statement without support or citing someone with no medical background or authority to advise American citizens on health matters.

In the following paragraph, the author uses expert testimony to convince his readers that lead vocalist Edward Kowalczyk and his band, Live, are headed for national success.

After only two albums, the four farm boys from York, Pa., are being groomed for the big leagues. "We look for artists that we think can go to the next level," says MTV's senior vice president of music and programming, Andy Schoun, who helps pick bands for *Unplugged.* "In the case of Live, they've got what it takes."

—Jeff Gordinier, "Live through This"

Definition

Writers use *definition* to explain and clarify. Thus, when you define something, you tell your reader what it means. A good definition has two parts: first the term being defined is placed in a general category, and then an explanation of how it fits within that category—a discussion of its distinguishing features—follows. For example, to define the term *skydiving,* you might first define it generally as a risky sport and then go on to explain what distinguishes skydiving from other risky sports, such as rock climbing and hang gliding.

In the following paragraph, the writer first defines the Sierra Club's Inner City Outings (ICO) program and then goes on to describe its activities. He thus categorizes the topic generally as a type of community-outreach program before pointing out its distinguishing feature: that it takes disadvantaged young people out of the city and into the "natural world" for a time.

> **HOW TO Develop a Paragraph**
>
> • Write a topic sentence that supports your thesis statement.
>
> • Support each topic sentence with details that increase interest and help the readers understand your main point.
>
> • Use methods of development such as description, narration, comparison and contrast, classification, process, examples, definition, and cause and effect.
>
> • Add or delete sentences to improve your paragraph.
>
> • Write a concluding sentence.

Now in its 23rd year of operation, ICO is one of the Sierra Club's longest-running and most successful community-outreach programs. Its dedicated corps of volunteer leaders works year-round to get disadvantaged young people of diverse ethnic and cultural backgrounds out of their concrete-and-asphalt environs and into the natural world.

—Mark Mardon, "City Kids Go Wild"

Cause and Effect

When you use *cause and effect,* you explain why something happened (the cause) and the result of it (the effect). Writers use cause and effect to show a necessary or logical connection between two things. It is not enough to say that two things happened at the same time. For example, if a freeze ruins the orange crop, and orange prices go up, that's cause and effect. If there also happens to be a full moon on the night of the freeze, that's a coincidence. It is the freeze, not the full moon, that ruins the crop.

In the following paragraph, the author explains the problems that arise when people unfairly stereotype each other. He shows a clear and logical connection between the cause—stereotyping—and the effect—a loss of individuality.

Hence, quite aside from the injustice which stereotypes do to others, they impoverish ourselves. A person who lumps the world into simple categories, who type-casts all labor leaders as "racketeers," all businessmen as "reactionaries," all Harvard men as "snobs," and all Frenchmen as "sexy," is in danger of becoming a stereotype himself. He loses his capacity to be himself—which is to say, to see the world in his own absolutely unique, inimitable and independent fashion.

—Robert L. Heilbroner, "Don't Let Stereotypes
Warp Your Judgments"

ACTIVITY 7

Developing Ideas. Following are several topic sentences. For each one, first decide whether you will use process, examples, definition, or cause and effect as the primary method of development. Then use that method to develop the topic sentence into a brief paragraph.

1. The meaning of "love" differs from person to person.

    Primary method of development: _____

    _____

    _____

    _____

    _____

    _____

2. With the right tools, it's easy to change a flat tire.

    Primary method of development: _____

    _____

    _____

    _____

    _____

    _____

3. The rating system for television shows, developed by the major networks, has failed children and parents alike.

   Primary method of development: _____

   _____

   _____

   _____

   _____

   _____

4. Because of stereotyping in the media, cheerleaders are often considered superficial and vain.

   Primary method of development: _____

   _____

   _____

   _____

   _____

   _____

ORGANIZING PARAGRAPHS

You must organize the ideas in your paragraphs. If you don't, your readers won't be able to follow what you're saying, they'll become frustrated, and they'll stop reading. You can organize your ideas using these methods: general-to-specific order, topic-illustration-explanation order, progressive order, directional order, question-and-answer order, and specific-to-general order.

General-to-Specific Order

General-to-specific order is one way to organize ideas in a paragraph. Whereas general statements are broad, specific statements are more focused. For example, the statement "I love dogs" is general because it refers to all dogs. But the statement "I love my dog Rupert because he's smart, funny, and affectionate" is specific because it cites a particular dog and several details.

In general-to-specific order, the most general idea is given at the beginning of the paragraph in the topic sentence. The more specific ideas that follow help support and explain the general statement. Notice this pattern of general to specific in the following paragraph.

> The *quinceañera,* or coming-out party, is a tradition for many young Latinas. In this ritual, parents proudly present their fifteen-year-old daughter to their community. The ceremony consists of a Mass followed by a dinner and dance. Fourteen young couples serve as the girl's court. Long formal dresses, tuxedos, live music, and video cameras are all part of the spectacle.

Topic-Illustration-Explanation Order

The *topic-illustration-explanation (TIE) order* is used to organize paragraphs that contain examples such as facts and expert testimony. As in general-to-specific order, the paragraph starts with a topic sentence. You can organize the paragraph in this way:

- State the topic.
- Give an illustration (such as a fact or expert testimony).
- Explain the significance of the illustration.

The TIE method of organization is used in the following paragraph about an American cultural symbol—the T-shirt. Notice that the writer states the topic, gives an illustration, and then explains why the illustration is important.

> T-shirts with political or controversial statements can require the viewer to think about the message. A few years ago the slogan "A woman's place is in the House" was seen on many T-shirts. To understand this slogan, the viewer had to know the original saying, "A woman's place is in the home," and then realize that the word *House* on the shirt referred to the House of Representatives. The House of Representatives, a part of Congress, has always had fewer female than male members. A person wearing

this T-shirt, then, advocated electing more women to political office.

In this paragraph, the topic is stated in the first sentence: T-shirts with political statements may require some thought. To illustrate, the writer uses a slogan—"A woman's place is in the House"—and then explains the significance of the slogan.

Progressive Order

Another way of organizing the ideas in your paragraphs is to use *progressive order,* in which ideas are arranged from least to most important. Since the final idea in a paragraph (or in an essay, for that matter) is the one that readers tend to remember most readily, ending with the most important idea is usually very effective. Thus, rather than presenting your examples randomly, you can arrange them progressively to emphasize the most important one.

Here's another paragraph from the essay about the American T-shirt. Notice that the writer uses progressive order to illustrate the various functions that the T-shirt serves in our culture.

> The common, ordinary T-shirt tells us much about the American culture. The T-shirt is a product of our casual lifestyle. People have been known to wear T-shirts under blazers at work and under evening dresses at the Academy Awards. The T-shirt is also associated with sexuality—think of the Calvin Klein ads in magazines and on buses. Most importantly, the T-shirt gives us a way to express ourselves. It tells others about our favorite schools, sports teams, or cartoon figures. It can also let others know our political views—whether or not they care to know.

In this paragraph, the most important function of T-shirts is stated at the end. The writer emphasizes this function with the introductory words *most importantly.*

Directional Order

When you use *directional order,* you describe something from one location to another, such as left to right, down to up, or near to far. For example, suppose you want to describe a photograph of your brother taken while he was in the air force. To organize your description, you might use top-to-bottom directional order, as in the following example.

This is my brother Antonio in his air force uniform. His face is clean-shaven, and his haircut is regulation-style. He's smiling his big lopsided smile. He has an athletic build, like a bodybuilder's. He wears his uniform proudly. It is perfectly pressed, and every brass button is perfectly shined. The crease in his pants is as sharp as a blade. His shoes are like black mirrors.

Question-and-Answer Order

Question-and-answer order is another method for organizing ideas in a paragraph. It involves asking a question at the beginning of the paragraph and then answering that question in the rest of the paragraph. In the following paragraph, the writer uses the question-and-answer method when discussing the causes of homelessness.

What's the root of the homeless problem? Everyone seems to have a scapegoat: Advocates of the homeless blame government policy; politicians blame the legal system; the courts blame the bureaucratic infrastructure; the Democrats blame the Republicans; the Republicans, the Democrats. The public blames the economy, drugs, the "poverty cycle," and the "breakdown of society." With all this finger-pointing, the group most responsible for the homeless being the way they are receives the least blame. That group is the homeless themselves.

—L. Christopher Awalt, "Brother, Don't Spare a Dime"

Specific-to-General Order

In *specific-to-general* order, the most specific ideas are stated first and the general idea appears at the end of the paragraph. Use this pattern when you want to position a topic sentence at the end of a paragraph.

In the example that follows, the writer organizes ideas from the most specific to the most general.

The audience gasps as colors explode in the night sky—red, blue, yellow, green. The explosions grow bigger and bigger until they cover the night sky, and then they slowly disintegrate like silvery rain. Although everyone enjoys a fireworks spectacle on the Fourth of July, few understand the origin of this ritual celebration. The Fourth of July commemorates America's fight for independence, and the fireworks are to remind us of the historic battles that ended the Revolutionary War.

HOW TO **Organize a Paragraph**

The **topic sentence** states the main point of the paragraph. **Support sentences** include details that support your topic sentence arranged using one of these methods: general-to-specific, topic-illustration-explanation, progressive, directional, question-and-answer, specific-to-general order. The **concluding sentence** restates the main point of the paragraph.

• Indent the first line of each paragraph five spaces.

• Use margins of one inch on each side of the page.

• Check that each sentence is a complete thought and ends with a period (.), question mark (?), or exclamation mark (!).

ACTIVITY 8

Identifying Patterns of Paragraph Organization. With your classmates, identify the pattern of organization in each of the following paragraphs as general-to-specific, topic-illustration-explanation (TIE), progressive, directional, question-and-answer, or specific-to-general. Some patterns may overlap.

1. With about a half-billion passengers a year boarding scheduled U.S. flights, air travel has become so routine that it's easy for people to forget what's outside their cabin cocoon. The atmosphere at 35,000 feet won't sustain human life. It's about 60 degrees below zero, and so thin that an inactive person breathing it would become confused and lethargic in less than a minute.

   —"Breathing on a Jet Plane," *Consumer Reports*

   Pattern: _____

2. When you need a new car, do you go to the nearest auto dealer and buy the first car you see? Most of us don't. We shop and compare features, quality, and price. We look for the best value for our money.

   —O. M. Nicely, "Using Technology to Serve You Better"

   Pattern: _____

3. When you go on a hike in the desert, the least of your worries is snakes and scorpions. If you stay away from them, they'll stay away from you. Instead of worrying about reptiles and bugs, worry about the sun. To avoid a serious burn, apply sunscreen to exposed skin and wear a hat. Most importantly, bring plenty of water—at least a gallon per person.

   Pattern: _____

4. Many dogs, when they hear the words "Let's go on a hike!" can't contain their excitement. They wag their tails, jump up and down, and even bring their leashes to their owners. Most dogs love to hike, and their owners love to take them. Just as with humans, though, dogs need to be prepared for a rigorous day on the trail.

   Pattern: _____

5. Almost everyone knows that smoking is bad for one's health, yet more and more young people are smoking every day. According to the National Cancer Institute, one million Americans begin to smoke each year, and most of them are teenagers. Experts believe so many young people are taking up smoking because they think smoking will make them look "cool."

   Pattern: _____

ACTIVITY 9 (GROUP)

Finding Patterns of Paragraph Organization. Working in a group, analyze the way ideas are organized in paragraphs from textbooks for your other courses. Find as many examples as you can of paragraphs that use the patterns discussed in this chapter: general-to-specific, topic-illustration-explanation (TIE), progressive, directional, question-and-answer, and specific-to-general. Make copies of your group's sample paragraphs to share with the rest of the class.

SPECIAL TYPES OF PARAGRAPHS

In addition to focusing on topic sentences and paragraph unity, development, and organization, you need to keep in mind the special requirements of two different but important types of paragraphs: introductions and conclusions.

Introductions

First impressions are important. In a job interview, employers prefer someone who is well spoken and neatly dressed over someone who mutters and is dressed to go to the gym. Similarly, the *introduction* to an essay provides the readers with a good first impression of your ideas.

In a short essay (two to three pages), the introduction usually consists of only the first paragraph; longer essays often have introductions that are several paragraphs in length. A good introduction has three characteristics: it gets the readers' attention, narrows the topic, and states the thesis.

GET THE READERS' ATTENTION. The technique of getting your readers' attention is often called the *hook*. You want your introduction to grab your readers and pull them into your essay, just as a hook lures a fish to bite on the line. In addition to getting the readers' attention, the hook contains information relevant to the topic of your essay. A hook can consist of a question, an interesting fact, a brief story, or a vivid image.

When readers encounter a question at the beginning of an essay, they want to read on to find the answer. In the following introduction, the author uses a question to begin her essay about her father's heroism during World War II.

> "Who is your hero and why do you admire him?" is the question my son, Andy, had to answer on his application to a private school. The school's headmaster made an eloquent speech linking the growing incidence of drug abuse, suicide and violence among teen-agers to the absence of heroes in contemporary life.
>
> —Irina Hremia Bragin, "What Heroes Teach Us"

An interesting fact can also get the readers' attention, as in this essay on how to drive safely.

> The first automobile crash in the United States occurred in New York City in 1896, when a car collided with a bicyclist. We've had 100 years since then to learn how to share the road, but with increasingly crowded and complex traffic conditions, we're still making mistakes, mostly because we assume that other drivers—and their vehicles—will behave the way we do.
>
> —Carolyn Griffith, "Sharing the Road"

Most readers would be intrigued by the date of the first car accident and would want to read more about this topic.

A third way to hook readers is to tell a brief story related to the topic.

> The Hollywood blockbuster had been playing for about 20 minutes when one of the characters took a gunshot in the face, the camera lingering on the gory close-up. Fifteen rows from the big screen, a little girl—no more than six years old—began shrieking. Her mother hissed, "Shut up," and gave her a stinging slap.
>
> —Alvin Poussaint, "Let's Enforce Our Movie Ratings"

In addition to getting readers' attention, this story illustrates the writer's point that movie ratings need to be enforced.

Because readers like to imagine scenes, a vivid image is another effective way to hook readers.

> A woman in a left-turning Dodge zooms through two pedestrians like a football running back. A man in a Mitsubishi flosses his teeth—at 30 m.p.h.—grabbing the steering wheel between string tugs. An ambulance, siren screaming, races through traffic, with a man in a Jaguar sneaking behind it all the way.
>
> —William Ecenbarger, "America's Worst Drivers"

This lively description of out-of-control drivers introduces the topic of bad driving.

NARROW THE TOPIC. An introduction announces the general topic of the essay and then narrows the subject to the more specific point stated in the thesis. Just as a photographer focuses the lens on a specific object for greater clarity, a writer narrows the scope of the essay.

In the following example, the writer introduces the general topic of ethnic diversity (in the first paragraph) before focusing on his main point of ethnic conflict.

> The history of the world has been in great part the history of the mixing of peoples. Modern communication and transport accelerate mass migrations from one continent to another. Ethnic and racial diversity is more than ever a salient fact of the age.
>
> But what happens when people of different origins, speaking different languages and professing different religions, inhabit the same locality and live under the same political sovereignty? Ethnic and racial conflict—far more than ideological conflict—is the explosive problem of our times.
>
> —Arthur Schlesinger Jr., "The Cult of Ethnicity, Good and Bad"

By gradually narrowing his topic to ethnic and racial conflict, Schlesinger prepares his readers for his thesis that "ethnic and racial conflict . . . is the explosive problem of our times."

STATE THE THESIS. After getting readers' attention and narrowing the topic, you're ready to state your thesis. Generally, the thesis appears at the end of the introduction; depending on the length and complexity of the essay, it can range from one sentence to several sentences long. As you read in Chapter 2, the thesis of an essay states the topic and explains its significance.

Do you need more information about thesis statements? See p. 36.

In the following introduction, notice how the writer attracts readers' attention, narrows her topic, and then states her thesis (italicized).

"Welcome to Rio Bravo Grill! Can I get y'all a margarita?" With those words I began my stint as a full-time waitress, apartment renter and bill payer in downtown Atlanta. It was the first time I had ever truly been on my own, with no help from my parents except for the occasional sardonic words of advice or chastisement. At that time I had no idea what I wanted to do with my life. I had recently been forced to leave the United States Air Force Academy, and I didn't know what to do next. My life had always been planned around a career in the air force, and I had never pictured myself as anything else. *My leaving and subsequent return to the academy, as well as my experiences during the time I was out, taught me a lot about myself, the world around me and where I want to go from here.*

—Andrea L. Houk, "The Honor Principle"

HOW TO Write an Introduction

- Use a hook such as a question, an interesting fact, a brief story, or a vivid image or description to get readers' attention.

- Narrow the topic to one main point.

- Write a thesis statement.

ACTIVITY 10

Unscrambling an Introduction. The following sentences are from the introduction of an essay about a young college student's reaction to the birth of his child. The sentences are out of order. With several other classmates, put the paragraph into the correct order.

- Also, I had to give up my dreams of graduating from college in four years.
- When I discovered I was going to be a father at age nineteen, I thought my life was over.
- Now, however, I can't imagine my life without my daughter.
- To begin, I needed to get a full-time job to support my new family.
- She has taught me that despite the responsibilities of parenthood, the joy and love make it worthwhile.
- In fact, I thought I had to give up going to college at all.

Conclusions

Often the last thing people read is what they remember the most. Therefore, your *conclusion* needs to be well written and memorable. The standard way to end an essay is to restate your thesis and broaden your focus.

RESTATE THE THESIS. By restating your thesis, you ensure that your readers remember your main point. However, don't use the same words you used in your introduction. Instead, vary your word choice so that your main point isn't unnecessarily repetitive. The restated thesis can appear at either the beginning or end of the conclusion.

STATEMENT OF THESIS IN INTRODUCTION	If we make it a point to be considerate of all the occupants of our roadways, from cars and trucks to motorcycles and pedestrians, we can make our streets much safer places to be.
RESTATEMENT OF THESIS (ITALICIZED) IN CONCLUSION	But no matter how much time elapses, the basic principles of sharing the road safely won't change much. Just watch out for *the big guys, cut the little guys some slack, pay attention to "vehicular diversity"* and above all, enjoy the ride.

—Carolyn Griffith, "Sharing the Road"

By varying her word choice, Griffith restates her thesis in an interesting way.

BROADEN THE FOCUS. In your introduction, you state the general topic and then narrow your focus until you give the thesis statement. In the conclusion, however, you want to broaden your focus—widen the lens of the camera—in order to tell your readers how your main point connects to other important ideas.

In his introduction to "The Cult of Ethnicity, Good and Bad," Arthur Schlesinger Jr. writes that "ethnic and racial conflict . . . is the explosive problem of our times." Notice that in his conclusion, Schlesinger broadens his focus by suggesting a solution to this conflict (italicized):

> The growing diversity of the American population makes the quest for unifying ideals and a common culture all the more urgent. In a world savagely rent by ethnic and racial antagonisms, *the United States must continue as an example of how a highly differentiated society holds itself together.*
>
> —Arthur Schlesinger Jr., "The Cult of Ethnicity, Good and Bad"

By ending his essay with the suggestion that the United States serve as a model of unity, Schlesinger leaves his readers with a sense that action must be taken.

HOW TO **Write a Conclusion**

- Restate the thesis to remind readers of the main point.

- Sum up what has been said in the essay.

- Broaden the focus or make an additional observation about the main point.

ACTIVITY 11 (GROUP)

Unscrambling a Conclusion. The following sentences are from an essay about a young college student's reaction to the birth of his child. The sentences are out of order. With a group of your classmates, put the sentences in the correct order.

- Because of her, I get angry when I hear people talk about how bad it is when young people have children.

- In fact, for some people it's the best thing that can ever happen to them.
- It's not always bad.
- My daughter has improved my life in many ways, from making me more responsible to teaching me what love really means.

Online Writing Labs

Share your introduction, thesis statement, and conclusion with a tutor in an online writing lab. Go to <www .bedfordstmartins.com/choices/> and click on "Annotated Web Links" and then choose one of the online writing labs.

ONE STUDENT'S PARAGRAPH

As you recall, the writing assignment for this chapter is to write a paragraph for your instructor and classmates in which you describe a photograph and explain what it reveals about your life. On the following pages you'll follow Elizabeth Fleming, a student writer, as she writes her paragraph for this assignment. Use Elizabeth's writing process as a guide to writing your own paragraph.

Elizabeth's Ideas

In her journal, Elizabeth freewrote about the assignment after she had looked through several photographs she had recently taken.

> I know I want to describe a photograph of my niece Nicole because she's the greatest thing that's happened to me this year, but I can't decide which one. I want the paragraph to be mostly about her, so I'll stick to one that just has her and maybe one other person. Or maybe one of her and our dog, Jake.

After selecting a photograph, Elizabeth brainstormed about it in her journal:

> Nicole's plump cheeks
>
> Her two front teeth just coming in
>
> She's grabbing Jake, leaning on him
>
> Jake looks away

His fur is so soft

Short, white, beige, brown fur

Fat little body on his short legs

The red T-shirt I gave her

Sunlight in her hair

My brother's legs in the background

In their backyard

What was she thinking when I took this?

I can almost hear her high voice — "Aunt Liz"

Highlight Your Text

As you read over the ideas you have gathered on your topic, highlight the blocks of text that you want to use in your discovery draft. Copy them to a separate file, and use that file to begin your discovery draft. Number or date your drafts so that you know which is your latest version and can turn in multiple drafts if required.

Elizabeth's Drafting

After studying the photograph again and referring to her brainstorming, Elizabeth wrote the following discovery draft. (Note that the example includes the types of errors that typically appear in a first draft.)

```
                    Nicole

    When I look at this photograph, I remember how much I
love my niece. I took this picture of her and our dog,
Jake, when she was two. Nicole is sitting [not really sit-
ting but I can't think of the right word] in the backyard
with her arms around Jake. She loves Jake so much he gets
angry because she bugs him alot. Sunlight on her hair.
She's wearing the red T-shirt I bought her when I went to
Martha's Vineyard but it's so long it practically comes
down her to her feet. She's smiling and her two little
front teeth show. Her cheeks are fat and pink. My brother's
```

legs are in the background. Jake is looking away like he
doesn't want to be with her. This photograph shows how
loving and adorable she is. And I'm so glad she's wearing
my T-shirt! I can't wait until I have a child of my own,
but I know that won't be for a long time.

Save Frequently

**When drafting on a computer, save your document
frequently to ensure that you have the most recent version
of your work. Keep a backup copy as a precaution.**

Elizabeth's Revising

Elizabeth read her paragraph aloud to several classmates, so they
could give her suggestions for revision. Because her classmates were
confused about her main point, Elizabeth decided to begin her paragraph with a topic sentence that would be supported by the rest of
the paragraph. Her classmates also suggested that Elizabeth organize
the sentences in the paragraph and include more description.

Here is Elizabeth's revised draft. (Because she focused on getting
down her ideas, you may spot editing errors she still needed to correct.)

Nicole

This photograph of my two-year-old niece Nicole reminds me how important she is in my life. I took this
photograph last year after I had returned from a trip to
Martha's Vineyard with a red T-shirt for her. In this
photo, she is stooping on the patio in the backyard of our
house, her arms are around our dachshund, Jake. The red
T-shirt is so long it covers practically her whole body.
She has turned toward the camera, with a smile on her face.
Sunlight in her light brown hair. Her cheeks are fat and
pink, her new front teeth peek out of her open mouth. Her
hands rest on Jake's back. Jake is looking away from her
because he doesn't like it when she grabs him. Nicole is
important to me because I get to see her experience life

for the first time. Because of the pressures of work and school, I often find myself focusing on what needs to be done and how little time there is to accomplish everything. Seeing her so happy to play in the sunshine makes me apreciate even the little things in life like sunshine or a new T-shirt. She reminds me that there are more important things in life than the next deadline. She has made me more responsible because when I baby-sit her I know how important it is to take good care of her. She is so precious to our entire family, so I must do everything possible to ensure that she is healthy and safe. Most of all, because shes in my life I know I want to have children of my own, but only when I'm old enough to really take care of them. Now I am focused on completing my degree in social work and getting a job as a caseworker. Someday I will also have children of my own to nurture and care for. It's funny how one little girl named Nicole could completely change my outlook on life.

Elizabeth's Editing

To help her edit her paragraph, Elizabeth sought help from a tutor at her college's writing center. She also used the spell-check on her word-processing program.

Here is Elizabeth's edited paragraph. (The underlining indicates where she corrected errors during the editing stage.)

Nicole

This photograph of my two-year-old niece Nicole reminds me how important she is in my life. I took this photograph last year after I had returned from a trip to Martha's Vineyard with a red T-shirt for her. <u>In this photo, she is stooping on the patio in the backyard of our house, her arms around our dachshund, Jake</u>. The red T-shirt is so long it covers practically her whole body. She has turned toward the camera, with a smile on her face. <u>Sunlight shines in her light brown hair. Her cheeks are fat and pink, and her new front teeth peek out of her open mouth</u>. Her hands rest on Jake's back. Jake is looking away from her because he doesn't like it when she grabs him. Nicole is important to me because I get to see her experience life for the first time. Because of the pressures of work and school, I often find myself focusing on what needs to be done and how little time there is to accomplish everything. Seeing her so happy to play in the sunshine makes me <u>appreciate</u> even the little things in life like sunshine or a new T-shirt. She reminds me that there are more important things in life than the next deadline. She has made me more responsible because when I baby-sit her I know how important it is to take good care of her. She is so precious to our entire family, so I must do everything possible to ensure that she is healthy and safe. Most of all, because <u>she's</u> in my life I know I want to have children of my own, but only when I'm old enough to really take care of them. Now I am focused on completing my degree in social work and getting a job as a caseworker. Someday I will also have children of my own to nurture and care for. It's funny how one little girl named Nicole could completely change my outlook on life.

Elizabeth's editing log:

9/17 — "Nicole"

INCORRECT	In this photo, she is stooping on the patio in the backyard of our house, her arms are around our dachshund, Jake.
ERROR	comma splice
CORRECT	In this photo, she is stooping on the patio in the backyard of our house, her arms around our dachshund, Jake.

INCORRECT	Sunlight in her light brown hair.
ERROR	sentence fragment
CORRECT	Sunlight shines in her light brown hair.

INCORRECT	Her cheeks are fat and pink, her new front teeth peek out of her open mouth.
ERROR	comma splice
CORRECT	Her cheeks are fat and pink, and her new front teeth peek out of her open mouth.

INCORRECT	apreciate
ERROR	misspelled word
CORRECT	appreciate

INCORRECT	shes
ERROR	contraction without an apostrophe
CORRECT	she's

Online Grammar Skills Practice

The *Choices* Web site includes practice exercises in grammar, spelling, and punctuation. Go to <**www.bedfordstmartins .com/choices/**> and click on "Exercise Central." After logging in, click on the topic area in which you'd like to practice your skills.

Elizabeth's Publishing

In a journal entry, Elizabeth explained how she published her paragraph.

My classmates liked my paragraph. Some of them have children or nephews or nieces, and they could understand what I was talking about. But the best way I published my essay was to give it to my brother and sister-in-law to read and keep until Nicole is old enough to read it herself. They said they really liked it.

ACTIVITY 12

Improving Elizabeth's Paragraph. Discuss the following questions with your classmates.

1. What changes did Elizabeth make from the discovery draft to the revised draft that most improved it?

_____

_____

_____

_____

_____

2. What else could Elizabeth do to improve her paragraph?

_____

_____

_____

_____

CHAPTER CHECKLIST

☐ Remember the phrase "one thing at a time" when you write paragraphs. The "one thing" you explain in each paragraph is stated in the topic sentence.

☐ Write effective topic sentences by breaking down your thesis statement into several specific supporting ideas; then write a complete thought for each specific idea.

☐ Maintain paragraph unity by sticking to the topic introduced in your topic sentence.

☐ Develop your ideas by using description, narration, comparison and contrast, classification, process, examples, definition, and cause and effect.

☐ Organize the ideas in your paragraphs by using one or more of these patterns:

    ☐ general-to-specific order

☐ topic-illustration-explanation (TIE) order
☐ progressive order
☐ directional order
☐ question-and-answer order
☐ specific-to-general order

☐ In an introduction, get the readers' attention, narrow your topic, and state your thesis.

☐ In your conclusion, restate your thesis and broaden your focus.

REFLECTING ON YOUR WRITING

Reflect on the paragraph you just wrote by answering the following questions.

1. In your description of a photograph, which stages of the writing process (gathering ideas, drafting, revising, editing, and publishing) did you find the easiest to do? Which were most difficult? Why?

2. What pleases you most about your paragraph?

3. If you had more time, what parts of your paragraph would you continue to revise? Why?

Using your answers to these questions, update the writing process report you began in Chapter 2.

Writing Process Report

Date:

Strengths:

Weaknesses:

Plans for improvement:

Once you complete this report, freewrite about what you learned in this chapter and what you still hope to learn.

Writing to Share Ideas

Writing provides a permanent record of our ideas. Writing also allows us to communicate with others and to share what we know in ways that entertain, inform, and persuade.

In Part Two, you'll learn how to improve your writing as you write to share your ideas. You'll experiment with different methods of gathering ideas and practice writing discovery drafts. You'll learn how to revise to develop and organize your thoughts. You'll improve your sentences and learn how to choose just the right word to communicate what you want to say. Finally, you'll edit your writing to ensure that you communicate your ideas clearly.

Change alone is unchanging. —HERACLITUS

CHAPTER 4

Showing the Ways We Change

In this chapter you will

- write about a significant person, event, or period in your life.

- gather ideas by brainstorming, freewriting, clustering, and relating aloud.

- learn to develop your ideas using description, narration, and examples.

- practice organizing your essay around a thesis statement.

- practice writing topic sentences and unified paragraphs.

- combine sentences with coordinating conjunctions.

- delete empty phrases.

- correct run-on sentences and comma splices.

- correct misspelled words.

- reflect on your writing.

We all have memories of the important people and events in our lives. Some of these memories are happy: a special grandfather or coach, a first kiss or date, the night following high school graduation. Others are less pleasant: a serious illness, an accident, or the death of a family member or friend.

Although the memories may be pleasant or unpleasant, the people and events changed who we are and how we now see ourselves. To a great extent, then, we are defined by the important people and events in our lives. By exploring them in writing, we can come to a deeper understanding of who we are and what is meaningful to us.

Once we have written about our personal history, we can share it with others so that they understand who we are and what is important to us. This is what good writing is about—communicating something important to our readers so that they are better informed. One good place to start is by helping them understand who we are as writers.

 **WRITING ASSIGNMENT**

For this assignment, write about a significant person, event, or period in your life. You or your instructor may decide to do this assignment in one of several ways.

- You may gather ideas on one, two, or three topics.
- You may write a discovery draft on one, two, or three of these topics.
- You may choose one discovery draft to develop into a polished essay.
- Or, you may combine your discovery draft ideas into a new topic for your essay.

After completing your essay, share it with your instructor and classmates.

 Other Students' Ideas

Read students' responses to this assignment on the *Choices* Web site. Go to <www.bedfordstmartins.com/choices/> and click on "Student Writing."

For more information on purpose and audience, see pp. 5–15.

ACTIVITY 1

Analyzing Your Purpose and Audience. Before you begin gathering ideas about your topic, think about your purpose and audience.

For this chapter's assignment, your audience is your instructor and classmates. Your responses to the following questions will help you decide how to approach your topic.

1. Does this assignment call for primarily expressive, informative, or persuasive writing?

   _____

2. What is the average age of your audience?

   _____

3. How many readers are female? How many are male?

   _____

4. What parts of the country or world are they from?

   _____

   _____

5. How many have had experiences similar to your own?

   _____

   _____

Given your responses to the preceding questions, ask yourself these questions:

6. In what ways are your readers similar to or different from you?

   _____

   _____

7. How will these similarities and differences with your readers affect the way you write your essay?

   _____

   _____

GATHERING IDEAS

Ways of gathering ideas are explained on pp. 30–34.

For this chapter's assignment, you may gather ideas (or prewrite) using any of the methods you learned in Chapter 2. The student writers in this chapter used brainstorming, freewriting, clustering, and relating aloud. You may also gather ideas by reading the following essays and noticing how these authors communicate their thoughts to the readers.

A Significant Person

Think about the significant people in your life. Who would you name? You might name your parents, for example, or a partner, a teacher, or a friend. You might even name an acquaintance or a stranger you met once but who nevertheless gave you a new perspective at a critical time in your life. Whomever you choose, the significant person should be someone who has helped you understand who you are and who you strive to be.

Dawn Sanders, in "Beth," tells us about an elementary school classmate who changed the way Sanders treats other people.

DAWN SANDERS
Beth

1   I used to see her walking alone in the crowded hallways. Sometimes a group of girls would follow behind whispering and giggling after her. Occasionally, boys would tease. Our eyes met once, but her gaze fell quickly to the floor, as if in shame. If she only knew that it was I, not she, who should have felt ashamed.

2   Beth did not graduate with my grade-school class, but we had been classmates through seventh grade. As I look back, I realize that those were the best years of my childhood, unburdened with cares and responsibilities. But even carefree, innocent children can be cruel.

3   From the very beginning, Beth was different, an outsider. Her physical appearance set her apart. Stringy blond hair framed her homely face and accentuated her long pointy nose. She had a bad overbite, probably caused by her incessant thumb-sucking. On her bony shoulders hung an old, faded sweater, out of shape from too many washings, and hopelessly out of style. With her

sallow complexion, she looked malnourished. We all thought she was dense. The ideas that were easy for us to understand seemed out of her reach. She remained at the bottom of the class, never seeming to benefit from the teacher's help.

We excluded Beth from our games. If we did let her join, it was so we could gang up and laugh at her. The boys all called her names, pulling her hair and stealing her food at lunch. At first, Beth fought back, but after a time she seemed to lose spirit. She became quiet and withdrawn.　　4

I remember one incident in particular. It was in the fifth grade. The class bully, Fred Washek, was also the teacher's son. Fred did whatever he wanted to do, which was normally something cruel. During Fred's reign of terror, Beth was his main target. He taunted and tormented her.　　5

One day, while Mrs. Washek was running an errand, Fred put a tack on Beth's chair. I don't know if she noticed it, but she hesitated to sit down. Fred commanded her to sit and threatened to knock her down if she disobeyed. Beth refused. Fred pushed her hard into the chair. Immediately, she jumped up, wincing in pain. Fred angrily pushed her down again and held her there. The class had been enjoying Fred's prank but became increasingly uneasy. Still, no one dared come to Beth's defense for fear of Fred's vengeance. Finally, the teacher returned and Fred calmly went back to his seat. In the meantime, Beth began to whimper. Mrs. Washek ignored her as usual, but as Beth's sobs became louder, she scolded her for being a crybaby and disturbing the class.　　6

That incident made me realize how terribly we all had been treating Beth. When the others teased her, I no longer joined in. But I did nothing to stop them. Nor did I become her friend. The term was nearly over by then and Beth's grades were so poor that she was held back. She was probably happy to get away from us. I think I was a little relieved to get away from her.　　7

Her being held back turned out to be the best thing for her. The class she moved into was more accepting. I saw her now and then over the next five years and saw her make friends and gain confidence. Her grades improved. She joined the varsity volleyball team and became assistant librarian. She got a part-time job and was able to get some stylish clothes.　　8

I came more and more to admire Beth. She cast off the label of loser that our class had given her and made something of herself. In fact, she always had been special; we just never noticed. We saw only the shell, not the person within.　　9

VOCABULARY WORDS: unburdened (2), accentuated (3), incessant (3), sallow (3), taunted (5), tormented (5)

ACTIVITY 2

Reading to Improve Writing. Discuss the following questions about "Beth" with your classmates.

1. How does Sanders describe Beth? Compare the description before and after Beth was held back a grade.

   _____

   _____

   _____

2. Why is Beth a significant person in Sanders's life?

   _____

   _____

3. What do you want to know about Beth that the writer doesn't reveal?

   _____

   _____

   _____

4. What details does Sanders use to show how Beth influenced her life?

   _____

   _____

   _____

ACTIVITY 3

Brainstorming to Gather Ideas about a Person. Think of a person who is (or has been) important to you. Write the person's name at the top of a blank page. Then brainstorm whatever comes to mind in response to the following questions.

1. How would you describe this person to someone who has never met him or her?

   _____

   _____

2. How would you describe some of the places you have visited with this person?

   _____

   _____

3. What special objects do you associate with this person? Why?

   _____

   _____

4. What song, book, or movie do you associate with this person? Why?

   _____

   _____

5. What holidays or other special occasions are memorable because of this person? Why?

   _____

   _____

6. How do you feel when you think of this person? Describe these feelings.

   _____

   _____

   _____

7. Why do you think this person is significant to you?

_____

_____

Here's how one student writer, Jesus Ramirez, responded to the first four questions of the preceding activity.

1. *My father*

5 feet, 6 inches tall	*kind*
green eyes	*understanding*
brown hair	*always tries to be helpful*
full head of hair	*soft-spoken, but firm!*
in good shape	

    doesn't talk much, but when he does everyone listens!

2. *We've been so many places together that it's hard to name only a few:*

baseball games	*grandparent's house*
church	*Uncle Jim's*
the mall	*fishing*
auto-parts store	*I could go on and on!*
Disneyland	

3. *Anything about baseball:*

his Cardinals' baseball cap	*TV remote control*
fishing gear	*favorite chair*
lawn mower	*newspaper*
'56 Chevy	*coffee mug*

4. *Field of Dreams* — *My dad loves baseball so much that if he had a cornfield he'd turn it into a baseball field, too.*

Brainstorm on Computer

To gather ideas through brainstorming, create a word-processing file and list the questions in Activity 3 to gather ideas about a significant person. Once you have entered the questions, brainstorm the answers and save your file.

ACTIVITY 4

Freewriting or Clustering to Gather Ideas about a Person.
Return to the material you generated in Activity 3. Evaluate your
responses to questions 2 and 5 about the times you shared with your
special person. Circle the one event that most fully reveals why this
person is significant to you. Then do some freewriting or clustering to
gather ideas about the event and person.

You now have some ideas about a significant person in your life.
Set this material aside for a time. Next, you want to turn to gathering
ideas on a different topic—an event that changed your life.

A Memorable Event

Along with the important people in your life are important events
that changed you in some way. Whether you worked to make these
events happen—such as achieving a goal or overcoming a personal
problem—or saw them change your life unexpectedly—such as winning a scholarship or needing surgery—such events have influenced
who you are. As you consider the many memorable events in your
life, choose one that has helped define who you are today.

In "The Dare," Roger Hoffmann describes the time when he
accepted a dangerous dare from a friend.

ROGER HOFFMAN

The Dare

The secret to diving under a moving freight train and rolling   1
out the other side with all your parts attached lies in picking the
right spot between the tracks to hit with your back. Ideally, you
want soft dirt or pea gravel, clear of glass shards and railroad
spikes that could cause you instinctively, and fatally, to sit up.
Today, at thirty-eight, I couldn't be threatened or baited enough
to attempt that dive. But as a seventh grader struggling to make
the cut in a tough Atlanta grammar school, all it took was a dare.

I coasted through my first years of school as a fussed-over   2
smart kid, the teacher's pet who finished his work first and then
strutted around the room tutoring other students. By the seventh

grade, I had more A's than friends. Even my old cronies, Dwayne and O.T., made it clear I'd never be one of the guys in junior high if I didn't dirty up my act. They challenged me to break the rules, and I did. The I-dare-you's escalated: shoplifting, sugaring teachers' gas tanks, dropping lighted matches into public mailboxes. Each guerrilla act won me the approval I never got for just being smart.

Walking home by the railroad tracks after school, we started playing chicken with oncoming trains. O.T., who was failing that year, always won. One afternoon he charged a boxcar from the side, stopping just short of throwing himself between the wheels. I was stunned. After the train disappeared, we debated whether someone could dive under a moving car, stay put for a 10-count, then scramble out the other side. I thought it could be done and said so. O.T. immediately stepped in front of me and smiled. Not by me, I added quickly. I certainly didn't mean that I could do it. "A smart guy like you," he said, his smile evaporating, "you could figure it out easy." And then, squeezing each word for effect, "I . . . DARE . . . you." I'd just turned twelve. The monkey clawing my back was Teacher's Pet. And I'd been dared.   3

As an adult, I've been on both ends of life's implicit business and social I-dare-you's, although adults don't use those words. We provoke with body language, tone of voice, ambiguous phrases. I dare you to: argue with the boss, tell Fred what you think of him, send the wine back. Only rarely are the risks physical. How we respond to dares when we are young may have something to do with which of the truly hazardous male inner dares—attacking mountains, tempting bulls at Pamplona—we embrace or ignore as men.   4

For two weeks, I scouted trains and tracks. I studied moving boxcars close up, memorizing how they squatted on their axles, never getting used to the squeal or the way the air fell hot from the sides. I created an imaginary, friendly train and ran next to it. I mastered a shallow, head-first dive with a simple half-twist. I'd land on my back, count to ten, imagine wheels, and, locking both hands on the rail to my left, heave myself over and out. Even under pure sky, though, I had to fight to keep my eyes open and my shoulders between the rails.   5

The next Saturday, O.T., Dwayne, and three eighth graders met me below the hill that backed up to the lumberyard. The track followed a slow bend there and opened to a straight, slightly uphill climb for a solid third of a mile. My run started two hundred yards after the bend. The train would have its tongue hanging out.   6

The other boys huddled off to one side, a circle on another   7
planet, and watched quietly as I double-knotted my shoelaces.
My hands trembled. O.T. broke the circle and came over to me.
He kept his hands hidden in the pockets of his jacket. We looked
at each other. BB's of sweat appeared beneath his nose. I stuffed
my wallet in one of his pockets, rubbing it against his knuckles on
the way in, and slid my house key, wired to a red-and-white fish-
ing bobber, into the other. We backed away from each other, and
he turned and ran to join the four already climbing up the hill.

I watched them all the way to the top. They clustered   8
together as if I were taking their picture. Their silhouette resem-
bled a round-shouldered tombstone. They waved down to me,
and I dropped them from my mind and sat down on the rail.
Immediately, I jumped back. The steel was vibrating.

The train sounded like a cow going short of breath. I pulled   9
my shirttail out and looked down at my spot, then up the incline
of track ahead of me. Suddenly the air went hot, and the engine
was by me. I hadn't pictured it moving that fast. A man's bare
head leaned out and stared at me. I waved to him with my left
hand and turned into the train, burying my face in the incred-
ible noise. When I looked up, the head was gone.

I started running alongside the boxcars. Quickly, I found   10
their pace, held it, and then eased off, concentrating on each
thick wheel that cut past me. I slowed another notch. Over my
shoulder, I picked my car as it came off the bend, locking in the
image of the white mountain goat painted on its side. I waited,
leaning forward like the anchor in a 440-relay, wishing the baton
up the track behind me. Then the big goat fired by me, and I was
flying and then tucking my shoulder as I dipped under the train.

A heavy blanket of red dust settled over me. I felt bolted to   11
the earth. Sheet-metal bellies thundered and shook above my
face. Count to ten, a voice said, watch the axles and look to your
left for daylight. But I couldn't count, and I couldn't find left if
my life depended on it, which it did. The colors overhead went
from brown to red to black to red again. Finally, I ripped my
hands free, forced them to the rail, and, in one convulsive jerk,
threw myself into the blue light.

I lay there face down until there was no more noise, and I   12
could feel the sun against the back of my neck. I sat up. The last
ribbon of train was slipping away in the distance. Across the
tracks, O.T. was leading a cavalry charge down the hill, five very
small, galloping boys, their fists whirling above them. I pulled
my knees to my chest. My corduroy pants puckered wet across
my thighs. I didn't care.

VOCABULARY WORDS: cronies (2), implicit (4), ambiguous (4), heave (5), silhouette (8), convulsive (11), cavalry (12)

ACTIVITY 5

Reading to Improve Writing. Discuss the following questions about "The Dare" with your classmates.

1. Why did the author accept the dare?

   _____

   _____

   _____

2. Relate this sentence from paragraph 12 to the main point of the essay: "Across the tracks, O.T. was leading a cavalry charge down the hill, five very small, galloping boys, their fists whirling above them."

   _____

   _____

   _____

3. Compare how Hoffman feels about this event now—as an adult—with how he felt about it as a child.

   _____

   _____

   _____

4. Examine the description that Hoffman uses in paragraph 11. What specific details does he use? How does he get you to picture him under the moving train?

   _____

   _____

   _____

ACTIVITY 6

Brainstorming about Memorable Events. Spend a few minutes thinking about the course of your life. First brainstorm a list of happy events that have had a profound effect on who you are today. Then brainstorm a list of unhappy events that have affected you in the same way. You may find that some of the same events you associated with a significant person come to mind now as well, but you'll want to add others to your list.

One student writer, Karla, brainstormed the following list of significant events:

Happy events:

> the day I got my driver's license
>
> the day I graduated from high school
>
> when I fell in love for the first time
>
> when I got my own apartment near campus

Unhappy events:

> when I lost my close friend
>
> when I got a speeding ticket
>
> when my mom almost died
>
> when Greg dumped me last year
>
> my history class this semester

Karla then worked with a peer response group to see which event her classmates found most interesting and wanted to know more about. The group seemed most interested in the time Karla's mother almost died. Karla then related that event aloud, as one of her classmates took notes. This is Karla's story.

It all began on my first day in fifth grade. After I arrived home, I wanted to go shopping for school supplies. My mom didn't really want to take me, but I just had to get some things. My sister, Norma, and I jumped in the backseat of the car while my mom and older sister, Ana, got in front. Ana was going to drive since my mom has heart trouble and can't drive. It was then that we spotted another one of my sisters, Mary, driving my Dad's truck. There was only one place she could be going—to her boyfriend's house. My mom had forbidden Mary to see him because he was separated but not divorced. "Do you want me to follow her?" Ana asked.

My mother said yes. I was thinking, why does this always happen to me!

At last the truck stopped and Mary went to the front door of the house. Her boyfriend came out and hugged her. My mother was hysterical! "How could she? What does she think she's doing?" Then she leaped out of the car and ran toward the house, yelling at Mary, "Get in the car!" Mary yelled back, "I will not! I hate the way you treat me, the way you follow me, the way you are! I hate you." Then the moment I dreaded came. My mom sank to the ground. She began to gasp for breath. I remember the panicky look in my mother's eyes, the look of fear in Mary's eyes, and the blank look on Ana's face.

Mary's boyfriend called 911, and Mom was taken to the hospital. I prayed hard for my mom, and we all cried a lot. After a while, things turned out all right. She had had a heart attack, but she was going to live. While my mom was in the hospital, my sister Mary moved out. When mom came home, she talked to me more than she ever used to. We began to share our lives more, the way a mother and daughter should.

Karla's story prompted many questions from her peer response group. For example, one student asked, "Did your mom and sister make up?" Karla responded:

Yes, they had a long talk and they're trying to work out their differences.

Other group members asked, "Can you remember anything else that was said?" and "How did you feel during all of this?"

I remember Norma screaming and crying, "You killed Momma." Mary didn't say anything. She just stood with her boyfriend. She seemed frozen with fear. Ana was kneeling next to Mom saying, "It's going to be all right." I was really scared. I knew what was coming. My heart sank. I thought my mother was going to die.

Finally, someone asked Karla why this event was significant to her.

It made me realize how much I loved my mother. It also led to a better relationship between me and my mom.

Relating the event aloud and reading over the group member's notes helped Karla focus on the details and significance of the event. She now had useful description and dialogue to add to her piece. Relating aloud and answering the group's questions also helped Karla zero-in on her main idea: none of her family's difficulties were as significant as the possibility of losing her mother. This would become her thesis statement.

Relating Aloud. Working with a small group, relate your significant event aloud. The event may be a happy or sad one that has markedly affected who you are. Ask someone to take notes on your story or use a tape recorder. When you finish relating aloud, respond to the group's questions about your topic. Then read over the notes (or listen to the tape) to gather additional ideas.

Set your material on a memorable event aside for a time. You now want to turn to gathering ideas on a different topic—an important period in your life.

An Important Period in Your Life

Unlike an event, which occurs at a specific time or on a particular day (such as Karla's mother's heart attack), a period in your life includes events that take place over a stretch of time. For example, it could be a time when your life came together or fell apart, the year you lived in New York, your first year of marriage, or the months you spent in rehabilitation after a car accident.

Malcolm X, in "Prison Studies," describes the period in his life when he learned to love reading. He also describes the effect that reading had on his life.

MALCOLM X
Prison Studies

Many who today hear me somewhere in person, or on television, or those who read something I've said, will think I went to school far beyond the eighth grade. This impression is due entirely to my prison studies. 1

It had really begun back in the Charlestown Prison, when Bimbi first made me feel envy of his stock of knowledge. Bimbi 2 had always taken charge of any conversation he was in, and I had tried to emulate him. But every book I picked up had few sentences which didn't contain anywhere from one to nearly all of the words that might as well have been in Chinese. When I just skipped those words, of course, I really ended up with little idea of what the book said. So I had come to the Norfolk Prison Colony still going through only book-reading motions. Pretty soon, I would have quit even these motions, unless I had received the motivation that I did.

I saw that the best thing I could do was get hold of a dictio-   3
nary—to study, to learn some words. I was lucky enough to reason also that I should try to improve my penmanship. It was sad. I couldn't even write in a straight line. It was both ideas together that moved me to request a dictionary along with some tablets and pencils from the Norfolk Prison Colony school.

I spent two days just riffling uncertainly though the dictio-   4
nary's pages. I'd never realized so many words existed! I didn't know which words I needed to learn. Finally, to start some kind of action, I began copying.

In my slow, painstaking, ragged handwriting, I copied into   5
my tablet everything printed on that first page, down to the punctuation marks.

I believe it took me a day. Then, aloud, I read back, to my-   6
self, everything I'd written on the tablet. Over and over, aloud, to myself, I read my own handwriting.

I woke up the next morning, thinking about those words—   7
immensely proud to realize that not only had I written so much at one time, but I'd written words that I never knew were in the world. Moreover, with a little effort, I also could remember what many of these words meant. I reviewed the words whose meanings I didn't remember. Funny thing, from the dictionary first page right now, that "aardvark" springs to my mind. The dictionary had a picture of it, a long-tailed, long-eared, burrowing African mammal, which lives off termites caught by sticking out its tongue as an anteater does for ants.

I was so fascinated that I went on—I copied the dictionary's   8
next page. And the same experience came when I studied that. With every succeeding page, I also learned of people and places and events from history. Actually the dictionary is like a miniature encyclopedia. Finally the dictionary's A section had filled a whole tablet—and I went on into the B's. That was the way I started copying what eventually became the entire dictionary. It went a lot faster after so much practice helped me to pick up handwriting speed. Between what I wrote in my tablet, and writ-

ing letters, during the rest of my time in prison I would guess I wrote a million words.

I suppose it was inevitable that as my word-base broadened,   9
I could for the first time pick up a book and read and now begin to understand what the book was saying. Anyone who has read a great deal can imagine the new world that opened. Let me tell you something: from then until I left that prison, in every free moment I had, if I was not reading in the library, I was reading on my bunk. You couldn't have gotten me out of books with a wedge. Between Mr. Muhammad's teachings, my correspondence, my visitors—usually Ella and Reginald—and my reading of books, months passed without my even thinking about being imprisoned. In fact, up to then, I never had been so truly free in my life. . . .

As you can imagine, especially in a prison where there was   10
heavy emphasis on rehabilitation, an inmate was smiled upon if he demonstrated an unusually intense interest in books. There was a sizable number of well-read inmates, especially the popular debaters. Some were said by many to be practically walking encyclopedias. They were almost celebrities. No university would ask any student to devour literature as I did when this new world opened to me, of being able to read and understand.

I read more in my room than in the library itself. An inmate   11
who was known to read a lot could check out more than the permitted maximum number of books. I preferred reading in the total isolation of my own room.

When I had progressed to really serious reading, every night   12
at about ten P.M. I would be outraged with the "lights out." It always seemed to catch me right in the middle of something engrossing.

Fortunately, right outside my door was a corridor light that   13
cast a glow into my room. The glow was enough to read by, once my eyes adjusted to it. So when "lights out" came, I would sit on the floor where I could continue reading in that glow.

At one-hour intervals the night guards paced past every   14
room. Each time I heard the approaching footsteps, I jumped into bed and feigned sleep. And as soon as the guard passed, I got back out of bed onto the floor area of that light-glow, where I would read for another fifty-eight minutes—until the guard approached again. That went on until three or four every morning. Three or four hours of sleep a night was enough for me. Often in the years in the streets I had slept less than that.

I have often reflected upon the new vistas that reading   15
opened to me. I knew right there in prison that reading had

changed forever the course of my life. As I see it today, the ability to read awoke inside me some long dormant craving to be mentally alive. I certainly wasn't seeking any degree, the way a college confers a status symbol upon its students. My homemade education gave me, with every additional book that I read, a little bit more sensitivity to the deafness, dumbness, and blindness that was afflicting the black race in America. Not long ago, an English writer telephoned me from London, asking questions. One was, "What's your alma mater?" I told him, "Books." You will never catch me with a free fifteen minutes in which I'm not studying something I feel might be able to help the black man. . . .

Every time I catch a plane, I have with me a book that I want   16
to read—and that's a lot of books these days. If I weren't out here every day battling the white man, I could spend the rest of my life reading, just satisfying my curiosity—because you can hardly mention anything I'm not curious about. I don't think anybody ever got more out of going to prison than I did. In fact, prison enabled me to study far more intensively than I would have if my life had gone differently and I had attended some college. I imagine that one of the biggest troubles with colleges is there are too many distractions, too much panty-raiding, fraternities, and boola-boola and all of that. Where else but in prison could I have attacked my ignorance by being able to study intensely sometimes as much as fifteen hours a day?

VOCABULARY WORDS: emulate (2), painstaking (5), inevitable (9), engrossing (12), intervals (14), feigned (14), vistas (15), dormant (15)

ACTIVITY 8

Reading to Improve Writing. Discuss the following questions about "Prison Studies" with your classmates.

1. In what ways is the period of time spent reading significant in Malcolm's life?

   _____

   _____

   _____

2. How do you think this period in Malcolm's life affected him after his release from prison?

_____

_____

_____

3. Which details about Malcolm's prison life do you find especially interesting? Why?

_____

_____

_____

4. The writer says in paragraph 9, "I never had been so truly free in my life." What does he mean?

_____

_____

_____

ACTIVITY 9

Gathering Ideas about an Important Period in Your Life. So far in this chapter, you have used various methods for gathering ideas on a topic—brainstorming, freewriting, clustering, and relating aloud. Choose the one or two methods that work best for you and use them to gather ideas about an important period in your life.

DRAFTING

You have now gathered ideas on three topics—a significant person, a memorable event, and an important period in your life, each of which changed you in some meaningful way. You are ready to begin drafting. Here are some of your options:

To learn more about drafting, see pp. 34–39.

- You may select one of the three topics for your discovery draft.
- You may write drafts on two or three of the topics to see which one you prefer to continue working on.
- You may combine related topics in your discovery draft. For example, you might connect your significant person with a significant event or period in your life.

Be sure to choose a topic that interests you and that you have many ideas about. Before you begin drafting, write a preliminary thesis statement that indicates the main point of the essay. Keep your audience and purpose in mind but remember that your main goal at the drafting stage is to get your ideas down on paper. You'll have time later on to revise and edit your discovery draft.

As you write this draft, you might find that your thoughts take you in an unexpected direction. Follow the path that seems most interesting to you. When you write a discovery draft, you aim to explore possibilities rather than follow a map that's already been drawn.

Draft on Computer

If at all possible, use a word-processing program to draft your discovery draft. Having a draft on computer will make revising your essay much quicker and easier.

Use E-mail or Networked Discussion

E-mail your discovery draft to your fellow students for feedback. Alternatively, if you have access to a networked computer lab, discuss your draft online with other students in the class, on your campus, or even at different colleges. Whether you e-mail or discuss the draft online, ask your readers (1) what interested them the most about your draft, and (2) what they want to know more about. Use their responses to help you decide where to add supporting details.

Student writer Jesus Ramirez, whose brainstorming you saw earlier in the chapter, wrote the following thesis statement and discovery draft about a significant person. Notice that although Jesus decided to write about his father, he narrowed his topic to going to baseball games with his father. A more focused topic allowed Jesus to provide supporting details and thereby develop his ideas more fully in this short essay. (Note that Jesus's discovery draft includes the types of errors that typically appear in a first draft.)

<u>Preliminary thesis statement</u>: *There is more to baseball than a game; it is the sport through which my father taught me valuable lessons.*

Baseball Memories

I love this sport because of my father. My father is   1
the reason I love baseball. He cares for his family. He's always putting them above everything else. He works hard at his job to ensure that we have all of the necessities of life. He loves to rent videos for us to watch, too. Ever since I was two years old my father has taken me to baseball games. There is more to baseball than a game; it is the sport through which my father taught me valuable lessons.

On one occasion, a player struck out two times. He   2
threw his bat out on the baseball field. My father told me that the next time, he would strike out again. I didn't believe him when the player was at bat again, I was ready to disprove my dad. But he was right. I asked him how he knew that the batter was going to strike out. He told me that it is very hard to get things accomplished though anger or frustration because anger gets in the way of performance.

He also showed me the importance of not giving up.   3
During one ball game, a player struck out three times. As he stepped up to the plate for the fourth time, the crowd was booing and cursing him. I asked my dad, "Why are all these people being rude to this player?" He said that he was not doing too well. He was having a bad night. That did not make him a bad player, though.

But of all the times I went with my father to the ball   4
games, this one stands out. It was a warm afternoon when my father asked me to go with him. When we got there, it was very cold and the wind was blowing. My father had to put his arms around my bare legs to protect me.

My memories of my father at the ballpark will always   5
be special to me. He used baseball games to teach me about
life.

REVISING

*Why is revising impor-
tant? See pp. 39–41.*

When you revise a discovery draft, you focus not only on what
you want to communicate to your audience but also on how you
communicate it. In this stage, then, you concentrate on such tasks as
developing your ideas, organizing your essay, and polishing your sentences and words. As you learned in Chapter 2, writers often move
back and forth among the stages of the writing process. Thus, it's possible that as you revise you might need to return to the gathering
ideas stage. After you've gathered enough ideas, you can go back to
revising.

As you revise, always think about what your reader needs to know
in order to understand the significance of that special person, event,
or period in your life.

FAQs

The *Choices* Web site includes frequently asked questions
about topics in each chapter of the textbook. Go to **** and click on "FAQs."

Developing Your Ideas

When you wrote your discovery draft, you probably wrote the story
quickly, as Jesus did. Now, while you revise, you want to add details to
make your piece interesting and memorable. You need to go beyond
describing experiences in general ways to describing them in enough
detail that your readers feel as though they were there with you.

*More information on
description, narration,
and examples can be
found on pp. 65–70
and 73–74.*

For this chapter's writing assignment, you will develop your ideas
and support your topic sentences through using description, narration, and examples. These techniques serve several important functions in an essay:

- They increase the reader's interest in your topic.
- They help the reader understand your main ideas.
- They help to convince the reader to accept your viewpoint.

DESCRIPTION. As you learned in Chapter 3, when you use description, you create images by describing how something looks, sounds, smells, tastes, or feels. For example, Dawn Sanders, in "Beth," describes Beth's appearance this way. This description of how Beth looks increases the reader's interest in her.

> Stringy blond hair framed her homely face and accentuated her long pointy nose. She had a bad overbite, probably caused by her incessant thumb-sucking. On her bony shoulders hung an old, faded sweater, out of shape from too many washings, and hopelessly out of style. With her sallow complexion, she looked malnourished.

HOW TO Use Description

- Draw on all five senses: sight, sound, smell, taste, and touch. Instead of "the movie theater was dark," write "the dark movie theater smelled like popcorn and stale cigarettes."

- Be specific. Instead of "the room was nicely decorated," write "the room's light blue walls contrasted with the pearl white sofa."

- Make comparisons, such as "the baby's eyes are like gray marbles."

- Avoid common phrases, such as "as pretty as a picture" or "as cute as can be."

NARRATION. As you learned in Chapter 3, you use narration when you want to tell a story based on a series of events as they happened in time.

In the following example from "Prison Studies," Malcolm X summarizes in narrative form the series of events that resulted in his new vision for blacks in the United States.

> I have often reflected upon the new vistas that reading opened to me. I knew right there in prison that reading had changed forever the course of my life. As I see it today, the ability to read awoke inside me some long dormant craving to be mentally alive. I certainly wasn't seeking any degree, the way a

college confers a status symbol upon its students. My homemade education gave me, with every additional book that I read, a little bit more sensitivity to the deafness, dumbness, and blindness that was afflicting the black race in America. . . .

HOW TO Use Narration

- Tell a series of events that supports your thesis, usually in the order in which they occurred.

- Narrate only the most important events.

- Use descriptive details and dialogue to illustrate important points.

EXAMPLES. Examples (such as facts or details) illustrate or explain an idea. Examples can make your essay more interesting and convincing. Imagine that Roger Hoffman's "The Dare" contained this sentence:

Adults often dare each other to do things, though they don't directly state it.

What kinds of dares? How are the dares communicated? Instead of being vague, the author gave examples such as these:

We provoke with body language, tone of voice, ambiguous phrases. I dare you to: argue with the boss, tell Fred what you think of him, send the wine back.

These examples make the author's point clearer and livelier.

HOW TO Use Examples

- Use examples to support your ideas, in particular your topic sentences.

- To think of examples, ask *who, what, where, when, why,* or *how* about the topic.

- Give specific information or description in the examples.

ACTIVITY 10

Adding Details to Your Essay. Reread your discovery draft. Now add details (using description, narration, and examples) to make your essay interesting and memorable.

Organizing Your Essay

One way you communicate clearly is by organizing your essay so that your reader can easily understand your message. To organize, first look at your thesis statement to ensure that it is effective. Next, look at your topic sentences to ensure that they are effective. Then consider your paragraph unity.

WRITING EFFECTIVE THESIS STATEMENTS. In Chapter 2, you learned that an effective thesis statement

- announces the topic of the essay.
- shows, explains, or argues a point about the topic.
- gives a sense of what the essay will be about.

In her essay, "Beth," Dawn Sanders writes the following thesis statement about a significant person in her life: "If she only knew that it was I, not she, who should have felt ashamed." In addition to indicating the topic of the essay (Beth), this thesis statement shows a point (the author, not Beth, should be ashamed) and gives a sense of what the essay will be about (*why* the author, not Beth, should be ashamed).

For his discovery draft, Jesus Ramirez wrote the following preliminary thesis statement: "There is more to baseball than a game; it is the sport through which my father taught me valuable lessons." This is an effective thesis statement because it announces the topic (baseball and Jesus's father); shows a point about the topic (through baseball his father taught him valuable lessons); and gives a sense of what the essay will be about (the valuable lessons his father taught him).

Need more help writing a thesis statement? See pp. 36–37.

ACTIVITY 11

Revising Your Thesis Statement. Reread your thesis statement. Does it announce the topic, show a point about the topic, and give a sense of what the essay will be about? If necessary, revise your thesis statement to make it be more effective.

Topic sentences are also explained on pp. 59–60.

WRITING EFFECTIVE TOPIC SENTENCES. As you learned in Chapter 3, the "one thing" that you explain in a paragraph is stated in a topic sentence. To write effective topic sentences, you must

- break up your thesis statement into several specific supporting ideas.
- write a complete thought for each of these specific ideas.

Here are some of the topic sentences in "The Dare" and "Prison Studies." Notice how these topic sentences provide specific supporting ideas to develop the essay.

From "The Dare"

THESIS STATEMENT

Today, at thirty-eight, I couldn't be threatened or baited enough to attempt that dive. But as a seventh grader struggling to make the cut in a tough Atlanta grammar school, all it took was a dare.

TOPIC SENTENCES

Walking home by the railroad tracks after school, we started playing chicken with oncoming trains.

As an adult, I've been on both ends of life's implicit business and social I-dare-you's, although adults don't use those words.

The train sounded like a cow going short of breath.

I started running alongside the boxcars.

From "Prison Studies"

THESIS STATEMENT

Many who today hear me somewhere in person, or on television, or those who read something I've said, will think I went to school far beyond the eighth grade.

TOPIC SENTENCES

It had really begun back in the Charlestown Prison, when Bimbi first made me feel envy of his stock of knowledge.

I saw that the best thing I could do was get hold of a dictionary—to study, to learn some words.

I woke up the next morning, thinking about those words—immensely proud to realize that not only had I written so much at one time, but I'd written words that I never knew were in the world.

I suppose it was inevitable that as my word-base broadened, I could for the first time pick up a book and read and now begin to understand what the book was saying.

As you learned in Chapter 3, a topic sentence may fall anywhere in the paragraph. Most often, however, it comes first.

Notice in the following paragraph from "Beth" that the topic sentence (italicized) comes first and the rest of the paragraph tells us how Beth was different.

From the very beginning, Beth was different, an outsider. Her physical appearance set her apart. Stringy blond hair framed her homely face and accentuated her long pointy nose. She had a bad overbite, probably caused by her incessant thumb-sucking. On her bony shoulders hung an old, faded sweater, out of shape from too many washings, and hopelessly out of style. With her sallow complexion, she looked malnourished. We all thought she was dense. The ideas that were easy for us to understand seemed out of her reach. She remained at the bottom of the class, never seeming to benefit from the teacher's help.

ACTIVITY 12

Revising Your Topic Sentences. Reread your discovery draft. Underline your thesis statement and each topic sentence. If necessary, revise your topic sentences or write several more. First break up your thesis statement into several specific ideas. Then write a complete thought—a topic sentence—for each of these ideas.

Revise with Color

To help you examine particular aspects of your draft, use the "color" feature on your word-processing program. For instance, you can write your topic sentences in green typeface. This technique makes it easier for you to focus on one aspect of your text at a time. Of course, you need to return the typeface to black when you're preparing your final draft.

CREATING PARAGRAPH UNITY. As you learned in Chapter 3, once you have an effective topic sentence for each paragraph, you need to make sure that all other sentences within the paragraph relate to the topic sentence. In the following paragraph from "Beth," several

For more information on paragraph unity, see pp. 63–64.

irrelevant sentences—sentences that do not support the topic sentence—have been added (in italics); notice how these sentences detract from the topic sentence.

> We excluded Beth from our games. *I wish I were still a kid and could play some of those games; they were really fun.* If we did let her join, it was so we could gang up and laugh at her. The boys all called her names, pulling her hair and stealing her food at lunch. *This was in the days before there were individual canned servings of pudding and fruit, and all we ever got were apples and bananas or a little box of raisins.* At first, Beth fought back, but after a time she seemed to lose spirit. She became quiet and withdrawn.

When you revise, you need to eliminate such irrelevant sentences in order to achieve paragraph unity. Here is the same paragraph from "Beth" without the irrelevant sentences.

> We excluded Beth from our games. If we did let her join, it was so we could gang up and laugh at her. The boys all called her names, pulling her hair and stealing her food at lunch. At first, Beth fought back, but after a time she seemed to lose spirit. She became quiet and withdrawn.

ACTIVITY 13

Eliminating Irrelevant Sentences from Your Draft. Reread your discovery draft, looking for irrelevant sentences. Delete any that you find.

Save Your Drafts

As you revise, save copies of your drafts. You can do this by printing out copies, or you can save the drafts in separate files. Number or date the drafts to avoid confusion. These drafts can be included in a portfolio of your work to show your writing improvement. Also, many instructors like to examine students' drafts to evaluate their writing processes. Be sure to keep backup disks of your files.

Polishing Your Sentences and Words

Now that you have improved your thesis statement, your topic sentences, and your paragraph unity, you'll want to turn your attention to your sentences and words. When you wrote your discovery draft, you were busy getting your thoughts on paper, so your sentences may not have come out as clearly as you would like. An important part of the revision process, then, is to revise your sentences and words to be clearer and more interesting.

One way to ensure clear, interesting sentences is to consider sentence variety. Readers get bored easily if many of your sentences are short and sound alike. You may have noticed, for example, that Jesus's discovery draft contained many short sentences. To improve his discovery draft, Jesus used a technique known as sentence combining.

COMBINING SENTENCES USING COORDINATING CONJUNCTIONS. One way to combine short, closely related sentences is to use *coordinating conjunctions*. Here are seven coordinating conjunctions and their meanings:

for—because
and—in addition
nor—neither
but—opposite
or—alternatively
yet—opposite
so—as a result

Many people remember these coordinating conjunctions by thinking of the word "FANBOYS." This word is spelled with the first letter of the seven coordinating conjunctions.

See Sentence Coordination in the Handbook for more help with sentence combining.

Use an appropriate coordinating conjunction (or FANBOYS) to combine short, closely related sentences. Put a comma before the coordinating conjunction.

SHORT SENTENCES

Last Saturday I went to an outlet store to buy a business suit. I also saw a movie with my best friend.

COMBINED SENTENCE WITH *AND*

Last Saturday I went to an outlet store to buy a business suit, and I also saw a movie with my best friend.

SHORT SENTENCES

The plane was an hour late getting into the airport. I missed my connecting flight.

COMBINED SENTENCE WITH *SO*

The plane was an hour late getting into the airport, so I missed my connecting flight.

SHORT SENTENCES

I gave my girlfriend another chance to show her commitment to me. She started dating my best friend.

COMBINED SENTENCE WITH *BUT*

I gave my girlfriend another chance to show her commitment to me, but she started dating my best friend.

HOW TO Combine Sentences with Coordinating Conjunctions

- Be sure that the closely related sentences you're combining are complete. Check that each one has a subject and a verb and conveys a complete thought.

- Select an appropriate coordinating conjunction *(for, and, nor, but, or, yet, so).*

- Use a comma before the coordinating conjunction.

ACTIVITY 14

Combining Sentences. Combine the following sentences with an appropriate coordinating conjunction.

1. Baseball is a multimillion dollar business. It is also one of America's oldest organized sports.

   _____

   _____

2. Baseball is still popular. Other sports, such as basketball and football, have become more popular.

_____

_____

3. Hundreds of major-league players earn more than a million dollars a year. Many athletes are attracted to the sport.

_____

_____

4. Women's softball has increased in popularity. This game is played at many colleges and at the Olympics.

_____

_____

5. At this time, a softball player can't earn a living playing softball. Not many athletes are interested in the sport professionally.

_____

_____

ACTIVITY 15 (GROUP)

Writing Sentences with Coordinating Conjunctions. With several classmates, select an activity you all are familiar with, such as dealing with a difficult customer, studying for a test, going to a concert, or applying for a job. Then, collaborate on writing five sentences on that topic. Each sentence should consist of two short, closely related sentences combined with a coordinating conjunction. For the five sentences you write, use at least three different coordinating conjunctions.

EXAMPLE   *Applying for a job can be intimidating, but it's an unavoidable part of making a living.*

AVOIDING EMPTY PHRASES. Empty phrases cause wordiness because they take up space without adding meaning to the sentence.

WORDY   *Due to the fact that* my mother is an actress, I was introduced to the theater at an early age.

REVISED   Because my mother is an actress, I was introduced to the theater at an early age.

WORDY   Nancy was *very* pleased that her graduation was *really* well attended.

REVISED   Nancy was pleased that her graduation was well attended.

WORDY   *In the event that* I finish my master's degree, it will be an important milestone.

REVISED   If I finish my master's degree, it will be an important milestone.

Here is a list of some other empty phrases to avoid and their more precise substitutes:

WORDY	PRECISE
owing to the fact that	because
through the use of	with
in the neighborhood of	about
for the purpose of	for
in order to	to
until such time as	until
at the present time	now
by means of	by
as of that date	then

In addition, note that the phrases *in my opinion, I believe, I feel,* and *I think* are empty because they state the obvious. The fact that you are writing the statement means it is *your* thought or opinion or belief. You are not adding new information for your reader.

WORDY   *In my opinion,* the drinking age should be lowered to eighteen.

REVISED   The drinking age should be lowered to eighteen.

WORDY   *I think* all my hard work has finally paid off.

REVISED   All my hard work has finally paid off.

WORDY   *I feel* the food in the Student Union is getting better.

REVISED   The food in the Student Union is getting better.

ACTIVITY 16

Eliminating Empty Phrases. Revise the following sentences to eliminate empty phrases.

1. As of this date, we haven't received the letter.

   _____

   _____

2. I received an A on the test due to the fact that I studied up until the time the test began.

   _____

   _____

3. I refused to pay the bill for the reason that the service was so poor.

   _____

   _____

4. The fact that it was so cold didn't stop me from jogging every morning.

   _____

   _____

5. Jill will continue to drive her car until such time as her license is revoked.

   _____

   _____

6. In my opinion, you should save your money in the event that you lose your job.

   _____

   _____

7. I went to college for the purpose of getting a good job.

   _____

   _____

8. I think, in the final analysis, the person who works hard will be well rewarded.

   _____

   _____

9. I was late paying my rent owing to the fact that my paycheck was late.

   _____

   _____

10. I believe we should leave early so as to arrive at the movie on time.

    _____

    _____

ACTIVITY 17

Polishing Your Sentences and Words. Reread your discovery draft, looking for short, closely related sentences that can be combined with coordinating conjunctions. Also, examine your word choice. Is your vocabulary specific and clear? Can you delete any unnecessary words or phrases?

Jesus's Revised Draft

Before you read Jesus's revised draft, reread his discovery draft. Notice, in particular, how in the revision he has improved his thesis statement and topic sentences, developed his ideas, organized his essay, and polished his sentences and words. (You will still notice a few errors in the revised draft; these will be corrected when Jesus edits his essay later on.)

Baseball Memories

To some baseball is just a sport where someone tries to reach base before getting thrown out. To others it is "America's pastime," a baseball stadium filled with people cheering, eating hot roasted peanuts, and, when the seventh inning approaches, singing "Take Me Out to the Ball Game." To me, though, baseball will always be more than just a game because my father used baseball to teach me valuable lessons about life.

1   Introduction is more interesting.

From the time I was two years old, my father took me to baseball games. On one occasion, when we were at a game, a player struck out two times and threw his bat out on the baseball field. My father told me that the next time, the player would strike out again. I didn't believe him when the player was at bat again, I was ready to disprove my dad. But he was right. I asked him how he knew the batter would strike out again. He told me that it is very hard to get things accomplished though anger or frustration; anger gets in the way of performance. He added that I should not throw things when I get mad because this could hurt someone else or myself. Instead, he suggested that I take the time to think things over before I do something that I will regret later on.

2

The main point of the paragraph is clearer.

He also used baseball to show me the importance of not giving up. During one ball game, a player struck out three times. As he stepped up to the plate for the fourth time,

3

the crowd booed and cursed him. I asked my dad, "Why are all these people being rude to this player?" He replied, "He is one of the best players the team has, he is not doing too well. There are days when we are not ourselves we are humans and make mistakes. Just because he struck out three times does not make him a bad person. You should learn from his experience—life is made of strikeouts, but it doesn't matter how many strikeouts you have, what matters is that you get another chance to hit the ball. If you are confident, you will succeed, but if you are not confident and do not believe in yourself, you will fail."

Dialogue makes the father's advice easier to understand.

But of all the times I went with my father to the ball   4
games, one stands out. It was a warm afternoon when my father asked me to go with him. When we got there, it began to get very cold and the wind was blowing. I remember that I was just wearing shorts my legs were freezing. I told my father that I was cold, but I didn't want to leave. He then suggested that we move to another place where the wind didn't blow as hard. But when we moved to the new place, it was still cold, so my father sat in back of me and asked me to bend my knees toward my chest and lean back. Then he put his warm hands on my legs, like a duck protecting his duckling from bad weather or a predater that might hurt him. Not only did I feel warmed by my father, but I felt protected as well.

This description makes the essay more interesting and the point clearer.

My memories of my father at the ballpark will always   5
be special to me. He used baseball to teach me the importance of controlling my temper and of not throwing or hitting things when I become upset. He also used baseball to teach me to work toward goals without giving up. Like a batter facing that next pitch, he taught me to face life head-on.

The conclusion is more extended and doesn't leave the reader hanging.

ACTIVITY 18

Analyzing Jesus's Revised Draft. Use the following questions to analyze how Jesus has improved his draft through revision.

1. Is Jesus's introduction interesting? Why or why not?

   _____

   _____

   _____

2. What is Jesus's thesis statement? How did he improve it from his preliminary thesis statement?

   _____

   _____

   _____

   _____

3. How well does Jesus use topic sentences? After examining all of his topic sentences, focus on one paragraph. Identify the topic sentence and explain how the idea in the topic sentence is developed in the paragraph.

   _____

   _____

   _____

   _____

4. What details has Jesus included to improve his essay?

   _____

   _____

   _____

5. Look back at paragraph 1 of Jesus's draft (p. 119); he omitted two sentences in his revision. Why do you think he decided to omit these? Was it a good decision?

   _____

   _____

6. How has Jesus polished his sentences and words?

   _____

   _____

7. Does Jesus convince you—his reader—that his father is the most significant person in his life? Explain.

   _____

   _____

   _____

8. What other revisions could Jesus make to improve his draft?

   _____

   _____

   _____

   _____

ACTIVITY 19 (GROUP)

Using Peer Review. Form a group with two or three other students and exchange copies of your drafts. Read your draft aloud while your classmates follow along. Then ask your group members the following questions about your paper. Write down your classmates' responses. If you don't understand what a classmate is suggesting, ask for clarification before you write it down. You will want to read these notes later for suggestions on how to improve your draft.

1. What do you like best about my essay?

   _____

   _____

   _____

   _____

2. How interesting is my introduction? Does it make you want to continue reading my paper? Why or why not?

   _____

   _____

   _____

   _____

3. What is my thesis statement? Do I need to make the thesis clearer?

   _____

   _____

   _____

   _____

4. Examine my topic sentences. How well do they connect to my thesis and indicate the main idea of each paragraph?

   _____

   _____

   _____

   _____

5. Where in the draft could I better develop my ideas by using description, narration, and examples?

_____

_____

_____

6. Is each paragraph in my draft unified? Or do some paragraphs contain irrelevant sentences or words that need to be omitted?

_____

_____

_____

7. Where in my draft did my writing confuse you? How can I clarify my ideas?

_____

_____

_____

8. Have I followed all the instructions for this assignment?

_____

_____

_____

Use E-mail or Online Peer Review

E-mail your draft to several fellow students and ask them to answer the peer reviews in a return e-mail. Alternatively, if you have access to a networked computer lab, you may do peer review online. Send your suggestions for revision to the author's e-mail box.

Revising Your Draft. Taking your classmates' suggestions for revision into consideration, revise your draft on a significant person, event, or period in your life. Pay particular attention to the development of ideas and to improving your thesis statement, topic sentences, paragraphs, sentences, and words.

EDITING

Now that you have revised your draft, you're ready to edit it for correctness. Remember, the more your readers pay attention to the errors, the less attention they pay to what you have to say. As you edit, focus in particular on eliminating run-on sentences, comma splices, and misspelled words.

See Run-on Sentences in the Handbook for more help.

Correcting Run-on Sentences

A complete sentence contains a subject and a verb and expresses a complete thought.

Arizona has some of the hottest spots in the country.

Going to college while working full time has been hard.

I bought a minivan after I had my third child.

Student athletes often experience great pressures to do well.

A *run-on sentence* consists of two sentences blended together without punctuation.

Arizona has some of the hottest spots in the country don't visit it in August.

Going to college while working full time has been hard I never get enough sleep.

I bought a minivan after I had my third child for we needed the room.

Student athletes often experience great pressures to do well they might need extra support from their schools.

Correct run-on sentences in one of two ways.

• Make the run-on sentence into two sentences.

Arizona has some of the hottest spots in the country. Don't visit it in August.

HOW TO Correct Run-on Sentences and
Comma Splices

A run-on sentence consists of two sentences punctuated as one sentence. To correct a run-on,

- break it up into two sentences,

- or punctuate it correctly.

A comma splice consists of two sentences connected only with a comma. To correct a comma splice,

- replace the comma with a period to make the sentence into two sentences,

- or add a coordinating conjunction *(for, and, nor, but, or, yet, so)* before the comma,

- or replace the comma with a semicolon.

Going to college while working full time has been hard. I never get enough sleep.

- Punctuate the run-on sentence correctly.

I bought a minivan after I had my third child, for we needed the room.

Because student athletes experience great pressure to do well, they might need extra support from their schools.

ACTIVITY 21

Correcting Run-on Sentences. Seven of the following ten sentences are run-ons. Identify each run-on sentence and correct it by splitting it into two sentences or punctuating the sentence to make it correct.

1. My uncle has a glass eye he likes to take it out to frighten young children.

_____

_____

2. When there's a full moon our cat gets crazy he climbs the curtains and howls when we try to get him down.

_____

_____

3. My youngest daughter is only three she can already write her name.

_____

_____

4. Our new house almost burned down when I left a candle burning.

_____

_____

5. My father was treated for cancer he's doing well now.

_____

_____

6. Right after I turned sixteen, I got a job bagging groceries at the neighborhood market.

_____

_____

7. I'm returning to school to enter the health-care profession I plan to be a physical therapist.

_____

_____

8. Last year I started exercising an hour a day I lost sixty pounds.

_____

_____

9. Even though my boyfriend is Italian he doesn't know how to cook any pasta dishes.

_____

_____

10. I don't like to be alone at night I got a dog to keep me company.

_____

_____

 Online Grammar Skills Practice

The *Choices* Web site includes practice exercises in correcting run-on sentences. Go to <**www.bedfordstmartins .com/choices/**> and click on "Exercise Central." After logging in, click on "Run-on Sentences."

Correcting Comma Splices

Need more help? Go to Comma Splices in the Handbook.

A *comma splice* is an error that occurs when two complete sentences are combined only with a comma.

The day of the big sale was busy, we survived the rush of customers.

There are three ways to correct a comma splice.

- Replace the comma with a period to make two sentences.

  The day of the big sale was busy. We survived the rush of customers.

- Add a coordinating conjunction after the comma.

  The day of the big sale was busy, *but* we survived the rush of customers.

- Replace the comma with a semicolon.

  The day of the big sale was busy; we survived the rush of customers.

When using a semicolon, many writers include a conjunctive adverb such as *in addition, although, nevertheless, however, moreover, in fact,* and *for example.* The conjunctive adverb will tell your readers how the two parts of the sentence connect together. The conjunctive adverb comes after the semicolon and is followed by a comma.

The day of the big sale was busy; *however,* we survived the rush of customers.

Here's another example of a comma splice and how it can be corrected.

COMMA SPLICE   My boss doesn't pay me enough, he wants me to work too many hours.

CORRECT   My boss doesn't pay me enough. He wants me to work too many hours.

My boss doesn't pay me enough, and he wants me to work too many hours.

My boss doesn't pay me enough; in addition, he wants me to work too many hours.

ACTIVITY 22

Correcting Comma Splices. Seven of the following ten sentences contain comma splices. Identify the comma splices and correct them. Use each of the three ways of correcting comma splices at least once.

1. My next-door neighbor is great, she's always available to babysit my kids.

_____

_____

2. Because of the snowstorm, we were stuck in the airport for seven hours.

_____

_____

3. My high school football coach was tough on the outside, he was soft on the inside.

_____

_____

4. My trip to Paris was wonderful, it was also expensive.

_____

_____

5. Although spicy, Cuban black beans are delicious and nutritious.

_____

_____

6. People think being a model is glamorous, it's actually boring.

_____

_____

7. When I was in Rome, I saw the pope say Mass, it was inspiring.

_____

_____

8. My little brother used to drive me crazy, now he's a wonderful part of my life.

_____

_____

9. Because of the weather, our trip was delayed twice.

_____

_____

10. Having a concussion can be dangerous, it should be treated right away.

_____

_____

Online Grammar Skills Practice

The *Choices* Web site includes practice exercises in correcting comma splices. Go to <**www.bedfordstmartins .com/choices/**> and click on "Exercise Central." After logging in, click on "Comma Splices."

Correcting Spelling

While spell-checks are excellent tools, they won't catch all misspelled words. The following spelling rules will help you become a good speller.

CHANGING *Y* TO *I*. When adding an ending to a word that ends in *y*, change the *y* to *i*.

For more spelling rules, refer to Spelling in the Handbook.

apply	applied
easy	easiest
family	families
happy	happiness
study	studies

However, this rule doesn't apply to words ending with *-ing*.

apply	applying
dry	drying
study	studying

Do not omit the final *y* when a vowel *(a, e, i, o, u)* comes before it.

buy	buys
play	playful
stay	stayed

HOW TO **Be a Good Speller**

- Use a spell-check, but don't rely on it.

- Keep a list of words you often misspell.

- If a word doesn't "look right," look it up in a dictionary (print or electronic).

- Pay attention to how words are spelled when you read.

- Learn spelling rules.

- When you've spelled a word incorrectly, force yourself to write it ten times correctly.

- Carefully proofread your writing.

DROPPING THE FINAL SILENT *E*. When you add an ending that begins with a vowel, drop the final *e*.

age	aging
care	caring
fame	famous
remove	removable
use	usable

When you add an ending that begins with a consonant, keep the final *e*.

care	careful
lone	lonely
state	statement

Exceptions to this rule include *argument, judgment,* and *truly.*

ACTIVITY 23

Correcting Spelling. Correct the misspelled words in the following paragraph.

One of the best summers I ever spent was when I worked as a vulunteer for the National Park Service. I was sent to Big Bend

National Park, in southwest Texas, to repair trails. I had applyied
to be a campground host, so I was dissappointed when I was
handed a shovel and told to go to work. I worked with a group of
other volunteers on improveing the desert trails. The densness of
the cactus surprised me, and I often got pricked by sharp needles.
I discovered it was easyiest to just wear long, lose pants instead of
trying to avoid the cactus spines. Because it was so hot, I would
be soaked in alot of sweat after just a few minutes. However, I
found myself happy every night, knowing that I was helping to
improve that beatiful park.

Online Spelling Practice
The *Choices* Web site includes practice spelling exercises.
Go to <**www.bedfordstmartins.com/choice**> and click on
"Exercise Central." After logging on, click on "Spelling."

Jesus's Edited Essay

Using the Handbook in Part Four, Jesus corrected the errors in his
essay. His corrections are underlined here. Once he corrected them,
he recorded these errors in his editing log.

Jesus Ramirez

Professor Posey

English 0311

16 April 2002

Baseball Memories

To some baseball is just a sport where someone tries   1
to reach base before getting thrown out. To others it is
"America's pastime," a baseball stadium filled with people
cheering, eating hot roasted peanuts, and, when the seventh
inning approaches, singing "Take Me Out to the Ball Game."
To me, though, baseball will always be more than just a
game. My father used baseball to teach me valuable lessons
about life.

From the time I was two years old, my father took me   2
to baseball games. On one occasion, when we were at a game,
a player struck out two times and threw his bat out on the
baseball field. My father told me that the next time, the
player would strike out again. <u>I didn't believe him. When
the player was at bat again, I was ready to disprove my
dad</u>. But he was right. I asked him how he knew the batter
would strike out again. He told me that it is very hard to
get things accomplished <u>through</u> anger or frustration; anger
gets in the way of performance. He added that I should not
throw things when I get mad because this could hurt someone
else or myself. Instead, he suggested that I take the time
to think things over before I do something that I will
regret later on.

He also used baseball to show me the importance of not   3
giving up. During one ball game, a player struck out three
times. As he stepped up to the plate for the fourth time,
the crowd booed and cursed him. I asked my dad, "Why are
all these people being rude to this player?" He replied,
"<u>He is one of the best players the team has, but he is not
doing too well. There are days when we are not ourselves;
we are humans and make mistakes</u>. Just because he struck out
three times does not make him a bad person. <u>You should
learn from his experience--life is made of strikeouts,
but it doesn't matter how many strikeouts you have. What
matters is that you get another chance to hit the ball</u>.
If you are confident, you will succeed, but if you are not
confident and do not believe in yourself, you will fail."

But of all the times I went with my father to the ball   4
games, one stands out. It was a warm afternoon when my
father asked me to go with him. When we got there, it began
to get very cold and the wind was blowing. <u>I remember that
I was just wearing shorts, so my legs were freezing</u>. I told

my father that I was cold, but I didn't want to leave. He then suggested that we move to another place where the wind didn't blow as hard. But when we moved to the new place, it was still cold, so my father sat in back of me and asked me to bend my knees toward my chest and lean back. Then he put his warm hands on my legs, like a duck protecting his duckling from bad weather or a <u>predator</u> that might hurt him. Not only did I feel warmed by my father, but I felt protected as well.

My memories of my father at the ballpark will always be special to me. He used baseball to teach me the importance of controlling my temper and of not throwing or hitting things when I become upset. He also used baseball to teach me to work toward goals without giving up. Like a batter facing that next pitch, he taught me to face life head-on.

5

Jesus's Editing Log

To learn how to keep an editing log, go to pp. 41–42.

4/18 — "Baseball Memories"

INCORRECT	I didn't believe him when the player was at bat again, I was ready to disprove my dad. (2)
ERROR	run-on sentence
CORRECT	I didn't believe him. When the player was at bat again, I was ready to disprove my dad.

INCORRECT	though (2)
ERROR	wrong word
CORRECT	through

INCORRECT	He replied, "He is one of the best players the team has, he is not doing too well." (3)
ERROR	comma splice
CORRECT	He replied, "He is one of the best players the team has, but he is not doing too well."

INCORRECT	There are days when we are not ourselves we are humans and make mistakes. (3)
ERROR	run-on sentence
CORRECT	There are days when we are not ourselves; we are humans and make mistakes.
INCORRECT	You should learn from his experience—life is made of strikeouts, but it doesn't matter how many strikeouts you have, what matters is that you get another chance to hit the ball. (3)
ERROR	comma splice
CORRECT	You should learn from his experience—life is made of strikeouts, but it doesn't matter how many strikeouts you have. What matters is that you get another chance to hit the ball.
INCORRECT	I remember that I was just wearing shorts my legs were freezing. (4)
ERROR	run-on sentence
CORRECT	I remember that I was just wearing shorts, so my legs were freezing.
INCORRECT	predater (4)
ERROR	misspelled word
CORRECT	predator

ACTIVITY 24

Editing Your Essay. To edit, read your essay carefully, word-for-word, looking for errors in grammar, spelling, and punctuation. Also use a dictionary and the Handbook in Part Four of this book to help you correct the errors you find. Finally, record those errors in your editing log.

ESL Links

The *Choices* Web site includes links to useful ESL sites. Go to <www.bedfordstmartins.com/choices/> and click on "ESL Links."

PUBLISHING

Share your final essay with your instructor, friends, and classmates. Ask your reviewers to comment on the improvements you made after their review of your discovery draft. Don't be surprised if someone says, "I can't believe this is the same essay. It's so much better!"

CHAPTER CHECKLIST

- [ ] I analyzed my audience and purpose.
- [ ] I gathered ideas on my topic by brainstorming, freewriting, clustering, and relating aloud.
- [ ] I wrote a discovery draft after drafting a preliminary thesis statement.
- [ ] I revised my draft by
  - [ ] developing ideas by using description, narration, and examples.
  - [ ] revising the thesis and topic sentences.
  - [ ] improving paragraph unity.
  - [ ] combining short, closely related sentences with coordinating conjunctions.
- [ ] I edited my draft to correct errors, including run-on sentences, comma splices, and misspelled words.
- [ ] I published my draft by sharing it with my instructor and classmates.

REFLECTING ON YOUR WRITING

To help you continue to improve as a writer, answer the following questions about this assignment.

1. Did you enjoy writing an expressive piece, one in which you shared your thoughts and feelings?
2. Which method of gathering ideas worked best for you?
3. Which details most improved your essay?
4. If you had more time, what parts of your essay would you want to improve before sharing it with readers? Why?
5. Using your answers to these questions, update your writing process report.

Writing Process Report

Date:

Strengths:

Weaknesses:

Plans for improvement:

Once you complete this report, freewrite about what you learned in this chapter about your writing process and what you still hope to learn.

A Significant Person

If we're lucky, we find someone in our lives who teaches us what is truly important. In "My Favorite Teacher," *New York Times* foreign affairs columnist Thomas L. Friedman tells of such a person.

THOMAS L. FRIEDMAN
My Favorite Teacher

Last Sunday's *New York Times Magazine* published its annual review of people who died last year who left a particular mark on the world. I am sure all readers have their own such list. I certainly do. Indeed, someone who made the most important difference in my life died last year—my high school journalism teacher, Hattie M. Steinberg.

I grew up in a small suburb of Minneapolis, and Hattie was the legendary journalism teacher at St. Louis Park High School, Room 313. I took her Intro to Journalism course in 10th grade, back in 1969, and have never needed, or taken, another course in journalism since. She was that good.

Hattie was a woman who believed that the secret for success in life was getting the fundamentals right. And boy, she pounded the fundamentals of journalism into her students—not simply how to write a lead or accurately transcribe a quote, but, more important, how to comport yourself in a professional way and to always do quality work. To this day, when I forget to wear a tie on assignment, I think of Hattie scolding me. I once interviewed an ad exec for our high school paper who used a four-letter word. We debated whether to run it. Hattie ruled yes. That ad man almost lost his job when it appeared. She wanted to teach us about consequences.

Hattie was the toughest teacher I ever had. After you took her journalism course in 10th grade, you tried out for the paper, *The Echo*, which she supervised. Competition was fierce. In 11th grade, I didn't quite come up to her writing standards, so she made me business manager, selling ads to the local pizza parlors. That year, though, she let me write one story. It was about an Israeli general who had been a hero in the Six-Day War, who was giving a lecture at the University of Minnesota. I covered his

1

2

3

4

lecture and interviewed him briefly. His name was Ariel Sharon. First story I ever got published.

Those of us on the paper, and the yearbook that she also supervised, lived in Hattie's classroom. We hung out there before and after school. Now, you have to understand, Hattie was a single woman, nearing 60 at the time, and this was the 1960's. She was the polar opposite of "cool," but we hung around her classroom like it was a malt shop and she was Wolfman Jack. None of us could have articulated it then, but it was because we enjoyed being harangued by her, disciplined by her and taught by her. She was a woman of clarity in an age of uncertainty.

We remained friends for 30 years, and she followed, bragged about and critiqued every twist in my career. After she died, her friends sent me a pile of my stories that she had saved over the years. Indeed, her students were her family—only closer. Judy Harrington, one of Hattie's former students, remarked about other friends who were on Hattie's newspapers and yearbooks: "We all graduated 41 years ago; and yet nearly each day in our lives something comes up—some mental image, some admonition that makes us think of Hattie."

Judy also told the story of one of Hattie's last birthday parties, when one man said he had to leave early to take his daughter somewhere. "Sit down," said Hattie. "You're not leaving yet. She can just be a little late."

That was my teacher! I sit up straight just thinkin' about her.

Among the fundamentals Hattie introduced me to was *The New York Times*. Every morning it was delivered to Room 313. I had never seen it before then. Real journalists, she taught us, start their day by reading *The Times* and columnists like Anthony Lewis and James Reston.

I have been thinking about Hattie a lot this year, not just because she died on July 31, but because the lessons she imparted seem so relevant now. We've just gone through this huge dot-com-Internet-globalization bubble—during which a lot of smart people got carried away and forgot the fundamentals of how you build a profitable company, a lasting portfolio, a nation state or a thriving student. It turns out that the real secret of success in the information age is what it always was: fundamentals—reading, writing and arithmetic, church, synagogue and mosque, the rule of law and good governance.

The Internet can make you smarter, but it can't make you smart. It can extend your reach, but it will never tell you what to say at a P.T.A. meeting. These fundamentals cannot be downloaded. You can only upload them, the old-fashioned way, one by one, in places like Room 313 at St. Louis Park High. I only regret that I didn't write this column when the woman who taught me all that was still alive.

VOCABULARY WORDS: annual (1), lead (3), transcribe (3), comport (3), harangued (5), admonition (6), imparted (10), portfolio (10)

ACTIVITY 25

Reading to Improve Writing. Discuss the following questions about "My Favorite Teacher."

1. Select the one sentence in this essay that you think best captures the essence of Hattie M. Steinberg. Then, explain why you think this sentence best captures her essence.

_____

_____

_____

_____

2. Explain the significance of this sentence in your own words: "She [Hattie] was a woman of clarity in an age of uncertainty." (5)

_____

_____

_____

_____

3. Why does the author believe that Hattie's lessons are still important in the Internet age?

_____

_____

_____

4. Friedman writes at the end of his essay, "I only regret that I didn't write this column when the woman who taught me all that was still alive." Write a letter to someone who has influenced you. Tell that person how he or she influenced you and what it means to you.

A Memorable Event

Witnessing a car accident can be a traumatic experience, especially if the injuries are serious. However, even the worst accidents can bring out the best in people, as writer Debra Hotaling describes in "A Brief Assembly of Good Samaritans."

DEBRA HOTALING
A Brief Assembly of Good Samaritans

In the time it takes to dial 911, flames already lick out of the Plymouth's crushed body.   1

"I'm on the 405 northbound, south of Seal Beach Boulevard," I shout into my cell phone. "A car has hit the center divider. It's upside down. And, oh my God, it's on fire!" In the breath it takes to stutter out my phone number to the dispatcher, flames have quietly seized the vehicle. I never cry, but I'm crying now. And I'm thinking, there's someone in there. Someone is in there.   2

A moment ago I was—like every other urban commuter— swimming through the soup of afternoon traffic. Suddenly, a puff of black smoke explodes from the slow lane. Then, motion. Or echo of motion as motorists struggle to get out of the way of a car shooting full throttle across seven lanes of traffic. It hits the center divider with enough force to send the vehicle 10 feet into the air. The subcompact lands on its back, flames immediately unleashed from inside.   3

Where are the experts? My first-aid know-how dates back to the Girl Scouts. The contents of my first-aid kit include tiny bandages and hand wipes. We need experts. Fire trucks and ambulances and paramedics hauling red metal boxes loaded with things that save people's lives. Someone trained to think in a crisis instead of me, now shaking so hard I can't release the cell phone from my hand.   4

At that moment, a motorcycle cop with the Long Beach Po- 5
lice Department pulls up alongside the helpless car. OK, I think
to myself, someone who knows what he's doing. He kicks in the
window. The sound is muffled, like we're suddenly under water.
Kneeling down, he reaches inside the blazing wreck. All I can see
is his helmet glowing orange as he pushes his arms deeper into
the flames. A long moment later, the officer pulls back. No driver.

Nearby, a woman rifles through her trunk casting aside run- 6
ning shoes, a diaper bag, folding chairs. Finally she pulls out a
bottle of designer water. I turn this over in my mind. How odd,
serving refreshments to a burn victim. No. She's going to try to
put the fire out with it.

The ambulance, visible in the distance, is frozen in a sea of 7
stopped vehicles. No experts will come. No quick "MacGyver"-
style getaways fashioned from sticks and old tire parts. It's just
us, stranded on the freeway, and this horror.

I discover a small fire extinguisher my husband had stashed 8
under my seat. Cursing myself for not thinking of it sooner, I toss
it to the woman as she races back to the burning car with her
bottle of Evian.

Thick brown smoke now churns from the overturned car. I 9
can't tell if the fire is out, so I run down the freeway, shouting
from car to car, "Fire extinguisher? You got a fire extinguisher?"
Motorists shrug helplessly.

But others emerge from their cars to help. Like pioneers cross- 10
ing the wilderness, these commuters suddenly find themselves
banding together—an accidental community—to do whatever
is needed. Some surely do it out of instinct, others in the hope
that one day someone will come to their roadside aid. The scene
is too tragic to be glorious. But this brief assembly of good Samaritans does suggest that there is another story to tell about our
nation's freeways besides road rage and high-speed chases.

An out-of-state trucker leaps from his rig with a second 11
extinguisher and puts out whatever was left of the blaze. If this
were a movie, the police officer would pull out the motorist now.
But it's not. The car has to be turned over so the man's leg can be
released from where it's trapped.

These strangers have come to some kind of silent reckoning. 12
A handful of men, including one in a nice suit and another in
baggy pants, abandon their own vehicles to assist the officer as
he begins rocking the car, its torched frame blistering their bare
hands. It takes three tries before they right what's left of the
blackened wreck.

The officer pulls out the motorist. The victim's in bad shape 13
but still breathing. An R.N. has hopped the freeway's center

divider to do what she can for him. Another commuter begins directing traffic. The ambulance finally muscles its way to the accident scene. The red metal boxes have arrived. And as suddenly as this accidental community formed, it has now dispersed. There's nothing more to do here. My car stands in the way of 15 miles of stopped traffic. So I slide behind the wheel and slowly drive home.

The motorist dies on the way to the hospital. If it had been a high-speed chase, it would have led the 11 o'clock news. It doesn't. Here's what should have been reported: a man died. Strangers tried to help. In the heart of a difficult city, rush hour was briefly transformed by tragedy and goodness. 14

VOCABULARY WORDS: stutter (2), rifles (6), churns (9), Samaritans (10), reckoning (12)

ACTIVITY 26

Reading to Improve Writing. Discuss the following questions about "A Brief Assembly of Good Samaritans" with your classmates.

1. In your own words, write down the main point of this essay.

_____

_____

_____

_____

2. What effect did the car accident have on the author? How was she changed by it?

_____

_____

_____

_____

3. List five words that describe the different reactions of the witnesses to the crash.

4. Focus on a paragraph that contains many descriptive details. Explain how these details help the author express her point.

An Important Period in Your Life

In biology, a *metamorphosis* describes an animal changing form as it develops; for example, a caterpillar metamorphoses into a butterfly. We also use the word *metamorphosis* to describe someone who undergoes a major change. In "Metamorphosis," Peggy L. Breland tells of such a change.

PEGGY L. BRELAND
Metamorphosis

The time was 1982. The place was an old neighborhood in Baton Rouge known as "Old Goodwood." The people were an almost traditional family consisting of a mother (me), a father (Donnie), and two little boys. Alfie was thirteen, and athletic. Joey was twelve and a budding young musician.

We lived on a tree-lined street; every front yard had oak trees, so old and tall they formed a canopy over the street. There were big yards and plenty of boys for my sons to play with. Around the corner was a street known as the circle. If you wanted to find your kids, the circle was the first place to look. There was always something going on for the kids to do, and best of all, they had a father. My husband had adopted my boys shortly after we were married. Their own father had deserted them.

I liked being married and expected to grow old and die a married woman. In an age where marriage and family were looked upon as unfashionable and not worth the effort, I ranked marriage right up there with the Nobel prize. I enjoyed being a wife and mother and wouldn't have traded places with anyone. I also worked full time at a large medical clinic, didn't blow my paycheck, and did the yardwork. Actually, I should have been concerned about the fact that while I was doing the yardwork, my husband was playing with his guns and holding down his recliner. It never occurred to me that things were a little out of balance; all I knew was that I loved Donnie and he loved me and that made everything right.

Donnie was tall, handsome, funny, and looking back, crazy. Donnie was liked by everyone. He was a real homebody and I thought, very stable. Donnie had a more than casual interest in guns. He had guns, gun books, gun tools, and gunsmithing equipment all over the house, which drove me crazy. But, at least I knew where he was, unlike my first husband.

I'm a little slow about some things. I didn't worry too much about the M-16 on the porch. You see, Donnie's other interests included terrorists, mercenaries, and survivalists. As a matter of fact, he had a not so secret desire to go off to some godforsaken country and be a mercenary. We used to have coffee on the front porch in the evening after work, and there, in the corner, stood the ever-present M-16. I used to hope the neighbors didn't see it. Sometimes he had a .38 strapped to his ankle. One year, for our second wedding anniversary, he presented me with my very own .357 magnum. How's that for romance?

Donnie's jobs fluctuated between law enforcement and emergency medical services. Once he quit his job with the Sheriff's Department to pursue bounty hunting and private investigation. He and his partner went about it all wrong and didn't make any money, so he had to go back to the ambulance service.

One evening we were out taking a walk. It was late July, warm, and the air was fragrant with the smell of flowers and freshly gut grass. We were talking about everything and nothing, when he turned to me and said, "Oh, by the way, I have a female partner. Her name is Linda."

"No big deal, she has a job to do," I said. He and I worked together for an ambulance service while we were dating, so I understood the job and its demands. I always thought that was the way to hold on to a husband, by being his buddy as well as his wife. Right then, I asked him to promise me that if something were to happen between them, that if they ever became more than just partners, to tell me first. He tried to assure me that nothing like that would ever happen.

Three weeks later, Donnie informed me that he wanted a divorce.   9

"I don't think I'm in love with you anymore," he said.   10

"How long have you felt like this?"   11

"About six months."   12

I couldn't believe what I was hearing. I was the most married 13 person in the world. I'd always said I was living in the wrong time period, and that I belonged back in the forties and fifties when it was fashionable to be a wife and mother. Naturally, I blamed myself for everything. Women tend to do that. "What have I done? What have I not done? I'll change jobs, dye my hair, lose weight. We can move to Australia. Tell me what to do!"

He said, "It's not you, it's me. I can't handle the pressure and 14 responsibility of marriage and a family." A very interesting statement coming from a man who plays with the dog and balances the bank statement once a month. He didn't have to do anything else, but why should he? I did everything for him.

I said, "Who else knows about this?"   15

"Linda knows," he said.   16

"Why does Linda know?"   17

"She's my partner."   18

That night, I arranged for the boys to sleep over with a friend. 19 I had to fix this. We had to talk to somebody.

I couldn't go through another divorce. I held his mother in 20 very high regard and thought we should talk to her. So what if he's 6'4" tall and a grown man? She's his mother and mothers can fix anything.

Miss Betty didn't have any more success with him than I did. 21 She, like me, suggested a psychiatrist and a vacation. She talked and I talked and it was pointless. I don't think Donnie was even listening. He wanted out and nothing would change his mind.

We went home to a very quiet, empty house that was nor- 22 mally filled with noise and laughter. Usually, there were little boys in and out and Cub Scout meetings held on the back porch. Donnie was the Cub Scout leader for their troop. Now this house was like a morgue. Quite a change within just a few hours.

I stayed up all night, thinking, crying, and having my first 23 migraine, while in our room, in the king-sized bed that was his grandparents', Donnie slept. Had I just torn someone's heart out and wrecked his life, I don't think I would have been able to sleep. That should have told me something. Donnie never had any trouble sleeping. Especially during the winter storm of 1982, when the electricity went out and the house was so cold. I'm the one who drove to the store and wrote a rubber check so I could make soup and try to keep everyone warm. I was also the one outside trying to wrap the water pipes so that they wouldn't burst. Well, they did burst, and Donnie still slept.

Right away, my boys started asking questions, and I had to tell them their lives would be changing again. I had to tell them that Donnie and I were separating. Joey started crying.   24

Alfie just said, "I don't like it but there's nothing I can do about it."   25

I can still see their faces. So much pain for such little boys. And they were so good. Elderly people in the neighborhood always told me what good boys they were. This was so unfair. Their own father had deserted them. Now they would lose another father.   26

We always had music in the house. Donnie had been a drummer in a few rock and roll bands. He taught Joey how to play, and Joey lived for music. Alfie played football. This life was good for them. I could look at their school pictures and see happiness and confidence. Before, when we were on our own, I saw fear. Would I see that again?   27

I won't bore you with any more details about what a great wife I was and what a sweet deal he was giving up. I reasoned and suggested for three weeks, and, finally, I gave up when he told me he went into bounty hunting with the intention of getting "blown away" as a means of escape. At that point, I gave up.   28

I didn't want to get out of bed to go to work. I was so embarrassed. The great love affair of the century was all a big joke, and the joke was over. But the girls I worked with did everything they could to console me and were so supportive. Actually, they were just as shocked as I was.   29

With their help, I eventually stopped crying and started eating again. I'd dropped twenty pounds and looked awful. The girls kept me busy, and I had my boys to look after. I knew that with time, I would get over this. I prayed for strength and for time to pass quickly. And looking back, it did pass quickly, though at the time it seemed to stand still.   30

It took a long time for the grief to subside and longer still to learn to enjoy my freedom. I learned to enjoy lingering in bed on Sundays with my coffee and the newspaper. Realizing that I didn't have to be Superwoman took a few more years. I learned to enjoy a social life, joined an exercise class, started weightlifting, and even did private investigation part time for extra money. I received a promotion at work and began working for a surgeon.   31

I ran into Donnie one day, and he was still having his little daydream about saving the world from terrorism. He also had a   32 python and a boa constrictor as pets. He had married Linda and she liked his snakes, so I guess they were meant for each other.

One day, it hit me. I was relieved to be out of it. I was in my apartment enjoying the fact that it was decorated to my taste and not a single gun, gun book, or gun tool in the whole place, with the exception of my own gun placed discreetly under my bed. For the first time, I was enjoying seeing my things around me, my clothes, my make-up. My bedroom smelled like jasmine instead of gun oil. I was learning to feel as comfortable in a dress shop with my friends as I once felt in a gun store. 33

VOCABULARY WORDS: mercenary (5), fluctuated (6), bounty (6), morgue (22), console (29), subside (31)

ACTIVITY 27

Reading to Improve Writing. Discuss the following questions about "Metamorphosis" with your classmates.

1. List three phrases that describe Peggy, the author of this essay. Then, list three phrases that describe Donnie. What do these phrases indicate about this couple's troubled marriage?

_____

_____

_____

_____

_____

2. Why do you think Peggy didn't see the signs that Donnie wasn't happy in their marriage?

_____

_____

_____

_____

3. How did Peggy change—or metamorphose—as a result of her failed marriage with Donnie?

_____

_____

_____

_____

4. Describe the author's writing style in three words or phrases. In your view, how effective is this writing style in conveying the author's main point?

_____

_____

_____

_____

Satisfaction lies in the effort, not in the attainment. Full effort is full victory. —MAHATMA GANDHI

CHAPTER 5

Examining Cultures

In this chapter you will

- write about a cultural symbol, tradition, or hero.

- gather ideas by questioning, freewriting, clustering, brainstorming, and relating aloud.

- learn to develop your ideas using definition, process, and cause and effect.

- learn to use keywords and transitions.

- combine sentences using conjunctive adverbs and transitional phrases.

- learn to eliminate clichés.

- learn to correct sentence fragments and to use apostrophes.

- reflect on your writing.

Have you ever traveled to another country? Were you surprised at what you saw and heard? Did people drive on the left or right side of the road? Were prices higher or lower than in this country? Were you introduced to new foods or styles of dress? Although unsettling at times, such encounters enable us to learn not only about other cultures but also about our own. The term *culture* refers to the customs, beliefs, values, objects, and language shared by members of a particular group.

Many people grow up as part of a single culture — Chinese, American, or French, for instance. But more and more people are recognizing themselves as *multicultural,* or as having roots in more than one culture. Culture can refer not only to ethnic heritage but also to the beliefs and customs of a particular group. The "hippie" culture of the 1960s believed in social and personal rebellion, had a distinctive lifestyle, and represented itself with the peace symbol. Businesses typically have their own "corporate cultures." One corporate culture, for example, may encourage teamwork, whereas another may value competition.

What cultures do you belong to? Consider your ethnic heritage, age group, school, workplace, and pastimes. In what ways have these cultures contributed to the kind of person you are? What have you learned from the different cultures you belong to?

WRITING ASSIGNMENT

For this assignment, write about a cultural symbol, tradition, or hero. You or your instructor may decide to do this assignment in one of several ways:

- You may gather ideas on one, two, or three topics.
- You may write a discovery draft on one, two, or three of these topics.
- You may choose one discovery draft to develop into a polished essay.
- You may combine your discovery draft ideas into a new topic for your essay.

After completing your essay, share it with your instructor, classmates, and students who come from cultures other than your own. You might also want to send your essay via e-mail to a friend in another part of the country or world.

Online Writing Assignments

For additional assignments to be completed online, visit the *Choices* Web site at <www.bedfordstmartins.com/choices/> and click on "Assignments."

ACTIVITY 1

Analyzing Your Purpose and Audience. Before you begin gathering ideas about your topic, think about your purpose and audience. For this chapter's assignment, you'll explore a symbol, tradition, or hero that is important in your culture. Because some of your readers come from different cultures, you need to discover their current knowledge about your topic and their attitude toward it. Your responses to the following questions will help you decide how to approach your topic.

For more information on purpose and audience, see pp. 5 and 13.

1. Does this assignment call for primarily expressive, informative, or persuasive writing?

    _____

2. What is your reader's average age?

    _____

3. How many are female? _____ How many are male?_____

4. What parts of the country or world are they from?

    _____

    Given your responses to the preceding questions, ask yourself these questions:

5. What might my readers already know about my topic? If I asked them to list five words about my topic, which five might they list?

    _____

    _____

    _____

6. What do my readers need to know about my topic? Which terms and concepts do I need to define? Which objects or events do I need to describe in detail?

_____

_____

_____

7. How might my readers feel about my topic? Will they find it interesting, or will I have to work to get their attention?

_____

_____

_____

GATHERING IDEAS

For more information about gathering ideas, see pp. 29–34.

In the previous chapter, you gathered ideas by brainstorming, freewriting, clustering, and relating aloud. In this chapter, you will again use brainstorming, freewriting, clustering, and relating aloud, but you will also use questioning to gather ideas about a cultural symbol, tradition, and hero.

Cultural Symbols

A *symbol* is something that stands for or represents something else. For example, the American flag symbolizes the United States. It also stands for freedom and democracy. A skull symbolizes death, whereas a red rose stands for love. Cultural symbols tell us about a culture's values and lifestyle, what the people of the culture consider important.

In the following reading, "What's a Bagel?" Jack Denton Scott explains how the bagel, once considered an ethnic food, has been adopted by mainstream America.

JACK DENTON SCOTT
What's a Bagel?

If bread is the staff of life, the bagel may be the laugh of life. 1
"Brooklyn jawbreakers," "crocodile teething rings," even "dough-nuts with rigor mortis" are affectionate terms invoked by bagel aficionados.

For those who haven't tried one, the flavorful bagel is a shiny, 2
hard, crisp yet chewy roll with a hole in the middle, and it is booming in popularity. Eight million are consumed daily in the United States—worth about $400 million a year. Bakery experts call the phenomenon "the Americanization of the bagel." To bagel believers it's "the bagelization of America." In the past four years retail sales of bagels have about doubled. Over 80 percent of these sales are now to non-Jewish consumers, a dramatic soci-ological switch. Moreover, the "bagel belt," always on the East Coast, is starting to stretch across the country. In fact, the world's largest bagel bakery is now located in Mattoon, Ill., producing over a million rolls a day.

Walter Heller of *Progressive Grocer* magazine calls the bagel's 3
rise to stardom an example of "America's current love affair with ethnic foods." Yet, unless sliced in half, toasted and eaten warm, the bagel isn't easy to handle. It may make messy sandwiches and challenge the teeth. What's more, bagels become stale and hard after 12 hours—"something you can fight wars with," as one bagel expert said.

For the health-conscious, however, the bagel has a lot going 4
for it. The plain, two-ounce toaster-size has just 150 calories and one gram of fat. (The popular buttery croissant, by comparison, contains 235 calories and 12 grams of fat.) Furthermore, the plain bagel has no cholesterol, preservatives, or artificial color.

Bagels are made with unbleached, protein-rich, high-gluten 5
flour, lightly seasoned with malt, salt and sugar, and raised with yeast. They then get a brief bath in boiling water. This results in the shiny surface after they are baked. (Most are hearth-baked to give them a crusty exterior and chewy interior.)

Some U.S. bakeries still use the Old World method of rolling 6
and shaping the stiff dough by hand. This requires about six months to learn, but one expert bagel baker can whip out about 700 an hour. (One automated machine can turn out up to 9000 an hour.)

Where did this quirky roll originate? One version has the 7
bagel created by an Austrian baker in 1683, honoring the king of

Poland who had defeated Turkish invaders. It was first formed to resemble a stirrup (*beugel,* from the German *bügel,* for stirrup), because the king's favorite hobby was riding.

Another account puts the bagel in Cracow, Poland, in 1610, 8 where poor Jews, who normally ate coarse black bread, considered their uncommon white-flour roll a delicacy. Bagels were officially approved as presents for women after childbirth, and mothers used them as teething rings for their children. In the 1600s in Russia, bagels were looped on strings, and were thought to bring good luck and have magical powers.

Bagels were brought to New York City and New Jersey by 9 Jewish immigrants about 1910. Among the most successful immigrant bagel bakers was Harry Lender, who arrived from Lublin, Poland, in 1927 and settled in New Haven, Conn. His sons—Sam, Murray and Marvin—have almost made Lender's Bagels household words by using humor to push sales. For their bakery's 55th anniversary party, Murray and the executive staff attended a ballet class for two months; then, dressed in orange leotards and yellow tutus, they gracefully tiptoed to what was announced as "The Dance of the Bagels."

Today the baffling bagel surge to the top is even inspiring 10 bagel restaurants. They offer as many as 17 flavors, from raisin and honey to zippy onion, plus bagel sandwiches, burgers, clubs, grilled cheese, French toast, salad sandwich combos, an egg-and-sausage bagelwich and a rancher's bagel breakfast. Big also are bagelettes—one-inch bagels—served by the basket with dinners. Then there are hero, hoagie, pizza and taco bagels—even Bagel Dogs. Where there's a bagel, there's a way.

Bagel bakeries are opening in Alaska, England, Japan and 11 Israel. Ron Stieglitz, founder of the New York Bagels bakery in London, where few people had ever seen a bagel, had trouble raising money from banks. "A lot of them thought we were a football team," he said. But the bakery now supplies four large retail chains and many small shops and restaurants.

Lyle Fox, from Chicago, sees more potential for the bagel in 12 Japan than in the United States. Young Japanese view the bagel as trendy and upscale—so much so that he easily sells 6000 a day. Fox discovered that the Japanese associate the bagel with New York, and New York with fashion. Thus, a lot of his customers are young women who consider the bagel as "sort of another accessory." A long-time bagel lover, Fox says his stomach does a sickly flip when Japanese customers ask for lox and cream cheese on a cinnamon-raisin bagel.

Cashing in on the new bagel awareness, innovators have come up with some really neat twists. Three Philadelphians started Bagels in Bed, a home-delivery business. Mike Bretz, owner of Simon Brothers Bakery in Skokie, Ill., has borrowed an idea from Chinese fortune cookies. He stuffs slips with Yiddish wisdom into his Schlepper Simon's Yiddish Fortune Bagels. One cheerfully advises, "Smile, *bubeleh,* success is assured." 13

A spirited cookbook, *The Bagels' Bagel Book* (Acropolis Books), has recipes like "Mexicali Bagel Fondue," the "Kojak Bagel" with feta cheese and Greek olives, "Tofu Bagels," and "Delhi Bagels" with whipped cream cheese, curry and chutney. The book also captures some of the laughter inspired by baking's most remarkable roll. Here's comedienne Phyllis Diller: "President Reagan was so gung-ho to get ethnic votes, he went into a deli and ordered a bagel. The waiter asked, 'How would you like that?' Ronnie said, 'On rye.'" 14

What's a bagel? Fun you can eat. 15

VOCABULARY WORDS: aficionados (1), phenomenon (2), sociological (2), croissant (4), delicacy (8), immigrant (9), tutus (9)

ACTIVITY 2

Reading to Improve Writing. Discuss the following questions about "What's a Bagel?" with your classmates.

1. How does Scott define the bagel?

   _____

   _____

   _____

2. Where did the bagel originate?

   _____

   _____

   _____

3. Who considers the bagel to be "trendy and upscale"? Why has it spread in popularity?

_____

_____

_____

_____

4. Why does the author refer to the bagel as "baking's most remarkable roll"?

_____

_____

5. How does Scott use definition, process, and cause and effect to support his thesis statement?

_____

_____

_____

_____

ACTIVITY 3 (GROUP)

Collecting Contemporary Symbols. People tend to think of symbols as including only important and permanent representations, such as the flag of the United States. As you discovered reading "What's a Bagel?" symbols can be quite ordinary and represent any number of things.

Imagine that you and your classmates are collecting objects to put into a time capsule that will be opened a hundred years from now. What objects would you choose to symbolize contemporary American culture? Here are some examples.

school yearbook   daily newspaper

photograph of the president   Palm Pilot

bottle of purified drinking water   Ricky Martin poster

hot dog   backpack

What would you omit from this list? What would you add to it?

ACTIVITY 4

Questioning and Freewriting about a Cultural Symbol. Select an object that you think symbolizes contemporary American culture or some other culture. Then respond to the following questions about the object.

1. When was the last time you encountered or used the object?
2. Describe the object to someone who has not seen it before.
3. What ideas, events, or other objects do you associate with the object?
4. How does the object symbolize the culture's lifestyle or beliefs?

Keeping your responses to these questions in mind, freewrite about the object and the culture it symbolizes.

Here's how one student, Clara, answered some of the questions in Activity 4 and freewrote about the object she chose—an artificial Christmas tree.

1. *My mother and I used this artificial Christmas tree last Christmas after we moved out of our big house and into a small apartment.*

2. *The tree is about two feet tall, with pointed silver leaves. Little red balls hang from each branch.*

3. *The tree reminds me of Christmas, but not the kind of Christmas I had as a little girl, when we had a big, natural tree that smelled up the living room.*

4. *To me this tree symbolizes how artificial and commercial Christmas can be in our culture.*

I wish people would think more about the spirit of the Christmas season than about gifts. But that's not the way it happens. To me this artificial tree symbolizes the commercialism of Christmas. It doesn't look or smell like a real tree. It's just something to put gifts under. I know that having a real tree is impractical because our apartment is so small. But it almost seems that having no tree at all would be better than having one that looks so artificial.

Put your freewriting about a cultural symbol aside for now. Next, you want to gather ideas about another aspect of culture and another possible topic for your essay—cultural traditions.

Cultural Traditions

A *tradition* is an event or activity repeatedly performed in the same way, usually to celebrate a culture's heritage and bring people closer together. Many families develop traditions, such as Sunday dinner, that bring them together. A cultural tradition, however, extends beyond a family's tradition because it reflects the values of a whole culture.

Thanksgiving and the Fourth of July are cultural traditions unique to the United States. Other American cultural traditions have been adapted from other parts of the world and changed to suit American lifestyles and values. In Europe, the figure of St. Nicholas represents religious values, whereas in America St. Nicholas has become Santa Claus, a figure associated with the giving of gifts. New cultural traditions develop all the time. Kwanza, for instance, is an African American tradition that takes place during the final week of the year. In this tradition, African Americans remember their African heritage by celebrating the customs and beliefs of several African tribes.

One of the Navajo Indian cultural traditions is weaving rugs. In the following essay, Julia Duin describes the Navajos' efforts to preserve this tradition.

JULIA DUIN

Navajos Struggle to Keep Weaving Tradition Alive

Although there's a bull market for American Indian rugs, weavers earn little and few young people are learning the craft. Some say the tradition will die with this generation. Dressed in a traditional purple tribal dress with long sleeves and a flounced "broomstick" skirt, Nanaba Aragon is on a one-woman crusade to pass on the art of rug weaving to the children of the next millennium. "While I weave," she says, "kids sit very still, watching me. I tell them stories, how to string the loom, which colors to use and what they mean."

Aragon also has produced a how-to video, *Basic Navajo Weaving,* a radical notion for a craft where apprentices are expected to learn the art by sitting at the elbow of an experienced seamstress. But Indian weaving, like many traditions, is having to forge new paths to survive. "So much of the culture these days has been commercial culture, producing things for ready consumption," says Mae Lee, a coordinator for the Ramah Navaho Weavers Association in New Mexico. "There now seems to be a greater appreciation of things that are handmade."

Well over 90 percent of all Indian weavings, jewelry, sand paintings and other crafts pour into trading posts and rug auctions in Gallup, N.M., located quite conveniently near Interstate 40, one of America's major east-west travel routes. The city, which stretches 14 miles long and five blocks wide along the railroad tracks, has become the Southwest's center for Indian culture. An hour before the first gavel fell on a recent Friday, for example, tourists were pawing through piles of Indian jewelry, baskets, pots and rugs ranging in price from $25 to $12,000. "We did this to develop a market for quality Navajo weaving," says auctioneer John Hornbeck. "There was nothing available for the upper grade."

Collectors fear American Indian culture will die out with this generation—most of the weavers making the intricate rugs are well over 70, and the younger generation is slow to pick up the slack. As a result, woolly tapestries are enjoying a "bull market," according to *Business Week,* which reported a 200-year-old Navajo rug auctioned off for a record-setting $76,750 on May 26 at Sotheby's in New York. "They've been collector's items for years but more and more so as we see fewer weavers picking up the craft," says Mark Wilson, owner of rug galleries in Santa Fe and Newcomb, N.M., in the heart of the Navajo reservation.

Despite the bull market, weavers typically make less than $1,000 a month. The winner for best rug at this year's Inter-Tribal Indian Ceremonial—a 4-foot-by-6-foot tapestry by weaver Virginia Deal containing more than eight miles of hand-spun yarns—netted her a mere $15,000. She worked on it for 18 months. Indeed, rug making takes a long time. Weavers must shear their own sheep; clean, card, spin, wash, and dye their own wool; and construct a loom, all before starting the actual weaving. If they use natural vegetable and plant dyes, they will make about $1.30 an hour, according to the book *Rugs and Posts.*

For her weaves, Lee uses wool from Churro sheep, a Spanish
breed known for its long wool, and makes dyes from plants:
olive green from walnuts, orange from wild carrot, gold from the
Navajo tea plant, tan from sagebrush, blue from indigo, magenta
from prickly pear and red from boiled cochineal bugs. Most
moderns forsake the traditional ways for a quick wool purchase
at the local fabric store, but the end result is never the same,
maintain traditional weavers.

"This is more than a product," says Lee. "The whole process,
including the carding and spinning, focuses the individual into
doing just that thing. It's picking the dye plants, planning the
pattern, working with the wool. But the dominant society looks
at the product. The process is not as important to them." Weavers also must work off an Indian loom, constructed with two
upright pine-tree logs set at right angles to two crosspieces.
Woolen threads (the warp) are tightly strung between the crosspieces while the designing thread (the weft) is woven between
the warp.

Once a weaver decides to sell the piece, she may take it to the
queen of monthly Indian auctions at the Crownpoint Elementary School cafeteria in the reservation town of Crownpoint, 60
miles northeast of Gallup. There, visitors from around the world
can rummage through hundreds of Navajo rugs piled on long
tables. "We have all sorts of different cultures in Europe," says
Helmut Weber, in town to shop for rugs for his art gallery in
Munich. "But there are no galleries that show this."

Now that the demand is high, far-sighted Navajos are creating a labor pool among the younger set. Lee, whose Ramah
weavers group includes one man, says it's a stiff challenge, considering the rural nature of the craft. "The real work is to get the
younger people involved," she says.

VOCABULARY WORDS: radical (2), apprentices (2), forge (2), intricate (4), magenta (6), cochineal (6), dominant (7)

ACTIVITY 5

Reading to Improve Writing. Discuss the following questions
about "Navajos Struggle to Keep Weaving Tradition Alive" with your
classmates.

1. What did you learn about Navajo rug weaving from reading Duin's essay?

   _____

   _____

   _____

2. Who purchases Navajo rugs?

   _____

   _____

   _____

3. Why don't younger Navajos learn to weave rugs?

   _____

   _____

   _____

4. The author believes this cultural tradition will die out. Do you agree or disagree? Why?

   _____

   _____

   _____

   _____

5. How effective is the author's introduction?

   _____

   _____

   _____

ACTIVITY 6

Clustering and Questioning about a Cultural Tradition. Cluster on the topic of cultural traditions. Then choose one of those cultural traditions to write about. Use these questions to help you decide which tradition you know a lot about and are most interested in.

- When does this tradition take place?
- What happens during the tradition?
- Who participates in the tradition?
- What special clothes, food, music, or dance accompany the tradition?
- Why is the tradition important to the participants?

Figure 5.1 is a quick cluster of cultural traditions completed by one student, Sandra Cordero. From the traditions in her cluster, San-

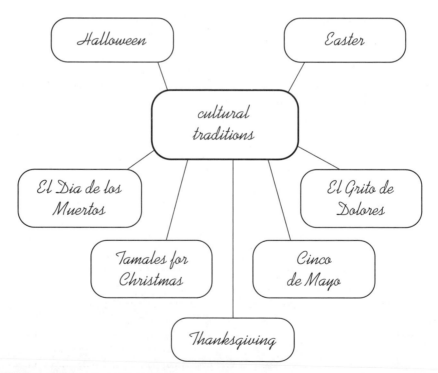

Figure 5.1. Sandra's Clustering

dra decided to answer the questions in Activity 6 by writing about "El Grito de Dolores."

1. *This tradition takes place in Mexico on the evening of September 15 and the morning of September 16.*

2. *During this tradition, the people reenact the time when Miguel Hidalgo told his people in Dolores to fight for freedom from Spain.*

3. *The governor of each city participates by pretending to be Hidalgo. Then the people of the city attend a parade.*

4. *Fireworks are set off on September 15; the next day a parade is held and some people dress in traditional costumes.*

5. *This tradition is important because the Mexican people celebrate their freedom from Spain.*

Put your writing about a cultural tradition aside for now. You want to explore one more possible topic—cultural heroes—for your essay.

Make a Chart

Use the drawing tools in your word-processing program to make a chart of the questions about a cultural tradition and your responses to them. If your ideas encompass more than one cultural tradition, the chart can also help you compare and contrast your responses.

Cultural Heroes

We all have personal heroes—family members, friends, teachers, or coaches—whom we admire because of their courage, dedication, or hard work and who serve as role models. *Cultural heroes,* people who inspire an entire culture, also serve as role models. Unlike personal heroes, however, cultural heroes are known by many people within the culture. Some cultural heroes come from the contemporary culture, whereas others are a part of a group's cultural heritage. Martin Luther King Jr., Abraham Lincoln, César Chávez, Princess Diana, Mother Theresa, and Eleanor Roosevelt are some examples of cultural heroes.

Many Americans consider Oprah Winfrey a contemporary cultural hero because of the way she triumphed over personal hardships and has encouraged others to do the same. In the following reading,

John Culhane describes one of Winfrey's most precious values: telling the truth.

JOHN CULHANE

Oprah Winfrey: How Truth Changed Her Life

In January 1984 a phenomenon hit the airwaves. Chicago's WLS-TV needed someone to take over its floundering morning program, which ranked third in local competition for the 9 a.m. slot. So it brought in a little-known news anchor from Baltimore. Her name was Oprah Winfrey.

Earthy, articulate and spontaneous, Oprah seemed to have a knack for connecting emotionally with her guests, her studio audience and her viewers. In a single season, she brought the show to the No. 1 spot in its time period. In 1985 the program was retitled *The Oprah Winfrey Show,* and in 1986 it was syndicated nationally. Oprah won an Emmy for the 1986–87 year, and her approximately 20 million loyal viewers have made her program television's most popular daytime show.

But hers is not the typical celebrity success story, by any means. Oprah actually calls her program "a kind of ministry." And there is something more, something intensely personal and powerful in the advice she often gives nervous guests before air time. "Just tell the truth," she says quietly, gazing directly into their eyes. "It'll save you every time."

It is a lesson Oprah learned against great odds. Significantly, this woman noted for the unflinching honesty of her interviews learned the value of truth only after she tried—and failed—to lie her way to happiness.

As Oprah explains: She was born January 29, 1954, in Kosciusko, Miss., to an unmarried 18-year-old farm girl. Vernon Winfrey, a soldier at Fort Rucker, didn't even know until much later that Vernita Lee had become pregnant with his child.

The infant was named after Orpah, the sister-in-law of Ruth in the Bible. (The midwife misspelled the name "Oprah" on the birth certificate.) Shortly after, Vernita Lee left Oprah in the care of the child's grandmother and headed for Milwaukee, where unskilled black women could find jobs as maids.

On the farm where she was reared, little Oprah began her broadcasting career declaiming to the pigs in the barnyard. At three, she was reciting in church. By the time her grandmother enrolled her in kindergarten, Oprah could already read and write well enough to send a note to her teacher: "Dear Miss New. I do not think I belong here." Agreeing, Miss New advanced her to the first grade, where envious classmates soon nicknamed her The Preacher.

"From the time I was eight years old," says Oprah, "I was a champion speaker. I spoke for every women's group, banquet, church function—I did the circuit. Anybody needed anybody to speak anything, they'd call me." Oprah begins to recite, in the commanding voice she's had since childhood, from the famous old poem "Invictus" by William Ernest Henley: 8

> *Out of the night that covers me,*
> *Black as the Pit from pole to pole,*
> *I thank whatever gods may be,*
> *For my unconquerable soul.*

Oprah grins. "Very impressive, especially when you're eight." 9

Between ages six and nine, Oprah lived part-time with her mother in Milwaukee, part-time with her father in Nashville. But then she moved in full-time with her mother. Perhaps her precociousness was one reason the relationship was difficult. In Oprah's words, "My mama really wasn't prepared to take on this child—me." 10

Oprah's childhood innocence came to a traumatic end when, at nine, she was raped by a teen-age cousin. "Three people abused me from the time I was nine until I was fourteen," she says. The horror of this sexual abuse would come out years later on one of Oprah's famous talk shows, but at the time she kept it secret, and it fed an enormous sense of shame and insecurity. 11

When Oprah was thirteen she decided new, octagon-shaped glasses would make her beautiful and popular. Her mother refused, telling Oprah they couldn't afford such an extravagance. The next day, after her mother had gone to work, Oprah smashed her old glasses on the floor. She pulled down the curtains, knocked over a table and threw things around the room. Then she called the police. 12

"I decided to be unconscious when they came in and to have amnesia." 13

At the hospital, the doctor brought her mother to her bed, but Oprah pretended not to recognize her. "All we know is that someone broke into the apartment, hit her over the head and broke her glasses," explained the doctor. 14

"Broke her *glasses*?" asked Vernita Lee. "Do you mind if I'm alone with the child for a few minutes?" 15

The mother glared at her daughter and counted to three. As Oprah tells it: "She got to two, and I knew she was going to kill 16 me. And so I said, 'It's coming back to me now . . . you're my mother!' She dragged me from the bed and we went home. Yes, I got the octagons."

But Oprah wasn't any happier. She ran away from home, only to be brought back.   17

She tells these stories on herself with her usual candor and humor, but it seems clear that the teen-age Oprah was using theatrical lies to win acceptance and love, just as she had won admiration in the past through her dramatic speaking roles.   18

Finally, Vernita Lee had had enough. "And that's how I ended up with my father."   19

Vernon Winfrey had married and grown into a responsible member of the community, a barber and pillar of the Baptist church. He and his wife, Zelma, were unsettled by the heavily made-up teen-ager with the tight skirt and belligerent expression. "You will not live in this house unless you abide by my rules," he told her. Those rules, and, more important, Vernon Winfrey's air of confidence and certainty, would change Oprah's life.   20

His first rule was that she had to be home by 11 p.m. Another was that she read a book a week and submit a written report on it. When she came home with C's on her report card, he told her: "If you were a child who could only get C's, then that is all I would expect of you. But you are not. So in this house, C's are not acceptable."   21

Oprah found herself getting home by ten minutes before eleven. And she became an honor student and president of the student council. But the most significant turn-around was her newfound honesty.   22

"I never told another lie. I wouldn't dream of making up a story to my Dad. Let me tell you, there is something about people who believe in discipline—they exude a kind of assurance and realism."   23

Five feet, seven inches tall, about 135 pounds, with the same dramatic eyes and magnetic presence we see today, Oprah entered a Nashville beauty pageant in high school. She figured she would be asked what she planned to do with her life, and calculated the best answer would be: "I want to be a fourth-grade schoolteacher."   24

But on the morning of the interview, she happened to watch the *Today* show, then featuring Barbara Walters. And when the judges asked her about her life's ambitions, she found herself stating firmly: "I believe in truth, and I want to perpetuate truth. So I want to be a journalist."   25

She won the contest and was offered a part-time news position at a local radio station. In an oratorical contest, sponsored   26 by the Elks, she won a four-year scholarship that she used to attend Tennessee State University in Nashville.

Once she was in college, the management of the CBS affiliate   27
in Nashville offered her a job on television.

In 1976, the year she should have graduated, Oprah still had   28
to make curfew—which her father had now extended to midnight. Later that year, she moved to Baltimore to join WJZ-TV;
"her primary motive," according to her official biography, "was
to escape her father's curfew." And in Baltimore, destiny—in the
form of a Chicago TV station searching for a talk-show host—
found her.

The topics on her nationally syndicated show have ranged   29
from overcoming weight problems (a longtime concern for Oprah,
who recently shed more than 60 pounds) to racism. For her most
famous show, in February 1987, she went to an all-white county
in Georgia and asked an audience composed entirely of white
residents some simple questions: "Why has Forsyth County not
allowed black people to live here in 75 years? What is it you're
afraid black people are going to do?" Though there were some
dissenters, Oprah found many in her audience who believed in
co-existence with blacks. The show made newspaper stories across
America.

Through her show, Oprah won a substantial victory over her-   30
self. Her lawyer had advised her against ever disclosing that she
had been sexually abused as a child, arguing that many people still
blame the victims of abuse. He didn't want his client to suffer
from that stigma. Oprah agreed. Nevertheless, during a program in
which victims of sexual abuse spoke of their experiences, Oprah
suddenly decided to tell her story. She put her arms around another
victim and wept with her. It was an honest, moving moment. . . .

Now there was just one more old fence to mend. Every time   31
she visited, her father warned her that she would not amount to
anything without a college degree. Oprah had left Tennessee
State without a diploma: she had finished all her course work,
but not her senior project.

Through a friend, Oprah made discreet inquiries: Would Ten-   32
nessee State University waive the senior-project requirement if
Oprah did independent work or study? TSU would not.

Oprah had to re-enroll and then put together a project to   33
fulfill her requirement in the media course. So she did it. TSU
informed her that she would receive her diploma at the 1987
commencement ceremonies and invited her to address the graduating class.

Vernon Winfrey was in the audience that packed Howard C.   34
Gentry complex on TSU's North Nashville campus. "Even though

I've done a few things in life, every time I've come home, my father has said, 'You need that degree,'" she told the crowd. "So this is a special day for my dad." With that, she announced she was establishing scholarships at the school in his name.

She was her father's daughter, too, in the advice she gave to fellow graduates: "Don't complain about what you don't have. Use what you've got. To do less than your best is a sin. Every single one of us has the power for greatness, because greatness is determined by service—to yourself and to others." 35

She was Oprah the graduating senior, and she was also Oprah the famous and wealthy entertainer. But she was still the Oprah they used to call The Preacher, who had herself learned the most valuable lesson of all: *Just tell the truth. It will save you every time.* 36

VOCABULARY WORDS: floundering (1), earthy (2), articulate (2), unflinching (4), precociousness (10), octagon (12), candor (18), belligerent (20), abide (20), dissenters (29)

ACTIVITY 7

Reading to Improve Writing. Discuss the following questions about "Oprah Winfrey: How Truth Changed Her Life" with your classmates.

1. What did you learn about Oprah Winfrey from this reading that you didn't already know?

   _____

   _____

   _____

   _____

2. Of the events that are described by Culhane, which one do you think had the most effect on Winfrey? Why?

   _____

   _____

_____

_____

_____

3. Why is telling the truth so important to Winfrey?

_____

_____

_____

_____

4. Do you admire Winfrey? Why or why not?

_____

_____

_____

_____

5. How does Culhane keep his audience interested in his topic?

_____

_____

_____

_____

ACTIVITY 8 (GROUP)

Gathering Ideas about a Cultural Hero. With your classmates, brainstorm a list of cultural heroes. Consider musicians, athletes, public officials, actors, entrepreneurs, celebrities, and ordinary citizens who are widely known because of their extraordinary talent, dedication, or achievements. Then freewrite on one of these heroes. Use these questions as a guide:

- What facts do you know about this person (age, accomplishments, and so on)?
- Which five words best describe this person?
- What do you most admire about this person?

Finally, talk about this person with one of your classmates. Explain why you believe this person is a cultural hero. How does your classmate feel about this person? What more does your classmate want to know about this person?

Here's how one student, Mark, gathered ideas about the reggae musician Bob Marley by freewriting in his journal.

Bob Marley was a great musician. He wrote songs that celebrated Jamaican music. His songs popularized Jamaican music for the rest of the world. He also celebrated his Jamaican heritage by reminding people of the beauty and strength of Jamaican culture. He died tragically at age thirty-six, but his spirit lives on in his music.

DRAFTING

Having trouble remembering the steps of the writing process? See p. 18.

You have now gathered ideas on three aspects of culture: cultural symbols, traditions, and heroes. You thus have a rich source of material for writing, but you need to decide how to proceed. Here are some of your options:

- You may select one of the three topics for your discovery draft.
- You may write drafts on two or three of the topics to see which one you prefer to continue working on.
- You may combine related topics in your discovery draft. For instance, you might describe a cultural symbol that is part of a cultural tradition.

The topic you choose should be one that interests you and that you are already fairly well informed about. Although you may need to collect such basic information as dates and names for your discovery draft, most of the information should come from your own knowledge and experience.

To review how to write a preliminary thesis statement, see p. 36.

Before you begin drafting, write a preliminary thesis statement that announces your topic and states its importance. As you draft, you may decide to revise your thesis as new ideas emerge. Keep your audience and purpose in mind, but remember that your main goal at the drafting stage is to get your ideas down on paper. You'll have time later on to revise and edit your discovery draft.

Here's the discovery draft written by Sandra Cordero about a cultural tradition. After reading the draft, discuss with your classmates what Sandra might do to revise it. (Note that the example includes the types of errors that typically appear in a discovery draft.)

El Grito de Dolores

I am proud to be part of the Mexican culture. The   1
Mexican culture honors events important to its history. To
celebrate Mexicos independence, Mexicans have "El Grito de
Dolores." "El Grito de Dolores" tells about what happened
the day when the fight for our independence was over. Every
Mexican participates in this event because it's the way we
thank our heroes and ancestors for giving us freedom.

Our celebration begins the night of the 15th of   2
September. The main event is celebrated in Mexico's
capital, which is "El Distrito Federal." The holiday is
celebrated everywhere in Mexico. Even the most little towns
have their own celebration. People get together in the Main
Plaza to celebrate the fiesta. Exactly at midnight the
governor of each city goes on top of the municipal building. "Viva Don Miguel Hidalgo!" he yells to give honor to
the person who made our independence possible. The words
"Viva Mexico, Viva Mexico, Viva Mexico!" give honor to our
country.

On the morning of the 16th of September, people get   3
together on the main street to see the parade. The parade
includes children, business leaders, government leaders,
clubs, police officers, and firefighters. Everyone under
the sun. On this day, everyone feels the freedom that this
day brought. Every town in Mexico has a street called "16
de Septiembre" where it begins and ends.

> We give honor to the men who made us free. Mexicans 4
> believe in traditions. By giving honor to the men who made
> us free, we thank them our ancestors for the freedom that
> they have given us.

REVISING

As you learned in Chapter 2, when you revise a discovery draft, you concentrate on clarifying and supporting your ideas. You should resist the urge to correct errors when revising; that is your concern during the editing stage.

In this chapter, you will learn several revision techniques for developing your ideas most effectively. You will also learn to write an introduction and conclusion, connect ideas, and combine short sentences.

Developing Your Ideas

Read about other ways to develop your draft on pp. 34–39.

In Chapter 3, you learned that your essay must be well developed in order to be convincing. In other words, you need to give information that supports your points. This information tells the reader that you are knowledgeable about your subject and makes your paper more interesting. Three methods of development—definition, process, and cause and effect—are especially appropriate for an essay on a cultural symbol, tradition, or hero.

DEFINITION. To define something is to explain what it means. *Definition* is a helpful strategy to use when developing your essay because it can clarify important points. When you define a term, place it in a general category and then explain how it fits within that category according to what sets it apart—its distinguishing features. For example, in her discovery draft Sandra Cordero defines "El Grito de Dolores" by placing it in a general category—events important to the history of Mexico. She then explains the characteristics of this holiday (the gathering in the main plaza and the parade), which highlights its distinguishing features.

In "What's a Bagel?" Jack Denton Scott begins his second paragraph with a simple definition to help his readers understand this symbol: He places it in the general category of "rolls," and explains what sets it apart from other rolls. "For those who haven't tried one, the flavorful bagel is a shiny, hard, crisp yet chewy roll with a hole in

Adding Definitions, Process, and Cause and Effect to Your Essay. Exchange your discovery draft with a classmate. Read your classmate's draft and underline any sections that contain narration. Then, in the margins write where you think more definitions, process, and cause and effect would help your classmate develop the ideas. Your classmate should do the same for your paper.

Organizing Your Essay

In Chapter 3 you learned how to organize your paragraphs using topic sentences. You also learned that essays, to be effectively organized, include an introduction and a conclusion. Readers expect essays to have not only well-developed ideas but also an interesting introduction and a forceful conclusion. Let's look first at introductions and how to make them more effective.

WRITING AN EFFECTIVE INTRODUCTION. The *introduction* to an essay serves three purposes: it gets your readers' attention, it narrows the topic, and it states your thesis statement. By using the opening sentences of your essay to hook your readers' interest, you convince them that your essay is worth reading. By narrowing your topic and presenting your thesis statement in the introduction, you give your readers a road map of sorts for reading your essay. Although introductions are often only one paragraph with the thesis statement at the end of the paragraph, they may be two, three, or more paragraphs.

How do you go about writing an introduction that gets your readers' attention, narrows your topic, and presents your thesis? One way is to hook your readers' interest while also leading up to the thesis statement. You may do this by using one of the four techniques described in detail in Chapter 3:

For help with revising your thesis, see p. 37.

1. question
2. facts
3. brief story or anecdote
4. description

Or, if you like, try using one of these additional techniques:

5. definition
6. classification

First let's review the four techniques described in Chapter 3.

Question. Posing one or more *questions* at the start of an essay can arouse readers' curiosity about your topic and encourage them to read on for the answers. In the revised essay "El Grito de Dolores," Sandra Cordero begins her second paragraph with a question to engage her readers.

> What is "El Grito de Dolores"?

Cordero uses the remainder of her essay to answer this question for her readers.

Facts. Introducing a topic with *facts*—statements that can be verified as true—has two important effects on readers. It signals them that you know your topic well, and it encourages them to read further to see what you have to say. This technique is used by Culhane in "Oprah Winfrey: How Truth Changed Her Life."

> In January 1984 a phenomenon hit the airwaves. Chicago's WLS-TV needed someone to take over its floundering morning program, which ranked third in local competition for the 9 a.m. slot. So it brought in a little-known news anchor from Baltimore. Her name was Oprah Winfrey.

These facts also convince his readers that Culhane knows his subject well.

Brief Story or Anecdote. Beginning with a *brief story* or an *anecdote* can help draw readers into your essay because most readers like to read about other people's lives. In the following introduction, the author uses a short story to engage her readers and to emphasize the importance of her topic: exercise. She then introduces her thesis in the first sentence of the second paragraph.

> "After the birth of my twins, I just ran out of energy," says Betsy Spratt, a full time mechanical engineer from Trafalgar, Indiana, and mother of three boys under the age of four. "Even though I was able to lose my pregnancy weight by dieting for a few months, I was constantly tired and getting sick. I knew I had to build up my strength. So once the twins were sleeping through the night, I started using exercise videos to do fifteen minutes of calisthenics and thirty minutes of aerobics in the evenings. I also got a double jogging cart so that after my husband gets home from work, he can watch our older son while I take the twins for a forty-five minute run. I've been following this regimen three to six times a week for year now and I'm healthier, I feel better and I look better. Best of all, I have so much more energy to take care of my boys. Exercising sure improved my life."

For many *Working Mother* readers like Spratt, exercise is an essential part of every week.

—Kalia Doner, "Fitting in Fitness"

Description. An introduction that contains vivid *description* sets the scene and draws readers into your essay. Julia Duin, in "Navajos Struggle to Keep Weaving Tradition Alive," sets the scene by using description as part of her introduction.

Dressed in a traditional purple tribal dress with long sleeves and a flounced "broomstick" skirt, Nanaba Aragon is on a one-woman crusade to pass on the art of rug weaving to the children of the next millennium.

Now, let's look at two new ways to introduce your topic.

Definition. You may remember that Jack Denton Scott defined the meaning of the word *bagel* in "What's a Bagel?" This type of introduction works well when you need to define an unfamiliar topic for your readers. In the following introductory paragraph, the writer uses definition to ensure her readers' understanding of her topic and thesis statement. Notice also that she uses humor in the definition to further engage her readers. Her thesis sentence is the last one in the paragraph.

As a lifelong crabber (that is, one who catches crabs, not a chronic complainer), I can tell you that anyone who has the patience and a great love for the river is qualified to join the ranks of crabbers. However, if you want your first crabbing experience to be a successful one, you must come prepared.

—Mary Zeigler, "How to Catch Crabs"

Classification. You may wish to use *classification* in an introduction when categorizing by types can help narrow your topic and focus your readers' attention on the one type discussed in your essay. For example, in the following introduction, the writer classifies various types of musicians before focusing attention on the essay's topic: the two types of musicians who play percussion instruments, "drummers" and "percussionists." The writer's thesis statement comes last in the introduction.

Quick—what do you call a person who plays a trumpet? A trumpeter, of course. A person who plays the flute is referred to as a flutist, or flautist, if you prefer. Someone who plays a piano is usually known as a pianist, unless of course he plays the player piano, in which case he is known as a player piano player rather than a player piano pianist. Got the hang of this yet? Okay, then, what do you call someone who plays that set of instruments belonging to the percussion family? Why, you call him a percussionist, don't you? Wrong! It's not quite as easy as all that. There are two types of musicians who play percussion instruments, "drummers" and "percussionists," and they are as different as the Sex Pistols and the New York Philharmonic.

—Karen Kramer, "The Little Drummer Boys"

ACTIVITY 10

Revising Your Introduction. Reread the introductory paragraph of your essay. Then rate your introduction on a scale of 1 to 4, as indicated in the list that follows.

1. Effective (forceful, attention-getting hook; clearly stated thesis statement)
2. Adequate (satisfactory hook; clearly stated thesis statement)
3. So-so (uninteresting hook; vague thesis statement)
4. Ineffective (no hook and/or no thesis statement)

Discuss your rating with your classmates. Then revise the introduction to your essay using one of the techniques discussed in this chapter. Also look at your thesis statement to see how you can make it more effective. It should announce your topic clearly and reveal its significance.

WRITING A POWERFUL CONCLUSION. Unlike elementary school writing where "The End" marks the conclusion of a story, the ending of a college essay requires the writer to create a natural sense of closure.

As you learned in Chapter 3, the *conclusion* serves two major functions in an essay: it makes clear that you have made the point you set out to make at the start of the essay, and it draws the essay to a satisfactory close. Thus, in the conclusion you do not introduce new material or end abruptly; instead, you wrap up what you have already said. Writers use various techniques to create effective conclusions. These techniques include the two standard ones discussed in detail in Chapter 3:

1. restating the thesis
2. making a suggestion

Or, if you like, try one of the following techniques:

3. using an effective quotation
4. asking a question
5. including a call for action
6. providing a summary

First let's review the two techniques discussed in Chapter 3.

Restate the Thesis. By *restating the thesis* in your conclusion, you remind readers of its significance and thereby give emphasis to your main point or idea. For example, look back at the introduction to "El Grito de Dolores" on p. 189. Then notice, in the following conclusion, how the Cordero restates her thesis.

> Sometimes Mexico is divided because of politics. It is not on this day, though. "El Grito de Dolores" brings the Mexican people together in a celebration of their ancestors who fought for freedom.

Make a Suggestion. By *making a suggestion* in the conclusion, you leave readers with a bit of useful advice about your topic. Because you have special knowledge of the topic, you can inform others about how to put the information you have provided to good use. In the conclusion to "Oprah Winfrey: How Truth Changed Her Life," Culhane reminds readers to heed the lesson of Winfrey's life.

> She was Oprah the graduating senior, and she was also Oprah the famous and wealthy entertainer. But she was still the Oprah they used to call The Preacher, who had herself learned the most valuable lesson of all: *Just tell the truth. It will save you every time.*

Use an Effective Quotation. With an *effective quotation* you can conclude an essay in an interesting, attention-getting way that emphasizes your main point. Earlier (p. 194) you read the introduction to "Fitting in Fitness." In the conclusion, Doner ends with a quotation from a working mom who recently ran a marathon, thus emphasizing the success of a woman who found time to exercise.

> When working moms make an effort to exercise and put sweat and tears into getting into shape, they're showered with benefits both immediate and long term. Right from the start they feel exhilarated and energized; and over time they gain self-confidence and a sense of accomplishment. "Think about it," says Irene Sang, an optometrist in South Pasadena, California, and a

single mother of two who went from being overweight and at risk for diabetes to running her first marathon this fall. "Exercise is guaranteed to make you feel more relaxed, more confident and healthier. How can you pass up such an opportunity?"

Ask a Question. By posing a meaningful *question* in the conclusion, you increase your readers' interest in the topic and leave them pondering its importance. In his essay "What's a Bagel?" Scott again asks the question.

What's a bagel?

He then provides an answer.

Fun you can eat.

Include a Call for Action. A *call for action* helps personalize your essay by asking readers to do something or to continue thinking about the topic after they read the essay. In the following example from an article about the popularity of collecting baseball cards, the writer concludes with a call for action by asking readers to consider joining a baseball card club.

After collecting baseball cards for several years, our greatest desire is to start a baseball card club in Los Angeles. If you would be interested in joining such a club, write to the above address with a note, "Count me in!"

Provide a Summary. For a lengthy and complex essay, a *summary* can pull ideas together and reinforce main points in the conclusion. The author of an essay on the New England clambake summarizes her important points about the clambake in her conclusion.

A clambake may remind you of Boston and Paul Revere's ride, but to ensure a successful meal, remember these important points: start early, dig a pit that is at least 2 feet deep, feed the charcoal fire with hardwood, and use seaweed-soaked canvas. While your clams are cooking, get out the iced-tea and beer and enjoy playing volleyball or strolling along the beach while taking part in this cherished New England tradition.

ACTIVITY 11 (GROUP)

Revising Your Conclusion. Reread the concluding paragraph of your essay. Then rate the conclusion on a scale of 1 to 4, as indicated in the list that follows.

1. Powerful (memorable closure; main points reinforced)
2. Adequate (interesting closure; main points reinforced)
3. So-so (uninteresting closure; main points reinforced)
4. Ineffective (no sense of closure; main points are not reinforced)

Discuss your rating with the members of your peer response group. Revise the conclusion to your essay using one of the techniques discussed in this chapter. Try to leave your readers with a lasting impression about your topic and its significance.

E-mail Your Introduction and Conclusion

E-mail your introduction and conclusion to several classmates. Ask them whether they found your introduction engaging enough that they would want to read the rest of the essay. Ask them whether your conclusion provides a sense of closure. Read their responses to help you improve your introduction and conclusion.

CONNECTING IDEAS. In addition to improving your introduction and conclusion when you revise your essay, you need to refine your thesis statement so that it clearly indicates the main idea of the essay. Examine your topic sentences: do they state the main idea of the body paragraphs? In addition, focus on paragraph development, organization, and unity. Finally, revise your essay to make the ideas flow by using keywords, transitions, and transitional paragraphs.

Keywords. One way to connect your ideas is to repeat *keywords,* words that pertain to the topic being discussed. By repeating a keyword, you keep your reader focused on the topic. In the following paragraph from "What's a Bagel?" for example, notice how the repetition of a keyword (underlined) contributes to the flow of ideas and keeps readers focused on the topic.

> For the health-conscious, however, the <u>bagel</u> has a lot going for it. The plain, two-ounce toaster-size has just 150 calories and one gram of fat. (The popular buttery croissant, by comparison, contains 235 calories and 12 grams of fat.) Furthermore, the plain <u>bagel</u> has no cholesterol, preservatives, or artificial color.

In addition to repetition of the same keyword, you can use *pronouns* and *synonyms* as keywords. A pronoun takes the place of the original word. In the following paragraph, notice how the use of pronouns and synonyms (underlined) for the keyword *T-shirts* helps connect the writer's ideas.

Another reason people like T-shirts is that they can purchase them at a variety of locations. They're sold at discount stores, flea markets, and garage sales. In fact, this is one item of clothing that many people don't mind getting second-hand. When people feel like going upscale, they can purchase T-shirts from a chic fashion designer. While these shirts might be made from the same fabric as the inexpensive shirts, people pay more money for them because of the designer's logo, strategically placed for all to see.

Transitions. Another way to connect your ideas is to use *transitions,* words that indicate the relationships between ideas. Here is a list of some common transitions and the relationships they express.

to add further information: also, additionally, in addition, too, furthermore, as well, and

to show differences: in contrast, on the other hand, whereas, but

to show similarities: in the same way, similarly, in comparison

to show time: then, since, meanwhile, at that time, by then, during, when, while, soon, until then, after, before, now, sometimes

to show cause and effect: because, as a result, consequently, therefore, thus, hence, thereby

to contradict or contrast: although, however, in contrast, nevertheless, but, or

to add emphasis: indeed, in fact, in truth, actually, moreover, furthermore, most important

to give an example: for example, for instance, specifically, such as

to show sequence: first, last, next, finally

Whenever you use a transition, be sure it expresses the correct relationship between ideas. Using transitions inappropriately can confuse your readers. Notice how transitions (underlined) are used in the following paragraph to connect ideas.

Another way people use T-shirts to express themselves is by wearing one that bears the name of a particular college. Sometimes the college is prestigious, such as Harvard. Are we to think that the wearer of the T-shirt actually went to Harvard? Or perhaps the wearer just wants us to think that? In contrast, when we see a T-shirt from a lesser-known or less prestigious school, we are more likely to assume that the wearer is simply showing school pride. In truth, a T-shirt is a mode of expression—but it's not always clear what's being expressed.

ACTIVITY 12 (GROUP)

Adding Keywords and Transitions. In the following paragraphs from *And the Beat Goes On: A Survey of Pop Music in America* by Charles Boeckman, keywords and transitions have been deleted. Work with your classmates to make the paragraphs coherent by adding the necessary keywords and transitions.

In the 1950s, a revolution began in America. There was nothing quiet about it. It had happened before most people woke up to what was going on. It has been one of the most curious things in our history. The young people banded together, splintered off into a compartment totally their own. They formed their own culture, economy and morals. A generation of young people was totally immersed in its own music. It symbolized, reflected, dictated the very nature of its revolution.

The stage was set. Out of the wings stepped a young Memphis truck driver with a ducktail hair style and a sullen, brooding expression—Elvis Presley with his rock'n'roll guitar. In 1954, a Black group, the Chords, had played the rock'n'roll style. In 1955, Bill Haley and a white group, the Comets, recorded the hit "Rock around the Clock." They lacked Elvis's charisma. They lacked his sex appeal. Elvis did more than sing. He went through a whole series of gyrations filled with sexual implications. It was just the thing for the mood of the hour. His voice trembled and cried out. His guitar thundered. His torso did bumps and grinds and shimmies. A whole generation of young people blew its cool.

Improve the Flow of Ideas

Try this method to improve the flow of ideas in your draft: Use the **bold** function to highlight the keywords in each paragraph. Check that your keywords pertain directly to the topic of the paragraph. Add, delete, or revise keywords as needed. Then use the *italic* function to highlight the transitions in each paragraph. Add transitions where the flow of thought seems disconnected or where there are no transitions in a long section. (Remember to remove the highlighting of keywords and transitions before printing your essay.)

Transitional Paragraphs. Another way to make your ideas flow smoothly is to write a *transitional paragraph,* or a paragraph that connects an idea in one paragraph to an idea in the next paragraph. This type of paragraph is usually from one to three sentences in length.

John Culhane uses a transitional paragraph in "Oprah Winfrey: How Truth Changed Her Life":

> She tells these stories on herself with her usual candor and humor, but it seems clear that the teen-age Oprah was using theatrical lies to win acceptance and love, just as she had won admiration in the past through her dramatic speaking roles.

In this transitional paragraph, the author concludes his discussion of Oprah's lies and begins relating how Oprah started telling the truth.

HOW TO Use Keywords and Transitions

Keywords and transitions provide a road map to help your readers connect ideas.

- Repeat keywords or use pronouns and synonyms to help readers follow your main idea.

- Use transitional words and phrases to move your readers to a new idea.

- Write a transitional paragraph of one to three sentences in length to move your readers from one major part of your essay to another.

ACTIVITY 13 (GROUP)

Finding Keywords, Transitions, and Transitional Paragraphs.
Working in a group, evaluate how well ideas are connected in your
textbooks for other courses. Make copies of several pages; then circle
the keywords, synonyms, and pronouns; underline the transitions;
and highlight transitional paragraphs.

Polishing Your Sentences and Words

So far in revising your paper, you have focused on developing
your ideas using definition, process, and cause and effect. You have
also helped your ideas flow by using keywords, transitions, and transitional paragraphs. Now you're ready to revise your sentences and
words.

For additional ways to combine sentences, see pp. 127–29, 269–73, 336–40, 412–15, and 476–78.

COMBINING SENTENCES USING CONJUNCTIVE ADVERBS.
As you learned in Chapter 4, by combining short, closely related sentences, you clarify the relationship between ideas, making them easier
to understand. Sentence combining also helps eliminate unnecessary
words and increase the different types of sentences you can use.

This section focuses on combining sentences using conjunctive
adverbs such as *however, therefore,* and *moreover* and transitional
phrases such as *for example, in other words,* and *to illustrate.* The following conjunctive adverbs are often used to combine two complete
sentences. Remember, a complete sentence has a subject and a verb.

HOW TO **Combine Sentences with Conjunctive Adverbs
and Transitional Phrases**

- Use a conjunctive adverb *(however, moreover, therefore)* to
combine short, closely related complete sentences.

- Use transitional phrases *(on the other hand, for example, in
conclusion)* to combine closely related complete thoughts.

- When using a conjunctive adverb or transitional phrase,
place a semicolon before the adverb or phrase and a comma
after it.

CONJUNCTIVE ADVERBS

also	meanwhile	specifically
besides	moreover	subsequently
consequently	nevertheless	then
finally	next	therefore
furthermore	otherwise	thus
however	similarly	

You can review a list of transitional phrases on p. 200.

While freewriting on "El Grito de Dolores," Sandra Cordero wrote several short sentences that need to be combined.

ORIGINAL   Every town in Mexico has a street called "16 de Septiembre." This is where the parade begins and ends.

REVISED   Every town in Mexico has a street called "16 de Septiembre"; consequently, this is where the parade begins and ends.

This revision, using a conjunctive adverb, shows the relationship between the two clauses: the parade begins and ends on this particular street because its very name represents the holiday. It is important to note that when you use a conjunctive adverb or transitional phrase between two complete thoughts, the adverb or phrase is preceded by a semicolon (;) and followed by a comma (,).

ORIGINAL   Every Mexican participates in this event. It's the way we thank our heroes and ancestors for giving us freedom.

REVISED   Every Mexican participates in this event; after all, it's the way we thank our heroes and ancestors for giving us freedom.

In this revision, using a transitional phrase, Sandra explains why Mexicans celebrate this holiday by showing the relationship between the event and what it represents.

ACTIVITY 14

Combining Sentences. Combine the following pairs or groups of sentences with conjunctive adverbs or transitional phrases. Don't forget to add a semicolon before the adverb or phrase and a comma after it.

1. Sports competitions are some of the most important cultural traditions throughout the world. International sports competitions increase national pride.

_____

_____

_____

2. In many countries soccer is the most popular sport. The World Cup tournament draws huge crowds of fans.

_____

_____

_____

3. An airline pilots' strike threatened to halt the 1998 World Cup when it was held in France. The French government quickly settled with the pilots' union.

_____

_____

_____

4. The French government had other concerns before the World Cup began. The construction of a new stadium was behind schedule.

_____

_____

_____

5. Many fans watched the games at neighborhood bars near the stadium. Some fans rioted in the streets.

_____

_____

_____

6. There was some fighting between fans of different teams. The games were still successful.

_____

_____

_____

7. French fans were delighted when France beat Brazil to win the World Cup. They celebrated for several days.

_____

_____

_____

ELIMINATING CLICHÉS. *Clichés* are overused expressions. You often hear them spoken in everyday conversation:

"I'm *as tired as a dog.*"

"That sales pitch *knocked his socks off.*"

"All weekend she was *as happy as a lark.*"

When most clichés originally appeared, they probably communicated ideas forcefully. The cliché *kick the bucket,* for example, came from a way of committing suicide: with a noose tied around the neck, a suicide victim would kick away the bucket he or she was standing on. But with overuse, clichés lose their meaning. Here are some other clichés to avoid in your writing:

easier said than done	crystal clear
playing with fire	almighty dollar
in a nutshell	silver lining
bite the dust	light as a feather
cool as a cucumber	crack of dawn
sick as a dog	goes without saying

Although clichés are acceptable in informal speech and writing, they're inappropriate in formal writing, including the writing you do in college and the workplace. If you find a cliché in a draft of your own writing, delete it and express the idea in your own words.

CLICHÉ	Thomas Jefferson lived to a *ripe old age.*
REVISED	Thomas Jefferson lived to be *eighty-three years old.*
CLICHÉ	Benjamin Franklin believed that you'll succeed if you *keep your nose to the grindstone.*
REVISED	Benjamin Franklin believed that you'll succeed if you *work hard.*
CLICHÉ	Even when Hillary Rodham Clinton was young, she was *no shrinking violet.*
REVISED	Even when Hillary Rodham Clinton was young, she was *not shy.*

ACTIVITY 15

Eliminating Clichés. Underline the clichés in the following sentences. Then rewrite each one, expressing the idea in your own words.

1. The great tennis player Billie Jean King always said what was on her mind. She was never one to beat around the bush.

   _____

   _____

2. Early on in his life, John F. Kennedy seemed to have the luck of the Irish.

   _____

   _____

3. The Fourth of July fireworks made my grandmother look like she'd seen a ghost.

   _____

   _____

4. Even though the demonstration nearly turned into a riot, Martin Luther King never lost his cool.

_____

_____

5. Cesar Chavez and his supporters burned the midnight oil planning for the farmworkers' protest against poor wages and dangerous working conditions.

_____

_____

_____

6. Benjamin Franklin invented bifocal eyeglasses because he was becoming as blind as a bat.

_____

_____

7. The little girl leading the parade looked as proud as a peacock in her Pilgrim costume.

_____

_____

8. Henry David Thoreau decided to quit the rat race and move to Walden Pond.

_____

_____

9. As a young girl, Chamique Holdsclaw wanted to play basketball every day of the week, but her grandmother put her foot down and wouldn't let her play on Sunday.

_____

_____

10. The Beatles' best album, *Sergeant Pepper's Lonely Hearts Club Band,*
    sold like hotcakes.

    _____

    _____

ACTIVITY 16

Polishing Your Sentences and Words. Reread your discovery
draft, looking for sentences that might be combined to eliminate
unnecessary words and to clarify the relationship between your ideas.
Also, make your writing lively by eliminating any clichés.

Sandra's Revised Draft

Before you read Sandra's revised draft, reread her discovery draft
(pp. 189–90). Notice, in particular, how Sandra has narrowed her thesis statement. She has also added examples, definitions, and cause
and effect. Her ideas are better connected and flow more smoothly as
a result. In addition, she has added information about the cultural
tradition that her readers may be unfamiliar with. (You will also
notice some errors in her revised draft; Sandra will correct these errors
when she edits her revised essay.)

El Grito de Dolores

"Viva Mexico! Viva Mexico! Viva Mexico!" hundreds of   1
people cry out at the same time. Gathered in the town plaza
at midnight on September 16, they are celebrating one of
Mexicos most important holidays, "El Grito de Dolores." The   Keyword *(holiday)* introduced.
holiday honors the men and women who fought for Mexico's
independence. On this day, Mexicans feel united as they
celebrate their history.

What is "El Grito de Dolores"? This expression means   2   Definition added.
"the cry from Dolores," and it refers to an important event
that happened early in the morning on September 16, 1810.   Transition *(at this time)* added.
At this time, Mexico was ruled by the Spanish king. But a

Cause and effect
added.

priest named Miguel Hidalgo called together his parishioners at his church in Dolores, Guanajuato, Mexico. In a
speech that was later called "El Grito de Dolores," Hidalgo
urged his people to fight for freedom. This was the begin-

Transition *(since then)*
added.

ning of the Mexican revolution against Spain. Since then,
the holiday is celebrated everywhere in Mexico. Even the
smallest towns have their own celebrations.

Repetition of key-
word *(celebration)*.

    The celebration begins in the main plaza exactly at   3
midnight the governor of each city goes on top of the
municipal building. "Viva Don Miguel Hidalgo!" he yells to
give honor to the person who began the movement for independence. ("Viva" means "long live.") The people shout

Transition *(then)*
added.
Repetition of key-
word *(celebrates)*.

"Viva Mexico! Viva Mexico! Viva Mexico!" Then fireworks
light up the night sky, and everyone celebrates the
countrys independence.

    The next part of the celebration is a parade held on   4
the morning of September 16. Held on the street called
"16 de Septiembre." Every town in Mexico has a street with

Examples added.

this name. The parade includes children, business leaders,
government leaders, members of clubs, police officers, and
firefighters. Green, red, and white streamers float through
the air. People waving little Mexican flags to show their
pride in their country.

    Sometimes Mexico is divided because of politics not on   5

Transition *(though)*
added.
Repetition of key-
word *(celebration)*.

this day, though. "El Grito de Dolores" brings the Mexican
people together in a celebration of their ancestors who
fought for freedom.

ACTIVITY 17

Analyzing Sandra's Revised Draft. Use the following questions to
discuss with your classmates how Sandra improved her draft.

1. Is the purpose of Sandra's draft clear? What is that purpose?

   _____

   _____

2. What is Sandra's thesis statement? Could it be improved?

   _____

   _____

   _____

   _____

   _____

3. Does Sandra tell her readers enough to understand the cultural tradition? Explain.

   _____

   _____

   _____

4. How effective is Sandra's introduction? Conclusion?

   _____

   _____

   _____

5. Are the paragraphs in Sandra's revision better developed than those in her discovery draft? Do the ideas flow together better? Explain, and give examples.

   _____

   _____

   _____

6. How could Sandra's revised draft benefit from further revision?

_____

_____

_____

ACTIVITY 18 (GROUP)

Using Peer Review. Form a group with two or three other students and exchange copies of your drafts. Read your draft aloud while your classmates follow along. Take notes on your classmates' responses to the following questions about your draft:

1. What did you like best about my essay?

_____

_____

_____

2. How interesting is my introduction? Do you want to continue reading the paper? Why or why not?

_____

_____

_____

3. What is my thesis statement? Do I need to make my essay's thesis clearer?

_____

_____

_____

4. Where in the essay could I add definitions, process, and cause and effect to help convey my message?

_____

_____

_____

5. How can I use keywords, transitions, and transitional paragraphs to make my ideas flow together better? Where can I combine sentences to improve the writing?

_____

_____

_____

6. What parts, if any, do not support my thesis and could be omitted? Are there any sentences or words that seem unnecessary?

_____

_____

_____

7. Where in the draft did my writing confuse you? How can I clarify my thoughts?

_____

_____

_____

8. How effective is my conclusion? Do I end in such a way that you know it's the end?

_____

_____

_____

Use Online Peer Review

If your class has a Web site, see whether the peer review questions are available on the site. If they are, you may be able to respond to your classmates' drafts electronically.

ACTIVITY 19

Revising Your Draft. Taking your classmates' suggestions for revision into consideration, revise your essay. In particular, focus on developing the ideas in your paragraphs effectively and using keywords, transitions, and perhaps a transitional paragraph to connect ideas. You might also consider combining closely related sentences and eliminating clichés. Finally, look for irrelevant or unnecessary material that can be omitted and experiment with moving sections of your draft to achieve the best presentation.

Online Writing Centers

For additional help with polishing sentences and words, visit the *Choices* Web site at <www.bedfordstmartins .com/choices/>. Click on "Annotated Web Links" and scroll to "Online Writing Labs (OWLS)."

EDITING

Now that you have revised your essay about a cultural symbol, tradition, or hero, you're ready to edit it for correctness. Remember, the fewer errors you make, the more your readers will focus on what you have to say. In Chapter 4, you focused on correcting run-on sentences and comma splices and punctuating dialogue. In this chapter, you will focus on correcting sentence fragments and checking apostrophes.

Correcting Sentence Fragments

A complete sentence contains a subject and a verb and expresses a complete thought. The subject tells who or what is doing the action, and the verb tells the action or links the subject to the rest of the sentence.

The following are complete sentences.

My *sister attended* graduation.
Jerry enjoys holidays.
I left class early.
He is my closest friend.

A *sentence fragment,* on the other hand, does not express a complete thought. A sentence fragment may be a *phrase,* a group of words that lacks a subject or a verb:

PHRASES

who attended graduation	(Who is attending graduation?)
Jerry's favorite holiday	(What about Jerry's favorite holiday?)
left class early	(Who left class early?)
my closest friend	(What about your closest friend?)

A sentence fragment may also be a *dependent clause,* a group of words that contains a subject and a verb, but doesn't express a complete thought.

DEPENDENT CLAUSES

when my sister attended graduation
because it was Jerry's favorite holiday
after I left class early
since Cheryl is my closest friend

HOW TO Correct Sentence Fragments

To identify a sentence fragment, ask yourself the following questions about each sentence in your essay:

- Does the sentence have a subject?

- Does the sentence have a verb?

- Does the sentence express a complete thought?

If you answer "No" to any of these questions, you have a sentence fragment. To correct the sentence fragment:

- Add the missing subject or verb.

- Combine the fragment with the sentence before or after it.

ACTIVITY 20

Correcting Sentence Fragments. Identify each of the following as a complete sentence or a sentence fragment. Then correct each sentence fragment by connecting it to the sentence before or after it or by rewriting it.

1. My favorite custom is hiding Easter eggs. Because it's fun for everyone.

   _____

   _____

2. Since I left home. My mother calls me every other day.

   _____

   _____

3. Approaching my home.

   _____

   _____

4. Never a dull moment.

   _____

   _____

5. We forgot to celebrate my birthday!

   _____

   _____

6. We visited family for the holidays. Which didn't surprise me.

   _____

   _____

7. Yom Kippur is a significant time in our family.

   _____

   _____

8. Whatever you do. Don't purchase fireworks for the Fourth of July.

   _____

   _____

9. Standing on the corner.

   _____

   _____

10. Whoever you saw. It wasn't my father.

   _____

   _____

Online Grammar Skills Practice

For additional practice eliminating sentence fragments, visit the *Choices* Web site at **<www.bedfordstmartins .com/choices/>** and click on "Exercise Central." After logging in, click on "Sentence Fragments."

Checking Apostrophes

Writers use *apostrophes* (') to show that something belongs to someone or something else. Add *'s* to a singular noun to show possession.

Sarah's favorite game is "Pin the Tail on the Donkey."
The *student's* mother came with her to orientation.

HOW TO Use Apostrophes

An apostrophe (') shows ownership or replaces a missing letter.

- To show possession, add *'s* to a singular noun. Add only an apostrophe (') to a plural noun that already ends in *s*. Add *'s* if a plural noun does not end in *s*.

- Be careful with *its* and *it's*. *Its* shows possession, and *it's* is the contraction for *it is*.

- Form a contraction by using an apostrophe (') to replace the missing letters.

If the noun is plural and ends in *'s,* just add an apostrophe after the *s*.

The *swimmers'* finished their laps.
The *students'* books were in the back of the room.

If the noun is plural, but does not end in *s,* then add *'s*.

The *children's* store is at the other end of the mall.
The *women's* store is at this end.

Apostrophes are also used to form contractions. The apostrophe takes the place of the omitted letters. For a list of contractions, see p. 700.

We *aren't* [are not] going because I *wouldn't* [would not] enjoy it.
She *doesn't* [does not] know he *hasn't* [has not] written yet.
It's [it is] about time that *she's* [she is] finishing her degree.

Notice that the apostrophe in *it's* forms the contraction for *it is*. Be careful not to use an apostrophe with the possessive pronoun *its*.

The whale slapped *its* tail against the waves.
The book has *its* good parts.

ACTIVITY 21

Checking Apostrophes. In the following sentences, underline the words in which apostrophes are missing. Add the apostrophes.

1. Janices fiancé comes to see her even if he doesnt stay long.

   _____

   _____

2. I cant imagine why Joes friends stick by him.

   _____

   _____

3. My relatives last names arent the same as mine.

   _____

   _____

4. Heres my favorite place to meet the Smiths.

   _____

   _____

5. Im determined to finish Joses ice cream for him.

   _____

   _____

6. Shell never go to her parents house again.

   _____

   _____

7. Theyve always been nice to the womans niece.

   _____

   _____

8. Wasnt that the best movie youve ever seen?

_____

_____

9. Well try to finish it because its so important.

_____

_____

10. Whos going to dinner?

_____

_____

Online Grammar Skills Practice

For additional practice using apostrophes, visit the *Choices* Web site at <**www.bedfordstmartins.com/choices/**> and click on "Exercise Central." After logging in, click on "Apostrophes."

Sandra's Edited Essay

You probably noticed that Sandra's revised draft contained errors in sentence structure and punctuation. Sandra corrected these errors in her edited essay. Her corrections are underlined here. Her editing log follows the essay.

El Grito de Dolores

"Viva Mexico! Viva Mexico! Viva Mexico!" hundreds of   1
people cry out at the same time. Gathered in the town plaza
at midnight on September 16, they are celebrating one of
<u>Mexico's</u> most important holidays, "El Grito de Dolores."
The holiday honors the men and women who fought for Mexico's

independence. On this day, Mexicans feel united as they celebrate their history.

What is "El Grito de Dolores"? This expression means "the cry from Dolores," and it refers to an important event that happened early in the morning on September 16, 1810. At this time, Mexico was ruled by the Spanish king. But a priest named Miguel Hidalgo called together his parishioners at his church in Dolores, Guanajuato, Mexico. In a speech that was later called "El Grito de Dolores," Hidalgo urged his people to fight for freedom. This was the beginning of the Mexican revolution against Spain. Since then, the holiday is celebrated everywhere in Mexico. Even the smallest towns have their own celebrations.

2

The celebration begins in the main <u>plaza. Exactly</u> at midnight the governor of each city goes on top of the municipal building. "Viva Don Miguel Hidalgo!" he yells to give honor to the person who began the movement for independence. ("Viva" means "long live.") The people shout "Viva Mexico! Viva Mexico! Viva Mexico!" Then fireworks light up the night sky, and everyone celebrates the <u>country's</u> independence.

3

The next part of the celebration is a parade <u>held on the morning of September 16 on the street called "16 de Septiembre."</u> Every town in Mexico has a street with this name. The parade includes children, business leaders, government leaders, members of clubs, police officers, and firefighters. Green, red, and white streamers float through the air. People <u>wave</u> little Mexican flags to show their pride in their country.

4

Sometimes Mexico is divided because of <u>politics. It is not</u> on this day, though. "El Grito de Dolores" brings the Mexican people together in a celebration of their ancestors who fought for freedom.

5

Sandra's Editing Log

INCORRECT	Mexicos (1)
ERROR	possessive noun without apostrophe
CORRECT	Mexico's

INCORRECT	The celebration begins in the main plaza exactly at midnight the governor of each city goes on top of the municipal building. (3)
ERROR	run-on sentence
CORRECT	The celebration begins in the main plaza. Exactly at midnight the governor of each city goes on top of the municipal building.

INCORRECT	countrys (3)
ERROR	possessive noun without apostrophe
CORRECT	country's

INCORRECT	Held on the street called "16 de Septiembre." (4)
ERROR	sentence fragment
CORRECT	The next part of the celebration is a parade held on the morning of September 16 on the street called "16 de Septiembre."

INCORRECT	People waving little Mexican flags to show their pride in their country. (4)
ERROR	sentence fragment
CORRECT	People wave little Mexican flags to show their pride in their country.

INCORRECT	Sometimes Mexico is divided because of politics not on this day, though. (5)
ERROR	run-on sentence
CORRECT	Sometimes Mexico is divided because of politics. It is not on this day, though.

ACTIVITY 22

Editing Your Essay. Read your essay word for word, looking for errors in sentence structure, grammar, spelling, and punctuation. Also ask a friend or classmate to help you spot errors you might have overlooked. Then use a dictionary and the Handbook in Part Four of this book to help you correct the errors you find. Finally, record those errors in your editing log.

Don't Rely Only on Spell-Check
The spell-check on your word-processing program will not catch spelling errors involving homonyms, or words that sound alike but are spelled differently (such as *there* and *their*). In addition to using a spell-check, take the time to search for spelling errors on your own.

PUBLISHING

After you edit your essay, you're ready to share it with your audience—your instructor, your classmates, and students who come from cultures other than your own (including, perhaps, students in your writing classroom and members of a campus club or organization for international students). You might also send your essay by e-mail to a friend. Finally, give some thought to the benefits of reading about and familiarizing yourself with other cultures.

CHAPTER CHECKLIST

☐ I gathered ideas on a cultural symbol, tradition, or hero by questioning, freewriting, clustering, brainstorming, and relating aloud.

☐ I developed the ideas in my paragraphs with definitions, process, and cause and effect.

☐ I made my ideas easier to understand by connecting them with keywords, transitions, and transitional paragraphs.

☐ I combined closely related sentences by using conjunctive adverbs and transitional phrases.

☐ I made my writing more interesting by eliminating clichés.

☐ I eliminated sentence fragments.

☐ I checked apostrophes.

☐ I shared my essay with readers from different cultures as well as with my instructor and classmates.

REFLECTING ON YOUR WRITING

To help you continue to improve as a writer, answer the following questions.

1. Did you enjoy writing about an aspect of your culture? Why or why not?
2. Which topic did you choose—a cultural symbol, tradition, or hero—and why?
3. What types of changes did you make when you revised?
4. If you had more time, what further revisions would you make to improve your essay? Why?

Using your answers to these questions, update your Writing Process Report.

Writing Process Report

Date:

Strengths:

Weaknesses:

Plans for improvement:

Once you complete this report, freewrite about what you learned in this chapter about your writing and what you still hope to learn.

Cultural Symbol

In the following reading, "Feather," Gerald Hausman writes about the symbolic importance of the feather in Native American life.

GERALD HAUSMAN

Feather

For decorations of war, worship, and as an expression of flight, the feather is the universal Native American symbol. In Arctic regions, the Indian sought water birds. On the North Pacific coast, they captured or killed ravens and flickers. In California, the tribes hunted woodpeckers, meadowlarks, crested quail, mallard ducks, blue jays, blackbirds, and orioles. Around the southwestern pueblos, hunters went after eagles, hawks, turkeys, and parrots. Using the feathers and skins and even bodies of birds, the tribes made clothes, masks, hats, blankets, and robes.

Parkas in the Arctic were made of water-bird skins sewn together, the feathers acting as insulation and waterproofing. Tribes to the south used the skins of young waterfowl, while still downy, and sewed them into robes. Eastern tribes cut bird skins into strips and wove them into blankets in the same way that western tribes used rabbit skins.

Captain John Smith and other early European settlers observed that the Indians of the East fashioned turkey robes: feathers tied in knots to form a network out of which beautiful patterned cloaks were wrought.

Fans and other accessories of dress were made of wings or feathers by the Iroquois. The western Eskimo sewed little sprays of down into the seams of garments. California tribes decorated their basketry with feathers; quills of small birds were incorporated into basketry in much the same way as porcupine quills. Of course, one of the most common uses of the feather was in arrow making. For giving directness in flight, arrow feathers were split so that halves could be glued to the shaft of the arrow in twos and threes.

An unusual use of bird scalps was practiced by certain California tribes, who used them as money, being both a standard of value and a medium of exchange.

The down feathers of birds have a special value to Native   6
Americans. Light and airy, fluffy and snowy, these feathers can
be seen as a bridge between the spirit world and Mother Earth, or
simply as messenger and prayer feathers. *Pahos,* as they are
called among the Hopi, are used to mark sacred sites and to
summon the deities as well as to ask their blessing.

The symbolism of the feather is a compression, so to speak,   7
of the bird. Humankind, seeing that birds can fly, has always
been desirous of flight. The mythology of angels, airborne deities
residing in heaven or heavens, is common to the collective
human tribe. The wish to fly, understood on its primary level, is
merely the desire to have something one does not or cannot
have. On a deeper philosophical level, however, flight is the
dreamlike movement of the unconscious, the freedom of will,
the connection between the spiritual and the material. In flight,
man releases his earthbound nature and is reborn in spirit. . . .

VOCABULARY WORDS: insulation (2), wrought (3), incorporated (4),
medium (5), summon (6), deities (6), compression (7), unconscious (7)

ACTIVITY 23

Reading to Improve Writing. Discuss the following questions
about "Feather" with your classmates.

1. What are some ways that Native Americans used feathers?

   _____

   _____

   _____

   _____

2. Why did down feathers have special value?

   _____

   _____

   _____

   _____

3. Why has the feather become the "universal Native American symbol" (1)?

_____

_____

_____

_____

4. Explain the author's meaning in this sentence: "In flight, man releases his earthbound nature and is reborn in spirit" (7).

_____

_____

_____

_____

5. How does Hausman use description to support his points about the feather in Native American culture?

_____

_____

_____

_____

Cultural Tradition

One of America's oldest cultural traditions is the Thanksgiving holiday, when people celebrate their heritage and give thanks. (Thanksgiving is also celebrated in Canada.) In the following essay, "Our Thanksgiving Tradition," William C. Brisick describes how the American Thanksgiving tradition began.

WILLIAM C. BRISICK

Our Thanksgiving Tradition

Thanksgiving is the quintessential American holiday, the   1
oldest, the most tradition-bound of our holidays. Oh, sure,
there's the Fourth of July, that red-white-and-blue day when we
Americans celebrate the sloughing off of our colonial servitude,
the commitment to our freedom, our independence. The backyard barbecues are busy every Fourth, no doubt about that, and
there's always a good deal of frolicking outdoors.

Thanksgiving, by contrast, is usually cast on a cold, wind-   2
swept, perhaps snow-swept, day—it's an indoor holiday. Yet its
muted warmth—from the fire of the hearth rather than from the
sun—casts its own spell, reminding us of how it was that America got started in the first place. It tells of immigrants in a new
land, grateful for a bountiful harvest after long and difficult
days; it speaks of settler and native breaking bread together in a
time of peace and understanding; and finally, pointing up a
more universal quality, it conjures images of friends and relatives
setting aside some moments to come together, to reconnect with
each other, to enjoy the pleasures of good food and drink.

For those of us who have experienced more than a few   3
Thanksgivings, the warm glow of holidays past suffuses—perhaps befogs—our memory. We're absolutely sure about the presence of turkey, reasonably sure of who was there to eat it, but a
bit uncertain about most everything else.

For the first Thanksgiving in 1621 we have only a few re-   4
corded facts from two sources: a letter written by Edward
Winslow, one of the participants, to a friend in England, and
Governor William Bradford's famous document, *Of Plimouth
Plantation.* We know that fifty-two Pilgrims, survivors of the
Mayflower voyage and the first winter/spring/summer, celebrated with ninety Indians, date unknown but sometime
between September 21 and November 9. Only four of the Pilgrim
wives were in attendance, the others having succumbed to the
rigors of life in the New World.

The Pilgrims, heirs to the English tradition of marking the   5
end of the harvest, were doing just that, but they were also setting aside a time to give thanks to God for blessings received. The
feast lasted three days, not one, and they ate cod and sea bass,
cornmeal, wild fowl, and deer brought by the Indians, pumpkins
(boiled, not in pies), and cranberries (pudding rather than sauce
because sugar was scarce). The wild fowl probably consisted of

ducks, geese, swans, and the staple of today's Thanksgiving table, turkey.

Until well into the 19th century Thanksgiving was a regional holiday, focused in the Northeast. There the states celebrated it during the fall but on varying dates; the governors, by proclamation, decided when it would take place. In each case it marked the boundary between the season of harvest with its arduous work schedule, and the onset of winter, a time of enforced leisure. People looked forward to it, prepared weeks in advance, and when the day finally arrived celebrated not only with the traditional dinner but with long walks or rides in the countryside, with indoor games and storytelling. Many New Englanders made it the occasion for weddings. 6

Sara Josepha Hale, editor of the journal *Godey's Lady's Book,* as early as 1846 began to campaign to make Thanksgiving a national holiday. Her letters to various presidents didn't bear fruit until Abraham Lincoln decreed in 1863 that the fourth Thursday in November would be set aside as a national holiday. That proclamation had only limited effect since the Civil War was still raging. In its aftermath the Southern states spent quite a few years adjusting to the celebration of what they considered a Yankee holiday. 7

But was it a Yankee holiday? There are some who believe that the first Thanksgiving actually occurred on Southern shores. The event took place December 4, 1619, on the banks of the St. James River shortly after the first landing of the English there. In affirmation, contemporary Virginians celebrate the gala Virginia First Thanksgiving Festival at the Berkeley Plantation on the first Sunday in November each year. 8

Not to be outdone, the Southwest has staked a claim of its own for a 16th-century Thanksgiving—April 1598, to be exact. A few weeks earlier a Spanish expedition under Don Juan de Oñate had ventured forth from Chihuahua in what is now Mexico, and after an arduous journey crossed the Rio Grande near present-day El Paso, Texas. Four hundred hardy souls they were, men and women; they netted fish from the river, shot ducks and geese, gave thanks and feasted—"a repast the like of which we had never enjoyed before," one participant wrote. 9

Historical one-upmanship aside, the act of getting together with family and friends for camaraderie and fellowship, a celebratory meal and an offering of thanks has been a tradition through the centuries. No doubt our cave-dwelling ancestors took the opportunity to relax and rejoice after a successful hunt. Happy to say, we've embellished the cuisine since then. 10

But whether or not our holiday fare reaches the highest standards of culinary art, the essence of what we do on the fourth 11

Thursday of November remains remarkably similar to what our forebears did on Thanksgivings past. They, like us, looked upon all sorts of weather outside, but managed, like us, to create a peculiar, very special warmth inside.

VOCABULARY WORDS: quintessential (1), sloughing (1), muted (2), conjures (2), suffuses (3), arduous (6), aftermath (7), hardy (9), embellished (10), cuisine (10)

ACTIVITY 24

Reading to Improve Writing. Discuss the following questions about "Our Thanksgiving Tradition" with your classmates.

1. What did you learn about Thanksgiving from reading Brisick's essay?

   _____

   _____

   _____

   _____

2. Why do Americans continue to celebrate Thanksgiving?

   _____

   _____

   _____

   _____

3. When do you think the first Thanksgiving took place?

   _____

   _____

   _____

4. Explain the first sentence from the essay: "Thanksgiving is the quintessential American holiday, the oldest, the most tradition-bound of our holidays."

_____

_____

_____

_____

5. How effective are the introduction and conclusion?

_____

_____

_____

_____

_____

Cultural Hero

Heroes don't always have to be well-known people. In the following essay, "Unforgettable Miss Bessie," Carl T. Rowan explains why one of his high school teachers is his hero.

CARL T. ROWAN

Unforgettable Miss Bessie

She was only about five feet tall and probably never weighed more than 110 pounds, but Miss Bessie was a towering presence in the classroom. She was the only woman tough enough to make me read *Beowulf* and think for a few foolish days that I liked it. From 1938 to 1942, when I attended Bernard High School in McMinnville, Tenn., she taught me English, history, civics — and a lot more than I realized.

1

I shall never forget the day she scolded me into reading *Beowulf.*   2

"But Miss Bessie," I complained, "I ain't much interested in it."   3

Her large brown eyes became daggerish slits. "Boy," she said, "how dare you say 'ain't' to me! I've taught you better than that."   4

"Miss Bessie," I pleaded, "I'm trying to make first-string end on the football team, and if I go around saying 'it isn't' and 'they aren't,' the guys are gonna laugh me off the squad."   5

"Boy," she responded, "you'll play football because you have guts. But do you know what *really* takes guts? Refusing to lower your standards to those of the crowd. It takes guts to say you've got to live and be somebody fifty years after all the football games are over."   6

I started saying "it isn't" and "they aren't," and I still made first-string end—and class valedictorian—without losing my buddies' respect.   7

During her remarkable 44-year career, Mrs. Bessie Taylor Gwynn taught hundreds of economically deprived black youngsters—including my mother, my brother, my sisters and me. I remember her now with gratitude and affection—especially in this era when Americans are so wrought-up about a "rising tide of mediocrity" in public education and the problems of finding competent, caring teachers. Miss Bessie was an example of an informed, dedicated teacher, a blessing to children and an asset to the nation.   8

Born in 1895, in poverty, she grew up in Athens, Ala., where there was no public school for blacks. She attended Trinity School, a private institution for blacks run by the American Missionary Association, and in 1911 graduated from the Normal School (a "super" high school) at Fisk University in Nashville. Mrs. Gwynn, the essence of pride and privacy, never talked about her years in Athens; only in the months before her death did she reveal that she had never attended Fisk University itself because she could not afford the four-year course.   9

At Normal School she learned a lot about Shakespeare, but most of all about the profound importance of education—especially, for a people trying to move up from slavery. "What you put in your head, boy," she once said, "can never be pulled out by the Ku Klux Klan, the Congress or anybody."   10

Miss Bessie's bearing of dignity told anyone who met her that she was "educated" in the best sense of the word. There was never a discipline problem in her classes. We didn't dare mess with a woman who knew about the Battle of Hastings, the Magna Carta and the Bill of Rights—and who could also play the piano.   11

This frail-looking woman could make sense of Shakespeare, Milton, Voltaire, and bring to life Booker T. Washington and   12

W. E. B. DuBois. Believing that it was important to know who the officials were that spent taxpayers' money and made public policy, she made us memorize the names of everyone on the Supreme Court and in the President's Cabinet. It could be embarrassing to be unprepared when Miss Bessie said, "Get up and tell the class who Frances Perkins is and what you think about her."

Miss Bessie knew that my family, like so many others during the Depression, couldn't afford to subscribe to a newspaper. She knew we didn't even own a radio. Still, she prodded me to "look out for your future and find some way to keep up with what's going on in the world." So I became a delivery boy for the Chattanooga *Times.* I rarely made a dollar a week, but I got to read a newspaper every day.

Miss Bessie noticed things that had nothing to do with schoolwork, but were vital to a youngster's development. Once a few classmates made fun of my frayed, hand-me-down overcoat, calling me "Strings." As I was leaving school, Miss Bessie patted me on the back of that old overcoat and said, "Carl, never fret about what you *don't* have. Just make the most of what you *do* have—a brain."

Among the things that I did not have was electricity in the little frame house that my father had built for $400 with his World War I bonus. But because of her inspiration, I spent many hours squinting beside a kerosene lamp reading Shakespeare and Thoreau, Samuel Pepys and William Cullen Bryant.

No one in my family had ever graduated from high school, so there was no tradition of commitment to learning for me to lean on. Like millions of youngsters in today's ghettos and barrios, I needed the push and stimulation of a teacher who truly cared. Miss Bessie gave plenty of both, as she immersed me in a wonderful world of similes, metaphors and even onomatopoeia. She led me to believe that I could write sonnets as well as Shakespeare, or iambic-pentameter verse to put Alexander Pope to shame.

In those days the McMinnville school system was rigidly "Jim Crow," and poor black children had to struggle to put anything in their heads. Our high school was only slightly larger than the once-typical little red schoolhouse, and its library was outrageously inadequate—so small, I like to say, that if two students were in it and one wanted to turn a page, the other one had to step outside.

Negroes, as we were called then, were not allowed in the town library, except to mop floors or dust tables. But through one of those secret Old South arrangements between whites of conscience and blacks of stature, Miss Bessie kept getting books

13

14

15

16

17

18

smuggled out of the white library. That is how she introduced me to the Brontës, Byron, Coleridge, Keats and Tennyson. "If you don't read, you can't write, and if you can't write, you might as well stop dreaming," Miss Bessie once told me.

So I read whatever Miss Bessie told me to, and tried to re-   19
member the things she insisted that I store away. Forty-five years later, I can still recite her "truths to live by," such as Henry Wadsworth Longfellow's lines from "The Ladder of St. Augustine":

> *The heights by great men reached and kept*
> *Were not attained by sudden flight.*
> *But they, while their companions slept,*
> *Were toiling upward in the night.*

Years later, her inspiration, prodding, anger, cajoling and   20
almost osmotic infusion of learning finally led to that lovely day when Miss Bessie dropped me a note saying, "I'm so proud to read your column in the Nashville *Tennessean.*"

Miss Bessie was a spry 80 when I went back to McMinnville   21
and visited her in a senior citizens' apartment building. Pointing out proudly that her building was racially integrated, she reached for two glasses and a pint of bourbon. I was momentarily shocked, because it would have been scandalous in the 1930s and '40s for word to get out that a teacher drank, and nobody had ever raised a rumor that Miss Bessie did.

I felt a new sense of equality as she lifted her glass to mine.   22
Then she revealed a softness and compassion that I had never known as a student.

"I've never forgotten that examination day," she said, "when   23
Buster Martin held up seven fingers, obviously asking you for help with question number seven, 'Name a common carrier.' I can still picture you looking at your exam paper and humming a few bars of 'Chattanooga Choo Choo.' I was so tickled, I couldn't punish either of you."

Miss Bessie was telling me, with bourbon-laced grace, that I   24
never fooled her for a moment.

When Miss Bessie died in 1980, at age 85, hundreds of her   25
former students mourned. They knew the measure of a great teacher: love and motivation. Her wisdom and influence had rippled out across generations.

Some of her students who might normally have been doomed   26
to poverty went on to become doctors, dentists and college professors. Many, guided by Miss Bessie's example, became public-school teachers.

"The memory of Miss Bessie and how she conducted her   27
classroom did more for me than anything I learned in college,"

recalls Gladys Wood of Knoxville, Tenn., a highly respected English teacher who spent 43 years in the state's school system. "So many times, when I faced a difficult classroom problem, I asked myself, *How would Miss Bessie deal with this?* And I'd remember that she would handle it with laughter and love."

No child can get all the necessary support at home, and millions of poor children get *no* support at all. This is what makes a wise, educated, warm-hearted teacher like Miss Bessie so vital to the minds, hearts and souls of this country's children.   28

VOCABULARY WORDS: civics (1), valedictorian (7), wrought-up (8), barrios (16), conscience (18), cajoling (20), osmotic (20)

ACTIVITY 25

Reading to Improve Writing. Discuss the following questions about "Unforgettable Miss Bessie" with your classmates.

1. Miss Bessie was Rowan's high school teacher, but how is she also a cultural hero?

   _____

   _____

   _____

2. How does Rowan's use of description help you picture Miss Bessie?

   _____

   _____

   _____

3. What did Miss Bessie teach Rowan besides English, history, and civics?

   _____

   _____

   _____

4. What strategies does Rowan use in his introduction and conclusion? Are they effective?

_____

_____

_____

_____

Give yourself something to work toward—constantly.

—MARY KAY ASH

CHAPTER 6

Investigating the Workplace

In this chapter you will

- gather ideas on workplace occupations, jargon, and problems.

- develop your ideas using classification and comparison and contrast.

- locate sources on your topic.

- learn to summarize sources.

- correctly use research material in your writing.

- combine sentences with subordinate conjunctions.

- learn to correct pronoun reference and agreement.

- reflect on your writing.

What do you want to be when you grow up?" Perhaps you remember being asked this when you were a child. This question shows the importance that people place on jobs. No doubt you want to find an occupation that is satisfying and rewarding; after all, you're likely to spend at least forty hours a week in the workplace. It's better to look forward to those forty hours instead of dreading them.

Most people will change occupations several times during their lives. Look at the occupations of America's presidents: Harry S Truman owned a clothing store, Jimmy Carter was a peanut farmer, Ronald Reagan starred in movies. You might already have had several occupations. Preparing for a particular occupation means not simply learning information from books. It means becoming aware of the culture of the profession—how people think, dress, behave, and communicate. It also means learning how people in that occupation go about solving the problems that they encounter.

In this chapter, you'll have the chance to learn about an occupation that interests you. You'll also investigate the kinds of jargon, or language, used in an occupation, as well as explain how to solve a problem you've encountered in the workplace.

WRITING ASSIGNMENT

For this assignment, you'll investigate the workplace by examining an occupation, analyzing kinds of language in the workplace, or explaining how to solve a workplace problem. You or your instructor may decide to do this assignment in one of several ways.

- You may gather ideas on one, two, or three topics.
- You may write a discovery draft on one, two, or three of these topics.
- You may choose one discovery draft to develop into a polished essay.
- Or, you may combine your discovery draft ideas into a new topic for your essay.

After completing your essay, you'll share it with your instructor and classmates. You might also share it with other students interested in the same occupation you are, or with current or future employers.

Other Students' Ideas

Read students' responses to this assignment on the *Choices* Web site. Go to <www.bedfordstmartins.com/choices/> and click on "Student Writing."

ACTIVITY 1

Analyzing Your Purpose and Audience. Before you begin gathering ideas about your topic, think about your purpose and audience. For this chapter's assignment, you'll write about a job in the workplace that interests you, kinds of language people use in a particular workplace, or a solution to workplace problems. Your responses to the following questions will help you decide how to approach your topic.

For more help on purpose and audience, see pp. 29–30.

1. Does this assignment call for primarily expressive, informative, or persuasive writing?

   _____

2. What types of jobs have your readers had in the past?

   _____

   _____

   _____

3. What types of jobs do your readers want to have, as a result of going to college?

   _____

   _____

   _____

4. How do your job interests resemble or differ from those of your readers?

   _____

   _____

   _____

5. How interested will your readers be in an essay that deals with the workplace?

_____

_____

_____

GATHERING IDEAS

These methods of gathering ideas are explained on pp. 30–34.

To gather ideas about your three workplace topics, select from among the techniques you learned in Chapter 2: brainstorming, freewriting, clustering, questioning, reading, consulting with others, relating aloud, and reflecting.

Investigating an Occupation

Many of us initially decide to pursue a particular occupation based on limited information. For instance, being an actor appears to be glamorous, until you realize that most actors are unemployed in their chosen profession. Or you might daydream of becoming a physician, until you remember that you feel faint at the idea of giving someone a shot. Before deciding on a particular job, you need to find out whether the job matches your interests, needs, and personality. The following article, "Career Profile: Science," describes what it's like to be a scientist.

THE EDITORS OF WEBFEET.COM
Career Profile: Science

So, you like science—the test tubes, the cool high-tech   1
equipment, the absolute certainty of knowledge—but you don't
want to spend the rest of your life rambling around the marble
hallways of a university. Those who've studied the pure sciences,
such as physics, chemistry, and biology, can find lucrative and
intellectually challenging careers in the private sector.

Scientists who work in the private sector are involved with applied research and development. While their work deals with the same concepts as scientists employed at universities, private-sector scientists generally cope with a more stringent time frame, and are more attuned to the bottom line. Scientists are in business to turn their ideas and hypotheses into products their companies can sell. 2

Of course, engineers also apply scientific principles to create products. But unlike engineers, applied scientists usually work on more fundamental research and are removed from the production lines. If you want to think of it in terms of a continuum, research scientists at universities deal with abstract principles of science. 3

Applied scientists use the same principles, but shape them into more specific ideas, materials, and equipment. Engineers then use such equipment to make products within a budget, on a timetable. 4

That doesn't mean the lines between science and engineering don't occasionally get blurred. As one industry insider with a PhD in physics put it, "When I first started in industry, I was hired to build a lot of equipment. At the time, I felt a lot more like a cross between a plumber and an electrician than a physicist. But after a while, I started to analyze the data and began feeling like a scientist again." 5

Scientists apply their skills to develop materials, products, equipment, and production methods in a variety of ways. Physicists, for instance, might be hired by biotechnology firms to design the equipment needed to work on materials at the molecular level; by semiconductor manufacturers to apply their knowledge of solid-state quantum mechanics (the study of crystalline solids such as silicon) to create computer chips that will run faster at lower temperatures; or by computer software firms to write and develop computer programs used to model complex processes, such as the blood flowing through a heart or money through a stock exchange. 6

Chemists work at such businesses as the Dow Chemical Co., of course, as well as at petroleum refining plants, pharmaceutical companies, paint manufacturers, and food-processing plants. 7

Many biological scientists work in the biomedical field and are known as medical scientists. They research infectious diseases (such as the common cold and AIDS) and develop vaccines, new drugs, and treatments. They may be employed by government agencies, such as the U.S. Centers for Disease Control and Prevention, or work for large drug companies such as GlaxoSmithKline. 8

Applied scientists need to be analytical thinkers and comfortable with math. There's a reason why scientists are often portrayed as people who speak in technical jargon impenetrable to the common ear: All fields of science require mastery of a host of precise terminology and complicated theories that have been piling up since the dawn of the Enlightenment. 9

Of course, that's not to downplay the role of solid communication skills. In today's business climate, scientists typically work in teams and need to be able to communicate efficiently what they've been doing and why it's important, especially if they're looking for a bigger budget. 10

To be sure, getting a well-rounded education is becoming especially important, because many scientists, both fresh out of school and those with experience, often decide they want a break, and find careers outside of laboratories. But getting a solid background in the sciences is rarely a waste of time. Increasingly, employers are realizing that the analytical skills and computer experience picked up learning science can be put to use in a host of other professions, such as technical writing, sales, marketing, and business consulting. 11

Of course, you can always teach high school or go back to academia to research or try to land a job as a professor. As one industry insider put it, "People are beginning to realize that someone who has mastered quantum physics usually treats something like analyzing the stock market or a complex business problem as an enjoyable break. Your options are really wide open." 12

VOCABULARY WORDS: private sector (1), hypotheses (2), infectious (8), jargon (9), analytical (9), impenetrable (9), academia (12)

ACTIVITY 2

Reading to Improve Writing. Discuss the following questions about "Career Profile: Science" with your classmates.

1. In your own words, describe what an applied scientist does.

_____

_____

_____

2. List five words or phrases that describe the skills an applied scientist needs.

_____

_____

_____

_____

3. In paragraphs 6, 7, and 8, the authors give examples of the types of work that scientists do. Give at least two reasons why they include these examples.

_____

_____

_____

4. Based on this essay, do you have the characteristics and skills to be a scientist? Why or why not?

_____

_____

_____

_____

ACTIVITY 3

Gathering Ideas about an Occupation. Gather ideas about an occupation you're interested in pursuing. Use the following questions to stimulate your thoughts:

1. When did you first become interested in pursuing this occupation?

2. If you're already in this occupation, in what way to do want to change, such as obtain a higher position or go into another specialty?

3. List three things that interest you about the occupation.
4. What aspects of your personality do you think will make you successful in this occupation?
5. What don't you like about this occupation?
6. List at least two things you want to learn about this occupation.

One student, Kathy, freewrote about her desire to become a pediatrician, a doctor who specializes in taking care of children.

> *I've wanted to become a pediatrician ever since I was a little girl. The doctor seemed so nice and knew so much. Then when my brother had to spend a week in the hospital, I got to see other pediatricians helping the sick children. My family is so grateful to the pediatricians who helped my brother get better. I know that being a pediatrician is hard. First you have to go through years of school. I guess I could handle that. But I'm not sure I could handle dealing with sick children all the time. It takes patience and dedication.*

Put your writing about an occupation away for the time being so that you can gather ideas about another aspect of the workplace.

Investigating Jargon in the Workplace

Every workplace develops its own jargon, which consists of specialized language known only to those who work in that occupation. For instance, a server writing down your order in a restaurant uses abbreviations that only other workers in that restaurant can decipher. Police officers use obscure terminology when referring to particular crimes, telemarketers label incoming and outgoing calls according to numerical codes, and attorneys write contracts difficult for others to understand. One of the first things a person just entering a profession needs to learn is the jargon, as medical student Perri Klass demonstrates in "She's Your Basic L.O.L. in N.A.D."

PERRI KLASS

She's Your Basic L.O.L. in N.A.D

"Mrs. Tolstoy is your basic L.O.L. in N.A.D., admitted for a   1
soft rule-out M.I.," the intern announces. I scribble that on my

patient list. In other words Mrs. Tolstoy is a Little Old Lady in No Apparent Distress who is in the hospital to make sure she hasn't had a heart attack (rule out a myocardial infarction). And we think it's unlikely that she has had a heart attack (a *soft* rule-out).

If I learned nothing else during my first three months of working in the hospital as a medical student, I learned endless jargon and abbreviations. I started out in a state of primeval innocence, in which I didn't even know that "s̄ C.P., S.O.B., N/V" meant "without chest pain, shortness of breath, or nausea and vomiting." By the end I took the abbreviations so for granted that I would complain to my mother the English Professor, "And can you believe I had to put down *three* NG tubes last night?"

"You'll have to tell me what an NG tube is if you want me to sympathize properly," my mother said. NG, nasogastric—isn't it obvious?

I picked up not only the specific expressions but also the patterns of speech and the grammatical conventions; for example, you never say that a patient's blood pressure fell or that his cardiac enzymes rose. Instead, the patient is always the subject of the verb: "He dropped his pressure." "He bumped his enzymes." This sort of construction probably reflects that profound irritation of the intern when the nurses come in the middle of the night to say that Mr. Dickinson has disturbingly low blood pressure. "Oh, he's gonna hurt me bad tonight," the intern may say, inevitably angry at Mr. Dickinson for dropping his pressure and creating a problem.

When chemotherapy fails to cure Mrs. Bacon's cancer, what we say is, "Mrs. Bacon failed chemotherapy."

"Well, we've already had one hit today, and we're up next, but at least we've got mostly stable players on our team." This means that our team (group of doctors and medical students) has already gotten one new admission today, and it is our turn again, so we'll get whoever is next admitted in emergency, but at least most of the patients we already have are fairly stable, that is, unlikely to drop their pressures or in any other way get suddenly sicker and hurt us bad. Baseball metaphor is pervasive: a no-hitter is a night without any new admissions. A player is always a patient—a nitrate player is a patient on nitrates, a unit player is a patient in the intensive-care unit and so on, until you reach the terminal player.

It is interesting to consider what it means to be winning, or doing well, in this perennial baseball game. When the intern hangs up the phone and announces, "I got a hit," that is not cause for congratulations. The team is not scoring points; rather, it is getting hit, being bombarded with new patients. The object of the game from the point of view of the doctors, considering the players for whom they are already responsible, is to get as few new hits as possible.

These special languages contribute to a sense of closeness   8
and professional spirit among people who are under a great deal of stress. As a medical student, it was exciting for me to discover that I'd finally cracked the code, that I could understand what doctors said and wrote and could use the same formulations myself. Some people seem to become enamored of the jargon for its own sake, perhaps because they are so deeply thrilled with the idea of medicine, with the idea of themselves as doctors.

I knew a medical student who was referred to by the interns   9
on the team as Mr. Eponym because he was so infatuated with eponymous terminology, the more obscure the better. He never said "capillary pulsation" if he could say "Quincke's pulses." He would lovingly tell over the multinamed syndromes—Wolff-Parkinson-White, Lown-Ganong-Levine, Henoch-Schonlein— until the temptation to suggest Schleswig-Holstein or Stevenson-Kefauver or Baskin-Robbins became irresistible to his less reverent colleagues.

And there is the jargon that you don't ever want to hear your-   10
self using. You know that your training is changing you, but there are certain changes you think would be going a little too far.

The resident was describing a man with devastating terminal   11
pancreatic cancer. "Basically he's C.T.D.," the resident concluded. I reminded myself that I had resolved not to be shy about asking when I didn't understand things. "C.T.D.?" I asked timidly.

The resident smirked at me. "Circling The Drain."   12

The images are vivid and terrible. "What happened to Mrs.   13
Melville?"

"Oh, she boxed last night." To box is to die, of course.   14

Then there are the more pompous locutions that can make the   15
beginning medical student nervous about the effects of medical training. A friend of mine was told by his resident, "A pregnant woman with sickle-cell represents a failure of genetic counseling."

Mr. Eponym, who tried hard to talk like the doctors, once ex-   16
plained to me, "An infant is basically a brainstem preparation." A brainstem preparation, as used in neurological research, is an animal whose higher brain functions have been destroyed so that only the most primitive reflexes remain, like the sucking reflex, the startle reflex, and the rooting reflex.

The more extreme forms aside, one most important function   17
of medical jargon is to help doctors maintain some distance from their patients. By reformulating a patient's pain and problems

into a language that the patient doesn't even speak, I suppose we are in some sense taking those pains and problems under our jurisdiction and also reducing their emotional impact. This linguistic separation between doctors and patients allows conversations to go on at the bedside that are unintelligible to the patient. "Naturally, we're worried about adeno-C.A.," the intern can say to the medical student, and lung cancer need never be mentioned.

I learned a new language this past summer. At times it thrills 18 me to hear myself using it. It enables me to understand my colleagues, to communicate effectively in the hospital. Yet I am uncomfortably aware that I will never again notice the peculiarities and even atrocities of medical language as keenly as I did this summer. There may be specific expressions I manage to avoid, but even as I remark them, promising myself I will never use them, I find that this language is becoming my professional speech. It no longer sounds strange in my ears—or coming from my mouth. And I am afraid that as with any new language, to use it properly you must absorb not only the vocabulary but also the structure, the logic, the attitudes. At first you may notice these new alien assumptions every time you put together a sentence, but with time and increased fluency you stop being aware of them at all. And as you lose that awareness, for better or for worse, you move closer and closer to being a doctor instead of just talking like one.

VOCABULARY WORDS: primeval (2), inevitably (4), metaphor (6), perennial (7), enamored (8), eponymous (9), locutions (15), jurisdiction (17), atrocities (18)

ACTIVITY 4

Reading to Improve Writing. Discuss the following questions about "She's Your Basic L.O.L. in N.A.D" with your classmates.

1. According to Klass, why do health professionals use jargon? Give at least three reasons.

_____

_____

_____

2. Why do the interns say "He dropped his [blood] pressure" instead of "His [blood] pressure dropped"?

_____

_____

_____

3. Explain the significance of the last sentence of the essay: "And as you lose that awareness, for better or for worse, you move closer and closer to being a doctor instead of just talking like one."

_____

_____

_____

4. Have you ever heard medical professionals use terminology you couldn't understand? If so, describe what this experience was like.

_____

_____

_____

_____

ACTIVITY 5

Gathering Ideas about Jargon in the Workplace. Choose a job you're familiar with. It can be a job you've had, or a job held by a friend or family member close to you. Alternatively, you can consider a sport (such as basketball), hobby (such as chess), or organization (such as a fraternity or church group). Brainstorm about the jargon that you've encountered by listing words and their definitions. Then, freewrite about why that jargon was used.

One student, Javier, brainstormed about the jargon used by the teachers in the elementary school where he was a teacher's aide.

TAAS test—the standardized test that the students have to take every year

ADD—attention deficit disorder

Hyper—a child with ADD

SW—the "student of the week" award, also known as the "sweet-heart" award

Sub—substitute teacher

Meeting with the Pal—a meeting with the principal

Sight words—common words, like dog or the, that students should know

Portfolio—a collection of student work

In-Service training—educational sessions to update experienced teachers

Eager Beaver—a new teacher who thinks he or she knows everything

Here is Javier's freewriting about the jargon used by teachers:

At first I was confused by the terminology and didn't know what the teachers were talking about. But now I'm pretty good at it. I guess that means I'm accepted by the teachers. (Not really!) The teachers use this jargon because it's a quick way to talk. It lets them give their opinion. One of the teachers always refers to one of the new teachers as an "eager beaver," and she rolls her eyes when she says this. The jargon also lets them show their affection for their students. Every teacher has pet names for their students—"sweet pea," "my special guy," and so on. Now that I think about it, teachers seem to use jargon most when they're talking about how much they like their students or when they're feeling frustrated.

Put the writing you've done on jargon in the workplace aside so you can consider another aspect of the workplace.

Investigating Workplace Problems— and Solutions

No matter how much you like your job, you're always going to encounter problems. Perhaps your boss is difficult to talk to, or one of your co-workers likes to gossip too much. Your commute to work might be too long, or you might object to a recent change in policy. To be successful, you need to be able to find solutions to problems such as these. In "All Stressed Out—And Off to Work We Go," Kathy Simmons recommends several solutions to a common work-related problem—too much stress.

KATHY SIMMONS

All Stressed Out—And Off to Work We Go

Is your job stressing you out? Don't feel alone. A recent Gallup   1
poll shows only 14 percent of workers are dissatisfied with their
jobs, while a whopping 34 percent are dissatisfied with how
much stress they face at work. Stress elicited the highest level of
dissatisfaction from a list of common problems—even exceeding
recognition, promotion opportunities, and salary!

Sadly, anxiety in the workplace is likely to increase. Stiff   2
competition, expanding roles, and demanding technological advances all blend together to form a heavy dose of stress on even
the heartiest employee. We're not just talking about management. No level of staff is immune. For instance, the days when
typing speed was the main challenge for office professionals are
long gone. Now, they are expected to master skills ranging from
high-tech office equipment, complex software, purchasing, and
communication with a wide range of cultures and personalities.

So what's the answer? Obviously you can't control technol-   3
ogy, the world's economy or even how your co-workers or boss
choose to behave. But you can master the way you filter stress so
that it takes a minimal toll on your attitude and physical health.
Following are some tips for keeping stress at bay:

Remember: Stress Is a Response

Picture this: Two co-workers' phones ring simultaneously.   4
One of them answers right away with a smile, eager to satisfy the
caller in a cheerful manner. The other grumbles loudly, protesting that *&%$# phone is ringing again. Her blood pressure rises
and she makes it vehemently clear to all within earshot how
much she resents the intrusion. What's the difference between
these two workers? One thing is for sure—*it's not the phone.*

Top performers don't come in contact with less potentially   5
stressful situations. Nor do they avoid challenges. They simply
have learned to monitor their responses so that they are in
control.

The next time you are faced with an irritable boss, traffic   6
jam, or pressing deadline, remember that the event does not
determine your response—only you can do that. Remaining
calm is sure to lead to a better outcome than succumbing to emotions such as fear or anger.

Learn to Laugh

Laughter is powerful. In the words of Mark Twain, "Against the assault of laughter, nothing can stand."   7

Psychologist Steve Wilson, author of *The Art of Mixing Work and Play* and *Super Humor Power,* knows the value of humor in stressful situations. Wilson explains, "Humor is a special phenomenon existing only in human beings. The immune effect of laughter stays with us for a lifetime. In light of the data about how stress defeats the immune system, the saying 'laughter is the best medicine' contains indisputable scientific backing."   8

A hearty laugh relaxes muscles, reduces levels of stress-creating hormones, and lowers blood pressure. Furthermore, people simply get along better and perform more creatively in a fun environment. Have you ever noticed how a finely placed joke can cut through tension and misunderstandings? So it is with stress.   9

You can drastically lower your personal stress level by taking a few laugh breaks. Sharpen your sense of humor and you are sure to dull the effects of stress.   10

Be Gentle with Yourself

You wouldn't remain friends for long with someone who constantly makes remarks such as, "You'll never finish," or "You can't handle that," would you? So why tolerate it in yourself? Negative self-talk doesn't do a thing for your self-esteem or stress level. A positive mindset is more than half the battle when it comes to managing stress effectively. When faced with a situation in which you are likely to feel defeated, repeat kind and positive words to yourself.   11

For example, let's suppose an unhappy customer verbally berates you. A natural response would be to lash out and become defensive. Or take the "whipped puppy" approach and feel like an undeserving victim. These responses will only cause the situation to become more stressful. Instead, take a deep breath and say something like, "I will remain calm. By the time we hang up, we will be having a friendly discussion." Treat yourself with care and concern—just as any supportive friend would. Practice positive self-talk at every opportunity.   12

Take a "Technology Holiday"

Technology was supposed to make our lives easier. What happened? Many have realized that it's actually increasing stress levels for most workers. Laptop computers, pagers and cellular phones have in essence created a 24-hour office for which there   13 is no escape. Surveys show that 60 percent of workers feel their levels of stress have increased since computers made their debut into the workplace. Nearly 50 percent feel their workload has increased since that time.

Eighteen years of practice in the field of occupational medi-   14 cine have enlightened Robert du Puis, M.D., author of *How to Avoid High Tech Stress,* of the dangers of technology. He encourages employees to take a technology holiday to reduce stress. "Putting technology in proper perspective as a useful tool but not allowing it to run our lives is becoming increasingly difficult," du Puis explains. He advises that escaping e-mail, voicemail, cell phones, and beepers even during the evening or lunch hours is a sound step toward lower stress.

Just Say No

The less control people have over their workday, the more   15 likely they are to suffer stress-related illnesses. Somewhere along the line, we convinced ourselves that saying no is rude. We fear people won't like us. Unfortunately, this logic carries a steep price tag in matters of stress.

Imagine you are staring at the last few hours of a pressing   16 deadline when a talkative co-worker comes to your office to chat. Do you entertain her, hoping she will run out of things to say eventually? If so, you are unnecessarily inviting stress into your life. If the deadline is missed, you will encounter stress. Even if your frantic efforts allow you to meet it, you will also encounter stress. It's basically a no-win situation when people cannot behave in an assertive manner.

The next time someone asks "got a minute?" try answering   17 politely, "Not right now. Can I get with you later?" You might be surprised how well they will take it—and how much more control you have over your workday.

Forgive and Forget

Choosing to be angry will cause your stress meter to sky-   18 rocket. Have you known co-workers who remained in perpetual states of resentment? Did they seem to have an elephant's memory when it came to injustices? Indeed, they probably took a perverse delight in repeating all the gruesome details to any willing audience. Talking about it over and over is far from healthy. In fact, studies show that reliving a negative experience carries an undesirable consequence—it forces the grudge-holder to relive the physiology that went along with the stressful moment. In other words, the stress is repeated as many times as they choose to walk down unpleasant memory lanes.

Is It Worth Dying For? How to Make Stress Work for You—   19
Not against You (Bantam Books, 1993) shares a unique "trick" for dealing with annoying co-workers. Use the brain tumor prescription for those impossible to get along with. Pretend the person has an incurable brain tumor that causes him or her to act in this manner. They aren't responsible for their irrational and upsetting behavior. You certainly can't do anything about it either—remember, it's incurable. So your only logical option is to avoid letting it get to you—and avoid taking their rudeness personally. It's that pesky brain tumor, after all.

Commit to unloading grudges and anger in order to reduce   20
your stress level. An added by-product is that you will be a much more pleasant person to be around!

These six tips are just a few ways to manage stress at work.   21
The best tip of all is to become an expert on the topic. You can do this by reading a multitude of excellent books and articles available. Or you can ask those you work with who are masters at stress-management about their secrets. One thing is for sure: stress is a choice you don't have to make. Your physical health, co-workers, family, and emotional well being will all thank you for learning the important life skill of strong stress-management.

VOCABULARY WORDS: elicited (1), immune (2), minimal (3), toll (3), succumbing (6), berates (12), perpetual (18), physiology (18)

ACTIVITY 6

Reading to Improve Writing. Discuss the following questions about "All Stressed Out—And Off to Work We Go" with your classmates.

1. Summarize the six tips that the author gives to reduce stress in the workplace.

   _____

   _____

   _____

   _____

2. Of the six tips given by the author, which one, in your view, is the most helpful? Explain your answer.

_____

_____

_____

_____

3. What writing strategies does the author use to keep her readers' attention?

_____

_____

_____

4. Do you agree with the author that the workplace has become more stressful? Why or why not?

_____

_____

_____

_____

ACTIVITY 7 (GROUP)

Freewriting and Relating Aloud. Freewrite about a problem you've encountered in the workplace. For instance, you can write about a problem with your work schedule, the attitudes of co-workers, or difficult customers. Then, read aloud your freewriting to several classmates. Ask your classmates to discuss ways that you can solve your problem. Take notes on their responses.

Here is student writer Alfredo's freewriting about a workplace problem:

Whenever I'm on the night shift at the restaurant where I work, I see other workers steal food. We're allowed to eat one meal after our shift, but what these people are doing goes way beyond that. They carry out bags of food! Nobody likes the owner, so maybe that's why the workers don't care about what they're doing. I don't like the owner either, but she's a small business owner who's working hard to make a living. She's never there when we close up so I don't think she knows what's happening. If I tell on the workers they might hate me, but if I keep quiet my conscience bugs me. What should I do?

Alfredo's classmates had these suggestions:

BRENDA: I think you should tell the owner. Who cares what the workers think? What they're doing is wrong.

JOE: But what if the other workers deny it? What if the owner doesn't believe Alfredo?

BRENDA: It's a chance Alfredo will have to take. It's the right thing to do.

ALFREDO: I make good tips at this job. I really don't want to lose it.

JOE: Maybe you can talk to the people who are stealing? Tell them they should knock it off.

RUDY: Maybe you can just change shifts. That way you won't see it being done.

Alfredo used his classmates' comments to gather more ideas about his topic.

DRAFTING

You have now gathered ideas on a workplace occupation, workplace jargon, and a workplace problem. You have a rich source of material for writing, but you need to decide how to proceed. Here are some of your choices:

- You may select one of the three topics for your discovery draft.
- You may write drafts on two or three of these topics to see which one you prefer.
- You may combine related topics in your discovery draft, or even choose a new topic for your essay.

Remember to select a topic you're interested in and that you have thought about or have some experience with. You may want to do some limited research on the topic. For instance, if you decide to write about an occupation you're interested in, you can consult the U.S. Department of Labor's *Occupational Outlook Handbook,* available on the Web at <http://www.bls.gov/oco>. This handbook contains useful information on a variety of occupations.

Before writing your discovery draft, write a preliminary thesis statement. Keep your audience and purpose in mind as you draft, but remember that your main goal at this stage is to get your ideas down on paper. You'll have time later on to revise and edit your discovery draft.

Want more information about how to write a draft? See pp. 117–20.

Use E-mail or Networked Discussion

E-mail your discovery draft to your fellow students for feedback. Alternatively, if you have access to a networked computer lab, discuss your draft online with other students in the class, on your campus, or even at different colleges. Whether you e-mail or discuss the draft online, ask your readers (1) what interested them the most about your draft, and (2) what they want to know more about. Use their responses to help you decide where to add supporting details.

Here's a discovery draft written by Kathy Chu, the student whose freewriting about her desire to be a pediatrician you read earlier in this chapter. (Note that the discovery draft includes the types of errors that typically appear in a first draft.)

```
                    Helping Children Heal

     Ever since I was a child, I wanted to be a pediatri-      1
cian, which is a doctor who specializes in children. I
hated going to the pediatrician when I was a child, but I
was also fascinated by the woman in the white jacket who
seemed to have all the answers. I want to be a pediatrician
so I can help children, make a good living, and have an
interesting job.

     Ever since I can remember, I've wanted to take care of   2
children. My little brother used to get earaches. I'd pre-
tend I was the doctor and hold a cup to his chest so I
```

could hear his heartbeat. In high school I volunteered at Providence Hospital in the children's wing. Seeing a sick child made me sad, but I felt better when I'd play with them and cheer them up.

As a pediatrician, I can make a good living. Making a good living is important to me. My parents have had to cope with many financial difficulties. I want to be able to provide for my parents when they get old. I want to take care of my own family, too.   3

I think pediatricians have exciting jobs. You never know what might be making a child sick. They might have a runny nose or something more serious. It's your job to make sure they get the right treatment so they can get well. The job might make me tired or stressed, but never bored.   4

For me, nothing beats helping a child get well.   5

REVISING

As you review your discovery draft, apply the skills you learned in previous chapters. Clarify and support your main ideas, organize your paragraphs, make your ideas flow smoothly, and write a good introduction, conclusion, and title. To help keep your audience in mind as you revise, review the audience analysis you completed in Activity 1. What information do your readers need to know to understand your topic? How can you keep your readers interested in your topic as they read your paper?

Developing Your Ideas

To help develop your ideas, consider using classification and comparison and contrast, as well as other methods of development. Also, you might want to locate and summarize one or two magazine articles on your topic.

CLASSIFICATION. To classify something, divide it into categories according to a certain principle. For instance, college students can be classified according to demographic information such as age, major, and economic class. Similarly, college students can be classified

When you revise, pay particular attention to improving your thesis. For ideas on what makes a good thesis, see pp. 36–37.

> **HOW TO** Use Classification
>
> - Decide on what basis you'll classify the topic. For example, the topic of "workplace stress" can be classified into "types of workplace stress."
>
> - Break the topic down into parts. "Types of workplace stress" can be grouped into "stress from co-workers," "stress from supervisors," and "stress from customers."
>
> - Give examples to support the classification.

More information on using classification is on pp. 70–71.

according to their participation in groups. For instance, students can be categorized according to their membership in fraternities or sororities, their participation in athletics, their memberships in clubs, and so on. Because classification breaks a large topic down into parts, it makes a topic easier to understand.

Classification can be used to develop an essay on a workplace occupation, workplace jargon, or workplace problem. The writers of "Career Profile: Science" classify scientists according to where they might work—biotechnology firms, pharmaceutical companies, and so on. Perri Klass, in "She's Your Basic L.O.L. in N.A.D," classifies medical jargon according to how it helps health care professionals communicate. In "All Stressed Out—And Off to Work We Go," author Kathy Simmons classifies ways to handle workplace stress, such as learning to laugh and "just saying no." By using classification, these authors order their ideas logically and clearly.

When you write a classification essay, discuss each category in a single section in the body of the essay. You may need to use more than one paragraph to explain the most important category.

Want more help with comparison and contrast? See p. 70.

COMPARISON AND CONTRAST. When you compare two things, you point out similarities; when you contrast two things, you focus on differences. We often use comparison and contrast in our daily life. We compare and contrast one job with another job or one boss with another. Comparison and contrast helps us explain our points more clearly and easily.

In "All Stressed Out—And Off to Work We Go," Kathy Simmons uses comparison and contrast in paragraph 4:

> Picture this: Two co-workers' phones ring simultaneously. One of them answers right away with a smile, eager to satisfy the caller in a cheerful manner. The other grumbles loudly, protest-

ing that *&%$# phone is ringing again. Her blood pressure rises and she makes it vehemently clear to all within earshot how much she resents the intrusion. What's the difference between these two workers? One thing is for sure—*it's not the phone.*

By contrasting two people's reactions to a ringing telephone, Simmons is able to convey her point that it's how you respond to events, not the events themselves, that causes stress.

When you write a comparison-and-contrast essay, you can order your ideas point by point or subject by subject. Point-by-point organization means that you explain two topics according to points of comparison. For instance, you can compare two co-workers by examining their work habits, personalities, and professionalism. Each section in the body of the essay focuses on one of the points.

First section: work habits

>   Explain work habits of co-worker 1

>   Explain work habits of co-worker 2

Second section: personalities

>   Explain personality of co-worker 1

>   Explain personality of co-worker 2

Third section: professionalism

>   Explain professionalism of co-worker 1

>   Explain professionalism of co-worker 2

Alternatively, you can organize your ideas subject by subject; each co-worker is discussed only once in the body of the essay.

First section: co-worker 1

>   Work habits, personality, professionalism

Second section: co-worker 2

>   Work habits, personality, professionalism

Use Color to Compare and Contrast

Use the color feature on your word-processing program when you compare and contrast. When you write about the first thing you're comparing, use a particular color. Then, when you write about the second thing you're comparing, use another color. This technique makes it easier for you to examine how well you support your points. Of course, you need to return the typeface to black before printing your final draft.

HOW TO Use Comparison and Contrast

- Use comparison to explain similarities and contrast to explain differences.

- Decide on what basis you will compare and contrast. For instance, you can compare and contrast a pediatrician and a family doctor on the basis of required training, types of patients, and salaries.

- Use point-by-point or subject-by-subject organization.

- Support the comparison and contrast with examples.

ACTIVITY 8 (GROUP)

Using Classification and Comparison and Contrast. With several classmates, brainstorm about ways to use classification and comparison and contrast with your topic. For instance, if your topic is dealing with a difficult supervisor, you might classify difficult supervisors into categories (supervisors who yell at you, supervisors who expect too much from you, and so on). You might also compare and contrast ways of dealing with difficult supervisors, such as trying to reason with the supervisor versus quitting your job. Use your classmates' suggestions when you revise your draft.

LOCATING SOURCES TO READ. To learn more about a particular topic dealing with work, consider reading several magazine articles. To locate articles on your topic, consult a library database or use the World Wide Web.

Assistance with library databases and keywords can be found in Chapter 11 on pp. 529–32.

A *library database* is available on a computer at the library or on your home computer through an Internet connection with your college library. A database contains thousands of references to articles, sorted by subject, keyword, title, or author. Many databases contain the full texts of articles, which means you can read the article on the computer screen instead of locating the printed version of the magazine. Use keywords, or words that pertain to your topic, to find useful articles. The wrong keywords can give you either too many or too few items from the database.

You also use keywords to find articles on the World Wide Web. Enter keywords into a search engine such as Alta Vista at <http://altavista.digital.com/>. However, be aware that the World Wide Web

Be sure to evaluate your sources! See pp. 534–35 in Chapter 11 for help.

HOW TO Use Keywords

- Narrow your search by connecting keywords using *and,* as in "engineers *and* jobs." You can substitute "+" for *and:* "engineers + jobs."

- You can also narrow your search by using *"not,"* as in "engineers *and* jobs *not* salaries." You can substitute "–" for NOT: "engineers + jobs – salaries."

- If your keywords don't result in enough items for you to examine, broaden your search by using *"or,"* as in "engineers *and* jobs *or* salaries."

- If you still can't find the right keywords, ask a reference librarian. He or she can help you find better keywords or check the subject headings in the database for you.

contains a great deal of material that you won't be able to use. For instance, if you enter the keywords "engineers and jobs" on a Web search engine, you're likely to find sites advertising engineering firms or promoting engineering products.

Keep in mind that an article or other source may not be useful, even if it's on your topic. Look for articles that contain facts or ideas that will help you explain one of the points in your own essay. For instance, if you're explaining an occupation, you might look for information about the salaries that people make and the amount of education they need.

ACTIVITY 9

Locating Articles on Your Topic. Find several articles on your topic in a library database and on the World Wide Web. Be sure that these articles directly support one or more of your ideas in your draft. Photocopy or print out copies of the articles.

Using Keywords

Practice a keyword search in *The English Research Room* Web site. Go to <www.bedfordstmartins.com/ english_research/> and click on "Interactive Tutorials."

SUMMARIZING WHAT YOU READ. A *summary* is a shortened version of a piece of text, written in your own words. A summary will always be shorter than the original because it explains the most important ideas while omitting details. By summarizing the articles you locate on your topic, you can select key ideas that will support your point.

Here's a summary of "She's Your Basic L.O.L in N.A.D."

> In "She's Your Basic L.O.L in N.A.D.," Perri Klass examines the jargon used in the field of medicine. This jargon includes abbreviations, special phrases, and comparisons. These expressions let health care professionals speak efficiently, express feelings, and keep an emotional distance from their patients' pain. New health care professionals must learn this jargon in order to understand and be accepted by other health care professionals.

ACTIVITY 10 (GROUP)

Practicing Summarizing. With several classmates, summarize either "Career Profile: Science" or "All Stressed Out — And Off to Work We Go" in four to six sentences. Compare your summary with the summaries by other groups of students. Which group best expressed the main ideas of the essay? Explain why you think it was the best summary.

HOW TO Write a Summary

- Read the text carefully. In your own words, take notes on the main ideas. These ideas usually appear in the thesis statement, the topic sentences, and the conclusion. Headings and subheadings also identify main ideas.

- Focus on the main points only. Leave out supporting details.

- Include the author and title of the text in the beginning of the summary.

- Write the summary in your own words. Avoid simply copying down the author's words.

ACTIVITY 11

Summarizing Articles. Write summaries of the articles on your topic that you located in Activity 9. Refer to these summaries to help you support your points when you revise your draft.

Organizing Your Essay

As you develop your ideas for your revised draft, you also need to consider how to organize them. If you use information from the articles you read on your topic in your essay, then it's important to pay special attention to where this information is included.

TENTATIVELY OUTLINE YOUR IDEAS. Before beginning your revised draft, make a rough outline of your major points, indicating where you'll add information from an article or a Web site. Remember that this outline is *tentative*—in other words, subject to change. As you write, you might think of other ideas or a better way to order your points. Don't hesitate to revise your outline as needed.

Your outline should include the ideas you plan to express in each paragraph. Follow the outline format that works best for you. If you're unsure of how to make an outline, follow the format used by student writer Kathy Chu in the following example. (Note that "P" stands for paragraph. Information from an article and a Web site is underlined.)

```
                    Helping Children Heal

P 1: Introduction of topic. Definition of pediatrician.
     Thesis: Pediatricians help children, make a good
     living, work hard, and enjoy challenges.

P 2: My desire to help sick children. Experiences I've had
     with my brother and at the hospital.

P 3: Pediatricians make a good living. Why this is
     important to me. Information about salaries from the
     online Occupational Outlook Handbook.

P 4: Pediatricians work long hours. This doesn't bother me.
     Information about number of hours per week and
```

> education requirements from the online *Occupational*
> *Handbook* and article from *Time*.
>
> P 5: Pediatric nurses also work with children, but they
> don't get to make decisions about treatment.
>
> P 6: Pediatricians face many challenges. This will keep me
> from getting bored. Quote from *Time* magazine from
> pediatrician about challenges.
>
> P 7: Conclusion. Go back to thesis. It's the job for me.

ACTIVITY 12

Tentatively Outlining Your Ideas. Outline your ideas for your revised draft. Use the format in Kathy's outline or a format of your own. Include the major ideas you'll express in each paragraph and any research that will help develop these ideas.

Use the Outline View

To help you organize your outline, use the outline view function found on many word-processing programs. This function will give you the option of outlining your ideas for the whole essay or for individual paragraphs. The "help" function of your program will lead you through the appropriate steps.

CORRECTLY USE RESEARCH MATERIAL. Keep these principles in mind if you use information from outside sources (articles, books, Web sites) in your paper:

Don't let the research take over your paper. You might be tempted to include long chunks of information in your paragraphs. Instead, select only the most pertinent ideas from the research to support your points. As a rule of thumb, limit information from outside sources to no more than 10 to 20 percent of your essay.

Use a quotation only to emphasize or explain an important point. A well-placed quotation can help you summarize an idea or express a thought in a distinct way. One or two quotations should be sufficient for a three-page essay.

Weave a quotation smoothly into your sentences. Use an introductory phrase, as Kathy does in her revised draft:

> *According to one pediatrician,* "I never know what I'll encounter with every patient I see. One child might just have a cold or flu. But the next child could have a bruise that won't heal. This could be a symptom of cancer" (Turner 53).

You can find more information on paraphrasing and quoting information in Chapter 11 (pp. 544–47).

Use paraphrases as well as quotations to support your ideas. When you paraphrase, you put the original words into your own words. Paraphrase—don't quote—information that consists of facts or statistics, as Kathy does in this example:

> Pediatricians don't have trouble finding jobs, and their median salary is $120,000 a year (*Occupational Outlook* 2).

Correctly document research material. Indicate where you obtained quoted or paraphrased material in the text of your essay and at the end of your essay.

- After paraphrased information, write the author's last name and the page number of the original article in parentheses.
- After a quotation, write the author's name and the page number of the original article in parentheses. But exclude the author's name if you already gave it when you introduced the quotation.
- At the end of the essay, include a Works Cited list that gives publication information for each source you used.

A sample Works Cited list is on p. 563 in Chapter 11.

Use Color for Research Material

Use the color feature on your word-processing program to highlight the quotations in your draft. Use another color to highlight paraphrased material. This technique will help you review the research material in your draft. For instance, if you have highlighted more than 10 to 20 percent of the draft, you know the research is taking over your own ideas. Be sure to return the typeface to black before printing the final draft.

HOW TO Use Research Material in an Essay

- Limit the amount of research material to no more than 10 to 20 percent of your essay.

- Use brief quotations only to emphasize or explain an important point.

- Introduce a quotation with a phrase such as *according to* or *in the words of . . .*

- Paraphrase, or put into your own words, information such as facts or statistics.

- Correctly indicate where you obtained any quotation or paraphrased information in the text of the essay and at the end of the essay.

ACTIVITY 13

Quoting, paraphrasing, and documenting information are essential. Otherwise, you can be accused of plagiarism. See pp. 535–36 in Chapter 11 for more help.

Quoting, Paraphrasing, and Documenting Information. The following is a paragraph about working while attending college.

Working your way through college has many advantages. Unlike students who depend on large checks from their parents, working students learn to be self-reliant and independent. Because they pay their own bills every month, they realize the value of a college education in getting a well-paid job. They learn how to manage time well, an important skill in the working world. They also gain excellent work experience for their résumés after they graduate. While they might be tempted to grumble about lack of free time or the old car they drive, working students have many advantages over students who don't work.

Here's a quotation on the same topic:

I believe the fact that my husband and I are happy and financially stable is a direct result of our learning how to manage time and money in college.

— "Pay Your Own Way! (Then Thank Mom),"
by Audrey Rock-Richardson, page 12 in
Newsweek on Sept. 11, 2000.

First, rewrite the paragraph by inserting this quotation into it. Be sure to introduce the quotation and correctly document the source in parentheses.

Then, rewrite the paragraph again. Rather than inserting the quotation into the paragraph, paraphrase the information instead by putting it into your own words. Be sure to correctly document the source in parentheses.

Finally, here is the correct Works Cited entry for this source:

> Rock-Richardson, Audrey. "Pay Your Own Way! (Then Thank Mom)." <u>Newsweek</u> 11 Sept. 2000: 12.

Using Research Material

For more help in using research material in your essay, visit *The English Research Room* Web site at <www.bedfordstmartins.com/english_research/>.

ACTIVITY 14

Quoting, Paraphrasing, and Documenting Information in Your Essay. As you revise your essay, check that you have correctly used quotations and paraphrases to develop your points. Make sure you have also documented information correctly in the essay and in the Works Cited list.

MLA Electronic Documentation

For the most recent information on documenting information from electronic sources, consult the Web site of the Modern Language Association, <www.mla.org>. Click on "MLA Style," then "FAQs about MLA Style."

Polishing Your Sentences and Words

Now that you have focused on developing and organizing your draft, you're ready to turn your attention to sentences and words. In this section, you'll concentrate on combining sentences using subordinate conjunctions.

See the Sentence Subordination section of the Handbook (pp. 682–85) for more assistance with sentence combining.

COMBINING SENTENCES USING SUBORDINATE CONJUNCTIONS. When you combine short, closely related sentences in your draft, you eliminate unnecessary words, clarify the connections between the sentences, and improve sentence variety. For now you'll focus on combining sentences using subordinate conjunctions. Here are some of the most frequently used subordinate conjunctions:

SUBORDINATING CONJUNCTIONS

after	before	that	where
although	even though	though	wherever
as	if	unless	whether
as if	since	until	while
as though	so that	when	
because	than	whenever	

When you combine two closely related sentences, one of them is going to be *subordinate* to—less important than—the other one. A subordinate conjunction tells the reader which idea is less important and which one is more important. The subordinate conjunction comes at the beginning of the less important sentence, which is called a *subordinate clause.*

In her discovery draft, Kathy had several short, closely related sentences that she combined with subordinate conjunctions in her revised draft. In the following examples, the less important sentence, or subordinate clause, is italicized.

ORIGINAL   *My little brother used to get earaches.* I'd pretend I was the doctor and hold a cup to his chest so I could hear his heartbeat.

REVISED   *When my little brother used to get earaches,* I'd pretend I was the doctor and hold a cup to his chest so I could hear his heart beat.

ORIGINAL   Making a good living is important to me. *My parents have had to cope with many financial difficulties.*

REVISED   Making a good living is important to me *because my parents have had to cope with many financial difficulties.*

As these examples illustrate, the subordinate clause can appear at the beginning or end of the sentence. When the subordinate clause comes at the beginning of the sentence, a comma divides it from the rest of the sentence. When the subordinate clause comes at the end of the sentence, no comma is used.

HOW TO **Combine Sentences with Subordinate Conjunctions**

- Combine sentences that are short and closely related in meaning.

- Decide which sentence is subordinate to or less important than the other.

- Turn the less important sentence into a subordinate clause by beginning it with an appropriate subordinate conjunction.

- When the subordinate clause begins the sentence, use a comma to divide it from the main clause. Don't use a comma when the subordinate clause is at the end of the sentence.

ACTIVITY 15

Combining Sentences Using Subordinate Conjunctions. Combine the following pairs of sentences. First, decide which sentence is less important in conveying the message; this will become the subordinate clause. Next select an appropriate subordinate conjunction to begin the subordinate clause, and then combine the two sentences. You may need to eliminate unnecessary words or move some words around.

SAMPLE

For many people, it's hard to decide on a career. There are so many careers to choose from.

For many people, it's hard to decide on a career because there are so many to choose from.

1. I'm studying to become a photojournalist. I like both photography and journalism.

    _____

    _____

2. I've always wanted to be a photojournalist. I remember wanting to be a photojournalist when I was a child.

_____

_____

3. A photojournalist takes photographs of current events. These photographs are published in magazines and newspapers.

_____

_____

4. Often people read a magazine just for the photographs. This is why photojournalists are important to magazine editors.

_____

_____

5. Photojournalists have exciting jobs. They get to travel and take pictures of important people.

_____

_____

6. A newspaper might hire only a few photojournalists. It might hire ten or twenty reporters.

_____

_____

7. Someone who wants to be a photojournalist needs a college degree. This is required to get a job.

_____

_____

8. Many photojournalists begin by working part time at a newspaper. They might be hired full time. This depends on how good they are.

_____

_____

9. I'm already working part time at the *Sun-News*. I might get be hired full time. This might happen after I get my degree.

_____

_____

10. I'll look for other jobs. This will happen if the *Sun-News* doesn't hire me full time.

_____

_____

ACTIVITY 16

Combining Sentences in Your Draft. As you revise your discovery draft, examine short, closely related sentences. Can any of them be combined using subordinate conjunctions? Remember that by combining sentences with subordinating conjunctions, you signal to the reader which ideas are most important.

Kathy's Revised Draft

Before you read Kathy's revised draft, reread her discovery draft (pp. 258–59). In particular, notice how she has used research from the *Occupational Outlook Handbook* and a magazine article to support her points. (You will also notice some errors in the revised draft; these will be corrected when Kathy edits her essay later on.)

Helping Children Heal

When I was a child, going to the doctor was both
frightening and exciting. I hated getting shots and seeing

1 Introduction is more interesting.

the crying babies. At the same time, the friendly doctor in the white jacket who seemed to have all the answers fascinated me. As an adult I still admire the doctor from my childhood. Now I know that she was a pediatrician, which is a doctor who specializes in the health needs of children. When I entered college and started to think of my future occupation, I thought more and more about becoming this kind of doctor. As a pediatrician, I can help children get well, make a good living, work hard, and enjoy challenges.

> Thesis is clearer.

Ever since I can remember I've wanted to take care of   2
children. When my little brother used to get earaches, I'd pretend I was the doctor and hold a cup to his chest as if I could hear his heartbeat. In high school I volunteered at Providence Hospital in the children's wing. Seeing a sick child made me sad, but I always felt better after playing with them and cheering them up. Being even a small part of a team that helped children heal, it made me feel worthwile.

> Sentences combined with subordinate conjunction *(ever since, when).*

> Example added.

As a pediatrician, I can make a good living. This is   3
important to me, because my parents have had to cope with many financial difficulties. I remember bill collectors calling us and my mother's care being repossessed. Pediatricians don't have trouble finding jobs, and their median salary is $120,000 a year (*Occupational Outlook* 2). This job security will let me provide for my parents when they get old, as well as take care of my own family.

> Sentences combined with subordinate conjunction *(because).*

> Information from Web site added.

Pediatricians work long hours. According to the *Occu-*   4
pational Outlook Handbook, published by the U.S. Department of Labor, more than one-third of all doctors work more than 60 hours a week (2). In addition, a pediatrician, like all doctors, must complete college, four years of medical school, and then three to eight years of further training in a hospital (Turner 54). It takes a high grade point

> Information from Web site and article added.

average and being especially good in science. Fortunately, I like to work hard. Right now I help take care of my family, carry a full class load at college, and work about 30 hours a week. I wouldn't know what to do with myself if I had free time!

Pediatric nurses also specialize in childrens' health care. While volunteering at Providence Hospital, I observed many pediatric nurses give children shots, examine their progress, and cheer up their patients. Pediatric nurses work one-on-one with children, while pediatricians spend less time alone with the patients. However, being a pediatrician appeals to me more than being a nurse because pediatricians diagnose children and decide on a treatment plan. Nurses have to carry out the decisions of doctors. I prefer to be the one who makes the decisions in the first place.

Finally, as a pediatrician I would encounter challenges every day. According to one pediatrician, "I never know what I'll encounter with every patient I see. One child might just have a cold or flu. But the next child could have a bruise that won't heal. This could be a symptom of cancer" (Turner 53). I look forward to helping children heal whether they have a runny nose or something more serious. The job might make me tired or stressed, but never bored.

While a pediatrician's job can be difficult, I think it's the job for me. Getting into medical school is tough, but I like to aim high. For me, nothing would be more satisfying than helping a child get well.

Examples added.

5   Comparison and contrast added.

Reasons added to support thesis.

6   Quotation used to support point.

7   Conclusion extended.

Works Cited

Occupational Outlook Handbook 2002-2003 Edition. U.S. Dept.
    of Labor. 14 Feb. 2002. <http:www.bls.gov/oco>.
Turner, Angela. "Pediatricians: An Endangered Species?"
    Time 7 Apr. 1999: 53-54.

ACTIVITY 17

Analyzing Kathy's Revised Draft. Use the following questions to discuss with your classmates how Kathy revised her draft.

1. How well has Kathy hooked the reader, given background information, and stated her thesis in her introduction?

   _____

   _____

   _____

   _____

2. What is Kathy's thesis statement? How well has it been improved compared to the thesis in her discovery draft? Could it be improved even more?

   _____

   _____

   _____

   _____

3. How has Kathy used classification and comparison and contrast to develop her points? Are these revisions effective? Explain.

   _____

   _____

   _____

   _____

4. What kind of research did Kathy conduct on her topic?

_____

_____

_____

_____

5. How well has Kathy used research in her essay? Is the research connected to the ideas before and after it? Are quotations introduced? Is the research documented in her essay and in her Works Cited list?

_____

_____

_____

_____

6. In your view, what point or points are best supported with facts, examples, and statistics? Is there any idea that needs more support?

_____

_____

_____

_____

7. How could Kathy's draft benefit from more revision?

_____

_____

_____

_____

ACTIVITY 18 (GROUP)

Using Peer Review. Form a group with two or three other students and exchange copies of your drafts. Read your draft aloud while your classmates follow along. Take notes on your classmates' responses to the following questions about your draft.

1. What did you like best about my essay?

   _____

   _____

   _____

2. How interesting is my introduction? Do you want to continue reading the paper? Why or why not?

   _____

   _____

   _____

3. What is my thesis statement? Do I need to make the essay's thesis clearer?

   _____

   _____

   _____

4. How well have I supported my points? Do I need to add facts, examples, or statistics to extend what I say? How can classification or comparison and contrast improve my supporting points?

   _____

   _____

   _____

5. How well have I used quotations and paraphrases from my research? Have I given the correct information about my sources in the text of my essay and in the Works Cited list?

_____

_____

_____

6. Where in the essay did my writing confuse you? How can I clarify my thoughts?

_____

_____

_____

7. How effective is my ending? Do I end in such a way that you know it's the end?

_____

_____

_____

 Use E-mail or Online Peer Review

E-mail your draft to several fellow students, and ask them to answer the peer reviews in a return e-mail. Alternatively, if your class has a Web site, see whether the peer review questions are available on the site. If they are, you may be able to respond to your classmates' drafts online.

ACTIVITY 19

Revising Your Draft. Taking your classmates' suggestions for revision into consideration, revise your essay. Consider using classification and comparison and contrast to help you explain your ideas. Think about adding research material for facts, examples, and statistics that can support your most important points. If you use research, correctly quote and paraphrase information from your sources. Identify your sources properly, both in the text of your essay and in a Works Cited list at the end.

EDITING

At this point you have worked hard to investigate a workplace occupation, workplace jargon, or a workplace problem. Now you're ready to edit your essay for correctness. Remember that the fewer errors you make, the more your readers will focus on what you have to say.

Correcting Pronoun Reference and Agreement

A *pronoun* takes the place of a noun. Here are some of the most common English pronouns:

Want more information on pronoun reference? See the Pronoun Reference section of the Handbook (pp. 664–67).

I, me, mine, we, us, our, ours

you, your, yours

he, him, his, she, her, hers

it, its

they, them, their, theirs

this, these, that, those

who, whom, whose, which, that, what

any, anyone, anybody, each, everybody, everyone, everything

someone, something

When you use a pronoun to refer to a noun, make sure the reference is clear, not vague. The pronoun should be close to the noun it takes the place of.

Here are two ways to correct vague pronoun reference.

- Replace the pronoun with the noun it refers to.
- Rewrite the sentence so the pronoun is no longer needed.

VAGUE   In the article "Dealing with a Difficult Boss," *it* said that good communication between boss and employee is essential. [What does *it* refer to?]

CLEAR   In the article "Dealing with a Difficult Boss," *the author* said that good communication between boss and employee is essential.

VAGUE   Ms. Ortiz told Rachel *she* was going to be late. [Does *she* refer to Ms. Ortiz or to Rachel?]

CLEAR   Ms. Ortiz said, "I'm going to be late."

VAGUE   In the art world, *they're* used to unusual behavior and clothing. [Whom does *they* refer to?]

CLEAR   People in the art world are used to unusual behavior and clothing.

VAGUE   Raymond loved traveling with his band and recording a CD last summer. *It* made him decide to make music a career. [Does *it* refer to traveling with the band, recording a CD, or both?]

CLEAR   Because Raymond loved traveling with his band and recording a CD over the summer, *he* decided to make music a career.

To check for *pronoun agreement,* make sure that the pronoun agrees in number with the noun it takes the place of. To maintain pronoun agreement, use a singular pronoun to refer to a singular noun and a plural pronoun to refer to a plural noun. Pronouns such as *any, anyone, anybody, each, everybody, everyone, everything, someone,* and *something* are singular.

Here are two ways to correct pronoun agreement.

- Make the pronoun and noun agree in number.
- Rewrite the sentence to eliminate the problem.

NO PRONOUN AGREEMENT   A successful job applicant will prepare for *their* job interview.

PRONOUN AGREEMENT   A successful job applicant will prepare for *his or her* job interview.

PRONOUN AGREEMENT   Successful job applicants will prepare for *their* job interviews.

NO PRONOUN AGREEMENT   To get a good job, *everyone* should try to get the best education *they* can afford.

PRONOUN AGREEMENT   To get a good job, *everyone* should try to get the best education *he or she* can afford.

PRONOUN AGREEMENT   To get a good job, *young people* should try to get the best education they can afford.

For more help, see the Pronoun Agreement section of the Handbook, pp. 667–70.

As these examples illustrate, you may wish to use a plural noun (such as *young people*) to avoid saying *he or she* or *his or her* throughout an essay.

> **HOW TO** **Correct Pronoun Reference**
> **and Agreement**
>
> - Identify the pronouns in each sentence of your draft.
>
> - Identify the noun that each pronoun replaces. Make sure the noun is easy to identify and is close to the pronoun.
>
> - Check to see that the noun and pronoun agree in number. Remember that the pronouns *any, anyone, anybody, each, everybody, everyone, everything, someone,* and *something* are singular. Use singular nouns with them.

ACTIVITY 20

Correcting Pronoun Reference and Agreement. Correct the problems with pronoun reference and agreement in the following paragraph.

Whenever I tell anyone my college major is food science, they get a puzzled look on their face. Most people haven't heard of it. I first read about food science in a magazine article about the invention of different varieties of corn for undeveloped countries. They said that scientists spend years in the laboratory and in greenhouses trying to get plants to grow in extreme climates or different types of soils. They take years to develop. Last semester in my Introduction to Food Science course they had us experiment with making a type of yogurt that doesn't need refrigeration. It isn't available to consumers in poor countries. It didn't taste very good, but it was interesting to make. My ultimate goal is to contribute to the elimination of starvation throughout the world.

Online Grammar Skills Practice

The *Choices* Web site includes practice exercises for correcting pronoun reference and agreement. Go to <**www.bedfordstmartins.com/choices/**> and click on "Exercise Central." After logging in, click on "Pronoun Reference" and "Pronoun Agreement."

ACTIVITY 21

Correcting Pronoun Reference and Agreement in Your Draft. As you're revising your draft, examine each pronoun to make sure its reference is clear and that it agrees in number with the noun it's replacing.

Kathy's Edited Essay

You probably noticed that Kathy's revised draft contained errors in grammar, spelling, and punctuation. Kathy corrected these errors in her edited essay. Her corrections are underlined here. Her editing log follows her essay.

```
Kathy Chu

Professor Mangelsdorf

English 0311

1 Oct. 2002


               Helping Children Heal

     When I was a child, going to the doctor was both        1

frightening and exciting. I hated getting shots and seeing

the crying babies. At the same time, the friendly doctor

in the white jacket who seemed to have all the answers

fascinated me. As an adult I still admire the doctor from

my childhood. Now I know that she was a pediatrician,

which is a doctor who specializes in the health needs of
```

children. When I entered college and started to think of my future occupation, I thought more and more about becoming this kind of doctor. As a pediatrician, I can help children get well, make a good living, work hard, and enjoy challenges.

Ever since I can remember I've wanted to take care of children. When my little brother used to get earaches, I'd pretend I was the doctor and hold a cup to his chest as if I could hear his heartbeat. In high school I volunteered at Providence Hospital in the children's wing. <u>Seeing sick children made me sad, but I always felt better after playing with them and cheering them up</u>. Being even a small part of a team that helped children heal made me feel <u>worthwhile</u>.

This essay shows how to give information about your sources in the body of the essay and in the Works Cited list. You can find another sample essay on pp. 559–63.

As a pediatrician, I can make a good living. <u>This is important to me because my parents have had to cope with many financial difficulties</u>. I remember bill collectors calling us and my mother's <u>car</u> being repossessed.

Pediatricians don't have trouble finding jobs, and their median salary is $120,000 a year (*Occupational Outlook* 2). This job security will let me provide for my parents when they get old, as well as take care of my own family.

Pediatricians work long hours. According to the *Occupational Outlook Handbook*, published by the U.S. Department of Labor, more than one-third of all doctors work more than 60 hours a week (2). In addition, a pediatrician, like all doctors, must complete college, four years of medical school, and then three to eight years of further training in a hospital (Turner 54). <u>People who want to be accepted to medical school must have a high grade point average and be especially good in science</u>. Fortunately, I like to work hard. Right now I help take care of my family, carry a full class load at college, and work about 30 hours a week. I wouldn't know what to do with myself if I had free time!

Pediatric nurses also specialize in <u>children's</u> health care. While volunteering at Providence Hospital, I observed many pediatric nurses give children shots, examine their progress, and cheer up their patients. Pediatric nurses work one-on-one with children, while pediatricians spend less time alone with the patients. However, being a pediatrician appeals to me more than being a nurse because pediatricians diagnose children and decide on a treatment plan. Nurses have to carry out the decisions of doctors. I prefer to be the one who makes the decisions in the first place.

5

Finally, as a pediatrician I would encounter challenges every day. According to one pediatrician, "I never know what I'll encounter with every patient I see. One child might just have a cold or flu. But the next child could have a bruise that won't heal. This could be a symptom of cancer" (Turner 53). I look forward to helping children heal whether they have a runny nose or something more serious. The job might make me tired or stressed, but never bored.

6

While a pediatrician's job can be difficult, I think it's the job for me. Getting into medical school is tough, but I like to aim high. For me, nothing would be more satisfying than helping a child get well.

7

Works Cited

<u>Occupational Outlook Handbook 2002-2003 Edition</u>. U.S. Dept.
of Labor. 14 Feb. 2002. <http://www.bls.gov/oco/>.
Turner, Angela. "Pediatricians: An Endangered Species?"
<u>Time</u> 7 Apr. 1999: 53-54.

To learn how to keep an editing log, turn to pp. 41–42.

Kathy's Editing Log

10/05 — "Helping Children Heal"

INCORRECT	Seeing a sick child made me sad, but I always felt better after playing with them and cheering them up. (2)
ERROR	Pronoun agreement (*child* and *them*)
CORRECT	Seeing sick children made me sad, but I always felt better after playing with them and cheering them up.

INCORRECT	worthwile (2)
ERROR	spelling
CORRECT	worthwhile

INCORRECT	This is important to me, because my parents have had to cope with many financial difficulties. (3)
ERROR	Comma before a subordinate clause that ends a sentence
CORRECT	This is important to me because my parents have had to cope with many financial difficulties.

INCORRECT	care (3)
ERROR	wrong word
CORRECT	car

INCORRECT	It takes a high grade point average and being especially good in science. (4)
ERROR	Vague pronoun reference (what does *it* refer to?)
CORRECT	People who want to be accepted to medical school must have a high grade point average and be especially good in science.

INCORRECT	childrens' (5)
ERROR	apostrophe after the *s*
CORRECT	children's

ESL Links

The *Choices* Web site includes links to useful ESL sites. Go to <www.bedfordstmartins.com/choices/> and click on "ESL Links."

ACTIVITY 22

Editing Your Essay. Read your essay word for word, looking for errors in grammar, spelling, and punctuation. Also ask a friend or classmate to help you spot errors you might have overlooked. Pay particular attention to eliminating errors in pronoun reference and agreement. Use a dictionary and the Handbook in Part Four of this book to help you correct the errors you find. Finally, record those errors in your editing log.

PUBLISHING

After you edit your essay, you're ready to share it with your audience—your instructor and classmates, as well as others interested in your topic. For example, if you wrote about a workplace problem, you could share your essay with others in your workplace who also have that problem. If you wrote about an occupation you want to pursue or about jargon in the workplace, you might show your essay to others interested in the same subjects.

CHAPTER CHECKLIST

- ☐ I gathered ideas on a workplace occupation, workplace jargon, and a workplace problem by brainstorming, freewriting, answering questions, and relating aloud.
- ☐ I developed ideas using classification and comparison and contrast.
- ☐ I located sources on my topic to help support ideas.
- ☐ I summarized sources on my topic.
- ☐ I wrote a tentative outline before I revised.
- ☐ I correctly used quotations and paraphrases in my draft.
- ☐ I documented quotations and paraphrases in the text and at the end of the draft in a Works Cited list.
- ☐ I combined short, closely related sentences using subordinate conjunctions.
- ☐ I corrected errors in pronoun reference and agreement.
- ☐ I shared my essay with readers interested in the topic.

REFLECTING ON YOUR WRITING

To help you reflect on the writing you did in this chapter, answer the following questions.

1. What did you learn from writing on your topic?
2. If you used research in your essay, what about the research process was hardest? What was easiest?
3. Compare and contrast writing this essay with writing previous essays.
4. If you had more time, what further revisions would you make to improve your essay? Why would you make these revisions?

Using your answers to these questions, update your Writing Process Report.

Writing Process Report

Date:

Strengths:

Weaknesses:

Plans for improvement:

Once you complete this report, freewrite about what you learned in this chapter about your writing and what you still hope to learn.

Workplace Occupation

In the following reading, "Lessons in Shrimping," Tamera Helms describes an occupation that is a mystery to many people: being a shrimper.

TAMERA HELMS

Lessons in Shrimping

"It's stupid to throw fish to those gulls," the captain said for the dozenth time.   1

"But Daddy, they're hungry," I cried.   2

"All right, Sis, but you're gonna regret it."   3

Two fish later I learned what he'd meant when a big white sea gull returned with a fish, like the ones I'd so generously thrown to him, only in a smellier and more liquid form. This was one of the many lessons I learned during the summers I worked on my father's shrimp boat. Shrimping, I was soon to learn, was much more complicated and interesting than just pulling up a net full of shrimp.   4

A shrimper's day starts long before sunrise, usually between 3:30 and 5 AM, depending on how far out the boat's headed that day. There are even times when a captain will keep the boat out overnight so as to have first crack at the prior day's hot spots. In Texas, where I learned about shrimping, the first "drag" (as pulling the net underwater is called) can't be started until the sun has fully crossed the horizon, but in the light before full sunrise the captain or a deckhand puts the net into the water to be rinsed and soaked. The net ranges in length from twenty to forty feet on an average sized boat, which is itself forty to fifty feet long. At this hour many shrimpers use a miniature net to look for the best spot to begin the first drag. This mini net, called a "try net," gives shrimpers some idea of what they'll catch without having to waste much time or fuel.   5

As soon as the sun is up and the captain has chosen a spot, they "put over the big rig." Having already put the net in the water, they need only to put in the huge wooden "doors" (which resemble the doors on an ancient castle) to spread open the mouth of the net and hold it underwater. It is, however, a sizeable task,   6

289

since the doors may weigh in excess of 150 pounds. A winch is used to lift the doors up off the deck. Then the captain must swing the doors out over the water by revving the engine and causing the boat to jump quickly forward. At that exact moment, he must release the winch brake, dropping the heavy doors into the water. If he fails to get the doors out over the water they could very easily put a hole in the deck or be damaged themselves. Next he must adjust the length of cable let out. If he doesn't let out enough, the net will catch only fish; if he lets out too much, the net may bog down in mud, or, worse, hit an old wreck and maybe destroy the net. Each time shrimpers put the rig over, they are risking two or three thousand dollars of equipment.

It would seem that the next hour or two would be just a waiting period, but instead the captain must monitor the cables and depth finder closely. Many shrimpers also monitor their catch with a try net to avoid pulling for shrimp that aren't there. After an hour or two the captain usually picks up the net, although three-hour drags are not uncommon. Using the winch again, he pulls the doors to the top of the water and, using a method similar to the one for dropping the doors, places them back in their rack. Then, using a rope tied to the bag of the net, he pulls the net up beside the boat. Using another rope and the winch again, he lifts the bag of the net up over the deck and unties the end, letting all the contents spill out. At this point the captain decides, from looking at the catch, whether to put it back over or to look for a better place.

7

Once the first catch of the day is pulled up, the real work starts. "Culling," as most people refer to it, is the art of separating the shrimp from the myriad ocean creatures pulled out of the water. The majority of these creatures are harmless: croakers, spots, blow fish, baby flounder, trout, and whiting. Others, however, pose dangers to the culler. Crabs, sting rays, eels, jelly fish, hard heads, and sea leeches must be avoided, and thus slow the culler down.

8

The most dangerous of them is the hard head. Hard heads are saltwater catfish, usually from two inches to a full foot in length, all equally threatening. What makes these fish so dangerous is the poisonous barbs around their head. These very sharp barbs can cut skin badly, shooting a poisonous venom into the cut. This poison causes the wound to swell enormously and painfully. Some people even become sick to their stomach and may run a slight fever. When struck by a hard head, the experienced culler will immediately try to force the wound to bleed and thus push out the poison.

9

There is, of course, more to culling than just avoiding hard   10
heads. Depending on the ratio of fish to shrimp and the size of
the shrimp, there are three different culling procedures. Each
begins, however, with the clearing out of the crabs. The pile of
shrimp and fish and other creatures is turned over again and
again with a shovel to free any crabs that might be lurking
underneath. Then the majority of them are pushed out the scupper holes in the side of the railing. Next the deckhand decides
whether to cull from the deck of the boat or on a table (which
usually doubles as an ice box). If the shrimp are big and easy to
see and grab, culling is usually done on the deck by picking up
the shrimp and raking the "trash fish" overboard. If the shrimp
are small and there are not too many of them, the deckhand
shovels loads of the mix onto the table top, picks the fish out of
the shrimp, and throws them over the side. He then rakes the
remaining shrimp into baskets at his feet. The last method, and
the most ingenious, is for a load that has just as many fish as
shrimp in it. The deckhand uses an invention called a "salt barrel" to separate the fish from the shrimp. A salt barrel is a tub of
seawater with a large amount of extra salt dissolved in it. The
excess salt causes the fish to float to the top of the water, where
they can be scooped out and thrown back into the bay. Then,
using the net, the deckhand dips deep into the barrel and pulls
out the remaining shrimp. Any fish that are left are picked out
and thrown over. When the culling is finished, the shrimp are iced
down and the deck is cleaned of all remaining ocean creatures.

Then, depending on the speed of the deckhand, there may be   11
time to rest a few minutes before the next load is brought up. And
so the work continues until sundown, at which time the captain
pulls up the last drag of the day and turns the boat toward the
port, to sell the day's catch.

At the dock they unload the catch into metal tubs, with   12
holes at the bottom. The shrimp are washed to melt any ice that
might add weight to the scales and are then weighed and
counted. The "count" indicates the size of the shrimp and is
determined by counting the number of shrimp to a pound.

It is at this time that shrimpers find out if they've made any   13
money for the day, or if they've just broken even with the boat's
overhead expenses. Despite what people may believe, shrimpers
don't make a very prosperous living. It could cause one to wonder why they continue to work under these conditions. Some are
trapped into it due to lack of a formal education. They know
shrimping, and so that's what they do. Others, such as my father,
do it because they love nature. They are addicted to the salt air,

the freedom of being on the water, the beautiful sunrises and sunsets. These shrimpers pass their respect and love for nature on to their children. Often this is as simple as warning them to watch for bird bombs. Whatever their reasons for shrimping, they each deserve respect and admiration. The work they do is much harder than most of us will ever know.

VOCABULARY WORDS: winch (6), culling (8), hard heads (9), barbs (9), lurking (10), scupper (10), ingenious (10), overhead (13)

ACTIVITY 23

Reading to Improve Writing. Discuss the following questions about "Lessons in Shrimping."

1. Give three reasons why shrimping is a difficult profession.

   _____

   _____

   _____

2. Why do people remain in such a difficult job?

   _____

   _____

   _____

3. Explain the title of the essay.

   _____

   _____

   _____

4. Why does the author explain the process of shrimping in such detail? In your view, is this level of detail effective or ineffective? Explain your answer.

_____

_____

_____

Workplace Jargon

Jargon helps people in the workplace communicate quickly and effectively. Until you understand this jargon, you'll be at a disadvantage. In "American Workplace Slang and Jargon," Rita Warren Hess writes a story that will help you understand some of the jargon used in the business world.

RITA WARREN HESS

American Workplace Slang and Jargon

Have you mastered the English language? Good! Can you also comfortably speak business-ese, the sometimes-unusual words and phrases like those in the following fictional American workplace?   1

Mega Music is a **brick and mortar** business (a traditional company with an actual building or store location, rather than an e-commerce business). Mega struggles to compete with online retailers, sometimes called *click and mortar* businesses. To remain financially sound, Mega Music used **headhunters**, paid recruiters who match hiring companies with employees or executives, to find a new CEO. The headhunter found a young energetic Yankee named Bill Black. (A **Yankee** is a person from the northeastern region of the United States. The name originated during the Civil War, because Yankees were soldiers from the north.)   2

Mega hired Bill because he possessed excellent **soft skills** *(people skills)*. He interacted well with the public, was an excellent motivator and a good conversationalist. Soft skills are sometimes more important than hard skills (hands-on abilities) like programming or building cars.   3

The headhunter also located a **bean counter** to handle the company's funds (beans). People often refer to *accountants* as bean counters. The bean counter suggested Mega managers do some **number crunching** (shrinking certain numbers) by lowering budget estimates or postponing planned projects. Mega's new   4 accountant further recommended **across the board** budget cuts (reductions that applied to everyone equally). Slashing budgets by 10% across the board meant *every* department received a 10% budget cut.

When budget projections still did not align with income esti-   5 mates, Mega Music **downsized** (went from one size to a smaller size by reducing the number of employees through terminations or retirements). Downsizing put department managers in a **Catch 22** situation, where each had to make a choice between unappealing options. Janet had to reduce her engineering staff of four people by one. Each person was an excellent worker and played an important role in the group. Deciding which one to fire put her in a Catch 22 situation.

All department managers were uncomfortable knowing cer-   6 tain employees would receive a **pink slip** (termination notice). A person being fired (also known as *getting the axe*) does not actually receive a pink slip terminating his/her employment. This term is one of many unusual phrases adopted by businesses.

One Mega employee reacted unfavorably to termination and   7 charged the company with age discrimination. This was expected since the company had **deep pockets**, meaning they were a large and reasonably successful business. People contemplating litigation (legal charges) often target companies with deep pockets because they anticipate a large financial settlement.

Other employees welcomed the termination. They were tired   8 of the **rat race**—methodically getting up, going to work, performing job duties, going home, sleeping, and repeating the process over again. They never felt refreshed, although they escaped the rat race on weekends by catching up on **R and R** (rest and relaxation).

What else did Mega Music do to prevent **going under** (going   9 out of business)?

Bill, the new CEO, believed saving the company meant iden-   10 tifying previous mistakes. He invited all managers to a **Monday morning quarterback** session. This phrase originated after weekend football games, when fans discussed what the quarterback (an important player on a football team) *should* have done or *could* have done differently to change the game's outcome. Bill felt that by evaluating past failures, they could avoid the same mistake(s) in the future.

Following Bill's Monday morning quarterback session, his   11 staff presented a list of ideas for improvement.

First, they found their method of valuing and managing   12 warehouse products was a disaster. They switched to **FIFO**, an inventory term meaning first-in-first-out and placing a value on items sold by using the cost of the oldest items first. FIFO was chosen over another inventory valuation method called the LIFO (last-in-first-out).

Bill and his team also decided to decrease their inventory by using a process called **JIT (Just-in-time)**, in which they would stock little, if any, surplus goods or materials. Instead, buyers ordered items from suppliers to arrive just in time, or just before needed.   13

An internal investigation revealed that Mary, the Warehouse Manager, was receiving **kickbacks** (illegal payments made between two parties to give one person an unfair advantage over competitors). Mary routinely sent bid packages to obtain quotes on CD cases. John Jones, an employee at a plastics company that manufactures CD cases, paid Mary $500 cash each time she arranged it so that his company got the contract to supply the cases.   14

Besides firing Mary, Mega Music **outsourced** purchasing, meaning they hired an independent firm to provide the service rather than using employees on the company payroll. Financially, it benefited the company to outsource the function rather than having it done **in-house** (done by employees on the company payroll).   15

Bill's team also found that filling product orders was very **labor-intensive**, meaning labor costs were disproportionately high. They devised a plan to ship inventory twice as fast with fewer employees by **working smarter** (getting the work done more efficiently). Working smarter is different from working harder. For example, if your job is to move bricks from Pile A to Pile B all day, you could work harder and move more bricks. But if you load them in a wheelbarrow, push them across the yard, then go back for another load, you are working smarter.   16

Finally, Mega Music changed their advertising strategy by studying the **benchmark**, the best in their industry. Their largest competitor, Today's Tunes, had the ultimate advertising campaign for reaching young male audiences. Today's Tunes set the benchmark (the standard), so Mega used a similar format to devise a halftime Super Bowl Sunday commercial.   17

Mega encountered obstacles during the **eleventh (11th) hour**, the timeframe just before a deadline, but not necessarily the *hour* before. After spending six months preparing the new commercial, they made several changes during the last three weeks (their 11th hour) before the spot aired.   18

Mega's CEO wondered if the company's efforts would be in vain. If the Super Bowl advertisement did not bring the anticipated returns, the company would **take a bath** (an unfavorable   19 way of describing a person or group of people who did not fare well in some undertaking) and might face bankruptcy.

Bill worried needlessly. Millions of viewers watched Mega   20
Music's halftime commercial and the company telephones rang non-stop on Monday morning with new orders.

VOCABULARY WORDS: business-ese (1), retailers (2), projections (5), align (5), termination (6), inventory (12), surplus (13), disproportionately (16)

ACTIVITY 24

Reading to Improve Writing. Discuss the following questions about "American Workplace Slang and Jargon" with your classmates.

1. What is the author's purpose in this essay? Is this purpose stated directly? If it is stated directly, where does it appear? If it's not stated directly, why not?

   _____

   _____

   _____

   _____

   _____

2. Describe the audience that the author is writing for. (Hint: this article first appeared on a Web site called <*New2USA.com*>.)

   _____

   _____

   _____

   _____

   _____

3. Why did the author decide to write a fictional story—rather than a standard essay—to explain jargon in the business world?

_____

_____

_____

4. Among the business terms defined in this article are *pink slip, deep pockets,* and *rat race.* How do you suppose these terms came to be? Select at least one other jargon phrase and guess (or research) its origin.

_____

_____

_____

_____

Workplace Problem

As many people realize, the demands of the workplace can have a negative effect on family life. In "The Company Man," Ellen Goodman describes a typical "company man" and his relationship to his family.

ELLEN GOODMAN

The Company Man

He worked himself to death, finally and precisely, at 3:00   1
A.M. Sunday morning.

The obituary didn't say that, of course. It said that he died   2
of a coronary thrombosis—I think that was it—but everyone
among his friends and acquaintances knew it instantly. He was a
perfect Type A, a workaholic, a classic, they said to each other
and shook their heads—and thought for five or ten minutes
about the way they lived.

This man who worked himself to death finally and precisely   3
at 3:00 A.M. Sunday morning—on his day off—was fifty-one
years old and a vice-president. He was, however, one of six vice-
presidents, and one of three who might conceivably—if the president died or retired soon enough—have moved to the top spot.
Phil knew that.

He worked six days a week, five of them until eight or nine   4
at night, during a time when his own company had begun the
four-day week for everyone but the executives. He worked like
the Important People. He had no outside "extracurricular interests," unless, of course, you think about a monthly golf game
that way. To Phil, it was work. He always ate egg salad sandwiches
at his desk. He was, of course, overweight, by 20 or 25 pounds.
He thought it was okay, though, because he didn't smoke.

On Saturdays, Phil wore a sports jacket to the office instead   5
of a suit, because it was the weekend.

He had a lot of people working for him, maybe sixty, and   6
most of them liked him most of the time. Three of them will be
seriously considered for his job. The obituary didn't mention that.

But it did list his "survivors" quite accurately. He is survived   7
by his wife, Helen, forty-eight years old, a good woman of no
particular marketable skills, who worked in an office before mar-
rying and mothering. She had, according to her daughter, given
up trying to compete with his work years ago, when the children
were small. A company friend said, "I know how much you will
miss him." And she answered, "I already have."

"Missing him all these years," she must have given up part of   8
herself which had cared too much for the man. She would be
"well taken care of."

His "dearly beloved" eldest of the "dearly beloved" children   9
is a hard-working executive in a manufacturing firm down
South. In the day and a half before the funeral, he went around
the neighborhood researching his father, asking the neighbors
what he was like. They were embarrassed.

His second child is a girl, who is twenty-four and newly mar-   10
ried. She lives near her mother and they are close, but whenever
she was alone with her father, in a car driving somewhere, they
had nothing to say to each other.

The youngest is twenty, a boy, a high-school graduate who   11
has spent the last couple of years, like a lot of his friends, doing
enough odd jobs to stay in grass and food. He was the one who
tried to grab at his father, and tried to mean enough to him to
keep the man at home. He was his father's favorite. Over the last
two years, Phil stayed up nights worrying about the boy.

The boy once said, "My father and I only board here."   12

At the funeral, the sixty-year-old company president told the   13
forty-eight-year-old widow that the fifty-one-year-old deceased
had meant much to the company and would be missed and
would be hard to replace. The widow didn't look him in the eye.
She was afraid he would read her bitterness and, after all, she
would need him to straighten out the finances—the stock options
and all that.

Phil was overweight and nervous and worked too hard. If he   14
wasn't at the office, he was worried about it. Phil was a Type A, a
heart-attack natural. You could have picked him out in a minute
from a lineup.

So when he finally worked himself to death, at precisely 3:00   15
A.M. Sunday morning, no one was really surprised.

By 5:00 P.M. the afternoon of the funeral, the company presi-   16
dent had begun, discreetly of course, with care and taste, to
make inquiries about his replacement. One of three men. He
asked around: "Who's been working the hardest?"

VOCABULARY WORDS: obituary (2), thrombosis (2), Type A (2), conceivably (3), executive (9), board (12), discreetly (16)

ACTIVITY 25

Reading to Improve Writing. Discuss the following questions
about "The Company Man" with your classmates.

1. Why is "the company man" not given a name until the third
   paragraph?

   _____

   _____

   _____

   _____

2. Describe the relationship "the company man" had with his wife
   and children.

   _____

   _____

_____

_____

3. Explain the significance of the last sentence of the essay: "He asked around: 'Who's been working the hardest?'"

_____

_____

_____

4. In your view, does this essay accurately depict the modern workplace? Why or why not?

_____

_____

The unexamined life is not worth living. —SOCRATES

CHAPTER 7

Evaluating Your World

In this chapter you will

- evaluate a product, performance, or place.
- write a thesis statement that expresses a judgment.
- base your judgment on criteria.
- support your judgment with evidence and comparisons.
- keep a balanced perspective.
- combine sentences using relative clauses.
- eliminate sexist language.
- present titles correctly.
- reflect on your writing.

Evaluating your world is something you do every day. In the morning you may decide that a new brand of breakfast cereal tastes better than your old brand. During the school day you may realize that this semester's chemistry instructor explains new terms more clearly than your previous instructor did. In the evening you may channel-surf to find a show that is worth watching.

When you evaluate something, you decide its value, worthiness, or merit. An evaluation is based on standards: a breakfast cereal should taste good and be good for you, a chemistry instructor should be an effective communicator, and a television show should divert you from your everyday worries. When you evaluate, you apply standards like these to your subject. You taste the cereal and examine the nutritional label on the box. You listen to see how well your chemistry instructor explains new terms. You examine television shows for amusing plots or interesting settings.

After applying the appropriate standards to your subject, you can make a decision about its value, worthiness, or merit. Once you have evaluated your subject, you are ready to write a convincing essay in which you share what you have decided with others.

WRITING ASSIGNMENT

For this assignment, write an essay in which you evaluate a product, performance, or place. You or your instructor may decide to do this assignment in one of several ways.

- You may gather ideas on one, two, or three topics.
- You may write a discovery draft on one, two, or three of these topics.
- You may choose one discovery draft to develop into a polished essay.
- Or, you may combine your discovery draft ideas into a new topic for your essay.

After completing your essay, you'll share it with your instructor, classmates, and perhaps others who are interested in your topic, such as fellow consumers, students, co-workers, friends, and family members.

Other Students' Ideas

Read students' responses to this assignment on the *Choices* Web site. Go to <www.bedfordstmartins.com/choices/> and click on "Student Writing."

ACTIVITY 1

Analyzing Your Purpose and Audience. Before you begin gathering ideas about your topic, think about your purpose and audience. As you gather ideas, remember that your audience will include people directly affected by your topic. If you plan to evaluate a product, your readers will include consumers interested in purchasing that product. If you aim to evaluate a play, movie, or television show, your readers will be people interested in seeing the show. And if you plan to evaluate a shopping mall, museum, or tourist attraction, your audience will include people who would enjoy visiting that site. Your responses to the following questions will help you decide how to approach your topic.

Want more help with audience and purpose? Go to pp. 29–30.

1. Does this assignment call for primarily expressive, informative, or persuasive writing?

   _____

2. What are some consumer products your audience might be interested in reading about?

   _____

   _____

3. What movies, television shows, music groups, and books are your readers familiar with?

   _____

   _____

   _____

4. What places—restaurants, shopping malls, museums, amusement parks—do your readers visit regularly?

   _____

   _____

   _____

5. How interested will your readers be in an essay that evaluates a product, performance, or place? How can you make sure you keep your readers' interest as they read your essay?

_____

_____

_____

GATHERING IDEAS

These methods of gathering ideas are explained on pp. 30–34.

To gather ideas to evaluate a product, performance, or place, select from among the various techniques you learned in Chapter 2. The student writers in this chapter will use brainstorming, freewriting, and questioning.

Evaluating a Product

As a consumer, you evaluate products before purchasing them. If the product is inexpensive, such as a can of soup, your evaluation might be as simple as reading the label. If the product is a major purchase, such as a stereo system or a car, you might consult friends, read a magazine such as *Consumer Reports,* and comparison shop. Even after you purchase the product, you probably continue to evaluate it to see whether you made a good choice.

In "Hummer: Still a Rich Man's Toy," Al Haas evaluates the Hummer sport-utility vehicle. As you read, notice how the writer explains and supports his evaluation.

AL HAAS

Hummer: Still a Rich Man's Toy

Here's a news flash: The Hummer isn't for people who don't like to be noticed. So, if you do wet work for the CIA or are paid to spy on married people playing musical beds, you probably don't want to drive to the job site in this huge, thinly veiled military vehicle.   1

Civilian Hummer

With a price tag of $85,961 on the Hummer I tested, you also   2
could say this is not a vehicle for those of us who clip food
coupons from our newspaper.

As a matter of fact, the Hummer is quite literally a rich man's   3
toy: The people who buy it are almost all men who earn in excess
of $250,000 a year. In some cases, like that of actor Arnold
Schwarzenegger, who purchased five, the buyer earns well in
excess of $250,000 a year.

For those who spent the last six years backpacking in the   4
shadow of the North Pole, the Hummer is the civilian version of
an incredibly sure-footed military pack animal called the humvee
(for high-mobility, multi-purpose wheeled vehicle).

Weighing in at more than three tons and half again as wide   5
as many cars, the humvee was developed for the Army by AM
General Corp. The military uses the four-wheel-drive vehicle in
100 configurations, ranging from personnel carriers and ambulances to mobile mountings for rocket launchers.

AM General started building the humvee at its plant in South   6
Bend, Ind., in 1985. It began offering the Hummer seven years
later. This civilian rendition is available in several hard- and soft-
top models, including the hard-roofed four-door pickup I tested.

There is little essential difference between the Hummer and   7
the military vehicle. The Hummer is painted with automotive
gloss finishes instead of the flat olive drab and camouflage employed on the humvee, and it has passenger car amenities such

as air conditioning and a stereo. But structurally and mechanically, it is the same critter.

While Hummers, like other sport-utility vehicles, spend al-   8
most all their time on the road, they make a particularly wonderful rich man's plaything if Mr. Portfolio happens to be an
off-road enthusiast.

The Hummer is arguably the finest production off-road ve-   9
hicle in the world, and certainly the best I've ever driven. I had
the thing in deep sand and on hideously rutted trails, and I never
got close to sticking it.

Most of the Hummer's off-road facility is evident just from   10
looking at it. It has 16 inches of ground clearance, which is
about twice that of a conventional sport-ute. The all-terrain tires
on the test vehicles were the biggest I've ever seen. At 37 inches
in diameter, they weren't so much tires as rubber-coated Ferris
wheels. Also, the Hummer's short front and rear overhang give it
extraordinary angles of approach and departure.

Indeed, this vehicle will perform stunning feats. Because it is   11
so wide and stable it can traverse grades that would send ordinary four-wheelers rolling down the hill. Its great clearance
allows it to climb 22-inch steps without bottoming out. It can
also ford a creek 2½ feet deep.

Driving the rather hard-riding Hummer on the road is less   12
impressive. You are constantly aware of its width on narrow city
streets, and of the decibel level of its 6.5-liter General Motors
diesel V-8.

The folks at AM General made much of the fact that the huge   13
diesel had been quieted down with additional sound insulation
since the first time I drove the Hummer in early 1996. Presumably, we should be thankful for small things. Instead of being
seated in the fourth row at the heavy metal concert, we now
have tickets for row seven.

Because the vehicle is so wide and has such a large drivetrain   14
tunnel, the driver feels light years away from the front-seat passenger. Granted, that minimizes fresh behavior on the first date.
But when you couple that great distance with the engine's great
noise, you also minimize first-date conversation.

Some of the comfort and convenience touches that have   15
been installed on the Hummer—including air conditioning—
are welcome. Others, such as the clearance-diminishing running
boards on the test vehicle, are dumb. And still others, including
the ersatz wood trim on the tester's dashboard, have the effect of
emasculating the most macho vehicle in the world.

Personally, I don't want the Hummer to get too civilized. I   16
don't want them to teach Genghis Khan to use the right fork.

VOCABULARY WORDS: configurations (5), personnel (5), rendition (6), amenities (7), arguably (9), facility (10), traverse (11), ersatz (15), emasculating (15)

ACTIVITY 2

Reading to Improve Writing. Discuss the following questions about "Hummer: Still a Rich Man's Toy" with your classmates.

1. What is Haas's opinion of the Hummer? Where in the evaluation does he state this opinion?

   _____

   _____

   _____

2. In addition to describing the Hummer's good qualities, why does Haas describe the drawbacks to the vehicle?

   _____

   _____

   _____

3. Why does Haas compare the Hummer to other sport-utility vehicles?

   _____

   _____

   _____

4. How does Haas attempt to keep his audience interested in his topic?

   _____

   _____

   _____

ACTIVITY 3

Gathering Ideas about a Product. Gather ideas about a product you want to evaluate. Consider writing about a product you use every day—a car, a backpack, a cell phone. Think of your audience as people interested in purchasing the product. Your evaluation will affect their decision to purchase (or not to purchase) the item. Use the following questions to stimulate your thinking.

1. What is your overall opinion of the product? Why do you have this opinion?
2. What is good about the product? What is bad about it?
3. What experiences have you had with the product that formed your opinion of it?
4. Compare the product with other similar products. How is it better? How is it worse?
5. What research could you do to learn more about the product?
6. Who would be interested in reading about the product? Why would they be interested?

One student, Janice, decided to write about the CD player, a Fitzhugh 6000, she recently purchased. To gather ideas about her topic, Janice answered the questions in Activity 3.

1. *My overall opinion is that the Fitzhugh 6000 is the best CD player on the market in its price range because of its excellent sound quality, convenience, and reliability.*

2. *What's good about it—how it sounds, that it's easy to use, that it never breaks down, and that it's a good value. What's bad about it—it doesn't have a remote volume. Also, some of my friends don't think it sounds as good as I think it does.*

3. *I've had this CD player for over a year, and I've listened to it nearly every day. I've never had any problems with it. It always sounds good. It even works well with some of my discs that are scratched.*

4. *I've listened to the same CDs on the Packer 250, which costs about the same, but its sound quality isn't as good.*

5. *I could listen to some CDs on other CD players and compare how they sound. I could also read about CD players in music magazines.*

6. *A lot of people either own a CD player or are interested in purchasing one. I think these people would want to read my paper.*

Put your writing about a product aside for now, so you can gather ideas for another type of evaluation—a performance.

Evaluating a Performance

Before investing your hard-earned money in a movie ticket, you decide to read a review of the movie in a newspaper. If the review is positive, you're more likely to see the film. Newspapers and many magazines carry reviews of movies, music concerts, art shows, dance performances, museum exhibits, books, television shows, and sporting events.

In "Blood and Circuses," critic Brian D. Johnson evaluates the movie *Gladiator.* As you read the essay, notice how Johnson uses comparisons with other movies to support his evaluation.

BRIAN D. JOHNSON

Blood and Circuses

For a certain generation, the thrill of discovering the movies began at the close of the 1950s, with the so-called sandal epics of *Ben-Hur* and *Spartacus*—spectacles with monumental sets, casts of thousands and bronzed warriors goring one another in mix'n'match ensembles of loin cloths, leathers and chains. Since then, the genre has fallen out of fashion, but with *Gladiator,* the first major sandal epic in 40 years, director Ridley Scott makes an extravagant bid to restore its faded glory.

Gladiator is a blockbuster movie about the culture that originated the thumbs-up/thumbs-down school of reviewing blockbuster entertainment: ancient Rome, city of bread and circuses. Yes, it's violent, and perhaps too graphic for some, but a gladiator movie without a decapitation or two would seem as inappropriate as *The Godfather* or *GoodFellas* without a garrotting. Scott, the visual adventurist who directed *Blade Runner, Alien* and *Thelma & Louise,* has engineered a grandiose spectacle that is not half as smart as it pretends to be. It wields its religiosity, and its democratic morality, with the subtlety of a broadsword. But this is a ferociously entertaining spectacle, with thrilling action sequences, eye-popping art direction and uniformly powerful performances.

Gladiator is a long film about killing: the story of an untarnished hero fighting for truth, vengeance and the Roman way. Russell Crowe stars as Maximus, a devoted general who just wants to go back to the farm and see his wife and family after years of fighting on the front lines. But the dying Emperor Marcus Aurelius (Richard Harris) calls upon him to assume the throne after his death and replace a corrupt empire with a republic ruled by the Senate. The emperor's jealous son, Commodus (Joaquin Phoenix), has other plans. Hastening his father's death, he proclaims himself heir and orders Maximus and his family killed—Maximus escapes only to be sold into slavery. Groomed as a gladiator, he works his way back to Rome until, as a star contender, he is face-to-face with Emperor Commodus at the Colosseum.

The movie opens with a massive battle between Romans and   4
barbarians in the woods of Germania. Shot in a grey, wintry light, with volleys of flaming arrows piercing the gloom, the scene recalls the opening assault in *Saving Private Ryan*. There is the same digital grain to the bloodshed, an impression of intimate carnage. And throughout the film, Scott shoots the fighting in close, cutting so fast that the editing and the swordplay become synonymous. It can get confusing—as at a sports event, you want to be able to follow the play—but the visceral excitement of the scenes is undeniable.

Although Scott's bombastic direction, buoyed by Hans Zim-   5
mer's Wagnerian sound track, constantly threatens to overwhelm the movie, Crowe keeps grounding its realism with the same tenacity and rage that he brought to *The Insider*, while his co-stars flesh out the script's stereotypes. Phoenix artfully toys with the campy inflections of his ready-for-therapy villain, an unloved wimp with incestuous designs on his sister—sharply portrayed by Connie Nielsen. Richard Harris and Derek Jacobi add a dash of Brit dignity, which we've come to expect from ancient Romans. And Oliver Reed, who drank himself to death near the end of the shoot, uncorks a robust swan song as the farm-team slave trader who becomes head coach to the gladiators. "Win the crowd," he tells them, "and you'll win your freedom."

Gladiator is mass entertainment about mass entertainment.   6
When Scott offers an aerial shot of the Colosseum, it's hard not to think of the Goodyear blimp drifting over the Super Bowl. And although this is not exactly a movie of ideas, the script likes to draw modern links between politics and marketing. "The beating heart of Rome is not in the marble of the Senate, but in the sand of the Colosseum," says one character, reminding us that the box office conquers all. At one point, a sarcastic Maximus turns to the mob and yells: "Are you not entertained?" Yes, we are. And we'd prefer not to feel guilty about it.

VOCABULARY WORDS: genre (1), decapitation (2), garroting (2), grandiose (2), untarnished (3), synonymous (4), visceral (4), bombastic (5), tenacity (5), incestuous (5)

ACTIVITY 4

Reading to Improve Writing. Discuss the following questions about "Blood and Circuses" with your classmates.

1. What is Johnson's opinion of *Gladiator*? Does he express this opinion in a single sentence? If so, indicate what sentence this is.

   _____

   _____

   _____

   _____

2. What reasons does Johnson give to support his point?

   _____

   _____

   _____

   _____

3. Why does Johnson make comparisons to other movies?

   _____

   _____

   _____

4. Explain the meaning of the last sentences of Johnson's evaluation: "At one point, a sarcastic Maximus turns to the mob and yells: 'Are you not entertained?' Yes, we are. And we'd prefer not to feel guilty about it."

   _____

   _____

   _____

ACTIVITY 5

Gathering Ideas about a Performance. Gather ideas about a performance you want to evaluate. The performance may be a live one—such as a concert, comedy show, sporting event, dance recital, or play—or one that has been recorded—such as a movie or television show. Select a performance that you remember well and know something about. (If you select a movie or television show, you have the advantage of being able to watch it more than once on a VCR.) Think of your audience as consisting of people interested in attending or viewing the performance. Use the following questions to stimulate your ideas.

1. What is your overall opinion of the performance? Why do you have this opinion?
2. What is good about the performance? What is bad about it?
3. Compare the performance with other similar performances. How is it better? How is it worse?
4. What research could you do to learn more about the performance?
5. Who would be interested in reading about the performance? Why would they be interested?

Here's how one student, Gus, used the questions in Activity 5 to brainstorm about the play *Steel Magnolias*. On his computer screen, he made a chart for his responses. Here's a sample:

Overall opinion: The play is excellent and shouldn't be missed, even if you've already seen the movie.

What was good: The acting made me feel for the characters. The humor was great.

What was bad: A little too long.

Comparison: The play was better than the movie because the actors were better.

Research: I could read the play so I could quote lines in my evaluation.

Audience: People interested in seeing the play, comparing it to the movie, or even acting in the play might want to read my review.

Put your ideas about a performance aside for now, so you can gather ideas for one more type of evaluation.

Evaluating a Place

A new shopping mall opens near your town, and you spend an afternoon visiting the stores, examining the layout, and sampling products from the food court. Afterwards, you decide that you like the mall but wish it had a parking garage. You have just evaluated a place. Other places you might evaluate include a museum, park, college or office building, apartment, classroom, theater, store, library, and restaurant.

In "Mix Blends Tasty Food with Classy Ambience," Max Romero evaluates a restaurant. As you read the essay, notice how the writer supports his evaluation with descriptive details. (You may also notice that Romero intentionally uses some sentence fragments because he is writing in a humorous, informal way.)

MAX ROMERO

Mix Blends Tasty Food with Classy Ambience

For a split-second after walking into the Mix, I wondered if I should have worn "The Disguise." 1

You know . . . "The Disguise," that time-honored set of camouflage clothing worn by slackers since beatniks first found out they couldn't ALL make a living writing whacked-out poetry. Slacks (a subtle slap of irony there). Shoes without a hint of Velcro. A shirt with buttons that go from top to bottom with a collar. If you're really going into "deep cover," then you may need to strap on that modern-day noose known as a necktie. 2

Surrounded as I was by beautifully tiled floors, elegantly simple furnishings and the sense that maybe I had wandered into an art gallery by mistake, jeans and a T-shirt didn't seem as if it would cut it. 3

But, true to its name, Mix isn't afraid of stirring all sorts of ingredients into its culinary melting pot. 4

The slightly upscale restaurant is a little dash of something different itself (not to mention different from its sister restaurant Downtown, La Norteña, a nouveau Mexican food eatery also brought to you by owner Mick Lynch). Parked on one end of the fabled string of restaurants in the Kern Place area, Mix is beyond the bar-and-grill types of eateries populating the strip. There is a bar, but it's mostly someplace to sit while waiting for your table, not necessarily where you'd watch the game. 5

And your table's where you want to be. Not only does the service make you feel more than welcome, but the menu will make 6 you feel as if someone's rolled out the red carpet. There is a classy variety of appetizers to choose from, as well as a number of soups and salads for those who have a little more room in the basement.

Don't close that door yet. Once you've polished off appetizers (in this case, an order of the roasted corn—plus a handful of grilled veggies tossed together into something more like a relish) and had a chance to absorb the floor show (this night: black turtlenecks and people wearing sunglasses), it's time for the entree. 7

Two tips for making the most out of dinner at Mix: make sure you've got enough dough, and skip lunch—you want to make sure you'll be able to afford the slightly pricey meals and you want to make sure you've saved your appetite. 8

Especially if you have a bowl of soup first. The cream of tomato concoction served at Mix is an experience. The soup is a generous serving of a "special-sauce" looking combination of garlic (lotsa garlic), tomato, and a little more garlic. If you don't like garlic, you won't like this soup (one diner decided it was "a little too much" and left it unfinished), but if you love garlic, you'll want to give this soup a name and marry it. 9

But don't commit just yet—there's still dinner to be had. This night we decided to go with the pork chops stroganoff and the crispy half chicken, and we weren't disappointed. The chops, served on a mound of creamy pasta and joined by a glop of "smashed" potatoes, were cut thick and came in pairs. They also could have been a little bit juicier, but not much, and besides, the rich sauce more than makes up for it. 10

The chicken, on the other hand, hit a perfect balance, sporting a crispy outside and a surprisingly moist inside. 11

But make sure to chew. The reason it's called the crispy half chicken is because it's a crispy chicken split right down the middle—WHACK!—leaving behind some chicken shrapnel, namely some rib and breast bone bits. Eat carefully, especially since the stuffing of onions, thyme and sage will have you shoveling faster than a ditchdigger on a rainy day. 12

Finally, it was time for dessert. Unfortunately, it was near closing and the kitchen was closed, limiting dessert choices. Fortunately, this meant ordering what turned out to be a huge, honking piece of cheesecake garnished with whole sliced strawberries. The cheesecake was superior, almost crumbly on the fork but rich and creamy on the palate. It was also generous enough a serving that could be shared, and no one felt left out. 13

Which is a lot like Mix itself; plenty for everyone, and everyone's welcome to have a taste for themselves. 14

And you don't even have to wear a tie. 15

VOCABULARY WORDS: camouflage (2), slackers (2), culinary (4), nouveau (5), concoction (9), shrapnel (12), garnished (13)

Reading to Improve Writing. Discuss the following questions about "Mix Blends Tasty Food with Classy Ambience" with your classmates.

1. What does Romero like about this restaurant?

_____

_____

2. How does Romero introduce his review? Why does he introduce it this way?

_____

_____

_____

3. Why does the writer describe in detail the dishes served at the restaurant?

_____

_____

4. How does Romero keep his audience interested in his evaluation?

_____

_____

Gathering Ideas about a Place. Gather ideas about a place you want to evaluate. Choose a place that is important to you and that others might want to know about, such as a new restaurant close to campus or an entertainment park that recently opened. Use the following questions to stimulate your thinking.

1. What is your overall opinion about the place? Why do you have this opinion?
2. What is good about the place? What is bad about it?
3. Compare the place with other similar places. How is it better? How is it worse?
4. What research could you do to learn more about the place?
5. Who would be interested in reading about the place? Why would they be interested?

One student, Jody, decided to evaluate her dorm. Here is part of her freewriting:

> *Dryden Hall is such a rip-off, I can't believe it. My room looks like a hospital room—no carpet, plain furniture, a small window that looks out at a brick wall. My roommate and I are squished together like rats. There aren't any social activities, and every time you turn on your computer or hair dryer you never know if there's going to be a blackout. If this place were cheap, it might be okay, but it's one of the most expensive dorms on campus! I wish I could live in Johnson Hall, which looks a lot nicer, has a lot of activities, and is cheaper.*

DRAFTING

You have now gathered ideas to evaluate a product, performance, and place. At this point, you must decide how to proceed. Here are some of your options:

- You may select one of these topics for your discovery draft.
- You may write drafts on two or three of these topics to see which one you prefer to continue working on.
- You may combine related topics in your discovery draft, or even choose a new topic for your essay.

Because you will write a persuasive essay in which you make an evaluation, select a topic about which you can make a judgment.

For more information about writing a discovery draft, see pp. 34–35.

Before you begin writing your discovery draft, narrow your topic and write a preliminary thesis statement. As you write, follow your train of thought, even if it means revising your thesis statement later on. Keep your audience and purpose in mind, but remember that your main goal at the drafting stage is to get your ideas down on paper. You'll have time later to revise and edit your discovery draft.

Here's the discovery draft written by a student, Jody Albert, whose freewriting you read earlier. In this draft, Jody evaluates her college dorm. After reading the draft, discuss with your classmates what Jody might do to revise it. (Note that the example includes the types of errors that typically appear in a first draft.)

Avoid Dryden Hall

1 I was away from home for the first time, eager to move into my home away from home--Dryden Hall. I excitedly opened the door to my new dorm room. What I saw disappointed me. It was a little room with no carpeting and a window with a view of a brick wall. This was only the first of many disappointing things about this dorm.

2 Dryden Hall is one of the most expensive dorms on campus, but you'd never know it by looking at it. Repainting is needed. The colors are drab and the walls are chipped. The furniture in the lobby looks like they got it at a flea market. The rooms look like hospital rooms, with plain cupboards and dirty white tile. Dryden Hall is unattractive. It has shabby furniture and a stained carpet.

3 Dryden Hall also needs to be renovated because so many students now use computers to get into the library's resources and to talk to each other on e-mail. Right now, the dorm isn't plugged into the campus computer system, so you can't do any of these things. The dorm also has an out-of-date intercom phone system. This is useless because most residents have telephones. Sometimes the electricity goes out because the electrical wiring can't take all of our microwaves, televisions, and VCRs.

4 Socially Dryden Hall is bad. It is a disaster. When I came here, I didn't know anyone. I thought that living in a dorm would help me make friends. Not in Dryden Hall! Yes, I have gotten to know my roommate and a few of the other

girls on my floor. The social events are completely inadequate. These are the social events that are planned in advance. The monthly pizza party only lasts about fifteen minutes because we run out of food and drinks so quickly. The other regular social activity is a Sunday morning breakfast from 8-10 a.m. Most of us sleep later than that.

One thing that is good about Dryden Hall is the number 5 of study rooms, several on each floor. These rooms have comfortable furniture. Also, tutors are available in most of the study rooms in the evenings. The dorm is usually quiet, so it's pretty easy to study even in your own room.

If I could do it all over again, I'd choose Johnson 6 Hall, which is older than Dryden Hall but which has recently been renovated. It has attractive rooms, many good social activities, and is less expensive compared to Dryden Hall. Choosing Dryden Hall was definitely a mistake.

Gather Ideas during Drafting

If you run out of ideas while drafting, press "enter" a couple of times and begin to use one of your favorite techniques for gathering ideas, such as freewriting or brainstorming. When you think of something you can use, cut and paste it into the draft.

REVISING

For more help revising paragraphs, go to pp. 39–41.

When you revise your draft, use the skills you acquired in the preceding chapters. Support and clarify your main ideas, organize your paragraphs, make your ideas flow smoothly, and write an effective introduction, conclusion, and title.

FAQs

The *Choices* Web site includes frequently asked questions about topics in each chapter of the textbook. Go to <www .bedfordstmartins.com/choices/> and click on "FAQs."

Developing Your Ideas

Most writers find that their discovery draft needs additional information to make it more interesting and informative. As you revise, consider how you will develop your ideas so that you communicate more effectively.

EXPRESS A JUDGMENT. As you may recall from Chapter 2, the thesis statement announces the topic of your essay, shows, explains, or argues a particular point about the topic, and gives the reader a sense of what the essay will be about. For your evaluative essay, the thesis statement argues a particular point. Specifically, it expresses your judgment of the topic. Let's look at each of these qualities in more detail.

Express an Opinion. A judgment is an opinion about the value or merit of something. It's not a fact. Notice the difference between fact and judgment in these statements:

FACT   The Ford Mustang was among the most popular cars of the 1960s.

JUDGMENT   The Ford Mustang was one of the best cars made in the 1960s.

The first statement is factual because it can be verified by statistics concerning best-selling cars in the 1960s. The second statement expresses an opinion about the worthiness of the car. Some but not all people will agree with this statement.

Focus on the Subject. A judgment focuses on the subject being evaluated, not on the writer.

FOCUS ON THE WRITER   I really like my new Hungarian sports car.

FOCUS ON THE SUBJECT   The new Hungarian sports car is surprisingly fast and economical.

In the first example, the first-person *I* shows that the focus is on the writer. In the second, the first-person *I* has been replaced by the third-person *it*—the car. This change reflects the shift in emphasis, from the writer to the subject being evaluated.

Be Moderate, Not Extreme. A good thesis statement for an evaluative essay gives a sensible opinion about the subject. A sensible opinion is moderate rather than extreme.

EXTREME   Central College's library is the best college library in the country.

MODERATE   Central College's library has one of the best library computer systems in the area.

The extreme statement cannot be proven without visiting every college library in the country, whereas the moderate version is much easier to support.

A judgment is a type of thesis. For more help with thesis statements, see pp. 36–39.

Be Clear and Specific. A good thesis statement for an evaluative essay also expresses a judgment that is immediately understandable. If your readers can't understand your thesis statement, they won't understand the rest of your essay either. To make your thesis statement clear, use standard written English.

UNCLEAR   The new Student Union building is gross.

CLEAR   The new Student Union building is a disappointment because of its plain facade and cold, gray cinderblock interior.

The nonstandard *gross* (in this context) has been replaced with *disappointment,* a more precise word, and details have been added to explain the judgment.

A good thesis statement also tells why you have reached your judgment so that your readers can better understand your opinion about the topic.

VAGUE   The Georgia O'Keeffe show at the Art Institute was excellent.

SPECIFIC   The Georgia O'Keeffe show at the Art Institute was excellent because it displayed some never-before-seen paintings.

The first statement leaves readers asking why the show was excellent. The second statement answers that question.

HOW TO **Write a Thesis Statement for an Evaluative Essay**

- Express an opinion about the value or merit of something.

- Focus on the subject, not yourself.

- Use a moderate tone.

- Be clear and spec ific.

ACTIVITY 8 (GROUP)

Revising Judgments. Working with your peer response group, review the characteristics of a good thesis statement for an evaluative essay. Then determine the fault in each of the following thesis statements. Finally, revise each thesis statement accordingly.

1. The worst jeans ever made are manufactured by Salisbury, Inc.

    Fault(s): _____

    _____

    Revision: _____

    _____

2. Julia Roberts is an OK actor.

    Fault(s): _____

    _____

    Revision: _____

    _____

3. The Super Bowl is seen by millions of people around the world.

    Fault(s): _____

    _____

    Revision: _____

    _____

4. The Smithsonian is my favorite museum.

    Fault(s): _____

    _____

    Revision: _____

    _____

5. The Bradley running shoe is one of the newest shoes on the market.

Fault(s):   _____

_____

Revision: _____

_____

_____

ACTIVITY 9

Revising Your Judgment. Revise the thesis statement for your essay so that it meets the requirements for an evaluative essay: it expresses an opinion about the value or merit of your subject; focuses on the subject; is moderate, not extreme; and is clear and specific.

GIVE CRITERIA. As in other types of essays, you must support your thesis statement in an evaluative essay as well. You do this by informing your readers of the criteria on which you base your judgment. Criteria are the standards on which a judgment is based. For example, Al Haas, in "Hummer: Still a Rich Man's Toy," uses off-road facility as one criterion. For the Hummer to be evaluated highly, it must be able to perform well off-road. Remember, you should include enough criteria to inform your reader, your criteria should suit the topic, and if your criteria are not already obvious, you should explain them.

Include Enough Criteria. An effective evaluation is based on having enough criteria. In most cases, an effective evaluative essay has between three and five criteria. Judging a subject on the basis of only one or two criteria may not be enough to persuade your readers to accept your judgment. Imagine, for instance, if Brian D. Johnson had evaluated *Gladiator* only on the action scenes. As readers, we would

Highlight Your Criteria

To make it easier to determine whether you have enough criteria, highlight them in your draft using a particular color. The highlighting will show you whether you need additional criteria.

have been left with questions about the film's acting and plot, and we would have doubted the writer's judgment of the movie.

Use Suitable Criteria. The criteria on which your judgment is based should be suitable for your subject. Max Romero, for example, in "Mix Blends Tasty Food with Classy Ambience" does not claim that Mix is a good restaurant because of the color of paint on the walls. Rather, the criteria Romero uses—quality food, good service, classy atmosphere—are appropriate because most diners are concerned about such features in a restaurant.

Suppose, however, that Romero was writing his review for an audience of interior designers. In this case, the interior design elements—including the color of the walls—would be suitable criteria. In other words, what are "suitable" criteria depends on the characteristics or interests of your intended readers.

HOW TO Select Criteria

- Fill in the blanks: "I think that _____ is good/bad because _____ ."

- Think of as many reasons as you can for your opinion.

- Review your reasons to make sure they're suitable for the topic and audience. Limit yourself to three or four reasons.

ACTIVITY 10

Determining Whether You Have Enough Suitable Criteria. Following is a list of subjects and criteria. For each subject, an audience is given. Circle any criteria that are not suitable for evaluating the subject. Then determine whether there are an appropriate number of criteria for each subject. Add suitable criteria where necessary.

1. Subject: sports car
   Audience: readers of *Consumer Reports*
   Criteria: handling, power, style, cleanliness, price,

2. Subject: shopping mall
   Audience: readers of *Ladies' Home Journal*
   Criteria: types of stores, number of pay phones, location,

   _____

3. Subject: apartment
   Audience: readers of the classified ads in your local newspaper
   Criteria: lighting, number of rooms, spaciousness,

   _____

4. Subject: amusement park
   Audience: readers of *Parents* magazine
   Criteria: safety of park, price of admission, number of vending
                machines,

   _____

5. Subject: gym
   Audience: readers of *Fitness for Everyone*
   Criteria: number of weight machines, quality of weight ma-
                chines,

   _____

ACTIVITY 11

Examining the Criteria in Your Essay. Examine the criteria in
your own draft. Keeping your audience in mind, determine if you
have enough suitable criteria. Make any necessary changes.

Explain Your Criteria. When your readers might not understand
your criteria, you'll need to explain them. For example, in an evaluation of a computer, you would probably need to explain the importance of the computer's memory. Similarly, in evaluating a fashion
show, you would explain why music is essential to the show's success.

But not all criteria require explanation. In evaluating Mix, Max
Romero did not need to explain why one of his criteria for a good
restaurant is good food. Similarly, in evaluating a movie, Brian D.

HOW TO Explain Criteria

- Will your readers automatically see why your criteria are suitable to your subject? If not, you need to explain the criteria.

- For readers familiar with your subject, include a brief explanation of the criteria (such as, "A pair of jeans needs to be comfortable because they're worn so frequently").

- For readers unfamiliar with your subject, include a more detailed explanation of the criteria (such as, "All the seats in a sports arena should give spectators good visibility. You shouldn't have to sit behind a post that partially obstructs your view").

Johnson doesn't need to explain why good acting is a necessary criterion. Only when you think readers may have questions about a particular criterion should you explain it.

ACTIVITY 12 (GROUP)

Explaining Your Criteria. Work with several other students to explain the criteria for each of the following subjects.

1. Subject: a notebook computer

   Criterion: A notebook computer should weigh under seven pounds.

   Explanation: _____

   _____

   Criterion: A notebook computer should have a large hard drive.

   Explanation: _____

   _____

Criterion: A notebook computer should have a high-resolution monitor.

Explanation: _____

                 _____

                 _____

2. Subject: the Student Union at your college
   Criterion: The Student Union should offer a variety of food services.

   Explanation: _____

                 _____

                 _____

   Criterion: The Student Union should offer different activities and programs.

   Explanation: _____

                 _____

   Criterion: The Student Union should offer comfortable places to relax.

   Explanation: _____

                 _____

                 _____

3. Subject: a television documentary
   Criterion: A television documentary should be well researched.

   Explanation: _____

                 _____

Criterion: A television documentary shouldn't sensationalize topics in order to get high ratings.

Explanation: _____

                    _____

                    _____

Criterion: A television documentary should be on a topic relevant to many viewers.

Explanation: _____

                    _____

Do Group Activities Online

Group activities can be done online if you have access to a networked computer lab. Send your responses to a particular activity to your classmates' e-mail boxes.

ACTIVITY 13

Explaining the Criteria in Your Essay. Examine the criteria in your essay. Which criteria are obvious? Which criteria need to be explained? Add any necessary explanations.

PROVIDE EVIDENCE. An evaluative essay consists largely of evidence in support of a judgment. In other words, you need to explain to your readers how well your subject measures up to the criteria you apply. To do this, writers often use examples, facts, and expert testimony as types of evidence to explain how a subject measures up to the criteria.

Examples. Using examples to support your judgment makes your essay more interesting to read as well as more convincing. In "Mix Blends Tasty Food with Classy Ambience," Romero gives many examples to illustrate his points. For instance, he gives examples to show that the décor is indeed classy:

For more information on how to develop the paragraphs in your essay, see pp. 65–70.

Surrounded as I was by beautifully tiled floors, elegantly simple furnishings and the sense that maybe I had wandered into an art gallery by mistake. . . .

Romero also gives examples of the dishes as evidence that the menu is varied and tasty:

The cream of tomato concoction served at Mix is an experience.

This night we decided to go with the pork chops stroganoff and the crispy half chicken, and we weren't disappointed.

. . . a huge, honking piece of cheesecake garnished with whole, sliced strawberries.

Facts. Facts are a highly persuasive form of example, primarily because they can be verified by readers. They also demonstrate your knowledge of the topic. In "Hummer: Still a Rich Man's Toy," Haas uses facts to demonstrate his knowledge of the vehicle. He begins by stating the price of the Hummer:

With a price tag of $85,961 on the Hummer I tested, you also could say this is not a vehicle for those of us who clip food coupons from our newspaper.

He supports his point that the Hummer is a "rich man's toy" with another fact:

The people who buy it are almost all men who earn in excess of $250,000 a year.

Expert Testimony. Expert testimony—the opinion of people knowledgeable about a subject—can be used as a type of example to confirm a judgment. In evaluating a product, for instance, you might

HOW TO Generate Evidence

- List examples that support your criteria.

- Identify facts that support your criteria by observing the subject carefully.

- Refer to expert testimony. Look in a library database and on the World Wide Web for articles on the subject you're evaluating.

refer to *Consumer Report's* rating of the product. In evaluating a performance or a place, you could check a magazine or newspaper to see whether your subject has been evaluated by others. Awards can be considered a form of expert testimony because they're given by experts in a particular field. If a movie wins an Oscar for best director, it means that a team of successful movie directors thought highly of the film's director.

ACTIVITY 14 (GROUP)

Identifying Types of Evidence. Work with your peer response group to identify the types of evidence used in the following paragraphs.

1.　　The story of *Sex, Lies, and Videotape* is part of movie folk-lore: how Soderbergh, at twenty-nine, wrote the screenplay in eight days during a trip to Los Angeles, how the film was made for $1.8 million, how it won the Palme d'Or at the 1989 Cannes Film Festival, as well as the best actor prize for Spader. I am not sure it is as good as the Cannes jury apparently found it; it has more intelligence than heart, and is more clever than enlightening.

　　　　　　　　　　　　—Roger Ebert, *Roger Ebert's Video Companion*

Type(s) of evidence: _____

2.　　The most expensive hotels . . . pile on the extras and charge accordingly. Rooms at the Four Seasons in downtown Philadelphia visited by our reporter feature reproduction antique furniture, feather pillows, huge towels, lots of fancy soaps and shampoo, a telephone in the bathroom, and a minibar. The staff doted on our reporter and his family. The children got free cookies and milk (or soft drinks and popcorn), movies, and Nintendo games—all delivered to the room.

　　　　　　　　　　　　—*Consumer Reports,* "The Best Hotels"

Type(s) of evidence: _____

3.　　The AMC Grand's parking lot, which AMC says it has expanded to include 2,200 spaces, can still be a headache for customers. The entrances and exits create irritating traffic tie-ups, and customers often have to walk several blocks to the box office. By that time, a cold drink seems more a necessity than an indulgence.

　　—Philip Wuntch, "Dallas' Two New 'Megaplexes' Size up Nicely"

Type(s) of evidence: _____

4.   As cosmetics go, lipstick is the cheapest and most popular product on the market. That doesn't mean you can't spend a fortune on the stuff, however. Enter Princess Marcella Borghese's Superiore State-of-the-Art lipstick. Cost: $20 for 0.15 ounce. That comes to $133 an ounce. The same amount of Wet 'n' Wild or Artmatic lipstick, at less than $1 a tube, costs about $7. Of course, the Borghese lipstick has much prettier packaging. But you may want to save the $126 you'd spend for an ounce of this lipstick, and get yourself a whole line of beauty products instead.

— *Consumer Reports,* "Choosing a Lipstick"

Type(s) of evidence: _____

Using Keywords

Use keywords to locate articles on your subject in a library database or on the World Wide Web. Practice a keyword search in *The English Research Room* Web site. Go to <**www.bedfordstmartins.com/english_research/**> and click on "Interactive Tutorials."

ACTIVITY 15

Charting Your Criteria and Evidence. To help you visualize the connections between your criteria and evidence, list them in a two-column chart. First, write your thesis statement at the top of the page (to remind you of your judgment). Then, in the left column, list the criteria that you will use to make your judgment. In the right column, list the evidence that supports your judgment. (You should include several pieces of evidence for each criterion.)

Here's an example of a chart for "Hummer: Still a Rich Man's Toy":

CRITERIA	EVIDENCE
expensive	price of $85,961; purchased by men who earn more than $250,000
rugged	civilian version of the humvee; weighs more than three tons; twice as wide as cars
car amenities	gloss finishes; air conditioning; stereo
off-road	never stuck during test drive; 16 inches of ground clearance; 37-inch tires; short front and rear overhang; climbs 22-inch steps, fords a 2½-foot deep creek

on-road	wide for narrow streets; loud with 6.5 liter diesel V-8; great distance between driver and front-seat passenger
comfort	air conditioning; running boards; wood trim

Chart Your Criteria and Evidence

Use the drawing feature of your word-processing program to chart your criteria and evidence. Create two columns with a line drawn between them. Place your criteria in the first column and the evidence across from them in the second column.

ACTIVITY 16

Examining Your Evidence. Examine the evidence you use in your draft. Is your judgment supported by examples, including facts and expert testimony? Where can you include additional evidence to make your points more convincing? Add evidence where needed.

Write on Two Screens

Use a separate window when gathering evidence. Then use the cut-and-paste function to move your evidence to the main screen that contains your draft.

MAKE COMPARISONS TO SIMILAR SUBJECTS. Another way to support your judgment is to make comparisons between your subject and other similar subjects. In his evaluation, for example, Brian D. Johnson compared *Gladiator* with *Ben-Hur* and *Spartacus,* other movie spectacles that were set in ancient Rome. These comparisons make Johnson appear knowledgeable about his topic.

When making comparisons, be sure you focus on similar subjects. In evaluating the new campus recreation center, for example, you would not compare it to the college library. Instead, you might compare the new center with the old center to point out the improvements that have been made.

ACTIVITY 17

Finding Similar Subjects for Comparison. Work with your class-mates on the following list of subjects. For each main subject, identify two or three similar subjects that could be used to make a compari-son. Here's an example:

SUBJECT   Ford Explorer

SIMILAR SUBJECTS   Chevrolet Blazer, Nissan Pathfinder, GMC Jeep

1. Subject: The movie *Star Wars*

   Similar Subjects: _____

2. Subject: McDonald's

   Similar Subjects: _____

3. Subject: Häagen-Dazs Ice Cream

   Similar Subjects: _____

4. Subject: Wal-Mart department store

   Similar Subjects: _____

ACTIVITY 18

Using Comparisons in Your Essay. For your topic, list one or more similar subjects. Then consider how you might use these similar sub-jects to make a comparison and thereby support the judgment you make in your essay.

Organizing Your Essay

You organize an evaluative essay using the same organization that you learned in previous chapters. In an evaluative essay, however, you must balance your evaluation by providing both the positive and negative aspects. Let's see how this is done.

KEEP A BALANCED PERSPECTIVE. Readers know that few subjects are all good or all bad. Informing readers of both the negative and the positive aspects of your subject makes your evaluation more balanced. A balanced judgment shows readers that your evaluation is fair, reasonable, and believable.

You may recall from the restaurant review by Max Romero that he tells us about Mix's flaws: the food is pricey, the chicken has bone bits, and at closing time the dessert menu is limited. By sharing this information with the reader, he maintains a balanced perspective and thereby strengthens his believability.

You don't have to give equal space in an evaluative essay to the strengths and weaknesses of your subject. If your judgment about the subject is positive, briefly describe the negative aspects, as Romero does in his essay. If your judgment about the subject is negative, briefly describe the positive aspects.

ACTIVITY 19 (GROUP)

Analyzing for a Balanced Perspective. Work with a group of students to determine how Al Haas maintains a balanced perspective in "Hummer: Still a Rich Man's Toy" (pp. 306–8). First, create a two-column chart with the headings "Positive Aspects" and "Negative Aspects" at the top. Then, referring back to the reading as needed, list the positive and negative comments that Haas makes about the Hummer.

POSITIVE ASPECTS	NEGATIVE ASPECTS

Finally, analyze your findings by answering these two questions:

1. By showing both positive and negative aspects of the Hummer, how does Haas strengthen his evaluation?

2. What effect does this balanced perspective have on you as the reader?

_____

_____

_____

ACTIVITY 20

Charting the Positive and Negative Aspects of Your Subject. Gather ideas about the positive and negative aspects of your subject in a two-column chart. Label the columns "Positive Aspects" and "Negative Aspects." Then list the positive and negative features of your subject. Number the items in each column in the order that you plan to use them in your essay. As you revise your draft, use this chart to maintain a balanced perspective.

Polishing Your Sentences and Words

Now that you have improved the development and organization of your essay, you'll want to turn your attention to your sentences and words. Remember, an important part of the revising process is to revise your sentences and words to be clearer and more interesting.

COMBINING SENTENCES USING RELATIVE CLAUSES. In earlier chapters, you learned to combine short, closely related sentences in order to increase sentence variety and clarify the relationship between ideas. Another way to combine sentences is by using *relative clauses*. A relative clause begins with a *relative pronoun:*

RELATIVE PRONOUNS

who   which

whose   that

Who and *whose* refer to people. *Which* refers to people and animals. *That* refers to people and things.

A relative clause

- contains a subject and a verb.
- begins with a relative pronoun (who, whose, which, that).

- cannot stand alone as a sentence.
- appears in the middle or at the end of a complete sentence.

Here's how Jody revised two pairs of short sentences in her discovery draft by using relative clauses.

ORIGINAL   The dorm also has an out-of-date intercom phone system. This is useless because most residents have phones.

REVISED   The dorm also has an out-of-date intercom phone system *that is useless because most residents have phones.*

ORIGINAL   The social events are completely inadequate. These are the social events that are planned in advance.

REVISED   The social events *that are planned in advance* are completely inadequate.

By combining these sentences, Jody eliminated unnecessary words and communicated her thoughts more clearly.

Don't use commas when a relative clause identifies who or what it is referring to, as in the following example.

The book *that's on the table* belongs to Wilbur.

No commas are used before or after the relative clause because it's a necessary part of the sentence: it tells which book—the book on the table—is the one that belongs to Wilbur.

See the Sentence Subordination section of the Handbook (pp. 682–85) for more help combining sentences using relative clauses.

> ## HOW TO Combine Sentences with Relative Clauses
>
> - A relative clause contains a subject and verb, is not a complete sentence, and begins with a relative pronoun: *who, whose, which,* and *that.*
>
> - A relative clause can be added to the middle or end of a complete sentence.
>
> - Use a comma or commas when the relative clause adds information not necessary to the meaning of the sentence.
>
> - Don't use commas when a relative clause adds information that identifies the word it's referring to.
>
> - Don't use commas when the relative clause begins with *that.*

In contrast, use commas when the relative clause gives information that's *not* essential to understanding the sentence.

The book, *which is on the table,* is by one of my favorite authors.

Commas are used in this example because the relative clause—*which is on the table*—is simply adding information. The sentence makes sense without it: *The book is by one of my favorite authors.*

Avoid using commas with relative clauses that begin with *that:*

The bicycle *that's been sitting in the garage* is too small for my children to ride.

ACTIVITY 21

Combining Sentences. Combine the following pairs of sentences using relative clauses. You may need to eliminate unnecessary words or move words around. Use a comma or commas when the relative clause is unnecessary for the sentence to be understood.

1. *North by Northwest* is one of my favorite movies. It was directed by Alfred Hitchcock. It was made in 1959.

   _____

   _____

2. Cary Grant plays an advertising executive. His name is Roger Thornhill.

   _____

   _____

3. Cary Grant is framed for killing a U.N. diplomat. He is mistaken for a man named George Kaplan.

   _____

   _____

4. James Mason plays a foreign spy. The spy's name is Phillip Van-damm. James Mason was a British actor.

_____

_____

5. Eva Marie Saint plays a beautiful blonde woman. The woman's name is Eve Kendall. Eve Kendall is actually Phillip Vandamm's lover.

_____

_____

6. Cary Grant falls in love with Eva Marie Saint on a train. He's trying to escape from Mason.

_____

_____

7. One of the most famous scenes in the film is when Cary Grant is chased by a small plane. The small plane is flying above a corn-field in the Midwest.

_____

_____

8. Cary Grant, James Mason, and Eva Marie Saint eventually end up at Mount Rushmore. Mount Rushmore provides a unique setting for the movie's finale.

_____

_____

9. *North by Northwest* is typical of many Hitchcock movies. It has mistaken identities, a cool blonde woman, and a man. The man is chased by people he doesn't know.

_____

_____

_____

10. *North by Northwest* is one of the greatest thrillers. It is one of the greatest thrillers Alfred Hitchcock ever made.

_____

_____

AVOIDING SEXIST LANGUAGE. Another way to polish your sentences and words is to look for sexist language in your essay. Sexist language unfairly excludes or denigrates women or men. Nonsexist language, in contrast, either makes no mention of sex or includes both sexes.

Inexperienced writers often use the masculine pronouns *he, his,* and *him* to refer to both men and women. Today, this usage is recognized as sexist because it excludes women. Instead, use both masculine and feminine pronouns, such as *his or her,* or rewrite the sentence, using a plural pronoun such as *they, theirs,* or *them.*

SEXIST	The student was looking forward to his spring break.
NONSEXIST	The student was looking forward to spring break.
NONSEXIST	Students were looking forward to spring break.
SEXIST	Because his job involves travel, a basketball player should receive travel pay.
NONSEXIST	Because his or her job involves travel, a basketball player should receive travel pay.
NONSEXIST	Because their jobs involve travel, basketball players should receive travel pay.
SEXIST	Everyone has a right to his own opinion.
NONSEXIST	Everyone has a right to his or her own opinion.
NONSEXIST	People have a right to their own opinions.

Another kind of sexist language occurs when we refer to occupations that traditionally excluded women or men. Because of changes in the workplace, terms that imply that only men or women pursue these occupations are no longer accurate. Use terms that include both women and men. Here are some examples:

SEXIST LANGUAGE	NONSEXIST LANGUAGE
stewardess	flight attendant
actress	actor

HOW TO Avoid Sexist Language

- Don't use *he, his,* and *him* to refer to both men and women.

- Use plural pronouns whenever possible: *they, theirs,* or *them.*

- Don't use terms that exclude women or men, such as *chairman, salesman,* or *waitress.*

- Use terms that include both men and women: *chairperson, salesperson,* or *server.*

fireman	firefighter
policeman	police officer
chairman	chairperson or chair
congressman	member of Congress; congressional representative
salesman	salesperson
weatherman	weather forecaster
waitress	server

Similarly, substitute a nonsexist term for *man* and *mankind* when these words are used to refer to both sexes.

SEXIST	the average man in the street
NONSEXIST	the average person
SEXIST	what's good for all of mankind
NONSEXIST	what's good for all of humanity
SEXIST	man-made fabric
NONSEXIST	synthetic fabric

Use Search and Replace

If you realize you have used sexist language several times in an essay, use the search function on your word-processing program to locate and revise the language. For instance, if you used *man* instead of *person,* you could do a search for *man* and replace it with a more suitable word.

ACTIVITY 22

Eliminating Sexist Language. Revise the following sentences as needed to eliminate sexist language.

1. Airline stewardesses are responsible for passengers' safety.

   _____

   _____

2. Every student should bring his book to class.

   _____

   _____

3. The weatherman reported an 80 percent chance of rain.

   _____

   _____

4. Because a salesman spends so much time traveling, he should have a good car.

   _____

   _____

5. Mankind has a long history of warfare.

   _____

   _____

6. Each graduate was happy he was finally getting a job.

   _____

   _____

7. Employees and their wives are eligible for the free trip.

_____

_____

8. For many years Barbara Boxer was a congressman from California.

_____

_____

9. Has everyone done his homework?

_____

_____

10. A new secretary needs to be trained to use her computer.

_____

_____

Jody's Revised Draft

Before you read Jody's revised draft, reread her discovery draft (pp. 319–20). Notice, in particular, how Jody has improved the evaluation of her subject in the revision. (You will also notice some errors in the revised draft; these will be corrected when Jody edits her essay.)

Avoid Dryden Hall

I walked down the long, gray hall, looking for room 315--my room for the school year. My arms ached from carrying my two heavy suitcases. I put the key in the lock, turned it, and opened the door. I couldn't believe my eyes. The room looked as if it belonged in a hospital. The vinyl floor was scuffed and dull, the window had a view of a

1   Introduction is more interesting.

Judgment is more
specific.

brick wall, and the walls were painted a drab green. This was only the first of many disappointments I've had with my dorm. Dryden Hall is an overpriced dorm that lacks many of the amenities found in less expensive dorms. The inside of the building is unattractive, the wiring is outdated, and the social events are unsuccessful.

Criteria are
explained.

Where a person lives is important to his well-being.   2
Since so many students live in dorms, the college should try to make them attractive. The rooms should be clean, the walls painted an uplifting color, and the furniture fairly new. A dorm should also have updated facilities so that a student can plug into the college computer system in his own room. How else can students examine the library records or talk to their instructors on e-mail? A dorm should also offer opportunities for students to meet other people. Because many students are away from home for the first time. Finally, a dorm should be a good place to study.

Unattractive from the first floor to the top floor,   3
Dryden Hall has shabby furniture and a stained carpet. One of the couches even has its stuffing hanging out. The halls are painted a dark gray that makes them seem like tunnels, many of the rooms have walls with chipped paint or that need cleaning. The walls in my room, for example, are filled with holes from where former occupants have hung pictures. The kitchen on the top floor has rusty cupboards and an ancient sink.

Examples and facts
are added.

Dryden Hall also needs to be modernized. Part of our   4
fees pays for an out-of-date telephone intercom system that is useless because most residents have their own telephones. Sometimes the electricity goes out because the wiring can't take all of our microwaves, televisions, and VCRs. Most importantly, Dryden Hall isn't plugged into the campus computer system. Unlike students in other dorms, I can't use my computer to search the library records or communi-

cate with instructors or students on e-mail. This is a major inconvenience when I'm working late at night on an assignment.

Socially as well, Dryden Hall is a disaster. When I came here, I didn't know anyone. I thought that living in a dorm would help me make friends. Not in Dryden Hall! The social events that are planned in advance are completely inadequate. The main event here is a monthly pizza party. Unfortunately, they run out of pizza after about fifteen minutes, so no one stays around to meet anyone else. The dorm also serves donuts and coffee in the lobby every Sunday from 8 to 10 a.m. Way too early for me and many others. Surely some of the money we pay to stay in Dryden Hall could be used for more, and better, social events.

It is true that Dryden Hall is a good place to study. Each floor has several study rooms (all of them in need of repainting, of course). Tutors are available in most of these study rooms in the evenings. Because there's not much socializing, the dorm is usually quiet, so it's easy to study whenever necessary.

As I sit in my dorm room, staring at the cracked ceiling and the brick wall outside my window, I'm reminded of the mistake I made when I moved into Dryden Hall. I wish I had chosen to live in Johnson Hall, which is less expensive than Dryden Hall. It has been renovated inside and out and has alot of parties. I only hope that the word gets out about Dryden Hall so that other students don't make the same mistake.

5   Additional facts are added.

Facts support judgment.

6   Balanced perspective is given.

7   Comparison strengthens judgment.

Conclusion restates judgment.

ACTIVITY 23

Analyzing Jody's Revised Draft. Use the following questions to discuss with your classmates how Jody has improved her draft.

1. How has Jody improved her introduction?

   _____

   _____

   _____

2. Why is her thesis more effective now?

   _____

   _____

   _____

3. What criteria does Jody use to evaluate Dryden Hall? Does she use enough suitable criteria? Are they obvious or need explanation?

   _____

   _____

   _____

4. How well does Jody support her judgment with examples, facts, and expert testimony?

   _____

   _____

   _____

5. Does the comparison with Johnson Hall further support Jody's judgment? Why or why not?

   _____

   _____

   _____

6. Does Jody maintain a balanced perspective? Explain.

_____

_____

_____

7. How could Jody's revised draft benefit from further revision?

_____

_____

_____

ACTIVITY 24 (GROUP)

Using Peer Review. Form a group with two or three other students and exchange copies of your drafts. Read your draft aloud while your classmates follow along. Take notes on your classmates' responses to the following questions about your draft.

1. What did you like best about this essay?

_____

_____

_____

2. How interesting is my introduction? Do you want to continue reading the paper? Why or why not?

_____

_____

_____

3. What is my thesis statement? Is it effective? Does it express an opinion about the value or merit of my subject? Is it focused on the subject? Is it moderate rather than extreme? Is it clear and specific?

_____

_____

_____

4. What are my criteria? Are there enough of them, and are they suitable? Are they obvious, or do I need to explain them?

_____

_____

_____

5. How well do I support my judgment with examples, facts, and expert testimony?

_____

_____

_____

6. Do I maintain a balanced perspective? Why or why not?

_____

_____

_____

7. Do I make effective comparisons? Explain.

_____

_____

_____

8. How effective is my ending? Do I conclude in such a way that you know it's the end?

_____

_____

_____

Use Online Peer Review

If your class has a Web site, see whether the peer review questions are available on the site. If they are, you may be able to respond to your classmates' drafts electronically.

ACTIVITY 25

Revising Your Draft. Taking your classmates' suggestions for revision into consideration, revise your essay. In particular, focus on improving your thesis statement, criteria, evidence, and comparisons. Also work to maintain a balanced perspective. You may decide to omit unnecessary material or to rearrange parts of your essay more effectively as well.

Comment on Your Draft

Use the "comment" function of your word-processing program to insert suggestions for revision in your draft. The suggestions for revision (or "comments") will appear as highlighted words in your text, similar to your instructor's or classmates' handwritten comments.

EDITING

At this point you have worked hard to write an evaluation of a product, performance, or place. But before you can share your essay with your audience, you must edit it for correctness.

Presenting Titles Correctly

Learn more about what words need to be capitalized on pp. 715–17 of the Handbook.

In your evaluation, you probably referred to titles, such as those of movies, museums, or CDs. In a title, capitalize all words except for articles *(a, an, the)*, coordinating conjunctions *(and, but, or, for, nor, so)*, and prepositions *(of, on, in, at, with, for)*, unless they are the first or last word of the title.

Me Talk Pretty One Day   *Gone with the Wind*
Malcolm in the Middle   *The House on Mango Street*

Titles of short works or titles of parts of longer works are put in quotation marks. These include songs, short stories, book chapters, essays, articles in magazines or newspapers, and episodes of television shows. Do not, however, put the title of your own essay in quotation marks.

One of my favorite songs is "You've Lost That Loving Feeling."

I just watched an episode called "Never Say Never" of my favorite television show.

The magazine article you should read is "Five Symptoms of Skin Cancer."

Underline or italicize titles of longer works, including books, magazines, films, television shows, newspapers, magazines, computer software, and music albums or CDs.

Meet the Parents is a hilarious movie.

I have the most recent version of *Encarta* on my computer.

I read the *Cleveland Plain-Dealer* every morning.

HOW TO Present Titles

- Capitalize all words except for articles *(a, an, the)*, coordinating conjunctions *(and, but, or, for, nor, so, yet)*, and prepositions *(of, on, in, at, with, for)*, unless they are the first or last word of the title.

- Put in quotation marks the titles of short works such as the names of newspaper or magazine articles, episodes of television series, songs, book chapters, and essays.

- Underline or italicize the titles of longer works such as books, movies, television shows, magazines, newspapers, computer software, and music albums or CDs.

ACTIVITY 26

Presenting Titles. Correctly present the titles in the following sentences. Some sentences are correct.

1. One of my favorite records is o brother, where art thou?, and my favorite song on that album is o death.

   _____

   _____

2. I love that episode on I love Lucy that's called the Camping Trip.

   _____

   _____

3. Have you read "the silicon boys and their valley of dreams"? It's a great book about the development of the silicon valley.

   _____

   _____

4. Microsoft released windows ME with a great deal of publicity.

   _____

   _____

5. I can't get Shirley Jackson's story *The Lottery* out of my mind.

   _____

   _____

6. Some people find *There's Something about Mary* an offensive movie, but I think it's funny.

   _____

   _____

7. *Battleship Earth* with John Travolta is one of the worst movies ever made.

_____

_____

8. The movie Pretty Woman featured the song Pretty Woman by Roy Orbison.

_____

_____

9. Businesspeople of all kinds often consult the "Wall Street Journal."

_____

_____

10. My favorite work of William Shakespeare is Romeo and Juliet.

_____

_____

Online Grammar Skills Practice

The *Choices* Web site includes practice exercises for capitalizing titles. Go to <**www.bedfordstmartins.com/ choices/**> and click on "Exercise Central." After logging in, click on "Capitalizing Titles."

Jody's Edited Essay

You might have noticed that Jody's revised draft contained errors in grammar, spelling, and punctuation. Jody corrected these errors in her edited essay. Her corrections are underlined here. Her editing log follows her edited essay.

Jody Albert

Professor Rowley

English 0311

19 March 2002

Jody used correct MLA format for her paper. See pp. 359–63 for another example of correct MLA format.

Avoid Dryden Hall

    I walked down the long, gray hall, looking for room
315--my room for the school year. My arms ached from
carrying my two heavy suitcases. I put the key in the lock,
turned it, and opened the door. I couldn't believe my eyes.
The room looked as if it belonged in a hospital. The vinyl
floor was scuffed and dull, the window had a view of a
brick wall, and the walls were painted a drab green. This
was only the first of many disappointments I've had with my
dorm. Dryden Hall is an overpriced dorm that lacks many of
the amenities found in less expensive dorms. The inside of
the building is unattractive, the wiring is outdated, and
the social events are unsuccessful.

    Where a person lives is important to <u>his or her</u> well-
being. Since so many students live in dorms, the college
should try to make them attractive. The rooms should be
clean, the walls painted an uplifting color, and the
furniture fairly new. A dorm should also have updated
facilities so that <u>students</u> can plug into the college
computer system in <u>their own rooms</u>. How else can students
examine the library records or talk to their instructors on
e-mail? <u>Because many students are away from home for the
first time, a dorm should also offer opportunities for
students to meet other people</u>. Finally, a dorm should be a
good place to study.

    Unattractive from the first floor to the top floor,
Dryden Hall has shabby furniture and a stained carpet. One
of the couches even has its stuffing hanging out. The halls

1

2

3

are painted a dark gray that makes them seem like tunnels, and many of the rooms have walls with chipped paint or that need cleaning. The walls in my room, for example, are filled with holes from where former occupants have hung pictures. The kitchen on the top floor has rusty cupboards and an ancient sink.

Dryden Hall also needs to be modernized. Part of our   4 fees pays for an out-of-date telephone intercom system that is useless because most residents have their own telephones. Sometimes the electricity goes out because the wiring can't take all of our microwaves, televisions, and VCRs. Most importantly, Dryden Hall isn't plugged into the campus computer system. Unlike students in other dorms, I can't use my computer to search the library records or communicate with instructors or students on e-mail. This is a major inconvenience when I'm working late at night on an assignment.

Socially as well, Dryden Hall is a disaster. When I   5 came here, I didn't know anyone. I thought that living in a dorm would help me make friends. I was wrong. The main social event here is a monthly pizza party. Unfortunately, the organizers run out of pizza after about fifteen minutes, so no one stays around to meet anyone else. The dorm also serves donuts and coffee in the lobby every Sunday from 8 to 10 a.m., which is way too early for me and many others. Surely some of the money we pay to stay in Dryden Hall could be used for more, and better, social events.

It is true that Dryden Hall is a good place to study.   6 Each floor has several study rooms (all of them in need of repainting, of course). Tutors are available in most of these study rooms in the evenings. Because there's not much socializing, the dorm is usually quiet, so it's easy to study whenever necessary.

As I sit in my dorm room, staring at the cracked
ceiling and the brick wall outside my window, I'm reminded
again of the mistake I made when I moved into Dryden Hall.
I wish I had chosen to live in Johnson Hall, which is less
expensive than Dryden Hall. It has been renovated inside
and out and has <u>a lot</u> of parties. I only hope that the word
gets out about Dryden Hall so that other students don't
make the same mistake.

7

Jody's Editing Log

For more information on how to keep an editing log, see pp. 41–42.

3/20 — "Avoid Dryden Hall"

INCORRECT — Where a person lives is important to his well-being. (2)

ERROR — sexist language

CORRECT — Where a person lives is important to his or her well-being.

INCORRECT — A dorm should also have updated facilities so that a student can plug into the college computer system in his own room. (2)

ERROR — sexist language

INCORRECT — A dorm should also have updated facilities so that students can plug into the college computer system in their own rooms.

INCORRECT — Because many students are away from home for the first time. (2)

ERROR — sentence fragment

CORRECT — Because many students are away from home for the first time, a dorm should also offer opportunities for students to meet other people.

INCORRECT — The halls are painted a dark gray that makes them seem like tunnels, many of the rooms have walls with chipped paint or that need cleaning. (3)

INCORRECT — comma splice

CORRECT — The halls are painted a dark gray that makes them seem like tunnels, and many of the rooms have walls with chipped paint or that need cleaning.

INCORRECT   Not in Dryden Hall! (5)

ERROR   sentence fragment

CORRECT   I was wrong.

INCORRECT   Unfortunately, they run out of pizza after about fifteen minutes, so no one stays around to meet anyone else. (5)

ERROR   vague pronoun reference

CORRECT   Unfortunately, the organizers run out of pizza after about fifteen minutes, so no one stays around to meet anyone else.

INCORRECT   Way too early for me and many others. (5)

ERROR   sentence fragment

CORRECT   The dorm also serves donuts and coffee in the lobby every Sunday from 8 to 10 a.m., which is way too early for me and many others.

INCORRECT   alot (7)

ERROR   misspelled word

CORRECT   a lot

Online Grammar Skills Practice

The *Choices* Web site includes practice exercises in grammar, spelling, and punctuation. Go to <www.bedfordstmartins .com/choices/> and click on "Exercise Central." After logging in, click on the topic area in which you want to practice your skills.

ACTIVITY 27

Editing Your Essay. Using the Handbook in Part Four of this book as a guide, edit your revised essay for errors in grammar, spelling, and punctuation. Your classmates can help you locate and correct errors you might have overlooked. Add the errors you find and their corrections to your editing log.

Create an Error File

Create a file in which you list the types of errors you tend to make. Review this file when you edit your essay.

PUBLISHING

You're ready to share your essay with your audience—your instructor and classmates, as well as others interested in your topic. For instance, if you evaluated a product, consider sharing your essay with someone interested in purchasing the product. If you evaluated a movie, share your essay with someone who has also seen the film and then discuss your different viewpoints. If you evaluated a place, share your essay with someone who is familiar with that place and ask the person for feedback. You might also send your essay to someone who can take action on the issues related to your topic. Jody, for example, sent a copy of her evaluation of Dryden Hall to the person in charge of maintaining the residence halls on campus. A few months later, Dryden Hall was repainted.

CHAPTER CHECKLIST

- ☐ I gathered ideas for evaluating a product, performance, and place.
  - ☐ I wrote a thesis that expressed an opinion or judgment about the value or merit of the subject; focused on the subject, not the writer; was moderate, not extreme; and was clear and specific.

- ☐ I gave the criteria on which the judgment is based.
  - ☐ I used enough suitable criteria and explained those criteria that weren't obvious.
  - ☐ I provided evidence—examples, facts, and expert testimony—to support the judgment.
  - ☐ I made comparisons between my subject and other similar subjects to support the judgment.
  - ☐ I gave both the positive and negative aspects of my subject to maintain a balanced perspective.

- ☐ I combined short, closely related sentences with relative clauses.
- ☐ I revised to eliminate sexist language.
- ☐ I edited to eliminate incorrect presentation of titles and other errors in grammar, punctuation, and spelling.

REFLECTING ON YOUR WRITING

To help you reflect on the writing you did in this chapter, answer the following questions.

1. Compare your experience writing an evaluation with writing an expressive or informative essay. What did you find easiest and most difficult about these assignments?
2. What did you learn from writing this essay?
3. How will your audience benefit from reading your essay?
4. If you had more time, what more would you do to improve your essay before sharing it with readers?

Using your answers to these questions, update your Writing Process Report.

Writing Process Report

Date:

Strengths:

Weaknesses:

Plans for improvement:

Once you complete this report, freewrite about what you learned in this chapter about your writing and what you still hope to learn.

Evaluation of a Product

In the following essay, "The Game Room," author Peter Cohen evaluates three computer games that were released in 2001.

PETER COHEN

The Game Room

The game industry moves fast. The shelf life of many computer games is now measured in weeks—heck, some console games get discounted faster than dented cans of tomatoes. But low prices can be deceiving, because they don't necessarily indicate low value. If you look in the right places, you'll find some terrific games out there that cost next to nothing—and some that come absolutely free. 1

All three of the hard-to-find gaming treasures I'm about to share with you have a few things in common. They're inexpensive or free; they don't demand ridiculous amounts of memory or processor performance to operate effectively; and they're safe for the whole family—you won't find excessive violence, sex, or foul language here. 2

I Remember MCP When It Was a Chess Program

As a youth, I whiled away many an hour in my local videogame arcade, listening to Duran Duran cassettes on my Walkman. Back in the 1980s, Disney released *Tron*—a movie that gave me (and countless other young nerds) a totally different idea of what one could do with computers. The film mixed computer animation with live action footage to tell the story of a programmer unwittingly placed inside the world of a computer. Although it wasn't the greatest story ever told, the graphics—painstakingly rendered on a Cray supercomputer—were absolutely stunning. 3

Thanks to the advances in graphics and processing power over the intervening two decades, any PC or Mac can now render graphics of even better quality than the Cray could 20 years ago. That's opened the door for programmers such as Andreas Umbach, who introduced *GLtron* (an open-source game that uses OpenGL graphics). And thanks to Mac programmer Darrell 4

Walisser, *GLtron* has come to the Macintosh. Walisser provides regular updates, too.

In *GLtron,* you and your computer opponents pilot light-   5
cycles across a vast, flat, gridlike arena. As you ride, light barriers stream behind you. Make contact with a barrier—yours or your opponents'—and it will blast you to smithereens. Essentially, the game is a 3-D version of *Snake,* in which your goal is to trap your opponents and avoid their traps. *GLtron* gets a bit repetitive after a while, but it's a great deal of fun—perfect for a quick pickup game, and you can't beat it for the price (free).

Even though *GLtron* has sophisticated animation, it can run   6
at high frame rates, even on slower systems. This should appeal to users of older iMacs and other systems with only modest 3-D-graphics acceleration. A separate team is working on a Mac OS X version of *GLtron,* so if you've updated your system software, you're in luck.

Seeing the Forest for the Trees

Another gem I love is *Bushfire.* It comes from two brothers,   7
Aaron and Adam Fothergill, who have started a game-publishing and -developing firm called Strange Flavour. *Bushfire* is straight-up, old-school, side-scrolling fun.

You pilot a helicopter, and your goal is to put out fires in the   8
last forest populated by the rare, endangered goose spruce tree. You control the blaze by commanding parachuters to jump out of your helicopter and by dropping water from tanks on its underside. You have the ability to pick up your jumpers and transport them elsewhere, and you can refill your tanks by landing in forest streams. The challenges become progressively more difficult with each level. Eventually you must dodge airborne hazards such as flying lava rocks and panicked fowl, try to trap mad arsonists, and rescue civilians whose aircraft have crashed in the woods. One cool feature is an Extras folder full of Easter eggs and other goodies. The more you play, the more you're rewarded.

If you're familiar with classics such as *Choplifter* or *Armor*   9
Alley, you'll understand what the brothers Fothergill are attempting here; but the goal in *Bushfire* is the opposite—you aim to preserve, not to destroy. *Bushfire* is an extraordinary bargain at $3, given the hours you can spend playing it. It's perfect for a PowerBook and your idle commuting time on the train. Best of all, *Bushfire* is Carbonized, so it should run on Mac OS X without a hitch, despite previous compatibility problems in the course of development. The most current version as of this writing—1.10—works solidly in both Mac OS 9.1 and Mac OS X.

C'est Fromage

For a game with a completely cheesy plot that's lots of fun, try   10
out *Captain Bumper.* This comic action title comes from MacRun
Games, a new Mac game developer based in France.

Captain Bumper strongly evokes the game style made popu-   11
lar by the 16-bit video-game consoles (such as Super NES and
Sega Genesis) ubiquitous in early-nineties households, but the
game's design is all modern Mac. You take control of a square-
jawed hero piloting a spaceship on a mission to save a damsel in
distress (of course). With his bomber jacket, aviator glasses, and
jack-o'-lantern smile, Captain Bumper makes his way through
space, into labyrinthine caverns, and across inhospitable terrain,
all the while fending off the attacks of vicious green alien critters
bent on destroying him. You can collect power-ups, recharge
your fuel and weapons supply, and boost your shields as you
make your way toward the princess.

Captain Bumper is ideal for families in search of addictive   12
fun. The game has cartoonish graphics and rich, colorful backgrounds with great detail. The core engine, developed by Richard
Soberka, runs silky-smooth, just like a console title. The music is by
Jens Nilsson, who also produced the music for Pangea's *Nanosaur.*

Captain Bumper's licensing works a bit differently from that   13
of the other games mentioned here: MacRun takes advantage of
distribution on the Internet even though it's a commercial game.
You can download a two-level demo version from the company's
Web site, and if you decide you like it, you pay the $25 licensing
fee. In return, you receive a serial number and access to the complete version.

If I have any complaint about *Captain Bumper,* it's that the   14
game is too short. I'd love to see a level editor, or more add-ons
that would continue the fun. Then again, that's what sequels
were invented for. In this initial version, Mac OS X compatibility
is limited to the Classic environment.

Cheap, Wholesome Entertainment

For me, the three words above pretty much summarize these   15
three games. One is free, another is next to free, and the third is
less expensive than many games out there—that means *GLtron,*
Bushfire, and *Captain Bumper* will eat up less of your money and
more of your leisure time. And the best part is, you can download all three and try them right now.

VOCABULARY WORDS: console (1), unwittingly (3), fowl (8), arsonists (8), evokes (11), ubiquitous (11), labyrinthine (11), terrain (11)

ACTIVITY 28

Reading to Improve Writing. Discuss the following questions about "The Game Room" with your classmates.

1. What criteria does the author use to make his evaluation of the three computer games?

   _____

   _____

   _____

2. How does the author show that he's knowledgeable about the topic?

   _____

   _____

   _____

3. List three facts and examples that the author uses that you think are effective in supporting his evaluation. Explain why you think they're effective.

   _____

   _____

   _____

   _____

4. Did this essay make you want to play any of these computer games? Why or why not?

   _____

   _____

   _____

Evaluation of a Performance

One of the most popular television shows in the 1990s, *Seinfeld* was "a show about nothing"—the everyday experiences of Jerry, George, Elaine, and Kramer. Unlike many viewers, television critic Mary Ann Watson finds little to laugh about in this show.

MARY ANN WATSON
Seinfeld

It's been called "the defining sitcom of our age." Let's hope   1
that's hype. But, sadly, there's probably a big kernel of truth in it. Plenty of evidence confirms we're living in a self-absorbed, cynical era in which real creeps are often elevated as colorful nonconformists and the good-hearted and hard-working are dismissed as dull chumps.

For most of television history, the conventional wisdom has   2
been that television characters were surrogate friends and family. Therefore, they had to be people we cared about enough to worry about. In the 1980s, for instance, Gary David Goldberg, producer of *Family Ties,* explained that three things had to happen for his show to be successful: "One is the audience has to want to be part of that family. Then, the second thing is, they have to see themselves in that family. And, the third thing, and a very important thing, is that the audience has to begin to want to watch because they think they can learn how to be a better family."

Seinfeld totally rejected that mode of thinking. It is inten-   3
tionally a series without a moral center. In 1983, when *Buffalo Bill* broke the basic rule of episodic TV—that the lead character must be likable—there were supporting characters whose warmth juxtaposed with the caustic star and conveyed the message that core values count. But when it comes to *Seinfeld,* well, just call Western Union.

It's almost always a funny show but never a humane one—   4
kind of like a really well-told offensive joke. It's easy to appreciate it on one level yet naggingly troublesome on another. A recent article in the *National Review* speculated that the phenomenal popularity of *Seinfeld* is "an explicit rebuke to PC pieties." I'll buy that explanation. All of us—even those who feel we make genuine efforts to put ourselves in other people's shoes and see the world from their perspectives—have been stung by a charge of insensitivity at one time or another. The knee-jerk

reaction is to complain that political correctness has run amok rather than try to understand an unfamiliar point of view.

When George takes Kramer's advice to park in a space re-   5
served for the handicapped, a disabled woman who needed that space ends up in an accident. Their inconsiderate act is small potatoes, though, compared to the angry mob that destroys George's father's car. The PC do-gooders are the real villains. They cramp our style.

Seinfeld gives viewers who are tired of walking on eggs license   6
to laugh at deaf people, midgets, and the "boy in the bubble"—a child with an immune deficiency. Only the self-righteous and humorless would take offense. Screw 'em if they can't take a joke.

The lives of the principal cast members are regularly incon-   7
venienced by immigrants, aliens, and people of different cultures. Why can't they just ladle the soup, clean the sidewalk, park the car, empty the trash baskets, and show us to our table pleasantly? Wouldn't it be nice if they would just do their work and disappear? *Seinfeld* gives expression to feelings we've all had. But instead of feeling ashamed of our arrogance and intolerance, we're validated by the callousness of the prime-time gang.

The *Encyclopedia of Television* describes *Seinfeld* as "one of   8
the most innovative and inventive comedies in the history of American television." I'll buy that as well. The humor drawn from the quotidian and trivial is groundbreaking. I've enjoyed many good hard laughs of recognition and have great admiration for the talent and skill involved in producing the series. But, for me at least, the laughs that felt right became overshadowed by the ones that didn't. Some people will argue that there's no such thing as a bad laugh—or a bad orgasm. Beware of anyone over thirty who still believes it.

The *Seinfeld* season finale in May 1996 made me feel physi-   9
cally sick. George's fiancee Susan dies after licking toxic envelope glue on their wedding invitations. George is relieved since he was trying to weasel out of the marriage anyway. Upon learning the shocking news at the hospital, Elaine, Jerry, and Kramer are unmoved. They shrug in "that's life" resignation and urge George to join them for coffee.

I know, I know, it's supposed to be absurdist farce. I took   10
"Intro to Theater," too. But I just decided I didn't want any part of it. Maybe I'm not sophisticated enough to appreciate it. So be it.

I always thought a good litmus test for gauging the value of   11
a friendship is whether or not you're a better person for spending time together. I want my friends in real life and on TV to appeal to my better angels. And for those who don't—no matter how funny, attractive, or popular—I haven't the time.

So I didn't watch *Seinfeld* for a couple of seasons. Occasionally 12
I'd be left out of coffee-break conversation in the office lounge,
but never missed those guys. They certainly didn't miss me or the
handful of other viewers I've met who made the same decision to
stop watching the show because it just made them uneasy.

The popular press has kept us all abreast of the raises the 13
stars received, the phrases they introduced to the American lexicon, and the scores of web pages they inspired. And now, the end
of the show's nine-year run is generating a tidal wave of copy,
commentary, and ballyhoo.

The NBC affiliate in Detroit, WDIV, ran a sweeps weeks series 14
called "*Seinfeld* Extravaganza." A very good reporter, who could
have been investigating a story of real importance to the station's
viewers, was instead sent off to New York City to be a cheerleader
for the network's two-million-dollar-per-thirty-second-spot final
episode. The first of the five installments included an interview
with the man who inspired the character of Kramer. When asked
to give a hint about the sign-off plot, he would only guarantee
with a smile "there's not going to be any moral message here. It's
just going to be four despicable people living their despicable
lives, even more despicable than you ever saw them before."

Long after we're gone, when historians analyze America in 15
the 1990s, the good ones won't overlook *Seinfeld* as a clue to
what contributed to our collective character. Larry David, co-cre-
ator with Jerry Seinfeld, summarizes the show's guiding principle as "no hugging, no learning." It's the perfect formula for an
empty life turned into "Must See TV."

VOCABULARY WORDS: nonconformists (1), surrogate (2), juxtaposed (3), caustic (3), pieties (4), validated (7), quotidian (8), lexicon
(13), affiliate (14), despicable (14)

ACTIVITY 29

Reading to Improve Writing. Discuss the following questions
about *Seinfeld* with your classmates.

1. What criteria does the author use to support her evaluation?

_____

_____

_____

2. List three facts or examples that the author uses to support her evaluation. Explain how effective you found this evidence.

_____

_____

_____

3. Explain the significance of the phrase "no hugging, no learning" as applied to *Seinfeld*.

_____

_____

_____

4. Do you agree with the author's evaluation of *Seinfeld*? Why or why not?

_____

_____

_____

_____

Evaluation of a Place

One of the most popular museums in the United States is the Rock and Roll Hall of Fame and Museum in Cleveland, Ohio, which contains exhibits about rock and roll from its birth in the 1950s to the present. In "A Palace of Rock," Nicholas Jennings evaluates this museum soon after it opened in 1995.

NICHOLAS JENNINGS
A Palace of Rock

As museum pieces, they are the most humble of artifacts: a   1
few report cards, a black leather jacket, a pair of government-

issue eye glasses. Yet for many, the three objects are priceless. Once the property of John Lennon, those treasures are now on display at the recently opened Rock and Roll Hall of Fame and Museum in Cleveland, Ohio, where they are already among its most popular exhibits. Looking at the articles, it is easy to see why: each of them brings the viewer closer to the real Lennon. His elementary school report card reveals that one of his teachers found rock's future genius "hopeless," while the well-worn, sloppy jacket somehow perfectly captures the musician's irreverent charm. And Lennon's wire-rimmed spectacles trigger a flood of emotions because they are so evocative of the artist, who was fatally shot by a crazed fan in December, 1980. "Rock music has a power that makes you want to be a part of it," says museum director Dennis Barrie. "Hopefully, we represent some of that."

Judging by the scores of fans who flooded into the facility during its Labor Day weekend opening—an estimated 8,000 on the first day—Barrie need not worry: despite a once-shaky history, the Rock and Roll Hall of Fame and Museum is now a resounding success. Visitors can feast on more than 3,500 items, ranging from posters, album jackets and handwritten lyric sheets to movies and interactive exhibits that play requested songs and videos. Among the most memorable displays: a replica of the old Sun Studios in Memphis, Tenn., where Elvis Presley made his first records; a piece of Otis Redding's private airplane, which crashed in 1967; and the 1945 Magnavox tape recorder that pioneering musicologist Alan Lomax used to record blues legends such as Lead Belly and Muddy Waters. And Hall of Fame inductees Neil Young and The Band are reminders that rock has also thrived in Canada.

Meanwhile, hundreds of photographs, instruments and costumes—including Michael Jackson's famed sequinned glove and Madonna's gold bustier—are also housed in the museum's impressive, seven-level structure, a $123-million geometric shrine designed by New York City-based architect I. M. Pei, whose other accomplishments include the additions to the National Gallery of Art in Washington and the Louvre in Paris. From the air, the lakefront building resembles a record player with turntable, tonearm and a stack of 45s. But from the ground level, the elaborate structure is a cheeky mix of pyramid-like facades, rectangular towers and trapezoidal extensions that boldly jut out over Lake Erie.

The contents of the museum, like the all-star concert that launched it on Sept. 2—the roster of performers included Chuck Berry, James Brown, The Kinks, Creedence Clearwater Revival, Robbie Robertson and Bruce Springsteen—reflect rock in all of its ragged glory. For some, the very idea of chronicling the history of rock 'n' roll in a serious, curated institution is offensive. They argue that, like caging a wild beast, it runs counter to the laws of nature, as though rock music should always be allowed to roam free of commerce and academia. "Absolute nonsense," scoffs Rob Bowman, a professor of rock at Toronto's York University. "Rock has been institutionalized for at least the last 40 years, by record companies, radio stations and other media. Anyone who doesn't understand that is a hopeless romantic." Still, it is difficult to ignore some of the contradictions raised by the museum. Thirty years ago, The Who's Pete Townshend was smashing his guitar in a display of anarchic frenzy, yet the museum has one of his instruments respectfully encased in a glass cabinet. The irony is not lost on Ron House of the Columbus, Ohio-based band Thomas Jefferson Slave Apartments. The musician has written a punk protest song called "RnR Hall of Fame" that angrily tackles the subject. "I don't want to see Eric Clapton's stuffed baby/I don't want to see the shotgun of Kurt Cobain," sings House. "I don't want to see the liver of David Crosby/Blow it up before Johnny Rotten gets in."

Although Rotten's Sex Pistols have yet to be inducted by the   5
Hall of Fame Foundation (artists become eligible 25 years after their first recording), the British punk band is part of the museum's "Blank Generation" exhibit, which examines punk's birth in London and New York City between 1975 and 1980. Included is an 11-inch Sid Vicious doll, complete with chains, ripped T-shirt and swastika, that was used as a prop in the 1980 documentary, *The Great Rock 'n' Roll Swindle,* made a year after his death from a heroin overdose.

In fact, the museum strives mightily to keep up to date with   6
rock's more recent developments, charting the rise of rap music and Seattle's grunge scene. According to chief curator James Henke, a former editor at *Rolling Stone,* the museum's collection will be in constant flux. That is partly due to the fact that most display items are on loan, partly due to the nature of its subject matter. Says Henke: "Like the music, it'll always be evolving."

However, the collection is shamelessly skewed to the past.   7
Above the entrance to the main exhibition area is a neon sign quoting Chuck Berry: "Roll Over Beethoven." Berry and other such pioneers as Little Richard and Presley are well represented in a noisy, arcade-like space that includes small cinemas, record booths and computer screens. Amateur musicologists can trace the 500 songs that the museum has deemed to have shaped the history of rock 'n' roll. Among the oldest entries: Woody Guthrie's

1956 folk anthem "This Land is Your Land" and Louis Jordan's jump-blues classic "Caldonia," written in 1945. But the most revealing exhibit is The Beat Goes On, which traces musical family trees. Touch-screen computers allow museum-goers to click on images of musicians and discover their influences through video clips and songs. In some cases, the technology bridges generations. Lucy Schlopy, an 82-year-old visitor from Bradford, Pa., found that her favorite artist, Roy Orbison, had in turn influenced one of her great-niece's musical heroes, Bruce Springsteen. "I'm learning all kinds of things," said Schlopy.

Responses like that, says director Barrie, who previously 8 worked at the Smithsonian Institution in Washington and Cincinnati's Contemporary Arts Center, prove that the museum is a success. "People are actually reading, taking in the content of the exhibits," he beamed. "They're not just looking at the glittery costumes, which is very gratifying." At the same time, the costumed mannequins throughout the museum are proving to be among the biggest draws. Especially popular are Presley's leather stage outfit from his 1968 comeback TV special, Lennon's lime-green Sgt. Pepper's uniform and the "butterfly dresses" of Motown's The Supremes. For the kids, rock's schlock meister Alice Cooper, standing next to a guillotine and a bloody, severed head, is an awesome, cartoonish highlight.

By contrast, the actual Hall of Fame, housed on the top floor, 9 is a model of decorum. To get there, visitors climb a long, spiral staircase to reach a darkened room honoring the inductees (123 so far). Images of such legends as Buddy Holly and Bob Marley dissolve on tiny video screens like ghosts, while their signatures, etched on backlit glass plaques, seem to float in the ether. After the musical cacophony and video chaos downstairs, the Hall of Fame is a welcome sanctuary.

For the Hall of Fame's creators, the museum was a pipe 10 dream that almost never materialized. Founders Jann Wenner, editor of *Rolling Stone,* and Ahmet Ertegun, president of Atlantic Records, steered the project through three directors and one site change before the groundbreaking two years ago. Cleveland was chosen over Memphis and New York after residents collected 600,000 signatures and local businesses raised $87 million. But the city had already earned a place in rock history: Alan Freed, its famous deejay, popularized the term rock 'n' roll in the 1950s.

At the museum's ribbon-cutting ceremony, Jimi Hendrix's 11 version of "The Star Spangled Banner" played over the loudspeakers. The guitarist's rendition, conceived as an anti-Vietnam statement at Woodstock in 1969, is full of feedback and guitar distortions designed to simulate war sounds. But suddenly, Hendrix's tortured notes were punctuated by the real-life sounds of two Marine Corps Harrier jets flying overhead. The irony was not lost on some in the crowd, including Wenner, who later addressed the issue of how rock has now joined the establishment. The hall, said Wenner, standing next to Lennon's widow Yoko Ono, was built to remind people of the "power of innocence, rebellion and youth," but also the value of "maturity and growth and perspective." Rock 'n' roll, once scruffy and rebellious, is all grown up. Although it will strike some as contradictory, a hall of fame and museum is simply a natural step in its evolution.

VOCABULARY WORDS: artifacts (1), irreverent (1), replica (2), roster (4), contradiction (4), anarchic (4), inducted (5), skewed (7), sanctuary (9), scruffy (11)

ACTIVITY 30

Reading to Improve Writing

1. What is the author's evaluation of the Rock and Roll Hall of Fame and Museum? Where in the essay is this evaluation expressed?

_____

_____

_____

_____

2. What criteria does the author use to support his evaluation?

_____

_____

_____

3. Explain in your own words what the author means when he writes in paragraph 4 that "it is difficult to ignore some of the contradictions raised by the museum." What are these contradictions? Give an example.

_____

_____

_____

_____

4. Rock and roll artists can be inducted into the museum twenty-five
   years after their first recording. In your opinion, what current
   rock and roll groups or performers will be inducted into the Hall
   of Fame when they become eligible?

_____

_____

_____

Free speech is the whole thing, the whole ball game. Free speech is life itself. —SALMAN RUSHDIE

CHAPTER 8

Debating the Limits of Free Expression

In this chapter you will

- gather ideas about free expression in the schools, in the media, and on the Internet.

- make an argumentative claim.

- generate pro and con points to support your claim.

- order your argumentative points.

- learn to recognize faulty logic.

- combine sentences using introductory phrases.

- eliminate unnecessary repetition.

- learn to use correct subject-verb agreement and to avoid shifts in verb tense.

- reflect on your writing.

Freedom of expression is a fundamental right in the United States. In fact, it is a part of the First Amendment to the Constitution:

> Congress shall make no law respecting an establishment of religion, or prohibiting the free exercise thereof; or abridging the freedom of speech, or of the press; or the right of the people peaceably to assemble, and to petition the Government for a redress of grievances.

The First Amendment gives the people of the United States the right to attend the church of their choice, to protest against the government's actions, and to express themselves freely.

But can freedom of expression be taken too far? Because of the First Amendment, Nazis demonstrate in the streets and the Ku Klux Klan publicly burns crosses. Some of the most popular music in the country advocates abusing women. Hard-core pornography is readily available. Children are exposed to acts of violence on television, which some experts believe promotes actual violence. Clearly, freedom of expression comes in many forms.

Rather than advocate total freedom or no freedom of expression, some people suggest a middle road: freedom of expression should be permitted unless the welfare of society is endangered. Yet who decides when society is endangered? And how will freedom of expression be restricted?

WRITING ASSIGNMENT

For this assignment, write about your views on freedom of expression—in schools, in the media, or on the Internet. You or your instructor may decide to do this assignment in one of several ways.

- You may gather ideas on one, two, or three topics.
- You may write a discovery draft on one, two, or three of these topics.
- You may choose one discovery draft to develop into a polished essay.
- You may combine your discovery draft ideas into a new topic for your essay.

After completing your essay, you'll share it with your instructor and classmates, as well as with others directly affected by your topic, such as parents, friends, teachers, television producers, or government officials.

ACTIVITY 1

Analyzing Your Purpose and Audience. Before you begin gathering ideas about your topic, think about your purpose and audience. For this chapter's assignment, you'll give your opinion on one aspect of free expression. Remember that your audience includes your instructor and classmates as well as other people directly affected by your topic. For example, the audience for an essay about banning books from school libraries might include parents, teachers, and librarians, whereas the audience for an essay on regulating language use on the Internet might include Internet users and government officials. Your responses to the following questions will help you decide how to approach your topic.

Read more about purpose and audience on p. 5.

1. Does this assignment call for primarily expressive, informative, or persuasive writing?

   _____

2. What is your readers' average age? Approximately how many readers are male and how many are female?   How many are parents, teachers, and librarians?

   _____

   _____

   _____

3. What parts of the country or world are they from?

   _____

   _____

4. What, if anything, do you know about your readers' political views? Would most readers have conservative, moderate, or liberal views? Give examples.

   _____

   _____

   _____

GATHERING IDEAS

Read more about gathering ideas on pp. 29–34.

To gather ideas about free expression in schools, in the media, and on the Internet, select from among the various techniques you have practiced in the preceding chapters: brainstorming, freewriting, clustering, questioning, reading, interviewing, relating aloud, and reflecting.

Free Expression in Schools

In elementary and high school, free expression is an important issue. The subjects taught and the books students read are regulated by parents, teachers, school administrators, and school board members.

As you probably know, even such books as *Huckleberry Finn* and *Catcher in the Rye* have been banned in certain parts of the country. In recent years, certain books supposedly about satanism, or devil worship, have also been banned from school libraries. One school librarian, Kerry Leigh Ellison, addresses this issue in "Satan in the Library: Are Children in Danger?"

KERRY LEIGH ELLISON

Satan in the Library: Are Children in Danger?

Last Halloween, in New Castle, Pennsylvania, school librarian Nancy Prentice faced accusations of practicing satanism after she read the folk ballad "Tam Lin" to a group of fifth graders. A few months later, library aide Debbie Denzer of Kalispell, Montana, lost her job for lending her own books on the history of witchcraft to two seventh grade girls. The single largest category of book challenges last year consisted of religious objections, primarily the mention of witchcraft, satanism, and the occult.   1

Are our children in danger from books on satanism, Halloween, magic, and New Age religions?   2

I have no doubt that satanism is practiced here in America and that—in some groups at least—children who are born into it or attracted to it suffer horribly. I know this because I was raised in a family that practiced satanism. The horrors that survivors describe really do happen. I am a witness to these crimes,   3 as are other members of my family who have made the long journey out of the cult.

As a survivor and a professional, I take an active interest in the intellectual freedom of the children I serve. In my experience, indoctrination into satanic belief and practices involves a very rigid way of thinking: children must learn to see the world as inherently chaotic, satan as more powerful than God, the cult as omnipresent, and love as a sign of weakness.

Cult activities take place behind a wall of secrecy and denial. In the "daytime" world, children must act as if nothing is wrong, all the while experiencing a "nighttime" reality of abuse and sexual exploitation. In our cult, we were taught that the leaders could see our every move, even when we were alone. We were taught that no outsider would believe us if we told and that any breach of secrecy was punishable with death.

Like the children of Jonestown, we were taught to never question authority. Like the children in the compound at Waco, Texas, we were not allowed to make choices for ourselves. Fear, ignorance and "magical thinking" kept us in line.

But in the daytime world—at school and in the public library—I could make choices. Once I discovered the world of books, I chose to read everything I could get my hands on.

One of my first books was Johanna Spyri's *Heidi*, which I read over and over. The freedom of her life in the mountains was so delicious. Then there were those terrible months in Frankfurt with the ailing Klara. In a way I could not have described at the time, I felt understood and less alone when I was with Heidi. . . .

In fantasy novels such as Madeleine L'Engle's *A Wrinkle in Time* (Farrar, 1962), I aligned myself with good in the fight against evil, and learned that love is more powerful than hate or fear. C. S. Lewis's *The Lion, the Witch and the Wardrobe* (Macmillan, 1988) gave me the vicarious experience of a benevolent deity, one who protects and heals children, rather than abuses them.

Reading Louise Fitzhugh's *Harriet the Spy* (HarperCollins, 1964), I saw a child like myself struggle with the confusing values of her parents and with classmates who could not understand her.

Early on, I crossed over into the adult section of the library where I found a mirror for many of my feelings in Anne Frank's *Diary of a Young Girl*. Here was the horror, the hiding, and the tenacious hope. Hope, too, is what I gleaned from *Fahrenheit 451* (Buccaneer, 1990). Ray Bradbury's hero questions accepted values and makes up his own mind about the burning of books. In the end, he helps keep learning alive, if only in his heart and mind.

George Orwell's *1984* (Dutton, 1950) gave me a basis for   12
understanding the double-talk that permeates cult thinking.
("Do what thou wilt is the only law," really means complete sexual license for a few adults. A child who speaks the truth about
what is happening is told she is "lying," "talking crazy," and
"cruising for a bruising.") . . .

I may have felt unhampered in my reading as a child, but   13
the truth is that children's libraries are not, and perhaps never
should be, totally free of censorship. The distinction between
"book selection" and "censorship" is primarily semantic. We all
know of books that we would never put in a grade school library
or read out loud to children. Wise choices must be made that
take into account their interests and developmental needs. Most
five-year-olds, for instance, are not ready to handle the scary stories that so delight middle graders.

The real question is: On what basis will we make our   14
choices? Will we limit children's access to information out of
fear of angering one group or another? Should we try to keep
controversy out of the library? Can reading about witches, magic,
and demons really hurt children? . . .

Halloween is a time when small groups of perverts enact   15
black masses—where truly horrible things are done—but it is
much more. It is the eve of All Saints' Day, an important Christian
holiday, and Mexico's *los Días de los Muertos*, when loved ones
who have died are honored with flowers and ofrendas [offer-
ings]. For most children, Halloween is a time of parties, laughter,
and fun. And for getting scared and practicing being brave.

Satanists don't own Halloween any more than Hallmark   16
owns Mother's Day. How we choose to celebrate—or not—is
what counts. . . .

If we kick out all the witches, we would lose Donna Jo   17
Napoli's *Magic Circle* (Dutton, 1993), and with it the most moving description of the state of grace I have yet to see in children's
literature. We would lose, too, Monica Furlong's intelligent and
moral portrayal of both good and evil practitioners of England's
pre-Christian religion in *Wise Child* (Knopf, 1987).

If we ban the mention of satan from young adult collections,   18
we would lose Otfried Preussler's *The Satanic Mill* (Macmillan,
1991). This cautionary fantasy shows a young man's seduction
into the "dark arts." It also shows how evil eventually enslaves
him and how he breaks free, once again through the power of
love.

If we fear even the depiction of controversy, we miss *Save*   19
Halloween! (Morrow, 1993) by Stephanie Tolan. In the story, a

community is polarized when the daughter of an evangelical minister is asked by her teacher to write a class play on the history of Halloween. Tolan treats all of her characters with respect, and shows, in the end, that in our pluralistic society we can accommodate different viewpoints while preserving individual rights.

Certainly we must respect the very different backgrounds   20
and beliefs of the families we serve. In most cases, we can accomplish this by encouraging parents to be involved in their own child's reading choices and by discussing books with children as they read.

But if we let every parent remove any book that offends, our   21
libraries will quickly be stripped of their worth. This was brought home to me recently when a father complained about a book he had been reading to his daughter.

"How can you recommend this for children?" he demanded.   22
"Halfway through, the girl gets down on her knees and prays to God. I don't want my children exposed to that garbage!"

The book this parent found so offensive was *Heidi*.   23

VOCABULARY WORDS: occult (1), indoctrination (4), inherently (4), omnipresent (4), breach (5), benevolent (9), tenacious (11), semantic (13), pluralistic (19)

ACTIVITY 2

Reading to Improve Writing. Discuss the following questions about "Satan in the Library: Are Children in Danger?" with your classmates.

1. How does Ellison feel about removing books related to satanism, Halloween, and magic from school libraries?

---

2. What reasons does Ellison give to support her position?

_____

_____

_____

_____

_____

3. Why does Ellison tell us about her own experiences with satanism as a child?

_____

_____

_____

_____

4. Do you think the writer's argument is effective? Explain.

_____

_____

_____

ACTIVITY 3

Gathering Ideas about Free Expression in Schools. Gather ideas about free expression in schools. Use the following questions to stimulate your ideas.

1. Should students be taught sex education? If so, what type of sex education would be most appropriate?
2. Should certain books be banned from school libraries? If so, which books?

3. Should certain types of clothing be banned from school? If so, which types of clothing?

4. Should school newspapers be censored? If so, what type of coverage should be affected?

5. Should students be allowed to protest school policies if they disagree with them? Is there any type of protest that should be banned?

One student, Reginald, freewrote about an unpopular ad that ran in his college newspaper:

A school newspaper ad states that blacks should not receive reparations (a method of making up for past injustices) for slavery. There were ten reasons given for why blacks aren't entitled to damages for the effects of slavery. As you can imagine, a lot of people were really worked up about this ad and wanted the paper to apologize. But the editor of the paper said that he wouldn't, stating freedom of speech as his reason. Well, I don't agree with the ad, either, but I agree with the editor that the paper doesn't have to apologize.

Put your writing on free expression in schools aside for now. You want to gather ideas about another aspect of free expression.

Free Expression in the Media

One of the most controversial issues in the United States today is free expression in the media. An increasing number of television shows and movies depict graphic violence, contain sexually oriented material, and use obscene language. To some viewers, violence, sex, and obscene language make the shows more realistic; other viewers argue that such portrayals are unnecessary and potentially harmful.

The music industry is also involved in the free-expression controversy. Some popular song lyrics contain language that expresses obscenities or prejudice against certain racial groups. Other songs describe, and even advocate, violent acts against women and other groups of people. Should these songs be banned? Should they be labeled as containing offensive words? Members of Congress have introduced bills that would require record companies to label CDs that contain objectionable song lyrics. Many who work in the music industry, on the other hand, oppose laws that require record companies to label CDs. In the following testimony before a Senate subcommittee, later published on the Internet, Danny Goldberg, CEO of

Artemis Records, argues that the government doesn't have the right to ban or label music lyrics.

Testimony of Danny Goldberg, CEO and Co-owner, Artemis Records, before the Senate Commerce Committee

Chairman McCain, Senator Hollings, and Members of the Committee. I am pleased to have the opportunity to testify before you today.

I am the CEO and co-owner of Artemis Records, a year old independently owned record company. Our current roster includes Rickie Lee Jones, Steve Earle, Warren Zevon, and the Baha Men. During the nineteen-nineties I was the president of three major record labels, Atlantic, Warner Bros, and Mercury.

I am speaking not only as a long time record executive, but also as a father of a ten year old girl and a six and a half year old boy. I do not believe either government or any entertainment industry committee has any business in telling me and my wife what entertainment our children should be exposed to.

The United States is a diverse country with hundreds of divergent religious beliefs, ethnic backgrounds, regional traditions, and opinions about art and entertainment. Unlike the visual media, the record business is being asked to categorize and label groups of words. For the same reason there is no ratings system for books, or for that matter congressional testimony, with one narrow exception, it is virtually impossible to "rate" words.

For example, on the subject of violence, what kind of system can distinguish between the words "I want to kill you" said in an affectionate, sarcastic or ironic way from those same words being used literally? Song lyrics are by their nature impressionistic and are often used symbolically. No one really thought that the words to "killing me softly with his song" referred to murder.

The one exception are the so-called seven dirty words, and for fifteen years record companies, including my independent company Artemis Records, have been placing "parental advisory" stickers on albums that have a lot of curse words. Please note, senators, distinguished from the movie business and contrary to the sloppy and inaccurate remarks of the president and vice-president earlier this week, record companies have never suggested an age limit for albums with "parental advisory" stickers. We placed such a sticker on our current album *Spit* by the heavy metal band Kittie because the teenage girls in the band use several curse words over the course of the album. There is nothing illegal about this, and I and critics across the country and the half a million people in the U.S. who have bought the album are morally comfortable with it as well. I know that there are many Americans who are offended by curse words and don't want children exposed to them. However, those people have no moral or legal right to impose such a standard on my family or the millions of other Americans who, like George Bush, are comfortable with cursing.

The parental advisory sticker informs retailers and parents   7
that such words are on the album. Other than that there is no universal criteria for categorizing words in lyrics, books, magazines, newspapers, etc. There are, of course, subjective criteria. It is the function of critics to criticize, of preachers to preach and of people like myself to exercise personal moral judgments about what my company releases. However people of good will often have different opinions about entertainment. I respect the fact that many parents don't want their kids to watch R rated movies but I prefer a deeper analysis of each movie and I recently recommended the R rated *Erin Brockovich* to our ten year old daughter Katie who is a passionate feminist and environmentalist because I had seen the film and knew the rating was because of cursing. Others may disagree but this country will cease to be free the day that one group of parents can tell all other parents how to raise their children.

Song lyrics are not literal. Listening to the blues often makes   8
people happy. Angry weird songs often make adolescents feel less lonely and more connected to other kids. Millions of these teens and young adults feel ostracized when politicians and academics who obviously have no real understanding of their culture make sweeping generalizations about their entertainment, conveniently overlooking the fact that literally every generation has embraced entertainment with sexual and violent themes. Gangsta rap is the direct descendent of the gangster movies of the thirties and forties, the TV westerns of the fifties, and critically acclaimed films like *The Godfather.*

Mr. Chairman, I don't like every record. Spike Lee criticizes   9
much of the rap culture in his new movie *Bamboozled.* Criticism and immoral argument is appropriate and an integral part of the entertainment culture. In an internet world, there will be ever increasing ways for parents to find like minded groups who can advise them on entertainment through the prism of their own particular values. However so-called self-regulation achieved by political intimidation is the equivalent of censorship.

It has become commonplace to assert that popular culture is   10
popular against the wishes and values of its fans. But popular
culture gets that way precisely because the balance of consumers—not record makers, not rule makers, but everyday people—
enjoy it.

Mr. Chairman, make no mistake, their tastes, their values,   11
and their morality are under assault every bit as much as the
entertainment executives who occupy the hot seat today.

Washington is a culture of legislation and policy. Asking the   12
FTC or the Washington media or the Congress to analyze popular
entertainment makes about as much sense as going to Hollywood
to re-structure Medicare. From Ralph Nader to Pat Buchanan,
Washington political leaders, who are out of touch with the real
dynamic of the ways young people process entertainment, con-
demn youth culture. The only result of demonizing pop culture
is to drive millions of young people away from politics. In the
last congressional election in 1998, less than 17 percent of 18–25
year olds voted, less than half the rest of the population. I believe
that fifteen years of youth culture entertainment bashing in
Washington has greatly contributed to alienation and apathy on
the part of young people from politics.

VOCABULARY WORDS: exposed (3), divergent (4), impressionistic
(5), symbolically (5), subjective (7), literal (8), integral (9), demonizing (12), alienation (12)

ACTIVITY 4

Reading to Improve Writing. Discuss the following questions
about Goldberg's Senate testimony with your classmates.

1. What is Goldberg's position on "rating" song lyrics?

   _____

   _____

   _____

   _____

2. What reasons does Goldberg give to support his position?

_____

_____

_____

_____

3. Why does Goldberg use his own experience as a father to support his claim?

_____

_____

_____

4. Do you think Goldberg's argument is effective? Explain.

_____

_____

_____

ACTIVITY 5

Gathering Ideas about Free Expression in the Media. Gather ideas about free expression in the media. Use the following questions to stimulate your ideas.

1. Should there be any attempt to regulate sex and violence in the media? Why or why not?
2. How effective are the rating systems used for movies and videos? What changes in the systems, if any, do you suggest?
3. How effective are warning labels on television shows and CDs? What changes in the labeling system, if any, do you suggest?
4. Should there be less violence and sexual content in shows aimed at young children? Explain your position.

5. Are magazines and newspapers containing sexual material too accessible to children? If so, what can be done to limit their accessibility?

Here's how one student, Toraino, brainstormed about violence in movies:

slit throats

assault rifles

blood

brains spilling

sometimes this is life

who takes it seriously

why take it seriously

kids in the movie theater

ratings not enforced

parents should be more responsible

Put your ideas about free expression in the media aside for now so you can gather ideas about one more aspect of freedom of expression.

Free Expression on the Internet

Computer technology has introduced a new player in the debate over the limits of free expression. Some popular video games, for example, contain violent material—bloody battles, sadistic villains, mutilated bodies—that some experts fear may encourage children to perform violent acts. Social scientists report that children who spend hours playing violent video games may be more prone to violence than children who do not play the games.

Most recently, the Internet has become part of the free-expression controversy. The Internet consists of thousands of computer networks accessible to anyone—including children—with a computer and a modem. Some users have introduced sexually explicit material, including pornography, onto the Internet. Although some people believe the government should regulate the Internet, others view government regulation as an infringement of free expression. In the following, "Symposium: Two Views on the Installation of Internet Filters in Public Libraries and Schools," Richard Glen Boire argues that public libraries should not be required to install Internet filtering software. (See pp. 440–43 for a different view.)

RICHARD GLEN BOIRE

Symposium: Two Views on the Installation of Internet Filters in Public Libraries and Schools

Under a new law passed by Congress on Dec. 15, 2000, public libraries and schools are required to install expensive, unreliable, content-filtering software on all of their computers capable of accessing the Internet. A library that fails or refuses to install filtering software can be stripped of much-needed federal funding.

The new law was cast as a way to protect children from pornography, but its scope is much broader than keeping little Johnny's eyes away from digital centerfolds. By ordering public libraries to install blocking software on their Internet computers, the new law treats adults like children and turns public libraries into censorial agents of the government.

Far more than pornographic sites are blocked by today's content-filtering software. One test of the librarian edition of a filtering software package called X-Stop showed that sites such as those of the American Association of University Women, the AIDS Quilt, the Heritage Foundation, the Banned Books page at Carnegie Mellon University and the University of Chicago's censorship-tracking Fileroom Project were being blocked by the software. Another test conducted by the antifiltering-software group Peacefire (www.peacefire.org) found that Websites of Amnesty International and 29 other human-rights organizations were blocked by popular filtering software. Access to these sites was blocked because the filtering software categorized them as sexually explicit or as pertaining to drugs, violence or hate speech.

Banning access to certain information in public libraries violates the Constitution in at least two ways. First, restricting expression based on its content is a glaring violation of the First Amendment. The ban violates the First Amendment right to expression of those people whose Websites are barred from such important venues as the nation's public libraries. Second, the ban violates the rights of citizens who are denied access to the suppressed information. The Supreme Court has held that the right to receive ideas is protected by the First Amendment.

By ordering libraries to install content-blocking software, the federal government is effectively deputizing libraries as new public departments of censorship; the libraries, in turn, ultimately place this censorship power in the hands of about a half-dozen software companies that sell Internet-filtering software.

Yet, three years ago, the American Library Association presciently issued a sharply worded resolution stating its objection to Internet-filtering software, effectively putting Congress on notice that public libraries were not to be transformed into censorship agents. Evidently, Congress wasn't listening.

Internet-filtering software is specifically designed to block information based on its content and to prevent access to certain viewpoints. This is done in one of two ways. One method is to block the specific addresses of Websites whose content is deemed unacceptable. The second method blocks sites based on scanning for specific keywords. Most software-filtering programs currently use a combination of these techniques.   6

Both techniques are problematic. Vendors of filtering programs consider their preprogrammed list of blocked sites to be proprietary information and a trade secret. Thus, sellers of content-filtering software refuse to reveal which specific sites are blocked by their software. As a result, the new law vests the companies that sell filtering software with the unchecked power of censoring specific Websites without ever having to reveal exactly what information is denied or which sites are being blocked.   7

Using keywords to filter content also is problematic. None of the filtering packages are very good at determining the context of any given keyword. This leads to a sort of blind censorship by machine, as the filtering software spots a keyword such as "breast" and, in addition to blocking pornographic sites, blocks sites that convey information about breast cancer. The result is that much more than pornographic sites are blocked from the eyes of curious children.   8

Mandating the filtering of certain information on the Internet is equivalent to the government banning digital books of which it disapproves. The Supreme Court has explained that from the readers' viewpoint the Internet is comparable to a vast library including millions of readily available and indexed publications. In fact, more and more documents are added to the Internet every day, many of which do not exist in printed form. Consequently, denying Internet access to these digital documents via public venues constitutes an information blackout.   9

A truly inquisitive mind knows no borders; nor should it. Certainly, the government should not be in the business of policing the minds of Americans by policing their access to certain information at public libraries. Earlier this month, the American Association of University Professors recognized that Internet-filtering devices are a contradiction of the academic library mission to further research and learning through exposure to the broadest possible range of ideas and information. The professors   10 went on to say that such content filters in academic libraries are a fundamental violation of intellectual freedom.

While the more affluent users of university facilities are thereby supported in their pursuit of knowledge, the new filtering law limits the range of accessible information to those (often less affluent) people who rely on public libraries. By providing free information access to people of all income levels, ethnicities and locations, public libraries perform an important social role in our democracy—a role that is abdicated when materials are screened according to an arbitrary standard of acceptability that suppresses certain points of view by denying access to them. 11

In an awkward concession to the unconstitutional nature of the info-ban, the new law permits public libraries to disable the filtering software for an adult with a bona fide research or other lawful purpose. Yet, this is no protection at all. First, the disabling function is left completely to the library's discretion. Libraries are not obligated to have a system for turning off the filter. Second, who is to decide what is and what is not bona fide research? And why must one be devoted to serious work, as opposed to idle interest, in order to access information on certain topics? Will adults have to plead their case before a librarian who then has complete authority to decide whether to grant that person access to the uncensored Internet? Third, what happens to privacy in such a scenario? In many libraries, patrons already are required to leave their library card with the librarian while using an Internet-connected computer. With the new law, an adult who seeks access to the uncensored Internet not only is required in many cases to disclose his or her identity, but also will be required to disclose the topic of his or her research. 12

Imagine the outcry that would ensue if federal agents swept libraries clean of all books that did not meet the government's seal of approval or if the government directly banned certain Websites. Since 1999, the People's Republic of China has attempted to do just that: It has blocked the Websites of U.S. media outlets, human-rights groups and other sources of information deemed harmful by the Chinese authorities. 13

By exploiting the fear of the Internet as corrupter of the morals of America's youth—and by making libraries do the dirty work with self-righteous software that goes by names such as Cyber Patrol, NetNanny, CYBERsitter, X-Stop and Cyber Snoop— the new law is a similar attack on intellectual freedom. 14

Perhaps Congress needs a reminder that the United States, unlike China, has a First Amendment. Rather than utilize the same sort of censorship tactics employed by repressive governments, the federal government should recognize that access to 15

information and freedom of expression on all topics are necessary elements of a healthy democracy. Ordering public libraries
to censor the Internet is incompatible not only with intellectual
freedom, but with freedom itself.

VOCABULARY WORDS: censorial (2), venues (4), presciently (5), proprietary (7), mandating (9), inquisitive (10), repressive (15)

ACTIVITY 6

Reading to Improve Writing. Discuss the following questions
about Boire's essay with your classmates.

1. According to Boire, should filtering software be installed in public
   libraries?

   _____

   _____

   _____

2. Which reasons does Boire give to support this claim?

   _____

   _____

   _____

   _____

   _____

3. What is the strongest argument made in this essay? What is the
   weakest argument?

   _____

   _____

Newspaper Ad Sparks Controversy

An advertisement ran in last weeks school newspaper   1
that shocked a number of students and faculty. The title
was "Ten Reasons Why Reparations for Blacks Is a Bad Idea
for Blacks--and Racist." The ad stated a number of reasons
why blacks should not receive any damages for the effects
of slavery. Some of the reasons given were that not all
blacks have suffered because of slavery and that welfare
and affirmative action has served as reparations. Boy, did
this ad rile everyone! Some people wanted to burn all of
the newspapers, some wanted an apology from the editor, and
some said the paper should never plan to run this ad in the
first place. I don't like the ad and don't agree with what
it says, but I do believe in freedom of speech. For this
reason, I defend the right of the school newspaper to run
this ad.

The constitution of the United States provides for   2
freedom of expression. If we value our Constitution, then we
must protect it even if it means protecting "hate speech."

Universities are supposed to be a place where ideas   3
are debated. If we eliminate every piece of writing that
someone finds offensive, we will no longer have a free
exchange of ideas. There are many examples of books that
people would like to ban. If colleges had to remove from
the library shelves every book that was offensive to
someone, there would be few books left!

Burning the newspapers would be a crime just as burn-   4
ing books is. There are better ways to protest. Students
could run an ad themselves or write to the author of the ad.

Rather than burning newspapers or demanding an   5
apology, students should discuss the ideas expressed in the
ad and not just refuse to run it. We must attack these
ideas with better ideas of our own.

REVISING

When you revise your draft, use the skills you acquired in the preceding chapters. Support and clarify your main ideas, organize your paragraphs, make your ideas flow smoothly, and write an effective introduction, conclusion, and title. Where needed, combine sentences and improve your word choice. Also, consider conducting primary or secondary research to gather more information about your topic.

In this chapter, you'll focus on writing a persuasive argument. You'll learn how to make an argumentative claim, develop reasons to support that claim, respond to opposing arguments, avoid faulty logic, and organize your points. You'll also work on connecting ideas by combining sentences and eliminating unnecessary repetition.

Developing Your Ideas

To be persuasive, your essay must be well developed. In other words, it must contain sufficient supporting details to convince your readers that your position is valid. First, though, you need to make an effective claim.

MAKING A CLAIM. A claim is a statement asserting that something is true. In persuasive writing, a claim is a type of thesis statement. As you may recall from Chapter 2, the thesis statement announces the topic of your essay; shows, explains, or argues a particular point about the topic; and gives readers a sense of what the essay will be about. For an argumentative essay, you announce your topic and the point that you will argue. Let's look at each of the qualities of an effective claim in more detail.

Express an Opinion. An effective claim expresses an opinion, not a fact. An opinion is an idea that some but not all people share. In contrast, a fact is something that can be verified as true by an objective observer.

FACT   There is a rating system for movies.

OPINION   Because it's not uniformly enforced, the rating system for movies should be changed.

The first statement can be verified by checking advertisements for movies. There's no need to prove that it's true. The second statement, however, is a claim because some people will disagree with it. Notice that the claim includes the word *should*. Similar words used in claims include *needs to, ought,* and *must.*

Relate to Your Readers. An effective claim also seeks to persuade readers by pointing out how the topic relates to their lives. A claim that conveys only your personal interests, tastes, or experiences is not likely to persuade or interest readers. Rather, connect the claim to some aspect of your readers' lives.

PERSONAL   Protesters should never burn the American flag because it means so much to me.

PERSUASIVE   Because the American flag symbolizes what this country stands for, it should be illegal to burn it in protest.

The first statement focuses on the writer. But the second statement relates the topic—burning the American flag—to a concept relevant to readers' lives.

Narrow the Focus. An effective claim focuses the topic so that it can be fully developed and supported. If your claim isn't sufficiently focused, you won't be able to discuss it in detail in your essay.

UNFOCUSED   There's too much violence on television.

FOCUSED   The excessive use of guns on *Cops and Gangs* glamorizes a deadly use of force.

To support the claim made in the first example, you would have to cover all types of violence on all types of television shows—a topic better suited for a book than an essay. The second claim requires only that you focus on one type of violence—the use of guns—on one television show—*Cops and Gangs*. Because it's better focused, this claim could be fully supported in an essay.

In addition, a focused claim does not leave readers with unanswered questions.

UNFOCUSED   Pornography should be banned.

FOCUSED   To stop the growth of child pornography, Congress should pass a law banning child pornography on the Internet.

In the first example, readers might ask: "What type of pornography? How should it be banned? Why should it be banned?" In the second, readers are told the type of pornography, how it could be banned (through federal legislation), and why it should be banned.

HOW TO Make a Claim

- Express an opinion.

- Be persuasive by relating the claim to readers' lives.

- Keep the claim narrowly focused.

ACTIVITY 8 (GROUP)

Revising Claims.   Working in a group of several students, review the three parts of an effective claim. Then determine why each of the following claims is weak. Finally, revise each claim accordingly.

1. On the Internet you can find information on how to build a bomb.

   Fault(s): _____

   _____

   Revision: _____

   _____

   _____

2. Because of the First Amendment, we shouldn't attempt to regulate violence on television.

   Fault(s): _____

   _____

   Revision: _____

   _____

   _____

3. Certain radio shows should be censored.

Fault(s): _____

_____

Revision: _____

_____

_____

4. Some high school newspapers advertise events that minors are not allowed to attend.

Fault(s): _____

_____

Revision: _____

_____

_____

5. I believe in total freedom of expression.

Fault(s): _____

_____

Revision: _____

_____

_____

ACTIVITY 9

Revising Your Claim. Revise the claim for your essay so that it expresses an opinion, relates to your readers' lives, and is sufficiently focused.

GENERATING PRO POINTS. Once you have an effective claim, you need to concentrate on developing support for that claim—your reasons or pro points (*pro* means "in favor of"). Pro points tell readers why you believe your claim is true or valid. You develop pro points from three sources: your experience, observation, and research.

Experience. When trying to persuade others, we often look first to our own experience with the topic. This is what Danny Goldberg does when he describes his experience as a father in his testimony before the Senate Commerce Committee.

Suppose, for example, that you're writing about violent and obscene lyrics in rock music and that you believe the lyrics are harmless because listeners tend to focus on the music, not the words. This is true for you and for many of your friends. Thus, you have one pro point:

> Because most listeners focus on the music, not the lyrics, violent or obscene lyrics don't have a negative impact in rock music.

Pro and con points are usually stated in topic sentences. Read about topic sentences on p. 59.

How would you support this pro point? You could detail your own experiences with music. For instance, you could point out that you can't remember the lyrics to your favorite song. However, keep in mind that what might be true for you may not be true for others. In addition to describing your own experiences, then, you might conduct a survey to obtain the opinions of others, or you might research the topic.

Observation. You may have no personal experience with an issue that concerns you, but you may have observed how it affects others. In this case, you may base your pro points on observation, as Richard Glen Boire does in his essay about installing Internet filters on library computers. His argument is based partly on his observations that filtering software also blocks useful information.

Imagine, for instance, that you're arguing against censoring literature in high schools. Books weren't censored in your high school, but your niece attends a school that has banned several classics, including Steinbeck's *Of Mice and Men* and Orwell's *1984*. Because she is unable to study these books in school, she will be less well prepared for her college entrance exams. From observing your niece's experiences, you generate this pro point:

> Censoring important works of literature can limit students' opportunities in higher education.

You can support this point by describing your niece's experience with censorship. However, what happened to your niece might not happen to everyone. Thus, to strengthen your case, you could interview other students about their experiences with censorship or conduct research to collect facts and statistics that support your position.

Research. To learn more about your topic, you can conduct primary or secondary research. To argue against regulation, for example, Boire did research to learn about tests conducted on Web sites that were blocked by filtering software.

Say you're also arguing against government censorship of material on the Internet. You could also research software programs that prevent a computer from accessing sites on the Internet containing sexual material. From your research, you generate the following pro point:

> Rather than have the government censor the Internet, let computer owners censor whatever material they find obscene.

To support this pro point, you could describe a software program that individuals can purchase to prevent certain material from being downloaded onto their computer.

Generate Pro Points

If you have a class listserv or Internet discussion group, you can post your claim and ask fellow students to add pro points in support of it. Refer to your classmates' ideas when revising your essay.

ACTIVITY 10 (GROUP)

Generating Pro Points. Working in a group, generate pro points from experience, observation, and research for each claim that follows.

1. Claim: The excessive violence in cartoons and children's television shows can make children become overly aggressive.

   Pro point from experience: _____

   _____

   _____

Pro point from observation: _____

_____

_____

Pro point from research: _____

_____

_____

2. Claim: Sex education courses should focus on teaching abstinence, not on teaching "safer sex."

    Pro point from experience: _____

    _____

    _____

    Pro point from observation: _____

    _____

    _____

    Pro point from research: _____

    _____

    _____

3. Claim: Dress codes in high school can do more harm than good.

    Pro point from experience: _____

    _____

    _____

    Pro point from observation: _____

    _____

    _____

Pro point from research: _____

_____

_____

ACTIVITY 11

Generating Pro Points for Your Claim. Develop several pro points in support of the claim you make about free expression in your discovery draft. Draw on your experience, observation, and (if you wish) primary or secondary research.

SUPPORTING PRO POINTS. You support pro points with the same techniques used to support a thesis statement: description, narration, comparison and contrast, classification, process, examples, definition, and cause and effect. Not all supporting material is equally effective, though. The best supporting information is recent, relevant, and easily understood by readers.

Use Recent Material. Because you're probably writing about a current topic related to free expression, be sure to use supporting material that is up-to-date. By using recent material, you show your readers you're knowledgeable about the topic.

Keep in mind that your own experiences might be dated. If you're arguing for dress codes in high schools, use your own experiences only if you're a recent high school graduate. If you're discussing the burning of the American flag, find out about the last Supreme Court ruling on the issue. If your topic concerns the Internet, make a point of obtaining current information about this rapidly changing technology.

Use Relevant Material. The material you use to support your pro points must be directly related to your topic. If your research isn't relevant, your readers will easily dismiss it. For example, if your topic is the banning of cigarette advertisements, don't use unrelated advertisements for cigars or chewing tobacco as supporting material. Similarly, in an essay about censoring music lyrics, you would not use unrelated information about censoring books.

Use Understandable Material. Remember that you probably know more about your topic than your readers do. You may need to explain the plot of a book, the meaning of a term, or the lyrics of a song to readers who lack your familiarity with the subject. Consider finding more understandable material to support your points if your explanation becomes too long and detailed.

Use a Newsgroup

Consider joining a newsgroup, or Internet bulletin board, that focuses on issues related to your topic. For a list of newsgroups on various topics, refer to **<http://groups .google.com>**. Before using information from these sources, be sure that it is reliable.

ACTIVITY 12 (GROUP)

Evaluating Supporting Material. Working in a group, examine the following claim and determine whether the supporting material given for it is up-to-date, relevant, and easily understandable.

CLAIM   The current rating system for movies needs to be improved.

1. More and more television shows are showing scenes of graphic violence.

   _____

   _____

2. Owners of movie theaters are reluctant to enforce the current rating system.

   _____

   _____

3. In 1988, half of all profitable movies contained sexually oriented material.

   _____

   _____

4. The profit margin for R-rated movies is almost 21 percent of all movies when aggregated.

_____

_____

5. When I sold movie tickets, I almost never checked people's IDs.

_____

_____

6. Movie producers avoid the R rating by making two versions of the same movie: a milder version for movie theaters, and a more "hard-core" version for video stores.

_____

_____

ACTIVITY 13

Evaluating Your Supporting Material. Evaluate the supporting material in your discovery draft. Is it recent, relevant, and easily understood? Make any necessary changes to improve it.

RESPONDING TO CON POINTS. An argumentative essay is most persuasive when you anticipate readers' objections and argue against them. Therefore, in addition to presenting pro points, you need to argue against the con points (*con* means "against"). To do this, put yourself in the place of the readers who might not agree with your pro points. What might their objections be? How would they state these views? Now, consider how you would respond to these objections.

List Con Points. First, you need to identify the most important con points. To do this, imagine that you disagree with your claim, and then think of reasons you disagree with it.

Suppose that this is your claim:

Sex education should focus primarily on abstinence, not on contraception or "safer sex."

Now, imagine that you disagree with this claim—that you think sex education should focus on contraception and sexually transmitted diseases. Here are two arguments against this claim:

1. Many teenagers will have sex, no matter how often they're told to be abstinent.

2. Information about contraception and sexually transmitted diseases can prevent the tragedies of unwanted pregnancy and death from AIDS.

These are your con points—the points against the claim you make. You don't have to list all con points, just the most important ones. Depending on your topic, you might end up with two or three con points.

 Generate Con Points
If you have a class listserv, or Internet discussion group, you may post your claim and ask students to list con points. Refer to this list when revising your essay.

ACTIVITY 14

Listing Con Points.   For each of the following claims, list two con points.

1. English should be designated the official language of the United States.

   Con: _____

   _____

   Con: _____

   _____

   _____

2. Dress codes in high schools unfairly restrict students' right to express themselves through their choice of clothing.

   Con: _____

   _____

Con: _____

_____

_____

3. An amendment to the Constitution should ban burning the American flag in protest.

Con: _____

_____

Con: _____

_____

_____

ACTIVITY 15 (GROUP)

Listing Con Points for Your Claim. Read your claim to the students in your group. Ask those who disagree with your claim to explain their views on the topic. Use their responses to list several con points for your claim.

REFUTING CON POINTS

To refute means to argue against something. In your essay, you want to refute or respond to the con points to convince readers to accept your claim. To refute a con point, acknowledge what, if anything, is true about the con point, and then explain what you think is not true about it.

Let's return to the essay on sex education. This is your claim:

Sex education should focus primarily on abstinence, not on contraception or "safer sex."

Here's your first con point:

Many teenagers will have sex, no matter how often they're told to be abstinent.

Now, here's what you can say to refute, or argue against, this point:

It's true that we can't prevent all teenagers from having sex. But as more and more teenagers understand the benefits of abstinence, more and more of them will be willing to wait to have sex.

Notice that you first point out what is right about the con point—"We can't prevent all teenagers from having sex." Then, you express what you think is wrong about the con point.

Here's your second con point:

Information about contraception and sexually transmitted diseases can prevent the tragedies of unwanted pregnancy and death from AIDS.

Here's one way to refute this con point:

Information about contraception and sexually transmitted diseases is appropriate for mature couples. However, many teenagers are so impressionable that they interpret this information to mean that having sex is acceptable.

Again, notice that you point out what's right about the con point—that the information is appropriate for mature couples—before stating what's wrong with it.

ACTIVITY 16 (GROUP)

Debating an Issue. Working in a group, debate an issue related to freedom of expression. Follow these guidelines for organizing the debate and using pro and con points:

1. Choose a topic and make a claim. Here are some examples:
   - Rock lyrics should/should not be censored.
   - Advertisements for smoking should/should not be banned.
   - Sex education should/should not teach contraception and "safer sex."
   - Burning the American flag should/should not be illegal.
2. Elect a moderator.
3. Divide the group into two sides—a pro side (students in favor of the claim) and a con side (students against the claim).
4. Allow each side ten minutes to brainstorm reasons to support its position.

5. A volunteer on the pro side states a pro point in support of the claim.

6. A volunteer on the con side refutes this pro point.

7. Another student on the pro side states a pro point in support of the claim.

8. Another student on the con side refutes this pro point.

9. This interchange continues until everyone on both sides of the debate has had the opportunity to participate.

Debate on a Computer

If your class has access to a computer terminal as a group, hold a debate onscreen. Identify your claim and one pro point. Leave the screen on. When it's convenient, other students can read what you have posted and add a pro point, add a con point, or refute a con point.

If you're in a class where students are online simultaneously, carry on an online debate. This online exchange can give you the opportunity to think about your pro and con points before you debate them with others.

ACTIVITY 17

Refuting Your Con Points. Return to the list of con points you generated in Activity 15 for your essay. Refute each con point in the space provided here.

1. Con point: _____

_____

Argument against the con: _____

_____

_____

2. Con point: _____

_____

Argument against the con: _____

_____

_____

3. Con point: _____

_____

Argument against the con: _____

_____

_____

Organizing Your Essay

Now that you've developed the ideas in your draft, you're ready to begin organizing those ideas. If you order your pro and con points in a logical way, your readers will become more convinced of your claim as they read your essay.

ORDERING PRO POINTS. Some of your pro points will be more persuasive than others. Save your most convincing pro point for last so that you leave readers thinking about it. You might begin a paper with the least convincing pro point and slowly build up to the most convincing one. Or, you might begin with the second most convincing point, save the less convincing points for the middle, and end with the most convincing one.

ARRANGING CON POINTS. Where should you put the con points in your essay? You have several options. You may put con points at different spots in an essay, particularly when certain con points are closely connected to certain pro points. This pattern can help make the pro and con points flow smoothly in an essay.

> ## HOW TO Organize Pro and Con Points
>
> PRO POINTS
>
> - Save your most convincing pro point for last.
>
> - Begin your essay with the least convincing pro point and build up to the most convincing point.
>
> - Or begin with a fairly strong point, put the weaker points in the middle, and end with the strongest point.
>
> CON POINTS
>
> - Connect each con point to the related pro point.
>
> - Or begin with con points and then refute them with pro points.
>
> - Or save con points for near the end of the essay and refute them all at one time.

You may also begin an essay with the con points. After refuting them, give your pro points. Kerry Leigh Ellison uses this strategy in "Satan in the Library: Are Children in Danger?" She begins by describing the dangers of satanism (the con points), and then goes on to say that censorship won't stop these dangers (the pro points). Finally, you may save your con points until the end of the essay, but only when you can refute those points well. You don't want readers to finish your essay agreeing with the opposition. In his testimony before the Senate Commerce Committee, Danny Goldberg saves his con points until the fourth to last paragraph (9), where he writes: "Mr. Chairman, I don't like every record. Spike Lee criticizes much of the rap culture in his new movie *Bamboozled*." In other words, even though Goldberg doesn't like all popular music, he doesn't believe any of it should be rated or banned.

ACTIVITY 18 (GROUP)

Ordering Pro and Con Points. Working in a group, order the pro and con points in Reginald's discovery draft (p. 393). Finally, compare your group's ordering of the pro and con points with the order that

Reginald uses in his revised draft (pp. 418–20). Notice how Reginald improved his pro and con points in the revised draft.

Claim: _____

_____

_____

Pro points: _____

_____

_____

_____

_____

_____

_____

_____

_____

_____

Con points: _____

_____

_____

_____

_____

ACTIVITY 19

Ordering Your Pro and Con Points. Think about the pro and con points for your essay about freedom of expression. List your pro points in the order in which they should appear in your revised draft. Then decide where you can include your con points and add them to your list.

Move Your Pro and Con Points

Use the cut-and-paste function of your word processor to create several different lists of your pro and con points. Compare the various lists to determine the most effective ordering of the points for your revised draft.

AVOIDING FAULTY LOGIC

A persuasive essay makes sense to readers. An essay that is not persuasive usually is based on faulty logic, or flawed reasoning. Let's look at three common forms of faulty logic.

Hasty Generalization. A hasty generalization is a conclusion drawn from too little evidence. Suppose, for example, that you once had a bad experience dealing with a salesperson at a particular store. Based on that single experience, you conclude that all salespeople in that store are rude. Your conclusion, based on insufficient evidence (your one experience), would be a hasty generalization. Just because one salesperson was rude doesn't mean that all others are rude. One instance can't prove a point.

Here's another example: you argue that violence in children's programming has no harmful effects because it didn't harm you as a child. Your conclusion is based on insufficient evidence (only one example). More convincing evidence would include studies conducted to determine the effects of television violence on children or surveys of children and their parents.

Faulty Either-Or Reasoning. Faulty either-or reasoning proposes only two possible alternatives even though more than two options actually exist. For instance, you would use faulty either-or reasoning if you said, "Either I lose ten pounds or I won't get a date." The reasoning is faulty because more than these two alternatives exist. You might get a date without losing any weight. Or you might lose ten pounds and still not get a date. Or you could lose five pounds and get several dates.

A writer who argues "Either we regulate cigarette advertisements or more and more people will die from lung cancer" is using faulty logic because other alternatives also exist, such as efforts to decrease smoking through public service announcements and educational programs. Because of these efforts, fewer people might get lung cancer, whether or not cigarette advertising is regulated.

Faulty Cause-and-Effect Reasoning. Faulty cause-and-effect reasoning attributes an event to an unrelated cause. Superstitions are based on faulty cause-and-effect reasoning, such as when we blame the black cat that crossed our path, the salt we spilled, or the broken mirror we gazed into for a bad day. Logically, these events couldn't have caused the bad day because they were unrelated to what we experienced. Thus, we cannot assume that one event was caused by another event simply because one took place before the other.

Political candidates often use faulty cause-and-effect reasoning: "Since my opponent has been in the Senate, your taxes have increased." However, just because taxes went up after the senator was elected doesn't mean that the senator raised the taxes. Perhaps they were increased by the previous Congress. Similarly, an essay writer who argues "Ever since certain types of music have become popular, violence against women has risen" fails to acknowledge other possible causes for the rise in violence against women. Unless the writer provides evidence to support this point, the argument is based on faulty cause-and-effect reasoning.

ACTIVITY 20

Eliminating Faulty Logic. Exchange your draft with a partner. Ask your partner to point out hasty generalizations, faulty either-or reasoning, and faulty cause-and-effect reasoning in your draft.

Polishing Your Sentences and Words

After improving your essay's development and organization, you're ready to begin polishing your sentences and words. In this section, you'll combine sentences and eliminate unnecessary repetition.

COMBINING SENTENCES USING INTRODUCTORY PHRASES. As you know from previous chapters, sentence combining is a good way to connect closely related, short sentences. Sentence combining can make your writing clearer and more interesting.

One way to combine short, closely related sentences is to use introductory phrases. A phrase is a group of words that lacks a subject, verb, or both. It cannot stand alone as a sentence. In Reginald's discovery draft, "Newspaper Ad Sparks Controversy," Reginald wrote two sentences to describe his opinion of the ad.

> I don't like the ad and don't agree with what it says, but I do believe in freedom of speech. For this reason, I defend the right of the school newspaper to run this ad.

In his revised draft, he combined these two sentences using an introductory phrase and eliminating unnecessary words to create a stronger thesis statement.

> As a supporter of freedom of speech, I defend the right of the school newspaper to run this ad whether I agree with it or not.

ACTIVITY 21

Combining Sentences. Use an introductory phrase to combine the following pairs or groups of sentences. You may need to eliminate unnecessary words, change words, or move words around.

1. I took part in a boycott a few years ago. This was when I was in high school.

   _____

   _____

2. We were protesting a closed campus. We were against it.

   _____

   _____

3. We couldn't leave campus at lunchtime. We needed special permission from the principal.

   _____

   _____

4. We thought this limited our freedom too much. We organized a boycott.

   _____

   _____

5. We wanted to be prepared. We made signs, wrote chants, and told everyone we knew about the boycott.

   _____

   _____

6. We decided to boycott our first-period classes. We wanted to get the administration's attention right away.

   _____

   _____

7. The first-period bell rang. About thirty of us left our seats and gathered outside the main door.

   _____

   _____

8. We chanted. We also walked up and down and held up signs. We attracted a great deal of attention. We made the local news.

   _____

   _____

9. Everyone who participated in the boycott was suspended for at least three days. We missed several tests. Missing these tests lowered our final grades.

   _____

   _____

   _____

10. We felt that our right to free expression under the First Amendment of the Constitution was violated. This was because we were punished for boycotting our classes.

_____

_____

ELIMINATING UNNECESSARY REPETITION. Saying the same thing twice—unnecessary repetition—can make readers lose interest in your writing. Sometimes the repetition is in the form of synonyms or words that have the same meaning.

WORDY   In my opinion, I disagree with the movie rating system.

REVISED   I disagree with the movie rating system.

WORDY   The petition showed and demonstrated how angry the students were about the new uniform policy.

REVISED   The petition showed how angry the students were about the new uniform policy.

WORDY   When compared to each other, the rating systems for movies and records are both similar.

REVISED   The rating systems for movies and records are similar.

The following phrases are repetitious. There is no need, for example, to say "past history" because history is necessarily about past events.

past history	new beginning
at this point in time	connect together
end result	end product
true fact	blue in color
personal opinion	serious tragedy
invited guest	preplan

ACTIVITY 22

Eliminating Unnecessary Repetition. Revise the following wordy sentences as needed to eliminate unnecessary repetition.

1. The positive benefits of the Internet are really and truly great.

   _____   _____

   _____

2. Constant and continual monitoring of the Internet is a required necessity.

   _____

   _____

3. The final completion of the list of approved books will come during this semester's time period.

   _____

   _____

4. The parents were so tired and exhausted from debating and arguing about the book list that they quit early.

   _____

   _____

5. At this point in time the incomplete book list hasn't been finished.

   _____

   _____

6. After a frank and honest exchange, the senators decided to delay making a decision on the issue of rating song lyrics.

   _____

   _____

7. The senators need to have more advance planning in the future to come.

   _____

   _____

8. They required and needed more hard work and labor from everyone involved.

   _____

   _____

9. The true facts of the student demonstration will be proved con-
   clusively at the hearing scheduled at 7 p.m. in the evening.

   _____

   _____

10. The public official urged her fellow colleagues to cooperate to-
    gether to eliminate altogether obscene language.

    _____

    _____

HOW TO Avoid Unnecessary Repetition

Read each sentence in your essay. Check that each part of each
sentence

- relates to your main point.

- adds details of interest to your readers.

- is specific.

- does not restate what you have already said.

On occasion, you may wish to restate an idea to give it emphasis,
such as when you restate a thesis statement in your conclusion.
Check that the idea

- needs to be restated.

- adds interest to your essay.

- is stated in different words from the original.

Read about integrating research into your essay on pp. 266–69 and in Chapter 11.

ACTIVITY 23

Polishing Your Sentences and Words. Reread your discovery draft, looking for short, closely related sentences that can be combined. Then look for unnecessary repetition to eliminate.

Reginald's Revised Draft

Before you read Reginald's revised draft, reread his discovery draft (p. 393). Notice how his argument is stronger in the revision. (You will also notice some errors in the revised draft; these will be corrected when Reginald edits his essay later on.)

Newspaper Ad Sparks Controversy

An advertisement, "Ten Reasons Why Reparations for   1
Blacks Is a Bad Idea for Blacks--and Racist" ran in last
weeks school newspaper. A reparation is a repayment for
damage done in the past. This ad stated a number of reasons
why blacks should not receive repayments from the United
States government because of the damages done by slavery.
Some of the reasons given were that not all blacks have
suffered because of slavery and that welfare and affirmative action has served as reparations. This ad, which some
call a "hate" ad, upset a number of students and faculty.
Some people wanted to burn all of the newspapers, some
wanted a formal apology from the editor, and some said the
paper should never plan to run the ad in the first place.
As a supporter of freedom of speech, I defend the right of
the school newspaper to run this ad whether I agree with it
or not.

Because the Constitution of the United States provides   2
for freedom of expression, the editor of the school newspaper doesn't have to apologize for this ad. The First
Amendment to the Constitution states, "Congress shall make

Introduction is more interesting.

Claim is more specific.

A strong pro point comes first.

ACTIVITY 24 (GROUP)

Analyzing Reginald's Revised Draft. Use the following questions to discuss with your classmates how Reginald has improved his draft.

1. Is Reginald's claim more effective now? Why or why not?

   _____

   _____

2. How has Reginald improved his pro points?

   _____

   _____

   _____

3. How well has he refuted his con points?

   _____

   _____

   _____

4. In your view, how well does he organize his pro and con points?

   _____

   _____

   _____

5. How could Reginald's revised draft benefit from further revision?

   _____

   _____

   _____

ACTIVITY 25 (GROUP)

Using Peer Review. Form a group with two or three other students and exchange copies of your drafts. Read your draft aloud while your classmates follow along. Take notes on your classmates' responses to the following questions about your draft.

1. What do you like best about my essay?

   _____

   _____

   _____

2. How interesting is my introduction? Do you want to continue reading the essay? Why or why not?

   _____

   _____

   _____

3. How effective is my claim? Suggest an improvement.

   _____

   _____

   _____

4. How well do I support my pro points? Is that supporting material recent, relevant, and easily understood?

   _____

   _____

   _____

5. How well do I refute the con points?

_____

_____

_____

6. Are my pro and con points effectively organized? Can you suggest a better way to order them?

_____

_____

_____

7. Where in my draft should faulty logic be eliminated?

_____

_____

_____

8. Where in the draft does my writing confuse you? How can I clarify my thoughts?

_____

_____

_____

9. How clear is the purpose of my essay?

_____

_____

_____

Use Online Peer Review

If your class has a Web site with peer review questions listed, you may be able to respond to your classmates' drafts electronically.

ACTIVITY 26

Revising Your Draft. Taking your classmates' suggestions for revision into consideration, revise your essay. In particular, focus on making your claim more specific, supporting your pro points, refuting your con points, and eliminating faulty logic. You might also decide to rearrange parts of your essay to be more effective. Where appropriate, combine sentences and eliminate unnecessary repetition.

EDITING

At this point you have worked hard to persuade readers to accept your views on an issue related to freedom of expression. But before you can share your essay with your audience, you must edit it for correctness. In this chapter you'll focus on subject-verb agreement and avoiding shifts in verb tense.

Correcting Subject-Verb Agreement

You may recall that a complete sentence contains a subject and a verb. The subject tells who or what is doing the action, and the verb tells the action or links the subject to the rest of the sentence. To maintain *subject-verb agreement,* a *singular subject* must have a *singular verb* and a *plural subject* must have a *plural verb.*

INCORRECT   *Harry don't* care too much for the Internet.

CORRECT   *Harry doesn't* care too much for the Internet.

INCORRECT   We protested the banning of our favorite book, and the librarian said *it would remains* on the shelf.

CORRECT   We protested the banning of our favorite book, and the librarian said *it would remain* on the shelf.

When using the following singular pronouns as subjects, use singular verbs.

anybody	everything	somebody
anyone	nobody	someone
anything	no one	something
everybody	everyone	nothing

INCORRECT   *Anybody write* better than I do.

CORRECT   *Anybody writes* better than I do.

INCORRECT   *Someone need* to take care of this.

CORRECT   *Someone needs* to take care of this.

ACTIVITY 27

Using Correct Subject-Verb Agreement. Underline the correct form of the verb in the following sentences.

1. Everybody (needs, need) to support freedom of speech.

2. Everything (is, are) where I can find it easily.

3. Nobody (feel, feels) the way I do about this subject.

4. Someone (is, are) going to speak to the class on censorship.

5. Everyone I talk to (agrees, agree) with me on this.

Add a singular or plural verb to the following sentences as needed to create subject-verb agreement.

6. The book I wanted to read _____ been checked out.

7. My neighbor _____ like the kind of person who would wear a uniform.

8. We _____ to the movies every Friday night.

9. My favorite singer _____ Madonna.

10. Don't _____ me to change my mind about this topic.

Exercise Central

For additional practice avoiding shifts in verb tense, go to the *Choices* Web site at **<www.bedfordstmartins.com/ choices>**. Click on "Exercise Central."

Avoiding Shifts in Verb Tense

The *tense* of a verb tells the time of the verb's action. When writing about something that is happening now, use *present tense*. When writing about something that happened in the past, use *past tense*. And, when writing about something that will happen in the future, use *future tense*.

As a general rule, stay with the tense you began with at the start of a paragraph. Avoid shifting tenses unless the time of the action shifts.

CONFUSING   She *protested* at the campground to let others know how she felt about the draining of the lake. No water *means* no fish for the eagle whose nest *is* in the tree next to it. She *can't wait* to see the article on her protest that *ran* in the local newspaper.

REVISED   She *protested* at the campground to let others know how she felt about the draining of the lake. No water *meant* no fish for the eagle whose nest *was* in the tree next to it. She *couldn't* wait to see the article on her protest that *ran* in the local newspaper.

HOW TO Avoid Shifts in Verb Tense

Verb tense tells when the action is happening.

- Present tense: happening now

- Past tense: happened in the past

- Future tense: will happen in the future

Use the appropriate tense for what you are saying. Don't switch tenses unless the time of the action changes.

Correcting Awkward Shifts in Verb Tense. Rewrite the following paragraph to correct unnecessary shifts in verb tense.

My time on the Internet is precious to me. I spent over three hours online every night. This is valuable time to me because I learned so much each time I surf the Web. I have visited a number of sites that teaches me how to build model airplanes, my favorite hobby. I will encourage each and every one of you to try the Web for yourself. You won't regret it.

 Online Writing Centers

A number of college writing centers have online tutoring. Tutors will answer your editing questions electronically. For a list of such centers, go to the *Choices* Web site at **<www.bedfordstmartins.com/choices/>** and click on "Annotated Web Links" and then "Online Writing Centers (OWLs)."

Reginald's Edited Essay

You may have noticed that Reginald's revised draft contained errors in grammar, spelling, and punctuation. Reginald corrected these errors in his edited essay. His corrections are underlined here. His editing log follows the edited essay.

Reginald Jones
Professor Heller
English 1301
4 Mar. 2002

Newspaper Ad Sparks Controversy

An advertisement, "Ten Reasons Why Reparations for   1
Blacks Is a Bad Idea for Blacks--and Racist" ran in last

<u>week's</u> school newspaper. A reparation is a repayment for
damage done in the past. This ad stated a number of reasons
why blacks should not receive repayments from the United
States government because of the damages done by slavery.
Some of the reasons given were that not all blacks have
suffered because of slavery and that welfare and affirmative action <u>have</u> served as reparations. This ad, which some
call a "hate" ad, upset a number of students and faculty.
Some people wanted to burn all of the newspapers, some
wanted a formal apology from the editor, and some said the
paper should <u>never have run</u> the ad in the first place.
Linda Chavez, a writer for Creators Syndicate, says that
"the reparations debate has the potential of replacing
affirmative action as the most volatile race issue in
America, with Americans deeply divided on the topic" (6A).
If we value our Constitution, then we must protect it even
if that means using our campus newspapers as the showcase
for both sides of an issue. As a supporter of freedom of
speech, I defend the right of the school newspaper to run
this ad whether I agree with it or not.

2

The Constitution of the United States provides for
freedom of expression. The editor of the school newspaper
doesn't have to apologize for this ad. The First Amendment
to the Constitution states, "Congress shall make no law
respecting an establishment of religion, or prohibiting the
free exercise thereof; or abridging the freedom of speech,
or of the press; or the right of the people peaceably to
assemble, and to petition the Government for a redress of
grievances."

3

Universities are supposed to be a place where ideas
are debated. However, when David Horowitz, the founder of
the Center for the Study of Popular Culture, requested ad
space in 71 campus newspapers, only 21 would run the ad
(Chavez 6A). This is unfortunate. If we eliminate every

piece of writing that someone finds offensive, we will no longer have a free exchange of ideas. There are many examples of books that people would like to ban. Most recently, some people have called for the banning of the Harry Potter series of books because of their focus on wizardry and witchcraft. Some computer labs attempt to block students from visiting pornographic Web sites. If colleges remove every book and Web site that someone finds offensive, there would be few books or Web sites left for students to use.

To those students who propose burning the newspapers,   4
I remind them that this would be a crime. We don't want to encourage people to commit crimes just to ban material that makes them uncomfortable. There are better ways to protest. Students could run an ad themselves explaining their views on the topic of reparations for blacks, or they could write to the author of the ad to protest his views. On our campus, the topic has been debated as part of Black History month activities. We have set up debates and had students present both sides of the reparation argument.

Rather than burning newspapers or demanding an   5
apology, students should discuss the ideas expressed in the ad and not just refuse to run it. We must attack these ideas with ideas that are even stronger. Joan Bertin of the National Coalition against Censorship says, "While student protests are an appropriate way to explore controversy, when students take it upon themselves to suppress ideas that they find objectionable they fail to meet the challenge of a free society--to counter offensive ideas with more persuasive arguments of their own" (par. 4). At our most recent campus debate, we concluded that repara-tions are not likely to occur and that the discussion of them only divides Americans.

As students and teachers, we must protect freedom of   6

expression even if it means permitting some advertisements that we don't like to appear in our school newspapers. Instead of attempting to ban these advertisements, we must come up with constructive ways to encourage debate on the content of the ads themselves.

Use a separate page for your "Works Cited" entries. See p. 554.

Works Cited

Bertin, Joan. "Free Speech Groups Express Concern over Student Reaction to Controversial Ad." <u>NCAC on the Issues</u> 1 Mar. 2002. National Coalition against Censorship. 3 Mar. 2002 <www.ncac.org/issues/ reparationsad.html>.

Chavez, Linda. "Reparations Issue Could Be Divisive." <u>El Paso Times</u> 3 Mar. 2002: 6A.

Reginald's Editing Log

3/5 — "Newspaper Ad Sparks Controversy"

INCORRECT	weeks (1)
ERROR	missing apostrophe
CORRECT	week's
INCORRECT	Some of the reasons given were that not all blacks have suffered because of slavery and that welfare and affirmative action has served as reparations. (1)
ERROR	incorrect subject-verb agreement
CORRECT	Some of the reasons given were that not all blacks have suffered because of slavery and that welfare and affirmative action have served as reparations.
INCORRECT	Some people wanted to burn all of the newspapers, some wanted a formal apology from the editor, and some said the paper should never plan to run the ad in the first place. (1)
ERROR	unnecessary shift in verb tense
CORRECT	Some people wanted to burn all of the newspapers, some wanted a formal apology from the editor, and some said the paper should never have run the ad in the first place.

ACTIVITY 29

Make sure you refer to the Handbook to help you eliminate errors.

Editing Your Essay. Using the Handbook in Part Four of this book as a guide, edit your revised draft for errors in grammar, spelling, and punctuation. Your classmates can help you locate and correct errors you might have overlooked. Add the errors you find and their corrections to your editing log.

Switch Terminals to Edit

If your class has access to a computer terminal as a group, ask several classmates to read your essay on the computer terminal and to boldface the errors they find. The more student readers you enlist to help you spot errors in your draft, the more error-free it will be. If necessary, consult your instructor, a tutor, or the Handbook in Part Four of this book to verify the errors and help you correct them.

Be sure that you share your essay with those who can make a change.

PUBLISHING

You're ready to share your essay with your audience—your instructor and classmates, as well as others affected by your topic. If, for instance, you argue that a certain law should be enacted or repealed, you might send your essay to the appropriate government official, such as your senator or congressional representative. If you advocate a change in a television show, you could share your essay with the network on which the show appears. An essay on censorship in schools could be shared with local school superintendents, school board members, and others in charge of matters related to censorship.

CHAPTER CHECKLIST

- ☐ I wrote an effective claim, one that asserts something is true, expresses an opinion, relates to my readers' lives, and is focused.
- ☐ I used pro points, which came from experience, observations, and research, to support my claim.
- ☐ I supported pro points with material that is recent, relevant, and easily understood.
- ☐ I refuted or argued against con points, or objections, to a claim.

☐ I arranged pro and con points so that readers become more convinced of my claim as they read through my essay.

☐ I avoided faulty logic, or flawed reasoning, by eliminating hasty generalizations, faulty either-or reasoning, and faulty cause-and-effect reasoning.

☐ I combined short, closely related sentences to improve flow of ideas.

☐ I eliminated unnecessary repetition to keep readers' interest.

☐ I corrected errors in subject-verb agreement and awkward shifts in verb tense.

☐ I shared my essay with people affected by this topic.

REFLECTING ON YOUR WRITING

To help you reflect on the writing you did in this chapter, answer the following questions.

1. Compare your experience writing a persuasive essay with writing an expressive or informative essay. What did you enjoy most and least about these assignments?

2. What did you learn from writing this essay?

3. How persuasive do you think your essay would be to someone who strongly disagrees with your claim?

4. If you had more time, what more would you do to improve your essay before sharing it with readers?

Using your answers to these questions, update your Writing Process Report.

Writing Process Report

Date:

Strengths:

Weaknesses:

Plans for improvement:

Once you complete this report, freewrite about what you learned in this chapter about your writing and what you still hope to learn.

Freedom of Expression in Schools

In the following reading, "Is Harry Potter Evil?" Judy Blume presents her position on the controversy surrounding the Harry Potter series.

JUDY BLUME

Is Harry Potter Evil?

I happened to be in London last summer on the very day *Harry Potter and the Prisoner of Azkaban,* the third book in the wildly popular series by J. K. Rowling, was published. I couldn't believe my good fortune. I rushed to the bookstore to buy a copy, knowing this simple act would put me up there with the best grandmas in the world. The book was still months away from publication in the United States, and I have an 8-year-old grandson who is a big Harry Potter fan. 1

It's a good thing when children enjoy books, isn't it? Most of us think so. But like many children's books these days, the Harry Potter series has recently come under fire. In Minnesota, Michigan, New York, California and South Carolina, parents who feel the books promote interest in the occult have called for their removal from classrooms and school libraries. 2

I knew this was coming. The only surprise is that it took so long—as long as it took for the zealots who claim they're protecting children from evil (and evil can be found lurking everywhere these days) to discover that children actually like these books. If children are excited about a book, it must be suspect. 3

I'm not exactly unfamiliar with this line of thinking, having had various books of mine banned from schools over the last 20 years. In my books, it's reality that's seen as corrupting. With Harry Potter, the perceived danger is fantasy. After all, Harry and his classmates attend the celebrated Hogwarts School of Witchcraft and Wizardry. According to certain adults, these stories teach witchcraft, sorcery and satanism. But hey, if it's not one "ism," it's another. I mean Madeleine L'Engle's *A Wrinkle in Time* has been targeted by censors for promoting New Ageism, and Mark Twain's *Adventures of Huckleberry Finn* for promoting racism. Gee, where does that leave the kids? 4

The real danger is not in the books, but in laughing off those 5
who would ban them. The protests against Harry Potter follow a
tradition that has been growing since the early 1980's and often
leaves school principals trembling with fear that is then passed
down to teachers and librarians.

What began with the religious right has spread to the politi- 6
cally correct. (Remember the uproar in Brooklyn last year when
a teacher was criticized for reading a book entitled "Nappy Hair"
to her class?) And now the gate is open so wide that some parents
believe they have the right to demand immediate removal of any
book for any reason from school or classroom libraries. The list
of gifted teachers and librarians who find their jobs in jeopardy
for defending their students' right to read, to imagine, to question, grows every year.

My grandson was bewildered when I tried to explain why 7
some adults don't want their children reading about Harry Potter.
"But that doesn't make any sense!" he said. J. K. Rowling is on a
book tour in America right now. She's probably befuddled by the
brouhaha, too. After all, she was just trying to tell a good story.

My husband and I like to reminisce about how, when we 8
were 9, we read straight through L. Frank Baum's *Oz* series, books
filled with wizards and witches. And you know what those subversive tales taught us? That we loved to read! In those days I
used to dream of flying. I may have been small and powerless in
real life, but in my imagination I was able to soar.

At the rate we're going, I can imagine next year's headline: 9
"'Goodnight Moon' Banned for Encouraging Children to Communicate With Furniture." And we all know where that can lead,
don't we?

VOCABULARY WORDS: occult (2), zealots (3), suspect (3), sorcery
(4), bewildered (7), befuddled (7), brouhaha (7), subversive (8)

ACTIVITY 30

Reading to Improve Writing. Discuss the following questions
about "Is Harry Potter Evil?" with your classmates.

1. What is Blume's claim or position on banning Harry Potter books
   from school libraries?

   _____

   _____

2. Blume states, "I knew this was coming." How did she know?

_____

_____

3. What does Blume identify as the real danger? Do you agree or disagree with her point?

_____

_____

_____

4. How effective is Blume's argument? How could she improve it?

_____

_____

_____

Freedom of Expression in the Media

In the following reading, "Why We Crave Horror Movies," Stephen King claims that we watch horror movies to give free expression to our emotions.

STEPHEN KING
Why We Crave Horror Movies

I think that we're all mentally ill; those of us outside the asylums only hide it a little better—and maybe not all that much better, after all. We've all known people who talk to themselves, people who sometimes squinch their faces into horrible grimaces when they believe no one is watching, people who have some hysterical fear—of snakes, the dark, the tight place, the long drop . . . and, of course, those final worms and grubs that are waiting so patiently underground.

When we pay our four or five bucks and seat ourselves at
tenth-row center in a theater showing a horror movie, we are
daring the nightmare.

Why? Some of the reasons are simple and obvious. To show
that we can, that we are not afraid, that we can ride this roller
coaster. Which is not to say that a really good horror movie may
not surprise a scream out of us at some point, the way we may
scream when the roller coaster twists through a complete 360 or
plows through a lake at the bottom of the drop. And horror
movies, like roller coasters, have always been the special province
of the young; by the time one turns 40 or 50, one's appetite for
double twists or 360-degree loops may be considerably depleted.

We also go to reestablish our feelings of essential normality;
the horror movie is innately conservative, even reactionary. Freda
Jackson as the horrible melting woman in *Die, Monster, Die!* confirms for us that no matter how far we may be removed from the
beauty of a Robert Redford or a Diana Ross, we are still light-
years from true ugliness.

And we go to have fun.

Ah, but this is where the ground starts to slope away, isn't it?
Because this is a very peculiar sort of fun, indeed. The fun comes
from seeing others menaced—sometimes killed. One critic has
suggested that if pro football has become the voyeur's version of
combat, then the horror film has become the modern version of
the public lynching.

It is true that the mythic, "fairy-tale" horror film intends to
take away the shades of gray. . . . It urges us to put away our
more civilized and adult penchant for analysis and to become
children again, seeing things in pure blacks and whites. It may
be that horror movies provide psychic relief on this level because
this invitation to lapse into simplicity, irrationality, and even
outright madness is extended so rarely. We are told we may allow
our emotions a free rein . . . or no rein at all.

If we are all insane, then sanity becomes a matter of degree.
If your insanity leads you to carve up women, like Jack the Rip-
per or the Cleveland Torso Murderer, we clap you away in the
funny farm (but neither of those two amateur-night surgeons
was ever caught, heh-heh-heh); if, on the other hand, your insanity leads you only to talk to yourself when you're under stress or
to pick your nose on your morning bus, then you are left alone
to go about your business . . . though it is doubtful that you will
ever be invited to the best parties.

The potential lyncher is in almost all of us (excluding saints,
past and present; but then, most saints have been crazy in their
own ways), and every now and then, he has to be let loose to

scream and roll around in the grass. Our emotions and our fears form their own body, and we recognize that it demands its own exercise to maintain proper muscle tone. Certain of these emotional muscles are accepted—even exalted—in civilized society; they are, of course, the emotions that tend to maintain the status quo of civilization itself. Love, friendship, loyalty, kindness—these are all the emotions that we applaud, emotions that have been immortalized in the couplets of Hallmark cards and in the verses (I don't dare call it poetry) of Leonard Nimoy.

When we exhibit these emotions, society showers us with positive reinforcement; we learn this even before we get out of diapers. When, as children, we hug our rotten little puke of a sister and give her a kiss, all the aunts and uncles smile and twit and cry, "Isn't he the sweetest little thing?" Such coveted treats as chocolate-covered graham crackers often follow. But if we deliberately slam the rotten little puke of a sister's fingers in the door, sanctions follow—angry remonstrance from parents, aunts and uncles; instead of a chocolate-covered graham cracker, a spanking. **10**

But anticivilization emotions don't go away, and they demand periodic exercise. We have such "sick" jokes as, "What's the difference between a truckload of bowling balls and a truckload of dead babies?" (You can't unload a truckload of bowling balls with a pitchfork. . . . A joke, by the way, that I heard originally from a ten-year-old). Such a joke may surprise a laugh or a grin out of us even as we recoil, a possibility that confirms the thesis: if we share a brotherhood of man, then we also share an insanity of man. None of which is intended as a defense of either the sick joke or insanity but merely as an explanation of why the best horror films, like the best fairy tales, manage to be reactionary, anarchistic, and revolutionary all at the same time. **11**

The mythic horror movie, like the sick joke, has a dirty job to do. It deliberately appeals to all that is worst in us. It is morbidity unchained, our most base instincts let free, our nastiest fantasies realized . . . and it all happens, fittingly enough, in the dark. For those reasons, good liberals often shy away from horror films. For myself, I like to see the most aggressive of them—*Dawn of the Dead,* for instance—as lifting a trap door in the civilized forebrain and throwing a basket of raw meat to the hungry alligators swimming around in that subterranean river beneath. **12**

Why bother? Because it keeps them from getting out, man. It keeps them down there and me up here. It was Lennon and McCartney who said that all you need is love, and I would agree with that. **13**

As long as you keep the gators fed. **14**

VOCABULARY WORDS: grimaces (1), hysterical (1), province (3), innately (4), voyeur (6), mythic (7), immortalized (9), remonstrance (10), morbidity (12), subterranean (12)

ACTIVITY 31

Reading to Improve Writing. Discuss the following questions about "Why We Crave Horror Movies" with your classmates.

1. King claims that we watch horror movies to give freedom to our emotions. Which emotions is he referring to?

   _____

   _____

2. What pro points does King use to support his claim?

   _____

   _____

   _____

   _____

3. What con points does King use to refute this claim?

   _____

   _____

   _____

   _____

4. Do you watch horror movies? Why or why not? If you watch them, do you agree with King's analysis of why you watch?

   _____

   _____

   _____

Freedom of Expression on the Internet

In the following reading, "Symposium: Two Views on the Installation of Internet Filters in Public Libraries and Schools," Bruce Watson claims that it is time for Internet filters to be installed at libraries. This is the opposing view to Richard Glen Boire's article on pp. 387–90.

BRUCE WATSON

Symposium: Two Views on the Installation of Internet Filters in Public Libraries and Schools

How would you feel if your 11-year-old son went down to the public library and checked out *Deep Throat*, the hard-core pornographic video? Or your 9-year-old daughter stumbled across *Hustler* magazine during a research project in her classroom at school? 1

Most parents would experience something between shock and outrage, plus an element of pure surprise. But, of course, these are purely hypothetical examples—schools and libraries don't offer pornographic magazines and videos to kids. In fact, even for adults, it is almost unheard of for public libraries to have materials such as *Hustler* or *Deep Throat* in their print or video collections. 2

So presumably the same standards also would apply on the Internet, right? The answer, unfortunately, is not yet, which is why Congress took a step in this direction in December by passing the Children's Internet Protection Act (CIPA). The CIPA offers a simple deal: if federal funds are used to provide Internet access in schools and libraries, then part of those funds must be used to filter out the pornography. (More precisely, child pornography, obscenity and material defined legally as "harmful to minors" must be filtered for minors age 16 or younger. For adult access, only the first two categories apply, with disabling available by a supervisor for research or other bona fide purposes.) Although CIPA was tucked into an appropriations bill, there is no question it was a response to widespread concern: A national survey last fall by Digital Media Forum found an overwhelming 92 percent support for filtering pornography out of school computers. 3

The reasons for concern have little to do with coyly posed *Playboy* centerfolds. Even veteran pornographer Larry Flynt has 4 acknowledged that "There's an awful lot of material on the Internet that children should not have access to. There's material that even I, in my wildest imagination, would not consider publishing." And much of it is freely available to anyone who stumbles onto a porn Website.

A study last summer for the National Center for Missing and 5 Exploited Children found that one in four online youths ages 10 to 17 had an unwanted encounter with pornography in the previous 12 months. Children today are encountering these hard-core sites through misleading site names (such as whitehouse.com, a porn site), through invisible "metatags" misusing popular brand names such as Nintendo or Muppets, through unsolicited e-mail or simply by typing the word "porn" into an unfiltered Internet browser. Curiosity in children and teenagers is natural and healthy, but the distorted lens of hard-core porn offers a poor sexual role model.

Opponents of filtering say the software has too many anom- 6 alies, such as "overblocking" Websites for chicken-breast recipes or the county of Middlesex. Such examples often are based on first-generation word-association software rather than state-of-the-art products. They reflect the astonishingly persistent disinformation campaign waged by filtering opponents. Other examples, rather than confirming a sinister political agenda, have an almost hilariously random quality, such as the famous (and brief) blocking by one product of the Quaker church Website.

The real question is not whether filters are perfect—if you 7 use Windows, you know that perfection is an impossible standard in the world of computers and, thus, irrelevant. The real question is whether they work within a tolerable level of error. Experience in schools and libraries indicates that the good brands meet this test comfortably. The performance of the better products is one reason why the number of libraries using filters has doubled in the last two years. Approximately 25 percent of libraries now use at least some filtering, according to the National Commission on Library Science.

Besides, how can today's filtering software be described as a 8 one-size-fits-all solution when the industrial-strength products for schools and libraries typically have between 20 and 60 categories of customization available? Do the math—that's a dizzying range of permutations.

The American Civil Liberties Union (ACLU)/American Library 9 Association (ALA) strategy is fairly straightforward: By relentlessly publicizing the "anomaly of the week," they distract attention from the inherent absurdity of their own demand—that only a perfect filter is acceptable in the imperfect world of computers. They would have us believe that a single overblocked site is a more significant anomaly than an entire generation of school-children given free and easy access to the crudest of hard-core pornography. It's easy to see why 92 percent of the public disagrees with them.

The ALA's solution is to provide "acceptable-use policies" in each local library. The only problem is they don't work. More than 90 percent of public libraries already have such policies, yet former librarian David Burt's study, *Dangerous Access* (2000 Edition), found thousands of incidents of library patrons accessing pornography online. The more disturbing incidents included public masturbation, adults enticing children to view porn sites and trading in child pornography. Burt filed requests under the Freedom of Information Act for incident reports concerning Internet pornography but received only a 29 percent response rate after the ALA got involved. So much for open access to information.   10

A more serious concern, especially for conservatives, is whether it is necessary for the government to step in and require filtering. Part of the answer is that, if schools and libraries provide unfiltered access only, then public funds are being used to distribute pornography. When government funds are creating the problem, government funds should provide the solution. Requiring the feds to clean up their own mess is hardly a "big-government" proposition.   11

The other reason for a legislated approach is that the group that could help most—the ALA—is instead leading the opposition. Says Judith Krug, director of the ALA's Office of Intellectual Freedom: "Blocking material leads to censorship. That goes for pornography and bestiality, too. if you don't like it, don't look at it." This applies even for children. Their fetchingly titled manual, "The Censor Is Coming—Intellectual Freedom for Children," notes that, by formal policy, "the ALA opposes all attempts to restrict access to library services, materials and facilities based on the age of library users." The fierce opposition of ALA's Head Office is the principal reason why 75 percent of libraries use no filtering today.   12

When communities fret that this ivory-tower approach makes local libraries unsafe for children, Krug responds: "If you don't want your children to access that information, you had better be with your children when they use a computer." Former ALA president Ann Symons explains: "We do not help children when we simply wall them off from information and ideas that   13 are controversial and disturbing." The fallacy, of course, is to equate pornography with information and ideas. Hard-core pornography is simply not an intellectual matter; rather, like the Bill Clinton/Monica Lewinsky affair, the guiding impulse for porn comes from another part of the anatomy.

In conclusion, it is important to remember that parents still 14 have the primary responsibility for guiding their children on the Internet, just as they do on issues like smoking or drinking. The problem is that parents today carry all the responsibility, even though they usually are less computer-literate than their children. Parents need the support of the law, just as they do with smoking and drinking. Children's safety online involves parents and other gatekeepers, the Internet industry and the legal community. It would be irresponsible for any of these groups to claim a free ride by having someone else shoulder the entire burden.

VOCABULARY WORDS: hypothetical (2), obscenity (3), coyly (4), anomalies (6), sinister (6), tolerable (7), fallacy (13)

ACTIVITY 32

Reading to Improve Writing. Discuss the following questions about Watson's essay with your classmates.

1. Watson claims that government funds should be used to filter pornography in public libraries. Which sentence is his thesis statement?

   _____

   _____

   _____

2. What pro points does Watson use to support his claim?

   _____

   _____

   _____

3. What con points does Watson use to refute this claim?

_____

_____

_____

4. Do you agree with Watson? Why or why not?

_____

_____

_____

Injustice anywhere is a threat to justice everywhere.

—MARTIN LUTHER KING JR.

CHAPTER 9

Identifying Issues, Proposing Solutions

In this chapter you will

- write about a campus, regional, or national issue.

- provide evidence that the problem exists.

- propose a solution to the problem.

- learn to persuade readers by using logical, emotional, and ethical appeals.

- combine sentences using appositives.

- learn to maintain a reasonable tone.

- avoid shifts in person.

- use quotation marks correctly.

- reflect on your writing.

Think about some of the arguments you have been involved in. Did you ever become so angry that you couldn't discuss the issue at hand? Did you yell, stomp your feet, and leave the room, slamming the door behind you? Sometimes when we're angry, we don't think clearly, and afterwards we realize that we forgot to say something important or that we said something we wish we could take back. Seldom is anything accomplished as a result oı a heated argument.

At the center of any argument is an issue, something on which people disagree. Almost anything can be an issue—the clothes you wear, the books you choose to read, even your choice of friends. Larger issues, such as campus, regional, and national issues, affect many people.

Campus issues affect students, staff, and faculty on a college campus. Can you think of some issues on your campus? Do students need better advising? Is computer access adequate? Is the food served at the student center edible? Are there enough parking spaces? Regional issues affect the people of a town, city, state, or region of the country. Does Mason Township need a new animal shelter? Should more money be allocated to protect the Everglades? Is the California state income tax too high? National issues affect nearly everyone within a particular country. Does the United States need better gun-control laws? Does the welfare system need to be revamped? Should illegal immigrants receive social services?

WRITING ASSIGNMENT

For this assignment, write a persuasive essay about a campus, regional, or national issue that concerns you. You will state a problem and give your position on it, provide evidence that the problem exists, and propose a solution. You or your instructor may decide to do this assignment in one of several ways.

- You may gather ideas on one, two, or three topics.
- You may write a discovery draft on one, two, or three topics.
- You may choose one discovery draft to develop into a polished essay.
- You may combine your discovery draft ideas into a new topic for your essay.

After completing your essay, you'll share it with your instructor and classmates, as well as with others who can take action on the issue such as parents, friends, school administrators, television producers, or government officials.

As you think about these larger issues, consider your responsibility to your college, your region, and your country. What problems can you identify, and what solutions can you propose? By writing about a problem and possible solutions to it, you may help resolve an issue for yourself and others.

ACTIVITY 1

Analyzing Your Purpose and Audience. Before you begin gathering ideas about your topic, think about your purpose and audience. For this chapter's assignment, you will describe your views on an issue, propose a solution, and attempt to convince your audience to accept and take action on your proposal.

For more information on purpose and audience, see p. 5.

Keep in mind that in addition to your instructor and classmates, your audience will include someone with the authority to act on your proposal. For example, if you choose a campus issue, such as inadequate advising or unsafe parking lots at your college, your audience would include, respectively, the dean or the campus police chief. Similarly, for a local or regional issue, such as the need for a new local animal shelter or for adequate state prison facilities, your audience would include local government officials or the state governor. Finally, for a national issue, such as the federal government's proposed cuts in financial aid benefits to students, your audience would include your congressional representative and possibly the U.S. president.

Once you identify your audience and purpose, use the following questions to help you decide how to approach your topic.

1. Does this assignment call for expressive, informative, or persuasive writing?

   _____

2. What is your readers' average age?

   _____

3. What is your readers' average educational level?

   _____

   Ethnic background?

   _____

Economic level?

_____

Political orientation: conservative, moderate, or liberal?

_____

4. How might your responses to the previous three questions affect how you write your essay?

_____

_____

_____

GATHERING IDEAS

Read more about gathering ideas on pp. 29–34.

   To gather ideas about a campus, regional, or national issue, select from among the various techniques you learned in Chapter 2. The students in this chapter will use freewriting, reading, relating aloud, and reflecting on their topic.

A Campus Issue

   Think about some of the issues affecting students on your campus. What could be done to improve education or campus life? Perhaps you would like to see more courses offered in photography or more school spirit among students. Maybe you want the registration process streamlined or the campus parking situation improved in some way. Which issue do you complain about most often? Now is your chance to do something about it.

   You might ask, "But who will listen to me?" Despite many college students' assumptions that they can't change "the system," most college administrators are eager to listen to students. After all, you're their customers. However, they must be aware of problems and, more important, they must find solutions. As a student writer, you can play an important role in helping campus administrators perform these functions.

In the following essay, Tony Laure identifies a problem: students who spend too much time talking on cell phones. He then goes on to propose the solution: students should be less materialistic.

TONY LAURE

Students Caught Up in Cell Phone Craze

In a dimly lighted classroom at the University of Illinois at Chicago, students gather their belongings while listening to a professor wrap up a well-prepared lecture. With only a few minutes of class time remaining, a female student in the second row pulls a cellular phone from her coat pocket and holds it firmly in her hand. Seeing this, other students in the class start checking their phones with an urgency as contagious as yawning at the ballet. One by one, students pull out their treasured cell phones. Some are gold in color, some are silver, some even flip open and all are new and stylish. As the professor dismisses the class, students rush to check their messages.

OK, so at one point or another we all have been annoyed by somebody on a cell phone, either someone whose phone rang during class or a motorist swerving all over the road with a phone smashed between a shoulder and an ear. The fact is cell phones are everywhere. But lately it seems what once was an essential tool for important communication has become merely a toy for college kids and adults alike. And now, the accessibility and inexpensiveness of this useful technology has spawned a whole new breed of annoying Americans whose lack of cell phone etiquette clearly demonstrates the selfishness of today's youths.

It is evident the cell phone craze has swept UIC. Just walking around campus it's almost certainly easier now to find a person on a cell phone than someone holding a calculator or even listening to headphones. On campus, I've actually witnessed students decorate their cell phones with colored covers, play video games on the phone's display screen and even compare them with friends. Just the other day as I was lounging before a class, I was surprised to hear Beethoven's Fifth Symphony emanating from a student's pocket. Now I've heard plenty of bad cover songs, but none as bad as this brilliant piece being played as a series of beeps on a royal blue Nokia cell phone.

Sure, some people might read this and think, "It's just a phone. What's the big deal?" But I believe the significance of the cell phone is correlated with the values of today's youths. Ultimately, and unfortunately, this is the importance young people place on material goods and products. There is no doubt we are living in a visual age in which images encourage us to be good consumers. But we must realize we are living in a country where everything we consume is first researched by teams of experts whose main objective is increasing profits. This includes technologies such as cell phones, and today's youth are obliviously buying into the hype and filling in a void normally reserved for spirituality and even original thought.

It's funny how things change. Since the 60s, college students   5
are more concerned with updating their cell phones every two months and adorning their new cars with shiny chrome wheels than they are in fighting for a good cause. The cell phone culture certainly is a selfish one. Cell phones can be a convenience, but when they are used to detach the user from the environment, it simply is unnecessary and wrong. What better way to avoid interaction with the environment and the people in it than to shield your ear with a cell phone?

As the technology continues to progress, it is obvious young   6
Americans will continue to be obedient consumers. But ultimately it boils down to what is important to us, and I truly hope it's more than just the material.

VOCABULARY WORDS: craze (title), urgency (1), essential (2), spawned (2), emanating (3), obliviously (4), hype (4)

ACTIVITY 2

Reading to Improve Writing. Discuss the following questions about "Students Caught Up in Cell Phone Craze" with your classmates.

1. What is the author's thesis statement?

_____

_____

_____

_____

2. What evidence does he provide that the problem exists?

_____

_____

_____

3. What are the results of the problem?

_____

_____

_____

4. Do you agree with Laure's reasons for why students talk on cell phones?

_____

_____

_____

_____

5. What does Laure propose as a solution?

_____

_____

_____

6. List several problems that need attention on your campus.

_____

_____

_____

_____

ACTIVITY 3

Freewriting about a Campus Issue. Freewrite to gather ideas about the campus issue that most concerns and interests you. Use the following questions to stimulate your thinking.

1. What is your position on the issue?
2. What do you already know about it?
3. What more do you need to know about the issue?
4. What do you think should be done?
5. Who has the power to act on your proposed solution?

Li Chaing, a student writer concerned about the computer lab on his campus, did some freewriting in response to the questions in Activity 3. Here's what he wrote:

> I am concerned about the computer lab on campus. My position is that the computer lab does not serve the needs of students. Even though we pay a $50 user fee each semester, we don't get good service. I know quite a bit about the lab because I spend most of my spare time there. I don't own a computer and must use the lab to complete assignments. From my own observations, I know that the hardware is outdated, the software selection is inadequate, and the students who work there are not very helpful. However, I need to find out whether other students on campus agree with my position, as well as why the college administration has not made any attempt to improve the computer lab. I think part of the user fee students pay each semester should be used to update the computer lab on a regular basis. The vice president for academic affairs is the person in charge of this matter.

Put your material about a campus issue aside for now. You want to think about a regional issue that concerns you.

A Regional Issue

Your college campus is only one of the environments in which you live. When you leave the campus, you interact with family, friends, and other members of your local and regional community. As you interact, you cannot help but notice problems. Perhaps your neighbors don't show an interest in recycling. Maybe a local factory pollutes the air, or nearby cities are taking water needed to irrigate farms in your county.

Regional issues can be solved only by showing people that a problem exists and then persuading them to correct it. Sometimes a solution requires people to forgo comfort or personal gain for the good of the entire community. Then it becomes more difficult to persuade people to accept change. But if you succeed, you'll have benefited not only yourself but others who live in your region as well.

In the following essay, "An Act of Conscience," John Garrity identifies a problem—private golf club discrimination—and proposes a solution.

JOHN GARRITY

An Act of Conscience

1   I almost cheered when I read Friday morning's front-page headline in *The Kansas City Star:* WATSON QUITS CLUB, CITING BIAS. . . . Tom Watson, winner of eight major golf championships and 32 PGA Tour titles, had resigned from the ultra-restrictive Kansas City Country Club to protest the club's blackballing of tax-preparation tycoon Henry Bloch.

2   Bloch, the cofounder and chairman of H&R Block, Inc., is Jewish. Watson is not Jewish, but his wife, Linda, and their two children are. Watson said his conscience forced him to resign "out of respect for my family—my wife, my children and myself."

3   Those close to Watson say he is torn up by the decision, and little wonder. The Kansas City Country Club has been at the center of his universe since he first appeared on its fairways in short pants, learning golf at his father's side. His longtime coach, Stan Thirsk, is the club pro and a second father to Watson. For years, when other touring pros spent the winter sharpening their games in Arizona and Florida, Watson stayed home and hit practice balls into the snow from a mat in the course superintendent's shed.

4   There was no warning that Watson would step forward on this issue. As recently as last summer, when the Shoal Creek controversy brought the discriminatory practices of private clubs into focus, Watson defended the status quo. He said that people should "chill out" and that private clubs had the right to choose their members. Funny how some of the most important decisions in our lives come unbidden.

Those of us who know both Watson and the Kansas City Country Club have long wondered how he handled the competing loyalties of club and family. How did he insulate his wife, his kids and his brother-in-law, Chuck Rubin, who is also his manager, from the ethnic slurs sometimes voiced in the club's public rooms? 5

My own feelings about the Kansas City Country Club surely color these remarks. I caddied there a few times in my teens, and, thanks to the Kansas City Junior Golf Association, I even got to play there one Thursday every summer. My notions of upper-class golf were thus formed—from the bottom looking up. 6

Some of what I saw I liked: the rows of lofty elms and oaks, the steep-faced bunkers, the silky greens. There was more that I disliked: the clubhouse staff's arrogance, the rudeness of certain members and, most of all, the unmistakable message that I was there at their sufferance. It was at the Kansas City Country Club, coincidentally, that I first heard the word *kike.* 7

Today I live within walking distance of the club. Like most Kansas Citians, I regard it as a vestige of the mid-century, something from the era of Mr. and Mrs. Bridge, the fictional Kansas City couple created by novelist Evan Connell. The Bridges of this world, I have found, live lives stunted by their simple faith in the "right" neighborhoods, the "right" schools and, of course, the "right" clubs. 8

I was ticked off, though, when I read that Bloch's candidacy, which was sponsored by Hallmark Cards chairman Donald Hall and seconded by two other major corporate chairmen, never got to the club's board for a vote. Bloch was thwarted by a five-man membership committee. This star chamber is so secret that only the club's president and secretary know its composition. Its members may not wear hoods during their deliberations, but their performance this time was sufficient to embarrass not just the club but the city as well. 9

That's the galling part of the Bloch affair. I suspect that many—possibly most—of the club's members hold Henry Bloch in high regard and would welcome him as a member. Undoubtedly, others are comfortable with the idea of Hispanic, Asian or black members. But until now fear has kept decent people from speaking out. 10

Fear of what, you ask? Why, the greatest fear of all—that they will no longer be accepted by their peers. Sounds trivial, but social acceptance is the glue that binds a city's power elite. Mavericks don't get the big contracts, the special tax abatements, the school buildings named in their honor. 11

By their recent actions, Bloch's sponsors and Watson have 12 lifted that veil of fear. Already, prominent Kansas City Country Club members are publicly distancing themselves from the bigotry. Either Bloch or another Jewish candidate will be accepted soon, they say, or there will be more resignations. "It's going to change," vows one of the reformers. "I'm convinced of that."

The place to start, if an outsider may offer a suggestion, is with   13
that secret membership committee. Flush those scrofulous characters into the open, make them accountable for their actions, and they won't be so quick to smear and denigrate. Next, do whatever it takes to get Tom Watson back in the fold. A friend of the Watson family says, "He's hurting something fierce right now."

Watson's pain may ease when he realizes that in his chil-   14
dren's eyes, and in ours, this single act of conscience will one day count for more than all the trophies he has won with his clubs.

VOCABULARY WORDS: bias (1), discriminatory (4), insulate (5), arrogance (7), sufferance (7), vestige (8), thwarted (9) galling (10), bigotry (12), scrofulous (13)

ACTIVITY 4

Reading to Improve Writing. Discuss the following questions about "An Act of Conscience" with your classmates.

1. What regional problem does Garrity identify in his essay?

   _____

   _____

2. What is his position on this problem?

   _____

   _____

3. What supporting details does he use to convince his readers that the problem exists?

   _____

   _____

_____

_____

4. What is his proposed solution?

_____

_____

_____

_____

5. Does Garrity persuade you that this problem exists? Why or why not?

_____

_____

6. Do you think Garrity's solutions are practical? Why or why not?

_____

_____

7. List problems that exist in your region.

_____

_____

ACTIVITY 5

Reading to Gather Information. In the reference section of your library or on the World Wide Web, locate several magazine and newspaper articles on the regional issue you want to explore. Use these questions to evaluate the articles.

For additional help conducting research, see Chapter 11.

1. Do most of the articles support or oppose your position on the issue?

2. What supporting details do the authors use to convince readers of their views?

3. Can you add additional details to these arguments?

4. Do the authors propose any worthwhile solutions?

Search the Web

If you have access to the World Wide Web, you can use a search engine to find Web sites on your topic. After reading them online, you may wish to print the information that you will use for your essay. You may also access news magazines on the *Choices* Web site. Go to **<www .bedfordstmartins.com/choices/>** and click on "Annotated Web Links."

One student, Joy, decided to write about the death penalty in an attempt to persuade her governor that, in her view, capital punishment is a deterrent to violent crime. To learn more about the issue, Joy read several articles about crime. Here is how she answered the questions in Activity 5:

1. *As a resident of this state, I am concerned about the increasing violence in our cities and what can be done about it. Newspaper accounts of violence appear regularly. According to some articles I've read, capital punishment is one means to deter violent crime.*

2. *Most authors use crime statistics to support the view that crime is out of control. Since 1973, violence has more than doubled. The Department of Justice estimates that one out of every six people will be a victim of some form of crime.*

3. *In support of those statistics, I can cite several recent examples of violent crime in my area. On April 27, at 12:30 a.m., a local university student was shot to death for blowing his car horn in front of his girlfriend's apartment. A week later, a thirteen-year-old boy was set on fire for standing too close to a car.*

4. *The authors propose various solutions, including capital punishment. It would allow us to express indignation for certain heinous acts, such as capital murder. It would also send the message that violent crime will not be tolerated.*

Set your writing on a regional issue aside for now, so you can explore one more possible topic for your essay — a national issue.

A National Issue

National issues affect all of us in one way or another. Drugs, crime, welfare, educational reform, and taxation are all national issues. Usually more complex than local or regional issues, national issues can be more difficult to resolve. Americans' diversity is one of this country's greatest strengths, but it also contributes to the complexity of many national issues. People living in different parts of the country and who are ethnically, religiously, and economically diverse tend also to hold differing opinions about national issues.

Solutions to national problems often require imaginative ideas. In "Perils of Prohibition," Elizabeth M. Whelan identifies a problem: the legal drinking age of twenty-one encourages irresponsible drinking. She then proposes a surprising solution: lower the drinking age to eighteen and educate teens about alcohol abuse.

ELIZABETH M. WHELAN

Perils of Prohibition

My colleagues at the Harvard School of Public Health, where I studied preventive medicine, deserve high praise for their recent study on teenage drinking. What they found in their survey of college students was that they drink "early and . . . often," frequently to the point of getting ill.

As a public-health scientist with a daughter, Christine, heading to college this fall, I have professional and personal concerns about teen binge drinking. It is imperative that we explore why so many young people abuse alcohol. From my own study of the effects of alcohol restrictions and my observations of Christine and her friends' predicament about drinking, I believe that today's laws are unrealistic. Prohibiting the sale of liquor to responsible young adults creates an atmosphere where binge drinking and alcohol abuse have become a problem. American teens, unlike their European peers, don't learn how to drink gradually, safely and in moderation.

Alcohol is widely accepted and enjoyed in our culture. Studies show that moderate drinking can be good for you. But we legally proscribe alcohol until the age of 21 (why not 30 or 45?). Christine and her classmates can drive cars, fly planes, marry, vote, pay taxes, take out loans and risk their lives as members of the U.S. armed forces. But laws in all 50 states say that no alcoholic beverages may be sold to anyone until that magic 21st birthday. We didn't always have a national "21" rule. When I was in college, in the mid-'60s, the drinking age varied from state to state. This posed its own risks, with underage students crossing state lines to get a legal drink.

In parts of the Western world, moderate drinking by teen- 4 agers and even children under their parents' supervision is a given. Though the per capita consumption of alcohol in France, Spain and Portugal is higher than in the United States, the rate of alcoholism and alcohol abuse is lower. A glass of wine at dinner is normal practice. Kids learn to regard moderate drinking as an enjoyable family activity rather than as something they have to sneak away to do. Banning drinking by young people makes it a badge of adulthood—a tantalizing forbidden fruit.

Christine and her teenage friends like to go out with a group 5 to a club, comedy show or sports bar to watch the game. But teens today have to go on the sly with fake IDs and the fear of getting caught. Otherwise, they're denied admittance to most places and left to hang out on the street. That's hardly a safer alternative. Christine and her classmates now find themselves in a legal no man's land. At 18, they're considered adults. Yet when they want to enjoy a drink like other adults, they are, as they put it, "disenfranchised."

Comparing my daughter's dilemma with my own as an 6 "underage" college student, I see a difference—and one that I think has exacerbated the current dilemma. Today's teens are far more sophisticated than we were. They're treated less like children and have more responsibilities than we did. This makes the 21 restriction seem anachronistic. For the past few years, my husband and I have been preparing Christine for college life and the inevitable partying—read keg of beer—that goes with it. Last year, a young friend with no drinking experience was violently ill for days after he was introduced to "clear liquids in small glasses" during freshman orientation. We want our daughter to learn how to drink sensibly and avoid this pitfall. Starting at the age of 14, we invited her to join us for a glass of champagne with dinner. She'd tried it once before, thought it was "yucky" and declined. A year later, she enjoyed sampling wine at family meals.

When, at 16, she asked for a Mudslide (a bottled chocolate- 7 milk-and-rum concoction), we used the opportunity to discuss it with her. We explained the alcohol content, told her the alcohol level is lower when the drink is blended with ice and compared it with a glass of wine. Since the drink of choice on campus is beer, we contrasted its potency with wine and hard liquor and stressed the importance of not drinking on an empty stomach.

Our purpose was to encourage her to know the alcohol con-   8
tent of what she is served. We want her to experience the effects
of liquor in her own home, not on the highway and not for the
first time during a college orientation week with free-flowing
suds. Although Christine doesn't drive yet, we regularly reinforce
the concept of choosing a designated driver. Happily, that already
seems a widely accepted practice among our daughter's friends
who drink.

We recently visited the Ivy League school Christine will attend   9
in the fall. While we were there, we read a story in the college
paper about a student who was nearly electrocuted when, in a
drunken state, he climbed on top of a moving train at a railroad
station near the campus. The student survived, but three of his
limbs were later amputated. This incident reminded me of a tragic
death on another campus. An intoxicated student maneuvered
himself into a chimney. He was found three days later when frat
brothers tried to light a fire in the fireplace. By then he was dead.

These tragedies are just two examples of our failure to teach   10
young people how to use alcohol prudently. If 18-year-olds don't
have legal access to even a beer at a public place, they have no
experience handling liquor on their own. They feel "liberated"
when they arrive on campus. With no parents to stop them, they
have a "let's make up for lost time" attitude. The result: binge
drinking.

We should make access to alcohol legal at 18. At the same   11
time, we should come down much harder on alcohol abusers and
drunk drivers of all ages. We should intensify our efforts at alcohol education for adolescents. We want them to understand that
it is perfectly OK not to drink. But if they do, alcohol should be
consumed in moderation.

After all, we choose to teach our children about safe sex,   12
including the benefits of teen abstinence. Why, then, can't we—
schools and parents alike—teach them about safe drinking?

VOCABULARY WORDS: imperative (2), binge (2), predicament (2),
proscribe (3), per capita (4), tantalizing (4), disenfranchised (5),
dilemma (6), exacerbated (6), anachronistic (6), prudently (10)

ACTIVITY 6

Reading to Improve Writing. Discuss the following questions
about "Perils of Prohibition" with your classmates.

1. Why does Whelan believe the current legal drinking age is a problem?

    _____

    _____

    _____

    _____

2. What is her position on the issue?

    _____

    _____

    _____

    _____

3. What supporting details does she use to convince her readers that the problem exists?

    _____

    _____

    _____

    _____

    _____

4. What is her proposed solution to the problem?

    _____

    _____

    _____

    _____

5. Does Whelan persuade you that the problem exists? Why or why not?

_____

_____

_____

_____

6. Do you think Whelan's solution is practical? Why or why not?

_____

_____

_____

ACTIVITY 7 (GROUP)

Relating Aloud to Gather Ideas. Read your material about a national issue aloud to the members of your peer response group. One member should take notes on (or tape-record) your description of the problem and proposed solution. Respond to the group's questions about your topic. Then use the group's suggestions to gather additional ideas about your topic.

Post to the Internet

If you have access to the Internet, post your essay to a newsgroup, listserv, or bulletin board. Ask readers to respond to your essay by suggesting ways you can improve your appeals.

Here's how one student, Bruce, related his ideas about a national issue to his peer response group.

My biggest concern is how the welfare system seems to break up families. Did you know that if a teenage girl becomes pregnant, she can't receive welfare for her baby unless she moves out of her parents' home? Because of this law, teenage girls from poor families are forced to leave home and try to make it on their own. They not only have a rough time making it alone, but they also lose the emotional support of their family at a time they need it most. I would like to see this law changed. I don't think we want to encourage unwed mothers to have babies, but if they do and if their families are eligible, I think they should be able to remain with their families and still receive public assistance benefits.

In response to his group members' questions about his topic, Bruce admitted that he needed to do some additional research and reflecting on his issue.

I'll need to find more about why the welfare system is set up this way and how it could be changed without costing taxpayers more money. I'm sure the idea is to save money, but I'm not sure how this works. I think I'll call my congressional representative and see if she has any information. Then I'll rethink my position.

DRAFTING

You have now gathered ideas on campus, regional, and national issues. You have a rich source of material for writing, but you need to decide how to proceed. Here are some of your options:

- You may select one of the three topics for your discovery draft.
- You may write drafts on two or three of these topics to see which one you prefer.
- You may combine related topics in your discovery draft, or even choose a new topic for your essay.

Above all, choose a topic that concerns and interests you and that you know something about. In addition, make sure you narrow the topic if it is too broad to handle within the space of an essay. You would not be able to address world peace, pollution, or homelessness in one essay, but you could focus on one specific aspect of the problem. If you chose homelessness, for example, you could write about who the homeless are, why they are homeless, or ways to help the homeless in your city, but you might have difficulty writing about all three in one essay.

Before you begin writing your discovery draft, write a preliminary thesis statement. Keep your audience and purpose in mind as you draft, but remember that your main goal at this stage is to get your ideas down on paper. You'll have time later to revise and edit your discovery draft.

Here's a discovery draft written by Li Chaing, the student whose freewriting about the campus computer lab you read earlier. (Note that the example includes the types of errors that typically appear in a first draft.)

```
                Tollroad on the Information Superhighway

     I am one of thousands of students who doesn't yet own      1
a personal computer and must use the campus computer lab.
Due to the poor condition of this facility, I have been
forced to go elsewhere to use a computer. The equipment is
outdated, it breaks down often, and the lab staff doesn't
seem very helpful. What really makes me angry is that
students pay a $50 user fee as part of their tuition each
semester. You would think that this fee would entitle
students to first-rate computer facilities.

     Instead, we have to use old IBM 486 computers or        2
Macintosh computers. These computers aren't even powerful
enough to run the software that provides students access to
the Internet. There is a Macintosh G4. It is fast enough
and powerful enough for students to access the World Wide
Web on the Internet. What's more, on any given day, one-
third of the two hundred computers have Out of Order signs
on them. What gives? With thousands of students needing
these computers, they should all be kept in working order.
Also, the staff isn't very helpful. Who trains these clowns
anyway? They often sit around doing their homework instead
of offering to help students learn how to use the computers
and the software programs. We need more software, too.

     The college needs to upgrade the campus computer lab      3
or quit charging students to use campus computing facili-
ties. We questioned Dr. Bruhn. He is the vice president for
instructional technology. He responded that the majority of
the funds collected through the computer use fee were being
used to create a computerized telephone registration system.
```

Need a review of thesis statements? See p. 36.

```
We're being ripped off! The way it is now, we pay a toll,
but can't even get on the information superhighway.
```

As you review your discovery draft, use the skills you acquired in the preceding chapters. Support and clarify your main ideas, organize your paragraphs, make your ideas flow smoothly, and write an effective introduction, conclusion, and title. Also refer back to the audience analysis you completed in Activity 1. What does your audience need to know to understand the problem? How can you propose your solution so that your readers will act on it?

Developing Your Ideas

You'll now learn how to revise a problem-solution essay. You'll state the problem, provide evidence that the problem exists, propose a solution, persuade your readers, combine short sentences, and maintain a reasonable tone.

STATE THE PROBLEM. As you may recall from Chapter 2, the thesis statement announces your topic; shows, explains, or argues a particular point about the topic; and gives readers a sense of what the essay will be about. An effective thesis statement for a problem-solution essay

- describes a specific problem or issue.
- conveys your position on the issue.

Underline Your Problem and Position

To ensure that you have described a specific problem and stated your position, underline the problem and boldface your position. Is your position specific to the problem you underlined?

Here are some examples of vague and specific thesis statements:

VAGUE   Something should be done about students who cheat.

SPECIFIC Students caught cheating on their final exams should be expelled from this college.

VAGUE   City roads need improvement.

SPECIFIC Montana Road between the airport and the freeway should be resurfaced because of the many potholes.

VAGUE   Financial aid to students should not be cut.

SPECIFIC If Congress passes a bill to cut the Stafford Loan program, thousands of college students will not be able to continue their education.

ACTIVITY 8

Analyzing Thesis Statements. Rewrite each thesis statement that follows so that it defines the specific problem or issue at hand and clearly states your position on the issue.

1. Students shouldn't have to pay to attend football games.

   _____

   _____

2. The community sports arena doesn't offer a wide range of sports activities.

   _____

   _____

   _____

3. Cigarette taxes should be raised.

   _____

   _____

4. The welfare system must be abolished.

   _____

   _____

ACTIVITY 9

Revising Your Thesis Statement. Evaluate the preliminary thesis statement you wrote for your essay about a campus, regional, or national issue. Does it identify a specific problem and clearly state your position? Revise your thesis accordingly.

PROVIDE EVIDENCE. When writing a persuasive essay, simply stating the problem isn't enough. You need to convince readers that the problem is serious enough to require a solution. Evidence can help you do this. You may include a brief history of the problem, its causes, and the consequences of leaving it unsolved.

Suppose, for instance, that in her essay Elizabeth M. Whelan had stated her thesis without providing any evidence: "Prohibiting the sale of liquor to responsible young adults creates an atmosphere where binge drinking and alcohol abuse have become a problem."

A review of types of evidence is on p. 65.

You might ask: "Wouldn't fewer sales result in less binge drinking and fewer problems?" and "How does Whelan define 'young adults' and 'binge drinking'?" If you hadn't already read her essay, you probably wouldn't agree with her thesis. You would want evidence that prohibiting the sale of liquor to young adults encourages alcohol problems.

ACTIVITY 10

Recognizing Evidence of a Problem. Reread Whelan's essay (pp. 460–62). List the types of evidence she uses to convince readers that the problem requires attention.

_____

_____

_____

ACTIVITY 11

Examining Your Evidence. Examine the types of evidence you use in your draft to support your problem statement. Do you include sufficient supporting details to convince readers that the problem is serious and in need of a solution? Consider how you can revise to make your evidence more persuasive.

E-mail Your Supporting Details

To ensure that you have enough supporting details, send e-mail to your group members or use a class chat room to share your thesis statement and a list of your supporting details. Ask them to let you know what more you could add.

PROPOSE A SOLUTION. After you state the problem and provide evidence of it, you're ready to propose a solution. A good solution offers specific and practical action for correcting the problem or addressing the issue.

Let's look again at the solutions proposed in this chapter's readings. Notice that in each case, the writer identifies a specific and practical resolution to the problem.

LAURE'S ISSUE	Students spend too much time talking on cell phones.
LAURE'S SOLUTION	Students should be less materialistic.
GARRITY'S ISSUE	The Kansas City Country Club is prejudiced when selecting new members.
GARRITY'S SOLUTION	Force all membership decisions to be made in the open.
WHELAN'S ISSUE	The legal drinking age of twenty-one encourages irresponsible drinking.
WHELAN'S SOLUTION	Lower the legal drinking age to eighteen and educate teens about alcohol abuse.

Laure suggests that students should spend more time thinking about spirituality or important causes than talking on the phone. Garrity's solutions have been successfully implemented in other cities. Whelan makes her solution practical by telling us about its success in other countries. Your solution should be specific and practical, too, one that your readers will consider worthy of their attention.

HOW TO **Propose a Solution**

- Identify a problem.

- Provide evidence of the problem.

- Provide a specific solution.

- Make sure that the solution is practical.

ACTIVITY 12

Proposing Practical Solutions. Return to the four thesis statements you prepared in Activity 8. For each thesis, propose a specific solution to the problem. Then state why you believe the solution is practical.

1. _____

   _____

   _____

2. _____

   _____

   _____

3. _____

   _____

   _____

4. _____

   _____

   _____

_____

_____

ACTIVITY 13 (GROUP)

Revising Your Solution. Working with your peer response group, discuss the solution you propose in your draft about a campus, regional, or national issue.

1. Is the proposed solution to the problem specific? Why or why not?
2. Is the proposed solution practical? Why or why not?
3. How would you implement your solution?

   Use your classmates' feedback to revise your solution accordingly.

Organizing Your Essay

As you look at the organization of your persuasive essay, consider whether you have done all you can to persuade your readers.

PERSUADE YOUR READERS. In identifying a problem or issue and proposing a solution, you also aim to be persuasive. That is, you want your readers to understand the problem, accept your proposed solution, and perhaps take action on the issue. Three types of appeals—logical, emotional, and ethical—can help you be persuasive.

Logical Appeals. In a logical appeal, you provide believable evidence for your position on the issue. By providing logical, believable evidence, you convince your readers that you know your topic well and that your solution has merit. For example, let's look at an overview of Whelan's essay to see how she uses appeals to logic.

PROBLEM (PARS. 1–2)

- College students drink "early and . . . often."
- Research supports the writer's claim that the current laws are unrealistic.
- Prohibiting sales of alcohol encourages binge drinking.
- American teens don't learn how to drink safely.

EVIDENCE OF THE PROBLEM (PAR. 3)

- Studies show moderate drinking can be beneficial.
- Teens accept other adult responsibilities.
- In the 1960s, the drinking age varied by state.

ADDITIONAL EVIDENCE (PARS. 4–6)

- Teens in other countries learn to drink responsibly.
- American teens are forced to use false IDs to get into clubs or must hang out in the streets.
- Teens are more sophisticated today than in the 1960s and should be treated as adults.

RESULTS OF THE PROBLEM (PARS. 6–10)

- Teens with no prior drinking experience tend to abuse alcohol.
- Teens introduced to alcohol in a responsible way don't abuse it.
- Incidents of teenage alcohol abuse are evident on many college campuses.
- Such binge drinking results from lack of education about and exposure to alcohol.

SOLUTION (PARS. 11–12)

- Make alcohol legal at age eighteen.
- Crack down on alcohol abusers.
- Educate young people about alcohol.

ACTIVITY 14 (GROUP)

Identifying Logical Appeals. Working in a group, reread Laure's essay (pp. 451–52) and make a list of the writer's logical appeals. Then discuss how each appeal contributes to Laure's persuasiveness.

ACTIVITY 15

Improving Your Logical Appeals. Under the headings Problem, Evidence, and Solution, list the points you make in your draft. Review each point to ensure that it is presented logically. Then consider adding details to strengthen your logical appeals.

Emotional Appeals. Sometimes a logical appeal is not enough to spur readers to action. In this case, an emotional appeal may be more effective; it aims to make readers feel strongly about a problem or issue—compassionate, proud, sad, angry, or intolerant, for example. But be careful when using an appeal to emotion: readers dismiss appeals that are overly emotional because they assume that the writer is too close to the problem to propose an objective solution. Remember, too, that emotional appeals only add to a logical argument. You must always include logical evidence to support your thesis statement.

Garrity uses several emotional appeals in "An Act of Conscience." Even the title of his essay suggests Garrity's strong feelings about his topic. By relating his own experiences while working at the Kansas City Country Club, Garrity demonstrates his firsthand knowledge of the problem. He also points out how much Tom Watson's decision to quit the club has hurt Watson. With such appeals to emotion, Garrity hopes to foster a renewed conscience that will spur action.

ACTIVITY 16 (GROUP)

Recognizing Emotional Appeals. Working in a group, collect articles, editorials, and advertisements from newspapers and magazines and analyze their use of emotional appeals. Which emotions do the appeals aim to make readers feel? Do the emotional appeals effectively strengthen the logical argument? Which appeals seem overly emotional and, therefore, less effective? What conclusions can you draw about the emotional appeals used in articles and editorials versus those employed in advertisements?

ACTIVITY 17

Improving Your Emotional Appeals. Evaluate your draft to determine whether an appeal to emotion would make your logical appeals more persuasive. Where in your essay might you appeal to your readers' compassion, pride, anger, or some other emotion to spur them to action? Revise your draft accordingly.

Ethical Appeals. With an ethical appeal, you aim to demonstrate your genuine concern about the problem or issue, your commitment

> ## HOW TO Use Logical, Emotional, and Ethical Appeals
>
> - Use logical appeals to provide believable evidence for your position.
>
> - Use emotional appeals to help readers feel strongly about your problem.
>
> - Use ethical appeals to demonstrate your respect for your readers and your genuine concern about the problem.

to the truth, and your respect of others' differing opinions. You support your position with verifiable evidence such as examples, including facts, statistics, and expert testimony, and you ask readers to make a fair judgment based on that evidence.

Earlier in the chapter, you saw how several writers use ethical appeals in this way. Each demonstrates a genuine concern for the problem identified: Laure for students' excessive cell phone use, Garrity with the bigotry at the Kansas City Country Club, and Whelan with the effects of the current legal drinking age. These writers also provide verifiable evidence to demonstrate their commitment to the truth and show respect for their readers' opinions. In return, they ask us, as open-minded readers, to evaluate their arguments fairly.

ACTIVITY 18

Recognizing Ethical Appeals. Reread the essay by Laure, Garrity, or Whelan for additional ethical appeals. How does each author persuade you that he or she is qualified to write on this topic and a fair-minded person? How does each writer ask you, in return, to evaluate the argument fairly?

ACTIVITY 19

Improving Your Ethical Appeal. Evaluate the ethical appeals in your draft. Do they demonstrate your genuine concern about the issue, your commitment to the truth, and your respect for others' opinions? Revise your ethical appeal accordingly, and eliminate any details that are exaggerated or not factual.

Evaluating Appeals on the Web
Access a Web site for a product you enjoy using. Evaluate how the Web site uses logical, emotional, and ethical appeals to hold your attention.

Polishing Your Sentences and Words

Now that you have improved the development and organization of your paragraphs, you'll want to turn your attention to your sentences and words.

COMBINING SENTENCES USING APPOSITIVES. As you have learned, combining sentences can turn short, weak sentences into longer, stronger ones. Thus far, you have used several techniques for combining sentences. Another way to combine sentences is by using appositives. An appositive is a word or group of words, set off by commas, that define or rename a person or thing in the sentence.

Here's how Li revised some short sentences in his discovery draft.

ORIGINAL   There is a Macintosh G4. It is fast enough and power-ful enough for students to access the World Wide Web on the Internet.

REVISED   Only one computer, *a Macintosh G4,* is fast enough and powerful enough for students to access the World Wide Web on the Internet.

ORIGINAL   We questioned Dr. Bruhn. He is the vice president for instructional technology. He responded that the major-ity of the funds collected through the computer use fee were being used to create a computerized telephone registration system.

REVISED   When questioned about campus computing services, *Dr. Bruhn, the vice president for instructional technology,* responded that the majority of the funds collected through the computer use fee were being used to create a computerized telephone registration system.

HOW TO Combine Sentences with Appositives

- Eliminate the subject and verb in one sentence.

- Add the remaining phrase that describes the noun to the other sentence.

- Set off the phrase with commas.

ACTIVITY 20

Combining Sentences. Combine the following pairs of sentences using appositives. Then, reread your discovery draft looking for sentences to combine using appositives.

1. Jane is my sister. She is running for mayor.

   _____

   _____

2. The new campus plan is an improvement. It is called Student Access.

   _____

   _____

3. My biology book isn't difficult to understand. The title is *Life Science for Dummies*.

   _____

   _____

4. This holiday is important to Americans. It's called Martin Luther King Day.

   _____

   _____

5. Jerry asked that the campus cafeteria serve more fresh vegetables. He is short and heavyset.

   _____

   _____

6. Don't even ask my girlfriend to go with you to the city council session. Luisa isn't interested in the city's problems.

   _____

   _____

7. George jumped in over his head. He was always impulsive.

   _____

   _____

8. That park is ugly. It is the one with the standing water.

   _____

   _____

9. Ted is an outstanding state senator. At one time he couldn't even get our attention.

   _____

   _____

10. The national parks are beautiful gems. They are often underfunded.

   _____

   _____

USING A REASONABLE TONE. A writer creates tone through choice of words and their placement in sentences. You'll always want to strive for a reasonable tone, especially if you're proposing a solution. Earlier you saw several examples of an angry and snide tone in Li Chaing's discovery draft, "Tollroad on the Information Superhighway":

ANGRY TONE   "What really makes me angry . . ."
              "What gives?"

SNIDE TONE   "Who trains these clowns anyway?"
              "We're being ripped off!"

Venting your anger in writing has the same effect as raising your voice, stomping your feet, or slamming the door in an argument. Remember, your goal is to persuade your readers to acknowledge the problem and to accept your solution. A harsh, negative tone won't accomplish this nearly as well as a reasonable tone. To be persuasive, you must show respect for your readers' opinions by maintaining a reasonable tone.

ACTIVITY 21

Creating a Reasonable Tone. Revise the following angry or snide statements so that they convey a reasonable tone.

1. The mayor of our city is a real jerk.

   _____

   _____

2. Who came up with this stupid plan anyway?

   _____

   _____

3. I demand that something be done about this problem!

   _____

   _____

4. This is the worst senator in the history of our state.

   _____

   _____

5. Advising at our college is for the birds.

_____

_____

ACTIVITY 22

Improving Your Tone. Reread your draft, looking for angry statements or snide remarks that show a lack of respect for others' opinions. Revise as needed to create a reasonable tone.

Help Others Improve Tone
Ask your peer response group to send their essays to you electronically. Read for angry or snide statements. Boldface any statements that you think could be revised to improve the tone and then send the essay back to the author.

Li's Revised Draft

Before you read Li's revised draft, reread his discovery draft (pp. 466–67). Notice how Li has improved his tone and added evidence in the revision. (You will also notice some errors in the revised draft; these will be corrected when Li edits his essay later on.)

Tollroad on the Information Superhighway

Fact—logical appeal

Fact—logical appeal

Adjusted tone used to state the problem.

Thousands of students on our campus who don't yet own   1
a personal computer must rely on the campus computer lab
for their computing needs. Every student pays a $50 user
fee each semester for access to this lab. The college administration should be congratulated for providing these
computing services and for keeping the fee reasonable.
However, the computer hardware, software, and student
assistance provided in the campus computer lab are inadequate to meet students' needs. They should be improved or
the fee should be abolished.

The computer hardware is outdated and is often not working, my roommate, for instance, has been forced to go off campus to find a computer powerful enough to run the statistical program required in his Introduction to Statistics class. Only one computer, a Macintosh G4, is fast enough and powerful enough for students to access the World Wide Web on the Internet. The reason is because as the director of the computer lab states, "This lab was founded in 1999, and we are still using the same computers we did on the day we opened. I would love to be able to serve our students better, but there just isn't money to upgrade the equipment."

As if outdated equipment weren't bad enough, some of the existing hardware doesn't even work. A quick survey of the equipment one day this week revealed that of the 150 machines available in the computer lab, 48 of them had Out of Order or Off the Network signs on them. Meanwhile, hundreds of fee-paying students must either wait in line for the remaining machines or make other arrangements to use a computer.

The software offered in this lab is also inadequate. Yes, you can do word processing, if a machine is available, but what if you want to add graphics, charts, or diagrams? You're out of luck, because there are no desktop publishing, database, or spreadsheet programs available. What's more, with only one computer connected to the Internet, access to the information superhighway is severely limited. One student claims, "I have waited in line up to three hours to get on the Internet. On the day before Thanksgiving, the computer lab director actually had to call in campus security to maintain order because several students started fighting over this one computer."

In addition, the students hired to work in this lab are not friendly or helpful. On three separate occasions,

2 Example—logical appeal

Example—logical appeal

Expert testimony— logical appeal

3 Example—emotional appeal

Fact—logical appeal

Adjusted tone

4 Example—logical appeal

Question—emotional appeal

Fact—logical appeal

Expert testimony— logical appeal

5 Example—emotional appeal

Fact—logical appeal

I observed lab tutors doing homework even though they were waiting for help with the software program Microsoft Word. According to a survey reported in last Friday's campus newspaper, 60 percent of the students who use the computer lab are dissatisfied with the service offered. Most would prefer more assistance with computer hardware and software and would like to see this assistance offered twenty-four hours a day.

Expert testimony—logical appeal

When questioned about campus computing services, Dr.   6
Bruhn, the vice president for instructional technology, responded that the majority of the funds collected through the computer use fee were being used to create a computerized telephone registration system. Once this system is in place, the computer lab will be upgraded and services improved. When asked, he acknowledged that students had no input into the decision on how these computer use fees are spent. Meanwhile, students on campus make do with woefuly inadequate computing facilities.

Solution proposed

This situation is obviously unfair. Students are pay-   7
ing a fee for computing services that they are not receiv-

Adjusted tone

ing. This college needs to upgrade the campus computer lab or quit charging students for inadequate campus computing

Ethical appeal

facilities. If students are going to pay the toll, at least give them access to the information superhighway.

ACTIVITY 23

Analyzing Li's Revised Draft. Use the following questions to discuss with your classmates how Li improved his draft.

1. What is Li's thesis statement? Is it effective?

_____

_____

_____

_____

2. What kinds of evidence does Li provide to show a problem exists?

_____

_____

3. Does his solution seem practical?

_____

_____

4. How does Li appeal to his readers logically, emotionally, and ethically?

_____

_____

_____

_____

5. How has Li adjusted his tone to make it more reasonable than in his discovery draft?

_____

_____

_____

6. How could Li's revised draft benefit from further revision?

_____

_____

_____

ACTIVITY 24 (GROUP)

Using Peer Review. Read your draft aloud to the members of your peer response group. Take notes on your classmates' responses to the following questions about your draft.

1. What do you like best about this essay?

   _____

   _____

   _____

2. How effective is my thesis statement? Do I clearly state the problem?

   _____

   _____

   _____

3. Do I provide adequate evidence of the problem?

   _____

   _____

   _____

4. Do I propose a practical solution to the problem?

   _____

   _____

   _____

5. How could I improve my logical, emotional, and ethical appeals?

   _____

   _____

   _____

6. Where in my essay do I need to adjust my tone?

_____

_____

_____

7. How clear is the purpose of my essay?

_____

_____

_____

Use Online Peer Review
If your class has a Web site, see whether the peer review questions are available on the site. If they are, you may be able to respond to your classmates' drafts electronically.

ACTIVITY 25

Revising Your Draft. Taking your classmates' suggestions for revision into consideration, revise your essay. In particular, focus on improving your thesis, evidence, and solution. Also evaluate your use of logical, emotional, and ethical appeals, and adjust your tone as needed.

EDITING

At this point you have worked hard to communicate your position on a campus, regional, or national issue. Now that you're satisfied with the content of your revised draft, you're ready to edit it for correctness. Editing is important; an essay that contains errors distracts readers from focusing on the writer's ideas. It also creates the impression among readers that a careless writer is irresponsible. A clean, error-free essay, in contrast, implies that a careful writer probably is genuinely concerned about the topic and worthy of readers' attention. Therefore, edit your essay carefully before sharing it with your readers.

Avoiding Shifts in Person

Authors write in one of three persons: *first (I, we), second (you),* or *third (he, she, they).* Here is a complete list of singular and plural pronouns in first, second, and third person.

SINGULAR

First Person	*Second Person*	*Third Person*
I	you	he, she, it, one
me	you	him, her, it
my, mine	your, yours	his, her, hers, its

PLURAL

First Person	*Second Person*	*Third Person*
we	you	they
us	you	them
our	your, yours	their, theirs

As a general rule, avoid shifting from one pronoun to another because it confuses the reader.

CONFUSING   *I* never wanted to complain about the parking situation on campus. *You* know that it can be horrendous. *I* finally wrote to the school newspaper to express *our* views. *We* believed something needed to be done about this situation, and so *I* took action.

REVISED   *I* never wanted to complain about the parking situation on campus even though *I* know that it can be horrendous. *I* finally wrote to the school newspaper to express *my* views. *I* believed something needed to be done about this situation, and so *I* took action.

ACTIVITY 26

Correcting Unnecessary Shifts in Person. Revise the following paragraph to correct unnecessary shifts in person.

My favorite pastime is writing letters to the editor. I always have something to say about what's going on in our city. And there is plenty for you to write about: the lack of parks, potholes in the roads, and trash everywhere. They are always saying how much we need to improve. You can never take a beautiful city for granted. I know I will continue to let people know how we feel about changing things around here.

Exercise Central

For additional practice correcting unnecessary shifts in person, go to the *Choices* Web site at **<www .bedfordstmartins.com/choices>** and click on "Exercise Central."

Using Quotation Marks Correctly

For more on quotation marks, see p. 702.

There are specific rules for using *quotation marks* (" "), and as an effective writer, you will want to use them correctly. Use quotation marks to show that you are repeating a speaker's or writer's exact words.

According to my professor, "Students are afraid to talk to professors because students believe professors will discover how little they know."

In his essay on student cell phone use, Laure states, "The cell phone culture certainly is a selfish one. Cell phones can be a convenience, but when they are used to detach the user from the environment, it simply is unnecessary and wrong."

Use quotation marks to enclose the titles of articles, essays, book chapters, speeches, poems, short stories, and songs.

I love to read "My Turn" in *Newsweek* magazine.

My favorite essay in this textbook is "Perils of Prohibition."

Edgar Allan Poe's "The Raven" is required reading in most high school literature classes.

ACTIVITY 27

Using Quotation Marks Correctly. Revise the following sentences as needed to correct missing quotation marks.

1. Janie said,   Let's get out of this place.
2. My favorite song is   Yesterday   by the Beatles.

3. He wrote a poem entitled Forever Free.
4. My essay is entitled When Will They Ever Learn?
5. Chapter 4 is Showing the Ways We Change.

Li's Edited Essay

You probably noticed that Li's revised draft contained errors in grammar, spelling, and punctuation. Li corrected these errors in his edited essay. His corrections are underlined here. His editing log follows his essay.

Li Chaing

Professor Bledsoe

English 101

7 April 2002

Tollroad on the Information Superhighway

Thousands of students on our campus who don't yet own a personal computer must rely on the campus computer lab for their computing needs. Every student pays a $50 user fee each semester for access to this lab. The college administration should be congratulated for providing these computing services and for keeping the fee reasonable. However, the computer hardware, software, and student assistance provided in the campus computer lab are inadequate to meet students' needs. They should be improved or the fee should be abolished.

The computer hardware is outdated and is often not working. My roommate, for instance, has been forced to go off campus to find a computer powerful enough to run the statistical program required in his Introduction to Statistics course. Only one computer, a Macintosh G4, is fast enough and powerful enough for students to access the

World Wide Web on the Internet. As the director of the
computer lab states, "This lab was founded in 1999, and we
are still using the same computers we did on the day we
opened. I would love to be able to serve our students
better, but there just isn't money to upgrade the equipment" (Fagel, personal interview).

As if outdated equipment weren't bad enough, some of   3
the existing hardware doesn't even work. A quick survey of
the equipment one day this week revealed that of the 150
machines available in the computer lab, 48 of them had Out
of Order or Off the Network signs on them. Meanwhile,
hundreds of fee-paying students must either wait in line
for the remaining machines or make other arrangements to
use a computer.

The software offered in this lab is also inadequate.   4
Yes, students can do word processing, if a machine is
available, but what if they want to add graphics, charts,
or diagrams? They're out of luck, because there are no
desktop publishing, database, or spreadsheet programs
available. What's more, with only one computer connected to
the Internet, access to the information superhighway is
severely limited. One student claims, "I have waited in
line up to three hours to get on the Internet. On the day
before Thanksgiving, the computer lab director actually had
to call in campus security to maintain order because
several students started fighting over this one computer."

In addition, the students hired to work in this lab   5
are not friendly or helpful. On three separate occasions,
I observed lab tutors doing homework even though students
were waiting for help with the software program Microsoft
Word. According to an editorial in last Friday's campus
newspaper, 60 percent of the students who use the computer
lab are dissatisfied with the service offered. Most would

prefer more assistance with computer hardware and software and would like to see this assistance offered twenty-four hours a day.

When questioned about campus computing services, Dr. Bruhn, the vice president for instructional technology, responded that the majority of the funds collected through the computer use fee were being used to create a computerized telephone registration system. Once this system is in place, the computer lab will be upgraded and services improved. When asked, he acknowledged that students had no input into the decision on how these computer use fees are spent (Personal interview). Meanwhile, students on campus make do with <u>woefully</u> inadequate computing facilities.

6

This situation is obviously unfair. Students are paying a fee for computing services that they are not receiving. This college needs to upgrade the campus computer lab or quit charging students for inadequate campus computing facilities. If students are going to pay the toll, at least give them access to the information superhighway.

7

Works Cited

Bruhn, John. Personal interview. 1 April 2002.

"Computing Facilities Need Upgrade," Editorial. <u>The Centennial</u>. 15 Feb. 2002: B7.

Fagel, Jerry. Personal interview. 2 April 2002.

Li's Editing Log

5/9 — "Tollroad on the Information Superhighway"

Need information on keeping an editing log? See p. 41.

INCORRECT   The computer hardware is outdated and is often not working, my roommate, for instance, has been forced to go off campus to find a computer powerful enough to run the statistical program required in his Introduction to Statistics class. (2)

ERROR comma splice

CORRECT The computer hardware is outdated and is often not working. My roommate, for instance, has been forced to go off campus to find a computer powerful enough to run the statistical program required in his Introduction to Statistics course.

AWKWARD The reason is because as the director of the computer lab states, "This lab was founded in 1999, and we are still using the same computers we did on the day we opened." (2)

IMPROVED As the director of the computer lab states, "This lab was founded in 1999, and we are still using the same computers we did on the day we opened."

INCORRECT Yes, you can do word processing, if a machine is available, but what if you want to add graphics, charts, or diagrams? You're out of luck, because there are no desktop publishing, database, or spreadsheet programs available. (4)

ERROR inappropriate shift from third to second person

CORRECT Yes, students can do word processing, if a machine is available, but what if they want to add graphics, charts, or diagrams? They're out of luck, because there are no desktop publishing, database, or spreadsheet programs available.

INCORRECT On three separate occasions, I observed lab tutors doing homework even though they were waiting for help with the software program Microsoft Word. (5)

ERROR unclear pronoun reference; software title not underlined or italicized

CORRECT On three separate occasions, I observed lab tutors doing homework even though students were waiting for help with the software program <u>Microsoft Word</u>.

INCORRECT woefuly (6)

ERROR misspelled word

CORRECT woefully

ACTIVITY 28

Editing Your Essay. Edit your revised draft, looking for errors in grammar, spelling, and punctuation. If you know you often make a particular type of error, read the essay one time for only that error. Also ask a friend, family member, or classmate to help you spot errors you may have overlooked. Then use a dictionary and the Handbook in Part Four of this book to help you correct the errors you find. Finally, record those errors in your editing log.

PUBLISHING

You're ready to share your essay about a campus, regional, or national issue with your audience—your instructor and classmates, as well as with someone with the authority to act on your proposal.

According to an ancient Chinese proverb, "A journey of a thousand miles begins with one step." Perhaps your essay will be the first step in bringing about a needed change on your campus, in your region, or in your nation. You may be surprised by the power of your writing. If you receive a reply, share it with your instructor and classmates.

CHAPTER CHECKLIST

- [ ] I gathered ideas for a problem-solution essay.
- [ ] I stated a specific problem and position in a thesis statement.
- [ ] I gave evidence to persuade my readers that the problem exists and merits their attention.
- [ ] I proposed a practical solution to the problem.
- [ ] I used logical, emotional, and ethical appeals to persuade my readers to accept my position on the issue.
- [ ] I combined short sentences by using appositives.
- [ ] I used a reasonable tone.
- [ ] I eliminated unnecessary shifts in person and used quotation marks correctly.
- [ ] I shared my essay with people with the authority to act on my proposal.

REFLECTING ON YOUR WRITING

To help you reflect on the writing you did in this chapter, answer the following questions.

1. Why did you choose the issue you did?
2. How did you determine the audience for your essay?
3. Which supporting details in your essay do you think provide the strongest evidence for your position? Why?
4. Which type of appeal—logical, emotional, or ethical—do you think you use most effectively in your essay? Why?
5. If you had more time, what more would you do to improve your essay before sharing it with readers?

Using your answers to these questions, update your Writing Process Report.

Writing Process Report

Date:

Strengths:

Weaknesses:

Plans for improvement:

Once you complete this report, freewrite about what you learned in this chapter about your writing and what you still hope to learn.

A Campus Issue

In the following essay, "Scheduling Woes," a student writer identifies the problem of canceled classes and asks college administrators to work with students to find a solution.

Scheduling Woes

Last semester I was lucky enough to enroll in all five classes that I needed for general education requirements. All the course sections I had in my schedule were still open when I registered. I didn't have to worry about back-up classes since I figured my schedule was set.

By the end of the second week of the semester, three of my five classes had been canceled, due to a lack of the "necessary" enrollment. Then I was forced, along with many other students, to scrounge around for other classes, which was frustrating and difficult. I ended up getting into only two other courses, neither of which I would have taken by choice. Clearly, there's something wrong with the scheduling practice at the college, and students are suffering.

For the second semester now, the college has scheduled significantly more sections of general ed courses than have been "made." It appears the school, or deans, or whoever makes the enrollment decisions waits to see which sections reach the magic minimum of twenty enrollees, and then cancels all those with fewer than twenty. Students caught in the smaller classes are then compelled to seek out other sections or courses, with no guarantees that they'll be allowed in.

To make matters worse, sometimes smaller sections are "carried" through the second week in hopes of late enrollments, leaving students desperately seeking classes in the third week of the semester. Some instructors have a policy of not accepting any students after the second week of the semester, and the students are often treated as if they have no business trying to get into classes late!

The effects of sections being canceled are obvious. First, students are lulled into believing that their schedules are set for the semester, so they don't worry about "double enrolling" in additional courses to cover themselves, a practice the college frowns on. Second, they are left, often for two weeks into the semester, with the uncertainty and anxiety of not knowing which of their classes will "make" and which will be canceled. Third, once classes are canceled, students are left with the responsibility of finding other classes to fill their schedules, and the college guarantees them nothing. Finally, and most damaging, they often end up taking classes they didn't want or need, and taking fewer classes than they had planned, which could jeopardize their grant eligibility and lengthen their stay at the college.

I'm sure the college has its reasons for overscheduling sections of courses. It can see which sections fill and then cancel the smaller sections that are more costly. It can also list the instructors for most sections as "staff" and then place teachers in sections where there are the best enrollments. And the college knows that with many small sections being canceled, the enrollment in the sections that "make" will only get better. In short, the administrators are doing what's best financially for the college at the expense of the students.

The college's current practice of overscheduling sections of courses is very unfair to students. The number of sections offered any semester should reflect the number of classes that realistically should fill with at least twenty students. That number can be pretty well determined by checking the number of sections of a course that "made" the same semester of the previous year. A two- or three-year study, taking college enrollment fluctuations into account, might provide an even more accurate indicator. The excuse that the college can't really predict how many sections to offer in any given semester just doesn't wash.

Last semester, according to the college admissions office, twenty-four sections of general ed pattern courses were canceled due to small enrollment. That is a scandalously high number. I think anyone could understand four or five sections needing to be canceled or added, based on enrollment fluctuations, but twenty-four canceled sections indicates a clearly intended practice of overscheduling and canceling classes, strictly for the financial benefit and convenience of the school and at the expense of the students.

This practice needs to be stopped immediately, and I am asking the administration to meet with a student committee before next semester's schedule is published. We want to ensure that all of the classes scheduled, based on current overall enrollment, have a realistic chance of reaching minimum enrollment figures.

When that occurs, students' registration schedules will accurately reflect their load for the semester, students won't be forced to scrounge for classes after the semester begins, and students will have a better chance of getting the classes and the units they need. After all, the college is here for the students, and not the other way around.

VOCABULARY WORDS: scrounge (2), compelled (3), fluctuations (7), indicator (7)

ACTIVITY 29

Reading to Improve Writing. Discuss the following questions about "Scheduling Woes" with your classmates.

1. What problem does the student identify?

   _____

   _____

2. What evidence of the problem does the student provide?

   _____

   _____

3. What is the proposed solution?

   _____

   _____

4. Is the solution specific and reasonable?

   _____

   _____

   _____

   _____

5. Are there similar problems with scheduling classes at your college?

_____

_____

_____

A Regional Issue

In the following essay, "A City's Assault on Teen Pregnancy," Joe Loconte identifies the problem of teen pregnancy in Indianapolis.

JOE LOCONTE

A City's Assault on Teen Pregnancy

Eve Jackson taught "family life" classes to students in Hamilton Southeastern High School, a typical Indianapolis-area public school, for four years. They were troubling years for her Baptist conscience.

At the exact time when the hormones of adolescents are at flood tide, Jackson says, the most persuasive message they get about sex comes from their peers—and the message is: "Come on in, the water's fine." Other voices remain muffled. Teachers often ignore or play down a state requirement that they stress abstinence in sex-education classes. Church–state legal doctrine bans religious ideas about premarital sex from public schools. Says Jackson, "As much as I wanted to talk about God, I really couldn't."

And what she could talk about—responsible decision-making, peer pressure, self-esteem—had no more effect than a flashing yellow light on a lonely country road. "So many of them were sexually active. Every year I had a couple of students who had abortions," she says. "But I couldn't talk them out of being sexually involved." Jackson eventually left public education, developed a Bible-based abstinence program taught by high-school juniors and seniors, and brought it into 34 Catholic grade schools throughout the city.

Now the public schools—in a city with a teen pregnancy rate that has risen 40 percent over the last decade—want Jackson back. Mayor Steve Goldsmith has asked Jackson to bring her chastity program, "A Promise to Keep," into 150 public grade schools this fall. Stripped of its religious references, the program will recruit at least 100 high-school students to serve as advocates for abstinence. It's one of more than two dozen initiatives launched by the mayor in the last year, using his bully pulpit in an effort to reduce out-of-wedlock births. Citing its impact on crime, poverty, and welfare dependence, Goldsmith calls teen pregnancy "the most serious long-term issue facing this city. We can do nothing if we don't solve this problem."

Energize and Stigmatize

The mayor of the nation's 12th-largest city seems uninterested in expanding government services. Following a meeting last year that included the city's school superintendent, a juvenile-court judge, and a county health director, Goldsmith mapped out a 27-point strategy for city-wide action. His aim: energize public opinion, the courts, and church and community groups to stigmatize out-of-wedlock births while supporting teen mothers.   5

The mayor intends to treat casual attitudes about teen pregnancy with the same tolerance that actor Jean-Claude Van Damme brings to flabbiness: Since studies show that roughly half of all teenage moms are impregnated by males older than 18, Goldsmith wants prosecutors to crack down on statutory rape. He plans to enforce laws requiring women to establish paternity as a condition of receiving welfare. He intends to publish monthly reports of teen pregnancies in every high school in the city.   6

And while local Planned Parenthood clinics seek to build "creative self-expression" through dance, art, and painting classes, Goldsmith is pressuring schools to ban pregnant teens and boys who have fathered children from extracurricular activities. He even has floated the idea of sending pregnant girls to separate schools altogether.   7

"Philosophically we're not in agreement," says Kathleen Baldwin, Planned Parenthood's director of education in Indianapolis. "They would define the problem largely as illegitimacy, and we would define it as limited opportunities for achievement."   8

Esperanza Zendejas, the superintendent of Indianapolis's public schools, opposes some of the mayor's school-based sanctions, but applauds his broad-based approach to attacking the problem of illegitimacy. "The fact that the city, as a city, is looking at teen pregnancy is extraordinary," she says. "It should be happening in every city in the nation."   9

It wouldn't be happening in Indianapolis without the active support of the religious community, Goldsmith says. Indeed, the   10 mayor insists that the most dynamic partner in the assault on the culture of teen pregnancy—and all of the social problems it creates—will be churches and synagogues.

In February, he summoned 100 spiritual leaders—Protestant, Catholic, Jewish, Muslim, and Buddhist—to a summit on teen pregnancy. He asked them to speak out on the risks of sexual activity outside of marriage. More significantly, he challenged congregations to become personally involved with families on welfare by helping women to avoid more pregnancies, reunite with the father of their children, and get off of government assistance. "The whole notion is to be more of a mentor and support group, not a candy store," says Richard Wiehe, the executive director of the Faith and Families project, a new effort to link congregations with welfare families.   11

The mayor wants religious groups to fight this culture war almost everywhere—even in city parks. Indianapolis now has 16 congregations managing 30 contracts to maintain public parks. In exchange, churches can sponsor events in the parks with minimal bureaucratic hassle. Goldsmith's explicit hope is that people of faith will form relationships with children who live in surrounding neighborhoods. "We could put police officers on every corner of the city," he says, "but if our people did not believe in God and basic moral values, then we would still not have a safe community."   12

Crime statistics seem to side with the mayor: Juvenile crime in Indianapolis has increased nearly tenfold in the last decade, and 75 percent of those offenses were committed by fatherless children. Judge Jim Payne of the juvenile court of Marion County says at least 600 new juveniles enter the system each month. "Out-of-wedlock birth is driving every single rotten outcome in our city," says Krista Rush, Mayor Goldsmith's social-policy advisor.   13

At Goldsmith's request, the Indianapolis Training Center (ITC) set up shop in the city a few years ago to reach out to troubled youth and their families. Payne now refers kids headed for state detention centers to the Christian-based program, which houses about two dozen teens at a time in its residential center. To overcome objections by the Indiana Civil Liberties Union, Payne argued that the program's emphasis on character and family relationships could help reverse irresponsible and predatory attitudes toward sex that have become "incredibly common" among today's youth.   14

Center director Benny McWha says that many of the girls at the center were sexually abused as children, and are considered at high risk of teen pregnancy. Most of the boys come with no   15 experience of responsible fatherhood. Eight mentor families and about a hundred student volunteers work to keep the kids out of trouble.

"Our primary goal is to help teach them character," McWha   16
says, which includes "moral purity from a biblical perspective." The ITC staff also offers practical support—and a message of abstinence—to unmarried mothers in some of the city's toughest neighborhoods.

Modeling the Message

Communicating an effective abstinence message may be the   17
most difficult task facing the mayor, and the city's public schools are becoming a prime battleground. It is here where getting involved sexually is considered a badge of honor. And it is here where more and more pregnant teens are envied, admired, and applauded—but rarely shunned. "In many of our schools," Rush says, "there's a tremendous reward for getting pregnant."

Jackson, who coordinates adolescent-growth programs for   18
the Catholic Archdiocese of Indianapolis, cites three principles for overturning an ethos of sexual freedom: (1) Give kids a clear message of abstinence until marriage, (2) get the message to them early, and (3) recruit credible high-school students to deliver it.

"There's a real need to have some positive peer pressure for a   19
change," Jackson says. Young people are more likely to listen when student role models get involved. And, contrary to Planned Parenthood's news releases, finding chaste high schoolers is not a problem. Last year, Jackson recruited 200 peer mentors from six Catholic schools and six public schools to lead the workshops. She expects to train at least 50 students from Indianapolis high schools to work with kids in the city's middle schools this fall.

Though Jackson has removed all religious references from   20
her public-school program, the six-hour curriculum parallels its religious counterpart in stressing chastity until marriage. Jackson essentially has translated religious concepts about the benefits of marriage—and the risks of sexual permissiveness—into secular language.

Moreover, most of Jackson's high-school mentors come from   21
strong religious backgrounds. "We're finding that our peer mentors are people of faith," she says. "That faith component is essential, because it gives them a moral standard to live by. Otherwise, it's anything goes."

VOCABULARY WORDS: abstinence (2), chastity (4), bully pulpit (4), illegitimacy (8), explicit (12), chaste (19)

ACTIVITY 30

Reading to Improve Writing. Discuss the following questions about "A City's Assault on Teen Pregnancy" with your classmates.

1. What problem does Loconte identify?

    _____

    _____

2. What evidence of the problem does he provide?

    _____

    _____

3. What is the proposed solution?

    _____

    _____

4. Is the solution specific and reasonable?

    _____

    _____

    _____

5. What is the greatest problem facing your region?

    _____

    _____

    _____

A National Issue

In the following essay, "Some Actions Aren't Affirmative," Roger Hernandez identifies the problem of students receiving preferential treatment in college admissions because of their ethnicity.

ROGER HERNANDEZ

Some Actions Aren't Affirmative

In these days of hypersensitivity about all things ethnic, it seems bizarre that there are millions of Americans alive who could not attend a college of their choice because they were black. 1

Did that really happen here, in this great country, this American democracy of ours? 2

Yep. 3

The University of Georgia was one of those colleges. Until 1961, it refused to admit blacks. How many qualified, intelligent African-Americans were denied a college education because of that policy? What kinds of spiritual wounds were inflicted by the knowledge that an elite institution of higher learning wanted nothing to do with those of your race? 4

Not only bizarre. Barbaric. 5

Higher education has come a long way. Yet vestiges of those days endure in a different form. At the University of Georgia, black people are no longer deemed so inferior that they cannot be accepted. What officials there now believe is that African-Americans—and Hispanics, too—are so inferior that they need bonus points to be accepted. 6

Of course, it's not just in Georgia that this happens. Colleges throughout the United States routinely lower admission standards for students considered to be from a "minority group." But a series of recent court decisions is putting a stop to this type of affirmative action. The latest blow came when the 11th U.S. Circuit Court of Appeals in Atlanta ruled unanimously that the University of Georgia's policy that "mechanically awards an arbitrary 'diversity' bonus" to all black and Hispanic applicants was unconstitutional. 7

The court did not focus on the condescending notion that each and every applicant considered a member of a "minority group," even those from upper-middle-class families, needs those bonus points to gain admission. Rather, it concentrated on the definition of "diversity." 8

The ruling said that while "racial diversity may be one com- 9
ponent of a diverse student body, it is not the only component . . . a white applicant from a disadvantaged rural area in
Appalachia may well have more to offer a Georgia public university such as UGA—from the standpoint of diversity—than a non-
white applicant from an affluent family and a suburban Atlanta
high school."

And, not incidentally, that white kid from Appalachia is 10
more likely to need bonus points to get into a school such as UGA
than the affluent black or Hispanic kid from suburban Atlanta.

Such a premise is just beginning to be accepted at admissions 11
offices, but only because they are being forced by the courts. Why
are all blacks and Hispanics presumed to need extra help? Why
not those poor white kids from rural Appalachia? Or the kids of
a white truck driver in Brooklyn? Why is an immigrant from
Bolivia said to need help, but not an immigrant from Bosnia?

What's more, too many blacks and Hispanics are among the 12
first to defend the kind of affirmative action that is built on
those demeaning assumptions. They have built their ethnic identity on notions of ethnic inferiority and don't even know it.

Diversity—in all its forms, including ethnic diversity—is a 13
worthy goal for colleges (and also employers) to pursue. But taking pride in being a member of a helpless "minority" is bizarre.
Maybe through these court decisions America is getting closer to
a day when the kind of affirmative action that patronizes the
very people it is supposed to help will be torn down, left in ruins.
The wreckage of earlier, barbaric times.

VOCABULARY WORDS: elite (4), barbaric (5), vestiges (6), arbitrary
(7), condescending (8), demeaning (12), patronizes (13)

ACTIVITY 31

Reading to Improve Writing. Discuss the following questions
about "Some Actions Aren't Affirmative" with your classmates.

1. What problem does Hernandez identify?

_____

_____

_____

2. What evidence of the problem does he provide?

_____

_____

3. What is his solution?

_____

_____

4. Is his solution specific and reasonable?

_____

_____

_____

5. Do you agree with his solution to the problem? Why or why not?

_____

_____

_____

Writing for Different Situations

Whether writing for class, the workplace, or personal enjoyment, you can use specialized writing strategies to help you do an even better job when you write.

In Part Three, you'll practice some of these writing strategies. You'll learn to keep a journal as a way to gather ideas and practice your writing. You'll learn to conduct research to help you support what you have to say with interesting and informative details. You'll discover tips for doing your best on timed writing such as essay exams and standardized writing tests. And you'll learn how to showcase your writing by creating a portfolio.

The blank page gives the right to dream.
—GASTON BACHELARD

CHAPTER 10

Keeping a Journal

In this chapter you will

- discover why writers keep journals.
- learn how to keep a journal.
- practice keeping three types of journals.
- begin your own journal.
- reflect on your writing.

Imagine that you want to become a great musician or athlete. How would you go about it? First, knowing that it would take hard work and a long time, you would have to be motivated to achieve your goal. Then you would seek out a teacher or coach to work with you. Finally, you would do what great musicians and athletes do—practice: musicians rehearse and athletes work out. The same is true if you want to be a writer. But, you say, "I don't want to become a great writer, just a better one. I don't want to be another Shakespeare; I just want to write well enough to get better grades on my term papers or a promotion at work." The path is still the same, whether you're aiming for the major leagues, the minors, or a spot on your neighborhood sandlot team: you'll need to make a commitment, study, and practice.

You have demonstrated your motivation to improve your writing by enrolling in a writing course. In class, you'll have the opportunity to learn what you need to do to become a better writer. But to become a truly effective writer, you'll also need to practice what you have learned. Just as the musician practices scales and the athlete lifts weights, writers practice by writing. Often, writers do this in a journal, a notebook in which they express their thoughts and ideas.

You may ask, "Aren't some people just born musicians, athletes, or writers? Why should I bother to learn and practice if I wasn't born with this talent?" Some people may have more natural skill, but that doesn't mean the rest of us can't become better if we set our minds to it. Even people with natural talent must be willing to learn and practice to realize their potential. Musicians don't reach the concert hall, athletes don't reach the big time, and writers don't have their work published unless they are committed and are willing to study and practice.

WRITING ASSIGNMENT

Begin to keep a journal. You can either use a computer or write in a notebook. If you choose a notebook, be sure to use one that has at least one hundred pages so you can write in it daily.

You may choose to keep one or more of three types of journals: a personal journal, a dialogue journal, or a learning log. If a journal is required for one of your classes, your instructor may ask you to keep a particular type of journal. Once you decide which type you will keep, set aside some time each day to write in your journal.

WHY WRITERS KEEP JOURNALS

Let's think more about practice. Would a musician wait until the night before a concert to practice the music? Would a basketball player wait until the day before the big game to practice slam dunks? Of course not. The same is true with writing. If you want to write well, you must start practicing now. As a writer, your equivalent to the musician's instrument or the athlete's equipment is a journal, a notebook for jotting down your ideas, opinions, feelings, and memories. The more time you spend writing in your journal, the more practice you'll get as a writer.

Lucy Calkins, in *The Art of Teaching Writing,* describes how she uses her notebook journal as a place to try out ideas.

LUCY CALKINS

From The Art of Teaching Writing

1   I write to hold what I find in my life in my hands and to declare it a treasure. I'm not very good at doing this. When I sit down at my desk, I'm like my students. "Nothing happens in my life," I say. I feel empty-handed. I want to get up and rush around, looking for something Big and Significant to put on the page.

2   And yet, as a writer I have come to know that significance cannot be found, it must be grown. Looking back in my notebook I find a brief entry about how my son Miles uses one of my cotton T-shirts as his "pretend blanket," replacing the original blanket, which has disintegrated. My inclination is to dismiss the entry as trivial, or something only a mother could care about, but then I remember the writer Vicki Vinton saying, "It is an illusion that writers live more significant lives than non-writers; the truth is, writers are just more in the habit of finding the significance that is there in their lives."

3   Vicki's words hang over my desk, as do the words of the poet Theodore Roethke, who said, "If our lives don't feel significant, sometimes it's not our lives, but our response to our lives, which needs to be richer." It's not only these quotations that nudge me to believe I can find significance in my son's "pretend blanket." I'm also instructed by memories of times when I've begun with something small, and seen significance emerge on my page. From my experiences as a writer and from the experiences of other authors, I have developed a small repertoire of strategies to draw

on when I want to take a seed idea and grow it into a speech, a
story, a book. This, for me, is what the writing process is all about.

Use your journal as a place to plant seeds of ideas, experiment
with different ways of writing, and write without the pressure of
being evaluated. Journal writing can help you find topics for writing.
It can also help you clarify and organize your ideas. But most important, writing in a journal helps you become an active thinker, rather
than being a passive reader or listener. This, in turn, will help you
write better papers in college and get that promotion at work.

PERSONAL JOURNALS

A *personal journal* is a collection of your thoughts and feelings.
You write simply to express yourself. You need not be concerned
about grammar, spelling, or punctuation, and you need not write
in complete sentences. Just as the musician practices scales and the
sprinter runs laps to loosen up, you develop fluency and the ability to
express yourself smoothly and easily by writing in a personal journal.
In addition to written entries, you may include lists, pictures, draw-
ings, newspaper clippings—anything that gives you ideas for writing.

Because you do not share a personal journal, you can write without worrying about others' reactions to your writing. You can relax
and write in your own style, using language that is natural to you.

Here are some sample entries from student writer Alyssa's personal journal:

April 4
   Here I am on a cloudy day headed to my house. My mom is
driving at thirty-five miles per hour. She has always been a cautious
driver. Every other car seems to be passing us. Some of the drivers
turn, maybe wondering why my mother is driving so slow. Now we're
passing the old factory. Sometimes it looks nice, especially at night.
But today it looks really ugly. All the smoke is more noticeable
because it is cloudy, too. I get sick just thinking about how many
chemicals we breathe every day.
   As I look around, I notice that this town is desperately in need
of some trees. All I can see are poles, billboards, and dirt.

April 5
   I called to see if I can get my old job back again. It's not exciting,
but the pay's good and the people are nice. Maybe there'll be more

part-timers around my age now. I hope I hear soon because otherwise I've got to get to work on finding something else.

April 7
   I like this poem by Pat Mora.

   "Clever Twist"
      The best revenge
      is pouring the tears
      into a tall, black hat
      waving a sharp No. 2 pencil
      slowly over the blue echoes
      then gently, gently
      pulling out
      a bloomin' poem.

April 8
   Heard from APCO. Got my summer job. Wow! That takes a load
off of my mind.

ACTIVITY 1

Starting a Personal Journal. With your notebook in hand, you're
ready to begin your personal journal. Try keeping one for several
days. Write about what you observe around you and how you feel
about it. Clip articles, cartoons, and photographs that interest you,
and write about why you find them interesting. To help you loosen
up, try answering some of the following questions. Choose the questions that appeal to you.

- What are two things I would rather be doing right now?
- Am I well organized? How often must I search for something
  that I have misplaced?
- If I could change anything about the way I have been raised,
  what would it be?
- If I could take a one-month trip anywhere in the world (and if
  money were not a consideration), where would I go and what
  would I do?
- What do I most strive for in life: accomplishment, security, love,
  power, excitement, knowledge, or something else?
- Is there something I have dreamed of doing for a long time?
  Why haven't I done it?
- Do I have long-term goals? What is one such goal, and how do
  I plan to reach it?

- What is the greatest accomplishment of my life?
- What is my most treasured memory?

Keep a Personal Journal on Computer
You may prefer to keep your personal journal on disk. Set up a file called "journal" and then add entries to it each day, just as you would to a notebook. Enter text as quickly as you can, concentrating on your ideas and resisting the urge to backspace, delete, or correct your writing.

DIALOGUE JOURNALS

The *dialogue journal* is a written conversation—or dialogue—between you and another person. As in a personal journal, your primary concern in a dialogue journal is expressing your thoughts. Unlike a personal journal, however, what you write in a dialogue journal will be read by someone else. Therefore, you should record your thoughts and ideas more completely so that your reader will understand them. You need not be overly concerned with grammar, spelling, and punctuation, but you should take more care than in a personal journal to ensure your reader's easy reading of your dialogue journal. You may focus on one topic or change topics each time you exchange journals. You may also exchange your dialogue journal with one or more friends or classmates.

One advantage of a dialogue journal is that it helps you clarify your understanding of an idea or issue by explaining it to someone else. Another advantage comes from sharing your dialogue journal with someone who can respond to what you have written. Your reader can help you determine how clearly you communicate your thoughts to someone else. You may even ask specific questions of your reader.

In the following sample entry from a student's dialogue journal, Kirk writes about a school issue that concerns him. Because he is writing to get his thoughts down on paper, Kirk makes some errors in grammar and punctuation.

> *One incident that really upset me this past week was the fact that on tests people are always cheating. It makes me mad that people expect others to always do their work for them. This might have been okay in high school but this is college and that means everyone has to make it on their own. We don't go to college expecting to "just*

pass." Well maybe some people do and those who do feel that way have no business in college.

However what do my friends say. "Oh what a small classroom. Great for cheating. Come sit by me and let me see your paper, okay." What kind of people are they. They are wasting their parents money because it is obvious they don't plan to study or have a career.

Here's how Kirk's student reader, Michelle, responded to his journal entry:

Kirk, rather than thinking so much about other people's cheating, concentrate on your own goals. In the long run, the cheaters will be the ones who lose out for not doing their own work. Just don't let them cheat off of you. Concentrate on not cheating yourself—be honest to your own work, your own future.

And here's what Kirk's writing instructor had to say after reading the same journal entry:

Kirk, I can see that you have strong feelings about cheating. You may want to write a persuasive letter to the editor of the campus newspaper about the problem of cheating on campus. Why do you suppose students cheat? Why do you say that cheating might have been okay in high school? Is cheating acceptable sometimes, but not at other times? How would you solve this problem? What do you think should happen to students who are caught cheating?

ACTIVITY 2

Starting a Dialogue Journal. You begin a dialogue journal just as you would a personal journal, with one exception: because a dialogue is a conversation, you must first find someone to read and respond to it. Ask a classmate to exchange journals with you for a few days. Write about anything of interest to you. If you need help getting started, try answering a few of the following questions:

- What do I value most in a relationship?
- Do I judge others by higher or lower standards than I use to judge myself?
- When did I last yell at someone? Why? Did I later regret it?
- Do I find it hard to say no to family and friends? Why or why not?
- Who is the most important person in my life? Why?

- Are there people whose lives I envy enough to want to trade places with them? Who are they?
- Have I ever disliked someone? If so, why and for how long?
- What do I most regret not having told someone? Why haven't I told that person yet?
- What is my best advice for getting along with others?
- How important is family life to me? Do I think of family as including only those people related to me by birth? Or do I include close friends and neighbors as well?

Keep a Dialogue Journal Online
Dialogue online by posting your entries on the class listserv or Web site. Alternatively, dialogue by sending e-mails back and forth to your classmates and instructor.

LEARNING LOGS

A *learning log* is a journal that focuses on your response to course content. In it you summarize, synthesize, or react to a class lecture, discussion, or assigned reading. You may restate the objectives of each class or try to pinpoint what confuses you about a particular topic. By keeping a learning log, you'll improve not only your understanding of the subject but also your attitude toward the course in general. Asking questions and voicing your concerns in your log will help you become an active learner and contribute in class discussions. You'll also find yourself making connections between new ideas and previous knowledge.

Get into the habit of placing the letter *T* in the margin, next to learning log entries that you think might make good essay topics. What makes a good topic? A good topic is one that you're interested in and that others might also want to learn about. Consider, too, how much you already know about the topic and whether you can find additional information about it.

Student writer Tom's learning log entry is about his first-year college composition class. By writing about his own writing, Tom gains insight into how to become a better writer.

I am glad to hear that I am not expected to write excellently from the beginning. I now understand that everyone can improve their writing. I like the idea that we will be sharing our work with our classmates. I always thought that in college we would not have an opportunity to share.

Today we learned about freewriting, which means to write off the top of your head as fast as you can. We did freewriting in my English class. I liked it because it lets ideas flow out freely without worrying about grammar or punctuation. I'm glad we will be freewriting this semester.

The essays we have to do seem hard. I already feel the pressure of my first paper. Maybe freewriting will help me.

Tom keeps his learning log in a traditional full-page format. Some students, however, prefer to integrate their logs with their class notes in a double-column format. To do this, simply divide each page down the middle, with one column labeled Notes and the other Thoughts. In the Notes column, record key concepts, important details, and examples from class lectures and outside reading. In the Thoughts column, reflect on what you're learning: What does it mean to you? How do you feel about it? How will you use this information in the future? You may also summarize, keep a list of new vocabulary words, and jot down notes on upcoming assignments.

Keeping a two-column learning log helps you integrate what you're studying in college into the fabric of your own thinking and past experiences. Personal examples help you understand the course material and how it relates to your life. Whichever type of learning log you choose to keep, responding to your class notes will help you recall information when you need it for a class discussion or an exam.

Here's an entry from the two-column learning log that student writer Tammy kept for her psychology class.

Notes	*Thoughts*

Memory—
 Where information is held.
 3 types
   sensory
   short-term
   long-term
 sensory—all info that enters the senses
 short-term—where all conscious thought takes place
 long-term—representation of all that is known
	I never realized there were three kinds of memory. I'm not surprised that we forget so much sensory info—there's so much of it. Short-term memory is what I am thinking now, drawing on what is happening around me. I think of long-term memory kind of like a book in the library. If I want to retrieve it, I hope that it is there.

HOW TO Keep a Learning Log

- During class or as you read, take notes on the left-hand side of the paper.

- On the right-hand side, summarize, define words, connect to your own experiences, or jot down ideas about upcoming assignments.

- After class, write about what you learned using a full-page format or in a computer file.

ACTIVITY 3

Starting a Learning Log. Try keeping a full-page or two-column learning log for several days. To get started, select a course you're currently enrolled in, and during class take notes as you always do. After class, reflect in your log by asking yourself these questions:

- How can I summarize what I learned in class today?
- What parts did I not understand?
- How might I clarify this information?
- What new vocabulary words do I need to look up?
- What key points are likely to appear on an exam?
- Which ideas would make good future paper topics?
- Do I agree or disagree with what I have learned today?
- How can I apply what I learned to other classes?
- How can I apply what I learned to my work?
- How will I use this information in the future?

Keep a Learning Log on Computer

You may prefer to keep your class notes and learning log on a laptop computer. Using the format command, you can easily create a two-column learning log. Consider using a different font for summaries. Boldface new vocabulary words and concepts you don't understand so that you can look them up later.

HOW TO Select the Right Journal for You

- Keep a personal journal if you want to express thoughts and feelings privately and safely.

- Keep a dialogue journal if you want to exchange ideas with others.

- Keep a learning log if you want to increase what you learn in your college classes.

CHAPTER CHECKLIST

- [ ] I used a journal to jot down ideas, opinions, feelings, and insights.
- [ ] I kept a journal in a notebook or on a computer, adding entries regularly.
- [ ] I used one or more of three types of journals: the personal journal, the dialogue journal, and the learning log.
  - [ ] The personal journal is for my eyes only and contains personal thoughts and feelings.
  - [ ] The dialogue journal is shared with someone who reads and responds to it.
  - [ ] The learning log is kept for a particular course and contains class or reading notes and my own thoughts, sometimes in a two-column format.

REFLECTING ON YOUR WRITING

You have practiced writing three types of journals: a personal journal, a dialogue journal, and a learning log. To help you decide which one you want to continue to keep this semester, answer the following questions and then consult with your instructors.

1. Do any of my instructors require a journal? If so, which type of journal is required?

2. How will keeping a personal journal be worthwhile to me as a student?

3. How does a personal journal differ from regular class notes?

4. If I keep a dialogue journal, who will I ask to read and respond to it?

5. How does a dialogue journal differ from a personal journal?

6. For which course would I keep a learning log?

7. Would I prefer to keep a full-page or double-column learning log?

8. How does a learning log differ from a personal or dialogue journal?

9. How will keeping a journal help me discover topics for future papers?

10. How will journal writing give me practice as a writer?

Using your answers to these questions, update your Writing Process Report.

Writing Process Report

Date:

Strengths:

Weaknesses:

Plans for improvement:

Once you complete this report, begin your journal by writing on what you learned in this chapter about journals and what you still hope to learn. Continue to add entries daily.

I could spend the rest of my life reading, just satisfying my curiosity. —MALCOLM X

CHAPTER 11

Conducting Primary, Library, and Internet Research

In this chapter you will

- prepare to research a topic.

- learn to make observations, survey others, and conduct interviews.

- learn to locate sources of information in the library and on the Internet.

- learn to evaluate sources of information.

- learn to avoid plagiarism.

- learn to take notes.

- learn to quote, paraphrase, and summarize information.

- learn to document sources in your paper.

- reflect on your writing.

Imagine that you received the following writing assignments in your college courses:

- Describe the life cycle of the diamondback rattlesnake.
- Analyze Cesar Chavez's leadership of migrant farmworkers.
- Explain the origin of the Internet in the late 1970s.

How do you find information on these topics? Of course, you head to the library or the Internet. But then what?

If you had looked for this information in a library twenty-five years ago, you would have headed to the card catalog to see where a book on your topic was located. You also might have examined a large book that listed magazine articles on your subject. Today, however, computers contain this information—and much more. Because of computer technology, libraries can now access information from around the world in minutes. How do you sort through this information for what is most useful and valid? How do you use this material in an essay? This chapter will give you strategies for conducting research and using information in your own essays. You will also learn to find information by becoming a researcher yourself.

WRITING ASSIGNMENT   The International Students Office on your campus is holding a public meeting to help students from other countries adjust to their new surroundings. Your psychology instructor has volunteered your class to participate in this forum. To prepare for the forum, your instructor has broken the class into teams. Each team is to write a report with ideas on helping international students adjust to a new country and university. You and your classmates will present these reports at the forum at the end of the term.

PREPARING TO CONDUCT RESEARCH

To conduct research, you need to know what information you're seeking. Otherwise, you might spend a great deal of time finding information that doesn't pertain to your topic.

Narrow Your Topic

Before beginning your research, narrow your topic so that your ideas can be well developed. For the International Students Office forum, you could explain aspects of American culture that are important for international students to understand. You could also suggest how international students can increase their enjoyment of their new culture. Another choice would be to focus on the stress that people suffer when they encounter a new culture or setting—in other words, culture shock. Narrowing your topic to just one of these ideas will allow you to give sufficient detail in your report. It will also help you know exactly what information you should find to support your points.

Write Research Questions

After you narrow your topic, decide on the information you need to obtain by thinking of questions that you want answered. These *research questions* will guide you in conducting your research. For

HOW TO **Plan a Research Project**

- Choose a topic that interests you.

- Review your purpose and audience.

- Narrow your topic.

- State the following questions: who, what, when, where, why, how?

- Select a few of these questions to explore.

- Establish a timeline for conducting research to answer these questions and to complete the project. Allow plenty of time to work on each part of the project.

instance, if you are writing about culture shock, you might ask these questions:

- What is the definition of culture shock?
- Who gets culture shock?
- What are the emotional and physical effects of culture shock?
- How can culture shock be prevented?

As you research your topic, refer to your research questions to help you stay focused on the information you need.

PRIMARY RESEARCH

Research that you do on your own, rather than read about, is called *primary research*. Thus, when you conduct an experiment in science, you're doing primary research. When you ask friends to suggest a good movie, you're essentially taking a survey, another form of primary research.

Three common types of primary research involve making observations, surveying others, and conducting interviews. These types of primary research are used for different purposes:

- When you want to explain how something works or how something is done, consider making observations.
- When you want to explain your topic's importance in people's lives, consider conducting a survey.
- When you require specialized information or information known only to experts, consider conducting an interview.

Conduct Primary Research

Primary research can be conducted with relative ease using a computer. You can use the format options of your word-processing or desktop publishing program to produce professional-looking surveys or questionnaires. Ask your instructor for guidelines on how to use surveys and how to ask permission to include the results in your paper.

Making Observations

To *observe* something is to watch it closely. Observations enable you to explain your points clearly to your readers. For example, if you're explaining mitosis, you can observe cell division under a microscope. In your essay, you can describe what you saw to make the process come alive for your readers. Similarly, in an essay about the Internet, you might describe your observations of some online conversations and include a quotation that illustrates a key point.

HOW TO Make Observations

- Obtain permission to observe an event relevant to your topic, if necessary.

- Remain visible but do not participate in the event.

- Decide what to focus on when you observe.

- Take detailed notes as you observe the event.

- Ask questions about what you observe but may not understand.

Surveying Others

A *survey* contains information collected from many people about a certain topic. Newspapers often conduct surveys to find out how citizens plan to vote in an upcoming election. Manufacturers hire market research companies to survey users of their products and thereby learn how to improve the products. In writing, a survey can help you point out people's opinions or knowledge about an issue. For example, if your topic for the International Students Office forum is culture shock, you could survey people to determine how many of them know the definition of culture shock. Your research findings might support the point that although many people experience culture shock, not enough of them know what it is or how it can be alleviated.

Conducting a Survey on the Internet

A written survey can be sent to people who have access to the Internet. Be sure to include a deadline for responding. Consider posting the results of the survey for those who participated in it. If you want the opinions of people who may not have access to the Internet, though, a printed survey is a better choice.

HOW TO Conduct Surveys

- Decide how you will conduct the survey—with an *oral survey* or a *written survey.* In an oral survey, respondents reply immediately; however, the respondents do not have much time to think about the questions. The written survey generates more detailed responses, but many people may not have the time to fill out a questionnaire.

- Decide where you will conduct the survey. You want to find a place where many people come and go, such as the entrance of the college library or Student Union.

- Create five to ten survey questions. Make them as brief as possible and easy to understand. Also use various types of questions, such as yes-no questions mixed with questions that require short answers. Test questions on classmates for suggestions to improve.

- Decide whom you will survey. For instance, do you want to survey both men and women from various age groups? Avoid surveying only people you know.

- Decide how many people you will survey. The more people you include in a survey, the more reliable your results will be. But you need to consider your time limitations as well.

- If you conduct an oral survey, write out your questions ahead of time and take careful notes.

Conducting Interviews

In addition to making observations and surveying others, you can conduct an *interview* to learn more about a research topic. By interviewing a knowledgeable person, you can collect information and gain an expert's perspective on your topic. If you're writing an essay on water quality in your region, you could interview an environmental engineer who has studied this subject. For the topic of culture shock, you could interview international students who can describe what it's like to experience culture shock.

HOW TO Conduct Interviews

- Choose a knowledgeable person to interview. To determine whether someone is an expert on your topic, check his or her credentials, such as academic degrees, professional activities, and published works. In some situations, a person's personal experience with your topic is more relevant than formal credentials.

- Contact the person in advance to set up an appointment.

- Prepare your interview questions.

- Dress appropriately and arrive on time if you conduct the interview in person.

- Keep the conversation focused on your questions. Be considerate of your interviewee's limited time.

- Listen carefully, and take good notes. Put quotation marks around the person's actual words. You may tape-record the conversation only if you obtain the interviewee's permission beforehand.

- Ask the interviewee to clarify anything you do not understand.

- Send a thank-you note to the person soon after the interview.

Here's one more tip: if you're reluctant to contact a stranger for an interview, remember that most people enjoy talking about what they know and are especially eager to share their knowledge with interested students.

Interviewing others is a great way to gather information. For a review of how to consult with others, see pp. 32–33.

ACTIVITY 1 (GROUP)

Conducting Primary Research. Discuss your writing topics with students in other groups. Determine the type of primary research that will best suit each group's topic. Then use the appropriate set of questions to discuss how members of each group can go about making observations, surveying others, or conducting an interview.

QUESTIONS ABOUT MAKING OBSERVATIONS

1. What information do you need to obtain from your observations?
2. Where will you make the observations?
3. Do you need permission to observe? If so, from whom?
4. What questions might you expect to have about the event you want to observe?

QUESTIONS ABOUT SURVEYING OTHERS

1. What information do you want the survey to provide?
2. Do you want your respondents to answer orally or in writing? Why?
3. Who will your respondents be, and how many people will you survey?
4. Where will you conduct the survey?
5. What questions will you ask in the survey?

QUESTIONS ABOUT CONDUCTING AN INTERVIEW

1. What information do you hope to obtain from the interview?
2. Who could give you this information?
3. What questions will you ask?

 Using Chat Rooms, Bulletin Boards, and Listservs
Online chat rooms, bulletin boards, and listservs allow you to discuss your topic with others on the Internet. For a list of chat rooms, bulletin boards, and listservs where you can discuss your writing, go to the *Choices* Web site at **<www.bedfordstmartins.com/choices/>** and click on "Annotated Web Links."

SECONDARY RESEARCH

Secondary research involves reading what others have written about your topic. To conduct secondary research, you need to know how to locate relevant sources of information; how to evaluate sources; how to take notes and avoid plagiarism; how to quote, paraphrase, and summarize sources of information; and how to document the sources you cite in your research paper.

Locating Sources of Information

Traditionally, sources of information in libraries have been in print form, such as books or newspapers. Magazines, which are written by journalists for a general audience, and journals, which contain articles by experts for a more specialized audience, are other print sources. However, many materials that used to appear only in print now also appear in electronic form. To do secondary research, you need to know how to access both print and electronic sources.

PRINT SOURCES. To begin your search for information, consult an encyclopedia. You're probably familiar with such general encyclopedias as *Encyclopaedia Britannica,* but specialized encyclopedias are a better source of in-depth information because they cover specific fields. Some specialized encyclopedias are the *Encyclopedia of Computer Science and Technology, Encyclopedia of Psychology, Encyclopedia of Biological Sciences,* and the *Harvard Guide to American History.* You can locate specialized encyclopedias by checking the library catalog or consulting a reference librarian.

After consulting an encyclopedia, you can find further information by checking an *Index,* which lists magazine, journal, or newspaper articles by subject or author. After finding the title of a useful article in an index, you will need to locate it in your college's library using a *call number,* the number the library assigns to each item in its collection. Most libraries gather magazine and journal articles into volumes, which are then placed on the library shelves (called "stacks"). You can find books on your topic by consulting your college library's subject catalog; the books will be shelved in the stacks by call number.

ELECTRONIC SOURCES. In addition to the print versions, many encyclopedias, magazines, journals, and newspapers are available online. Indexes, or databases, contain titles of articles from thousands of magazines, journals, and newspapers. Some databases, such as *Periodical Abstracts* and *Readers' Guide Abstracts,* list magazine and journal articles, whereas others, such as *Newspaper 5 Full Text,* include only newspaper articles. A reference librarian can help you choose the databases that are most useful for your topic. Compared with print sources, computer databases are generally more current because they can be more easily updated. You may even be able to access your library's computer databases from your home or dorm computer. Many databases are also available on the World Wide Web.

HOW TO Use Keywords to Search

- Narrow your search by connecting keywords using *"AND,"* as in "culture shock AND education."

- You can also narrow your search by using "NOT," as in "culture shock NOT immigration."

- If your keywords don't result in enough items for you to examine, broaden your search by using *"OR,"* as in "culture shock OR cultural studies."

- If you still can't find the right keywords, ask a reference librarian. He or she can then check the subject headings in the database for you.

When consulting a database, use *keywords,* or words that pertain to your topic, to locate articles. The wrong keywords can give you either too many or too few items from the database.

For her report on culture shock, one student, Leslie Lozano, searched the database *Periodical Abstracts* using the keywords "culture shock." She received a list of 138 articles—too many for her to review. To narrow her search, she used the keywords "culture shock AND international students." These keywords produced no items for her to examine. On the advice of a librarian, she used "culture shock AND education." This produced 7 items for her to examine—a more manageable size than the initial 138. Leslie's search results are shown on p. 531.

A database often gives you an abstract, or brief summary, of each article it contains. This abstract will help you determine whether the article is likely to answer one of your research questions. Leslie Lozano checked the abstract of the first article the database had given her, "Culture Club." Based on the abstract, which is shown on p. 532, she decided she might be able to use it in her report on culture shock. She was in luck—the full article was included in the database, saving the time of retrieving it from the periodical section of the library. After reading the article, she printed it out so she could take notes on it at a later time.

Another electronic source of information is the World Wide Web, which is a system of linked computer files on the Internet. Because topics are linked together, the Web allows you to jump from one topic to another quickly and easily. Computer programs such as *Microsoft Internet Explorer* and *Netscape Navigator,* known as *browsers,*

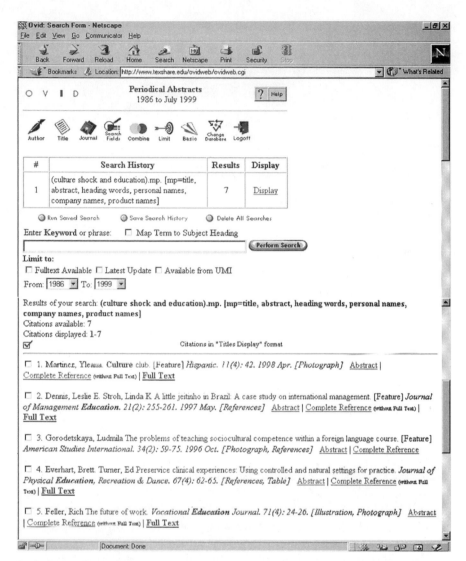

Leslie's search results

allow access to the Web. As with databases, use keywords to locate material on your topic.

OTHER SOURCES OF INFORMATION. Secondary research need not be limited to library sources. Check television listings for relevant documentaries or news shows. *All Things Considered,* broadcast daily on National Public Radio, is another excellent source of current news.

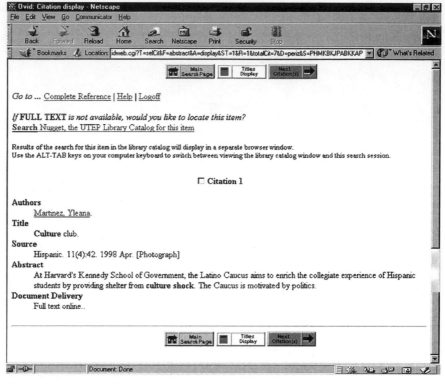

The abstract for Leslie's article

HOW TO Find Electronic Resources

- Identify a database, such as *InfoTrac,* on which to search for information. A list of databases is available at your campus library

- Enter keywords on your topic to access information.

- Read the abstract or summary to determine whether an article sounds useful.

- If the article seems useful, print or take notes on the information.

- Record the publication information for your Works Cited page.

ACTIVITY 2 (GROUP)

Conducting Library Research. Team up with a classmate to do some library research on your topic. First, explain to your partner the type of information you need to find. Then visit the campus library and, working together, locate specialized encyclopedias, magazine and newspaper articles, and books on your topics. Don't hesitate to ask a librarian for assistance if you can't find the sources you need. Finally, record here the titles and authors of the various sources you find on your topic.

1. Specialized encyclopedia (Give the title.)

   _____

   _____

2. Magazine article (Give the title of the article, the title of the magazine, and the author's name.)

   _____

   _____

3. Newspaper article (Give the title of the article, the title of the newspaper, and the author's name.)

   _____

   _____

Using Search Engines

When you explore the World Wide Web for information on your topic, use a *search engine,* which is a Web site that indexes other Web sites. Some common search engines are Yahoo! (<www.yahoo.com>), Alta Vista (<www.altavista.com>), Excite (<www.excite.com>), Google (<www.google.com>), and Lycos (<http://lycos.com>). You will need to use keywords to access Web sites on a search engine. Read the help screens for the search engine. They will help you to focus your keywords so that you will get a manageable number of sites.

4. Book (Give the title and the author's name.)

_____

_____

Sources of Information on the Web

A list of databases that include articles with information on your topic is available at your library. For additional sources of information, go to **<www.bedfordstmartins.com/ choices/>** and click on "Annotated Web Links." Scroll down to "Current Events, News, and Readings Online."

Evaluating Sources of Information

The credibility of the sources you consult is an important concern. A report isn't necessarily objective simply because it appears in print or on television. Many magazines have a political bias. *The National Review,* for instance, has a conservative slant, whereas *The Nation* is considered liberal. Recent sources (that is, those published within the last five years) are more up-to-date than older ones. If you gather information from television sources, be especially skeptical about what you watch. Many television news discussion programs also have a political bias, and some news-entertainment shows may exaggerate facts to make their stories more interesting to their audience. Avoid using material from a talk show unless you are certain it's not hearsay or gossip.

Evaluating sources you find on the World Wide Web is especially important. For the most part, no independent person or agency screens material before it is put on the Web. Therefore, *you* need to screen the material. When accessing information on culture shock, for instance, you might find Web pages advertising a therapist's treatment for culture shock, a site dedicated to a rock band named "Culture Shock," or a high school student's research paper on this topic.

ACTIVITY 3 (GROUP)

Evaluating Web Sites. With several of your classmates, evaluate several Web sites that deal in some way with culture shock. (To access these Web sites, use a search engine such as AltaVista, Yahoo!, Infoseek, or Lycos and type in the keywords "culture shock.") Which sites would be appropriate for an essay on culture shock? How did you determine their appropriateness?

Using Favorites and Bookmarks

Use the favorites feature in *Microsoft Internet Explorer* or the bookmarks feature in *Netscape Navigator* to help you quickly access Web sites you plan to examine more than once. These features allow you to "mark" a site rather than typing in the entire URL address. You can return to the site by choosing it from your list of favorites or bookmarks.

HOW TO Evaluate Web Resources

- Determine who put the information on that Web site. Does this person have credentials, such as college degrees or university affiliations? If no author is named, or if the author's credentials aren't given, find another source of information.

- Is the Web site trying to sell you something? If so, it might not contain objective information.

- Be cautious when accessing Web sites with "com" in their addresses, as in <www.elvispresley.com>. "Com" is an abbreviation for "commercial"; most of these Web sites are connected to commercial companies that are trying to sell you something.

- Web sites with "edu" in their addresses, as in <www.lib .iastate.edu>, are usually maintained by a college or university, and Web sites with "gov" in their addresses, as in <www.lcweb.loc.gov>, are sponsored by a governmental agency. Information provided on such sites is likely to be reliable, although you still need to determine the author of the site and its purpose.

Avoiding Plagiarism

A very serious offense, *plagiarism* is the use of another writer's ideas or words without giving credit to that writer as the source. Handing in someone else's work with your name on it is an obvious

HOW TO Avoid Plagiarism

- When you reproduce a writer's exact words, use quotation marks to enclose the quote. Be sure to name your source.

- When you restate an author's words in your own words, omit the quotation marks, but you must still name your source.

- List all of the sources named in your paper on the Works Cited page.

act of plagiarism. But using another writer's words or ideas in your paper without indicating where they came from, even if you do so unintentionally, is also an act of plagiarism.

Therefore, you must be careful to avoid plagiarism. Always identify your sources when you borrow ideas, information, or quotations so that your readers can clearly distinguish between what has been borrowed and what is your own.

The following sections on taking notes and on quoting, paraphrasing, summarizing, and documenting sources will also help you avoid plagiarism.

ACTIVITY 4 (GROUP)

Talking about Plagiarism. Plagiarism can come in many forms. Discuss the following situations with your classmates.

1. Because of her busy work schedule, Anne puts off writing a research paper until the night before the deadline and, as a result, doesn't take the time to identify the sources of borrowed words and ideas in her paper. A week later, her instructor calls her into his office and tells her that she has plagiarized.

   Why is this plagiarism? _____

   _____

   _____

How should Anne respond? _____

_____

_____

How should Anne be penalized? _____

_____

_____

2. Joanne belongs to a sorority that keeps a file of term papers written by its members. Looking in that file, she finds a paper on the same topic as an English paper she's writing. She copies several paragraphs from the paper, word for word, without indicating where they came from. Later, Joanne's instructor asks her why part of her paper sounds as if someone else wrote it.

Why is this plagiarism? _____

_____

_____

Should Joanne offer to rewrite the paper? _____

_____

_____

How should Joanne be penalized? _____

_____

_____

3. Co-workers Sam and Eloise are asked by their supervisor to write a report on the company's recent sales figures. Eloise volunteers to draft the report, and Sam agrees to revise, edit, and submit it to the supervisor. The report that Sam submits, however, has only his name on it.

Why is this plagiarism? _____

_____

_____

What should Eloise do? _____

_____

_____

How should Sam be penalized? _____

_____

_____

4. Frank and Joe are roommates. Frank is enrolled in the same history course that Joe took last semester. Frank comes across one of Joe's old notebooks, and in it is the history paper that Joe wrote for last semester's course. Frank retypes the paper and submits it as his own.

Why is this plagiarism? _____

_____

Do you think Frank's plagiarism of Joe's paper will be discovered?

_____

_____

_____

If it is discovered, how should Frank be penalized? Or, if it isn't, how might Frank's experience influence his behavior in the future?

_____

_____

_____

What advice would you give Frank if you could?

_____

_____

_____

Taking Notes

Once you locate a book, an article, or another source on your topic, skim it to see if it answers any of your research questions. To skim a source, simply read the introduction, the headings and sub-headings, and the conclusion. If it answers any of your research questions, take notes. You can also photocopy the relevant pages and highlight the important ideas. However, highlighting shouldn't replace taking careful notes. Note-taking forces you to select only what is useful from a source, to restate the information in your own words, and thereby to reflect on its meaning.

Consider using index cards for your notes. Because they're small, index cards help you focus on the information you need. Also, you can arrange the cards in various ways, which can be helpful in organizing your ideas during revision. Take notes for only one source per notecard.

 Take Notes on Computer

If possible, use a computer to take notes; this will make writing your essay easier because you won't have to retype your notes when you write your paper. To take notes on a computer, you can create a directory or folder for your essay and then use separate files within the directory or folder for your notes. For example, the directory or folder can be called "Culture Shock" and the files can be called "Effects of Culture Shock" or "How to Prevent Culture Shock."

For each source you use, be sure to record the author's name, the title, and the publication information you will need for your Works Cited page at the end of your essay. This information varies depending on the type of source you consult. For magazine, journal, and newspaper articles, encyclopedia entries, books, and Web sites, you must record the following information for each source you use:

MAGAZINE ARTICLE

title

author

name of magazine

date of publication (month and year)

page numbers of the whole article or printout

page numbers for the information you used

(If you accessed the article on a CD-ROM or Web database, also write the electronic date of publication, the name of the database [such as *Periodical Abstracts*], and the name of the company that produced the database [such as InfoTrac or ProQuest].)

JOURNAL ARTICLE

title

author

name of journal

volume number

date of publication (month and year)

page numbers of the whole article or printout

page numbers for the information you used

(If you accessed the article on a CD-ROM or Web database, write the date of electronic publication, the name of the database, and the name of the company that produced the database.)

NEWSPAPER ARTICLE

title

author

name of the newspaper

date of publication (month, day, and year)

section and page numbers of the article or printout

page numbers for the information you used

(If you accessed the article on a CD-ROM or Web database, write the date of electronic publication, the name of the database, and the name of the company that produced the database.)

ENCYCLOPEDIA ARTICLE OR ENTRY

title

author (if given, it usually appears at the end of the entry)

HOW TO Take Notes

- Refer frequently to your research questions to keep you focused on your topic.

- Don't just copy information from sources. Add your own thoughts. You might note, for instance, where you could use the information in your essay.

- Use quotation marks to indicate where you record an author's exact words. Write the rest of your notes completely in your own words. When you change a source's words and sentence structure into your own words, you are *paraphrasing* the source. Most of your notes should be paraphrased.

name of the encyclopedia

year and place of publication

volume and page number (if the encyclopedia is not arranged alphabetically)

BOOK

title

author

city and name of publisher

year of publication

page numbers

WEB SITE

title

author

name of any institution or organization associated with the site

date of publication

date of access

address (the URL, or Uniform Resource Locator)

An example of a notecard written by Leslie Lozano based on the article "Culture Club" follows on the next page. This article helped Leslie answer her research question, "What can students do to help them cope with culture shock?"

ACTIVITY 5

Practicing Taking Notes. Imagine that you're writing an essay on culture shock and that one of your research questions is "What can be done to help people cope with culture shock?" To answer this question, take notes on an index card on the following essay called "Cross-Cultural Perspective: Culture Shock." This piece appeared in a book called *Psychology* by Philip C. Zimbardo and Ann L. Weber, published in 1994 by HarperCollins, a publisher located in New York City. It appears on p. 332 of that book.

Compare your notecard with a classmate's. Did you answer the research question without giving unnecessary information? Did you put quotation marks around the authors' exact words? Did you record the necessary publication information for the source?

PHILIP ZIMBARDO AND ANN WEBER

Cross-Cultural Perspective: Culture Shock

Many people can point to a part of their culture that they consider *home*. Their feelings of "home" include positive emotions, familiarity, knowledge about ways to satisfy everyday needs, and attachment to others who demonstrate acceptance and affection. Feelings that people have about home often are associated with the length of time they spend in one place. Because time spent in one place is connected to feelings of home, some people may not react positively to the concept of "home." For example, the chil-   1

Side one of notecard

The information Leslie will need for her Works Cited page. ———→

This information helps answer one of Leslie's research questions. ———→

Author's exact words in quotation marks ———→

para. = paragraph numbers

An interesting fact Leslie learned from the article ———→

"*Culture Club*" *by Yleana Martinez.* <u>Hispanic</u>*. Vol. 11, April 1998.* <u>P. 14</u>*. Periodical Abstracts. Ovid. April 1999*

At Harvard's Kennedy School of Government, Latino students formed the Latino Caucus to help Latino students cope with the "inevitable culture shock." (para. 2)

The Latino Caucus also is an "advocacy group" and fights for causes like bilingual education. (para. 2)

Out of 700 students at the Kennedy School, only about 20 are Latino! (para. 2)

Leslie's notes on "Culture Club"

dren of migrant workers or the children of military families may never have lived in one place long enough to consider it home.

For those people who do have strong emotional ties to a home, moves from their familiar surroundings can cause stress. Consider a time in your own life when you were away from home and felt discomfort because of your move. This may have occurred when you first went away to college. It could have occurred in years past when your family relocated due to a job transfer by one of your parents, or when you left home in the summer to attend summer camp or visit distant relatives. What were your feelings? Did you feel lonely, out-of-step with others, frustrated at your inability to satisfy everyday needs, or clumsy because you did not know how to behave in acceptable ways? With these thoughts in mind, consider the following situations. 2

1. *An 18-year-old Navajo female from rural Arizona, who had won awards as a high-school basketball player, begins studies at one of the large state universities on an athletic scholarship.*

2. *An African-American businessman accepts a vice-presidential position in a large company where 95 percent of the upper-level executives are male Caucasians.*

3. *A student participates in a study-abroad program in Europe.*

4. *An American businesswoman travels to Japan to establish joint trade agreements for the marketing of computer hardware and software.*

What do these experiences (including your own) have in common? All of these experiences involve moves away from familiar surroundings and the need to adjust to many new social situations. All of the individuals involved moved on their own, without others who had long shared their respective support groups. When faced with everyday demands such as finding food, housing, and local transportation, these people had only their own resources to help them cope. Often, such individuals feel overwhelmed in their new surroundings and experience high levels of stress (Barna, 1991). *Culture shock* is the term commonly used to describe the stress experienced by people who move to unfamiliar surroundings. 3

The term "culture shock" was originally coined to explain the intense experiences of people who found themselves on overseas assignments in roles such as diplomats, international students, 4 technical assistance advisers, or businesspeople (Oberg, 1960). Over the last thirty years, the term has expanded to include other types of experiences people have when they move across cultural boundaries *within any one country.* Occasionally, culture shock is used to explain reactions to the new and the unfamiliar. Examples include going away to college, getting married, or being forced to go on welfare after years of productive employment.

The complaints people have when experiencing culture shock   5 are very similar, whether they are international students, overseas businesspeople, or members of an underrepresented ethnic group (Furnham & Bochner, 1986). Such individuals experience a sense of frustration and helplessness at their inability to meet their everyday needs. They feel lonely and find it hard to meet people and to develop good interpersonal relationships. Victims of culture shock often become suspicious of others and come to believe that others are "out to get them." People also report a predictable set of physical symptoms. They complain of stomachaches, inability to sleep, diarrhea, headaches, lack of sex drive, general feelings of tiredness, mild depression, and a lack of enthusiasm for life.

Many organizations now sponsor programs to help prepare   6 people for life's transitions. Most commonly called "cross-cultural training programs" (Brislin, 1993), one of the goals of such curricula is to introduce people to the various experiences they are likely to encounter. During the programs, participants are commonly told that the experiences associated with "culture shock" are normal and are to be expected. Knowledge of what culture shock is, how frequently it is experienced, and effective coping strategies can aid in reducing people's stress.

Quoting Information

As a general rule, use quotations sparingly. But when an author uses an especially memorable phrase, you might want to quote it directly in your paper. You also might use quoted material to emphasize a point or sum up an idea. These should be brief quotations of one or two sentences.

You should include an introductory phrase to tell your readers the source of each quotation. After the quoted information, put the page number of the source in parentheses. Here are some examples:

Refer to p. 703 in Part Four for guidelines about punctuating quotations.

According to psychologists Philip Zimbardo and Ann Weber, "Knowledge of what culture shock is, how frequently it is experienced, and effective coping strategies can aid in reducing people's stress" (332).

Psychologists Philip Zimbardo and Ann Weber write, "Knowledge of what culture shock is, how frequently it is experienced, and effective coping strategies can aid in reducing people's stress" (332).

"Knowledge of what culture shock is, how frequently it is experienced, and effective coping strategies can aid in reducing people's stress," write psychologists Philip Zimbardo and Ann Weber (332).

Also notice in the examples how the quotations are punctuated.

When you use a quotation, you can't just drop it into a paragraph. You need to explain its relevance to your topic or point. In the following paragraph from a student essay on culture shock, for example, the writer quotes a phrase from the Zimbardo and Weber essay and then explains its relevance to his point:

> When you think of people experiencing culture shock, you might picture immigrants moving to a new land or students studying in foreign countries. Not everyone who experiences culture shock, though, is in a foreign country. According to psychologists Philip Zimbardo and Ann Weber, "Over the last thirty years, the term has expanded to include other types of experiences people have when they move across cultural boundaries *within any one country*" (332). Therefore, people may experience culture shock when they leave home to go to college, lose their jobs, or move to a much bigger or smaller city.

Note, too, as this paragraph demonstrates, that the topic-illustration-explanation (TIE) pattern of organization is often used in paragraphs containing quotations.

For more information about using the TIE method of paragraph organization, refer to p. 78.

HOW TO Quote Information

- Use quoted information to draw upon memorable phrases, to emphasize a point, or to sum up.

- Include a phrase that provides the source of the information.

- Add quotation marks at the beginning and end of the quoted material.

- Explain why the quotation is relevant to your topic.

ACTIVITY 6 (GROUP)

Quoting Sources. Working with several other students, write a paragraph about one of the main ideas in "Cross-Cultural Perspective: Culture Shock." Use a quotation from the essay to help you develop the paragraph. Then create an introductory phrase for the quotation, and consider using the TIE pattern of paragraph organization. Compare your group's paragraph with those written by the other groups in the class.

Paraphrasing Information

To *paraphrase* is to restate a source in your own words. By paraphrasing information, you simplify complicated information and use your own writing style.

A paraphrase should be about the same length as the original passage and express the same ideas. Although when paraphrasing you might be tempted simply to substitute keywords with synonyms (words that have the same meaning), this can lead to plagiarism. Use your own writing style instead. This might mean changing the sentence structure or word order. Here's an example of an original passage, a poor paraphrase, and a good paraphrase. In the poor paraphrase, words from the original are in **boldface type**:

ORIGINAL
"Over the last thirty years, the term has expanded to include other types of experiences people have when they move across cultural boundaries *within any one country*" (Zimbardo and Weber 332).

POOR PARAPHRASE
Over the last thirty years, the concept has broadened to **include other** kinds **of experiences people have when they** cross **cultural boundaries *within any one country*** (Zimbardo and Weber 332).

GOOD PARAPHRASE
The meaning of this concept has broadened during the last three decades. Now it encompasses what happens to people crossing cultural borders *within a single country* (Zimbardo and Weber 332).

HOW TO Paraphrase Information

- Read the material you want to paraphrase. Then put it away. Write down the information or idea, using your own words and writing style.

- After the paraphrase, provide the name of the author whose ideas you have borrowed (if you haven't already given the author's name) and the page number of the source on your note.

- Reread the original passage to make sure you have accurately captured the author's information or ideas without plagiarizing.

When paraphrasing, you don't need to use quotation marks because the words are your own. You must, however, indicate the source of the idea or information.

Here is the same student paragraph on culture shock you saw on p. 545, except here the quotation is replaced with a paraphrase (in boldface type):

> When you think of who experiences culture shock, you might picture immigrants moving to a new land or students studying in foreign countries. Not everyone who experiences culture shock, though, is in a foreign country. **The meaning of this concept has broadened during the last three decades. Now it encompasses what happens to people crossing cultural borders *within a single country*** (Zimbardo and Weber 332). Therefore, people may experience culture shock when they leave home to go to college, lose their jobs, or move to a much bigger or smaller city.

Notice, too, that the TIE (topic-illustration-explanation) method of paragraph organization is used with the paraphrased information.

Need more information about using the TIE method of paragraph organization? Refer to p. 78.

ACTIVITY 7 (GROUP)

Paraphrasing Sources. Working with a group of students, paraphrase one or two paragraphs from "Cross-Cultural Perspective: Culture Shock." Compare your group's paraphrases with those of the other groups in your class.

Summarizing Information

A *summary* is a condensed version of a piece of text that contains that text's key ideas. A summary is always much shorter than the original because it omits details.

Summary writing is one of the most common types of writing used in college and the workplace. On the job, you might write a summary of sales over the past six months. In college courses, you might be asked to write summaries of lectures, lab experiments, or journal articles. In an essay, information summarized from primary or secondary research can provide good supporting examples, observations, definitions, facts, statistics, and expert testimony.

Depending on your purpose for writing, a summary may be as short as a sentence or as long as a paragraph. Here's a one-sentence summary of "Cross-Cultural Perspective: Culture Shock."

> In "Cross-Cultural Perspective: Culture Shock," Philip Zimbardo and Ann Weber explain what culture shock is, who experiences it, how it affects people emotionally and physically, and what people can do to cope with it.

Here's a longer summary of the same article:

> In "Cross-Cultural Perspective: Culture Shock," Philip Zimbardo and Ann Weber define culture shock as "the stress experienced by people who move to unfamiliar surroundings" (332). According to

HOW TO Summarize Information

- Reread the source and write down the main ideas. These ideas are usually expressed in the thesis statement, the topic sentences, and, at times, the conclusion. If the source has headings and subheadings, they may express main ideas as well.

- Focus on the main points only and omit the details.

- At the beginning of your summary, give the title and author of the source.

- Write the summary in your own words. Use a quotation only to emphasize an important point that cannot be conveyed as powerfully in your own words.

the authors, people may experience culture shock when they move to a new country or to a new place within their own country. A sudden life change, such as the loss of a job, can also create culture shock. This condition produces a variety of emotional problems, such as depression, loneliness, and unreasonable suspicions of other people. Culture shock can also cause physical problems, including stomach disorders and insomnia. Many programs now exist to help people about to undergo a life change that could result in culture shock.

When you summarize information in your essay, remember that your ideas come first. Summarized information should only be used to support your own points.

ACTIVITY 8

Analyzing Summaries.   Read the following two summaries of "Cross-Cultural Perspective: Culture Shock." How can they be improved?

1. In "Cross-Cultural Perspective: Culture Shock," Philip Zimbardo and Ann Weber explain that culture shock is "the stress experienced by people who move to unfamiliar surroundings." People who might have culture shock are a Navajo student who moves to a large university, an African-American businessman who takes a job in a company where the workers are 95% Caucasians, a student who travels to Europe to study, and an American businesswoman who travels to Japan for her job.

2. According to Philip Zimbardo and Ann Weber in "Cross-Cultural Perspective: Culture Shock," many people feel attached to a place that they call "home." When they leave this comfortable place, they often experience stress, which is called culture shock. They have problems doing ordinary things such as shopping or finding a place to live. When the term *culture shock* was coined, it referred to the stress felt by people who lived abroad.

ACTIVITY 9 (GROUP)

Writing a Summary.   Working in a group, read the following excerpt from an essay by Keiko Nozoe, "The Japanese Syndrome," about Japanese students in the United States. Then write a summary of the essay that includes one or two quotations. Compare your group's summary with those written by the other groups in your class.

KEIKO NOZOE

The Japanese Syndrome

"Japanese people never want to make friends with people from other countries," said my host-mother's father to me the other night at a party at her house. "They're always gathering around other Japanese, even when they're away from home." 1

I was quite shocked at this statement, and initially quite upset as well. I have always thought that the Japanese are the politest and friendliest people in the world. But when I analyzed my own behavior, and that of my fellow foreign students, I recognized that there was some truth to what my host-mother's father said. The Japanese do tend to stick to themselves, for a number of reasons. As a result, they do not easily make friends with people of other cultures. 2

There are a number of factors causing this Japanese syndrome. The first is that most Japanese students are very self-conscious about their English-speaking skills, which they feel are inadequate. Most Japanese students in the United States studied English throughout junior high and high school back home. However, our teachers—who were themselves Japanese—did not speak English well. They emphasized grammar and vocabulary, not conversation or listening skills. As a result, when we came to the United States, we felt lost and disappointed. We had thought that because we had studied the language for six or more years and earned good grades, we would have no problems with our classes here. But we discovered that because of our pronunciation, Americans often could not understand what we said! Thus we could not express our ideas. This made us lose much of our self-confidence, especially as we come from a culture that stresses perfection. Even after taking ESL classes, we tended to avoid situations where we would have to talk to non-Japanese people. 3

The role of the student in the Japanese educational system also explains why we are unwilling to speak in learning situations. Japanese students are taught not to talk during class. In 4 fact, few classes in Japan are set up to allow students to discuss class materials and express their opinions. They are supposed to be silent in class and listen carefully to the lecture. The teachers are happier this way. They feel that a student's silence is a mark of respect. That is why it is so hard for a Japanese person to speak up in class or even with a boss.

Next, certain differences in racial characteristics add to this 5 problem. The Japanese are not good at talking to people they have just met. Compared with Americans, we are much more reserved. Americans can often converse immediately with strangers on a bus or in a restaurant. This is very uncommon in Japan. For example, when I first rode a bus in the United States, I was surprised to hear people talking to the driver and to the other passengers. Not only were they making small talk, they were even discussing personal problems, like trouble with a boyfriend or girlfriend, or even divorce! I could not imagine behaving in this way with strangers on an Osaka bus.

Again, unlike most Americans, who are trained to be individualistic, most Japanese have a strong need to belong to a 6 group. This is because Japanese society always emphasizes the value of the group, and the importance of working for the group. Groups exist everywhere—in schools, at work, in neighborhoods. For example, from my elementary school days, I was part of a group of friends. We went everywhere together and did everything together. Everyone I knew belonged to a similar group. If they do not belong to a group, most Japanese tend to feel anxious and isolated. Therefore, as soon as we arrived in the United States, we looked for a group of Japanese students with whom we would feel comfortable, and we stayed with them.

One last explanation for this clustering tendency in Japanese 7 students is that we have always been used to a homogeneous society. In Japan, unlike the United States, almost everyone is the same. Japan has the same race, language and culture throughout its four islands. Most people even have the same religion, as there are only two major ones, Buddhism and Christianity. Although there are people of other cultures living in Japan, such as Koreans and Chinese, they are treated as outsiders. We do not try to mix with them. We do not make an effort to make friends with them or talk to them or get to know them. Many Japanese feel uncomfortable with these "foreigners," even if they have been living in the country for generations. Some feel that Japanese culture is superior to the foreigners' cultures. When we come to the United States, many of us bring these attitudes about foreigners with us, and thus we are not comfortable mingling with people of other cultures and customs here.

My host-mother's father's comments have alerted me to a   8
problem that a Japanese person faces in the United States. Having thought about it, I can see how complex the causes of this
problem are. But understanding them has made me want to
change my behavior patterns. Otherwise I will never be able to
speak up and let people know what I think. I will never be able
to communicate and learn through friendship with people from
other countries, or teach them about Japan. I may go back to
Japan without really improving my English skills or increasing
my knowledge of other cultures. Then my trip to the United
States will have been a wasted opportunity.

ACTIVITY 10

Summarizing Sources for Your Research Essay. Refer to the
research questions you prepared at the start of your primary and secondary research. Answer these research questions by writing summaries of your sources. Use this summarized information when you
revise your essay.

Documenting Sources

Documentation of sources is an important aspect of the research
paper. To *document* is to refer your reader to your primary or secondary research sources. Proper documentation allows readers to
locate and verify your sources for their own future research. It also
keeps you from inadvertently plagiarizing others' words or ideas.

You document sources both in the essay itself—where you identify the author and page number for quotations, paraphrases, and
summaries—and in a list of sources at the end of the paper, called a
Works Cited page.

IN-TEXT DOCUMENTATION. You need to document whenever
you quote, paraphrase, or summarize a secondary research source in
the text of the paper itself. For each source you refer to, you will write
a citation. Follow these guidelines for writing citations.

- Identify the author in an introductory phrase and give the page
  number in parentheses.

  As psychologist Liu Chang has noted, "Students experiencing
  culture shock will benefit from participating in support
  groups" (107).

- If you don't give the author's name in an introductory phrase, include the author's last name along with the page number in parentheses.

  > It is also true that "students experiencing culture shock will benefit from participating in support groups" (Chang 107).

- If the source has two or three authors, include all of the last names in the citation.

  > According to Johnson and Hall, "Culture shock is an inevitable result of traveling to a new place" (189).

  > Psychologists now understand that "culture shock is an inevitable result of traveling to a new place" (Johnson and Hall 189).

- If the source has four or more authors, either give the names of all the authors or give the name of the first author followed by *et al.*, which is an abbreviation for "and others."

  > As Gibson et al. have noted, "Culture shock can ultimately become a beneficial experience" (233).

  > Experts point out that "Culture shock can ultimately become a beneficial experience" (Gibson, Emerson, Chang, and Zimmerman 233).

- If no author is given for a source, give the title in an introductory phrase or a shortened version of the title in parentheses.

  > According to "Tips for Success for New Students," a brochure produced by the International Students' Office, culture shock will not "derail students' dreams of academic success" as long as they learn about this condition (3).

  > Culture shock will not "derail students' dreams of academic success" as long as they learn about this condition ("Tips for Success" 3).

- If you're using an article reprinted from an electronic database, no page numbers will be given. In this case, use the paragraph number or the screen number, if available.

  > Professor Caroline Edmunds has indicated that "even students who move away from home to attend a university only an hour away" can still experience culture shock (par. 5).

  > In fact, "even students who move away from home to attend a university only an hour away" can still experience culture shock (Edmunds, par. 5).

  > In fact, "even students who move away from home to attend a university only an hour away" can still experience culture shock (Edmunds, screen 3).

- Remember that you need to include in-text documentation for paraphrased or summarized information, in addition to quoted information.

  > In fact, students can experience culture shock even if they enroll in a university that's only sixty minutes from their homes (Edmunds, par. 5).

- Use transitions or keywords to connect the documented material to the point being made. Some keywords and transitions used in the above examples are "It is also true that," "psychologists now understand," and "in fact."

- Finally, study the format of the above examples. Notice that only the number of the page is given; don't abbreviate "page." Also, put the period after the parentheses.

WORKS CITED PAGE. The *Works Cited* page is a list of sources that appears at the end of your paper. Every source you mention in your essay should be included in the Works Cited list.

Different fields of study use different formats and titles for the Works Cited list. The following discussion and sample entries are based on the format established by the Modern Language Association, or MLA for short.

HOW TO Use MLA Format

- Put the Works Cited list on a separate page at the end of your paper.

- Arrange the source entries alphabetically by the authors' last names, or by title if the author is not named.

- Double-space the entries.

- The first line of each entry should line up with the left-hand margin. The other lines of each entry should be indented five spaces or ½ inch.

- Underline the titles of books, journals, magazines, and newspapers.

- Put the titles of magazine and newspaper articles in quotation marks.

MLA format also requires that you present the information about your sources in a specific way. Books, magazines, journals, and newspapers require different formats. Encyclopedias are different still, and there is a particular way to list an interview. Also, the form varies slightly when a source has more than one author. Here are some sample MLA-style entries.

BOOK WITH ONE AUTHOR

> Pedersen, Paul. <u>The Five Stages of Culture Shock</u>. Westport:
>   Greenwood, 1995.

BOOK WITH MORE THAN ONE AUTHOR

> Furnham, Adrian, and Stephen Bochner. <u>Culture Shock:
>   Psychological Reactions to Unfamiliar Environments</u>.
>   New York: Methuen, 1986.

CHAPTER OR ARTICLE FROM AN EDITED BOOK

> Burton, Robert S. "Talking across Cultures." <u>Understanding
>   Others: Cultural and Cross-Cultural Studies and the
>   Teaching of Literature</u>. Ed. Joseph Trimmer and Tilly
>   Warnock. Urbana: NCTE, 1992. 115-213.

MAGAZINE ARTICLE (PRINT SOURCE)

> Plagens, Peter. "These Days, It's the 'Old of the Shock.'"
>   <u>Newsweek</u> 29 Dec. 1997: 89.

JOURNAL ARTICLE WHEN JOURNAL IS PAGED CONTINUOUSLY (PRINT SOURCE)

Pages are numbered consecutively from the first page of the first issue to the final page of the last issue within a volume. Generally, a volume includes the articles produced in a year by that journal. For this kind of citation, include only the volume number.

> Schwarz, Adam. "Culture Shock." <u>Far Eastern Economic Review</u>
>   34 (1997): 63-68.

In this example, "34" refers to the volume number.

JOURNAL ARTICLE WHEN EACH ISSUE IS PAGED SEPARATELY

Include both the volume and issue numbers.

> Meyer, Lisa. "Academic Acculturation for Foreign Graduate
>   Students: Meeting New Concepts of Research and
>   Writing." <u>College ESL</u> 5.2 (1995): 83-91.

In this example, "5.2" refers to volume 5, issue 2.

NEWSPAPER ARTICLE (PRINT SOURCE)

> Newman, Bruce. "From the Land of Private Freeways Comes Car
> Culture Shock." <u>New York Times</u> 16 Oct. 1997: G8.

If the article appears on more than one page, and the pages are not consecutive, add a plus sign after the number of the first page: "C4+."

ENCYCLOPEDIA ARTICLE (PRINT SOURCE)

> "The Characteristics of Culture." <u>Encyclopaedia Americana</u>.
> 1998 ed.

PERSONAL INTERVIEW

> Wucinich, Sophia. Personal interview. 10 Jan. 2002.

TELEPHONE INTERVIEW

> Schroeder, Niels. Telephone interview. 14 Apr. 2002.

To cite a source you obtained from a CD-ROM or Web database, give the same information you would give if you had used a print format. Additionally, give the name of the database, the medium (CD-ROM or online), the name of the company producing the database, and the date of electronic publication.

ARTICLE FROM A COMPUTER DATABASE ON CD-ROM

> Harvey, Steve. "A Case of Culture Shock, or a Polish Joke
> Gone Awry?" <u>Los Angeles Times</u> 23 July 1997: B3.
> <u>Newspapers 5 Full Text</u>. CD-ROM. ProQuest. Sept. 1997.

INFORMATION FROM A WEB SITE

If you used information from a Web site on the World Wide Web, give the author's name (if included), the title of the site, the date of electronic publication, the name of any institution or organization associated with the site, the date you accessed the site, and the URL (or address) in angle brackets. If the URL won't fit on one line, separate it only after a slash.

> Do, Thi Thuan. <u>Asian American Students' Culture Shock</u>.
> 2 Jan. 1998. U of California, Irvine. 6 Nov. 1998
> <http://www.ics.uci.edu/~tdo/ea/Asian.html>.

For more information on how to document sources, consult the *MLA Handbook for Writers of Research Papers,* 5th edition (1999) or the *MLA Style Manual and Guide to Scholarly Publishing* (1998); both are available in the reference section of your library.

MLA Web Site

You can access the MLA's guide to citing electronic sources by visiting the *Choices* Web site. Go to **<www .bedfordstmartins.com/choices/>** and click on "Annotated Web Links."

ACTIVITY 11

Creating a Works Cited Page. Write up a Works Cited page in the MLA format for the following five sources. All necessary information is given (as well as unnecessary information you need not use).

1. *The Art of Crossing Cultures* by Craig Storti. Page 89. 1990. International Press, located in Yarmouth, Maine.

2. Interview by telephone with Helen Mar, who is Chinese, about her experiences as an international student. Boise, Idaho. June 30, 2002.

3. "Culture Shock" by Toni Mack, p. 188. Published in *Forbes* magazine in May 1997 on pp. 188–190.

4. Michael Ennis's article called "Shock Therapy," which appeared in *Texas Monthly* in June 1997 on pp. 88–93. Obtained on June 1, 1999 from *Periodical Abstracts,* which is produced by a company called OVID. Published on *Periodical Abstracts* in August 1997.

5. "The Role of the Physical Environment in Culture Shock," by Azrza Churchman and Michael Mitrani. Published in a journal called *Environment and Behavior,* vol. 29, issue 1, in January 1997 on pp. 64–86. Appeared in *Periodical Abstracts,* which is produced by Ovid and available online in April 1997.

SAMPLE RESEARCH PAPER

The following essay was written by student writer Leslie Lozano for the international students' forum on her campus. She used the writing process—gathering ideas, drafting, revising, and editing—before presenting this paper to the audience at the forum. (We have reproduced the essay in a narrower format than you will have on a standard eight-and-a-half- by eleven-inch sheet of paper so that we could annotate it.)

½"

Lozano 1

1"

Leslie Lozano

Professor Lee

Psychology 101

1 May 2002

Culture Shock

1"   People who have the opportunity to live and study in   1"

a new country usually are eager to master a new language,

taste different foods, and see new sights. But after a

while they might begin to feel lonely and confused. They

don't understand others, and others don't understand them.

Nothing tastes right. They get lost easily. They have

trouble doing even simple things such as shopping or

taking a bus. They realize that the way they speak, act,

and perceive things is different from other people in

their new environment. They are experiencing culture

shock.

   People do not have to travel to another country

to experience culture shock. At one point or another,

everyone becomes uncomfortable in an unfamiliar

environment or in the presence of people different from

themselves. However, international students, in

particular, are likely to experience culture shock because

their culture and the host culture can be so different.

Because culture shock can affect students' academic

success, it is important for them to understand the four

stages of culture shock: the honeymoon stage, the crisis

stage, the recovery stage, and the adjustment stage. These

Note proper heading.

Note double-spacing throughout.

The introduction tries to attract the reader's attention. It also defines culture shock.

Thesis is given.

Lozano 2

stages were first described by anthropologist Kalervo
Oberg in 1960 (Thomas and Althen 213).

    The honeymoon stage takes place when people first
arrive in their country. They feel excited about the new
and different environment. After a few weeks, though, they
become more aware of how different the new country is
compared to their home country. They also begin to feel
homesick. This is when the crisis stage begins. During
this stage, students feel confused because they are
confronting new behaviors and lifestyles (Thomas and
Althen 221). Sometimes students disapprove of the values
and beliefs of the new country. According to psychologists
Philip R. Harris and Robert T. Moran, "Traditions provide
people with a 'mindset' and have a powerful influence on
their moral system for evaluating what is right or wrong,
good or bad, desirable or not" (135). Because of their
negative evaluations of the new culture, students can feel
alienated from their surroundings. Other symptoms of the
crisis stage include depression, boredom, lack of focus,
and inability to sleep ("Culture Shock," par. 4).

    How can students help themselves during the crisis
stage? They can begin by making friends with other
international students at events organized by the
International Students Office. They could even create an
organization for international students experiencing
culture shock. This is what Latino students at Harvard did
when they formed the Latino Caucus, which helps Latino
students overcome loneliness and homesickness as well as
serving as an advocate for other Latino students

This citation shows where Leslie learned this information.

Source is paraphrased and cited.

Last name of authors and page number are given in parentheses.

Quote is introduced.

Quotation is used to support the concept of negative evaluations.

Page number follows quotation.

Source is paraphrased, and cited.

Paragraph number is cited for an electronic source without page numbers.

Note that most of the essay consists of Leslie's ideas rather than information from the research.

Source is paraphrased.

Lozano 3

(Martinez). Sharing feelings with others in groups such as these can reduce loneliness. Also, students can always go to the campus counseling center for one-on-one help from a counselor.

No page number is given because the article was retrieved from an electronic database.

Although getting together with other international students is helpful, it doesn't mean that the new culture should be ignored. In fact, students will get over culture shock faster if they learn as much as they can about the new culture. Christina Bernal, a Mexican student advisor from the Office of International Programs, suggests that international students "should be like a sponge and absorb as much information as possible." Students suffering from culture shock should read local newspapers, watch television, and listen to the radio to learn about customs and habits that are foreign to them. They can also take advantage of opportunities to get to know people from the new culture. For instance, this university sponsors a host family program in which international students are paired up with families who get together with them regularly. This type of program allows the international students to educate members of the new culture about where they are from, which encourages mutual understanding and tolerance.

Quote is introduced.

These ideas are Leslie's, so no citations are needed.

After a month or so, international students' anxieties begin to lower and they enter the recovery stage. During this stage, they still experience the symptoms of culture shock but not as intensely. The final stage of culture shock is the adjustment stage, when students begin to relax and enjoy being in the new culture, though they still can experience confusion and

This information is summarized from the article by Thomas and Althen.

Lozano 4

worries every once in a while (Thomas and Althen 221). By the time people reach the adjustment stage, they are usually more flexible and open-minded about cultural differences than they were before entering the new culture.

This is an important idea, so Leslie uses a quotation for emphasis.

Although culture shock can feel overwhelming at times, students need to remember that it "usually passes if a person stays in a new culture long enough to understand it and get used to its ways" (Kottak). In the long run, the benefits of living in a different culture-- such as being fluent in a second language, understanding a new value system, and getting around in a totally different environment--far outweigh the hardships.

1"

½"

Lozano 5

Works Cited

1"

Bernal, Christina L. Personal interview. 25 Mar. 2002.

"Culture Shock." 14 Jan. 1998. International Students

    Office of Loyola U. 2 Apr. 1999 <http://

    www.loyno.edu/isa/culture.shock.html>.

Harris, Philip R., and Robert T. Moran. <u>Managing Cultural</u>

    <u>Differences</u>. 4th ed. Houston: Gulf, 1996.

Kottak, Conrad Phillip. "Culture." <u>The World Book</u>

    <u>Encyclopedia</u>. 1996 cd.

Martinez, Yleana. "Culture Club." <u>Hispanic</u> 11 (1998): 42.

    <u>Periodical Abstracts</u>. CD-ROM. Ovid. Apr. 1998.

Thomas, Kay, and Gary Althen. "Counseling Foreign

    Students." <u>Counseling across Cultures</u>. 3rd ed. Eds.

    Paul B. Pedersen, Juris G. Draguns, Walter J. Lonner,

    and Joseph E. Trimble. Honolulu: U of Hawaii P, 1989.

    205–41.

1"

Source from an interview.

Note double-spacing throughout.

Web site source.

Source from a book with 2 authors.

Encyclopedia source: no page number is needed.

Source from an article that came from a database.

Source from an edited book.

CHAPTER CHECKLIST

- ☐ I narrowed my topic before beginning research.
- ☐ I wrote research questions to help keep the research process focused.
- ☐ I conducted primary research by observing, surveying, and interviewing.
- ☐ I conducted secondary research by reading what others have written about my topic in books, magazines, journals (or specialized magazines), newspapers, encyclopedias, and other sources.
- ☐ I used a computer to access magazine, journal, and newspaper articles electronically.
- ☐ I avoided plagiarism by documenting sources.
- ☐ I used note-taking as an effective research tool.
- ☐ I used quotation marks to indicate an author's exact words.
- ☐ I used a paraphrase to put an author's ideas into my own words.
- ☐ I used a summary of the main ideas to condense a lengthy passage.
- ☐ I documented sources properly by identifying them in the essay and listing them on a Works Cited page at the end of the essay.
- ☐ I included a Works Cited entry with full publication information for every source cited in my essay. I formatted these entries correctly.

REFLECTING ON YOUR WRITING

To help you continue to improve as a writer, answer the following questions about the writing assignment for this chapter.

1. What was the easiest part of doing research?
2. What was the hardest part of doing research?
3. Compare writing a researched essay with writing an essay that doesn't contain research.
4. What information about your topic did you learn from conducting research?
5. If you could do the research for your essay over again, what would you do differently?

Using your answers to these questions, update your Writing Process Report.

Writing Process Report

Date:

Strengths:

Weaknesses:

Plans for improvement:

Once you complete this report, freewrite about what you learned in this chapter and what you still hope to learn.

A problem is a chance for you to do your best.

—DUKE ELLINGTON

CHAPTER 12

Taking Timed Writing Tests

In this chapter you will

- learn how to prepare for and take essay exams.

- learn how to prepare for and take in-class timed writings in response to readings.

- learn how to prepare for and take multiple-choice writing tests.

- reflect on your writing.

It's getting close to midterm, and you're feeling confident about your classes; everything seems to be going well. As you read your syllabi, though, you begin to panic. You discover that in the next week you have three tests; two of them include essay exam questions, and the other is an in-class timed writing assignment in response to a reading you haven't even seen yet. You might have the same reaction as student writer Sherman, who wrote in his journal:

> Three tests in a week. Help! I've done all of the work (most of the reading), but I don't write well under pressure. How will I ever survive? I'm stressed out just thinking about all of these tests.

The most common type of timed writing you will do in college is the essay exam. But you may also be asked to do an in-class timed writing in response to a reading or to take a multiple-choice exam on sentence structure, grammar, and punctuation.

The good news is that you can use everything you have already learned about writing to help you do well on these timed writing tests. For example, you can use the process of gathering ideas, drafting, revising, and editing when answering essay exam questions or writing in response to a reading. And you can use everything you have learned about grammar, spelling, and punctuation to help you do well on multiple-choice writing tests.

For this assignment, write an essay for your instructor and classmates in which you describe how you feel about taking exams. How do you reduce test anxiety, and what do you do during the test to ensure that you do your best? Share your responses with your classmates as a way to begin discussion about how best to prepare for and take timed writing tests.

THE ESSAY EXAM

To review the writing process, see Chapter 2.

An essay exam includes questions to which you must respond in writing. Your responses must be written in paragraphs and complete sentences and should reflect your thoughts in an organized, clear way. The main difference between writing an essay outside of class and an in-class essay exam is that you must work through the first four stages of the writing process (gathering ideas, drafting, revising, and editing) in the time allowed for the exam.

Preparing for an Essay Exam

LEARN ABOUT THE TEST. You will do your best on an essay exam if you know what to expect when you walk into class on exam day. If possible, find out what type of essay questions will be on the test, how long you will have to complete the test, and how it will be graded. You can find out about the test by reading your syllabus, asking your instructor, and talking with former students. If your instructor permits, obtain copies of old essay test questions or ask your instructor to provide sample test items.

Online Exam Questions

Ask your instructor if there is a class Web site or other online source of sample essay test questions and student responses. If yes, access this source to learn as much as you can about the instructor's essay exams.

ANTICIPATE THE QUESTIONS. Whether or not you can look over copies of old essay test questions, anticipate the questions for your upcoming exam. Remember, your instructor will probably ask only a few essay questions, so they will most likely be on the most important topics in the course. If your instructor provides a review session or gives you a study guide, check these for possible essay questions. Most instructors take test items directly from these reviews or study guides. Reread your class notes and mark the topics that your instructor devoted the most time to in class. For example, if your history instructor spent a week discussing the Bill of Rights, you could anticipate an essay question on this topic. If this same instructor defined the First Amendment to the Constitution and then gave you a list of First Amendment rights, you could expect an essay question on this topic.

Sherman, the student who wrote the journal entry above, knew that one of his upcoming exams was in psychology. His instructor had spent a week lecturing on the topic of Abraham Maslow's "hierarchy of needs." The textbook assignment also contained several pages on this topic. Because of the amount of class time devoted to this topic, Sherman predicted that there would be an essay question on it. He was right. The instructor included this essay question on the test:

> Define Maslow's hierarchy of needs, classify these needs, and briefly describe each.

DEVELOP A STUDY ROUTINE. If you manage your study time wisely, you should have no difficulty studying for essay exams. You can manage your time wisely by setting aside two to three hours of study time a week for each hour that you are in class. During this time, review your lecture notes, read your textbooks, and complete any other assignments.

You might also consider forming a study group. Research suggests that studying in groups can increase your knowledge of course material because you and your classmates share the information you have learned. To form a study group, ask a few of your classmates to meet with you a week or two before a major exam. Share your class notes and discuss the textbook readings.

As a group, discuss and write down what you expect the essay exam questions to be. Then, write your individual responses to these possible essay questions. Discuss the strengths and weaknesses of each response so that each group member leaves the study session with a better idea of how to respond to possible essay questions.

ACTIVITY 1

Preparing for an Essay Exam. Take a moment to reflect and freewrite on how you have prepared for an essay exam in the past. What were your study strengths? What were your weaknesses? Now, how could you improve? If you were to form a study group, how could you best help others? How could they best help you? Which classmates might you ask to study with you?

Taking the Essay Exam

ANALYZE THE QUESTIONS. Most students have had the experience of writing an excellent answer that received no credit because it didn't answer the question asked. To prevent this from happening to you, use these strategies to help you analyze the questions: Quickly read over the exam. Notice the kinds of questions asked and the point value of each, and estimate the amount of time you will need to complete each response. With this information in mind, plan your answers, allowing the most time for the questions with the most point value.

As you read each essay question, be sure that you understand what is expected of you. One way to be sure that you understand the question is to mark it. Marking the question forces you to concentrate on what it is you need to do, reducing the chances that you will forget to answer part of the question or, even worse, write a response that doesn't answer the question at all. To mark the question, underline the keywords that indicate what the essay should be about and then circle the words that explain how you should develop and organize your response. Here is how Sherman marked the psychology question on Maslow's hierarchy of needs:

> (Define) Maslow's hierarchy of needs, (classify) these needs, and briefly (describe) each.

You probably noticed that the words *define, classify,* and *describe* used in this essay question are all words you recognize as methods of development. Just as you develop and organize paragraphs using description, narration, dialogue, comparison and contrast, classification, process, examples, definition, and cause and effect, you can develop and organize paragraphs in your essay exam responses using these same methods.

Here are some words you might see in essay exam questions. Notice how each points to which method to use.

See pp. 65–76 for additional information on the methods of development.

Description

    Describe the following . . .

    Explain . . .

    Illustrate . . .

    Give details of . . .

    Discuss . . .

Narration

    Relate the events . . .

    Tell what happened . . .

Dialogue

    Tell what a character said . . .

    Describe the exchange between . . .

Comparison-contrast

    Compare and contrast . . .

    Discuss the similarities . . .

    Discuss the differences . . .

Classification

    List the types of . . .

    Analyze the parts of . . .

    List the kinds of . . .

Process

    Provide the steps for . . .

    Outline the sequence of events in . . .

    Give the procedure . . .

    Analyze the following stages in . . .

Examples

    Give examples of . . .

    Support with evidence of . . .

    Provide support for . . .

    Explain . . .

    Describe what the author says . . .

Definition

    Define . . .

    Give the meaning of . . .

    Identify . . .

Cause and Effect

    Give the reasons for . . .

    Discuss the causes of . . .

    Describe the consequences of . . .

    Discuss the effects of . . .

    Explain why . . .

To review how to brainstorm and cluster, see pp. 30–33.

GATHER IDEAS. Once you have analyzed the essay question, you might be tempted to begin writing your response right away. If you look at students around you, some of them may have already started writing. Resist the urge to begin writing before you gather ideas. Taking the time to gather ideas first will help you write an organized essay. Set aside five minutes to brainstorm a list of the points you want to make or to create a cluster of your main ideas and supporting details. Once you have a list or cluster, number the key points in the order that you would like to write about them.

Here is an example of the list that Sherman brainstormed as he prepared to respond to the psychology question:

I *need* to do well on this test!

Abraham Maslow—1970 I think

Described needs as part of a hierarchy

A hierarchy is something arranged in ranks or stages

Maslow's hierarchy

 Hunger, thirst

 Need to feel safe and secure

 Need to feel loved

 Need for recognition

 Need to be all you can be!

But what are the stages? Help!

 Physiological (sp?)

 Safety

 Belongingness

 Esteem

 Self-actualization

How would I define these needs?

Priorities to be met.

WRITE YOUR RESPONSE. Now that you have taken five minutes to brainstorm or cluster your ideas, you'll want to draft quickly, but carefully. Organize your essay response just as you would an essay that you write outside of class. Begin with a brief introduction that includes a thesis statement that directly answers the exam question. Write your essay using complete sentences and paragraphs. Each paragraph should include a topic sentence or main idea, and each paragraph should include at least one or two specific details to support the topic sentence. Write a brief conclusion or concluding statement to sum up your essay.

More information on organizing an essay can be found on pp. 34–39.

REVISE AND EDIT YOUR RESPONSE. When you have completed your essay exam, you may want to turn it in right away. However, you should allow five to ten minutes to reread the questions and

> ## HOW TO Write an Essay Exam
>
> - Read the exam. Divide your time according to the point value of each question.
>
> - Mark up the question. Underline keywords that tell you what your essay should be about. Circle words (such as *classify*) that indicate how your essay should be organized.
>
> - Take a few minutes to gather and organize ideas in a rough outline form.
>
> - Write the essay. Include a brief introduction with a thesis statement that directly answers the exam question, body paragraphs with supporting details, and a short conclusion.
>
> - After you finish writing, take a few minutes to read over the exam and make quick corrections.
>
> - Keep track of the time.

your responses to be sure that you have answered the questions completely. If you wish to add content, write it neatly in the margin or at the bottom of the page and draw an arrow to the place where it belongs. For deletions or corrections, draw a line through the material to be deleted or corrected and write in the correction above the text. Where appropriate, you may wish to add transitions such as *then, however, moreover,* or *in conclusion* to help your instructor follow your train of thought.

For a complete list of transitions, see p. 200.

As you reread your response, also proofread for errors in grammar, spelling, and punctuation. Remember, your responses are judged not only for content, but also for how clearly they are written. Too many errors may make it difficult for your instructor to understand what you have written, resulting in a lower test grade. One more thing—be sure your name is on your exam before you turn it in.

Sample Essay Question and Student Response

Remember the psychology essay exam question: "Define Maslow's hierarchy of needs, classify these needs, and briefly describe each." Here's how Sherman responded to this question. Notice that he made additions, deletions, and corrections neatly.

Abraham Maslow described five needs that each person has [1]
and ranked them in order of importance. This order is a hierarchy
because a person must fulfill each need in order beginning with the
most basic one. These needs are hunger and thirst, ~~love, safety,~~ safety, love,
self-esteem, and the need to reach full potential.

The most basic need is hunger and thirst. What this means is that [2]
a person who is hungry or thirsty can't think of anything else. This
was demonstrated during World War II when a researcher, Keys, fed
36 volunteers just enough food to maintain their weight and then
cut their food in half. The effects showed that Maslow was correct.
The men became obsessed with food and lost all interest in social
activities.

The second need is for safety. A person who doesn't feel safe [3]
can't worry about the higher needs of love, ~~love,~~ self-esteem, and
reaching full potential. People must feel they can predict what will
happen and that they have some control over it.

The third need is love. Humans form relationships with other [4]
people and like to hang on to those relationships. That is why when
we meet people at school or on vacation we always promise to keep in touch. Most people
like to be with other people. If they are deprived of this need, they
often become depressed.

The ~~next~~ fourth need is self-esteem. A person needs to feel capable of [5]
achieving something in life and needs the respect of other people.
Motivation is what causes a person to ~~fear~~ work to earn other people's respect.
Intrinsic motivation is when a person does something just for the
challenge of it. Extrinsic motivation is when a person does something to be
rewarded or out of fear of punishment.

Maslow called the fifth need self-actualization. When Maslow [6]
studied people who had very successful lives, he discovered that
they were open and loving and didn't worry about what other people
think. They usually had a mission in life and had a few very good
relationships instead of a lot of not so meaningful ones.

Maslow's hope was that developing this hierarchy would help [7]
others think about how to motivate people to do their best.

ACTIVITY 2 (GROUP)

Taking an Essay Exam. Read and mark the following essay exam questions. Select one and brainstorm or cluster to gather ideas for a response. Then draft, revise, and edit your response. Share your response with members of your peer response or study group. What suggestions do they have for improving your response?

1. Explain the stages of the writing process as described in *Choices: A Basic Writing Guide with Readings*. Describe how you have used this process to improve your writing.

2. Compare and contrast an informative essay and a persuasive essay.

3. List the three types of journals. Give the advantages and disadvantages of each type.

4. Describe the process of preparing for and taking an essay exam.

IN-CLASS TIMED WRITING IN RESPONSE TO A READING

Instructors occasionally ask students to read a short article or essay just before or during class and to respond to a question or questions about this reading during class. This type of timed writing assignment requires that you read and write well under pressure.

Preparing for In-Class Timed Writing in Response to a Reading

DEVELOP A READING ROUTINE. You will be most successful writing in response to a reading if you are already an active reader. Active readers think as they read. They ask questions, challenge the author, and look for the author's next point. They also know why they're reading, either for entertainment or for information, and stay focused on that purpose. Often active readers write notes in the margins summarizing or commenting on what they have read.

Working with a study group can also help you become a more active reader. Ask study group members to help you summarize readings, discuss difficult passages, and define unknown vocabulary words. Reviewing your reading assignments as a group will help each of you better understand the content.

KEEP A READING JOURNAL. Keeping a reading journal is yet another way to become an active reader. Writing in a journal helps you explore your ideas more extensively than if you just think or talk about a text. By writing down your ideas, you can understand the reading more thoroughly. Reading journals also provide a place to reflect on what you have read. Writing in a reading journal helps you formulate questions and clarify ideas. Your journal is a place to collect and arrange your thoughts, draw conclusions, and evaluate what you have learned.

To begin keeping a reading journal, find a notebook that is comfortable to write in. One of the most effective types of reading journals is the two-column learning log. You write down the main points of the reading selection in one column and your thoughts about it in another column. The advantage of the two-column learning log is that the two columns make it easier both to summarize and to think about the reading.

Need more information on learning logs? See pp. 514–16.

Keep a Reading Journal on Computer

You may choose to keep a reading journal in a computer file. If you are keeping a two-column learning log, use the word-processing feature that sets up columns. When it's time to review for an in-class timed writing, you may want to print out your file.

KEEP A VOCABULARY LIST. The larger your vocabulary, the greater your chances of understanding even the most difficult reading. As you read a text, circle unfamiliar words. Then look them up in a dictionary, or ask someone in your study group to tell you the meaning. Keep a list of these words and review the list once a week. In addition to writing the definition of the word, use the word in a phrase or a sentence to help you remember it.

ACTIVITY 3

Preparing for In-Class Writing. Take a moment to reflect and freewrite on how you have read in the past. What are your strengths as a reader? What are your weaknesses? How could you improve your reading to ensure that you would do your best on an in-class timed writing in response to a reading?

Performing In-Class Timed Writing in Response to a Reading

Although active readers already have an advantage when assigned to write in class, all students can benefit from following these steps:

READ CAREFULLY. Good readers don't necessarily read faster than others or fully understand what they read the first time through, but they have ways of improving their understanding. Important reading strategies include previewing, distinguishing between main and supporting ideas, annotating the text, and learning how to read confusing passages.

To fully understand a piece, you should preview it first. Quickly scan the entire reading selection for clues about the author's main ideas. Previewing helps you begin to think about the most important ideas even before you begin to read carefully. To preview:

1. Examine the title to determine what it suggests about the topic.
2. Look at the author's name. Do you know anything about this author?
3. Read the headnote at the beginning of the reading. What does it suggest about the topic?
4. Examine the headings and any illustrations. These are clues to what the author considers important.
5. Read the first paragraph.
6. Look at the first sentence of each remaining paragraph. This is where the author most often puts the topic sentence: the main point of the paragraph.
7. Read the conclusion. Authors often restate their main points in their conclusions.

To review main ideas and supporting details, see Chapter 3.

Once you have previewed the reading selection, read it carefully to distinguish main ideas from supporting details. The main ideas are the writer's general points, whereas the supporting ideas are the more specific details that explain or justify the main ideas. For example, one of the main ideas of this section is that you can use specific strategies to improve your understanding of a reading; a detail is that previewing is one of these strategies. Once you can distinguish between main ideas and supporting details, you can more effectively respond to a reading selection.

Another strategy is to annotate the text. Just as you read and mark essay exam questions, you can read and mark the article or essay you are reading for a timed in-class writing. As you read, underline the main ideas. Once you have read the article, look back at what you have underlined. Which is the author's thesis statement? Which are the main ideas and supporting details that help explain or justify the thesis statement? In the margin, you may also wish to write brief phrases restating key ideas, noting unfamiliar words to look up in the dictionary, and expressing your own thoughts about the reading.

One of the most difficult things to learn is how to read a confusing passage. You might be tempted to skip over it, or you might panic and stop reading altogether. Instead, use these strategies to help you:

- Reread the confusing section again, sentence by sentence. Also, reread the paragraph just before and the one just after to provide you with a context.

- Underline words and phrases that seem significant.

- If permitted, use a dictionary to look up words that you don't know.

- If possible, ask your instructor for clarification of the confusing passage.

WRITE YOUR RESPONSE. Now that you have actively read the essay or article your instructor has assigned, you are ready to write a response to the question or questions that accompany the reading. Follow the same steps that you use when answering essay exam questions:

1. Analyze the question by marking it.
2. Gather ideas by brainstorming or clustering.
3. Write your response in an essay format.
4. Revise and edit it by making additions and deletions neatly.

Sample In-Class Writing Question and Student Response

Ofelia read this essay entitled "Freedom from Choice."

BRIAN A. COURTNEY
Freedom from Choice

As my friend Denise and I trudged across the University of Ten-   1
nessee campus to our 9:05 a.m. class, we delivered countless head
nods, "Heys" and "How ya' doin's" to other African-Americans we

passed along the way. We spoke to people we knew as well as people we didn't know because it's an unwritten rule that black people speak to one another when they pass. But when I stopped to greet and hug one of my female friends who happens to be white, Denise seemed a little bothered. We continued our walk to class, and Denise expressed concern that I might be coming down with a "fever." "I don't feel sick," I told her. As it turns out, she was referring to "jungle fever," the condition where a black man or woman is attracted to someone of the opposite race.

This encounter has not been an uncommon experience for me. That's why the first 21 years of my life have felt like a never-ending tug of war. And quite honestly, I'm not looking forward to being dragged through the mud for the rest of my life. My white friends want me to act one way—white. My African-American friends want me to act another—black. Pleasing them both is nearly impossible and leaves little room to be just me.

The politically correct term for someone with my racial background is "biracial" or "multiracial." My mother is fair-skinned with blond hair and blue eyes. My father is dark-complexioned with prominent African-American features and a head of woolly hair. When you combine the genetic makeup of the two, you get me—golden-brown skin, semi-coarse hair and a whole mess of freckles.

Someone once told me I was lucky to be biracial because I have the best of both worlds. In some ways this is true. I have a huge family that's filled with diversity and is as colorful as a box of Crayolas. My family is more open to whomever I choose to date, whether that person is black, white, biracial, Asian or whatever. But looking at the big picture, American society makes being biracial feel less like a blessing than a curse.

One reason is the American obsession with labeling. We feel the need to label everyone and everything and group them into neatly defined categories. Are you a Republican, a Democrat or an Independent? Are you pro-life or pro-choice? Are you African-American, Caucasian or Native American? Not everyone fits into such classifications. This presents a problem for me and the many biracial people living in the United States. The rest of the population seems more comfortable when we choose to identify with one group. And it pressures us to do so, forcing us to deny half of who we are.

Growing up in the small, predominantly white town of Maryville, Tenn., I attended William Blount High School. I was one of a handful of minority students—a raisin in a box of corn-flakes, so to speak. Almost all of my peers, many of whom I've known since grade school, were white. Over the years, they've commented on how different I am from other black people they know. The implication was that I'm better because I'm only *half* black. Acceptance into their world has meant talking as they talk, dressing as they dress and appreciating the same music. To reduce tension and make everyone feel comfortable, I've reacted by ignoring half of my identity and downplaying my ethnicity.

My experience at UT has been very similar. This time it's my African-American peers exerting pressure to choose. Some African-Americans on campus say I "talk too white." I dress like the boys in white fraternities. I have too many white friends. In other words, I'm not black enough. I'm a white "wanna-be." The other day, an African-American acquaintance told me I dress "bourgie." This means I dress very white—a pastel-colored polo, a pair of navy chinos and hiking boots. Before I came to terms with this kind of remark, a comment like this would have angered me, and I must admit that I was a little offended. But instead of showing my frustration, I let it ride, and I simply said, "Thank you." Surprised by this response, she said in disbelief, "You mean you agree?"

On more occasions than I dare to count, black friends have made sweeping derogatory statements about the white race in general. "White people do this, or white people do that." Every time I hear them, I cringe. These comments refer not just to my white friends but to my mother and maternal grandmother as well. Why should I have to shun or hide my white heritage to enhance my ethnicity? Doesn't the fact that I have suffered the same prejudices as every other African-American—and then some—count for something?

I do not blame my African-American or white friends for the problems faced by biracial people in America. I blame society for not acknowledging us as a separate race. I am speaking not only for people who, like myself, are half black and half white, but also for those who are half white and half Asian, half white and half Hispanic, or half white and half whatever. Until American society recognizes us as a distinct group, we will continue to be pressured to choose one side of our heritage over the other.

Job applications, survey forms, college-entrance exams and the like ask individuals to check only *one* box for race. For most of my life, I have marked BLACK because my skin color is the first thing people notice. However, I could just as honestly have marked WHITE. Somehow when I fill out these forms, I think the employers, administrators, researchers, teachers or whoever sees them will have a problem looking at my face and then accepting a big x by the word WHITE. In any case, checking BLACK or WHITE does not truly represent me. Only in recent years have some private universities added the category of BIRACIAL or MULTIRACIAL to their applications. I've heard that a few states now include these categories on government forms.

One of the greatest things parents of biracial children can do   11 is expose them to *both* of their cultures. But what good does this do when in the end society makes us choose? Having a separate category marked BIRACIAL will not magically put an end to the pressure to choose, but it will help people to stop judging us as just black or just white and see us for what we really are—both.

Ofelia then responded to the following questions: "What is the main point of Courtney's essay? Provide examples of the evidence he uses to support his main point. Do you agree or disagree with him? Explain your answer." Here's Ofelia's response:

Courtney's main point is that American society forces us to   1
identify ourselves as members of one race. Having to choose keeps
many people from identifying themselves as biracial or multiracial.

Courtney uses many examples as evidence. For example, he   2
describes his friend Denise's reaction to his hugging a white girl.
Denise accuses him of having "jungle fever." Yet, his black friends
say he is too white because he dresses in chinos and hiking boots.
He also points out that he must choose one race when he fills out
job applications, college entrance exams, and surveys.

I agree with Brian Courtney that Americans place too much   3
emphasis on race and ethnicity. As Courtney says, this comes
from Americans' obsession with pigeonholing each person. I am a
Mexican-American, but I could refer to myself as a Cholo, a Latino,
a Chicano, a Hispanic, a Mexican, or an American. But the point is I
am constantly pressured to choose.

If each of us refused to be pigeonholed, then we could take the   4
first step toward ending the obsession with labeling. And once we
quit labeling, maybe some of the problems Courtney and I have
experienced will begin to disappear.

HOW TO Take a Writing Test in Response
to a Reading

- Preview the reading for clues about the main ideas. Examine the title, headings, first paragraph, topic sentences, and conclusions.

- Read the text, distinguishing between main and supporting ideas.

- Annotate the text by taking notes in the margins about the main ideas. Look up unfamiliar words and reread confusing passages.

- Before writing your response, analyze the question, gather ideas, and outline your answer.

- Use an essay format.

- After you write, take a few minutes to make corrections.

- Keep track of the time.

ACTIVITY 4 (GROUP)

In-Class Timed Writing in Response to a Reading. Actively re-read the essay "Freedom from Choice." Respond in writing to this question: "Do you agree or disagree with Courtney's idea of including 'biracial' or 'multiracial' on forms that ask for ethnicity? Why or why not?" Share your response with members of your peer response or study group. What suggestions do they have for improving your response?

MULTIPLE-CHOICE WRITING TESTS

Some colleges require that students take multiple-choice writing tests for placement purposes or to advance to higher-level courses. Some writing instructors also administer multiple-choice writing tests as a way to determine each student's need for additional help with writing skills. For such tests, you may be asked to read a short passage and then determine the author's purpose and audience, to recognize main ideas and supporting details, and to recognize effective organization. A test on sentence structure may require that you identify sentence fragments, run-on sentences, incorrect subject-verb agreement, and incorrect word choice. You may also have to identify sentences that are poorly constructed because of too many words, misplaced words, or too few words. A test of grammar and punctuation skills requires that you identify standard sentence structure and standard punctuation.

Just as there are strategies for taking an essay exam and a timed in-class writing in response to a reading, there are strategies for doing your best on multiple-choice writing tests.

Preparing for a Multiple-Choice Writing Test

LEARN ABOUT THE TEST. Review the skills that will be tested. For example, if you are not sure of the parts of speech or what is meant by the phrases *standard sentence* or *standard punctuation,* you should review these. One way to review is to find out if there is a study guide for the test. Check with your college bookstore, tutoring center, or instructor. If a guide is available, review it before taking the test. Identify other resources, such as textbooks (including the handbook in this book), workbooks, and worksheets that may be available to help you practice. Find out if you will be able to use any aids such as a dictionary or thesaurus during the test.

Online Study Guides

If the test is standardized, there may be a computerized study guide available that tests and scores your present skills and tutors you on those you need to practice. Check on the World Wide Web for the study guide you need.

ANTICIPATE THE QUESTIONS. Answer any sample test questions provided in study guides or provided by your instructor. Then score yourself on these sample questions. If you answer a question incorrectly, review the study materials to determine how you should have answered it. Using your overall score as a guide, assess your strengths and weaknesses, and plan a strategy for overcoming them.

DEVELOP A STUDY ROUTINE. Consider the amount of time you have before the exam, the resources you have on hand, and the availability of instructors and tutors to help you. Then develop a study plan. To prepare for an essay exam, you focus on a few general topics, but to prepare for a multiple-choice writing exam, you must review everything that will be on the exam. Consequently, you may need to schedule several review sessions.

Preparing for a Multiple-Choice Writing Test. Take a moment to reflect on and freewrite about how you have prepared for multiple-choice writing tests in the past. What were your study strengths? What were your weaknesses? How could you improve?

Taking a Multiple-Choice Writing Test

ANALYZE THE QUESTIONS. When taking a multiple-choice writing test, read the instructions carefully. Often there are both general instructions for taking the test and specific instructions for completing each part. Read each set carefully; if you don't understand any of these instructions, ask for clarification.

Read over the test items. Notice the kinds of questions asked and the point value of each. Estimate the amount of time you will need to complete each part of the test. With this in mind, plan your strategy, allowing the most time for the questions with the greatest point value.

CHOOSE YOUR RESPONSES. Once you begin the test, glance at your watch occasionally to ensure that you are working at a steady pace. Read each question carefully and select the best answer to the question. To best manage your time, skip questions you can't answer right away. If there is a separate answer sheet, be sure that the number of the question on the test and the number on the answer sheet match.

When you have answered all the questions you know, return to the questions you skipped. If you are not penalized for guessing, choose the one that seems most reasonable. Having read and answered all the other questions may provide clues to the answers to the questions you skipped. If time still remains, double-check all your answers.

Taking a Multiple-Choice Writing Test. Read the following passages. Then read the questions that follow each passage and choose the one best answer. (Note that the questions refer to the numbered sentences or word groups in the passages.)

HOW TO **Take a Multiple-Choice Writing Test**

- Use study guides to learn about the types of questions that will be asked.

- Study for the test by reviewing what will be on it.

- When taking the test, read and follow the directions carefully.

- Save the most time for the questions with the highest point value.

- Skip questions you don't know and return to them later.

- Keep track of the time.

¹Archeologists are probably best known for discovering buried relics and ruins of ancient civilizations in faraway lands. ²Many archeologists work right here in the United States, however. ³Scholars have learned much about human history from studying the remains of past societies, not only the origins of modern humans but also the origins of our own country. ⁴Even though the original colonies and settlements that became the United States are young when compared to the centuries-old Mayan and Egyptian civilizations, there are still many questions left to be answered about what life in colonial America was like. ⁵By investigating questions and researching evidence found at the sites of old European settlements, archeologists and historians alike hope to find enough evidence to answer their many questions.

⁶Among the questions to be answered is the nature of the relationship between the European settlers and the Native Americans. ⁷Some people believe that the relationship between these two groups was usually hostile, while others believe it was often peaceful. ⁸Building foundations, fragments of pottery, and bits of trash is the pieces of evidence archeologists are using to help learn more about how colonists and Native Americans got along. ⁹Evidence discovered at the site of Jamestown Colony in Virginia suggests that the relations between the settlers and Native Americans were at times peaceful and at other times hostile.

¹⁰Although written records from colonial settlements have survived, these documents alone cannot tell the entire story.

1. Which of the following versions of sentence 5 eliminates the unnecessary repetition in the original?

   A. By investigating questions and researching evidence found at the sites of old European settlements, archeologists hope to find evidence to answer their many questions.

   B. Archeologists and historians, by investigating and researching evidence found at the sites of old European settlements, hope to find enough evidence to answer their many questions.

   C. By investigating and researching artifacts found at the sites of old European settlements, archeologists and historians alike hope to answer many questions about the settlements.

   D. Archeologists and historians alike hope to find evidence at the sites of old European settlements to answer their many questions.

2. Which of the following corrections should be made in the second paragraph?

   A. Sentence 6: Change "European" to "european."

   B. Sentence 7: Change "usually" to "usual."

   C. Sentence 8: Change "is" to "are."

   D. Sentence 9: Change "discovered" to "discovering."

3. Which of the following sentences is the best choice to use as a conclusion for the third paragraph?

   A. To find evidence, historians must always dig things up.

   B. Sometimes, three-hundred-year-old garbage can be just as instructive as what has been written down.

   C. Nobody can trust the written word at all, because the person writing it is always biased.

   D. Archeologists have a difficult and valuable job to perform.

Read the passage below, which has been taken from a student's essay, and answer the questions that follow.

   [1]Aldo Leopold (1887–1948) was a well-known ecologist who believed that all life benefits when humans live in balance with nature and respect the environment. [2]His *Sand County Almanac,* a book of essays, is one of the most important books on ecology and conservation. [3]Observing the environment, the interconnected relationships among the animals, and the disruptions to the web of life caused by humans. [4]Leopold reached a number of important conclusions.

⁵After receiving a master's degree in forestry from Yale University, Leopold began his career by working for the Forest Service in the Southwest. ⁶While there, he helped to establish the first protected wilderness area, the Gila National Forest in New Mexico. ⁷He was also interested in landscape processes, such as fire and erosion, and the role of predators such as wolves in the wild. ⁸Both interests helped shape his view of the natural world as an interconnected system, "a foundation of energy flowing through a circuit of soils, plants, and animals."

⁹<u>Several years later</u>, he bought and restored <u>an abandoned farm</u> where he worked on the land and studied nature. ¹⁰He also <u>pioneered an effort</u> to re-create Wisconsin's <u>prairie-savanna ecosystem</u>.

¹¹In 1948, as Leopold set out from his farm to help a neighbor put out a fire, he suffered a heart attack and died at 61.

_____

_____

4. Which of the word groups from the first paragraph is not a complete sentence?

   A. Word group 1

   B. Word group 2

   C. Word group 3

   D. Word group 4

5. Which of the following sentences would best fit after sentence 11, as a conclusion for this passage?

   A. He had a wife and five children.

   B. His influence is greater than ever, though, and his book has sold over 1.5 million copies since its publication in 1949.

   C. The chicken coop on Leopold's farm, where he lived and worked, still exists.

   D. Leopold was born in Iowa in 1887.

6. Which of the underlined words in the third paragraph should be replaced by more precise or appropriate words?

   A. "Several years later"

   B. "an abandoned farm"

   C. "pioneered an effort"

   D. "prairie-savanna ecosystem"

Read the passage on page 589, written in the style of a science textbook. Then answer the questions that follow.

[1]Alzheimer's disease, an illness that slowly deprives people of their memory, reasoning, judgment, and language skills, causes the gradual destruction of a person's brain cells. [2]For over ten years, scientists have known that this disease starts with the action of an enzyme. [3]This enzyme, beta secretase, divides a protein that sticks out from brain cells in two. [4]Then, gamma-secretase, another enzyme, further divides the resulting protein fragments. [5]This action creates the toxic A beta protein. [6]Theoretically, scientists could stop the production of A beta by blocking either enzyme, both enzymes have been difficult to block. [7]Recently, however, a group of researchers have found the gene that causes cells to make beta-secretase. [8]Using a process of elimination, they started with a pool of one hundred genes and narrowed it down to one. [9]Having found this, scientists hope to be able to prevent Alzheimer's or slow its progress with medicine that can block beta-secretase. [10]Unfortunately, this next step may still be years away.

7. Which sentence is a comma splice?

    A. sentence 2

    B. sentence 4

    C. sentence 5

    D. sentence 6

8. Which of the following changes is needed in this paragraph?

    A. Change "causes" to "caused" in sentence 1.

    B. Change "then" to "also" in sentence 4.

    C. Change "Having found this" with "With this finding" in sentence 9.

    D. Change "slow" to "slowing" in sentence 9.

CHAPTER CHECKLIST

☐ I prepared for an essay exam by learning about the test, anticipating the questions, and developing a study routine.

☐ When taking an essay exam, I analyzed the question, gathered and outlined ideas, used an essay format, and made corrections.

☐ I prepared for an essay exam in response to a reading by developing a reading routine, keeping a reading journal, and making a vocabulary list.

☐ I wrote an essay exam in response to a reading by previewing the essay, taking notes on the main ideas, and using the writing process.

☐ I prepared for a multiple-choice writing test by learning about the test, anticipating the questions, and developing a study routine.

☐ I took a multiple-choice writing test by following the directions, reading the questions carefully, and selecting the best responses.

☐ For all tests, I spent the most amount of time on items with the highest point value and always kept track of the time.

REFLECTING ON YOUR WRITING

You have practiced taking three types of timed writing tests: an essay exam, an in-class timed response to a reading, and a multiple-choice writing test. To help you reflect on your test-taking skills, answer the following questions.

1. Which type of timed writing test do you prefer to take? Why?
2. Does your college require such a test for placement?
3. Do any of your instructors give timed writing tests? If so, what do you know about the tests?
4. How will you study for each of these tests?
5. What strategies will you use during the test?

Using your answers to these questions, update your Writing Process Report.

Writing Process Report

Date:

Strengths:

Weaknesses:

Plans for improvement:

Once you complete this report, freewrite on what you learned and what you still hope to learn.

Good writing excites me, and makes life worth living.

—HAROLD PINTER

CHAPTER 13

Assembling a Writing Portfolio

In this chapter you will

- discover why writers keep writing portfolios.

- complete a writing portfolio.

- consider other audiences for your portfolio.

- reflect on your writing.

Artists, photographers, models, and others use portfolios to show-case their talents and accomplishments. Imagine an artist's port-folio with some of the artist's best sketches, a photographer's portfolio with a selection of best photographs, or a model's portfolio with pho-tographs of best poses. These professionals choose from among all their works only the very best ones for their portfolio. By organizing a portfolio, they not only demonstrate their abilities but reveal other things about themselves as well. A well-designed portfolio can reveal a person's creativity, organizational skills, thoroughness, neatness, and competence.

For a review of purpose and audience, see pp. 5–15.

Now, imagine a writer's portfolio with some of the writer's best writing. A writer's portfolio serves the same purpose as other portfo-lios: a showcase for best works and a place to reveal something about the writer as a person.

More information on the Writing Process Report appears on p. 55.

Throughout this book you have written essays and reflected on your writing strengths and weaknesses in Writing Process Reports. You probably have essays that you are especially proud of or that oth-ers especially enjoyed reading. Now you're ready to pull these best works together into a writing portfolio and to reflect on what it reveals about you.

Once you have completed a portfolio, you'll be able to use it for several purposes: for example, to apply for employment or submit as a writing sample for admission to other colleges. Creating a portfolio can also be a rewarding way to end a writing class because it gives you the opportunity to reflect on all of the commitment, study, and prac-tice you have done to become an effective writer.

WRITING ASSIGNMENT Complete a writing portfolio and reflect on what you have learned about writing and your own writing process. After completing your portfolio, share it with your instructor and classmates. Also consider how you might revise the contents of your portfolio to suit other, future audiences.

HOW TO Use Your Writing Portfolio

Create a writing portfolio to

- showcase your best writing.

- present yourself for employment or admission to college programs.

- reflect on your writing.

ACTIVITY 1

Analyzing Your Purpose and Audience. Just as you have done for the essays you have written, think now about your purpose and audience for a writing portfolio. Answer the following questions.

1. Is your portfolio primarily designed to express, inform, or persuade?

   _____

2. Who is the primary audience for your writing portfolio?

   _____

   _____

Given your responses to the preceding questions, ask yourself these questions:

3. What writing qualities would I like to demonstrate through my portfolio?

   _____

   _____

   _____

4. How can I best demonstrate these qualities in my portfolio?

   _____

   _____

   _____

5. What other qualities would I like to demonstrate through my portfolio?

   _____

   _____

   _____

6. How can I best demonstrate these other qualities?

_____

_____

_____

SHOWCASING YOUR WRITING

The Contents

The contents of your portfolio will vary depending on your audience. You'll begin by sharing your portfolio with your instructor and classmates; therefore, you should include pieces that will interest them. But remember that your purpose is to persuade your audience that you have become a skilled writer as a result of your work throughout this book. You may demonstrate your growth as a writer by including a broad range of topics and formats in your portfolio. In addition, you want to demonstrate your creativity through your portfolio. Your writing portfolio should include

- a table of contents.
- a cover letter.
- your best essays.
- selected Writing Process Reports.
- other types of writing you have done.

SELECTED ESSAYS. Although you might be tempted to include all the essays you have written during the term, your portfolio should include only your best writing. Most likely, you'll choose three or four essays as examples of your best work.

How do you choose which essays to include? You want to demonstrate your skill as a writer as well as your creativity. Your most creative essays are probably those you most enjoyed working on and were eager to share with readers. To demonstrate your writing skills, select essays that include

- a lively title.
- an effective introduction.
- unified and coherent paragraphs.

- good supporting details.
- smooth transitions.
- a powerful conclusion.

ACTIVITY 2

Selecting Your Best Essays. Using the criteria for essay selection just discussed, choose from among the many essays you have written for the term the three or four essays that best demonstrate your skill as a writer for inclusion in your writing portfolio.

SELECTED WRITING PROCESS REPORTS. In addition to demonstrating your writing skills, you want your portfolio to show your growth as a writer. You recorded interesting discoveries about your writing process and reflected on your commitment to writing in your Writing Process Reports. By including some of these entries in your writing portfolio, you can demonstrate this growth to your readers.

Begin by reviewing your Writing Process Reports. How did your strengths, weaknesses, and plans for improvement change? How did your writing improve? Look for entries that reflect those improvements, reveal your growth as a writer, or indicate a new understanding about your writing process. Revise and edit the ones you plan to include in your portfolio, correcting any errors in grammar, spelling, and punctuation.

One student, Patrick, selected the following Writing Process Reports for his portfolio. The reports demonstrate his growth as a writer, his ability to handle a difficult writing task, his work with other students, and his approach to the writing process.

```
              Chapter Four Writing Process Report

     I have always had trouble writing about my personal
feelings. When I was asked to write an essay about an
incident that changed my life, I decided to write about my
grandfather's death. I wrote the essay "An Idea Whose Time
Has Gone," which is about my grandfather's willingness to
face death. At first, I was afraid I wouldn't be able to
write on this topic because it would bring back many
painful memories.
```

Many thoughts crossed my mind, but I finally put all my feelings into this essay. Not only did I want to show myself that I could write about my feelings, but I also wanted to understand why I was feeling the way I did. Never have I opened up to anybody as I did when I wrote this essay.

When I read it aloud to some friends, they told me they had never heard anything so moving. My peer response group also thought it was a good essay because it expressed my thoughts and feelings well. My group asked questions that helped me see the need for more specific details about my grandfather's death. This essay helped me open up and express my feelings in writing.

I think the essay is well written. When I read it to my dad, he felt like he was experiencing my grandfather's death all over again. Others reacted strongly, too; some cried and others just stayed silent. I remembered from class that a good expressive essay should move the reader. I knew I had done this because I had written the essay from my heart.

Chapter Five Writing Process Report

I signed up for this writing class thinking it would be just another class in which the professor lectures and gives assignments to take home, write about, and then turn in for a grade. Was I wrong! Taking this course has made me enjoy writing for the first time. Of the essays I've written so far, I think the one about rap music is my favorite. Not only did I look forward to writing this essay, but I also acquired a greater appreciation for this form of music as a result.

Writing this essay didn't seem like an assignment for me when I realized I wanted to share my excitement for rap with my classmates. The writing process I used for this essay was easy and simple. On the day the essay was assigned, I began reading and interviewing people about rap music, and I continued working on it every day until the deadline. First, I concentrated on what I wanted to say; then I revised, adding more description and dialogue to make the essay more interesting. Near the end of the process, I concentrated on deleting unnecessary paragraphs and sentences and editing to eliminate errors. This essay is a good piece of writing because of the effort and dedication I put into it.

ACTIVITY 3

Selecting Writing Process Reports. Select several Writing Process Reports in which you reflect on your growth as a writer or on your writing process. Revise and edit the entries to improve their readability and appearance. Then add them to your writing portfolio.

OTHER WRITING. In addition to the essays and Writing Process Reports, your portfolio may include other types of writing that show a broader range of your work. For example, you might include a term paper or summary you wrote for another course or a short story or poem you wrote for your own pleasure. By including other types of writing in your portfolio, you can demonstrate your ability to write well on a wide range of topics and in various different formats.

Patrick included the following poem in his portfolio to showcase his ability to write descriptively and concisely:

Composure

Her head leaned
against the creamy plaster wall;
her arms hung at her sides,
tense.
Her shoulders rigid,
taut with anticipation.

```
Her eyes, full of love

and sweet expectation,

watched her baby sleep.
```

ACTIVITY 4

Selecting Other Types of Writing. Review the other writing you have done on your own or for other courses. Select several examples for your portfolio that demonstrate your ability to write well in a range of formats.

COVER LETTER. After you assemble your best essays, Writing Process Reports, and other writing for your portfolio, consider whether including a business or informal cover letter is appropriate given your purpose and audience. A cover letter might briefly explain the contents of your portfolio and how it represents your growing skills in various writing formats. (If you include a cover letter, list it on your Contents page.)

Patrick included in his portfolio the cover letter to his writing instructor shown on the next page. Notice that his letter uses a business-letter format with single-spaced copy.

ACTIVITY 5

Writing a Cover Letter. Write a cover letter to introduce your portfolio. In it describe the contents of your portfolio and explain how the selections reflect on you as a writer—your skills, growth, and ability to handle diverse writing situations.

TABLE OF CONTENTS. You should include a table of contents in your portfolio. It tells readers what they can expect to find in the portfolio. It also demonstrates your ability to organize your work.

The table of contents should appear on a separate page, headed Contents, at the start of your portfolio and should include your name. Organize the table of contents in three columns for easy reference (see the example on p. 602). In the first column, give headings for the types of writing and the titles of the essays in your portfolio. In the second column, give the date you wrote each selection. In the third column, give the appropriate page numbers for the selections in the portfolio. (The pages of your portfolio should be numbered sequentially.) Notice, in the accompanying example, how Patrick prepared a table of contents in this way for his portfolio.

Patrick Callahan
1203 Devonshire
Salt Lake City, Utah 17032
December 15, 2002

Ms. Deborah Smith
Department of English
Salt Lake City College
Salt Lake City, Utah 17036

Dear Ms. Smith:

As you requested, I have compiled the following portfolio
of my best writing. Included in this portfolio are three
essays, two Writing Process Reports, and one poem.

Explains contents of the portfolio.

The three essays demonstrate my skill and range as a
writer. I chose one expressive, one informative, and one
persuasive essay to demonstrate that I can write for a
variety of purposes and to several different audiences.
In each one, I develop my ideas well and present them in
an interesting, informative way.

Demonstrates skill in writing for different purposes.

I have also included two Writing Process Reports to show
how I have grown as a writer and how I have come to enjoy
writing as a result of this course. I used to dread having
to communicate in writing, but I now feel more confident
in my ability to handle writing assignments in all of my
courses.

Demonstrates growth as a writer.

Finally, I have included one of my favorite poems to
demonstrate that I can write descriptive poetry as well.
I have always enjoyed writing poetry and welcome this
opportunity to share my poem with you and my classmates.

Demonstrates range of writing skills.

If you have any questions or comments about my portfolio,
please contact me.

Sincerely,

Patrick Callahan

Patrick Callahan

```
                               Contents

                                    Date Written      Page

Cover Letter                            12/15           1

Essays

   "An Idea Whose Time Has Gone"

      (expressive writing)              9/30            2

   "Local Rap Group Makes Headlines"

      (informative writing)            10/24            5

   "Capital Punishment: Your State Tax

      Dollars at Work" (persuasive writing)  11/5      10

Writing Process Reports

   Chapter Four Entry                   9/18           14

   Chapter Five Entry                  10/7            15

Other Writing

   "Composure" (poem)                   6/2            16
```

ACTIVITY 6

Creating a Table of Contents. Create a table of contents for your portfolio by following these directions.

1. Create a portfolio title that includes your name.
2. Divide the page into three columns.
3. Label the types of writing you included in your portfolio.
4. List the title of each selection under the appropriate heading.
5. List the date you wrote each selection.
6. Give the appropriate page number for each selection.

Assemble a Portfolio

If you have saved your files to a disk, you can now choose to print those you wish to include in your portfolio.

Polishing Your Portfolio

Think again about the impression you want to make with your portfolio. You want to persuade your readers that you're a skilled writer by including selections that demonstrate your writing skills and creativity. But you also need to present your work neatly.

First, you want to ensure that your work communicates well. Reread the summary that appears at the end of each chapter of this book. Then reread each selection in your portfolio and make any final revisions that may be needed. For instance, you might reword an ineffective introduction or conclusion, add supporting details, or revise an unclear sentence.

Need additional suggestions on revision? See pp. 39–41.

Turn next to your editing log. Reread the entries, and then check your portfolio selections for errors you may have overlooked. If you're unsure about a grammar or punctuation rule, refer to the Handbook in Part Four of this book for help. Finally, look at the manuscript format for each selection in the portfolio. Use a consistent format, and retype or reprint selections as needed to produce clean, error-free copies.

To review the editing log, see pp. 41–42.

ACTIVITY 7

Revising and Editing Your Portfolio. Reread each portfolio selection and make any final revisions now. Then edit your work to eliminate errors in grammar, spelling, and punctuation, and retype or reprint any selections that are not clean and neat.

Finally, revise your Contents page so that it accurately lists the selections within your portfolio. Check that the columns are aligned, that all dates are included, and that the page numbers are correct.

Binding Your Portfolio

Once you assemble your portfolio, you'll need to bind it in some way. The size of your portfolio will determine whether you should use a folded piece of construction paper or a sturdy three-ring notebook. When choosing a binding, select one that is attractive and holds the pages in a way that makes them easy to read.

Use divider pages to mark each section of your portfolio, and add tabs to the divider pages to match the headings given in your table of contents. Some students choose to decorate the cover of their portfolios with photographs of themselves or of their classmates, family, or friends. Others use markers and other art supplies to design a creative cover.

ACTIVITY 8

Binding Your Portfolio. Assemble and bind your portfolio. Divide the sections of the portfolio and, if you wish, decorate the cover.

Design a Cover

If you have access to a desktop publishing program, use it to design an attractive cover and divider sheets for your portfolio.

USES FOR YOUR PORTFOLIO

You're now ready to share your portfolio with your instructor and classmates. But before you do, let's consider several other uses for your portfolio.

Presentation

Your writing portfolio is a permanent record of the writing that you have done in this course. In sharing it with your instructor and classmates, you can demonstrate your writing skills. Save your portfolio for use with future audiences, including employers and colleges.

EMPLOYERS. When you apply for a job, particularly one requiring writing skills, you may want to present your portfolio to your prospective employer. Before presenting your portfolio, though, consider your audience and revise your portfolio accordingly. If Patrick, for instance, were applying for a summer job in an insurance office, he would replace the poem in his portfolio with business letters he had written. He might also include a résumé listing his job skills, work history, and education.

COLLEGES AND UNIVERSITIES. Some colleges and universities ask applicants to submit samples of their writing with their application for admission. If you transfer to another school or apply to a specific program, you may wish to use your portfolio. Again, you'll want to consider the specific requirements of the university. If Patrick were applying to another school, he would probably replace the poem in his portfolio with a term paper that he wrote for one of his courses.

When you complete your portfolio, congratulate yourself—no one knows as much about your writing as you do. In Chapter 1, we asked, "What comes into your mind when you think of a writer?" Your answer should now be "I do."

Place Your Portfolio on the World Wide Web

If you have access to the World Wide Web, you may be able to place your writing portfolio on a Web site. Check with your instructor or Internet service provider to see if this is an option.

CHAPTER CHECKLIST

- ☐ I showcased my skill and growth as a writer and my ability to write in a range of formats.
- ☐ I demonstrated my organizational skills, creativity, thoroughness, and neatness in my portfolio.
- ☐ I included my best writing: essays, Writing Process Reports, other writing, a table of contents, and a cover letter.
- ☐ I revised and edited my portfolio to ensure that my work communicates well, is free of errors, and is clean and neat.
- ☐ I bound my portfolio in a way that is attractive and easy to read.
- ☐ I used my portfolio to reflect on how to improve my writing.
- ☐ I varied the contents and cover letter of my portfolio for different purposes and audiences, such as applying for employment or for admission to other colleges.

REFLECTING ON YOUR WRITING

By now, you should have a fairly good idea of what works best for you when gathering ideas, drafting, revising, and editing. Knowing this will help you complete writing assignments in other courses as well as in the workplace. Now that you have assembled your portfolio, you can use it to reflect on how you have grown as a writer during your work in this course. Reflect on what you have learned about your writing process. Use the following questions as a starting point.

1. What are your writing strengths? Your writing weaknesses?
2. How can you continue to improve your weak areas?

3. Which selections in your portfolio were the easiest for you to write? Which were the most difficult?

4. How did you accomplish these difficult assignments?

5. Are there any types of writing that you haven't done, but that you would like to add to your portfolio? Explain.

6. Do you now consider yourself an effective writer? Why or why not?

PART FOUR

Handbook with Exercises

When you write, you want to communicate your ideas as clearly as possible. Using correct grammar, punctuation, and spelling helps your readers understand what you mean.

You'll probably use this Handbook in various ways. You may consult it during the editing stage as well as when you add entries to your editing log. You may complete certain sections to help you target specific problem areas in your writing. If you're a multilingual writer, you may consult the Guidelines for Multilingual Writers and Grammar for Multilingual Writers to help you write in English.

Above all, you should use this Handbook to help you recognize and eliminate errors to do the best possible job of communicating your message to your reader.

HANDBOOK TOPICS

Parts of Sentences

When you're working on your writing, you need to understand the basic structure of the sentence. You may have studied sentence grammar before, but if you didn't apply what you learned to your own writing, chances are you didn't see much improvement in your papers even if you always earned A's on grammar tests. The activities in Part Four will help you learn how to use grammar correctly. But the most important activity for you will be to apply what you learn to your own writing.

Parts of Sentences

For additional practice with the parts of sentences, go to **<www.bedfordstmartins.com/choices/>**. Click on "Exercise Central," and after logging in, click on "Parts of Sentences."

WHAT IS A SENTENCE?

A *complete sentence* consists of a subject and a verb and expresses a complete thought. Usually the subject is a *noun*—a person, place, or thing. But a subject can also be a *pronoun*—a word that takes the place of a noun. The *subject* tells who or what is doing the action.

Mary works.

She is a hard worker.

The *verb* in a sentence conveys the action or links the subject to the rest of the sentence.

Flowers *bloom* in the spring.

Roses *are* my favorite flower.

Sometimes a sentence may have more than one subject.

Marty and *Susan* work at Kmart.

Sometimes a sentence may have more than one verb.

They *stock* shelves and *help* customers.

ACTIVITY 1

Identifying Subjects and Verbs. Circle the subjects and underline the verbs in the following sentences.

1. I walk five miles a day.

2. My dog walks with me.

3. We walk along an abandoned railway trestle.

4. Great Western built the railroad here in 1856.

5. The trains stopped in 1982.

6. Mountain bikers and hikers travel the railroad tracks now.

7. I found a rusted railroad spike on the trail.

8. We worked with Rails to Trails.

9. It organizes groups of hikers.

10. The hikers build wilderness paths on the old railroad easements.

SUBJECTS

To understand the basic structure of a sentence, you need to be able to identify its *subject*. Often the subject is easy to spot because it consists of one word. Other times, though, the subject can be hard to detect.

Tips for Multilingual Writers

Be careful to include a subject in each sentence.

INCORRECT   I love math. Is my favorite subject.

CORRECT   I love math. *It* is my favorite subject.

INCORRECT   Walks to the store.

CORRECT   *My mother* walks to the store.

Tips for Multilingual Writers

Remember, you can't include a pronoun that refers to the subject as part of the subject.

INCORRECT   *Henry he* stayed up late.

CORRECT   *Henry* stayed up late.

INCORRECT   *Barbara Jordan she* was a great member of Congress.

CORRECT   *Barbara Jordan* was a great member of Congress.

Subject Pretenders

Sometimes the subject of a sentence is difficult to identify because a word in a prepositional phrase is pretending to be the subject. But the subject of a sentence is *never* found in a prepositional phrase. A prepositional phrase is a group of words that begins with a preposition.

COMMON PREPOSITIONS

about	beside	inside	since
above	between	into	throughout
against	by	like	to
among	despite	near	toward
as	down	next to	under
at	during	of	until
before	except	off	up
behind	for	on	upon
below	from	out	within
beneath	in	past	without

ACTIVITY 2

Identifying Prepositions. Underline the prepositions in the following paragraph.

Leticia went into her bedroom and took her journal from her bedside table. She sat in her favorite chair while recording her thoughts. Throughout the day she had felt tense. During breakfast she had studied for her chemistry test. At school she couldn't find a parking spot. Despite all of her studying, she felt unprepared for the test. After the test, she had gone to the Student Union where she had spilled ketchup on her white blouse. Now she was happy to put the day behind her and just write in her journal.

A *prepositional phrase* consists of the preposition and its object (a noun or pronoun). Here are some examples:

PREPOSITION	OBJECT	PREPOSITIONAL PHRASE
into	her bedroom	into her bedroom
after	the test	after the test
in	her journal	in her journal

ACTIVITY 3

Writing Prepositional Phrases. Complete each sentence that follows by adding a prepositional phrase.

EXAMPLE   He ironed his shirt <u>with an old iron.</u>

1. She put her books _____.

2. He made dinner _____.

3. The dog ran _____.

4. Jane watched television _____.

5. Harry felt sick _____.

6. _____ May parked the car.

7. _____ he knocked on the door.

8. Li hid the gift _____.

9. Yvette walked _____.

10. I received an A _____.

Because you know that the subject of a sentence is never in a prepositional phrase, you can find the subject of the sentence easily. First, cross out all of the prepositional phrases; then decide which of the remaining words is performing the action.

She applied (for a job) (as a short-order cook) (at Gino's). [The subject is *she*.]

One (of my favorite comic strips) (in the Sunday paper) is Doonesbury. [The subject is *one*.]

ASK YOURSELF: How Do I Identify a Sentence?

- Identify the subject, which is a noun or pronoun that tells who or what is doing the action. Cross out prepositional phrases before you identify the subject.
- Identify the verb, which is a word that shows the action or links the subject to the rest of the sentence.
- Check that the sentence expresses a complete thought.
- Check that the sentence begins with a capital letter and ends with a period, question mark, or exclamation mark.

ACTIVITY 4

Identifying Prepositional Phrases and Subjects. In the following paragraph, cross out the prepositional phrases and circle the subjects.

Some students in our writing class published their stories in the school newspaper. An essay on Eileen's travels to Mexico was on the front page. One of her poems was on the second page. Donna, another student, wrote about her childhood in Alaska. Bob's essay on playing in the band was in the Entertainment section. Luther described his trip through Australia. Jeremy's stories about the floods were so good that they also appeared in national news magazines.

Tips for Multilingual Writers

Prepositions that show time, such as *for, during,* and *since,* may have differences in meaning.

For refers to an exact period of time, one that has a beginning and an end:

I went to college *for* six years.
It has been raining *for* two hours.
I've been cooking *for* a long time.

During refers to an indefinite period of time:

Several times *during* the semester I was very busy.
I plan to visit my parents sometime *during* the summer.
It snowed *during* the night, but I don't know exactly when.

Since refers to time that has elapsed.

I've gained weight *since* last year.
Since April, Joe's been looking for a job.
Pete has been so happy *since* the birth of his daughter.

VERBS

Action and Linking Verbs

An *action verb* conveys the action of the subject.

Veronica *races* her bike.

The train *left* for Chicago.

Our family *met* Dave in Dallas.

A *linking verb* connects the subject to a word that renames or describes it. The most common linking verbs include the forms of *to be: am, are, is, was, were, be, been, being.*

Amanda *is* seventeen.

We *are* lost.

I *am* happy.

Certain other words can also act as linking verbs. Most of these other words have to do with our senses:

appear	grow	smell
become	look	sound
feel	remain	taste
get	seem	

Notice how such words act as linking verbs in the following sentences:

The coffee *tastes* bitter.

She *grows* taller every year.

My feet *feel* tired.

However, these same words can act as action verbs, as in the following sentences:

She *tastes* the hamburger special.

My sister *grows* tomatoes in her garden.

He *feels* the rough edges of the desk.

How can you tell whether one of these words is acting as a linking verb or an action verb in a sentence? Try replacing the verb with one of the forms of *to be* to see if the sentence still makes sense. If you can substitute a *to be* verb (as in "The coffee *is* bitter"), then the word is acting as a linking verb. If you cannot exchange a *to be* verb (as in "She *is* the hamburger special"), then the word is acting as an action verb.

Identifying Action and Linking Verbs. In each of the following sentences, underline the verb and identify it as an action verb or a linking verb.

1. My parents went home on Sunday. _____

2. In this part of the country, the sun shines nearly every day.

   _____

3. She is with her best friend. _____

4. Sam and Louise were brother and sister. _____

5. The store appears to be abandoned. _____

6. Harry felt the cold rain on his face. _____

7. The lasagna smells delicious. _____

8. The children danced shyly in front of their parents. _____

9. I was late for the third time this month. _____

10. Anna felt the sting of the cold air. _____

Helping Verbs

In addition to action verbs and linking verbs, sentences may contain helping verbs. A *helping verb* may indicate the time of other verbs in the sentence.

- *to be* verbs: *am, are, is, was, were, be, been, being*
- *to have* verbs: *have, has, had*
- *to do* verbs: *do, does, did*
- *may, might, must*
- *can, could, shall, should, will, would*

I *should* wash my car. [The helping verb *should* indicates that the action, *wash*, needs to be completed in the future.]

Jorge *had* finished the job. [Here the helping verb *had* indicates that the action, *finish*, was completed in the past before some other action.]

Tron *will* drive the car. [Here the helping verb *will* indicates that the action, *drive*, will be completed in the future.]

Tips for Multilingual Writers

When you write questions and negative statements in the past tense using the helping verb *do*, put only *do* in the past tense. Don't change the main verb to the past tense.

INCORRECT	When *did* she *left* the movie?
CORRECT	When *did* she *leave* the movie?
INCORRECT	I *did* not *washed* my clothes.
CORRECT	I *did* not *wash* my clothes.

ACTIVITY 6

Identifying Helping Verbs. Circle the helping verbs in the following sentences. (Note that some sentences may not contain helping verbs.)

1. I must finish studying for this test before I go to the party.

2. This customer can pay with a credit card.

3. The dog chased its tail.

4. May I close the door?

5. You might not want to go shopping today.

6. Jane could take a nap after lunch.

7. April smoothed out the wrinkles in her skirt.

8. The snow is not going to stop soon.

9. My computer needs more memory.

10. Before his shift is over, Deion should return all the phone calls.

ACTIVITY 7

Identifying Action, Linking, and Helping Verbs. Underline the action verbs, circle the linking verbs, and put brackets around the helping verbs in the following paragraph.

I should have registered for my classes earlier. I registered during late registration. Most of the classes were full. The only English class I could take is at 6:30 in the morning. My math class will meet on Saturdays. I did ask for an overload in algebra. Biology classes were completely full. I could have signed up for my classes earlier. I will remember my early registration date next semester. I have a difficult schedule for the next four months.

Regular and Irregular Verbs

Regular verbs form the past tense and past participle by adding *-ed*.

COMMON REGULAR VERBS

Verb	Past Tense	Past Participle
cook	cooked	cooked
measure	measured	measured
study	studied	studied
walk	walked	walked

Irregular verbs form the past tense and past participle in a variety of ways.

COMMON IRREGULAR VERBS

Verb	Past Tense	Past Participle
to be	was, were	been
begin	began	begun
catch	caught	caught
choose	chose	chosen
come	came	come
do	did	done

COMMON IRREGULAR VERBS

Verb	Past Tense	Past Participle
drink	drank	drunk
eat	ate	eaten
feel	felt	felt
fly	flew	flown
get	got	gotten
go	went	gone
leave	left	left
ride	rode	ridden
see	saw	seen
sleep	slept	slept
take	took	taken
write	wrote	written

Past participles are used with *has, have,* or *had,* as in the following examples:

I *have eaten* a big dinner.

Joan *has caught* two fish.

The children *had done* their chores.

ACTIVITY 8

Using Regular and Irregular Verbs. Write the correct form of the verb in the space provided. If necessary, consult your dictionary for the correct form.

1. Janice _____ more than ten hours last night. (*sleep*)

2. The doorbell has _____ three times in the last hour. (*ring*)

3. I only _____ thirty minutes for the test. (*study*)

4. The turkey _____ all afternoon. (*cook*)

5. My brother and I have _____ three fish today. (*catch*)

6. Last night Sam _____ so much he woke up with a hangover. (*drink*)

7. My favorite book is *One* _____ *Over the Cuckoo's Nest.* (*fly*)

8. Someone has _____ my purse. (*steal*)

9. Yesterday I _____ my favorite pair of pants in the wash. (*place*)

10. My best friend and I have _____ each other for ten years. (*know*)

ACTIVITY 9

Identifying Subjects and Verbs.   Circle the subjects and underline the verbs in the following paragraph.

Every night at my grandmother's house, I would go to sleep to the whirring sound of the sewing machine. My grandmother was a seamstress. She didn't work during the day. During the day, she slept. But she worked all night. Sometimes my mother and my aunt would help her. Then they would stay awake all night. After those nights, my brother and I would fix ourselves breakfast. Then we would quietly watch cartoons. In the afternoons, the customers would come for their dresses. They would hand my sleepy grandmother checks and cash and step out of the door full of life into the beautiful sunlit days.

Tips for Multilingual Writers

The verb tense must agree with any phrase such as *now, yesterday,* or *a week ago* that indicates when the action takes place.

INCORRECT	Yesterday I *catch* two fish.
CORRECT	Yesterday I *caught* two fish.
INCORRECT	Tomorrow my sister *leave* for China.
CORRECT	Tomorrow my sister *will leave* for China.

> **Tips for Multilingual Writers**
>
> Always include a verb in every sentence, even if the meaning is obvious without it.
>
> | | |
> |---|---|
> | INCORRECT | Bernard a hard worker. |
> | CORRECT | Bernard *is* a hard worker. |
> | | |
> | INCORRECT | The Rocky Mountains steep and rugged. |
> | CORRECT | The Rocky Mountains *are* steep and rugged. |

Verb Pretenders

Like subject pretenders, verb pretenders look like verbs but do not act as verbs in sentences. The most common verb pretenders are *verb + -ing* and *to + verb* combinations.

rowing	to rest
singing	to climb
talking	to go

When an *-ing* verb appears in a sentence without a helping verb, it modifies, or describes, other words in the sentence.

We could hear Dad *singing* in the shower. [The *-ing* verb modifies *Dad*.]

Yelling loudly, Peter hailed the cab. [The *-ing* verb modifies *Peter*.]

We can spot the crew *rowing* toward shore. [The *-ing* verb modifies *crew*.]

When an *-ing* verb appears in a sentence with a helping verb, it forms a complete verb.

He *was singing* "She Loves Me." [The complete verb is *was singing*.]

Peter *was yelling* for the cab. [The complete verb is *was yelling*.]

The crew *is rowing* toward shore. [The complete verb is *is rowing*.]

ACTIVITY 10

Identifying *-ing* Verbs. In the space provided, indicate whether the *-ing* verb in each sentence functions as a modifier or as a verb.

1. Alice was studying with me. _____

2. Studying together, Alice and I learned most of the equations.

   _____

3. The swimming pool is green from algae. _____

4. I was swimming when the phone rang. _____

5. Nicole loves the cartoon with the dancing bears. _____

6. Working as a team, we finished the project in an hour.

   _____

7. She was mowing the lawn when Fred came home. _____

8. The changing room at the gym is filthy. _____

9. My mother was shocked to see me lighting a cigarette.

   _____

10. That barking dog is driving me crazy. _____

ACTIVITY 11

Using Verbs and Verb Pretenders. For each of the following *-ing* verbs, write two sentences. In the first sentence, use the word as a verb. In the second sentence, use the word as a modifier.

> EXAMPLE   listening
> Verb: I was listening to the beautiful music.
> Verb pretender: Listening to the music, I forgot about the time.

1. boiling

   Verb: _____

   Verb pretender: _____

   _____

2. growing

   Verb: _____

   Verb pretender: _____

   _____

3. dripping

   Verb: _____

   Verb pretender: _____

   _____

4. sleeping

   Verb: _____

   Verb pretender: _____

   _____

5. trembling

   Verb: _____

   Verb pretender: _____

   _____

The *to + verb* combination also looks like a verb but does not act as a verb in a sentence; rather, it can act as either a noun or a modifier.

I can't wait *to open* my gifts. [Because *to* appears in front of the verb *open, to open* does not act as a verb. Rather, it acts as a modifier.]

I *opened* my gifts. [Here *opened* acts as a verb.]

Susan went to the store *to buy* apples. [Because *to* appears in front of the verb *buy, to buy* does not act as a verb. Rather, it acts as a modifier.]

Susan *bought* apples at the store. [Here *bought* acts as a verb.]

To study would be the sensible thing to do. [Because *to* appears in front of the verb *study, to study* does not act as a verb. Rather, it acts as a noun.]

I *studied,* which was the sensible thing to do. [Here *studied* acts as a verb.]

ASK YOURSELF: How Do I Find the Verb in a Sentence?

- Look for a word that shows action or links the subject to the rest of the sentence.
- Check that the word is not a verb pretender. Verb pretenders are *-ing* verbs *(dancing)* without a helping verb or *to* verbs *(to open)*.

ACTIVITY 12

Using *to* + *Verb* Combinations. Complete each sentence with a *to + verb* combination.

EXAMPLE   Joe waited until June to buy a car.

1. Erin didn't want _____

2. _____ was boring, according to Ned.

3. Joss decided _____

4. My friends desired _____

5. After being on my feet all day, I couldn't wait _____

6. _____ said Hamlet.

7. I love _____

8. After two days on the road, we need _____

9. My favorite hobby is _____

10. _____ is Matilda's greatest wish.

ACTIVITY 13

Identifying Subjects and Verbs. Circle the subjects and underline the verbs in the following paragraph.

Amanda waited to study until the night before the test. After studying all night, she slept late the next morning. Waking late, she had ten minutes to drive to school. She arrived at class just as the bell started to ring. The teacher was handing out the tests. Amanda took a deep breath before picking up the questions. She hoped to make at least a C+ on the test. During the test, her mind kept wandering. Running late for school, she hadn't had time to eat breakfast. Leaving the classroom after the test, Amanda promised to improve her study habits.

ADJECTIVES AND ADVERBS

Adjectives modify nouns by describing or adding information about them.

He prepared her *favorite* meal.
The *yellow* pansy stood out in the *beautiful* flower bed.
My *new* car really impresses my *classy* friends.
He looked at the *dilapidated* bus and wondered if he dared get on it.

Adjectives may also be used to show comparison. When comparing two things, add -*er* or *more*. When comparing three or more things, add -*est* or *most*.

Mary is *shorter* than Joan.
He was *more* fearful of the lion than she was.
Mary is the *shortest* of her three friends.
He was the *most* fearful of the lion of all his friends.

Tips for Multilingual Writers

Some adjectives are forms of verbs that end with *-ing* or *-ed*. A verb form that ends with *-ing* modifies a person or thing *causing* an experience. A verb form that ends with *-ed* modifies a person or thing *undergoing* an experience.

> INCORRECT   The movie is *interested*.
>
> CORRECT   The movie is *interesting*.

The first sentence is incorrect because the movie isn't experiencing interest. The second sentence is correct because the movie is causing interest.

> INCORRECT   After the tournament, the tennis player was *exhausting*.
>
> CORRECT   After the tournament, the tennis player was *exhausted*.

In these examples, the first sentence is incorrect because the tennis player isn't causing exhaustion. Instead, the tennis player is experiencing exhaustion. Thus, the second sentence is correct.

ACTIVITY 14

Identifying Adjectives. Underline the adjectives in the following sentences.

1. My Aunt Jamie is a lovely person.

2. My flighty niece, however, is a chatterbox.

3. They usually serve honey-roasted peanuts on overseas flights.

4. He gave her the biggest piece of cake.

5. The old dog jumped onto the plaid sofa and slept away the sunny afternoon.

6. The cold weather forces me to wear my warm overcoat.

7. His was the smaller of the two suitcases.

8. Susan decided to buy the red dress.

9. This was the most expensive item on the menu.

10. The wrecked car was parked next to the curb.

Tips for Multilingual Writers

Do not make adjectives plural even when the nouns they modify are plural.

INCORRECT	The *browns* shoes need to be polished.
CORRECT	The *brown* shoes need to be polished.
INCORRECT	I found three *larges* boxes.
CORRECT	I found three *large* boxes.

Adverbs modify verbs, adjectives, or other adverbs by describing or adding information about them. Adverbs usually answer the questions *how, when, where, why,* or *how often.*

The coach ran *toward* the swimmers. [modifies the verb]

The swimmers returned to the pool *very* slowly. [modifies the adverb]

The swimmers were *frequently* late getting to practice. [modifies the adjective]

Adverbs may also be used for comparison. When comparing two things, add *more.* When comparing three or more things, add *most.*

Jan spends her money *more wisely* than Betty.

Among Jan, Betty, Lisa, and Helena, Jan spends her money *most wisely* of all.

ASK YOURSELF: What Are the Main Parts of Speech?

- Noun
- Pronoun
- Verb
- Adjective
- Adverb
- Preposition
- Conjunction

Identifying Adverbs. Underline the adverbs in the following sentences.

1. The birds chirped noisily at my bedroom window.

2. The hike was very worthwhile.

3. The cat was more likely to lie in the sun than the dog.

4. The gasping, perspiring runner quickly dropped out of the race.

5. He ran swiftly toward his mother.

6. Tammy stepped to the door and listened silently.

7. He was the most respected professor on campus.

8. He seldom cared for horror movies.

9. I was surprised that I had done well on the exam.

10. We carefully opened the door.

Tips for Multilingual Writers

When comparing two things, put the word *than* between the adverb or adjective and the second thing.

INCORRECT	Mike is smaller Roberto.
CORRECT	Mike is smaller *than* Roberto.
INCORRECT	My cat Freckles runs faster my dog Murphy.
CORRECT	My cat Freckles runs faster *than* my dog Murphy.

CLAUSES

Clauses are the building blocks of sentences. There are two kinds of clauses: independent and dependent.

Independent Clauses

An *independent clause* is a group of words with a subject and a verb that expresses a complete thought. In other words, it can stand alone as a complete sentence. All sentences contain at least one independent clause. Some sentences consist of two or more independent clauses.

Marty enjoyed his first year of college. [This sentence is an independent clause because it contains a subject and a verb and expresses a complete thought.]

He learned how to study, and he learned how to manage his time. [This sentence consists of two independent clauses.]

He had time to complete his schoolwork properly and time to spend with his friends. [This sentence consists of one independent clause.]

ACTIVITY 16

Identifying Independent Clauses. Underline the independent clauses in the following paragraph.

My high school English teacher taught me a lot about writing. In the beginning I didn't think all that writing helped. When we finally started our research papers two months before the end of school, my writing had improved. I also felt more confident as a writer because she encouraged us to write about our interests. My final research paper earned an A. It was also fun to write.

Dependent Clauses

A *dependent clause,* as its name implies, depends on other information to make a sentence complete. Although a dependent clause contains a subject and a verb, it does not express a complete thought and cannot stand alone as a sentence. Two types of dependent clauses are *subordinate clauses* and *relative clauses*.

SUBORDINATE CLAUSES. A subordinate clause contains a subject and a verb and begins with a *subordinate conjunction*.

after	even though	until
although	if	when
as	since	whenever
as if	so that	where
as though	that	whereas
because	though	wherever
before	unless	while

Because the electricity went out, I couldn't study for my chemistry test. [The subordinate clause at the beginning of the sentence contains a subject and a verb, but it does not complete the thought and cannot stand alone.]

Before the week was over, I'd received two job offers. [This sentence also starts with a subordinate clause.]

I'd never known extreme heat *until I visited Phoenix in the summer.* [This subordinate clause comes at the end of the sentence.]

When a subordinate clause begins a sentence, a comma separates it from the rest of the sentence. When a subordinate clause ends a sentence, no comma is used.

ACTIVITY 17

Identifying Subordinate Clauses. Underline the subordinate clauses in the following paragraph.

This year's football team has been a huge disappointment. We've struggled with our passing game after our quarterback was injured. Until he comes back, we have to rely on our running game. Although our running backs are experienced, they fumble the ball too much. Because the kicker is a freshman, our kicking game has been poor. Unless the team gets better, we might end up with our worst record since we finished last in our division in 1990.

RELATIVE CLAUSES. Another type of dependent clause is a *relative clause*. A relative clause contains a subject and a verb and begins with a *relative pronoun:*

that	who
whose	whom
whoever	which

Who, whose, and *whom* refer to people. *Which* refers to things and animals. *That* refers to people and things.

The person *who left crumbs on the table* should wipe them up. [This relative clause describes a *person,* the subject of the sentence.]

I read all three books, *which were equally interesting and informative.* [Here the relative clause modifies the object of the sentence, *books.*]

Don't use commas when a relative clause is necessary to identify who or what it is referring to, as in the following example.

The spaghetti *that her aunt made* was the best Martha ever ate.

No commas are used before or after the relative clause because it's a necessary part of the sentence: it tells which spaghetti—the spaghetti her aunt made—was the best Martha ever ate.

In contrast, use commas when the relative clause is giving information that's *not* essential to understanding the sentence.

Spaghetti, *which I eat at least once a week,* is my favorite food.

Commas are used in this example because the relative clause—*which I eat at least once a week*—is simply adding information. The sentence makes sense without it: *Spaghetti is my favorite food.*

Don't use commas with relative clauses that begin with *that.*

The spaghetti *that's been sitting in the refrigerator* is too old to eat.

ACTIVITY 18

Identifying Relative Clauses. Underline the relative clauses in the following paragraphs.

When I first enrolled in college, I expected it to be like high

school. However, college teachers who care about their students

expect you to work hard. They also expect you to think critically.

If you don't want to work hard and try new things, I wouldn't suggest college.

My college composition class is filled with students who did well in high school English. Our teacher, who is young and strict, asks us to revise our papers. In high school the papers that I wrote always received good grades. Here in college all of my papers, which usually required some research, were revised at least twice. After I began to revise, my grades improved. I feel my writing, which I was never confident about, has improved since I started this class.

ASK YOURSELF: How Do I Identify the Type of Clause?

- Determine whether a clause is independent or dependent.
- To determine if a clause is independent, check whether the clause has a subject and verb and can stand alone as a complete sentence.
- To determine if a clause is dependent, check whether the clause has a subject and a verb but can't stand alone as a sentence because it begins with a subordinating conjunction such as *although, because,* or *since* or with a relative pronoun such as *that, which,* or *who.*

CONJUNCTIONS

Coordinating Conjunctions

Coordinating conjunctions connect two words, phrases, clauses, or sentences that are equally important. Use a coordinating conjunction when you want to combine short, closely related sentences. Be sure to put a comma before the coordinating conjunction.

I went to school, *and* my husband left for work.
Julie laughed at the movie, *but* Jeremy didn't think it was funny.
I either need to study now, *or* I'll have to do it this weekend.

These are the most commonly used coordinating conjunctions:

for   but   yet
and   or   so
nor

ACTIVITY 19

Using Coordinating Conjunctions. Using coordinating conjunctions, combine the following short sentences.

1. Next year I plan to leave for graduate school. I want to get a Master's of business administration degree.

   _____

   _____

2. John went to the doctor to get a flu shot. Surprisingly, it didn't hurt at all.

   _____

   _____

3. Hannah won't leave for the islands any time soon. She won't leave for Europe either.

   _____

   _____

4. I wanted to go to the movies. My friend didn't want to go with me.

   _____

   _____

5. Beth lives on the next street. She might live two streets over.

   _____

   _____

6. My father loves my mother. I never see them kissing in public.

_____

_____

7. Jackson was happy to have a cat. He bought another one!

_____

_____

8. I think I'll pass physics. I could be wrong.

_____

_____

9. Don't bother to shut the door. I'll be leaving shortly.

_____

_____

10. This is your last chance to read this book. You had better get busy.

_____

_____

Subordinating Conjunctions

Subordinating conjunctions connect two clauses or sentences that are not equally important. Use a subordinating conjunction when you want to combine short, closely related sentences by making one sentence a dependent clause. If the dependent clause begins the sentence, use a comma to separate it from the independent clause. If the dependent clause is at the end of the sentence, don't use a comma.

I went to school *so that* I could learn to care for children.
Because it was funny, Julie laughed at the movie.
I need to study now *if* I want to be prepared for the test.

These are the most commonly used subordinating conjunctions:

after	even though	until
although	if	when
as	since	whenever
as if	so that	where
as though	than	wherever
because	though	whether
before	unless	while

ACTIVITY 20

Using Subordinating Conjunctions. Using subordinating conjunctions, combine the following short sentences. You may need to eliminate words or move words around.

1. My father joined the army. He didn't feel he had any other choice.

   _____

   _____

2. Jamie can have this dessert. She is practicing going off her diet.

   _____

   _____

3. I attended the game. My husband went to the concert.

   _____

   _____

4. Carol's hair looks great. She goes out in the wind.

   _____

   _____

5. I don't like the idea of abusing animals. I still wear fur.

_____

_____

6. He left me at the altar. I didn't really matter to him.

_____

_____

7. I moved to this city. I've been extremely happy.

_____

_____

8. My dog learns new tricks. I can't really take him to the show.

_____

_____

9. Fall is a great time of year. The first freeze changes everything.

_____

_____

10. I've never missed an appointment. I have been late a few times.

_____

_____

Conjunctive Adverbs

Conjunctive adverbs, often called *transitions*, indicate the connection between two closely related sentences (or independent clauses) when they are combined with a semicolon.

A new manufacturing center just opened. More people will have jobs.

A new manufacturing center just opened; *as a result,* more people will have jobs.

My sister is raising three children. She goes to college full time.

My sister is raising three children; *in addition,* she goes to college full time.

Use a conjunctive adverb when you add an idea, show a contrasting or similar point, emphasize a key concept, show a consequence, or point out a sequence.

TO ADD AN IDEA

also	in addition
furthermore	moreover

TO SHOW A CONTRASTING POINT

however	nevertheless	nonetheless
instead	otherwise	

TO INDICATE A SIMILAR POINT

likewise	similarly

TO EMPHASIZE A KEY CONCEPT

indeed	undoubtedly	certainly	in fact

TO SHOW A CONSEQUENCE

as a result	therefore
consequently	thus

TO POINT OUT A SEQUENCE

finally	meanwhile	next

Note that the conjunctive adverb can come at the beginning, in the middle, or at the end of the independent clause. Put a comma after a conjunctive adverb that begins or ends the independent clause. Put a comma before and after a conjunctive adverb that appears in the middle of the clause.

The country is in a recession; *however,* the economy should improve soon.

The country is in a recession; the economy, *however,* should improve soon.

The country is in a recession; the economy should improve soon, *however.*

ACTIVITY 21

Using Conjunctive Adverbs. Using conjunctive adverbs, combine the following short sentences.

1. Most people have many jobs during their lives. Many people change jobs as often as once every three years.

   _____

   _____

2. In high school I worked at a fast-food restaurant. I also worked at a car wash.

   _____

   _____

3. Fast-food restaurants hire many teenagers for low wages. They often pay only minimum wage.

   _____

   _____

4. Minimum wage is fine for a young person still living at home. For people on their own, it's not enough to survive on.

   _____

   _____

   _____

5. When you don't make much money, you can barely afford to pay rent. You need to pay for food, clothes, and utilities.

_____

_____

_____

6. You empty out your bank account to pay one bill. Other bills arrive in the mail.

_____

_____

7. The only answer is to get a job that pays better. This is hard to do without a college degree.

_____

_____

8. Many people enroll part time in college. They keep working at their jobs.

_____

_____

9. Many colleges help students take out loans. They help students apply for scholarships.

_____

_____

10. A college education takes time and money. It's well worth the effort.

_____

_____

Correct Sentences

SENTENCE FRAGMENTS

A *sentence fragment* is a group of words that looks like a sentence — the first letter is capitalized and the word group ends with a period — but is not a sentence. At times, writers use fragments intentionally for emphasis or in dialogue. The science fiction writer Ray Bradbury, for instance, uses sentence fragments to describe the destruction of a house in his short story "August 2026: There Will Come Soft Rains." In the same way that the house is in pieces, the writing is in pieces — or fragments.

> The crash. The attic smashing into kitchen and parlor. The parlor into cellar, cellar into sub-cellar. Deep freeze, armchair, film tapes, circuits, bed, and all like skeletons thrown in a cluttered mound. Smoke and silence.

Sentence fragments may be used by writers in dialogue to reflect people's tendency to speak in fragments. Here's an example from Stephen King's memoir, *On Writing:*

> Uncle Oren let me undo the big latches. The common tools were all on the top layer of the box. There was a hammer, a saw, the pliers, a couple of sized wrenches and an adjustable; there was a level with that mystic yellow window in the middle, a drill (the various bits were neatly drawered farther down in the depths), and two screwdrivers. Uncle Oren asked me for a screwdriver.
>
> "Which one?" I asked.
>
> "Either-or," he replied.

In most other writing situations, however, and especially in the writing you do in college or at work, sentence fragments may be considered errors. To avoid unintentional sentence fragments, you first have to understand the components of a complete sentence. A complete sentence has a subject and a verb and expresses a complete thought. Usually, the subject tells who or what is doing the action. The verb conveys the action or links the subject to the rest of the sentence.

The *ball is* red.
I danced at the party.
Douglas gave his speech.
I moved back home.

ACTIVITY 1

Identifying Sentence Fragments. In the space provided, indicate whether each group of words is a sentence fragment or a complete sentence.

1. My dog loves to hike. _____

2. On Caroline's birthday. _____

3. The oldest dinosaur known to exist. _____

4. When will you come home tonight? _____

5. That cupcake is loaded with empty calories. _____

6. My daughter, the smartest student in the class. _____

7. Running as fast as she could. _____

8. Today of all days. _____

9. The restaurant smelled of cigarette smoke and barbecued meat.

_____

10. Splashed water all over the bathroom floor. _____

Correct Sentences

To practice correcting errors in sentences, go to **<www .bedfordstmartins.com/choices/>**. Click on "Exercise Central," and after logging in, click on "Correct Sentences."

Phrases

If a group of words lacks a subject or a verb or both, it's a *phrase*. A phrase is not a complete sentence. Notice the difference between phrases and sentences in these examples:

PHRASE   To make my house safe from burglars.

SENTENCE   I need to make my house safe from burglars.

PHRASE   Making a quilt.

SENTENCE   Elaine spent weeks making a quilt.

PHRASE   Including a new computer.

SENTENCE   My goal is to buy new equipment, including a computer.

PHRASE   Walking through the mall.

SENTENCE   We spent the day walking through the mall.

ACTIVITY 2

Turning Phrases into Sentences. Rewrite each of the following phrases to make it a complete sentence.

1. Running after the ball

   _____

   _____

2. After the delicious Thanksgiving dinner

   _____

   _____

3. Divided up my time equally

_____

_____

4. Because of the traffic jam

_____

_____

5. To avoid the freezing temperatures up north

_____

_____

6. Having to go out of town

_____

_____

7. Jane's smiling face

_____

_____

8. The Olympic games held in Salt Lake city, Utah

_____

_____

9. This expensive but beautiful coat

_____

_____

10. Drinking the coffee as fast as I could

_____

_____

Dependent Clauses

Sometimes a group of words contains a subject and a verb but doesn't express a complete thought. This group of words, called a *dependent clause,* can't stand alone as a sentence. Therefore, it is a sentence fragment.

FRAGMENT   Because my family is very close.

The fragment doesn't express a complete thought, so it can't stand alone as a sentence.

SENTENCE   Because my family is very close, we always get together on holidays.

The sentence can stand alone. It contains a subject *(we),* a verb *(get together),* and it expresses a complete thought.
Here's another example:

FRAGMENT   When we ate our Sunday dinner.

The fragment doesn't express a complete thought, so it isn't a sentence.

SENTENCE   Darkness had fallen when we ate our Sunday dinner.

The sentence contains a subject *(darkness),* a verb *(had fallen),* and it expresses a complete thought, so it can stand alone.

ACTIVITY 3

Turning Dependent Clauses into Sentences. In the space provided, rewrite each of the dependent clauses to make it a sentence.

1. Before I went home for the last time

   _____

   _____

   _____

2. Although my family had to struggle to pay for my tuition

   _____

   _____

   _____

3. When you drive down rutted mountain roads

   _____

   _____

4. Where each of her children had been born

   _____

   _____

5. That I finished high school at the top of my class

   _____

   _____

6. Unless you get home before midnight

   _____

   _____

7. While Eunice waited for the bus

   _____

   _____

8. Where you put your dirty laundry

_____

_____

9. Because I was so hungry

_____

_____

10. Although the election was still a month away

_____

_____

Many dependent clauses begin with a relative pronoun such as *who, whom, whose, which, whoever,* or *whomever.*

FRAGMENT	Whose purse was stolen
SENTENCE	Janet, not Beverly, is the student whose purse was stolen.
FRAGMENT	Which was very spicy
SENTENCE	Steve eagerly ate the chili, which was very spicy.
FRAGMENT	Who was always there for me
SENTENCE	I miss my best friend, who was always there for me.

ACTIVITY 4

Turning Dependent Clauses into Sentences. Rewrite each of the following dependent clauses to make it a complete sentence.

1. Who knew my cousin Jim

_____

_____

2. Who ate my homework

_____

_____

3. Whose clothes are on the floor

_____

_____

4. Whoever left the phone off the hook

_____

_____

5. Which was her last meal

_____

_____

6. Whose bookbag was stolen from the library

_____

_____

7. Whoever did the dishes last

_____

_____

8. Who left the front door open

_____

_____

9. Who sang "The Star-Spangled Banner" at the baseball game

_____

_____

10. Whose car ran out of gas on the freeway

_____

_____

Correcting Sentence Fragments

How do you correct a sentence fragment? One way is to connect it to the sentence that comes before or after it.

FRAGMENT   *After eating the last piece of chicken.* Matt smiled guiltily.

SENTENCE   *After eating the last piece of chicken,* Matt smiled guiltily.

FRAGMENT   My family consists of my brother, two sisters, and grandmother. *And, of course, my mother.*

SENTENCE   My family consists of my brother, two sisters, grandmother, *and, of course, my mother.*

Another way to correct a sentence fragment is to revise it into a complete sentence.

FRAGMENT   *To leave my sister at home alone.*

SENTENCE   It was a crime *to leave my sister at home alone.*

FRAGMENT   *Not to vote.*

SENTENCE   I decided *not to vote* because I didn't like either of the candidates.

ASK YOURSELF: How Do I Identify a Sentence Fragment?

1. Determine whether the sentence has a verb. (Keep in mind the difference between a verb and a verb pretender.) If the answer is no, it's a fragment. If the answer is yes, go to the next item.

2. Determine whether the sentence has a subject. (Usually the subject comes before the verb.) If the answer is no, it's a fragment. If the answer is yes, go to the final question.

3. Decide whether the sentence expresses an incomplete thought. Check whether it begins with a subordinate conjunction such as *after, although, because,* or *since* or with a relative pronoun such as *who, whose,* or *whomever.* If either answer is yes, it's a fragment.

ACTIVITY 5

Correcting Sentence Fragments. Identify each of the following items as a complete sentence or a sentence fragment. Then correct each sentence fragment by connecting it to the sentence that comes before or after it or by rewriting it as a complete sentence.

1. Both of my father's parents lived past their ninetieth year. His mother to 104 and his father to 95.

   _____

   _____

   _____

2. Driving through the deserted town. I remember the stories my grandfather told me.

   _____

   _____

3. To spend time with my grandmother. I decided to move to my father's hometown.

   _____

   _____

4. Before I'd heard about my grandmother's trip to Mexico in the 1920s. I was afraid to travel alone.

   _____

   _____

5. It is very important. Remembering where you came from.

   _____

   _____

6. My mother enjoys watching the flowers bloom each spring. She planted our yard with bulbs and flowers that bloom from April to July.

_____

_____

7. I walk for an hour each evening. Because we spent so much time walking the fields of our parents' farm. I need my evening walks to clear my head.

_____

_____

8. Any change is both good and bad. I understand that.

_____

_____

9. After I returned to my hometown and found most of the Main Street stores closed. I realized that my parents' dream of a country life for their children had disappeared.

_____

_____

_____

_____

10. Seeing my sisters for the first time in two years and laughing with them about how much we had changed.

_____

_____

_____

ACTIVITY 6

Correcting Sentence Fragments. Rewrite the following paragraph to eliminate the sentence fragments.

My father floats three feet above the ground. His eyes look directly out at me. From this photograph taken of him his first year on the college football team. His hair, what there is left of it, sticks up less than a half-inch from his head. A cut that he would keep all his life. No grass stains spoil his white jersey. His shoes are polished. If I could see the spikes that fly out behind him. I feel certain I wouldn't find any old mud or grass clinging to the steel. His arms are spread wide and his mouth is set in a determined grimace. In a darker gray than either the grass or sky in this black and white photograph. The number on his jersey says 49. My favorite picture of my father. He is young and strong, and he is flying. If only for a moment.

RUN-ON SENTENCES

A *run-on sentence* contains two or more independent clauses that run together without a connecting word or punctuation. A run-on sentence is difficult to read because it is unclear where one idea ends and another begins. Unlike a complete sentence, which consists of a subject and a verb and expresses a complete thought, a run-on sentence expresses more than one complete thought without the correct punctuation or connecting word.

Here is an example:

RUN-ON SENTENCE   I gave my dog Ralph the bone he liked it so much that it was gone in a minute.

This sentence is confusing because its two independent clauses are not separated. To correct this run-on sentence, separate the independent clauses with a period, a semicolon, or a comma and a coordinating conjunction (such as *and, but, or, nor, for, yet,* or *so*).

CORRECTED WITH A PERIOD	I gave my dog Ralph the bone. He liked it so much that it was gone in a minute.
CORRECTED WITH A SEMICOLON	I gave my dog Ralph the bone; he liked it so much that it was gone in a minute.
CORRECTED WITH A COMMA AND A COORDINATING CONJUNCTION	I gave my dog Ralph the bone, *and* he liked it so much that it was gone in a minute.

ASK YOURSELF: How Do I Correct a Run-on Sentence?

- Decide whether there are two independent clauses (groups of words each with a subject and verb that could stand alone as sentences).
- Separate these independent clauses with a period, a semicolon, or a comma and a coordinating conjunction.

ACTIVITY 7

Correcting Run-on Sentences. Correct the following run-on sentences by separating the independent clauses with a period, a semicolon, or a comma and coordinating conjunction.

1. It was a dark and stormy night isn't it always dark and stormy when something bad happens?

    _____

    _____

    _____

2. Mary stood close to the doorway, her hand resting on her hip a child peered out from behind her.

_____

_____

_____

3. My teacher tried to get me to make more friends she would give me assignments that required group work.

_____

_____

_____

4. Once I realized I could no longer live in a city, I searched for communities less than a hundred miles away I couldn't live in a city but I did want to visit now and then.

_____

_____

_____

5. His blond hair, cut at awkward angles and sticking straight up from his skull, formed an eerie halo around his head whether that halo told of good or evil, I couldn't tell.

_____

_____

_____

6. Keith's upper arms are covered in intricate purple and yellow floral designs his left eyebrow is accentuated with a small gold hoop a small black chain is etched into the skin of his right ankle.

_____

_____

_____

7. Although no music pounded out of the huge speakers on either side of the raised platform, the noise from the crowd was deafening then the stadium lights went out.

_____

_____

_____

8. Maria spends a lot of time driving to work and school she teaches aerobics classes three times a week and attends the community college three days a week.

_____

_____

_____

_____

9. In 1974, I was content to sit in front of the television for hours watching *The Brady Bunch* or whatever mindless programming the networks presented to kids home from school I'm not content to let my daughter waste her time watching reruns of *Roseanne* or *Beverly Hills 90210.*

_____

_____

_____

_____

10. The coach's eyes narrow and his jaw tightens he looks ready to bolt as he watches his student prepare for her dismount on the uneven bars.

_____

_____

_____

ACTIVITY 8

Eliminating Run-on Sentences. Eliminate the run-on sentences from the following paragraph by using a period, a semicolon, or a comma and coordinating conjunction as needed.

Up north we had a saying for girls like Jessica whose hair was teased impossibly high. Makeup was plastered in layer after layer her eyelashes were matted in thick clumps. Her fingernails were long, hard, and a bright red. Her lipstick matched her fingernails. She wore panty hose even in the heat of summer she wore high heels even if she had to stand all day. In Boston, we looked at girls like that and said, "Hey, Revere." We didn't mean Paul Revere we were referring to a small suburb east of Boston known for its beautiful girls. Of course, we assumed some lack of intelligence with those girls from Revere who in their right mind would wear hose when it's 106 degrees outside? I never really knew any girls from Revere when I was growing up, so I never corrected the assumption that Revere girls weren't the brightest bulbs on the tree Jessica corrected that assumption for me. She constantly scored higher on zoology tests than I did. Unlike me, she could focus the microscopes in zoology lab her fingernails were even useful during some of our more difficult dissections.

COMMA SPLICES

A *comma splice* contains two independent clauses separated by a comma. But the comma, which indicates only a slight pause, is not a strong enough punctuation mark to separate the two independent clauses. A comma splice is similar to a run-on sentence in that it expresses more than one thought without the correct punctuation.

Here is an example:

COMMA SPLICE   My sister is still in law school, she expects to finish in June.

To correct this comma splice, separate the two independent clauses with a period, a semicolon, or a comma and a coordinating conjunction *(for, and, nor, but, or, yet, so).*

CORRECTED WITH   My sister is still in law school. She expects to
A PERIOD   finish in June.

CORRECTED WITH   My sister is still in law school; she expects to
A SEMICOLON   finish in June.

CORRECTED WITH   My sister is still in law school, *but* she expects
A COMMA AND A   to finish in June.
COORDINATING
CONJUNCTION

ASK YOURSELF: How Do I Identify a Comma Splice?

- Decide whether there are two independent clauses (groups of words, each with a subject and verb, that could stand alone as sentences).
- Check whether the two independent clauses are separated only by a comma. If they are, you have found a comma splice.
- Separate these clauses with a period, a semicolon, or a comma and a coordinating conjunction.

ACTIVITY 9

Correcting Comma Splices. Correct the following comma splices by separating the two independent clauses with a period, a semicolon, or a comma and coordinating conjunction as needed.

1. I first met Angie in high school, we were in the same class.

   _____

   _____

2. He asked the instructor to repeat herself, then he pushed his hair back from his forehead.

   _____

   _____

3. Someone once told me that I shouldn't say bad things about myself, he said there were enough people around to do that for me.

   _____

   _____

   _____

4. When I first got married, I cooked dinner every night, now, more often than not, we heat microwave dinners and eat them in front of the television.

   _____

   _____

   _____

5. Brian pulls his English notebook from his backpack, I catch a glimpse of black ballet slippers next to his biology book.

   _____

   _____

   _____

   _____

6. Meredith's auburn hair always looks a bit unkempt, she dresses in clothes that look several sizes too large for her lanky body.

_____

_____

_____

7. She took an egg out of the refrigerator and cracked it into a bowl, it still looked fresh.

_____

_____

_____

8. When I was twelve, a boy named Derrick used to make fun of me, the next year he asked me to the junior high homecoming.

_____

_____

_____

9. Once Dan had decided to decline the football scholarship, he was relieved that he'd finally made up his mind, however, he was afraid his father wouldn't help him with his college expenses.

_____

_____

_____

10. I became active in the homeless shelter four blocks away from my house, what I've learned since going to work there has helped me understand the homeless.

_____

_____

_____

ACTIVITY 10

Eliminating Comma Splices. Eliminate the comma splices from the following paragraph by using a period, a semicolon, or a comma and coordinating conjunction as needed.

When I went from a small community college to a large university, I actually forgot to go to my classes. I remembered to go to Philosophy: Humans and the Universe for the first six weeks because the first book we read was *Alice's Adventures through the Looking Glass,* I remembered to go to my other philosophy class because the professor was cute. Somehow, though, I only made it to art history three or four times during the semester, I even liked art history, but the class was on Friday at one o'clock, by then I was usually on my way back to my hometown to spend the weekend with my boyfriend. About halfway through the semester, I stopped attending all of my classes. My boyfriend and I were breaking up, I felt out of place at such a big school. I hadn't made any friends. I had a job at the library, I stopped going to work, too. After I realized I couldn't keep a decent grade point average if I didn't go to class, I called the registrar and dropped all my classes. I went home for the summer, applied to a smaller state college, and, in the fall, I went to a smaller pond, I wasn't so afraid the big fish would swallow me there. I guess I'm lucky I was able to withdraw before a line of failures appeared on my permanent records, on the other hand, my tuition wasn't refunded.

SUBJECT-VERB AGREEMENT

In a complete sentence, the subject tells who or what is doing the action, and the verb conveys the action or links the subject to the rest of the sentence. To maintain *subject-verb agreement* in a sentence, a *singular subject* must have a *singular verb* form and a *plural subject* must have a *plural verb* form.

INCORRECT   *John don't* like anchovies. [singular subject; plural verb form]

CORRECT   *John doesn't* like anchovies. [singular subject; singular verb form]

INCORRECT   The *boat skim* the top of the lake. [singular subject; plural verb form]

CORRECT   The *boat skims* the top of the lake. [singular subject; singular verb form]

INCORRECT   *We was* going to order a sausage pizza. [plural subject; singular verb form]

CORRECT   *We were* going to order a sausage pizza. [plural subject; plural verb form]

To check for subject-verb agreement, you must first identify the subject of the sentence. Prepositions, dependent clauses, and other words sometimes occur between the subject and verb. Once you identify the subject, you can add the correct verb form.

INCORRECT   The *book* above the desks *need* to be put away. [singular subject; plural verb form]

CORRECT   The *book* above the desks *needs* to be put away. [singular subject; singular verb form]

INCORRECT   The *girl* from my hometown *run* every day. [singular subject; plural verb form]

CORRECT   The *girl* from my hometown *runs* every day. [singular subject; singular verb form]

INCORRECT   *Men* who don't know me very well *thinks* that I'm unfriendly. [plural subject; singular verb form]

CORRECT   *Men* who don't know me very well *think* that I'm unfriendly. [plural subject; plural verb form]

INCORRECT   Movie *theaters* located in the center of town *is* not for me. [plural subject; singular verb form]

CORRECT   Movie *theaters* located in the center of town *are* not for me. [plural subject; plural verb form]

ACTIVITY 11

Identifying Subject-Verb Agreement. Underline the correct verb form in each sentence that follows.

1. The books found in the parking lot (*was, were*) mine.

2. This book of jokes (*is, are*) very funny.

3. The man who lives next to the Parkers (*goes, go*) for a walk each day.

4. The flowers among the baskets (*is, are*) beautiful.

5. The swimming pool, crammed with swimmers, (*was, were*) dangerous.

6. Mr. Smith, along with his sons, (*hikes, hike*) in the summer.

7. Those dogs on the side of the yard (*looks, look*) friendly.

8. My best friend (*swims, swim*) every day.

9. Don't (*sits, sit*) on that chair.

10. We (*plays, play*) the saxophone.

When using the following singular pronouns as subjects, use singular verbs.

anybody	everything	somebody
anyone	nobody	someone
anything	no one	something
everybody	none	
everyone	nothing	

INCORRECT	*Anybody carry* books more easily than I do.
CORRECT	*Anybody carries* books more easily than I do.
INCORRECT	*Someone like* me!
CORRECT	*Someone likes* me!
INCORRECT	*No one study* as hard as I do.
CORRECT	*No one studies* as hard as I do.

INCORRECT   *Something* always *happen* when I'm least expecting it.

CORRECT   *Something* always *happens* when I'm least expecting it.

ASK YOURSELF: How Do I Identify Errors in Subject-Verb Agreement?

- Identify the subject. Do not select a subject pretender such as a prepositional phrase.
- Identify the verb. Do not select a verb pretender such as a verb + *-ing* or *to* + verb.
- Decide whether the subject is singular (one) or plural (more than one).
- Check that the verb matches the subject, using a singular verb for a singular subject and a plural verb for a plural subject.

ACTIVITY 12

Identifying Subject-Verb Agreement with Singular Pronouns. Underline the correct verb form in each sentence that follows.

1. Everybody (*wants, want*) to go to the park.

2. No one (*cares, care*) whether I finish my soda.

3. Everything about my life (*is, are*) wonderful!

4. Nothing (*bothers, bother*) me anymore.

5. Something in the boxes (*is, are*) missing.

6. Nobody who knows me well (*believes, believe*) that.

7. Somebody (*like, likes*) me.

8. Anything they do (*helps, help*) us learn.

9. Someone we know (*is, are*) coming over.

10. Everyone we meet (*shakes, shake*) our hand.

ACTIVITY 13

Identifying Subject-Verb Agreement. Underline the correct verb form in each sentence that follows.

1. The players (*is, are*) on the varsity basketball team.

2. The book (*doesn't, don't*) tell us much about life at the end of the nineteenth century.

3. Everyone in that class (*like, likes*) to write.

4. I (*listen, listens*) to Irish folk music.

5. We (*was, were*) happy to receive our varsity letters.

6. None of the band members (*listen, listens*) to other popular music.

7. The woman who wore that red dress on Monday (*doesn't, don't*) have good taste.

8. The coach of the losing team (*sit, sits*) with his head in his hands.

9. The coaches from both teams (*study, studies*) the plays of the top college teams.

10. Nobody (*appreciate, appreciates*) big band jazz anymore.

ACTIVITY 14

Correcting Subject-Verb Agreement. Revise the following paragraph as needed to correct errors in subject-verb agreement.

Steve play on a local roller hockey league. On Sunday nights, just as other families are sitting down to their last weekend meal, Steve opens his trunk and load about fifty pounds of hockey equipment. The equipment that he takes with him protect him from injuries and help him play a better game. Kevin, the enthusiast who started the league, drive fifty miles to get to the local rink. Anyone, even people who doesn't play hockey, are welcome, but most of the players grew up, like Steve, playing ice hockey. "Roller hockey is a kinder, gentler sport than ice hockey," Steve say. "In high school, we wasn't trying to hurt each other, but players got hurt anyway. Here we're just happy to play. No one ever get hurt." Anyone who watches ice hockey know the aggressiveness of the sport, but is roller hockey really less aggressive? Kevin's broad scar indicate just how rough roller hockey can be.

PRONOUN USAGE

A *pronoun* takes the place of a noun. Here are some of the most common English pronouns:

I, me, mine, we, us, our, ours
you, your, yours
he, him, his, she, her, hers
it, its
they, them, their, theirs
this, these, that, those
who, whom, whose, which, that, what
all, any, another, both, each, either, everyone
few, many, most, nobody, several, some, such
myself, yourself, himself, herself, itself
ourselves, themselves, yourselves

Pronoun Reference

When you use a pronoun to refer to a noun, make sure the reference is clear, not vague. To correct vague pronoun references, follow these guidelines:

- Replace the pronoun with the noun it refers to.
- Or, rewrite the sentence so the pronoun is no longer needed.

VAGUE	In the article "Jobs for the Twenty-first Century" *it* said that computer skills will be important. [What does *it* refer to?]
CLEAR	I read in the article "Jobs for the Twenty-first Century" that computer skills will be important.

VAGUE	Regina told Nicole *she* was going to the store. [Does *she* refer to Regina or Nicole?]
CLEAR	Regina said, "Nicole, I'm going to the store."

VAGUE	In New York *they're* used to crowds. [Who does *they* refer to?]
CLEAR	New Yorkers are used to crowds.

VAGUE	Last summer Joe loved being a camp counselor and working outdoors. *It* made him change his major to elementary education. [Does *it* refer to being a camp counselor, working outdoors, or both?]
CLEAR	Because Joe loved working with children last summer, he's changed his major to elementary education.

ASK YOURSELF: How Do I Correct Pronoun Reference?

- Identify the pronouns in each sentence.
- Be sure that each pronoun clearly refers to only one noun.
- Be sure that the noun is stated.
- Be sure that the pronoun is close to the noun.

ACTIVITY 15

Correcting Vague Pronoun Reference. Correct vague pronoun reference as needed in the following sentences. Note that some of the sentences may be correctly written; mark these "Correct."

1. Whenever Frank tries to speak German with George, he makes many mistakes.

_____

_____

2. In France, they're very proud of their language.

_____

_____

3. My father made the tuna casserole and the salad. It was delicious.

_____

_____

4. In the morning paper, it said that today was going to be hot.

_____

_____

5. The brakes are wearing out, but it has never been in a wreck.

_____

_____

6. Mark told Pablo that he needed to spend more time studying and less time partying.

_____

_____

7. In my nutrition textbook, they say that Americans eat too much fat.

_____

_____

8. Grandmother told Lisa that she wanted to spend more time reading.

_____

_____

9. Yesterday I cleaned out the closets and washed all the windows. It left me exhausted.

_____

_____

10. In Seattle they aren't used to snow, so yesterday's storm took everyone by surprise.

_____

_____

Pronoun Agreement

A pronoun should agree in number with the noun it replaces. To maintain pronoun agreement, use a singular pronoun to refer to a singular noun, and a plural pronoun to refer to a plural noun. To correct errors in pronoun agreement, follow these guidelines:

- Make the pronoun and noun agree in number.
- Or, rewrite the sentence to eliminate the problem.

NO PRONOUN AGREEMENT	A *student* should bring *their* books to class. [*A student* is singular, but *their* is plural.]
PRONOUN AGREEMENT	A *student* should bring *his or her* books to class.
	or
	Students should bring *their* books to class.

You may wish to use the plural to avoid saying *his or her* throughout an essay.

NO PRONOUN AGREEMENT	Mrs. Rowley asked *everyone* to raise *their* hands. [*Everyone* is singular, but *their* is plural.]
PRONOUN AGREEMENT	Mrs. Rowley asked *everyone* to raise *his or her* hand.
	or
	Mrs. Rowley asked the students to raise *their* hands.

NO PRONOUN AGREEMENT	*No one* wanted to hand over *their* wallets. [*No one* is singular, but *their* is plural.]
PRONOUN AGREEMENT	*No one* wanted to hand over *his or her* wallet.
	or
	The spectators didn't want to hand over *their* wallets.

ASK YOURSELF: How Do I Correct Pronoun Agreement?

- Identify the pronouns in each sentence.
- For each pronoun, identify the noun that the pronoun replaces. Is the noun easy to identify? Is it stated?
- Be sure that the pronoun is close to the noun.
- Be sure that the noun and pronoun agree in number. Use a singular pronoun with a singular noun and a plural pronoun with a plural noun.

ACTIVITY 16

Correcting Errors in Pronoun Agreement. Correct the errors in pronoun agreement as needed in the following sentences (or write "Correct" if the sentence contains no error).

1. A veterinarian studies for many years to earn their degree.

   _____

   _____

2. The coach asked her players, "Has everyone finished their warm-ups?"

   _____

   _____

3. Somebody in the back office keeps forgetting to turn their lights off at night.

_____

_____

4. No one was willing to volunteer his or her time to pick up litter.

_____

_____

5. An older student usually makes school their top priority.

_____

_____

6. A politician should keep their word.

_____

_____

7. Did anyone leave the lights on in their car?

_____

_____

8. A college graduate will earn much more money in their lifetime than someone without a college education.

_____

_____

9. A person is trusted if he or she never breaks a promise.

_____

_____

10. The instructor asks that everyone bring their homework to the main office.

_____

_____

SHIFTS IN PERSON

When you write, you have a choice of *first-person (I, we), second-person (you),* or *third-person (he, she, they)* pronouns in the singular and plural. In an expressive essay in which you share your personal history, you would probably choose to write in the first person. However, in an informative essay in which you give "how-to" directions, you would probably use the second person. In most other types of informative essays, the third person might be more appropriate. Finally, in a persuasive essay you might combine the third person (such as when quoting others) with the first person (such as when you use your own experience as evidence for your position).

Here is a complete list of singular and plural pronouns in the first, second, and third person.

SINGULAR

First Person	*Second Person*	*Third Person*
I	you	he, she, it, one
me	you	him, her, it
my, mine	your, yours	his, her, hers, its

PLURAL

First Person	*Second Person*	*Third Person*
we	you	they
us	you	them
our	your, yours	their, theirs

As a general rule, stay with the pronoun you begin with at the start of a paragraph. Avoid shifting from one pronoun to another unnecessarily as these shifts may confuse your reader.

CONFUSING   She loves to go to the mountains in the spring. You never know what wildlife one can see when hiking those trails. She finds that one never gets tired of see-

	ing deer, elk, and bobcats. You just can't help but love the outdoors.
REVISED	She loves to go to the mountains in the spring. She never knows what wildlife she'll see when hiking those trails. She finds that she never gets tired of seeing deer, elk, and bobcats. She just can't help but love the outdoors.
CONFUSING	You begin by mixing the dough by hand. Then one rolls the dough out on a wooden board. You allow it to dry a bit, and then one places it into the pasta machine. You'll find the results very satisfactory.
REVISED	You begin by mixing the dough by hand. Then you roll the dough out on a wooden board. You allow it to dry a bit, and then you place it into the pasta machine. You'll find the results very satisfactory.

ACTIVITY 17

Correcting Unnecessary Shifts in Person. Revise the following paragraphs as needed to correct unnecessary shifts in person.

1.　Although the sport is dangerous, bull riding has taught me to overcome my fear and learn from my mistakes. You have to do what you think is best and not what others think you should do. Bull riding has brought my family back together. They support me by watching me ride sometimes and telling me what I'm doing wrong. I feel bull riding is a hobby, yet I will use the experience with everything I do. It gives you the determination to succeed.

2.　They wanted to go to law school, but one has to have a high grade point average to be accepted. You just never know whether you'll be able to cut it until you send in that application. Then they wait and wait for the word on whether they've been accepted.

You are so disappointed if you are turned down, but what's one to

do? They can't just give up.

SHIFTS IN VERB TENSE

The *tense* of a verb tells the time of the verb's action. If you're writing about something that is taking place now, use the *present tense*. If you're writing about something that has already happened, use the *past tense*. To show that something will happen in the future, use the *future tense*.

As a general rule, stay with the tense you begin with at the start of a paragraph unless the time you are talking about changes. Avoid shifting from one verb tense to another unnecessarily, as these shifts may confuse your reader.

CONFUSING   He *went* to Massachusetts every fall, and this year *is* no exception. He and his friend always *enjoyed* jumping in the piles of leaves that the neighbors *are* raking up. Those leaves *will make* a wonderful playground. He *couldn't wait* to get at them.

REVISED   He *goes* to Massachusetts every fall, and this year *is* no exception. He and his friend always *enjoy* jumping in the piles of leaves that the neighbors *are* raking up. Those leaves *make* a wonderful playground. He *can't wait* to get at them.

ACTIVITY 18

Correcting Awkward Shifts in Verb Tense. Rewrite the following passage to correct unnecessary shifts in verb tense.

A lot of people have a special person who influences their life,

such as a parent, sibling, or friend. In my case, the person who

has influenced me the most is my ex-boyfriend. He is special

because of the times we spend together and the things we did. For

example, we will go to the movies, dinner, and graduation parties.
I have stuffed animals, letters, and pictures that remind me of him.
All of these warm and wonderful memories remind me of how we used to be.

DANGLING AND MISPLACED MODIFIERS

A *dangling modifier* is a phrase or clause that is not clearly linked to the word or words it modifies. The result is often an unclear or comical sentence.

DANGLING MODIFIER	Walking to class, snow was everywhere. [The snow seems to be walking.]
REVISED	Walking to class, we noticed snow was everywhere.
DANGLING MODIFIER	Having fleas, my sister said I couldn't keep the dog. [The sister seems to have the fleas.]
REVISED	Because the dog had fleas, my sister said I couldn't keep him.
DANGLING MODIFIER	Waiting for the bus, my handbag fell open. [The handbag seems to be waiting for the bus.]
REVISED	As I was waiting for the bus, my handbag fell open.

A *misplaced modifier* is a phrase or clause that is separated from the words it modifies, resulting in an unclear or comical sentence.

MISPLACED MODIFIER	There is a swimming pool in the backyard full of water. [The backyard seems to be full of water.]
REVISED	There is a swimming pool full of water in the backyard.
MISPLACED MODIFIER	He borrowed the suit from his friend with pinstripes. [The friend seems to have pinstripes.]
REVISED	He borrowed the suit with pinstripes from his friend.

MISPLACED MODIFIER   Maria took her dress to the seamstress that needed to be altered. [The seamstress seems to need to be altered.]

REVISED   Maria took her dress that needed to be altered to the seamstress.

ACTIVITY 19

Correcting Dangling and Misplaced Modifiers. Underline the dangling and misplaced modifiers in the following sentences. Then rewrite each sentence, moving the modifier to its correct position in the sentence.

1. Having left his apartment fifteen minutes late, getting to school on time was difficult for Brad.

   _____

   _____

2. Painted by her brother, Sue treasured the small portrait.

   _____

   _____

3. His book was finally found by looking under every bed in the house.

   _____

   _____

4. She drove the car over the bridge with the windows open.

   _____

   _____

5. Reading the e-mail notice, a grin appeared on Frank's face.

   _____

   _____

6. After flooring the brakes, the bottles in the back of my car crashed into the front seat.

   _____

   _____

7. Embarrassed but determined to overcome his shyness, Marcel asked the girl to have dinner with him in a red dress.

   _____

   _____

8. Fresh from the oven, he enjoyed the biscuits his mother had made.

   _____

   _____

9. My brother has read every book written by him, who has always enjoyed Stephen King.

   _____

   _____

10. My English paper was done after staring into the computer until three this morning.

    _____

    _____

ACTIVE VERSUS PASSIVE VOICE

In a sentence in the *active voice,* the subject of the sentence is also the actor. In a sentence in the *passive voice,* the receiver of the action is the subject. Most readers prefer the active voice because they expect the subject to do the action of the verb.

PASSIVE   A home run was hit over the stadium wall by Jerry.

ACTIVE   Jerry hit a home run over the stadium wall.

PASSIVE   The textbook was read by everyone in the class.

ACTIVE   Everyone in the class read the textbook.

ASK YOURSELF: How Can I Use the Active Voice?

Using active voice is clearer and more direct.

- Identify the subject and the verb.
- Decide whether the subject is doing the action or receiving the action.
- If the subject is receiving the action, revise the sentence so that the subject comes first and is doing the action.

ACTIVITY 20

Using the Active Voice. Rewrite the following passive voice sentences in the active voice.

1. The new movie was enjoyed by us all.

   _____

   _____

2. Sue's hours had been posted by the manager.

   _____

   _____

3. First place in the tournament was won by the home team.

   _____

   _____

4. A candlelight vigil was held by the students on May 2.

   _____

   _____

5. The dog was walked around the block by their daughter.

   _____

   _____

6. The dinner was made by Tony, but the dessert was prepared by his son.

   _____

   _____

7. The appointment had been made a month earlier by her husband.

   _____

   _____

8. The university was designed by an architect from Atlanta.

   _____

   _____

9. The sound track was written by Sting, and the songs were performed by other artists.

   _____

   _____

10. The child was rocked to sleep by his mother.

   _____

   _____

SENTENCE COORDINATION

Short, closely related sentences can be combined using *sentence coordination*. Use sentence coordination when you combine sentences that are equally important in meaning. When combining sentences, you can use a comma and a coordinating conjunction, a semicolon, or a semicolon and a conjunctive adverb.

Comma and Coordinating Conjunction

One way to form coordinate sentences is to use *coordinating conjunctions*. Here are seven coordinating conjunctions and their meanings:

for—because
and—in addition
nor—neither
but—opposite
or—alternatively
yet—opposite
so—as a result

Use the appropriate coordinating conjunction to express the relationship between the ideas in the sentences you want to combine. Put a comma before the coordinating conjunction.

SHORT SENTENCES	The thunderstorm delayed my plane by three hours. I also lost my luggage.
COMBINED SENTENCE WITH *AND*	The thunderstorm delayed my plane by three hours, *and* I also lost my luggage.
SHORT SENTENCES	I spent the night in the airport. The next day I felt tired and dirty.
COMBINED SENTENCE WITH *SO*	I spent the night in the airport, *so* the next day I felt tired and dirty.
SHORT SENTENCES	I dreaded the return trip home. The flight was smooth and on time.
COMBINED SENTENCE WITH *BUT*	I dreaded the return trip home, *but* the flight was smooth and on time.

Semicolon

Another way to form coordinate sentences is to connect short, closely related sentences with a semicolon.

SHORT SENTENCES	Dreams often reveal our subconscious desires. They are interesting to analyze.
COMBINED SENTENCE	Dreams often reveal our subconscious desires; they are interesting to analyze.
SHORT SENTENCES	I write my dreams down in my journal. I've found that no dream is exactly the same.
COMBINED SENTENCE	I write my dreams down in my journal; I've found that no dream is exactly the same.
SHORT SENTENCES	In many dreams I'm looking for something. I think this searching shows my restless nature.
COMBINED SENTENCE	In many dreams I'm looking for something; I think this searching shows my restless nature.

Semicolon and Conjunctive Adverb

A third way to form coordinate sentences is to use a semicolon and a conjunctive adverb (or transition). Here are some common conjunctive adverbs and their purposes:

TO ADD AN IDEA

also	in addition	moreover
furthermore	for example	

TO SHOW A CONTRASTING POINT

however	nevertheless
instead	otherwise

TO INDICATE A SIMILAR POINT

likewise	similarly

TO EMPHASIZE A KEY CONCEPT

indeed	undoubtedly	certainly	in fact

TO SHOW A CONSEQUENCE

as a result   therefore

consequently   thus

TO POINT OUT A SEQUENCE

finally   meanwhile   next

SHORT SENTENCES	The Academy Awards ceremony was very long. It was entertaining.
COMBINED SENTENCES WITH *HOWEVER*	The Academy Awards show was long; it was, *however,* entertaining.
SHORT SENTENCES	Whoopi Goldberg made a funny entrance. She kept the ceremony from getting too serious.
COMBINED SENTENCE WITH *IN ADDITION*	Whoopi Goldberg made a funny entrance; *in addition,* she kept the ceremony from getting too serious.
SHORT SENTENCES	The actors were beautifully dressed. I enjoyed seeing them accept their awards.
COMBINED SENTENCE WITH *AS A RESULT*	The actors were beautifully dressed; *as a result,* I enjoyed seeing them accept their awards.

Note that when the conjunctive adverb appears at the beginning of the independent clause, it is followed by a comma. When the conjunctive adverb comes within the clause, a comma comes before and after it. A few conjunctive adverbs, such as *however,* can appear at the end of the clause, in which case the conjunctive adverb is preceded by a comma.

ASK YOURSELF: How Do I Use Sentence Coordination?

Combine short, closely related sentences that are equal in importance with

- a comma and a coordinating conjunction *(for, and, nor, but, or, yet, so).*
- a semicolon.
- a semicolon and a conjunctive adverb (such as *in addition, however, therefore*).

ACTIVITY 21

Sentence Coordination. Combine each of the following pairs of sentences with a comma and a coordinating conjunction, a semicolon, or a semicolon and a conjunctive adverb.

1. Many people dislike doing housework. It's a necessary part of life.

   _____

   _____

2. Women do more housework than men. This inequality has existed for many years.

   _____

   _____

3. A recent study found that people don't care as much about a clean house as they did in the past. This is true for both women and men.

   _____

   _____

   _____

4. Men and women both have jobs. They don't have time for housework.

   _____

   _____

5. Many people prefer to spend time with each other instead of cleaning house. They like to relax at home.

   _____

   _____

   _____

6. Some people don't mind dusty furniture or dirty dishes. They just want to enjoy themselves after a hard day at work.

_____

_____

_____

7. Other people clean house no matter how tired they are. They hire a cleaning service.

_____

_____

8. To some people, a house should always be clean. They can't live any other way.

_____

_____

9. Other people find cleaning to be relaxing. They think it's good exercise.

_____

_____

10. Years ago women were expected to keep a clean house. This expectation has certainly changed.

_____

_____

SENTENCE SUBORDINATION

You can use *sentence subordination* to combine short, closely related sentences by adding a *subordinate conjunction:*

after	even though	until
although	if	when
as	since	whenever
as if	so that	where
as though	than	wherever
because	though	whether
before	unless	while

When you combine the two sentences, one of them is going to be *subordinate* to — less important than — the other one. The subordinate conjunction tells the reader which idea is less important and which one is more important. The subordinate conjunction comes at the beginning of the less important sentence, or *subordinate clause.*

SHORT SENTENCES	Making my sister a birthday cake was an adventure. I had never baked before.
COMBINED SENTENCE WITH *BECAUSE*	*Because* I had never baked before, making my sister a birthday cake was an adventure.
SHORT SENTENCES	The cake tasted pretty good and was low-calorie. I used fruit juice instead of sugar.
COMBINED SENTENCE WITH *SINCE*	The cake tasted pretty good and was low-calorie *since* I used fruit juice instead of sugar.
SHORT SENTENCES	I had tried to bake. I hadn't realized how complicated baking can be.
COMBINED SENTENCE WITH *BEFORE*	*Before* I had tried to bake, I hadn't realized how complicated baking can be.

ASK YOURSELF: How Do I Use Sentence Subordination?

- Examine two short, closely related sentences. Decide which sentence is subordinate to, or less important than, the other.

- Turn the less important sentence into a subordinate clause by beginning it with an appropriate subordinate conjunction.

- When the subordinate clause begins the sentence, use a comma to separate it from the rest of the sentence. Don't use a comma when the subordinate clause is at the end of the sentence.

As these examples illustrate, the subordinate clause can appear at the beginning or end of the sentence. When the subordinate clause comes at the beginning of the sentence, a comma separates it from the rest of the sentence. When the subordinate clause comes at the end of the sentence, no comma is used.

ACTIVITY 22

Sentence Subordination. Using sentence subordination, combine the following pairs of sentences.

1. More and more young adults are living with their parents. This happens when they are in their twenties.

   _____

   _____

2. College can be very expensive. More people are going to college.

   _____

   _____

3. They graduate from college. They might live with their parents for several years.

   _____

   _____

4. Despite some inconveniences, they live at home. They save money or pay off loans.

   _____

   _____

5. They also have money to spend. They do this when they live with their parents.

   _____

   _____

6. They might decide to buy a nice car or take long vacations. They might do this before they live on their own.

_____

_____

7. They get a place of their own. They're responsible for all the bills.

_____

_____

8. The grown children finally leave home. Some parents have the "empty nest" syndrome.

_____

_____

9. Some people in their twenties miss living with their parents. They are still children.

_____

_____

10. Parents and grown children need to separate. It can be painful.

_____

_____

Punctuation

If you have ever taken a lengthy road trip, you know that you depended on road signs to help you get from one place to another. Without road signs, you would have become hopelessly lost and unable to continue without asking directions. In writing, punctuation marks act as road signs, guiding readers through the text. If the writing is incorrectly punctuated, readers may become confused or lost and unable to understand the writer's meaning. Writers use punctuation to communicate more effectively, and readers depend on punctuation to help them understand the writer's meaning.

Punctuation

To review punctuation rules and to practice using punctuation correctly, go to **<www.bedfordstmartins.com/choices/>**. Click on "Exercise Central," and after logging in, click on "Punctuation."

COMMAS

The *comma* (,) is used in many writing situations:

- To set off an introductory word, phrase, or clause.
- To separate three or more words, phrases, or clauses used in a series.
- To separate two independent clauses joined by a coordinating conjunction.
- To separate a descriptive phrase that interrupts the flow of the sentence.
- To separate transitional words and phrases from the rest of the sentence.

- To separate the day of the month from the year.
- To separate a street address from the name of a city and to separate the name of a city from the name of a state.
- To set off dialogue or a direct quotation.

Use a comma to separate an introductory word, phrase, or clause from the main sentence.

Ella, please go pick up some milk at the store.
According to Ella, there was enough milk in the refrigerator.
Although she didn't really want to go, Ella went to the store for more milk.

ACTIVITY 1

Using Commas with Introductory Words, Phrases, or Clauses.
Add commas as needed to the following sentences.

1. Listening to the hum of the subway beneath my apartment I wondered if I would be able to sleep without its familiar rumble.

2. When Jason turned the corner he fell over a window washer's bucket and into a flower cart.

3. For example the neighbors in small towns take more interest in your successes and failures.

4. In the barn at the back of his property my grandfather stores his collection of rusted steel and tin.

5. After we'd sat for twenty minutes without being waited on David said that we should leave.

Use a comma to separate three or more words, phrases, or clauses used in a series. (You may notice, however, that in newspapers and some business writing, the writers omit the comma before the *and*.)

Ella decided she would buy gum, bread, and hot dogs as well as milk.

Ella stopped to water the flowers, talk to a neighbor, and admire the sunset on her way to the store.

Ella went to the store, John went to the movie, and Chi decided to stay home.

ACTIVITY 2

Using Commas in a Series. For each of the following lists of items, write a complete sentence using the series comma.

1. a loaf of bread, a book of poems, a bottle of grape juice

   _____

   _____

   _____

2. lettuce, tomatoes, carrots, cucumbers, green onions

   _____

   _____

   _____

3. behind the gas station, under a tree, in an old tire

   _____

   _____

   _____

4. you lose your car keys, you forget to turn off the coffee pot, you spill coffee on your white shirt, you snag your panty hose

   _____

   _____

   _____

5. listening for crickets, smelling the jasmine, swatting mosquitoes

_____

_____

_____

Use a comma to separate two independent clauses that are joined by a coordinating conjunction *(and, but, or, nor, for, yet, so)*.

Ella didn't really want to go to the store, *and* she didn't want her sister to have to go either.

Ella didn't really want to go to the store, *but* her sister had asked her to get some milk.

ACTIVITY 3

Using Commas with Coordinating Conjunctions. Use a comma and a coordinating conjunction *(for, and, nor, but, or, yet, so)* to join the two independent clauses into a single sentence.

1. I could hear the rain outside. I was too tired to look out the window for damage.

_____

_____

2. The room buzzed with the voices and laughter of children five years old. It was time to graduate from kindergarten.

_____

_____

3. She waited on the corner. She kept a wary eye on the speeding traffic.

_____

_____

4. Mark kept his eyes closed. He wouldn't see how high he was when he reached the top of the roller coaster.

_____

_____

5. The sand stung my cheeks. The wind pushed me back toward the water.

_____

_____

Use a comma before and after a descriptive phrase or an apposi-tive (a noun that renames the noun right before it) that could be removed from the sentence without changing the meaning.

DESCRIPTIVE PHRASE   Ella, who loved her sister dearly, decided to go to the store.

APPOSITIVE   Ella's sister, Mary, insisted on having her milk right away.

ACTIVITY 4

Using Commas with Descriptive Phrases and Appositives. Add commas as needed to the following sentences.

1. Martha my best friend wasn't home when I called her.

2. The students in her English class hoping for an extension of the due date left the classroom disappointed.

3. The green floral dress which I had purchased for the party lay in a heap on the bottom of the closet floor.

4. The man a plumber named Jerry stood in the driveway.

5. Her hair as a result was frizzy.

Use a comma to separate transitional words and phrases from the rest of the sentence.

In addition, Ella stopped to mail some letters that she had in her purse.

When she arrived at the mailbox, however, she realized that she had forgotten the stamps.

ACTIVITY 5

Using Commas to Set Off Transitional Words and Phrases. Add commas as needed to the following sentences.

1. It wasn't until I'd walked into the bright light of day however that I felt I'd accomplished something important.

2. The restaurant on the corner on the other hand serves breakfast all day.

3. Moreover the coat smelled musty and stale.

4. Amanda meanwhile stared at her reflection in the storefront glass.

5. Consequently Jake refused to finish the run.

Use a comma to separate the day of the month from the year when the day follows the month in the sentence.

Ella went to the store on June 1, 2002.
The store had opened on December 15, 2001.

When the year comes in the middle of a sentence, a comma is needed after the year.

May 1, 1981, is her birthday.
On March 15, 1993, I was married.

ACTIVITY 6

Using Commas in Dates. Add commas as needed to the following sentences.

1. I hope to graduate on May 31 2004.

2. He headed back to Little Rock on June 2 1997.

3. September 15 1972 was the day my brother left the service.

4. January 25 1986 is a day I'll always remember.

5. I was born on August 8 1980.

Use a comma to separate a street address from the name of a city. Also use a comma to separate the name of a city from the name of a county or state.

Ella lived at 713 Washington Street, Chicago, Illinois.

My boyfriend sent the letter to 234 East Main, Los Angeles, California.

ACTIVITY 7

Using Commas in Street Addresses. Add commas as needed to the following sentences.

1. We mailed the letter to 1610 Main Street Los Angeles California.

2. We spent our vacation in Tijuana Mexico.

3. He lives in Hudspeth County Texas.

4. My favorite city is Portland Oregon.

5. My uncle lives at 500 Elm Street Chicago Illinois.

Use a comma to set off dialogue or a direct quotation in a sentence.

"I'm headed to the store," Ella said to her neighbor.

The author of this article says, "Don't forget to read to your children."

"He just won't do it," she exclaimed to her boss, "even though I've asked him several times."

According to Professor Blaugrand, "The best time to apply for financial aid is in the spring."

ACTIVITY 8

Using Commas with Dialogue and Direct Quotations. Add commas as needed to the following sentences.

1. "I'll meet you at ten o'clock" Jose said to his friend.

2. According to John Lantham "The trees are always at their most beautiful in October."

3. "Who cares if we don't get to go" she yelled at her father.

4. "I'll take you to the library" Leonore said "as soon as I finish my lunch."

5. Dr. Jones says "You can do whatever you set your mind to."

ASK YOURSELF: What Are the Most Important Comma Rules?

- Use commas with introductory words, phrases, or clauses.
- Use commas for a list of items in a series.
- Use commas with independent clauses joined by coordinating conjunctions.
- Use commas to set off transitional words and phrases.
- Use commas in dates and street addresses.
- Use commas at the end of an introduction to dialogue or a question.

Using Commas Correctly. Add commas as needed to the following paragraph.

My mother told me about an incident that happened to our family in Savannah Georgia on August 8 1923. She and my father were sharecroppers and food including staples was impossible to buy on their salaries. One day my father said to her "Naomi let's take these kids into town for a good time." My mother however was worried that they didn't have the money for a good time. She had just discovered much to her dismay that they were out of flour rice beans and milk. How could they spend money on entertainment when they didn't even have food? My father surprised her though with a small amount of money that he had stashed under the mattress and so we went into town to buy food and have a good time.

SEMICOLONS

Use a *semicolon* (;) to link two independent clauses that are closely related in meaning and are not joined by a connecting word (*and, but, or, nor, for, yet,* and *so*).

We went to the Little League playoffs; the Blasters won the game. The Blasters have always been a good team; their coach is one of the best in the league.

Use a semicolon to link two clauses that are joined by a conjunctive adverb that indicates a shift in topic, such as *however* or *in addition*.

The Blasters may have tougher competition next year; nevertheless, we think they can win.

Use a semicolon to separate items in a series when those items already include commas.

We had followed that team to Gainesville, Florida; Biloxi, Mississippi; and Shreveport, Louisiana.

ASK YOURSELF: What Are the Rules for Using Semicolons?

How do you decide whether to use a comma or a semicolon to connect ideas in a sentence?

- Use a comma, not a semicolon, when connecting two complete sentences (or independent clauses) with a coordinating conjunction (*and, but, or, nor, for, yet,* and *so.*)

  The nightclub had a good atmosphere, *but* the band was incredibly bad.

- Use a semicolon when connecting two complete sentences (or independent clauses) without using the connecting words *and, but, or, nor, for, yet,* and *so.*

  The nightclub had a good atmosphere; the band was incredibly bad.

- Use a semicolon to connect two complete sentences (or independent clauses) that are joined with a conjunctive adverb such as *however, in addition, therefore,* and *moreover.* Put a comma after the conjunctive adverb.

  The nightclub had a good atmosphere; *however,* the band was incredibly bad.

ACTIVITY 10

Using Semicolons Correctly. Use a semicolon to punctuate each of the following sentences correctly.

1. We were aware of the many dangers we might face nevertheless, we decided to hike the canyon.

2. I could hear the ocean throwing pebbles onto the sand the seagulls swirled above me.

3. I have been to all the major U.S. cities except New York, New York, Chicago, Illinois, and Miami, Florida.

4. We had forgotten to pack the Coleman stove as a result, we only spent one night at the campsite.

5. For the most part, the summer had been dry we were surprised, therefore, when it began to rain as soon as we'd set up our tent.

COLONS

Use a *colon* (:) after an independent clause to introduce a list, clause, or phrase that explains the clause. (Remember that the independent clause must be able to stand alone as a sentence.) Don't use a colon following a verb or with *such as*.

INCORRECT	The supplies we bought for class include: books, pens, and a calculator.
CORRECT	We bought the following supplies for class: books, pens, and a calculator.
CORRECT	The supplies we bought for class include books, pens, and a calculator.
INCORRECT	There are many ways to stay out of debt, such as: make a budget and stick to it, buy only what you need, and cut up those charge cards.
CORRECT	There are many ways to stay out of debt: make a budget and stick to it, buy only what you need, and cut up those charge cards.
CORRECT	There are many ways to stay out of debt, such as making a budget and sticking to it, buying only what you need, and cutting up those charge cards.

ACTIVITY 11

Using Colons Correctly. Use a colon as needed in the following sentences to introduce a list, clause, or phrase that explains the independent clause. If the sentence is correctly written, write "Correct."

1. For school, I need paper, pens, books, and a calculator.

2. Please do the following mop the floor, vacuum the carpet, and dust the furniture.

3. I've seen two good movies this year *A Beautiful Mind* and *Shrek*.

4. When I get home, I will study, cook dinner, and feed the cats.

5. He tried swimming strokes such as the butterfly, the crawl, and the backstroke.

END PUNCTUATION

End punctuation signals the reader that you have completed a thought and ended a sentence. End punctuation includes the period, the exclamation mark, and the question mark.

Use a *period* (.) to end a sentence, an indirect question, and a command.

He waited for her to come home.
He asked her where she had been.
Call me if you plan to be late again.

Use an *exclamation mark* (!) to give emphasis or to show emotion.

She was shocked that he would question her!
Don't ever talk to me like that again!

Use a *question mark* (?) to end a direct question.

Why didn't she understand that he was just worried about her?
How many times did she have to tell him?

ACTIVITY 12

Using End Punctuation Correctly. Insert the correct end punctuation mark at the end of each group of words.

1. It took a long time for me to realize that my mother and I were very much alike

2. When I returned to my hometown, I tried to find the house I lived in as a child

3. I realized then that Thomas had been telling the truth

4. When did your family stop spending Saturdays at the beach

5. Get a grip on yourself

ACTIVITY 13

Correcting Errors in End Punctuation. Revise the following paragraph to correct errors in end punctuation.

The porch swing groaned as my grandfather pushed gently forward and back in time to the music of the story he was telling. We'd sit and watch the garden grow, as he called it! What we were really doing, though, was storytelling? At twenty, I hadn't been around long enough to have interesting stories of my own. Every afternoon while I did my homework and he watched his soap opera, I'd ask myself the same question: What will he talk about tonight. We had this talk after dinner each night during the two years I lived with him. We'd sit out back, and he'd tell me the stories of his seventy-eight years. He talked about growing up on a farm, and he often complained about how lazy his brothers had been. They left him to do all the work! He talked about his year playing semipro baseball? He told me stories about my father and about my aunts and their many children! One night, by the time he finished telling his story, Grandma was in bed, and the bright moon of east Texas was high overhead. This story, more than any other, revealed my grandfather's gentle spirit as well as the harshness of his life! More than that, it told me more about east Texas and the oil business than any of my Texas history books had revealed. Who wouldn't have felt fortunate to have a living history book sitting across from them on the swing.

APOSTROPHES

Use the *apostrophe* (') to show possession. A possessive word is followed by a noun that names something that belongs to it. If the possessive word refers to just one person, use *'s.*

The *student's* notes were clearly written. [one person]
Jessie's golf swing was the best in the state. [one person]

If the possessive word refers to more than one person, use *s'.*

All of the *students'* notes were clearly written. [more than one person]
The *golfers'* scores were the best in the state. [more than one person]

Possessive pronouns, such as *his, hers, yours, its, theirs,* and *ours,* do not require apostrophes.

His book was more interesting than *theirs.*
Hers was a better cup of coffee than *yours.*

ACTIVITY 14

Using Apostrophes to Show Possession. In the following sentences, underline the words in which apostrophes are missing or misused. Then write the correct form of the word in the space provided.

1. Mary Smiths house is on the corner of Dodge and Elm.

2. Is this book your's?

_____

3. Michael tried to return the mans umbrella, but the man rushed out the door.

_____

4. The girls sweatsuits lay crumpled on the floor.

_____

5. Jerrys pets were always running around the yard.

_____

Use the apostrophe to form a contraction. A *contraction* is formed by combining two words with an apostrophe taking the place of the omitted letters. Here are some common contractions:

aren't	are not	she's	she is
can't	cannot	there's	there is
doesn't	does not	they'll	they will
don't	do not	they're	they are
hasn't	has not	they've	they have
haven't	have not	wasn't	was not
he'll	he will	we'll	we will
here's	here is	we're	we are
he's	he is	weren't	were not
I'm	I am	who's	who is
it's	it is	won't	will not
I've	I have	wouldn't	would not
she'll	she will	you're	you are

It's [it is] always a good idea to take notes.

I *don't* [do not] care if you *can't* [cannot] remember to carry your backpack.

Caution: Don't confuse the contraction *it's* (for *it is*) for the possessive pronoun *its*.

INCORRECT   The restaurant was known for it's wonderful entertainment.

CORRECT   The restaurant was known for its wonderful entertainment.

ASK YOURSELF: What's the Difference between *It's* and *Its*?

To determine whether you should use *it's* (the contraction for *it is*) or *its* (the possessive word), ask yourself whether you can change *its* to *it is* and still have the sentence make sense.

    Can you change *its* to *it is* in the following sentence?

    My truck has lost *its* bright blue color.

    No. Therefore, *its* is correct.

ACTIVITY 15

Using Apostrophes in Contractions. In the following sentences, underline contractions with missing apostrophes. Then write the correct form of the contractions in the space provided.

1. Because its sunny outside, Ive decided to take the dog for a walk.

   _____

2. We arent planning a vacation this year because we cant afford one.

   _____

3. Well put all the toys in the red basket.

   _____

4. If youre going to the store, please get hot dog buns.

   _____

5. Its better to ask a question when you dont understand something than to leave this class confused.

   _____

ACTIVITY 16

Using Apostrophes Correctly. The following paragraph contains several apostrophe errors. Revise the paragraph to correct those errors.

We wanted to stop by Daves house on the way to see Oliver Stones new movie, but we didnt have time. Dave had borrowed Amys English textbook, and Amys instructor had assigned reading over the weekend. I couldnt let Amy borrow my book because I hadnt finished my reading yet. Dave had Amys textbook for a week, so Amy hadnt been prepared for her last English class. Shed been embarrassed when her instructor called on her to discuss the days reading assignment. When we arrived at the theater, Amy called Dave from the pay phone. Hed gone out of town for the weekend. "Isnt that just my luck," Amy said. I told her that she didn't need to worry. We could study together over the weekend, and Id let her borrow my book for Tuesdays class.

QUOTATION MARKS

Use *quotation marks* (" ") to show a speaker's or a writer's exact words.

Homer declared, "The Beatles are back!"

According to the *Washington Post,* "The remaining Beatles have considered reissuing early Beatles songs."

Use quotation marks to enclose the titles of articles, essays, book chapters, speeches, poems, short stories, and songs.

John Deaver's newspaper column, "Close-Up," is the first one I read in the morning.

I especially liked the chapter entitled "What It Means to Be Free" in my sociology text.

Martin Luther King's "I Have a Dream" speech is well known.

Robert Frost's poem "Stopping by Woods on a Snowy Evening" is Alma's favorite.

My class read Katherine Anne Porter's short stories "María Concepción" and "Flowering Judas."

We sing "Amazing Grace" at least once a month at my church.

ASK YOURSELF: What Are the Rules for Using Quotation Marks?

- Always place periods and commas inside of quotation marks.
- Always put colons and semicolons outside of quotation marks.
- Put question marks and exclamation marks inside of quotation marks if they are part of the actual quotation.
- Put question marks and exclamation marks outside of quotation marks if they are not part of the actual quotation, but part of your own sentence.

ACTIVITY 17

Using Quotation Marks Correctly. Revise the following sentences as needed to correct missing quotation marks.

1. During that time, I read the short story The Fly by Katherine Mansfield.

2. We decided that Pink Floyd's song Comfortably Numb would be our song.

3. You didn't think I was stupid, did you? asked Jessica.

4. Well, my grandfather said, I guess it's about time for us to go.

5. Marta said, I feel better about myself when I dress up.

DASHES

Use *dashes* to signal an abrupt change in thought. A dash (—) is typed as two unspaced hyphens (—) with no space before or after it.

Use dashes sparingly, though. Too many dashes may suggest that you haven't thought carefully about how to use punctuation effectively.

John came to my house—much later than I expected—to return the books he'd borrowed.

Maria wanted to buy gifts for everyone—although money was tight—because she loved her friends so dearly.

It came to her in a daydream—she was going to move to New York City.

ACTIVITY 18

Using Dashes Correctly. Revise the following sentences as needed by supplying missing dashes.

1. Everything I did running, jumping rope, bicycling was exhilarating.

2. Where I come from Las Vegas, Nevada we don't worry about buying overcoats.

3. Our campus bookstore next to the Food Court has everything you need for your classes.

4. All of our needs food, lodging, and transportation were covered by the scholarship.

5. He does it just the way I would splendidly!

ITALICS OR UNDERLINING

Use underlining to indicate *italics* in handwritten or typewritten copy. Italicize (underline) the titles of books, magazines, films, television shows, newspapers, journals, computer software, music albums, or anything else that is not part of a larger collection.

I read *Moby Dick* in my literature course.

The *Los Angeles Times* is my favorite newspaper.

I have *Windows XP* on my office computer.

ACTIVITY 19

Using Italics Correctly. In the following paragraph, underline to indicate where italics should be used.

One of my favorite authors is Gary Larson, the author of The Far Side calendars. His cartoons are just as funny as the ones I read in the San Francisco Examiner. The only thing I find funnier is the movie Blazing Saddles. Larson is hilarious. I would recommend that you purchase one of his calendars.

Spelling

English spelling is difficult, partly because many English words come from other languages. However, several spelling rules can help you master some of the most commonly misspelled words. These rules tell you when to use *ie* versus *ei,* when to double the final consonant, when to drop a final silent *e,* and when to change *y* to *i.*

Spelling

To review spelling rules and to practice spelling correctly, go to **<www.bedfordstmartins.com/choices/>**. Click on "Exercise Central," and after logging in, click on "Spelling."

USING *I* BEFORE *E*, EXCEPT AFTER *C*

Write *i* before *e*

Except after *c*

Or when sounded like *ay*

As in *neighbor* and *weigh*

This rhyme can help you remember the rules for using *ie* and *ei.* Write *i* before *e*

believe	piece
fierce	priest
grieve	reprieve
niece	thief

Except after *c*

ceiling	deceit
conceited	receipt
conceive	receive

Or when sounded like *ay*

eight	neighbor
freight	weight

Here are some exceptions to this rule:

counterfeit	leisure
foreign	neither
height	seize
heir	weird

Because there are exceptions, check your dictionary or use your computer's spell-check feature to verify your spelling. Remember that spell-check will not catch all errors, so proofread carefully.

ACTIVITY 1

Using *i* before *e* except after *c*. In the space provided, correct the misspelled words or write "Correct" if the word is spelled correctly.

1. recieve   _____

2. decieve   _____

3. beige   _____

4. sleigh   _____

5. conciet   _____

6. concieve   _____

7. leisure   _____

8. relieve   _____

9. wieght _____

10. peice _____

DOUBLING THE FINAL CONSONANT

When adding an ending that begins with a vowel (such as *-ed* or *-ing*) to a word that ends with a consonant, double the consonant when it is preceded by a single vowel and ends a one-syllable word or a stressed syllable. (A *stressed syllable* is one that is accented. In the word *believe,* for example, the stress is on the second syllable. Say the word to hear the stressed syllable.)

Double the consonant when it's preceded by a vowel and ends a one-syllable word:

bet	betting
hop	hopping
quit	quitting
sad	sadder
win	winner

Double the consonant when it's preceded by a vowel and ends a stressed syllable:

commit	committed
control	controller
omit	omitted
prefer	preferred
refer	referring

However, this rule does not apply when the ending doesn't begin with a vowel, such as *-ment* or *-ness.*

commit	commitment
disappoint	disappointment
sad	sadness
wet	wetness

ACTIVITY 2

Doubling the Final Consonant. Add the specified ending to each word in the space provided.

1. stop + *ed*   _____

2. rid + *ance*   _____

3. dry + *ness*   _____

4. tip + *ing*   _____

5. plan + *ed*   _____

6. refer + *ence*   _____

7. repeat + *ed*   _____

8. occur + *ence*   _____

9. bet + *ing*   _____

10. labor + *ed*   _____

DROPPING THE FINAL SILENT *E*

When adding an ending that begins with a vowel, drop the final *e*.

age	aging
care	caring
desire	desiring
fame	famous
remove	removable
use	usable

When adding an ending that begins with a consonant, keep the final *e*.

care	careful
dense	denseness

lone   lonely
safe   safety
state   statement

Some exceptions to this rule include *acknowledgment, argument, judgment, ninth,* and *truly.*

ACTIVITY 3

Dropping the Final Silent *e*.   Add the specified ending to each word in the space provided.

1. achieve + *ment*   _____

2. remove + *able*   _____

3. desire + *ing*   _____

4. argue + *ment*   _____

5. hope + *ing*   _____

6. hate + *ful*   _____

7. judge + *ment*   _____

8. sure + *est*   _____

9. manage + *ment*   _____

10. write + *ing*   _____

CHANGING *Y* TO *I*

When adding an ending to a word that ends in *y*, change the *y* to *i*.

apply   applied
carry   carries
ceremony   ceremonies
easy   easiest

family	families
happy	happiness
marry	married
study	studies
worry	worried

However, this rule does not apply to words ending with *-ing*.

apply	applying
carry	carrying
dry	drying
study	studying

Also do not omit the final *y* when it is preceded by a vowel (*a, e, i, o,* or *u*).

buy	buys
play	playful
monkey	monkeys
stay	stayed

ACTIVITY 4

Changing *y* to *i*. Add the specified ending to each word in the space provided.

1. employ + *ment* _____

2. busy + *ness* _____

3. try + *ing* _____

4. apology + *s* _____

5. easy + *ly* _____

6. beauty + *ful* _____

7. dry + *ed* _____

8. play + *ing* _____

9. attorney + *s*   _____

10. stay *+ing*   _____

Tips for Multilingual Writers

Spelling varies somewhat among English-speaking countries.
Note, for example, how the following words are spelled
differently in American and British English.

AMERICAN	BRITISH
canceled	cancelled
center	centre
check	cheque
civilization	civilisation
color	colour
defense	defence
humor	humour
judgment	judgement
realize	realise
traveled	travelled

ACTIVITY 5

Correcting Misspelled Words. Correct the misspelled words in the
following paragraph.

Every Sunday my stepfather went to the garage, grabed a
fourty-pound bag of charcol, and dumpped it into the larg kettle
grill on the patio. Mom scrubbed the potatos, and my brother and
I set the table. We rarly ate dinner at the antiqe dinning room
table, so Sunday diners were an ocassion. I was responsible for
chosing the placemats and napkins; my brother polished the sil-
verware and the glases. Earlier that morning, my mother had
preparred her special secret marinate. I'm still not sure what

ingredients she used, but the smel of her herbs and spices and the thik T-bone steaks always got our mouths watering. When my stepfather came in to get the plate for the steaks, we knew it was time to sit down. The table would be crowded with fresh rolls, real buter, sour cream, and a huge green salad. We'd end our Sunday ritual siting arond the stereo listening to Jerry Clower albums and eating big peices of fresh fruit pie with ice cream.

ADDING *-S* OR *-ES*

Add *-s* to form the plural of most nouns.

chair	chairs
book	books
lamp	lamps

Add *-es* to nouns that end in *-s, -sh, -ch,* and *-x.*

fetus	fetuses
wish	wishes
church	churches
tax	taxes

ACTIVITY 6

Adding -s or -es. In the space provided, add *-s* or *-es.*

1. piece _____

2. weight _____

3. bell _____

4. neighbor _____

5. video _____

6. desk   _____

7. purse   _____

8. fax   _____

9. beach   _____

10. gigolo   _____

ASK YOURSELF: How Do I Become a Better Speller?

- Learn when to use *ie* versus *ei,* when to double the final consonant, when to drop the final silent *e,* when to change *y* to *i,* and whether to add *-s* or *-es.*
- Use your spell-check, keeping in mind that it won't catch all misspelled words.
- Pay attention to how words are spelled when you read.
- Keep a log of words you tend to misspell.
- Consult a dictionary frequently.

Mechanics

This section focuses on the correct use of capital letters, abbreviations, and numbers.

Mechanics

For additional practice with mechanics, go to **<www .bedfordstmartins.com/choices/>**. Click on "Exercise Central," and after logging in, click on "Mechanics."

CAPITALIZATION

Capitalize *proper nouns*—nouns that refer to a specific person, place, event, or thing. Do not capitalize *common nouns,* which refer to a general category of persons, places, events, or things.

COMMON NOUNS	PROPER NOUNS
a college	Smith College
a country	Venezuela
a day of the week	Tuesday
a holiday	Christmas
a house	the White House
a mother	Mom
a president	President Kennedy
a professor	Professor Lee
a war	the Civil War

Capitalize the names of organizations, institutions, and trademarks.

My uncle is a *Shriner.*
I'm neither a *Republican* nor a *Democrat.*
My next car will be a *Honda.*

ASK YOURSELF: What Words Should Be Capitalized?

- Proper nouns
- Names of organizations, institutions, and trademarks
- Words in titles except articles, conjunctions, and prepositions, unless they are the first or last words in the title

---

ACTIVITY 1

Correcting Errors in Capitalization. Correct the errors in capitalization in the following sentences.

1. I always thought Miami university was in Florida, so I was surprised to find out it was in Ohio.

2. My favorite museum is the smithsonian.

3. My Father retired last year.

4. All I have to drink is seven-up.

5. One of our most important holidays is veterans day.

6. My Great-Grandmother lived to be 101.

7. One of my favorite professors is professor garcia.

8. I wish we had more holidays like thanksgiving.

9. After work, Mike went to the chevrolet dealership.

10. When she was a girl, Leticia had been a girl scout.

In titles, capitalize all words except articles *(a, an, the)*, connecting words *(and, but, or, for, nor, so)*, and prepositions *(of, on, in, at, with, for)*, unless they are the first or last word of the title.

For Whom the Bell Tolls	*The Miseducation of Lauryn Hill*
Gone with the Wind	the *New York Times*
Party of Five	*The Sound of Music*
Pride and Prejudice	*Titanic*

ACTIVITY 2

Capitalizing Titles Correctly. Correct the errors in capitalization in the following sentences.

1. When *The favorite child* was published, it was received well by the *San Francisco Chronicle*.

2. One of my favorite magazines is *Sports illustrated*.

3. My grandfather's favorite show is *friends*.

4. One of my favorite songs is Bonnie Raitt's "the road's my middle name."

5. The orchestra practiced Franz Schubert's "Scenes from Child-hood."

6. We had a test on *the Scarlet Letter*.

7. In my psychology class we read *the man who mistook his wife for a hat*.

8. For financial news, read The *wall street journal*.

9. I loved reading *To Kill A Mockingbird* by Harper Lee.

10. *Shakespeare In Love* won Gwyneth Paltrow an Academy Award.

ABBREVIATIONS

An *abbreviation* is a shortened version of a word or phrase. Note that abbreviations consisting of all capital letters usually don't require periods.

Mr. Daniel Adams

Dr. Lin Chao

Linda Larson, *MD* (Medical Doctor)

Oscar Olivarez, *MBA* (Master of Business Administration)

GM (General Motors)

ABC (American Broadcasting Company)

CIA (Central Intelligence Agency)

FBI (Federal Bureau of Investigation)

MADD (Mothers against Drunk Driving)

NAACP (National Association for the Advancement of Colored People)

AIDS (acquired immunodeficiency syndrome)

RAM (random access memory)

ESP (extrasensory perception)

The first time you use the name of a company, organization, society, or special term, spell out the name and identify the abbreviation in parentheses. You may then use the abbreviation in subsequent references. For example:

> The computer teacher introduced us to the term *random access memory* (RAM). We were then instructed to check the RAM needed for the software we planned to run.

ACTIVITY 3

Using Abbreviations Correctly. Rewrite the following sentences, spelling out the name or using abbreviations as needed.

1. I had always hoped to go to work for the Federal Bureau of Investigation. My grandfather worked for the FBI.

_____

_____

2. Every time I hear someone from MADD talk about drunk drivers, I'm so glad that I don't drink. MADD has greatly influenced my life.

_____

_____

_____

3. Don't even tell me that you have ESP; I don't believe in ESP.

_____

_____

4. The National Broadcasting Company (NBC) is my favorite network. I watch more shows on NBC than on any other network.

_____

_____

_____

5. I've always wanted to join the National Association for the Advancement of Colored People because the goals of the NAACP appeal to me.

_____

_____

_____

NUMBERS

Spell out whole numbers from one through ninety-nine and use numerals for all remaining numbers.

He wanted to purchase *eighteen* hot dog buns for his cookout.
We collected *204* cans of food for the homeless shelter.

Spell out numbers that begin a sentence.

Eighty-six students protested the new curfew laws.
Two hundred and fifty horses roamed the field.
One thousand of us crowded into the stadium.

Use numerals to indicate decimals, percentages, page numbers, years, and time of day.

The rod is *3.45* inches in length.
My car has depreciated *11 percent* since I purchased it.
Please turn to *page 283* in your textbook.
The plane leaves Boise, Idaho, at *8:50 A.M.* and reaches Chicago, Illinois, at *2:30 P.M.*

ACTIVITY 4

Using Numbers. Using the preceding guidelines on formatting numbers, underline the correct form in each of the following sentences.

1. He counted (*45/forty-five*) freckles on her face.
2. She claimed to have only (*5/five*) freckles.
3. (*101/One hundred and one*) people came to see my father play the violin.
4. Taxes have risen an average of (*8 percent/eight percent*) in the last year.
5. (One by one/*1 by 1*), they filed into the classroom.

Guidelines for Multilingual Writers

In this section, you'll learn some characteristics of written English that your readers are likely to expect. You'll also find advice about increasing your English vocabulary.

Multilingual Writers

For additional practice, go to **<www.bedfordstmartins .com/choices/>**. Click on "Exercise Central," and after logging in, click on "For Multilingual Writers."

CHARACTERISTICS OF WRITTEN ENGLISH

In English, as with any language, writing style is influenced by cultural beliefs and customs. In the United States, freedom of expression is highly valued; as a result, people are able to state their own opinions freely. Americans greatly prize originality and directness in writing and often expect writers to question authority. Also, people are believed to "own" their thoughts and ideas if they are published or broadcast.

Be Original

Although no concept is truly original—we are too influenced by what's around us—people who read and write English value what is commonly referred to as *original thought.* Rather than imitate or copy the words of esteemed people, you are expected to produce your own thoughts and words. If you're writing on a topic that many others

721

have explored, try to come up with a new angle or focus. Use different arguments, supporting points, and styles to separate your writing from what has been previously written.

Be Direct

In English, writing that informs or persuades should be direct and to the point. Readers want to know your purpose for writing as soon as they begin reading. They value ideas that are easy to follow and understand, even if they happen to disagree. As a result, when writing informative or persuasive essays, state your thesis in the beginning, don't stray from the main point, and use clear and concise language.

Question Authority

Read more about argumentative writing on pp. 394–412.

When writing in English, don't be afraid to disagree with others, even if they're highly respected authorities. This is especially true in argumentative writing, when you're expected to express an opinion that others will disagree with. In fact, in argumentative writing you often have to argue against—or refute—the claims made by people you don't agree with. However, your arguments need to be expressed calmly and rationally.

Don't Plagiarize

Find out how to document your sources in Chapter 11.

In the United States and other English-dominant cultures, writers are perceived as "owning" their thoughts or words if they were published or broadcast on radio or television. As a result, you need to document your sources in the text of your essay and at the end of it. The documentation tells your readers that you borrowed these words and ideas from others.

ACTIVITY 1 (GROUP)

Compare Writing in Different Languages. With several classmates, compare what it's like to write in different languages. To what degree is original thought, directness, and the questioning of authority valued? How do these differences (or similarities) reflect cultural beliefs and customs?

VOCABULARY

Like other languages, English changed over the centuries as English-speaking people interacted with people from different cultures. As a result, many words in English have been formed from words in other languages. We can see these changes in the different parts of English words. A *word root* is the main part of the word, a *prefix* is added to the beginning of a word, and a *suffix* is added to the end of a word. Here are the meanings of some common English word roots, prefixes, and suffixes.

English Word Roots

ROOT	DEFINITION	EXAMPLES
audi	to hear	audience, audio
bene	to help	benefit, benevolence
geo	earth	geography, geometry
logo	word or thought	logic, biology
manu	hand	manufacture, manual
photo	light	photography, telephoto
tele	far away	telepathy, telegraph
vid, vis	to see	visit, vision, video

English Prefixes

PREFIX	MEANING	EXAMPLES
ante-	before	antebellum, antedate
anti-	against	antisocial, antibody
bi-	two	bilateral, bipolar
de-	from	declaw, desensitize
hyper-	over, more than	hypersensitive
mal-	bad	malpractice
post-	after	postwar, postscript
trans-	across	transport, transition
uni-	one	uniform, unicycle

English Suffixes

SUFFIX	MEANING	EXAMPLES
-acy	state or quality	democracy, privacy
-dom	place or state of being	kingdom, freedom
-en	cause or become	cheapen, blacken
-ish	having the quality of	clownish
-less	lack of, without	childless, humorless
-ology	the study of	psychology, anthropology
-ment	condition of	impediment, payment
-sion, tion	state of being or action	transition

ASK YOURSELF: How Can I Build My Vocabulary?

In addition to learning English word roots, prefixes, and suffixes, follow these suggestions:

- Keep a vocabulary list on index cards. Write the word and the definition, and then use the word in a sentence. Keep the index cards with you for easy study and reference.

- Say new words out loud. If you don't know how to pronounce a word, ask someone.

- Read, and then read some more. Constantly search for books, magazine articles, and newspapers that are interesting.

Over the centuries, as people who spoke different languages interacted with each other, words in one language developed similarities to words in another language. Such similar words are called *cognates*. For example, the Spanish word *aceptar* is similar to the English phrase "to accept." At times, however, cognates can be confusing. The Spanish word *asisir,* for instance, means "to attend," not "to assist."

Language Contrasts: Spanish and English words

Because Spanish comes from the same language background as English, many Spanish words are similar to English words. However, some of these similarities are deceiving. Sometimes a word in Spanish sounds like a word in English, but the meaning is different. Here are some examples of these "false friends":

SPANISH	ENGLISH
actual	current
conductor	driver
embarazada	pregnant
exito	success
lectura	reading material
libreria	bookshop
pretender	intend
propaganda	advertising
propio	own
sensible	sensitive
suburbio	slum

Grammar for Multilingual Writers

In this section, you'll review important grammatical concepts and learn how English differs from other languages and dialects.

Multilingual Writers

For additional practice, go to **<www.bedfordstmartins .com/choices/>**. Click on "Exercise Central," and after logging in, click on "For Multilingual Writers."

ARTICLES

English has three articles: *the, a,* and *an. The* is the definite article; *a* and *an* are indefinite articles.

The definite article *the* comes before nouns with this exception: if the noun is preceded by one or more adjectives, the article comes before the adjective.

- Use *the* with nouns that refer to one or more specific things.

  I love *the* beautiful Victorian house.
  (Here *the* is referring to a specific house.)

  I love beautiful Victorian houses.
  (No house in particular is being referred to.)

  The roses bloom in May.
  (Particular roses are indicated.)

Roses bloom in May.
(Roses in general bloom in May.)

- In many cases with *the*, the noun that is being referred to has been mentioned before.

In buying a car, Chon focused mainly on appearance. *The* car he purchased looked sleek and sporty.

- *A* or *an* comes before nouns not specifically known to the reader, perhaps because they haven't been mentioned before.

A bird swooped out of the sky.
(The reader has no prior knowledge of the bird.)

A factory can create both jobs and pollution.
(No factory in particular is being mentioned.)

A day in the sun would do me good.
(This article refers to some day in the sun, but not to a specific day.)

- *A* comes before words that begin with consonant sounds (such as *b, c, d, f, g*).

a book   a cat   a movie   a speech

My husband said he will never wear *a* tie again.
(The article doesn't indicate a particular tie.)

I plan to buy *a* dress at the store.
(No particular dress is referred to.)

- *An* comes before words that begin with vowel sounds (*a, e, i, o, u*) to make them easier to pronounce.

an effort   an honor   an illness   an opera

An elephant is *an* interesting animal to watch.
(The articles refer to any elephant among many animals.)

An umbrella would have been useful today.
(The article refers to any umbrella.)

When writing in English, don't forget to include the article before a noun when it's needed.

COUNT AND NONCOUNT NOUNS

Count nouns can be singular or plural: *computer* or *computers*. *Non-count* (or *mass*) *nouns* usually can only be singular, even though the meaning may be plural. Here are some noncount nouns:

advice	homework	honesty
equipment	evidence	humanity
mail	furniture	courage
education	anger	poverty
information	vocabulary	employment
knowledge		

- Don't use indefinite articles (*a* and *an*) with noncount nouns.

INCORRECT   Her mother gave Molly *an advice* about her career.

CORRECT   Her mother gave Molly *advice* about her career.

- Noncount nouns can't be made plural, so don't add *-s* or *-es* at the end.

INCORRECT   I need to buy *furnitures* for my apartment.

CORRECT   I need to buy *furniture* for my apartment.

- To express a quantity for a noncount noun, use *some, any,* or *more*.

CORRECT   Her mother gave Molly *some advice* about her career.

CORRECT   I need to buy *more furniture* for my apartment.

Language Contrasts: Articles

- In Spanish, an article can be masculine or feminine, plural or singular, depending on the noun it precedes.
- In Japanese and many Native American languages, there's no difference between count and noncount nouns.
- Turkish has no definite article, while Arabic has no indefinite article.
- In Russian, Chinese, Korean, Polish, Tamil, and some Native American languages such as Navajo, articles don't exist.

Adding Missing Articles. Revise the following paragraph to include the missing articles.

> When I walked into room, girl I used to know spotted me. As I sat down on furniture, she approached to begin conversation. As much as I tried, I couldn't remember who she was. She reminded me that her name was Joan and that we had met at *bat mitzvah* years ago. Then, it all came back to me. This was girl whose dress I had ruined when I spilled glass of wine all over her. I was embarrassed to see same girl again.

PREPOSITIONS

Prepositions always begin a *prepositional phrase*—that is, a phrase that includes a preposition and its object.

at her dinner   in her office   on his folder

In English, the most common prepositions are *in, on,* and *at.*

- *In* indicates an enclosed area or a specific time.

  in a box   in the car   in the fall
  in England   in the classroom   in 2002
  in June   in the evening   in winter

  In New Mexico, you can find Pueblo pottery *in* Santa Fe.
  He wanted to get the book *in* the desk *in* the math lab.
  In 2004, I will graduate from college.
  I hoped to take a short trip *in* June.

- *On* indicates on top of, a day of the week, or a specific date.

  You'll find the envelope *on* the desk.
  I prefer to live *on* a mountain.
  Let's go to a movie *on* Friday night.

On Wednesday, I have to finish my project.

I'll start my new job *on* September 18.

On January 1, I always exercise to start the New Year.

*Watch out for preposi-
tional phrases that act
as subject pretenders.
See pp. 611–14.*

- *At* indicates a specific address, a general location, or a specific time.

  I live *at* 100 Main Street.

  You'll find the snowshoes *at* 1206 Devonshire.

  He played on the slide *at* the park.

  I'll meet you *at* your favorite restaurant.

  I'll see you *at* 7:30 P.M.

  At midnight, Cinderella turned into a pumpkin.

ACTIVITY 2

Using *in, on,* and *at*. Fill in the blanks in the following paragraph, using *in, on,* and *at* correctly.

_____ May 15, the semester will be over. It went fast, and I have to say that my attitude about English has changed. _____ my class, which I attended Monday, Wednesday, and Friday, we worked _____ the computer lab _____ the fourth floor _____ the Liberal Arts building. Having the computer helped me do my very best. _____ 7:30 A.M. each morning, I went to the lab and started to work. _____ 9:30 A.M., I was ready to go to class.

The most common prepositions for showing time are *for, during,* and *since.*

- *For* refers to an exact period of time, one that has a beginning and an end.

  I went into the army *for* six years.

  It has been snowing *for* two hours.

  I've been jogging *for* three weeks.

- *During* refers to an indefinite period of time.

  Several times *during* the hike I stopped to catch my breath.
  I plan to climb Mt. Everest sometime *during* the summer.
  It hailed *during* the night.

- *Since* refers to time that has elapsed.

  I've gained weight *since* the holidays.
  Since last spring, Nicola has been working at the zoo.
  Pete's been so happy *since* last month when he quit smoking.

ACTIVITY 3

Using *for, during,* and *since.* Fill in the blanks in the following paragraph, using *for, during,* and *since* correctly.

It was an easy task. _____ six years, I had been putting off cleaning out the garage. _____ the winter, I was too busy with work, and _____ the summer, I just wanted to go to the beach. _____ the holidays, though, I felt that I just had to make time. Now that I've finished the job, I wonder why I waited _____ years to get this done.

- Some common expressions in English always have the same prepositions.

  according to   refer to   believe in
  get over   talk about   different from

- Notice that some expressions in English use different prepositions to mean different things.

  put on clothes (get dressed)
  put off (delay)
  put out (fire)

ASK YOURSELF: How Can I Learn to Use Prepositions?

Many prepositions in English aren't rule-governed; they're used in particular ways simply because that's how people began using them as the language evolved. Moreover, similarities between the use of prepositions in English and in other languages are very few. Follow these suggestions for learning to use prepositions correctly:

- Learn the rules for those prepositions that have rules, such as *in, on,* and *at* and *for, during,* and *since.*
- When listening to others or reading books, magazines, or newspapers, pay attention to how prepositions are used.
- Keep a list of expressions that contain prepositions. Use index cards or a small notebook so you can refer to the list wherever you are.

OMITTED OR REPEATED SUBJECTS

In English, every sentence has a *subject* and a *verb*. The subject tells who or what is doing the action; the verb expresses an action or a state of being.

Omitted Subjects

What is the subject of a sentence? Turn to pp. 609–11.

The subject of a sentence must be stated, even when the meaning of the sentence is clear without stating it.

My *sister* loves to read.

That poor *dog* ran all the way home.

She quickly gathered the berries for her pie.

The subject of a dependent clause in a sentence must also be stated. A dependent clause contains a subject and verb but can't stand alone as a sentence because it begins with a subordinating conjunction (such as *because* or *although*) or a relative pronoun (such as *who, that,* or *which*). In the following examples, the subjects of the dependent clauses are italicized.

I already knew that *I* liked cats.

I was late for the appointment because my *car* didn't start.

Since the *package* was empty, I threw it away.

The expressions *it is* and *there is* function as subjects of sentences or dependent clauses, so they can't be omitted.

INCORRECT   *Is* too late to hand in the paper.

CORRECT   *It is* too late to hand in the paper.

INCORRECT   *Are* three bottles on the shelf.

CORRECT   *There are* three bottles on the shelf.

ACTIVITY 4

Adding a Missing Subject. Add the missing subject of the following sentences or dependent clauses.

1. In the computer lab at 9:00.

2. Is open every evening.

3. Saw many types of cars that liked.

4. However, never finished her dinner.

5. He felt drowsy during the movie, so left early.

6. Jane ate the all the cookies because had skipped dinner.

7. Are many different types of food.

8. Horace tried to make the deadline, but failed.

9. A sang outside the window.

10. Taking the course.

Repeated Subjects

Be careful not to repeat a subject that has already been stated earlier in the sentence.

INCORRECT   The lady in the store she was rude.

CORRECT   The lady in the store was rude.

INCORRECT   Some people they like to go to parties.

CORRECT   Some people like to go to parties.

ACTIVITY 5

Eliminating Repeated Subjects. Place a line through the repeated subjects in the following paragraph.

The student who wrote the essay evaluating his favorite restaurant he knew that he had to get his audience's attention. But his fellow classmates they didn't seem to understand this. The instructor, however, she explained the concept of audience again in class. Then, all of the students they knew what they needed to do. The student who wrote the essay on the restaurant he even knew what to do now.

Language Contrasts: Pronouns

- In Spanish, Portuguese, Turkish, and Chinese, personal pronouns (*I, you, he, she, they*) are not used when they're the subject of a sentence.
- In Arabic, personal pronouns are repeated in sentences as parts of the verb.
- English is unlike any other language in the use of *it is* and *there is* as the subject of a sentence.

WORD ORDER

In English, the basic word order of a sentence is *subject, verb, object.*

Jordan sewed the dress.

Adjectives and adverbs are placed close to the words they modify.

Jordan quickly sewed the blue dress.

Language Contrasts: Word order

- In Japanese, Korean, Farsi, and Turkish, the basic word order is subject, object, verb.
- In spoken Arabic, the basic word order is verb, subject.
- Spanish, Italian, and German feature loose word-order patterns.
- In Spanish, words that are emphasized can be placed last. Adverbs can come before a direct object: *Dr. Montez speaks very well English.*
- Greek, Russian, and Polish have no fixed word order.

Misplaced Adjectives

In English, adjectives almost always come before the noun.

Read more about adjectives on pp. 625–27.

An *important* thing to remember is to stop at stop signs.
George prepared to take the *difficult* test.
Julie bought the *red* motorcycle.

In English, adjectives precede the noun in a particular order. Though exceptions exist, this order is usually followed:

- Begin with articles and pronouns: *a, an, the, I, you.*
- Then add:

  words that evaluate: *ugly, handsome, honest, appealing, flavorful*
  words about size: *big, small, large*
  words about length or shape: *small, big, round, square, wide, narrow*
  words about age: *old, young, new*
  words about color: *red, blue, yellow*
  words about nationality: *Irish, Mexican, Canadian, Chinese*
  words about religion: *Muslim, Buddhist, Protestant, Jewish*
  words about the material of the noun: *wooden, glass, brick, adobe, stucco*
  nouns used as adjectives: *bathroom* floor, *track* team

- Finally, end with the noun: *book, car, movie, church, bench, computer.*

The *handsome old* house sat at the top of the hill.
My *German Catholic* grandmother died last year.
The *square wooden* box sat on the table.

**ASK YOURSELF: When Do I Need to Use
                 Commas with Adjectives?**

Decide whether you need a comma between two or more
adjectives by checking whether you can place *and* between the
adjectives and not change the meaning. If so, then you need the
comma.

   Suppose you want to write this sentence:

The tall fragile rosebush was blooming.

   Do you need a comma between *tall* and *fragile*? Yes, because
you can say *the tall and fragile rosebush was blooming* without
changing the meaning. Therefore, the correct punctuation is a
comma:

   The tall, fragile rosebush was blooming.

ACTIVITY 6

Placing Adjectives Correctly. Revise the following sentences so
that the adjectives are placed correctly. If the adjectives are already in
the correct place, write "Correct." Revise the punctuation between
adjectives as needed.

1. My history final exam long and difficult was given last week.

   _____

   _____

2. How do you like my red new big car?

   _____

   _____

3. The wooden large ancient house burned down.

   _____

   _____

4. It was a long difficult paper to write.

_____

_____

5. I thought of a title short and cute before I began to write.

_____

_____

6. The dress long blue hung in the closet.

_____

_____

7. The clever big cat ate all the food.

_____

_____

8. The harsh Cuban long cigar made me cough.

_____

_____

9. I vowed to change my old useless ways.

_____

_____

10. I wanted the blue swimsuit least expensive.

_____

_____

Misplaced Adverbs

Learn more about
adverbs on pp. 627–28.

Adverbs that modify verbs can appear at the beginning or end of a sentence, before or after a verb, or between a helping verb and the main verb. Most often, the adverb appears as close as possible to the verb.

Hurriedly, we escaped out the back door.

The dog *frantically* scraped against the window.

Abner *eagerly* wrote the letter.

My brother has *often* stayed out after midnight.

Do not put an adverb between a verb and its direct object.

INCORRECT   Li *put quickly the package* on the table.

CORRECT   Li *quickly put the package* on the table.

INCORRECT   The hairdresser *cut carefully my hair.*

CORRECT   The hairdresser *carefully cut my hair.*

ACTIVITY 7

Placing Adverbs Correctly. The sentences in the following paragraph do not have adverbs. Revise the sentences, putting at least one adverb in each sentence.

Security has been increased in our city's airport. People stand in long lines waiting to go through the security checkpoints. The baggage inspectors ask some passengers about what they have in their suitcases. Many passengers have to unpack their suitcases for inspection. Other security people stop people at random to ask about their destinations and reasons for traveling. Family members wait for hours in the terminals to see their loved ones arrive. Despite the inconvenience, most passengers and family members are calm because they understand why the security is necessary.

> **Language Contrasts: Adjectives and adverbs**
>
> - In Swahili, Arabic, Spanish, French, and Italian, adjectives follow nouns. In English, adjectives usually come before nouns.
> - In Japanese, adjectives are sometimes treated as verbs; as a result, *to be* can be omitted: *The food good.*
> - In Spanish and German, the noun can be dropped after the adjective if the meaning is clear: *She offered me several dresses, and I bought two.*

VERBS

A verb conveys an action or a state of being. Depending on your language background, verbs in English can be particularly challenging to master. This section will help you correctly use verb tenses, helping verbs, and verbs followed by gerunds and infinitives.

Verb Tense

Three basic tenses in English are the *simple present, past,* and *future.* These must be distinguished from the *present perfect, past perfect, present progressive, past progressive,* and *future progressive* tenses.

PRESENT TENSE. The simple present tense shows an action taking place at the time it is expressed. The present tense can also show an action that occurs regularly.

Pierre *studies* at least five hours a day.

I *drive* my daughter to school every weekday morning.

PAST TENSE. The simple past tense indicates something that began and ended in the past. Except for irregular verbs, use the *-ed* form.

Irregular verbs are listed on pp. 618–19.

Yesterday I *passed* my driver's test.

When he *was* a student, he *walked* wherever he had to go.

(This action happened more than once in the past, but it's not happening now.)

FUTURE TENSE. The future tense shows action that will take place or will probably take place. The future tense requires the use of *will* or *be going to* and the present tense.

I *will spend* my summer in New York City.

These economic times *are going to continue* indefinitely.

In some very formal writing, *shall* is used instead of *will* for the first-person future tense.

We *shall* triumph over adversity.

PRESENT PERFECT TENSE. The present perfect tense shows action that occurred over time and that is now finished. Unlike the past tense, no specific time period is given. With this tense, use *has* or *have* and the past participle, which consists of the base form of a verb with *-ed* on the end, as in *liked, wanted, begged,* or *touched.*

Alex *has cooked* the dinner.

The lawyers *have argued* their case.

Many past participles, however, are irregular and end in *-d, -en, -n,* or *-t.* Here are some common irregular past participles:

More past participles are listed on pp. 618–19.

bought	eaten	said
broken	gotten	spoken
caught	kept	sung
done	led	taken
drunk	read	taught

Elise *has taught* her first class.

Tran *has spoken* eloquently.

When the words *since* or *for* are used, the present perfect expresses action that began in the past and continues into the present time. Again, use *has* or *have* and the past participle with this tense.

Susan *has played* the trumpet *since* she was a child.

(Susan has played in the past and continues to play in the present.)

They *have lived* in Seattle for three years.

(They lived in Seattle in the past, and they currently live there.)

PAST PERFECT TENSE. The past perfect tense indicates an action occurring in the past before another time in the past. With this tense use *had* and the past participle.

I *had learned* the formulas before I took the test.

They *had smelled* smoke before they saw the fire.

PRESENT PROGRESSIVE TENSE. The progressive tenses show continual action. Use the present participle (usually the *-ing* form of the verb) and the appropriate form of *to be* with the progressive tenses.

The present progressive tense indicates an action that is happening at the time it is expressed.

> Eduardo *is helping* move the furniture.
>
> Right now, I *am baking* the bread.

PAST PROGRESSIVE TENSE. The past progressive tense shows action that occurred in the past and that is now over.

> Over the summer I *was spending* my money mostly on food.
>
> Last night the sick man's words *were becoming* very faint.

FUTURE PROGRESSIVE TENSE. The future progressive tense indicates continual action in the indefinite future or at a specific time in the future.

> The judge *will be hearing* your case soon.
>
> Next week we *will be going* on vacation.

ACTIVITY 8

Identifying Verb Tense. Identify the verb tense used in the following sentences.

1. I am saving as much money as possible. _____

2. Joe ate the whole pie. _____

3. They have enrolled in the same classes. _____

4. Will you help me solve this problem? _____

5. The children will be happy to see you. _____

6. I always prepare for the worst. _____

7. Last year I was going to the gym regularly. _____

8. They had announced the time change long before they printed

   the brochures. _____

9. The musician has agreed to an encore. _____

10. I have eaten ice cream every day for a year. _____

Language Contrasts: Verb tense

- There are no tenses in Chinese and Vietnamese.
- In Arabic, no future tense exists. Verbs can be changed to show whether action has been completed.
- Turkish doesn't have the verb "to be" (*is, are,* and so forth).
- In Native American languages, the verb "to be" either doesn't exist or isn't often used.
- In Navajo, singular and plural are indicated only in the verb. In English, singular and plural are also shown in nouns, usually with -*s* at the end of the word.
- In Japanese, verbs can indicate the speaker's feelings about the action.
- In Spanish, the present tense sometimes refers to the future.
- In African American spoken English, the verb *be* is used for events that happen over time and are still incomplete.

Helping Verbs

For more information on helping verbs, see pp. 616–18.

A *helping verb* is a verb that cannot appear alone in a sentence. Instead, it must be combined with the *main verb*.

Micah *has left* the room. (*Has* is the helping verb; *left* is the main verb.)

You *must wait* for the train to leave the station. (*Must* is the helping verb; *wait* is the main verb.)

MODALS. Some helping verbs, known as *modals,* can only be used as helping verbs:

can	might	should
could	must	will
may	shall	would

When using a modal in a sentence, use the base form of the verb after it. The *base form* of a verb is the form that follows the word *to,* such as *to run, to sing,* or *to follow.* The base form has no *-ed, -ing,* or *-s* ending.

Luisa *might travel* to Thailand.

My sister *would sing* if she *could read* music.

Rupert *can carry* the suitcase.

Unlike other helping verbs, a modal does not change form to agree in number with the subject, and neither does the main verb that follows it.

INCORRECT   He wills leave.
             He will leaves.

CORRECT   He will leave.

Language Contrasts: Modals

English has more modals than most other languages do, including Spanish, Chinese, Korean, Malay, Farsi, Arabic, Russian, and Turkish.

DO, DOES, DID. Like modals, the helping verbs *do, does,* and *did* are followed by the base form of the verb. Use one of these verbs

- to ask a question:

  Do you want to dance?
  Did my brother pick up his suit?

- to show a negative meaning (when used with *not*):

  I *did not* request this car.
  Sammy *does not* eat broccoli.

- to emphasize a main verb:

  Once again, I *do* appreciate the gift.
  She *does* look beautiful.

Unlike modals, the helping verbs *do* and *does* change in number to agree with the subject of the sentence.

INCORRECT   He *do* not enjoy watching football.
CORRECT   He *does* not enjoy watching football.

Language Contrasts: The use of *done*

In spoken dialects in the American South and in African American spoken English, *done* is used in two ways:

- *Done* is used instead of *has* or *have*: *The driver done found the way.*
- *Done* can mean "really": *The price doesn't matter because she done spent all her money.*

When you write standard English, use *done* as the past participle of *do*, as in *I have done my homework.*

HAVE, HAS, HAD. The helping verbs *have, has,* or *had,* used to indicate the present or past perfect tenses, change form to agree in number with the subject.

INCORRECT   They *has* broken all the good plates.

CORRECT   They *have* broken all the good plates.

Active-voice and passive-voice sentences are explained on pp. 676–77.

PASSIVE-VOICE SENTENCES. Helping verbs are used in sentences in the passive voice, or sentences in which the person or thing performing the action appears at the end. Here are some examples:

Jonathan *was hit* by the flying glass.

The book *was written* by Tom Wolfe.

Parts of the city *have been closed* by the chief of police.

ACTIVITY 9

Using Verbs. Fill in the correct form of the verb in the following paragraphs. Decide first on the correct verb tense; then select an appropriate helping verb.

Schindler's List [to be] _____ one of the best films of the last fifty years. This movie about the heroism of Oscar Schindler [play] _____ in movie theaters and homes across the world. Oscar

Schindler [to be] _____ an ordinary Polish businessman who singlehandedly [save] _____ hundreds of lives during the Holocaust. Because of this movie, people [learn] _____ of this terrible time in history.

In addition to teaching us about the Holocaust, *Schindler's List* [demonstrate] _____ to us Steven Spielberg's artistic excellence. Before *Schindler's List,* Spielberg [make] _____ entertaining movies such as *E.T.* and *Close Encounters of the Third Kind.* After *Schindler's List,* fans and movie critics alike [praise] _____ Spielberg for his ability to make a movie that told such an important story. Without a doubt, critics [recognize] _____ Spielberg as one of the best moviemakers of his generation.

Verbs Followed by Gerunds or Infinitives

A *gerund* is a verb that ends in *-ing* and is used as a noun.

I enjoy *walking.*
Cooking is his favorite hobby.

In contrast, an *infinitive* is the base form of a verb with the word *to* in front of it.

I decided *to stop* my car.
I went home *to wash* my clothes.

The following verbs can be followed by either a gerund or an infinitive:

begin   like
can't stand love
continue   start
hate

Watch out for gerunds and infinitives that act as verb pretenders. See pp. 621–24.

I started *to like* him right away.

I started *liking* him right away.

Other verbs change meaning depending on whether they're followed by a gerund or an infinitive.

She stopped *smoking* cigarettes.

(She gave up the habit of smoking.)

She stopped *to smoke* a cigarette.

(She paused so she could light up a cigarette.)

George remembered *to buy* the gift.

(George purchased the gift.)

George remembered *buying* the gift.

(George recalled purchasing the gift.)

The following verbs may be followed by a gerund but not by an infinitive:

admit	escape	quit
appreciate	finish	recall
avoid	imagine	resist
deny	miss	risk
discuss	practice	suggest
enjoy	put off	tolerate

Jonah escaped *going* to the store.

My father missed *opening* the presents.

This next list contains verbs that may be followed by an infinitive but not by a gerund:

agree	expect	mean	promise
ask	have	need	wait
beg	hope	offer	want
decide	manage	plan	wish

She planned *to take* the 7 A.M. flight.

Fred asked *to leave* the room.

ACTIVITY 10

Using Verbs Plus Gerunds or Infinitives. Finish each of the following sentences with a gerund or infinitive.

1. Herbert had hoped _____.

2. I hate _____.

3. My little sister tries _____.

4. The student denied _____.

5. I put off _____.

6. The little boy pretended _____.

7. The dog is begging _____.

8. I love _____.

9. My roommate always avoided _____.

10. William finally finished _____.

TWO-PART VERBS. Many verbs in English consist of two words. Here are some of the most common ones:

ask out	give up	play around
break down	help out	put together
call up	keep up	shut up
clean up	leave out	wake up
drop in	make up	
get along	pick up	

INCORRECT   Susan picked her packages.
CORRECT   Susan picked up her packages.

INCORRECT	When buying gifts, James left his cousin.
CORRECT	When buying gifts, James left out his cousin.

ACTIVITY 11

Using Two-Part Verbs. Use a two-part verb to complete each of the following sentences.

1. Peter _____ his wife on the phone.

2. It took me an hour to _____ the picture frame.

3. I _____ at 6 A.M.

4. "You must _____ with your brother," my mother said.

5. Even though you feel discouraged, don't _____ your dream.

PARTICIPIAL VERBS USED AS ADJECTIVES. Verbs that refer to feelings or senses can be used as adjectives. Such verbs include the following:

interest	fascinate	disturb
disappoint	tire	encourage
excite	charm	frighten
bore	embarrass	confuse

When a person or animal is *having* the feeling, use the *past* participle form.

The *frightened* cat jumped on the shelf.
The *bored* student tried to stay awake.
The *confused* child began to cry.

When a thing or person is *causing* the feeling, use the *present* participle form.

The *frightening* movie scared the children.
The *boring* book was hard to read.

The *confusing* message was not conveyed.

INCORRECT   I was *interesting* in the show.
CORRECT   I was *interested* in the show.

INCORRECT   The story was *excited*.
CORRECT   The story was *exciting*.

ACTIVITY 12

Using Participial Verbs as Adjectives. Complete the following sentences by filling in the correct participial verb.

1. I was [fascinate] _____ by the butterfly collection.

2. The butterfly collection was [fascinate] _____.

3. Jane, who was [embarrass] _____ by all the attention, wanted to be left alone.

4. The children's play was [charm] _____.

5. I have never seen such a [disturb] _____ collection of artwork in my life.

6. The spectators enjoyed the [excite] _____ fireworks display.

7. Frankly, I found the speech rather [tire] _____.

8. The [disappoint] _____ viewers turned off the television.

9. I am [charm] _____ to meet you.

10. When will this [embarrass] _____ display of affection end?

ACKNOWLEDGMENTS

Judy Blume. "Is Harry Potter Evil?" Reprinted by permission of the author.

Richard Glen Boire. "Symposium: Two Views on the Installation of Internet Filters in Public Libraries and Schools" from *Insight*, February 5, 2001. Copyright © 2002 News World Communications, Inc. Reprinted by permission. All rights reserved.

Jean Borysenko. "Mind/Body Programming" from *Minding the Body, Mending the Mind* by Joan Borysenko. Copyright © 1987 by Joan Borysenko, Ph.D. Reprinted by permission of Perseus Books.

Peggy Breland. "Metamorphosis" from *Purpose and Process: A Reader for Writers* 4th edition by Stephen Reid. Copyright © 2001 by Peggy Breland. Reprinted by permission.

William C. Brisick. "Our Thanksgiving Tradition" from *Geico Direct*, Volume 8, Number 4, fall 1994: 32–33. Reprinted by permission of GEICO Insurance, K.L. Publications, and the author.

Peter Cohen. "The Game Room" from *MacWorld*, September 2001. <www.macworld.com>. Reprinted by permission of MacWorld.

John Cullane. "Oprah Winfrey: How the Truth Changed Her Life" from the *Reader's Digest*, February 1989 issue. Copyright © 1989 by The Reader's Digest Assn., Inc. Reprinted with permission.

Julia Duin. "Navajos Struggle to Keep Weaving Tradition Alive" from *Insight*, October 4, 1999. Copyright © 2002 News World Communications, Inc. Reprinted by permission. All rights reserved.

Kerry Leigh Ellison. "Satan in the Library: Are Children in Danger?" from *School Library Journal*, October 1994. Copyright © 1994. Reprinted by permission.

Thomas L. Friedman. "My Favorite Teacher" from *The New York Times*, January 9, 2001. Copyright © 2001 by The New York Times Company, Inc. Reprinted by permission.

John Garrity. "An Act of Conscience" from *Sports Illustrated*, December 10, 1990. Copyright © 1990, Time, Inc. All rights reserved.

Danny Goldberg. "Testimony of Danny Goldberg, CEO and Co-owner, Artemis Records" from *Television Quarterly*, Volume 29, Number 3, 1998. Copyright © 1998 by the National Academy of Television Arts and Sciences. Reprinted by permission.

Ellen Goodman. "The Company Man" from *Close to Home* by Ellen Goodman. Copyright © 1979 by The Washington Post Company. Reprinted with permission of Simon & Schuster.

Gerald Hausman. "Feather" from *Turtle Island Alphabet* by Gerald Hausman. Copyright © 1992 by Gerald Hausman. Reprinted by permission of St. Martin's Press, LLC.

Tamera Helms. "Lessons in Shrimping" from *The Great American Bologna Festival and Other Student Essays* by Elizabeth Rankin. Copyright © 1991 Bedford/St. Martin's. Reprinted by permission.

Roger Hernandez. "Some Actions Aren't Affirmative" from *The El Paso Times*, August 31, 2001, p.13-A. Copyright © 2001 Roger Hernandez. Reprinted with special permission of King Features Syndicate.

Rita Warren Hess. "American Workplace Slang and Jargon" From the Web site: <www.coming2american.com>. Reprinted by permission of the author. Author's Web site: <www.enidprofessionalwriters.org>.

Roger Hoffmann. "The Date" from "About Men" column in *The New York Times Magazine,* January 1, 1986. Originally titled, "There's Always the Dare." Copyright © 1986 by The New York Times Company. Reprinted by permission.

Debra Hotaling. "A Brief Assembly of Good Samaritans" from *Newsweek,* May 29, 1995. Copyright © 1995 Newsweek, Inc. Reprinted by permission. All rights reserved.

Nicholas Jennings. "A Palace of Rock" from *Maclean's,* Volume 108, September 18, 1995. Copyright © 1995. Reprinted by permission.

Brian D. Johnson. "Blood and Circuses" from *Maclean's,* May 15, 2001. Copyright © 2001. Reprinted by permission.

Stephen King. "Why We Crave Horror Movies" from *Playboy* (1982). Copyright © Stephen King. Reprinted with permission. All rights reserved.

Perri Klass. "She's Your Basic L.O.L. in N.A.D." from *Not An Entirely Benign Procedure* by Perri Klass. Copyright © 1987 by Perri Klass. Reprinted by permission of Putnam Berkeley, a division of Penguin Putnam, Inc.

Tony Laure. "Students Caught Up in Cell Phone Craze" from <www.chicagoflame.com>, March 7, 2002, the independent student newspaper online for the University of Chicago. Reprinted by permission.

Joe Loconte. "A City's Assault on Teen Pregnancy" from *Policy Review,* November/December 1996. Copyright © 1996. Reprinted by permission.

Carl T. Rowan. "Unforgettable Miss Bessie" from *The Reader's Digest,* March 1985. Copyright © 1985 by The Reader's Digest Assn., Inc. Reprinted with permission.

Jack Denton Scott. "What's a Bagel?" From *The Reader's Digest,* June 1988. Copyright © 1988 by The Reader's Digest Assn., Inc. Reprinted with permission.

Kathy Simmons. "All Stressed Out—And Off to Work We Go" from <www.careermag.com>. Courtesy of VerticalNet.

Bruce Watson. "Symposium: Two Views on the Installation of Internet Filters in Public Libraries and Schools" from *Insight,* February 5, 2001. Copyright © 2002 News World Communications, Inc. Reprinted by permission. All rights reserved.

Mary Ann Watson. "Seinfeld" from *Television Quarterly,* Volume 29, Number 3, 1998. Copyright © 1998 by the National Academy of Television Arts and Sciences. Reprinted by permission.

"Career Profile: Science" from The Editors of <www.webfeet.com>. Copyright © 2002 Wetfeet.com, Inc. Reprinted by permission.

Elizabeth Whelan. "Perils of Prohibition" from *Newsweek,* May 29, 1995, pp. 14–15. Copyright © 1995 Newsweek, Inc. Reprinted by permission. All rights reserved.

Malcolm X. "Prison Studies" from *The Autobiography of Malcolm X* by Malcolm X and Alex Haley. Copyright © 1964 by Alex Haley and Malcolm X. Copyright © 1965 by Alex Haley and Betty Shabazz. Used by permission of Random House, Inc.

Philip Zimbardo and Ann L. Weber. "Cross-Cultural Perspective: Culture Shock" from *Psychology* by Philip Zimbardo and Ann L. Weber. Copyright © 1994 by Allyn & Bacon. Reprinted by permission of Allyn & Bacon. All rights reserved.

PHOTO CREDITS. p. 2, Index Stock Imagery; p. 26, Susie Fitzhugh; p. 56, Rick Kopstein/photographer; p. 98, Elizabeth Mangelsdorf; p. 166, Elizabeth Mangelsdorf; p. 238, Joseph Schuyler/Stock, Boston; p. 302, Michael Kagan, photographer; p. 307, Courtesy, Am General Corp.; p. 372, Bob Daemmrich Photography, Inc./The Image Works; p. 446, Robert W. Kelley/TimePix; p. 506, Jeff Greenberg/Photo Researchers; p. 520, Karim Shamsi-Basha/The Image Works; p. 566, Jean Claude LeJeune/Stock, Boston; p. 592, Michael Hart, photographer.

INDEX